## solutions@syngress.com

With more than 1,500,000 copies of our MCSE, MCSD, CompTIA, and Cisco study guides in print, we continue to look for ways we can better serve the information needs of our readers. One way we do that is by listening.

Readers like yourself have been telling us they want an Internet-based service that would extend and enhance the value of our books. Based on reader feedback and our own strategic plan, we have created a Web site that we hope will exceed your expectations.

**Solutions@syngress.com** is an interactive treasure trove of useful information focusing on our book topics and related technologies. The site offers the following features:

- One year warranty against content obsolescence due to vendor product upgrades. You can access online updates for any affected chapters.
- "Ask the Author"™ customer query forms that enable you to post questions to our authors and editors.
- Exclusive monthly mailings in which our experts provide answers to reader queries and clear explanations of complex material.
- Regularly updated links to sites specially selected by our editors for readers desiring additional reliable information on key topics.

Best of all, the book you're now holding is your key to this amazing site. Just go to **www.syngress.com/solutions**, and keep this book handy when you register to verify your purchase.

Thank you for giving us the opportunity to serve your needs. And be sure to let us know if there's anything else we can do to help you get the maximum value from your investment. We're listening.

www.syngress.com/solutions

SYNGRESS®

# HACK PROOFING™ Your E-commerce Site

The Only Way to Stop a Hacker is to Think Like One

SYNGRESS®

| KEY | SERIAL NUMBER |
|---|---|
| 001 | AERAF43495 |
| 002 | VNA49FU4FJ |
| 003 | CAKL3956FM |
| 004 | BNA424TURT |
| 005 | BNTUR495QF |
| 006 | 596JFA3RRF |
| 007 | Y745T9TBLF |
| 008 | QW5VCD986H |
| 009 | BN3TE5876A |
| 010 | NVA384NHS5 |

PUBLISHED BY
Syngress Publishing, Inc.
800 Hingham Street
Rockland, MA 02370

**Hack Proofing Your E-Commerce Site**



Printed in the United States of America

1 2 3 4 5 6 7 8 9 0

ISBN: 1-928994-27-X

Technical edit by: L. Brent Huston
Technical review by: Kevin Ziese
Co-Publisher: Richard Kristof
Developmental Editor: Kate Glennon
Acquisitions Editor: Catherine B. Nolan
Copy edit by: Darren Meiss and Beth A. Roberts
Freelance Editorial Manager: Maribeth Corona-Evans
Index by: Robert Saigh
Page Layout and Art by: Shannon Tozier

Distributed by Publishers Group West in the United States.

# Acknowledgments

We would like to acknowledge the following people for their kindness and support in making this book possible.

Richard Kristof and Duncan Anderson of Global Knowledge, for their generous access to the IT industry's best courses, instructors and training facilities.

Ralph Troupe, Rhonda St. John, and the team at Callisma for their invaluable insight into the challenges of designing, deploying and supporting world-class enterprise networks.

Karen Cross, Lance Tilford, Meaghan Cunningham, Kim Wylie, Harry Kirchner, Bill Richter, Kevin Votel, and Brittin Clark of Publishers Group West for sharing their incredible marketing experience and expertise.

Mary Ging, Caroline Hird, Simon Beale, Caroline Wheeler, Victoria Fuller, Jonathan Bunkell, and Klaus Beran of Harcourt International for making certain that our vision remains worldwide in scope.

Anneke Baeten, Annabel Dent, and Laurie Giles of Harcourt Australia for all their help.

David Buckland, Wendi Wong, Daniel Loh, Marie Chieng, Lucy Chong, Leslie Lim, Audrey Gan, and Joseph Chan of Transquest Publishers for the enthusiasm with which they receive our books.

Kwon Sung June at Acorn Publishing for his support.

Ethan Atkin at Cranbury International for his help in expanding the Syngress program.

Joe Pisco, Helen Moyer, and the great folks at InterCity Press for all their help.

# Contributors

**Ryan Russell** (CCNA, CCNP) is the best-selling author of *Hack Proofing Your Network: Internet Tradecraft* (ISBN: 1-928994-15-6). He is MIS Manager at SecurityFocus.com, has served as an expert witness on security topics, and has done internal security investigation for a major software vendor. Ryan has been working in the IT field for over 11 years, the last 6 of which have been spent primarily in information security. He has been an active participant in various security mailing lists, such as BugTraq, for years. Ryan has contributed to four Syngress titles on the topic of networking. He holds a Bachelors of Science degree in Computer Science. Ryan wishes to thank Karen Mathews at the U.S. Department of Energy for her assistance in preparing Chapter 10.

**Mark S. Merkow** (CCP) has been an Information Systems professional since 1975, working in a variety of industries. For the last 12 years he has been working for a Fortune 50 financial services company in Phoenix, AZ. Mark holds a Masters in Decision and Information Systems from Arizona State University's College of Business and is completing his Masters of Education in Educational Technology at ASU's College of Education, specializing in developing distance learning courses. Today he serves as an e-commerce Security Advisor working with both internal and external Web designers and developers. Mark has authored or co-authored six books on computer technology since 1990, including *Breaking Through Technical Jargon*, *Building SET Applications for Secure Transactions*, *Thin Clients Clearly Explained*, *Virtual Private Networks For Dummies*, *A Complete Guide to Internet Security*, and *The ePrivacy Imperative*. In addition, Mark is a computer columnist for several local, national, and international print publications, along with an e-zine hosted at Internet.com.

**Robin Walshaw** (MCSE, DPM), author of *Mission Critical Windows 2000 Server Administration* (ISBN: 1-928994-16-4), is an independent consultant who architects security and infrastructure solutions for large corporations around the globe. By applying a combination of sound business sense and technical insight, Robin is able to design and deliver scalable solutions targeted at enabling the enterprise to effectively leverage technology. With a flair for developing strategic IT solutions for diverse clients, he has worked in the world of computers in 8 countries, and has traveled to over 30 in the last 10 years. A veteran of numerous global projects, Robin has honed his skills across a wide variety of businesses, platforms, and technologies. He has managed to scratch his head and look slightly confused in the world of security, network operating systems, development, and research.

Having traversed the globe and seen its many beautiful wonders, Robin is still captivated by the one thing that leaves him breathless—Natalie, his wife. She is a light against the darkness, a beauty whose smile can melt even the coldest heart.

**Teri Bidwell** (GCIA) has been involved in Internet security for over 10 years as an analyst, engineer, and administrator and is a SANS-Certified GCIA Intrusion Analyst. Her career began securing Unix networks at the University of Colorado and continued as a Cisco network engineer and DNS manager for Sybase, Inc. Today, Teri is a security analyst for a firm headquartered in Reston, VA. She is a key contributor to corporate security strategy and is an advisor for e-business development. Her specialties include policy creation, vulnerability assessment, penetration testing, and intrusion detection for corporate environments.

Teri received a Computer Science degree from the University of Colorado and sits on the SANS GCIA Advisory Board. She currently lives and works in Boulder, CO with her family, Clint, Wes, and Michael.

**Michael Cross** (MCSE, MCP+I, CNA) is a Microsoft Certified System Engineer, Microsoft Certified Product Specialist, Microsoft Certified Professional + Internet, and a Certified Novell Administrator. Michael is the Network Administrator, Internet Specialist, and a Programmer for the Niagara Regional Police Service. He is responsible for network security and administration, programming applications, and is Webmaster of their Web site at www.nrps.com. He has consulted and assisted in computer-related/Internet criminal cases, and is part of an Information Technology team that provides support to a user base of over 800 civilian and uniform users. His theory is that when the users carry guns, you tend to be more motivated in solving their problems.

Michael owns KnightWare, a company that provides consulting, programming, networking, Web page design, computer training, and other services. He has served as an instructor for private colleges and technical schools in London, Ontario Canada. He has been a freelance writer for several years and has been published over two dozen times in books and anthologies. Michael currently resides in St. Catharines, Ontario Canada with his lovely fiancée Jennifer.

**Oliver Steudler** (CCNP, CCDP, CSE, CNE) is a Senior Systems Engineer at iFusion Networks in Cape Town, South Africa. Oliver specializes in routing, switching, and security and has over 10 years of experience in consulting, designing, implementing, and troubleshooting complex networks. He has written articles on TCP/IP, networking, security, and data communications and also co-authored another Syngress title, *Managing Cisco Network Security* (ISBN: 1-928994-17-2).

**Kevin Ziese** is a computer scientist at Cisco Systems, Inc. Prior to joining Cisco, he was a senior scientist and founder of the Wheelgroup Corporation, which was acquired by Cisco Systems in April of 1998. Before founding the Wheelgroup Corporation, he was Chief of the Advanced Countermeasures Cell at the Air Force Information Warfare Center.

# Technical Editor and Contributor

**L. Brent Huston** earned his Associate of Applied Science degree in Electronics at DeVry Technical Institute (Columbus, Ohio) in 1994. He has more than 10 years of experience in IT, mostly in the areas of cyber security testing, network monitoring, scanning protocols, firewalls, viruses and virus prevention formats, security patches, and hacker techniques. As President and CEO of his own information security company, MicroSolved, Inc., he and his staff have performed system and network security-consulting services for Fortune 500 companies and all levels of governmental facilities. He is well versed in the use and implementation of all the major security tools and appliances. In the past, Brent developed "Passys"—a passive intrusion detection system for Unix and has also identified previously unknown security vulnerabilities in Ascom routers, Windows NT, and Linux operating systems.

Brent is an accomplished computer and information security speaker and has published numerous white papers on security-related topics. Recently he was involved in the laboratory testing of major firewall appliances at his company's central Ohio facilities. This testing was to prove the worthiness of each appliance as well as possible vulnerabilities that had not as yet been established by their parent companies. He reported his results both to the individual product companies and at a national security industry presentation. Brent is also currently engaged with the Office of Independent Oversight and Performance Assurance in Columbus, OH. He was responsible for designing and implementing a state-of-the-art cyber security testing and research lab for this office and several DOE national laboratories have utilized his expertise to perform network penetration and detection services. Such services have required a high security clearance from Brent. Brent is an Internet Security Systems Certified Engineer, Sidewinder Firewall Certified Administrator, IBM Secure Network Gateway Certified Administrator, and Phoenix Firewall Certified Administrator.

# Contents

**Understand the Goals of Security in the Commerce Process**

- Protect the privacy of the consumer at the point of purchase.
- Protect the privacy of the customers' information while it is stored or processed.
- Protect the confidential identity of customers, vendors, and employees.
- Protect the company from waste, fraud, and abuse.
- Protect the information assets of the company from discovery and disclosure.
- Preserve the integrity of the organization's information assets
- Ensure the availability of systems and processes required for consumers to do business with the company.
- Ensure the availability of systems and processes required for the company to do business with its vendors and partners.

**Damage & Defense Sidebars Provide You with Additional Information on Minimizing Risk**

**Damage & Defense... Configuration Management**

One method of instigating a DoS is by altering the configuration of key devices such as routers and servers. Routing tables, registry databases, and UNIX configuration files are just a few of the potential configuration databases that can be used against a business. It goes without saying, then, that all Internet-facing devices should undergo strict change control procedures and that a backup of the last known good configuration should be available on

**Know What You May Be Giving Away in Your HTML Code**

Each hidden tag can be used with forms on your site and includes a name and a value. When the form is submitted, the name and value in the hidden field is included with the results. For example, the following line of code shows an input value of $100.00 associated with a variable called "cost."

```
<input type=hidden
name="cost"
value="100.00">
```

Using a text editor or HTML editing program, a hacker could alter the value so that the value is changed to a lower amount. For example, the $100.00 could be changed to $1.00. This would allow buyers to purchase products at a significantly reduced amount.

**Learn How to Produce a Security Policy**

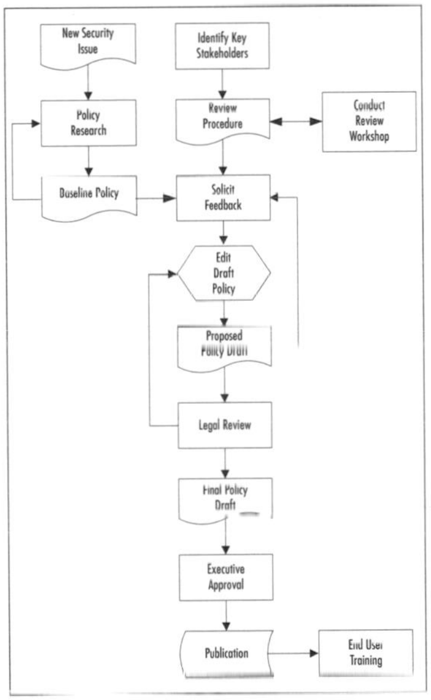

**Chapter 5 Answers All Your Questions About Implementing a Secure Site**

**Q:** How do I know if I am logging too much or too little information on my systems?

**A:** Log the information you feel that you need to make good decisions. If you have problems sifting through the logs to locate issues and you have had proper training, then you need to eliminate the log entries that you do not use to make decisions or keep those log entries and use an automated tool to select only the entries you are interested in. You are logging too little information if you do not have a picture of your systems' operations and your users' behaviors.

**Complete Coverage of Third Party Merchants' POS Systems.**

ICVERIFY's features include the following:

- Importing credit card transaction data from other PC applications, such as spreadsheets or databases.
- Offline group mode to submit a batch of transactions at one time for authorization.
- Support for Address Verification Systems (AVSs), Retail AVSs, CVV2s, and CVC2s to help reduce fraud due to stolen or fraudulent cards.
- Data import analysis of files for errors before import.

**Tools & Traps, Security Alerts, and Damage & Defense Sidebars Make Sure You Don't Miss a Thing:**

**Tools & Traps...Gauge Your Threat Level with a Honeypot**

A honeypot (in an information security context) is a system that is designed to be broken into. Setting up a honeypot will give you an opportunity to study tactics of attackers and possibly pick up a new attack or two along the way. Naturally, the attacker shouldn't be aware that he has broken into a honeypot, and he should think that he's gotten into an ordinary machine with no special monitoring. In fact, a honeypot machine typically has extensive monitoring in place around it, either on the machine itself or via the network. In order for the honeypot to be effective, as much information as possible must be collected about the attacker.

**Chapter 8 Answers All Your Questions About Disaster Recovery Planning:**

**Q:** How does e-commerce insurance pay out benefits when I incur a loss?

**A:** Types of insurance payout provisions are "Pay on Behalf" versus "Indemnification." Pay on Behalf takes care of expenses as they are incurred by the insured and works a bit like homeowner's insurance. If the policy covers your defense in a lawsuit, the legal fees will be paid as they are incurred. Indemnification reimburses the insured for covered expenses already incurred and works a bit like traditional health insurance. You pay for the covered expense and then apply for reimbursement from the insurer. Most insurance offerings for e-commerce are of the "Pay on Behalf" variety.

**Q:** What's the difference between a password and a passphrase?

**A:** A passphrase has spaces in it and is made up of multiple words. "ex&mpl3" is a password and "4 sc0re & s3v3n ye4r5 @go" is a passphrase.

## Understand Load Balancing and Security

For the most part, load balancers don't change security much, and in fact some can enhance it by acting as limited firewalls. However, in a few cases, security may be impacted.

Obviously the load balancer itself may have security problems—most products do. Attacks against the management interface or address of the load balancer may occur. In this sense, it's much like any system on your network, which might be compromised and give an attacker better leverage for other attacks. If an attacker manages to gain administrative control over your load balancer, they might be able to cause a "virtual defacement" by redirecting your Web traffic to a page of their choosing.

**Maintain a Chain of Custody List**

- Who was in custody (possession) of the evidence?
- Where was the evidence?
- What security measures are in place at that location?
- What items of evidence existed at that time?

# Foreword

*Hack Proofing Your E-Commerce Site* was written in response to requests from readers of our first book, *Hack Proofing Your Network: Internet Tradecraft*. Many of you asked us for more detail on how to protect e-commerce sites, given the unique risk and exposure such sites represent to organizations. We hope this book answers all of your questions on the topic and then some. If your organization engages in e-commerce, you will find this book invaluable, especially if security has been dealt with in a reactive fashion in the past. If you are a seasoned security professional, we believe that the level of detail in this book will be useful in covering topics such as customer privacy policies and securing financial transactions.

As practitioners, we encounter two types of networks: Those that haven't been hacked and those that have. Our goal is to provide you with the tools and resources to avoid seeing your network become part of the latter group. To that end, this book is thoroughly practical. We recognize that doing the "right" thing—creating a forensics laboratory and halting production to investigate each breach in painstaking detail—is beyond most staff resources, so we offer real-world solutions to approach that ideal within your limits.

We believe that for this book to be practical, it must also cover topics such as disaster recovery, load balancing, and performance optimization. We've tried to avoid the trap of recommending ill-defined "black-box" hardware solutions, a trap that other books in the field often fall into.

This book shares a feature in common with many Syngress books: It teaches *why* along with *how*. This is especially critical in the world of information security because technologies evolve at such a rapid pace and are also incredibly diverse. There are as many different ways to piece together an e-commerce site as there are e-commerce sites. It wouldn't be possible to anticipate any given reader's configuration. We present material that is designed to make you think. We want you to be able to take the information presented and adapt it to your situation.

We really hope you enjoy this book. You'll notice that Syngress offers an "Ask the Author" feature on their Web site for folks who have purchased the book. Please take advantage of that; we'd love to hear from you.

—*Ryan Russell, CCNA, CCNP*

# Chapter 1

# Applying Security Principles to Your E-Business

**Solutions in this chapter:**

- Security as a Foundation
- Applying Principles to Existing Sites
- How to Justify a Security Budget
- Security as a Restriction
- Security as an Enabler

☑ Summary

☑ Solutions Fast Track

☑ Frequently Asked Questions

# Introduction

Security in the virtual world of the Internet is even more confusing than in the real world we inhabit. Buzzwords and marketing hype only serve to add to the puzzle. Vendors and free products abound, but according to the experts, the Internet world is becoming more dangerous every day. How can that be? How can all these solutions from so many directions not solve even the basic problems?

The answer is not simple because the problems are so complex. Security is difficult to create and maintain. Security is messy. The problem is that the online world was built around a system of protocols and rules, but unfortunately, those rules are not always followed. The complexity of today's computer systems and software applications often creates programs that act in a manner unforeseen by the Internet's operational guidelines. Add to that scenario a few humans who insist on testing the rules and purposefully acting unexpectedly, and you have a huge potential for a rather large mess.

Attaining and maintaining suitable levels of security also requires resources. It requires people with the technical and business skills in balance. It requires time, energy, and of course, money. Security is not cheap. Products and training and doing things the right way are usually more expensive in the short term than taking shortcuts and cutting corners, but in the long run, security protects the assets that your organization depends on for survival.

Given all these dynamics, the concept of security can be seen as an ever-changing ideal that encompasses these threats and adapts as they adapt, like a living process. Security is most assuredly a journey and not a destination.

The easiest starting point on that journey is from the ground up. In the e-commerce world, those who benefit the most from security's elusive protections are those who started the process with security firmly in mind. While it is possible to apply security to existing sites, the implementation is often more difficult than starting the process anew.

In this chapter, we discuss how to bring security into focus from the start, what roles it should play, and how to get it included in the budget of a project. We also talk about how to justify its ongoing existence and measure its successes. For those of you who are tasked with defending an existing e-commerce site or other Web presence, we will explore the roles you should play in your organization and the process by which you can improve your site's security posture.

# Security as a Foundation

The easiest, and many agree, the best way to create a secure environment is to start with security in mind. This means applying the principles of secure operation as the foundation upon which the rest of the project will be built. The primary principles of security are confidentiality, integrity, and availability. To succeed, the project must address these principles in all phases and applications.

## Confidentiality

Confidentiality is the most widely known of the principles. Businesses have been dealing with confidentiality since commerce began. Today, it is a basic expectation of consumers that their personal information will be protected from disclosure. Vendors also expect a level of confidentiality to protect custom pricing, custom scheduling, and contractual details of their transactions with your company. Yet, as widely accepted as the concept of confidentiality is, it remains difficult to execute. Companies are in the news regularly because information about clients, vendors, or the politics of business relationships has become known.

Towards the end of 2000 a prominent U.S. hospital discovered that its security infrastructure had been breached and the confidentiality of 5,000 patient records had been violated. The risks to confidentiality do not stop with access to data; credit card details are illegally obtained from Internet facing systems, then used or sold, with alarming frequency. Some analysts have estimated that online credit card fraud incurs damages worldwide to the tune of $9 billion annually. Information is possibly one of the most valuable assets most companies possess; losing it or caring for it negligently could spell disaster and possibly even ruin.

If your company had exposed the records of these clients, what would the damage to your bottom line have been? How would your company deal with such a situation?

## Integrity

Integrity is perhaps the most difficult of the principles to achieve, yet it is the most vital of the three. Businesses must manage and maintain the integrity of the information with which they are entrusted. Even the slightest corruption of that data can cause complete chaos. The myriad of decisions based upon that integrity range from the basic business operation to the growth plans of the business long term. Over the centuries, various methods have evolved for building and maintaining the integrity of information. The double entry accounting system, the creation of jobs such as editors and proofreaders, and the modern checksum methods are all technical advances aimed at creating integrity. Yet, even with these modern tools and all the attention paid to the process over the years, integrity remains one of our greatest concerns. Integrity is something we almost take for granted. We assume that the database system we are using will maintain the records of our sales correctly. We believe that our billing system is smart enough to add the items on a customer's bill. Without some form of integrity checking, neither of these situations may be true. Integrity of information can have an even larger impact on an organization.

Imagine a computer virus that infected your accounting systems and modified all the sevens in your Excel spreadsheets, turning them into threes. What would the effect of those illicit modifications mean to your business? What steps would your organization take to recover the correct figures and how would you even discover the damage?

## Availability

Last, but not least, of the three principles is availability. Availability is the lifeblood of any business. If a consumer can't get to your business to purchase your goods, your business will soon fail. In the e-commerce world, where every moment can directly translate to thousands of dollars in sales, even downtimes of less than an hour can do immense financial damage to a company. Consider the amount of damage done to your company if your Web site became unavailable for four hours, which is the length of time that most vendors used as a benchmark for turnaround time in the pre-Internet world. Such an outage in e-commerce could cost tens of thousands of dollars, as we will see in Chapter 2. How long could your company continue to do business if your Internet presence was destroyed? How much money per hour would your organization lose if you could not do business online?

Security also entails a three-step process of assessment, revision, and implementation of changes (see Figure 1.1). This continual process of

**Figure 1.1** The Continual Security Assessment Process

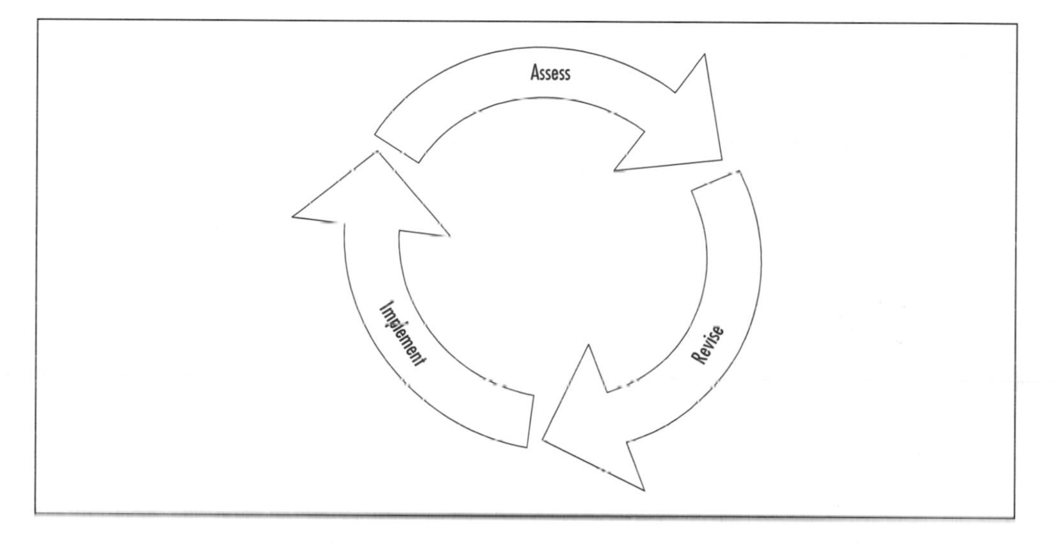


evaluation and feedback is necessary to adapt processes and products to the ever-changing conditions of the online world. As hackers examine existing software and hardware systems and discover new vulnerabilities, these vulnerabilities must be tested against your own systems and changes made to mitigate the risks they pose. The systems must then be tested again to ensure that the changes did not create new weaknesses or expose flaws in the systems that may have been previously covered. For example, it is fairly for common for software patches and version upgrades to replace configuration files with default settings. In many cases, this opens additional services on the box, or may re-enable protocols disabled by the administrator in a previous configuration. This ongoing process of evaluation strengthens the three principles and ensures their continued success.

Based on these ideas and the scenarios that can occur when the three principles are not managed well, you can see why building security from the ground up is so important. Building the three principles into a business certainly requires work and planning. Security is neither easy to accomplish nor easy to maintain, but with proper attention, it is sustainable.

# Presenting Security As More Than a Buzzword

Security must be more than a buzzword or a group within your organization. Security needs to be on the mind of every employee and in the forefront of the day-to-day operations. Security staff members need to work as partners or consultants to other groups within the company. They need to remain approachable and not be seen as "Net cops" or tyrants. They need to allow for dialogue with every employee, so that they can make suggestions or bring to their attention any events that seem out of place.

Security works best when all employees are attentive to situations that may expose customers to danger or the site to damage. The key to achieving this level of awareness is education. Education is the tool that disarms attackers who prey on miscommunication, poorly designed processes, and employee apathy. Such attacks, often called "social engineering" by hackers, can be devastating to a company and its reputation.

The best way to defend against these attacks is to educate your employees on your policies regarding security and customer privacy. They also need to see those policies being followed by all members of the team, from management down to the entry-level employees. They need reminders, refreshers, and periodic updates whenever changes to the procedures are made. In other words, security has to be an attitude from the top down. The highest levels of management must support the policies and their enforcement for long-term success to be achieved and maintained.

The security team also requires the support of management. A universal attitude of cooperation must be presented and maintained across all lines of business with the security group. Every employee needs to feel that the security group is approachable and they should have no fear of reporting things that seem suspicious. Employees need to know exactly whom to contact, and they need to be treated with respect instead of suspicion when they talk to the security team and its members.

Tools & Traps...

## Social Engineering

In the average business there are a number of avenues ripe for social engineering exploitation. With the security focus often turned to the more romantic notions of stealthy hacks and exotic code, the more prosaic methods of bypassing security are often neglected. Unfortunately, attempting to prevent social engineering can be a double-edged sword. Processes and procedures aimed at reducing the possibility of social engineering can do as much harm as good, driving users to ignore them due to their overly rigid and complex implementation. This said, there are a number of areas that are commonly open for abuse, including the following:

- **Passwords** Overly complex passwords are often written down and easily accessible. More memorable passwords, however, are often a greater risk because simpler passwords such as a husband's first name are easily guessed. Some companies employ strong authentication that requires the user to use a combination of a password and a number generated by a special token which the user possesses.

Continued

- **Support Services** When a user calls a help desk or a network engineer for support, the authenticity of the user is often taken for granted. A negligent help desk could easily respond to a request for a password change for a user's account without a guarantee that the caller is who he says he is. In this scenario the hacker typically leverages the anonymity provided by a telephone or e-mail message. Using a similar angle, a hacker could pretend to be part of the support services and during a phony "support" call obtain a user's logon ID and password.
- **Physical Access** Without adequate physical security a hacker or even a non-technical criminal with a confident bearing can walk directly into an office and begin using computer systems. In fact, a case reported in China detailed how a man walked into a securities firm posing as an employee and used an unsecured terminal to affect stock prices and the stability of the Shanghai stock market.

Since social engineering is such a dangerous weapon in the attacker's toolkit, it only makes sense to educate yourself about it. Here are some Web sites where you can learn more about social engineering:

- www.netsecurity.about.com/compute/netsecurity/cs/socialengineering
- www.cert.org/advisories/CA-1991-04.html
- www.pacbell.com/About/ConsumerInfo/0,1109,157,00.html

Remember, too, that social engineering may be used to attack more than your computer security. It is a wide-ranged tool used for fraud and privacy violations as well, or can be used to gather information to plan a larger attack.

# The Goals of Security in E-Commerce

Security plays a very important role in e-commerce, and is essential to the bottom line. While e-commerce done correctly empowers your company and the consumer, e-commerce done poorly can be devastating for those same participants. The goals of security in the commerce process must be to:

- Protect the privacy of the consumer at the point of purchase.
- Protect the privacy of the customers' information while it is stored or processed.
- Protect the confidential identity of customers, vendors, and employees.
- Protect the company from waste, fraud, and abuse.
- Protect the information assets of the company from discovery and disclosure.
- Preserve the integrity of the organization's information assets.
- Ensure the availability of systems and processes required for consumers to do business with the company.
- Ensure the availability of systems and processes required for the company to do business with its vendors and partners.

These goals are a starting point for the creation of a good security policy. A great security policy, as described in Chapter 4, will address all of these goals and lay out processes and practices to ensure that these goals are met and maintained. Think of your security policy as your first line of defense, because from it should come all the processes and technical systems that protect your business and your customer.

Any security measures you implement without a policy become de facto policies. A policy created that way was probably created without much forethought. The problem with unwritten policies is that you can't look them up, and you don't know where to write the changes.

## Planning with Security in Mind

Building the foundation from a secure starting point is very important. For this reason, the three principles have to be applied to the process from the beginning stages of planning. Examine the business plan and apply the aspects of confidentiality, integrity, and availability. Ask your staff and yourself questions such as:

- How are we going to ensure the confidentiality of our customers?
- How will we protect our business information from disclosure?
- What steps are we taking to double-check the integrity of our data gathering?
- What processes are we using to ensure that our data maintains integrity over time?
- How are we protecting ourselves against the loss of availability?
- What are our plans for failure events?

As the business plans begin to take shape, apply the three principles to them. Keep the principles involved continually as the planning evolves, and you will find that your questions give birth to scenarios, and those scenarios lead to solutions.

Spend time thinking about the threats to your site. Profile the flow of likely attacks and determine the probable ease of their success. For example, if an attacker wanted to gather customer financial information, could he or she simply compromise your Web server and gain access to it? There have been countless examples of situations exactly like this one, where what should have been a simple Web server compromise ended up exposing sensitive customer data to the attackers. Had those credit card numbers and other information been stored on a separate machine, or better yet, on a more protected network segment, the attacker may not have been able to harvest it. Avoid single points of failure. Ensure that compromise of one network component does not jeopardize your entire operation. Apply these scenarios to each step of the plans and revise them until you have resolved the apparent issues.

An example scenario for this process might include something like this: If an attacker used the latest exploit of the week to gain access to your Web server, what other systems could be easily compromised? In a recent, all too real example, a client called me when this had happened. The attacker had used the Unicode exploit (See Rain Forest Puppy's page at www.wiretrip.net/rfp/p/doc.asp?id=57&iface=6 for more details on Unicode.) against my client's Web server to gain access to the file system. After uploading a Trojan horse program, they quickly managed to grab the Repair password file and crack Administrator access to the system. Unfortunately, for my client, the attacker had compromised the system that they had designated to be the Domain Controller for all the Web server systems in the DMZ. They had chosen, unwisely, to deploy a Windows Domain for easier systems management of the Web servers and the server they used to allow vendors to pickup orders from their site. Also members of the same domain used their primary e-mail server and their ftp server. Each of these systems was, in turn, compromised by the attacker. By the time the damage had been discovered, each of these systems had to be removed from service and completely rebuilt. Their partners were advised of the damage, and they lost valuable time and money, not to mention confidence in their company by their partners. To date, that single mistake of making each of the systems a member of a Windows Domain instead of stand-alone servers has cost them thousands of dollars and several IT managers their jobs. Even small miscalculations can have large ramifications on security.

Understand that for every scenario and threat that you think of, dozens of others may exist or may come to exist in the future. Don't be alarmed if you feel like you have only thought of the most basic threats. This very act of preparation and scenario development will create large amounts of awareness to the issues encompassed in the three principles. In addition, your team's ability to handle security incidents down the road will be increased as you become more familiar with details of your business process.

At the end of this process, you should have some basic plans for your site. One of the best ways to organize this planned information is in a chart that details your risks and how you plan to mitigate them. An example is shown in Table 1.1. These examples are basic, and you should certainly have many more than this, but it is a start to give you the idea of a framework.

**Table 1.1** Sample Risk Mitigation Chart

| Phase of E-commerce Process | Explanation of the Risk | Strategy for Risk Mitigation |
|---|---|---|
| Consumer Check-out | An attacker could monitor the transmission of the credit card and consumer data. | We will use SSL encryption to protect the information as it travels across the Internet. |
| Credit Card Data Transfer to the ISP Credit Systems | An attacker could monitor our credit card batch file when we transfer it to the ISP credit card system each hour for processing. | We will use SecureFTP to send the data down an SSH tunnel to prevent sniffing attacks. |
| Any Phase | An attacker could compromise our database server that we use to store our client's personal information and purchase history. | We will protect the server by removing all unneeded services and installing a file system checksum program to alert us to changes. We will also locate the server in separate DMZ segment and only allow encrypted transfer through a SQL proxy to interact with the system. |
| Any Phase | An attacker could seek to shut us down by flooding our network. | We will protect ourselves by using redundant servers and a load balancing router. We will also be prepared to implement traffic blocking access control rules on the ISP router by calling their help desk line. |

# Security during the Development Phase

The steps involved in translating the plans established into actual products and processes can be very dangerous to the security principles. Often, compromises must be made to facilitate budgets, timeframes, and technical requirements. Many times, these compromises impact the overall security of a project.

The single best way to ensure that the underlying security of the project remains intact through the development phase is through continual involvement. As each process or product is defined, apply the three principles to it and revise the definition to answer the scenarios you created in the planning process. If compromises must be made that impact the security of the project, carefully profile those changes and create a list of the risks involved in them. This list of risks will become important in the implementation phase, as it gives you a worksheet for problems that must be mitigated through the combination of technology, policy, and awareness. Often, compromises in key areas will have a major impact on attempts to secure other dependent areas. Be sure that attempts to save a dollar when building an underlying component doesn't cost you ten in trying to patch the pieces sitting on top.

Each process and product must be carefully examined to define the various risk factors involved. Attention to detail is highly important in this step, as is the cross-examination of a process or product by the various team members. Each of the team members will have his or her area of concern, and thus will bring a different angle of examination to the table. This cross-examination, or "peer review," often creates stronger designs and more secure solutions. In fact, peer review can be a very helpful tool in your policy creation tool box as well. The whole concept is to pass each policy or development process by each team member allowing each to comment on the process or policy from their point of view. At the end, someone, usually the original author, edits all the commentary back into the policy or process to create a better end product. Peer review is often done across the board for policies, technical information, and new processes before they are released to the general public.

After each of the processes has been defined and developed, reconvene the examination team to review the complete procedure from beginning to end. Many times, during the combination of the various discreet processes into the overall product, security holes are created inadvertently through the communication and storage of information. Two components may not be insecure on their own, but can create a hole when they interact. An example might be two e-commerce systems that both store their information in encrypted databases but interact with each other, moving that same information over an unencrypted link. In this example, the vulnerability is not in the database servers, but in the method used to communicate with each other. Examine these types of scenarios carefully. Again, revise the processes as required, or note the accepted risks for mitigation during the implementation phase.

# Implementing Secure Solutions

The most important thing to remember as your business moves into the implementation phase is to only bring systems online *after* they have been thoroughly tested and established as being secure. The largest danger faced in this phase is that the systems will be rushed into operation before they have been thoroughly evaluated. Securing your systems after they have been brought online could leave you vulnerable for long enough to allow an attacker to plant a backdoor for later attack, or to compromise the system at that time. Securing an already compromised setup is not only futile, it is often very difficult to detect. The moral of the story is: Don't bring it online until you know it is ready for the world.

The evaluation of your systems involves using the tools and processes outlined in Chapter 8. Mainly, the process is to test your actual implementation against the three principles. Automated tools are used to examine each component and to determine the risks and weaknesses associated with them. Vulnerabilities may have been created through misconfigurations, last-minute technical revisions, or unforeseen issues with a software program or hardware device. Repair of these vulnerabilities may include applying patches, reengineering processes or network segments, or other changes. It is very important to evaluate each of these modifications in regard to the surrounding security and to reevaluate the systems from scratch once they have been applied.

Once you have successfully secured your environment and processes down to the level of your accepted risks, it is time to mitigate those issues through a combination of technology, policy, and awareness. Begin by using your list of accepted risks to create a policy to deal with them. Security policies are the backbone of your system of defense. These policies act as the basis for determining actions, system configurations, and the types of devices you will use to secure your network. They should be generated by your security staff, in conjunction with team members from Human Resources, your legal team, and the group that is developing and implementing your site. Involving these other teams in the policy creation will establish not only a sense of trust, but also a more open policy. It is easy to establish a restrictive, draconian security policy, but very difficult to create one that balances corporate, technical, and legal factors while still allowing the business to perform its needed functions.

Ensure that all of these issues are added to your security policy, and then implement technical systems to enforce those policies in real time. Systems such as firewalls, intrusion detection systems, and monitoring tools can be used to mitigate the risks you have accepted as an inherent part of your process.

Once you have mitigated your risks, you can begin to bring your systems online and offer access to the public. Many sites choose to roll out their systems in phases of deployment, while others release the entire site at once. Making this selection depends on your site and the level of staffing resources you have to handle situations as they arise. Remain attentive as the site begins to become popular. Carefully watch your processes and continue to evaluate your performance against the three principles. Remember, security is a journey and not a destination.

## Managing and Maintaining Systems in a Secure Environment

One of the most complicated issues surrounding an e-commerce site is the secure management and maintenance of the systems involved. Software systems require periodic patching as programmers repair security and functional problems. Hardware devices may require patches as well as physical maintenance. Log files have to be monitored, backups have to be performed, and the systems have to be administered for day-to-day operation. In addition, all of these events are expected to occur without compromising security or impacting the operation of the business.

In the pre-Internet days, data systems had scheduled outage times to handle maintenance and administration issues. However, in today's 24-hour consumer environment of the online world, sites must be available at all times to consumers or they will simply take their business elsewhere. Thus today, system operators and e-commerce businesses must strive for zero downtime and lower impact on the site to perform these management functions. This is made possible by hardware that is more powerful, faster networks, and redundancy for mission-critical systems.

Damage & Defense…

## Providing Mirrored Implementations for Administrators

Zero downtime is nearly impossible without creating a near duplicate environment for your system administrators to test their patches, fixes, modifications, and ideas. Ideally, this mirrored environment should be exactly like your production site. The smaller the variances between the test setup and the real site, the smaller the chance for problems or unpredicted behavior. While expense is often a factor in building such a mirrored lab, the long-term benefits are usually significant.

Mirroring your site or creating a test bed does not have to be cost prohibitive. If you cannot exactly duplicate your existing production systems, come as close as your budget will allow. At a minimum, allow your staff to create a test network segment with several systems that have swappable hard drives to allow them to be configured in a multitude of ways. With some imagination, using flexible hardware, you will find that you can simulate many varying environments.

Continued

I had the experience of assisting a client using Windows NT after they had neglected to use a test bed before applying a service pack. They had applied the service pack to a server upon which they had used Partition Magic to grow the main partition to larger than the Windows Disk Manager would allow. Everything worked fine before the service pack, but afterward the system would not boot. What had happened was this: Partition Manager had made the drive so large that the newer versions of the Windows NT software could not access them correctly and thus could not locate the kernel files for NT. While the solution in this case was simply to resize the partition back to less than the minimum, it also required moving data to the new extended partitions and reconfiguring several applications. The downtime for this system exceeded two hours, which was a costly timeframe for the company. However, they did learn an expensive lesson.

Patches and upgrades often have unexpected effects. Using a test bed or mirror site allows you to carefully test the process and the behavior of all modifications before you apply them to your real site.

Day-to-day management is mainly performed through automated processes on systems remote from the mission-critical systems to take advantage of speed and to reduce the danger of human error. Secure tunnels transfer log files and other monitoring information across our networks to prevent unauthorized observance and discovery. Devices communicate events back to common monitoring stations via communications bursts to alert operators and administrators that events have occurred or that they need attention. Administrators may then remotely access the systems across these secure tunnels or by physically visiting the machines if required.

Keep in mind that while the process of managing these machines seems largely automated, it still has inherent risks. Software packages require continual patching as vulnerabilities are discovered and repaired. Each of these patches could cause unexpected behavior in your environment. Vendors do test their patches, but the complexities and individualization of today's Internet sites make it impossible for them to test their software for every circumstance. In addition, the slightest change to your network components could also have a vast impact on the security of your site. As administrators change out equipment for maintenance or replace components or applications with new revisions. they may accidentally introduce misconfigurations or other weaknesses into your site.

The method used to avoid these issues is to continually evaluate your site against your known baselines. If new vulnerabilities or risks appear, changes may have been made. These changes may be the result of new vulnerabilities that have been discovered or the result of changes made to components. Either way, these vulnerabilities must be immediately mitigated through repair or by managing them through your combination of technology, policy, and awareness. The only way to ensure the long-term security of your site is to continually assess it, revise it, and implement the changes required to mitigate your risks. To help you maintain the process, the flow chart shown in Figure 1.2 can be used as a reference.

**Figure 1.2** Continuous Evaluation Process

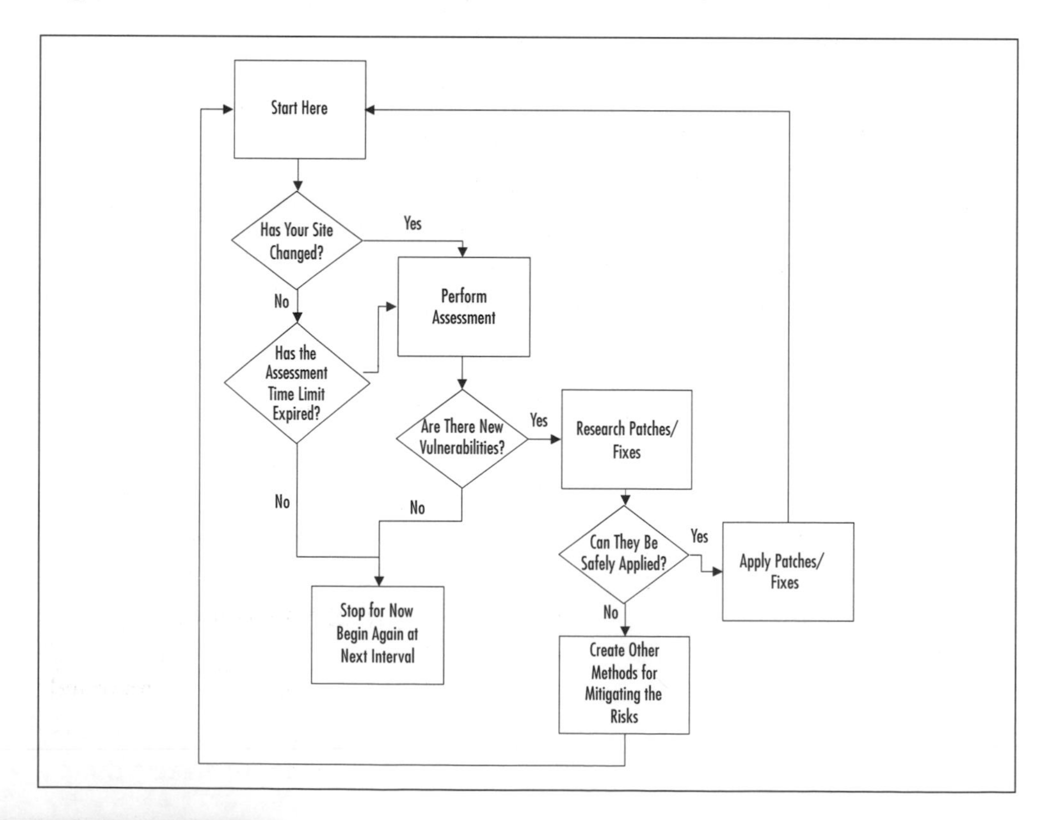

Tools & Traps...

## Sources to Learn The Basics

Security is a field that is both wide and deep. There are a lot of bases to cover when you are first getting started and a lot of places to look for good security information. Here is a list of some basic sites, mailing lists, and magazines that you might want to visit to widen your horizons or learn the ropes.

- **www.securityfocus.com** Site for general security news, also the host of Bugtraq, the world famous announcement mailing list for new vulnerabilities. SecurityFocus also has a very useful vulnerability database.
- **www.securityportal.com** Another great site for keeping up to date on security happenings. They also have excellent articles for beginners that cover the basics of security and hacking.
- **www.atstake.com/security_news/** Security news from the hacker's point of view.
- **http://phrack.infonexus.com** The immortal Phrack online Zine, which has years and years of hacker history, techniques, and insight. Read them all and learn to see inside the mind of your adversary.
- **www.defcon.org** The largest gathering of hackers in the world happens yearly in Las Vegas. Keep up to date on this site or better yet come and out and meet face to face with real, live hackers.
- **www.sans.org** The SANS page details training that is available to security professionals and gives insight into the status of threats from around the online world.

Continued

- **http://packetstorm.securify.com** The most popular site for hacker tools, toys, and exploits. The tools can come in handy for administrators and security professionals, but use caution.
- **www.astalavista.com** Search engine entrance to the underground. This is a very loosely organized search engine for finding hacking tools, exploits, and pirated programs (*warez*) from around the Web. Again, use your discoveries with caution because some of these programs may be more Trojan horse than useful utility.

# Applying Principles to Existing Sites

While it is optimal to begin the e-commerce process with security in mind, it is possible to apply the three principles of confidentiality, integrity, and availability to already operational sites as well. In fact, since much of the site development work is done, these sites are often able to apply greater time, effort, and money to securing their environment.

The process of applying the three principles to existing sites differs a bit from new sites, but many of the concepts are the same. Obviously, the principles themselves don't change, nor does the cycle of continuous security assessment. However, what does change is where and when these tools begin to be applied. For example, beginning the assessment process on your existing site could damage your production systems, so most sites begin by testing their development environment or a mirror of their production environment created just for the purpose of testing. They then begin to apply the revisions and patches to these test systems, giving them time to examine the impact before making these changes to the production site. Always remember, though, that security fixes are a race against the clock as attackers may be probing for those vulnerabilities while you are testing the fixes. The major effort here is to limit the size of this window of opportunity without causing damage to your site.

# It All Starts with Risk

Whether you choose to start with your test environment or take the risks of auditing your production site, the beginning point for applying the principles is to identify risks. The same tools from Chapter 8 are again used to perform an audit of your processes and applications to determine what vulnerabilities and risks already exist. Each of these risks must then be examined, and your site either fixed or revised to provide mitigation.

Depending on the complexity, nature, and size of your site, you may discover a few vulnerabilities, or thousands. Checkout www.cve.mitre.org for a dictionary of known vulnerabilities. Each of these vulnerabilities may vary in its significance, from allowing an attacker to gain information about your network to allowing someone complete access to your most critical systems at the highest level. The tools used to perform the audit should explain, in detail, the risks associated with each vulnerability. Keep in mind that in some circumstances, minor and medium vulnerabilities could be used to create major problems within your site, and could even be used to create denial of service (DoS) conditions.

Tools & Traps...

## Vulnerability Chaining

Vulnerability chaining is the name given to a situation in which certain vulnerabilities become more significant when combined with other vulnerabilities. An example of this is the classic echo/chargen attack.

Echo is a service that runs on most UNIX systems by default. Its behavior is just as expected: characters sent to the echo port are simply echoed back. Chargen is also a basic UNIX service and it simply generates characters continuously upon connection to its port. While the existence of either of these services alone poses little risk, together they can be used to cause a simple denial of service attack.

Continued

To perform the assault, the attacker spoofs a conversation between the two services and redirects the output of each service to the other, creating a rapidly expanding spiral of traffic. Essentially, the system begins to consume memory and processor power, eventually causing the whole device to become non-responsive to user commands.

By chaining together two minimal vulnerabilities, the attacker creates a serious issue for the target system. Many combinations such as this exist. Your vulnerability scanner should consider these situations when assigning levels of risk to a vulnerability.

## Fix the Highest Risks First

Once you have the report of your vulnerabilities and have examined the impact of the findings on your environment, begin to put the actions required for fixing them into order based on the levels of risk.

How do you know the level of risk for each vulnerability? Easy. Relate the risks to the real assets that your need to protect. By taking the time to identify company assets, the risk evaluation process gets much easier. Spend time thinking about your company and the business it does. What assets does the company hold that are valuable to it? Where are those resources located and how are they protected? Use the peer review process to create a detailed list of these assets and then relate the risks to that list. If any risk has even a remote possibility of compromising those assets then that risk gains the highest priority. Multiples of conditions that must be met to impact an asset gains the risk a medium level, while the lowest risk are those that have little impact on any critical asset. Again, use peer review to ensure that you have an accurate view of the priorities for the risks you have developed.

Fix those vulnerabilities with the highest risk first. Often, it is a good idea to mitigate these risks through additional means (such as by blocking the appropriate ports at the firewall or at border routers) while your staff works toward implementing the patches and modifications. In general, ensure that each and every process or application running on your production systems is up to the highest and most current patch levels and versions. Pay special attention to the popular services such as DNS, HTTP, SMTP, SNMP, FTP, POP, IMAP, and security-related applications such as firewalls or intrusion detection programs.

By repairing the highest risks first, you help your site to protect its mission-critical information and systems. When creating the priority of vulnerabilities, always remember to take into consideration other mitigation strategies and the criticality of the systems impacted and their data. In other words, if the audit tool reports a high risk vulnerability on a system that is not mission critical or that handles no mission critical data and/or is adequately protected by a firewall, it may fall in priority when compared to a vulnerability that allows an attacker access to a database that holds customer information for a short time during gathering and initial processing, but is accessible from the public Internet. For this reason, information from the audit tools must be parsed by comparing the actual impact to your environment.

After you have parsed and prioritized your work, begin the process of applying the fixes and revisions to your environment. Remember to allow sufficient time, traffic, and use to measure the impact of the changes before replicating them into your production environment. Then proceed through your list, applying the changes to the various affected systems. When you have finished and documented your work, then begin the process again to ensure that your modifications have not created new issues.

## Management and Maintenance during the Patching Process

The primary reason to test the modifications required to mitigate your risks is because of the unpredictability of computer programs and systems. Many times, the software or hardware fixes issued by a vendor or programmer affect the operation of those systems at a very deep level. In fact, the changes required may affect the very core processes or routines of the system. Because of this, these changes may actually create additional security risks or cause the system to perform in a new way.

Many examples have come to light in which software patches created by vendors to fix vulnerabilities have failed to solve the issue, resolved the problem incompletely, or created additional security problems. Discussions of these issues have found their way into many public forums such as Bugtraq and Usenet. The moral of the story here is that each patch really does need to be evaluated, and each system will require testing after applying the fixes. Failure to follow that model could result in disaster!

## Impact of Patching on Production Systems

Applying patches to your production systems does not have to be a major risk. The solution is to create an environment that mirrors your production site and test the fixes there first. However, in some cases, a vulnerability may be so dangerous as to require immediate action or risk damage to your customers and your business. In this case, it may be necessary to apply patches directly to your production systems—do so only if there is no alternative. If at all possible, at least test the installation procedure on a staging machine, which normally only takes a short amount of time.

In such times when you must patch your production systems without adequate testing of the fix, here are some steps to help you manage some of the risks you face:

1. First, before applying the patch, make a complete backup of the entire system.
2. Also before applying the patch, use cryptographic signatures or hash totals to validate the true authenticity of the patch code. Trojan horse patches are not unheard of.
3. After applying the patch, carefully monitor the CPU usage, memory statistics, and general operation of the server for a period of no less than one week. This will give the system time to experience variances of traffic and use that may exist.
4. Immediately after applying the patch, begin a complete automated scan of the system for new vulnerabilities or unexpected behaviors (remember to monitor the statistics above during the scan).

5. If the patch does not perform as expected, or the software behavior changes in a way that causes you concern, reload the backup data from step 1. Research the patch and test the process again before your next attempt.

If at any time you feel the system is behaving in an unexpected way or if the patch does not resolve the security problem immediately, stop and contact the vendor or programmer for support with the issues.

## The Never-Ending Cycle of Change

One thing is for sure: patches and security vulnerabilities are here to stay. As our systems and software programs grow in useful features and bells and whistles, they also grow in complexity. With so many lines of code and so many programmers working on the products today, bugs and vulnerabilities are a surety. As vendors and programmers scramble to respond to the security issues as they are discovered, there is more and more pressure on them to release patches in a shorter amount of time. Some vendors respond by publishing fixes that are not completely tested or that simply hide the problem instead of solving it.

While you can never be totally sure of the impact of a patch or modification, you can hedge your bet by implementing proper controls on the patching process. Steps such as creating a mirrored test network, authenticating the origins of a patch before installing it, and creating good communications channels with your vendors and staff members will take you a long way toward safety.

A large multi-national financial institution was in the process of upgrading their worldwide firewall infrastructure to a different product. Taking stability as a priority they decided to implement the most mature, but not most current, version of the firewall. During the global rollout a new and unexpected vulnerability was discovered, effectively exposing the institution to risk. The question now, was whether to halt the current upgrade cycle and patch the newly installed firewalls or to continue the implementation and instigate a patching regime after deployment. Before the deployment had even completed, a change cycle was required!

By assessing the risks and applying the basic security principles the company arrived at the conclusion that their best option was to complete the deployment and patch the deployed firewalls after completion. This decision turned out to be the right one, due in no small part to the fact that they understood how to patch their infrastructure and their levels of exposure.

## Developing a Migration Plan

Have a plan for performing these patches and modifications on your systems. Put into effect a framework for testing the patches, and create rules for what testing must be done before implementing the changes on your production systems. Such policies are called migration plans.

Migration plans also begin with risks, just like an assessment. The plan outlines which systems and components at your site are considered mission critical, and defines the systems that fit into lesser categories as well. The migration plan is used by to determine when a vulnerability is of the most urgent nature or when it resides lower in the queue. From there, the plan illustrates how the administrators should handle patches and modifications to each category of system. It defines the steps to be followed for authenticating a patch and backing up a system, as well as the testing required for a patch to be approved for implementation on the production site. It may also require peer review of the patched system, or documentation of the changes for archival by a systems management group. The migration plan is simply the administrator's guide to making changes in your organization.

Many frameworks for migration plans exist online today and can be used as templates for customizing the processes to your site. Microsoft offers some basic templates for use with their products to develop and publish migration plans. The Microsoft tools are available at www.microsoft.com/technet/iis/enfortem.asp. Using a search engine such as Google (www.google.com), it is easy to search for specific migration planning tools for your environment. Other resources include books on the subject and software packages that create the plans for you through interview style or electronic templates. Many sites include their migration plan in their security policies or their general employment policies as well. However you care to publish it, be sure that it exists and that your staff is following it.

# How to Justify a Security Budget

The most common problem with implementing security in any organization is finding the budget to get the people, tools, and time to perform the process. Security staff members are generally well compensated. Security tools and products are often expensive. In many organizations, the time required to apply security to processes is considered prohibitive. When security measures are working correctly, management generally doesn't have to worry about them. In the "New Economy," being first to market or timely in delivery is often more profitable in the short term than being secure. With all of these obstacles, how can you justify the budget you need to bring and maintain security at your site?

Over the years, several methods have been tried. Some have succeeded and many have failed. In many cases, what ultimately brings the security budget is an attacker. In most organizations, the knee-jerk reaction to a security incident is to throw money at the problem. This, however, is the wrong model to follow. The primary issue is that damage has usually already been done in one form or another, and the event may very well be a devastating one that causes a major loss of consumer confidence and thus an immense amount of financial damage.

The better solution is to use one of the strategies described in the next sections; these strategies build awareness of the security issues and make a case for the continued existence of information security in your organization, although they both can have negative possibilities. Let's call the first one the *yardstick approach*, and the second one the *fear tactic approach*.

## The Yardstick Approach

I have had the most success with this one. In this tactic, we use security and risk as yardsticks to measure the gains that security measures have made for the organization. Basically, we try to convert the security processes we have already created into a dollar amount versus the dollar amount of the damage that we might have faced should we have accepted those risks without mitigation. Dollar amounts seem to work the best, although I have also tried labor hours and other units of measure.

The first step in this process is to create a realistic risk profile for your site. Do this by examining the traffic flowing into your site from the Internet. One common method is to deploy an intrusion detection system outside of your firewall and use that to create baselines of the scans, probes, and attacks that you are seeing on a weekly basis. Extrapolate the data and calculate those figures into whatever timeframe you wish to use.

Next, review the attacks seen by the intrusion detection system (IDS) and estimate the amount of damage those attacks might have been able to do to the organization should they have been successful. Remember that IDSs are like virus scanners; they must be updated frequently to be effective. The easiest way to estimate the damage is to estimate the time required to rebuild the devices in the event of a compromise. If the device attacked is a mission-critical device or handles sensitive data, make a special note of that to use as collateral damages. You may be amazed to discover the amount of attacks that are actually going on. I have seen sites being probed several times a minute!

Lastly, throw into this mix the actual numbers estimated from any security incidents or damages that your site may have experienced in the last year or so. These numbers have extra leverage because your management is probably already painfully aware of the events and the damages that have been suffered. For these situations, show the processes that you have either implemented or plan to implement to mitigate these risks from reoccurring. Use real numbers instead of estimates where possible.

Now take these figures and chart them against your existing security budget. Develop the details into a full presentation and get in front of your upper management to explain them. If your numbers turn out as most do, you will be able to demonstrate that there is vast savings being generated through the risk mitigation steps that you have already taken. Don't forget to explain the probable damage from exposure of mission-critical systems or data to attack. Plot out worse-case scenarios and mention them, but don't be too strong with them. Your strategy here is to simply make a business case for your budget, not to cause fear or doubt. Figure 1.3 is an example of such a chart.

**Figure 1.3** A Security Budget Yardstick Slide from PowerPoint

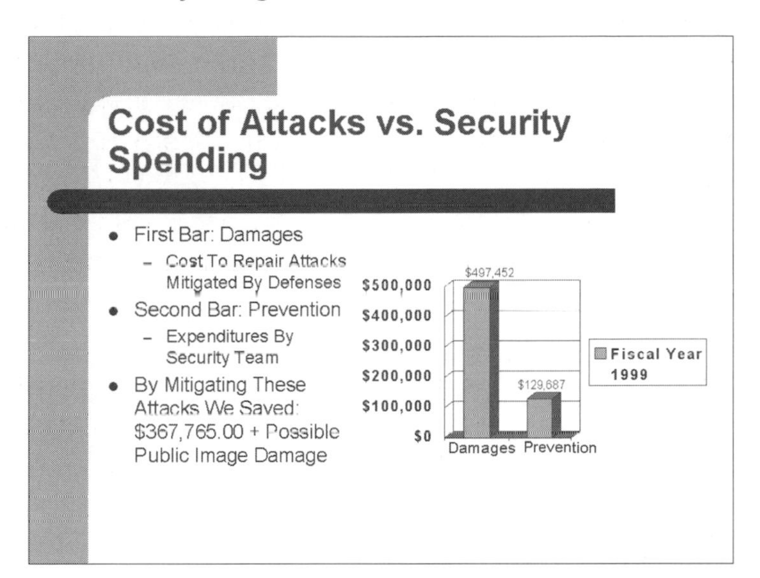


Using this method to build a business case for a security budget has worked in many companies of various sizes and markets. By appealing to the financial processes of the organization with clear, concise, and factual information, we bring a better view of the security situation to light, and we do so without causing fear and doubt, which can sometimes backfire on the security team.

## A Yardstick Approach Case Study

I once used the yardstick approach to assist in growing the security budget of a client with whom I was working. The client was a network facility for a major university and they were experiencing large numbers of attacks on a continual basis. They had deployed some basic security measures to protect the student, faculty, and business information of the school, but wanted additional funding to grow the security staff and build some protection systems for a new business-partnered research facility that they were building.

They already had a basic firewall and some internal IDS systems deployed in their organization, and these tools were mitigating most of the attacks. The only incidents they had experienced had been a compromise of a departmental e-mail system and a simple Web page defacement of a Web server in their demilitarized zone (DMZ) segment.

I followed the process of deploying an IDS outside of their firewall and discovered several interesting things:

- They were experiencing scans and probes on an average of one attack every half-hour.
- A UNIX system in their DMZ had been compromised and was being used as a distribution site for pirated software.
- Their internal routers and firewall were misconfigured and were passing nonroutable Internet Protocol (IP) addresses to the public Internet.

While the last item is simply a matter of network nicety, they were giving away the address schemes used behind the firewall. The real value, however, was the frequency of the detected attacks and the fact that they had a compromise in progress that could have caused a large amount of bad publicity and embarrassment to the school and its staff members.

We used the same formulas mentioned previously and estimated that attacks to the school would have cost the university in the neighborhood of half a million dollars in lost time and labor costs in the last year. We balanced this against the approximate costs of the firewall and the internal protection systems combined with the salary wages, taxes, and benefits for a total of approximately $130,000 over the last year. We created a short presentation from these figures and delivered it at the next budget meeting. The outcome was amazing. The university nearly doubled the security budget for the following year and provided for two additional team members to be hired. It was a complete victory.

## Possible Results of Failure

Not all of the attempts to use the yardstick approach have been successful. There are times when the approach has caused management to perceive that the security team had been less than effective. Sometimes the figures show that the security budget outweighs the threat levels and the value of the assets that are being secured. If this is the case, presenting the figures to management may be damaging to your team. You also should revisit the strategies you have used to secure your site, try to determine where the cost factors were too high, and evaluate the costs of keeping those solutions in place over time.

Another side effect of failing with this approach is that it often causes a loss of morale amongst your security team. They may feel devalued or unappreciated by the management team. The best way to combat this situation is to really work hard on building awareness in the coming year. You may need to create a "security evangelist" within your team and send him or her out to build excitement and educate the other members of your company.

Side effects of failure with this strategy are usually pretty easy to manage. They usually have less far reaching effects than the fear tactic approach. In addition, failing with this strategy often leaves room for another try during the following budget cycle, and you may find that you will achieve consistent victories, even after the first year of failure. It seems that this approach makes sense to management staff and that they often respond favorably to it. Consider trying this approach with your site, and use it before you attempt the fear tactic approach.

## The Fear Tactic Approach

The second strategy I have used to justify a security budget is the fear tactic approach. I have come to see this approach as a sometimes-necessary evil. This is a very common approach and it can be a very damaging situation if this strategy fails to convince the management team. In addition, I have seen even successful use of this tactic cause the end of careers for others in some organizations.

The whole point of this tactic is to use fear to raise awareness. Success depends on the reaction of management when confronted with a horrifying scenario or profile—the desired outcome is a knee-jerk reaction of providing resources to make the scenario go away. Occasionally, though, the opposite happens and the management team goes after the messengers, on the grounds that the security team has failed to protect them from these situations.

Even though this tactic raises the level of fear, uncertainty, and doubt in the organization, it is often very successful in raising the level of awareness. Tools such as penetration tests, real-life security incidents, and information warfare scenarios are the basis for this strategy. The bottom line here is to figure out what hurts an organization, and if it is a possibility, either exploit or explain it. The worst-case scenario is often easily understandable in the most basic of terms, and more times than not it will bring about the desired results.

**NOTE**

Use the fear tactic approach only as a last resort or when management will not respond to other methods. The results of the methods used in this approach are often controversial and may cause political damage to the security team if the process is not carefully managed, monitored, and controlled. While tools such as penetration testing and information warfare techniques may seem flashy, they can be dangerous if they are misused or get out of control. Always select qualified teams for this type of activity, create a well-defined scope of work, and maintain regular communication with participants.

## A Fear Tactic Approach Case Study

A few years ago I had a client that had tried many different approaches to raising security awareness in his company. He was a high-level director in the Information Technologies section of a software company, and he reported directly to a vice president. His company was a fast-growing firm, mainly through the acquisition of competing companies. Security had always been an afterthought for their organization, and he feared that things had gotten out of control.

Inside the company, several groups had created their own networks and private connections to the Internet. Additionally, as they acquired new companies, these groups were rapidly connected to the internal networks and allowed to maintain their own connections to the

Internet. Devices were popping up on the company networks at the rate of several systems a day, and they had no control over the deployment and no idea what all was out there. To make matters even worse, they had deployed no internal control methods, many of the employees in the purchased companies were openly hostile, and they were being rushed to market with a new e-commerce product offering. My client felt that things had to change before major damage occurred.

His team had tried, unsuccessfully, to raise awareness using the standard methods. They had created user groups, performed internal evangelism, hosted various security meetings, had outreach seminars for developers, and much more. Finally, as a last resort it was decided that they needed a vulnerability analysis and penetration test to give the company examples of the risks they were facing from the public Internet.

The tests began after all the contracts were finalized and the scoping of the testing was performed and agreed upon. Immediately, risks became vulnerabilities, and within hours, many systems were compromised. A software development group had left their systems unprotected and connected to the Internet. These systems were used as launching points to attack the internal network. Over the next few days, my team compromised many systems and thousands of accounts, finally ending with the capture and compromise of their newly deployed e-commerce systems.

In the weeks that followed, we created reports and gave presentations to many of their management teams and IT staff members. There were a few political situations, but overall management was responsive when confronted with the truth. The security group received their additional funding, and staff members were added as well as supplemented with consultants. Over the next year, the director rebuilt the network, deployed the e-commerce systems in a more secure fashion, and today is well on his way to regaining control and establishing safe management. New systems are no longer added to the network without appropriate migration planning, and connectivity is becoming centrally managed. They have added a complete incident response process and intrusion detection measures. While not all of the uses of this strategy end this successfully, this was one case where things turned out well.

## Possible Results of Failure

The fear tactic approach is not without its drawbacks. As expressed earlier, there are times when using this approach has come back against the security team itself as management ends up feeling that they have not functioned properly and blames them for the current problems. While this is not common, it is certainly a risk when dealing with this strategy.

Political problems often arise from this approach as well. Groups that are exposed as having been vulnerable are often blamed for the damages, or may become difficult to work with in the future. The best way to control this side effect is to continually reinforce that individuals are not to blame, but that the whole process requires change and better control. Extra effort to build relationships with the affected groups and offers of assistance with repair are often helpful as well.

Another problem with fear tactics is that sometimes management responds by creating a rush to "get secure." Often this problem leads to large-scale panic and chaos. The best method to avoid this problem is to create a step-by-step process for implementing the required solutions prior to presenting the results of the testing to the management team. In this way, you can better control the responses and demonstrate that you have a plan for resolving the issues without the need for panic. Careful application of the repair process can bring value to the security team and enhance its image within the company.

Additionally, a fear tactic often leads to a cycle of breaking systems to prove that they are insecure, rather than reaching a point where security operations happen proactively. The greatest danger here is to those systems that the team is not able to prove vulnerable—they may not be repaired despite your knowing that they may be vulnerable by an attacker with the proper skill level or resources. For example, your security team may not have the resources to properly design an exploit for a specific buffer overflow, but attackers may have access to a working tool outside of public knowledge. If you are caught in this cycle, you will need to break out of it by immediately stepping back and using an approach such as the yardstick method discussed earlier. Continuing to feed the "prove it or lose it" cycle only does your team and your organization a disservice.

Even with all the negatives this approach can provide, it is the most common method used for raising awareness in an organization. This often leads management to be distrustful of its results and methodologies, because they have heard similar scenarios many times and they often feel that the security team is crying wolf. If this is the case, you have to be able to demonstrate real-world exercises that lead to serious damage for the site and its clients. You also have to be able to deliver the solutions if they fund them, or you may find yourself polishing your résumé.

# Security as a Restriction

One of the largest challenges facing security teams today is the nature of how they are perceived. In many organizations, the history of the security team is intertwined with the roles of physical security guards. Many of these security teams are seen by their co-workers as little more than Net cops or computer guards. In addition, since the role of the security team members is often to work with the Human Resources team whenever a problem of usage occurs, the other employees of the company sometimes see the security team in a bad light.

These images and perceptions cause damage to the security process. By alienating the other employees, it becomes more difficult for the security team to perform its duties. The team members will receive less and less cooperation and will become unable to properly interface with the other groups.

The reason that this situation develops is that the wrong images are being portrayed to the other employees. The image is that security is a restriction. Often, this situation arises immediately after the implementation of controls or monitoring software is put into place to better manage the use of network resources or performance during business hours. While these technologies are not the cause, they are often seen as being a symptom of a "Big Brother" approach. No one likes to have their privacy violated, so remember to offer similar protections to your staff as you do to your clients. Doing so will let you avoid the dangers of playing "Net cop."

If a user makes a mistake and falls for a social engineering attack, and gives someone his or her password, you want him or her to be able to come tell you about it, and not be afraid of punishment.

# Security as an Enabler

To overcome the restrictive view of security, change the overall image of your team to be seen as enablers. Security as an enabler is best portrayed when the security team takes the role of consultant to the other members of your organization. When security is portrayed in this manner and the proper levels of awareness are in place, you will find that other groups begin to actually include your team in the planning and development stages of their projects.

By assuming a consultant role, your team is able to build rapport with the other groups and become a resource for them on which to depend. Often, the best way to create this situation is to continually work on awareness and use evangelism. Create informal challenges for the other groups that teach security principles (see the "Last Password Standing" sidebar for an example of a fun challenge).

Tools & Traps…

## The Last Password Standing Contest

In order to help a group of users understand the ideals of choosing strong passwords, create this contest for them to take part in:

- Set up a Windows NT Workstation and allow the users to create accounts for themselves and pick their ideas of strong passwords.
- Once your group has chosen their passwords, dump the passwords using L0pht Crack and begin to crack them.

Continued

- L0phtcrack is available from www.securitysoftwaretech.com.
- Award a prize to the last password cracked by the tool during a short seminar about choosing strong passwords.

Several companies have used this approach to create awareness of one of the most basic security problems. The majority of the companies using this approach saw a large improvement in the quality of the passwords being used by their employees. In fact, in one case where the same contest was tried again a year later, they found that the average time to crack the users' passwords had increased to more than double!

The other way that security can be seen as an enabler is by building awareness of how a secure environment can assist your employees with performing their jobs. Explain how tools such as Secure Shell and virtual private networks (VPNs) can allow them to perform their job duties remotely. Demonstrate and explain technical solutions that enable a greater range of services to be performed by your development groups by including secure tunneling and strong authentication. When other teams begin to see security as a flexible tool that creates options for their projects instead of a tight set of rules that they have to follow, you will have created a partnering image for your team.

Portraying your team as being enablers makes it much easier for your team members to perform. Organizations in which these types of partnerships exist between the security team and the other groups often have a much lower rate of incidents and a much higher rate of job satisfaction. Be seen as enablers instead of "Net cops" and you will find much more success in the e-commerce world.

# Summary

Understanding the basic principles of e-commerce security is the first step on your journey toward a sustainable protection of your business. By applying the three principles of security (confidentiality, integrity, and availability) to your e-commerce model, you can begin to understand the impact of different scenarios on your site. Additionally, by adding a system of continual assessment and revisions to your site, you can keep up with the ever-changing conditions of the online world, and even extend the principles to your daily business processes. Finally, by setting clear goals for security and integrating them into the planning, development, and implementation stages of your projects, you can ensure a sustainable security posture. Maintaining that posture over time requires a process for the managing and monitoring of your systems.

The methodology for adding security principles to an *existing* e-commerce site is very similar to the process of starting from the ground up. It begins with risk assessment, and then the setting of priorities for repairing the most critical vulnerabilities and weaknesses in your site; allowing you to bring your security posture to a higher level without impacting the day-to-day operation. Migration policy is used to manage the change process in our production networks and ensure that by adding these risk mitigation and vulnerability repairs, we do not prevent our site from doing business.

One of the most common problems for security teams and their managers is the justification of a budget for security operations. Two often-used strategies for doing this are taking the yardstick approach and by using a fear tactic approach to the justification. In the yardstick approach, information is gathered and presented that defines the costs of vulnerabilities and risks experienced by the organization and how the work done by the security team has saved the company substantial losses and expenditures. The fear tactic approach uses tools such as penetration testing to prove that the organization has vulnerabilities and exposures in the hope that by realizing the risks they face, the company will release budgeted resources to mitigate the risks. Each of these strategies has its positive effects and its drawbacks.

Security can be seen in two primary types of roles in an organization; the role of enabler, or the role of restrictor. In the role of enabler, the security team acts as consultants and works with the entire organization to raise security awareness and to improve the security posture over time. In the role of restrictor, the security team is often seen as a hindrance to the business process. The restrictor role often makes it very difficult to perform security tasks that require working with other teams from your organization. Take steps to always present your team as the security enabler. Build awareness and a sense of trust with your fellow employees.

# Solutions Fast Track

## Security as a Foundation

☑ The primary principles of security are confidentiality, integrity, and availability.

☑ Information is possibly one of the most valuable assets most companies possess; losing it or caring for it negligently could spell disaster and possibly even ruin. The risks to confidentiality do not stop with access to data; credit card details are illegally obtained from Internet facing systems, then used or sold, with alarming frequency.

☑ We assume that the database system we are using will maintain the records of our sales correctly. We believe that our billing system is smart enough to add the items on a customer's bill. Without some form of integrity checking, neither of these situations may be true.

☑ Availability is the lifeblood of any business. In the e-commerce world, where every moment can directly translate to thousands of dollars in sales, even downtimes of less than an hour can do immense financial damage to a company.

☑ Security also entails a three-step process of assessment, revision, and implementation of changes. This continual process of evaluation and feedback is necessary to adapt processes and products to the ever-changing conditions of the online world, as hackers examine existing software and hardware systems and discover new vulnerabilities.

☑ Once you have successfully secured your environment and processes down to the level of your accepted risks, it is time to mitigate those issues through a combination of technology, policy, and awareness. Begin by using your list of accepted risks to create a policy to deal with them. Once you have mitigated your risks, you can begin to bring your systems online and offer access to the public.

## Applying Principles to Existing Sites

☑ The process of applying the three principles of confidentiality, integrity, and availability to existing sites differs a bit from new sites, but many of the concepts are the same. What does change is where and when these tools begin to be applied. For example, beginning the assessment process on your existing site could damage your production systems, so most sites begin by testing their development environment or a mirror of their production environment created just for the purpose of testing.

☑ Fix those vulnerabilities with the highest risk first. Often, it is a good idea to mitigate these risks through additional means (such as by blocking the appropriate ports at the firewall or at border routers) while your staff works toward implementing the patches and modifications. Pay special attention to the popular services such as DNS, HTTP, SMTP, SNMP, FTP, POP, IMAP, and security-related applications such as firewalls or intrusion detection programs.

☑ Migration plans also begin with risks, just like an assessment. The plan outlines which systems and components at your site are considered mission critical and defines the systems that fit into lesser categories as well. The migration plan is used to determine when a vulnerability is of the most urgent nature or when it resides lower in the queue. From there, the plan illustrates how the administrators should handle patches and modifications to each category of system. It defines the steps to be followed for authenticating a patch and backing up a system, as well as the testing required for a patch to be approved for implementation on the production site.

## How to Justify a Security Budget

☑ The yardstick approach uses security and risk as yardsticks to measure the gains that security measures have made for the organization. Try to convert the security processes you have already created into a dollar amount versus the dollar amount of the damage that we might have faced should we have accepted those risks without mitigation (or use other units of measure such as labor hours).

☑ The fear tactic approach raises the level of fear, uncertainty, and doubt in the organization, it is often very successful in raising the level of awareness. Tools such as penetration tests, real-life security incidents, and information warfare scenarios are the basis for this strategy. The bottom line here is to figure out what hurts an organization, and if it is a possibility, either exploit or explain it.

## Security as a Restriction

☑ Perception in a company of security being a restriction arises immediately after the implementation of controls or monitoring software is put into place to better manage the use of network resources or performance during business hours. While these technologies are not the cause, they are often seen as being a symptom of a "Big Brother" approach. These images and perceptions cause damage to the security process.

## Security as an Enabler

☑ To overcome the restrictive view of security, change the overall image of your team to be seen as enablers. Security as an enabler is best portrayed when the security team takes the role of consultant to the other members of your organization. When other teams begin to see security as a flexible tool that creates options for their projects instead of a tight set of rules that they have to follow, you will have created a partnering image for your team and you will find that other groups begin to actually include your team in the planning and development stages of their projects.

# Frequently Asked Questions

The following Frequently Asked Questions, answered by the authors of this book, are designed to both measure your understanding of the concepts presented in this chapter and to assist you with real-life implementation of these concepts. To have your questions about this chapter answered by the author, browse to **www.syngress.com/solutions** and click on the **"Ask the Author"** form.

**Q:** How can I build a better sense of security awareness in my organization? I have tried putting up posters and publishing our policy, but it doesn't seem to be working.

**A:** Education is the primary means for building awareness. You have to spend time educating every member of your organization. From the top line managers, the development teams, and the customer service people—security needs to be on everyone's mind. They need to be aware of your security policy. They need to be aware of the impact that security has on an e-commerce company. Most of all, they need to understand the privacy policies that you extend to your customers. Consider popular methods such as having a security fair or undertaking a contest that teaches security principles. Functions that combine the teaching of security practices with fun activities have a very high success rate of improving awareness in an organization.

**Q:** What kinds of tools do I need to perform the assessments you discuss? Is this something my team should do, or should I hire someone outside my organization to perform them?

**A:** For more details on this, see Chapter 8, but as a minimum you need a vulnerability scanner, network monitoring tools, a packet analyzer, and a familiarity with the system monitoring tools of the operating systems you are using. Internal assessment versus hiring a team is often a complex issue. Using an internal team is great for first looks and initial testing, but hiring a skilled team to assess your site may prevent headaches in the long run. In addition, depending on your area of business, there may be regulations that require you to have an independent assessment performed by an accredited team. Make sure you have carefully read and understand any regulations that may apply to your business. An example of this type of problem is industries dealing with power distribution systems and the like. These systems are considered to be a part of the national infrastructure and require assessment on a periodic basis to meet the regulations placed on them by the U.S. government.

**Q:** Where can I get more information about creating my security policy?

**A:** Chapter 4 of this book explains more about developing a security policy. Other good starting points are the following Web sites: www.sans.org, www.cs.purdue.edu/coast, and csrc.nist.gov.

**Q:** Isn't the fear tactic approach too risky to use as a justification for a budget?

**A:** In some cases, yes. However, I only suggest that you use this approach as a last resort. It tends to leave a bad taste in the mouth of many managers, and it is difficult to use it as a long-term justification. In addition, if you do decide to use this approach, be extra careful about choosing your penetration team. If you are going outside of your company, be sure the proper contracts are in place, and check references for the team before hiring them.

**Q:** I am trying to hire a penetration team, and when I ask for references, they say they can't reveal the names of the people for whom they have worked. What should I do?

**A:** Don't walk away from that group—run away from them. Reputable penetration testing teams will be able to provide you with verifiable references and will have complete contracts, scoping documents, business insurance, and sample reports. If they don't, I suggest you take your business elsewhere.

Chapter 2

# DDoS Attacks: Intent, Tools, and Defense

## Solutions in this chapter:

- What Is a Distributed Denial of Service Attack?
- Why Are E-Commerce Sites Prime Targets for DDoS?
- What Motivates an Attacker to Damage Companies?
- What Are Some of the Tools Attackers Use to Perform DDoS Attacks?
- How Can I Protect My Site against These Types of Attacks?

☑ Summary

☑ Solutions Fast Track

☑ Frequently Asked Questions

# Introduction

Many pundits have described the current era as the information age—the dawn of a bright new future, a time when the barriers to communication have been dismantled, allowing the formation of virtual communities that span the globe. Businesses now have the ability to project their presence beyond the normal confines of geography, enabling them to reach out to a market that years earlier they would have, by necessity, ignored. Recreational users of the Internet share information and experiences almost instantly with people a world away. The application of Internet technology and the associated opportunities seem endless. And that is part of the problem.

With every opportunity comes risk. In the world of the Internet, this risk often materializes in the form of security. The Internet and security are inextricably linked—one should always accompany the other. Security should always be a byword when using the Internet, but some believe the mere use or integration with the Internet eliminates the ability to be secure in the first place.

Security is an evolving field where the good guys always seem to be one step behind the bad. The list of security risks a security officer or administrator may have to contend with reads like a science fiction novel. In a single week, they could be expected to counter threats posed by highly contagious viruses, trojans, worms and even be attacked by zombies. Recently one of the newer additions to the security officers' lexicon of despicable terms was the highly publicized Distributed Denial of Service (DDoS).

The end of 1999 brought to light a scenario that security experts around the globe had predicted but had hoped would not arise. New tools for performing Denial of Service (DoS) attacks on a massive scale were released to the Internet. These new tools were referred to as DDoS tools because of their distributed nature. They allowed an attacker to coordinate attacks against Internet sites from client machines (often called *zombies*) distributed around the world using a single client program. Given enough zombie machines, an attacker could bring any site to its knees.

As the security community scrambled to alert the world to the dangers these tools created, the assaults began. In just a few short days, the foundations of some of the largest Internet sites were rocked by massive coordinated attacks. The conditions that had set the stage for the spate of attacks had been in place for quite some time. Bandwidth had become a commodity, with broadband access offering high-speed Internet connectivity through cable modems and digital subscriber lines (DSL). Most computing communities were blissfully unaware of the dangers they faced. Penetrations began occurring at an alarming rate, leaving behind massive networks of DDoS zombies for later use. In addition, many of the largest sites on the Internet had failed to implement some of the most basic protection mechanisms. This confluence of technological advancement and circumstance allowed a single David to knock down several Goliaths with one powerful stone—DDoS.

# What Is a DDoS Attack?

To understand a DDoS attack and its consequences, we first need to grasp the fundamentals of DoS attacks. The progression from understanding DoS to DDoS is quite elementary, though the distinction between the two is important. Given its name, it should not come as a surprise that a DoS attack is aimed squarely at ensuring that the service a computing infrastructure usually delivers is negatively affected in some way. This type of attack does not involve breaking into the target system. Usually a successful DoS attack reduces the quality of the service delivered by some measurable degree, often to the point where the target infrastructure of the DoS attack cannot deliver a service at all.

A common perception is that the target of a DoS attack is a server, though this is not always the case. The fundamental objective of a DoS attack is to degrade service, whether it be hosted by a single server or delivered by an entire network infrastructure.

**NOTE**

The definition of a hacker and their activities has undergone many changes during the last twenty years. Originally a hacker was synonymous with individuals with a thirst for knowledge and the ability to develop elegant and ingenious pieces of code. They were instrumental in the development of the ideas and technologies that shaped the industry. The modern day understanding of the word hacker has taken a much more sinister turn, encompassing individuals who undertake activities on networks or systems that could be deemed to be detrimental to their owners. Hackers are often segmented into other more specific groups, including black hat or white hat hackers. In plain terms, a *white hat* hacker does not attempt to breach the integrity of computer systems in the pursuit of profit, personal gain, or mischief. *Black hat* hackers, or *crackers*, on the other hand, represent the darker side of the hacker community. For the purposes of this chapter, the term *hacker* will encompass all of these definitions.

## Laying the Groundwork: DoS

Before the DDoS hue and cry rose to almost thunderous proportions, DoS attacks had been tirelessly aimed at networks for some time. DoS attacks are conducted using software written to deliberately cause degradation in the target systems service levels. A number of well-documented types and variants of DoS attacks currently swirl around the backwaters of the Internet. One of the significant problems exacerbating DoS attacks is the number of freely available programs that turn this technical exploit into a task that requires the use of a mouse, a clicking finger, and a trivial amount of grey matter. This simplification can turn an Internet neophyte into a cyber criminal.

A DoS attack attempts to reduce the ability of a site to service clients, be they physical users or logical entities such as other computer systems. This can be achieved by either overloading the ability of the target network or server to handle incoming traffic or by sending network packets that cause target systems and networks to behave unpredictably. Unfortunately for the administrator, unpredictable behavior usually translates into a hung or crashed system.

Numerous forms of DoS attacks exist, some of which can be difficult to detect or deflect. Within weeks or months of the appearance of a new attack, subtle copycat variations along the same theme begin appearing elsewhere. By this stage, not only must defenses be deployed for the primary attack, but also for its more distant cousins.

Many DoS attacks take place across a network, with the perpetrator seeking to take advantage of the lack of integrated security within the current iteration of Internet Protocol (IP), IP version 4 (IPv4). Hackers are fully aware that security considerations have been passed on to higher-level protocols and applications. An attempt to rectify this problem has resulted in IP version 6 (IPv6), which includes a means of validating the source of packets and their integrity by using an authentication header. Although the continuing improvement of IP is critical, it does not resolve today's problems because IPv6 is not in widespread use.

DoS attacks do not only originate from remote systems, but also locally to the machine. Local DoS attacks are generally easier to locate and rectify because the parameters of the problem space are well defined (local to the host). A common example of a local based DoS attack includes fork bombs that repeatedly spawn processes to consume system resources.

Although DoS attacks do not in themselves generate a risk to confidential or sensitive data, they can act as an effective tool to mask other more intrusive activities that could take place simultaneously. Although administrators and security officers are attempting to rectify what they perceive to be the main problem, the real penetration could be happening elsewhere. In the confusion and chaos that accompanies system crashes and integrity breaches, experienced hackers can slip in undetected.

The financial and publicity implications of an effective DoS attack are hard to measure—at best, they are embarrassing and at worst, a death blow. In the world of e-commerce, a customer's allegiance is fleeting. If a site is inaccessible or unresponsive, an alternate virtual shop front is only a few clicks away. Companies reliant on Internet traffic and e-purchases are at particular risk from DoS and DDoS attacks. The Web site is the engine that drives e-commerce, and customers are won or lost on the basis of the site's availability and speed. A hacker, regardless of motive, knows that the real place to hurt an e-business is to affect its Internet presence in some way. Unfortunately, DoS attacks can be an efficient means of achieving this end; the next sections cover two elemental types of DoS attacks: resource consumption attacks (such as SYN flood attacks and amplification attacks) and malformed packet attacks.

## Resource Consumption Attacks

Computing resources are by their very nature finite (though we wish it could be otherwise!). Administrators around the world bemoan the fact that their infrastructure lacks network bandwidth, CPU cycles, RAM, and secondary storage. Invariably the lack of these resources leads to some form of service degradation the computing infrastructure delivers to the clients. The reality of having finite resources is highlighted even further when an attack is orchestrated to consume these precious resources.

The consumption of resources (and in this instance bandwidth is considered to be a resource) involves the reduction of available resources, whatever their nature, by using a directed attack. One of the more common forms of DoS attack targets network bandwidth. In particular, Internet connections and the supporting devices are a prime target of this type of attack due to their limited bandwidth and visibility to the rest of the Internet community. Very few businesses are in the fortunate position where they have too much Internet bandwidth (does such a thing exist?), and when a business relies on the ability to service client requests quickly and efficiently, a bandwidth consumption attack can drive home how effectively that bandwidth can be used to bring the company to its knees.

Resource consumption attacks predominantly originate from outside the local network, but do not rule out the possibility that the attack is from within. These attacks usually take the form of a large number of packets directed at the victim, a technique commonly known as *flooding*.

A target network can also be flooded when an attacker has more available bandwidth then the victim and overwhelms the victim with pure brute force. This situation is less likely to happen on a one-to-one basis if the target is a medium-sized e-commerce site because they will—in most cases—have a larger "pipe" than their attackers. On the other hand, the availability of broadband connectivity has driven high-speed Internet access into the homes of users around the world. This has increased the likelihood of this type of attack as home users replace their analog modems for DSL and cable modem technologies.

Another way of consuming bandwidth is to enlist the aid of loosely configured networks, causing them to send traffic directed at the victim. If enough networks can be duped into this type of behavior, the victim's network can be flooded with relative ease. These types of attacks are often called *amplification attacks*.

Other forms of resource consumption can include the reduction of connections available to legitimate users and the reduction of system resources available to the host operating system itself. Denial of service is a very broad term, and consequently some exploits cross the boundary into DoS attacks due to the circumstances surrounding their manifestation. A classic example of this scenario was the Melissa virus, which proliferated so swiftly that it consumed network resources resulting in a DoS in some cases. In short, a plethora of DoS attacks are available on the Internet, though for the purposes of this chapter we discuss only the more notorious and direct varieties.

## Damage & Defense...

### Configuration Management

One method of instigating a DoS is by altering the configuration of key devices such as routers and servers. Routing tables, registry databases, and UNIX configuration files are just a few of the potential configuration databases that can be used against a business. It goes without saying, then, that all Internet-facing devices should undergo strict change control procedures and that a backup of the last known good configuration should be available on demand.

## Anatomy of a SYN Flood Attack

In September 1996, a DoS attack caused a New York ISP to be unavailable for almost a week. The impact of the outage affected close to 6,000 users and 1,000 companies. The attack leveraged a technical vulnerability in Transmission Control Protocol/Internet Protocol (TCP/IP) that had been known for some time and was one of the first high-profile attacks to exploit SYN flooding.

A *SYN flood attack* achieves its desired impact by manipulating the mechanics of how a TCP connection is initiated. Unlike the User Datagram Protocol (UDP), communication streams established with the TCP protocol are connection-oriented. This means that a session must be established between the source and target computers before data can be exchanged between them. Establishing the session involves a three-way handshake, with each step commencing only when the previous one is complete.

The steps involved in the TCP three-way handshake between two machines (the *client* and *server*) can be described as follows:

1. **A SYN is sent from the client machine to the server.** A SYN (*synchronize*) packet is sent from a port on the client machine to a specific port on the server that is waiting for client connections. An Initial Sequence Number (ISN) is also submitted with the packet. TCP is a reliable protocol and consequently needs a mechanism for recovering from transmission failures and to help with packet reassembly. The ISN helps the recipient to sequence packets correctly.
2. **A SYN/ACK is sent from the server to the client.** The server responds to the client by sending back the client's ISN plus 1. The server's ACK *acknowledges* the clients SYN; the server's SYN indicates to the client that the server is able to establish a session with the client. The SYN sent from the server to the client contains the server's own ISN, which is different than the client's ISN.

3. **An ACK is sent from the client back to the server.** The client responds to the server's SYN/ACK with an ACK containing the server's ISN plus 1. The client and server have now established a TCP connection.

So, during the normal construction of a TCP session, the three-step process is followed, as depicted in Figure 2.1. A SYN flood attack works by starting the TCP handshake by sending a SYN to the target server. The most important difference between this SYN and one originating from a legitimate user is that the source address has been spoofed. A *spoofed* address is an address that has been changed from the original address to another address, usually for malicious or covert purposes. The nature of IPv4 ensures that after a spoofed packet has left the source host and begins to be routed, tracing it back is very difficult, making it a favorite technique employed by hackers.

**Figure 2.1** The Three-Way TCP Handshake

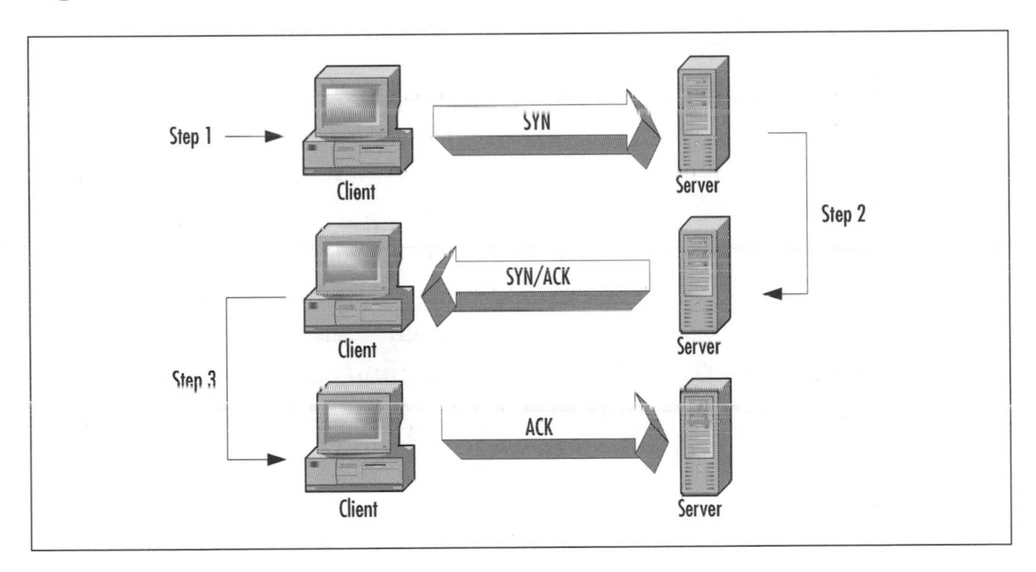


Now, this means that the SYN sent from the hacker's machine during Step 1 of the handshake does not contain his real address as the source of the SYN. The address used in forging the SYN is usually a nonexistent address or a nonroutable address. IP addresses not routable over the Internet include the private IP addresses in the Class A range from 10.0.0.1 to 10.255.255.254, in the Class B range from 172.16.0.1 to 172.31.255.254, and the Class C range from 192.168.0.1 to 192.168.255.254.

The server receiving the spoofed SYN then attempts to respond to the nonexistent address with a SYN/ACK. Due to the (sometimes unreliable) nature of network connections, many implementations of TCP/IP protocol stacks are configured to wait a certain period before assuming that the SYN/ACK will not receive a response. Because the source address included in the initial SYN was forged with a nonexistent address, the server will never receive an ACK in response. In other words, Step 3 in Figure 1.1 never happens in a SYN flood attack. The connection is then left in what can be termed a *half-open state.*

A connection queue is responsible for managing the attempted connections on the server, allowing only a certain number of half-open connections to build up before future attempts to connect to that port are discarded. Only a limited amount of resources are assigned to the number of SYN/ACKs that can be queued at any one time, and the connection queue is quickly exhausted and legitimate users can no longer establish a TCP connection. A successful SYN flood attack ensures that more spoofed SYNs are sent to the server than can be released from the connection queue, effectively causing the connection queue to overflow.

A SYN flood usually involves a number of packets being directed at the target server, consequently overloading the connection buffer. Unfortunately the SYN flood attack can be quite effective, primarily because it can be launched by a hacker with limited resources and has the added advantage of obscuring the source of the attack in the first place.

Other clever twists to the SYN flood attack can include spoofing the source of the SYN in Step 1 with a legitimate routable address. Administrators observing this behavior could then be forced to filter traffic emanating from the spoofed address, even though they are in fact *not* the originator of the attack. That could mean that an administrator may be faced with the task of filtering traffic coming from a branch office, partner, or legitimate user.

## Anatomy of an Amplification Attack

An *amplification attack* achieves its effectiveness by enlisting the aid of other networks that act as amplifiers for the attack. This allows hackers with limited resources to target victims with a considerable increase in resources. The networks used in the amplification attacks are usually oblivious to their part in the whole process. Two examples of amplification attacks are the whimsically named Smurf and Fraggle. Unfortunately, the only innocuous elements to these attacks are their names.

The Smurf attack gained its moniker from a program that leverages this particular attack methodology. A Smurf attack is staged by using a combination of loosely configured networks and the Internet Control Message Protocol (ICMP). As most administrators know, IP was not designed to be reliable and consequently requires a method of providing status and error information. This is where ICMP steps in. ICMP is used for, amongst other things, error control. The ubiquitous **ping** command uses ICMP to determine if a host is alive by sending an ICMP echo request to a host. If the host is up and running a TCP/IP stack, it replies with—not surprisingly—an ICMP echo reply.

A Smurf attack exploits this seemingly simple dialogue by spoofing the source address of the initial ICMP echo request. The first step in the process is for the attacker to place the victim's IP address in the source address field of the ICMP echo requests. The destination of the ICMP echo request can then be any "loosely" configured network that has a router that broadcasts to its subnet, and similarly, hosts that will respond to the echoes on the network broadcast address after they have passed through the router.

This may in itself sound relatively harmless, but a couple of factors exacerbate the problem. First, the attacker sends the ICMP echo not to a specific IP host, but to the broadcast address of the loosely configured network. Sending an ICMP echo request to a broadcast address of a network causes the echo to be processed by every machine on that network.

To illustrate this point, consider a scenario in which fifty hosts are assigned network addresses within the IP range 192.0.1.1 through to 192.0.1.254 and a subnet mask of 255.255.255.0. All machines on this network will respond with an ICMP echo reply, if the following simple command is issued:

```
ping 192.0.1.255
```

The single **ping** command then elicits 50 responses directed at the client deemed to have issued the command. In other words, the original message has been amplified 50-fold!

How does this form of amplification relate to the Smurf attack? The machines on the loosely configured network will then respond to ICMP echoes with an ICMP echo reply directed at the spoofed address. In other words, the victim becomes the recipient of the replies to the ICMP echo. Secondly, the attacker usually ensures that he sends a number of ICMP echoes. The victim then receives ICMP echo replies equivalent to the number of original ICMP echoes sent by the hacker, multiplied by the number of hosts on the broadcast address (see Figure 2.2). If two hundred hosts are on the broadcast address, then the attacker could magnify a single ICMP echo into 200 ICMP echo replies.

**Figure 2.2** A Smurf Attack

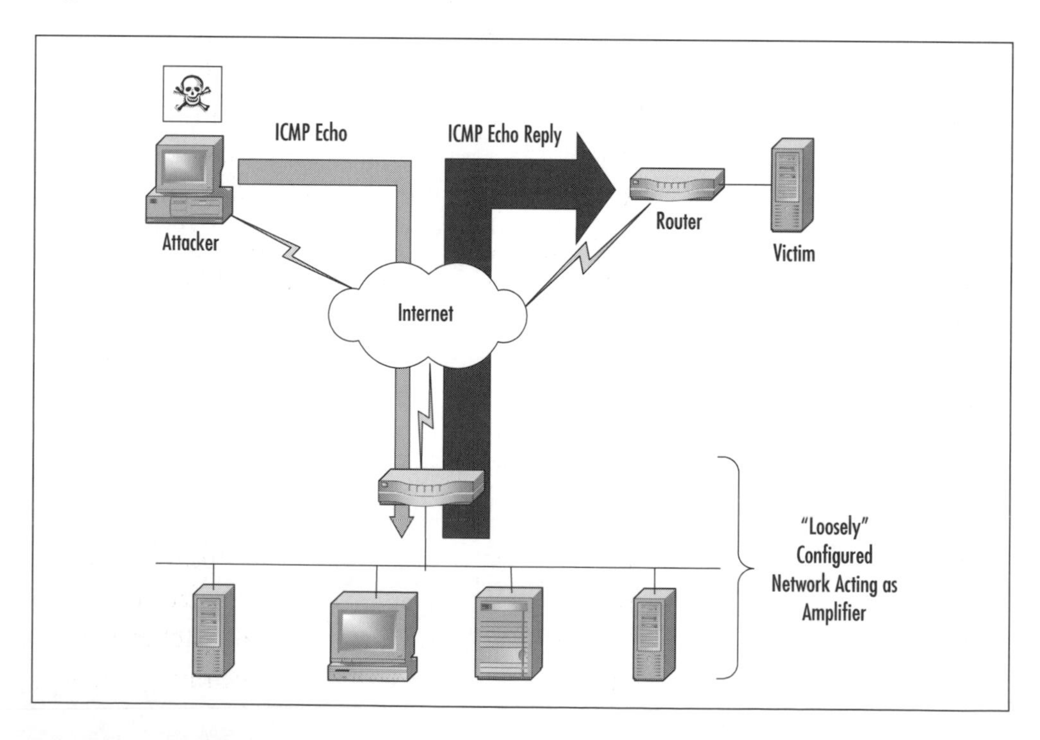

Note that in our example we have simplified the context of the attack by assuming that the hacker has used a single loosely configured network to act as an amplifier; if an attacker uses multiple networks, the traffic generated would be larger and more diverse (thus harder to filter).

The Fraggle attack is a variant to the Smurf, exploiting similar amplification methods by directing UDP packets to network broadcast addresses. Fraggle relies on the largely unused UDP services *chargen* and *echo*. The amplification network used by the Fraggle attack responds to the UDP packets by sending UDP messages to the spoofed address.

A side effect of amplification attacks is that they can affect two victims: the amplifier and the owner of the spoofed address. The network the attacker used to bounce the ICMP echo experiences similar problems as the final victim, such as network congestion, slow response, and possibly a total denial of service.

## Malformed Packet Attacks

Operating Systems (OSs) have a notorious reputation for falling over at the slightest provocation. Considering the variety of uses the modern OS is put to, they perform extremely well. Okay, perhaps just well—even though they are pushed through rigorous testing cycles and patched on a regular basis, they can behave unexpectedly when nonstandard events occur. For the hacker interested in DoS attacks, an unexpected situation hopefully leads to resource contention or a crashed system.

A *malformed packet attack* usually consists of a small number of packets directed at a target server or device. The packets are constructed in such a fashion that on receipt of the packet, the target panics. A *panic* is considered to occur when the device or operating system enters an unstable state potentially resulting in a system crash.

A classic DoS malformed packet attack is the Ping of Death. Most vendors of network hardware and software have been hardened to what was once the scourge of the Internet community. The Ping of Death consists of directing a large ICMP echo at the victim. The ICMP echo can be generated using the **ping** command, but the packet size must exceed 65535 bytes—which is the maximum size of an IP packet—or contain 65507 bytes of data. The ICMP packet is not transmitted "as is" and may be broken up because the underlying transport has a smaller maximum packet size. For example, the maximum packet size for Ethernet is typically 1500 bytes. On reassembly at the target, the ICMP echo overflows the OS buffer (which is not expecting a packet larger than 65535 bytes), causing the machine to crash or become unstable.

**NOTE**

As an exploit, buffer overflows are certainly not new. Part of the success of the Internet Worm that shut down 10 percent of systems attached to the Internet was due to the exploitation of buffer overflows in the finger service. A *buffer* is a continuous portion of memory used to store data of the same type. Many DoS attacks, such as the Ping of Death, attempt to overflow buffers in some way.

A typical **Ping of Death** command could look like this:

```
Ping -l 65515 victims.address.com
```

A number of variations along similar lines to the Ping of Death are in circulation, many of which vendors have supplied fixes for. Included in this list are:

- **Teardrop** This attack exploits a vulnerability during the reassembly of IP packets on target hosts. Large packets are fragmented into smaller packets that need to be reassembled at the target. The fragments include an offset to the beginning of the first packet that enables the entire packet to be reassembled. In the Teardrop attack, the offsets are changed, making it impossible for the target system to reassemble the packet properly. This unexpected situation causes the OS to become unstable.
- **Bonk/Boink** This attack exploits the reassembly of malformed UDP datagrams.
- **Land** This attack sends a malformed packet during the setup of the three-way TCP handshake. The initial SYN is sent to

the target with the victim's address detailed as both source and destination.

- **Malformed RPC** This attack utilizes malformed RPC packets to disable RPC services.

Tools & Traps...

## Physical and Indirect Attacks

DoS attacks come in a variety of subtle and surprising flavors, although most people expect them in the form of some devilishly ingenious method of electronic surprise attack. An often-neglected aspect of securing a site against DoS attacks is ensuring *physical* security. Spending large sums of money protecting digital assets and ensuring quality of service is all fine and well until someone just walks up to your servers and pulls the plug! Not only must the physical security of the servers be considered, but also the cabling and power infrastructures.

Indirect attacks could also become more relevant as DoS attacks attain greater subtlety. Consider a scenario in which a hacker decides to target your business indirectly. A savvy hacker could target the weakest link in your business chain instead of mounting a full frontal assault on the business itself. This could be any of the third parties that supply services or products critical to the continuing delivery of your own service. Examples include power companies, outsourcing partners, and credit and trading partners. An effective strategy against DoS attacks must not take an isolationist perspective—remember, your business depends on more than just itself to survive.

## Anatomy of a DDoS attack

Though some forms of DoS attacks can be amplified by multiple intermediaries, the first step of a DoS exploit still originates from a single machine. DDoS attacks advance the DoS conundrum one more painful step forward. DoS attacks have evolved beyond single-tier (SYN flood) and two-tier (Smurf) attacks. Modern attack methodologies have now embraced the world of distributed multi-tier computing. One of the significant differences in methodology of a DDoS attack is that it consists of two distinct phases. During the first phase, the perpetrator compromises computers scattered across the Internet and installs specialized software on these hosts to aid in the attack. In the second phase, the compromised hosts, referred to as *zombies,* are then instructed through intermediaries (called *masters*) to commence the attack.

Hundreds, possibly thousands, of zombies can be co-opted into the attack by diligent hackers. Using the control software, each of these zombies can then be used to mount its own DoS attack on the target. The cumulative effect of the zombie attack is to overwhelm the victim with either massive amounts of traffic or to exhaust resources such as connection queues.

Additionally, this type of attack obfuscates the source of the original attacker: the commander of the zombie hordes. The multi-tier model of DDoS attacks and their ability to spoof packets and to encrypt communications can make tracking down the real offender a tortuous process.

The command structure supporting a DDoS attack can be quite convoluted (see Figure 2.3), and it can be difficult to determine a terminology that describes it clearly. Perhaps one of the more understandable naming conventions for a DDoS attack structure and the components involved is detailed below.

Software components involved in a DDoS attack include:

- **Client** The control software used by the hacker to launch attacks. The client directs command strings to its subordinate hosts.
- **Daemon** Software programs running on a zombie that receives incoming client command strings and acts on them accordingly.

The daemon is the process responsible for actually implementing the attack detailed in the command strings.

**Figure 2.3** A Generic DDoS Attack Tree

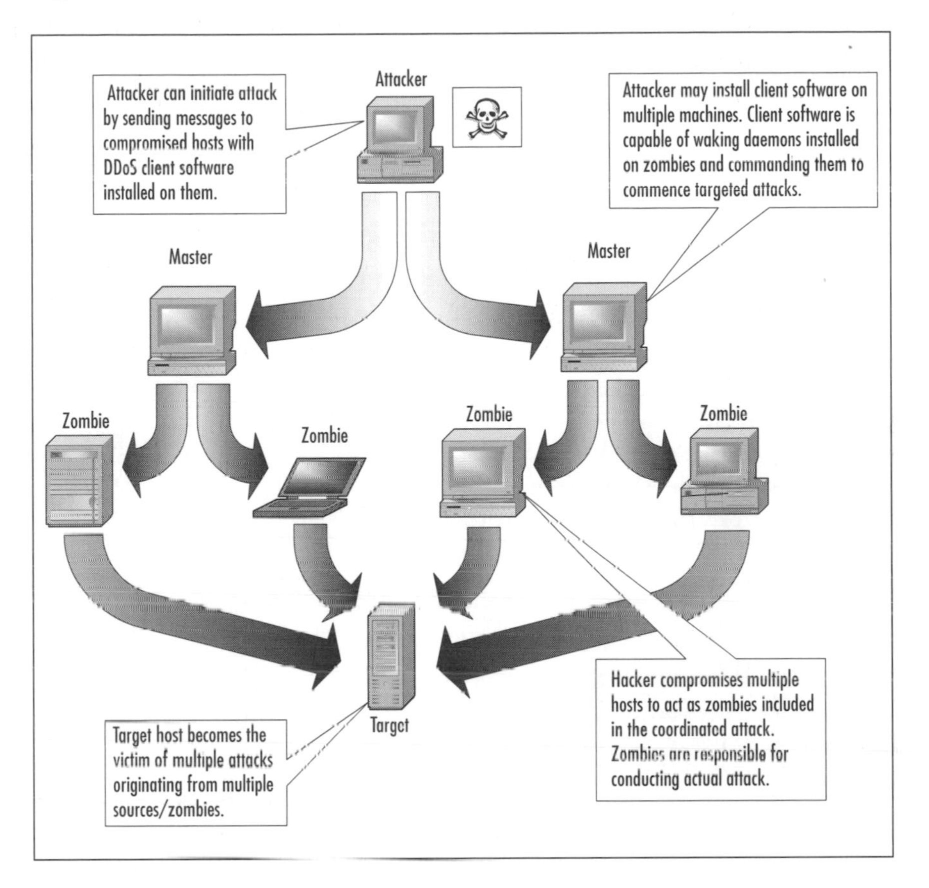


Hosts involved in a DDoS attack include:

- **Master** A computer from which the client software is run.
- **Zombie** A subordinate host that runs the daemon process.
- **Target** The recipient of the attack.

In order to recruit hosts for the attack, hackers target inadequately secured machines connected in some form to the Internet. Hackers use various inspection techniques—both automated and manual—to uncover inadequately secured networks and hosts. Automated trawling for insecure hosts is usually scripted and can, under the correct circumstances, be detected by a company's security infrastructure. Depending on the hackers' level of competence, manual inspection can be harder to identify because the attacker can adapt his approach accordingly, but it is also much more time consuming.

After the insecure machines have been identified, the attacker compromises the systems. Hackers gain access (root, usually) to a host in a startling variety of ways—most of which, quite sadly, are preventable. The first task a thorough hacker undertakes is to erase evidence that the system has been compromised and also to ensure that the compromised host would pass a cursory examination. The tools used to ensure that these tasks will be successful are sometimes collectively called *rootkits.*

Some of the compromised hosts become masters while others are destined for zombification. Masters are installed with a copy of the client software and are used as intermediaries between the attacker and the zombies. Masters receive orders that they then trickle through to the zombies for which they are responsible.

Available network bandwidth is not a priority for hosts designated to be masters. The master is only responsible for sending and receiving short control messages, making lower bandwidth networks just as suitable as higher bandwidth networks.

On the hosts not designated as masters, the hacker installs the software (called a *daemon*) used to send out attack streams and the host graduates to become a zombie. The daemon runs in the background on the zombie, waiting for a message to activate the exploit software and launch an attack targeted at the designated victim. A daemon may be able to launch multiple types of attacks, such as UDP or SYN floods. Combined with the ability to use spoofing, the daemon can prove to be a very flexible and powerful attack tool.

After the attacker has recruited what he deems are a sufficient number of zombies and has identified his victim, the attacker can contact the masters (either via his own methods or with a specially written program supplied with the DDoS program) and instruct them to launch a particular attack. The master then passes on these instructions to multiple zombies who commence the DDoS attack. After the attack network is in place, it can take only a few moments to launch a distributed attack. With similar speed, the hacker can also halt the attack.

The basic flow of the attack then becomes:

**For hosts:** Attacker ➔ Master ➔ Zombie ➔ Target

**For software:** Attacker ➔ Client ➔ Daemon ➔ Target

To provide a context for the possible scale of DDoS attacks, consider the attack mounted on the University of Minnesota by hundreds of zombies that denied network access to thousands of users for three days. In fact, during the writing of this book, Microsoft became next in the line of bemused businesses subjected to successful DDoS attacks.

The use and development of DDoS programs have piqued the interest of governments, businesses, and security experts alike, in no small part because it is a new class of attack that is extremely effective while simultaneously being hard to trace.

# The Attacks of February 2000

In the first weeks of February 2000, a media furor trumpeted the arrival of a new type of Internet attack—DDoS. A number of Internet stalwarts such as Amazon, eBay, CNN, Yahoo! and Buy.com became the first prominent victims of a new type of Internet attack that had degraded, and in some cases, temporarily shut down their Internet presence. Actual data on downtime is sketchy, but reports suggested that Yahoo! was inaccessible for three hours, with the other sites experiencing longer outages.

Yahoo! received in excess of 1GB per second of traffic during the peak of the malicious attack on one of their Californian data centers, while Buy.Com's chief executive reported that their site received traffic quantities approximating to eight times their site's total capacity. The attacks were thought to be of the Smurf and SYN flood variety.

The Fear-Uncertainty-Doubt (FUD) factor generated by the attacks on Yahoo! and other prominent Internet sites was overwhelming. The misery of the victims was compounded further by the media frenzy that ensued the attacks. Doom-laden prophecies such as "The Web at War!"

dominated headlines with the targeted companies receiving significant coverage—for all the wrong reasons.

To further add to their woes, it was generally well known that law enforcement agencies and Internet organizations had published a number of warnings about the possibility of these types of attacks and the tools that could be used to conduct them several months previously. Three months prior to the February attacks, the FBI National Infrastructure Protection Center (NIPC) issued an alert about Tribal Flood, a DDoS attack toolkit. Reported instances of Tribal Flood had been discovered in the mainstream community, with some of the compromised computers having access to high bandwidth Internet connectivity.

Damage & Defense...

### DDoS: The Hardest Way to Learn a Lesson?

Security professionals dogmatically emphasize the need to keep abreast of security exploits and hacking methods. A number of advisories exist that provide timely and valuable information on security developments. The hardest security lesson to learn is the one that you discover too late.

Accurate financial losses are particularly hard to ascertain during service loss in the Internet world. Incredibly, figures in the ballpark of $1 billion in damages were ascribed to the extended outages of February 2000. These figures were attributed to loss of commercial opportunity, bandwidth costs, response costs, and damage to corporate image. The following points provide an outline of the events leading up to and beyond the DDoS attacks that alerted the world to the full extent of their menace.

**February 8, 1996** Computer Emergency Response Team (CERT) releases advisory regarding UDP Port DoS attack.

**September 19, 1996** CERT releases advisory regarding TCP SYN flooding and IP Spoofing.

Continued

**January 5, 1998** CERT releases advisory regarding Smurf DoS attacks.

**October 21, 1999** David Dittrich releases comprehensive analysis of DDoS programs TFN and trinoo.

**November 18, 1999** CERT releases Incident Note warning of DDoS (TFN and trinoo) compromises.

**December 20, 1999** DDoS reports reach the popular IT press.

**December 28, 1999** CERT releases advisory regarding new DDoS tools.

**January 3, 2000** CERT releases advisory on DDoS developments; multiple zombies discovered.

**February 7, 2000** Yahoo! subject to DDoS attack. Site down for at least three hours.

**February 8, 2000** CNN, eBay, Buy.com, and Amazon hit by DDoS attacks.

**February 7–11, 2000** DDoS attacks attributed to hacker under pseudonym of "Mafiaboy."

**February 7–14, 2000** Media frenzy builds.

**April 15, 2000** Fifteen-year-old boy arrested in connection with Internet attacks.

**January 18, 2001** Defendant admits to being "Mafiaboy" and pleads guilty to 55 charges of mischief.

Yahoo! was the recipient of an ICMP flood attack; CNN was on the receiving end of a SYN flood attack. Interestingly, the CNN DoS was not a consequence of the Web servers failing but rather the border routers that filtered the incoming Web traffic.

Access Control Lists (ACLs) filter traffic traveling through a router, denying or allowing traffic based on certain criteria. This results in the examination of each packet intending to pass through the router. The attack in February 2000 bombarded the CNN routers with SYNs across a range of ports. Each of these packets had to be examined by the router resulting in buffer overflows. Unable to handle the quantities of traffic, the routers began to reboot continually, resulting in a DoS.

After the first attack, eBay learned from the experience and installed additional filters on their routers. A subsequent attack was repelled with the aid of the same filters.

When the smoke had settled, the FBI and other investigative bodies were called into action. Investigators uncovered an unexpected amount of data about the perpetrator of the attack. The data was a surprise find, because any hacker worth his salt would have cleaned up all available logs and muddied audit trails in an attempt to lead investigators down false trails. To compound his mistake, the hacker bragged about his achievements on Internet Relay Chat (IRC). A combination of the uncovered logs from the University of California at Santa Barbara and IRC conversations led the investigators to arrest a 15-year old Canadian boy. The young teenager did not possess the particular technical skills associated with real hackers (in fact he was considered to be a *script-kiddie*, a wannabe hacker in possession of only limited knowledge but also powerful automated hacking tools).

These types of scenarios, such as the real-life drama of February 2000, have the potential to convey a number of possible messages to the masses using the Internet as a tool and not as a technical playground. The message could be that e-commerce is immature, or perhaps that it is insecure. Or worse, that the companies involved in these types of outages are incompetent. By protecting, detecting, and responding effectively, you can ensure that your own site is not tarred with the same brush.

Tools & Traps...

### New Battle Frontiers: The Rise of Information Warfare

More could be at stake in the attacks staged across the Internet than merely what is involved with personal or commercial motives. It sounds very James Bond like, but the Internet may become another delivery mechanism for the modern equivalent of the cold-war weapons of mass destruction. Militants, armed forces, and government agencies could severely impact enemy states or organizations through the Internet by using DoS attacks.

A brief taste of the abilities of the Internet and DoS to be used during military and political campaigns is exemplified by the downing of NATO hardware during the campaign in Yugoslavia. The hardware in question this time was not a plane, but a NATO Web server downed by a Serb DoS attack. The progression from military activity to terrorism is in some eyes a very small step indeed. Cyber terrorists could hypothetically use DDoS programs to target governments, banks, or even air-traffic control systems. With the greater reliance of businesses, governments, and the military on the Internet, the DDoS attack could be the next cruise missile of the new century.

# Why Are E-Commerce Sites Prime Targets for DDoS?

Many companies may believe that their Web site is their portal to the rest of the world. The demand for e-commerce and the number of innovative commercial Web activities grows daily, driving highly complex technologies and large volumes of data onto the Internet. Web sites grow seemingly of their own accord, including information and opportunities from a number of different areas within the company. The added opportunities bring greater complexity to already difficult-to-maintain sites.

The more complex a site and the technologies it uses, the more difficult it is to maintain an aggressive security profile. Managing change control can be particularly troublesome for large sites, and each change has the potential to introduce vulnerability. If the technologies are complex and leading-edge, then the likelihood of new vulnerabilities coming to light in the near future are close to certain. Even well-established technologies are not immune to vulnerabilities, and it is safe to say that the discovery of vulnerabilities will continue for all software and network devices, regardless of maturity.

E-commerce sites are popular targets for attack for a number of reasons. As alluded to earlier, the complexity of the site can reduce security coverage through human error, design fault, or immature technology implementations. E-commerce sites have a large presence and are easy to access. A successful attack on a well-known e-commerce site is always more newsworthy than one targeting academia or nonprofit organizations.

## A Growing Problem

The precedents have been set and the battle lines drawn. The likelihood of an increase in the frequency of DDoS attacks is high, in part due to the unprecedented growth of computing infrastructure and the Internet. Huge volumes of hosts are connected to the Internet, with more being added daily. Internet technologies are not only being driven into our homes and businesses, but into almost every facet of our lives. Wireless networking and small-footprint access devices are truly making the Internet ubiquitous. Many of these devices have discouragingly weak security making them ideal candidates for a hacker. This situation is even more regrettable when the sites with weak security are compromised to mount attacks on more diligent sites with comprehensive security.

Even systems that have sound security infrastructure are not immune from attack or compromise. The increasing demand for software and the rapid decrease in development cycles means that new versions of software are installed on machines at an ever-faster pace. This often results in a softening in security focus and the introduction of new vulnerabilities.

Legislation involving technology misdemeanors and crimes is struggling to keep up with the Internet world. Minors and nationals of foreign countries are often involved in cyber crime and prosecution of the guilty parties can be a long and painful process. Add to the pot that DDoS programs are open source and in the hands of an alarming number of people, and the adage "may you live in interesting times" may become very true for the modern security professional.

## How the Media Feeds the Cycle

When the media reports on computer-related security issues, invariably some degree of trade-off exists between the technical accuracy of the report and its entertainment value. The media not only heightens the public perception of the severity of attacks by using leading reports such as "Satanic Viruses" and "WWW—World Wide War" but at times romanticizes the roles hackers play within the realm of electronic crimes and misbehaviors. Or, at the other end of the spectrum, they attempt to turn electronic forensic activities into a witch-hunt.

The media will continue to play a significant, though unintended, role in the ongoing DDoS saga. The attacks of February 2000 were intensely scrutinized not only by the IT press, but also by every conceivable TV station, newspaper, and magazine. Dramatic headlines screamed the news that multinational corporations were brought to their knees by a series of attacks perpetrated by wily hackers. The story broke across the world media almost simultaneously—no one could miss it.

Now, cast your thoughts to the silent Internet lurkers eagerly reading Hacking 101 white papers. All it takes to find the DDoS toolkits mentioned in every broadsheet and magazine across the land is a few brief minutes on any search engine. In possession of only the most rudimentary skills, they soon begin to cut their teeth on the automated tools used to orchestrate the renowned attacks declaimed in the press. Aware that many sites will have deployed fixes or workarounds for the current tools, they await the arrival of newer and less-known DDoS programs.

By striking early and fast using the latest DDoS tools, the young hacker achieves instant infamy worldwide. Claiming responsibility, the new Mafiaboy brags of his exploits on the Web, basking in the afterglow of his achievement. After all, he had brought international companies to their electronic knees. Other would-be hackers marvel at his skill and audacity while the media foam the waters as they feed on the Internet bodies left behind.

Now, cast your thoughts to the silent Internet lurkers eagerly reading Hacking 101 white papers…and so the cycle begins again.

# What Motivates an Attacker to Damage Companies?

Many people have voiced opinions regarding the motives governing DDoS attacks and hacking in general, and psychologists, economists, and academics have tried to propose sweeping theories. But the reality is that motivations are as unique as each individual behind the attack, with only a few general statements holding true in most cases.

Attempting to neatly segment the Internet community into well-defined categories is clearly at odds with the chaotic web of ideas and people that it is comprised of. We also have to realize that with the good things come the bad and also the downright ugly. The facts are irrefutable—attacks are on the increase. According to Attrition.org, a paltry five sites were defaced in 1995. This increased to a worrying 245 in 1998, then to 3,746 in 1999, until ballooning to an alarming 5,823 in 2000. To put a slightly different spin on this, if you do a search on the word *hacking* you can produce close to a dizzying 620,000 hits. Most companies are not asking if they will be attacked, or even when, just how and why.

## Ethical Hacking: A Contradiction in Terms?

The origins of hacking are partly founded in the quest for knowledge, a desire to satisfy an innate technological curiosity. Many hackers justify their activities by citing this ethos, intimating that they bring to light flaws and shortcomings in security.

## Damage & Defense...

### The Importance of Being an Alarmist

Reading through this chapter, you might think that the plight of security and the Internet is an irresolvable conundrum, so why bother preventing DDoS attacks in the first place? It's a failing of the profession unfortunately. Security officers and administrators are by their very nature alarmist (and need to be). Part of the job description is to be paranoid and pessimistic and to consider worst-case scenarios. We're the type of people who believe that when everything is going swimmingly, someone's up to something.

You may wonder that if the press feeds the attacking cycle, then what about this book? The purpose of this book is to arm professionals with the facts about security and the realities of protecting an e-commerce site. The full disclosure and sharing of information in the correct forums can constructively aid in the defense against malicious hacking activity.

Many regulated professions have a well-defined code of conduct (and/or ethics) describing what is deemed acceptable while practicing their profession. The public and industry can then take confidence that the members of that profession who subscribe to these codes can be judged by their own peers or even be prosecuted by the law. Other codes, such as the original hacker ethic, are much more informal and unstructured. Most people who are labeled hackers do not in fact comply with most of the original hacking ethos, preferring to target sites for reasons other than in the quest for knowledge and the wish to increase security awareness.

Ethical hackers target sites with the intent of raising the security awareness. This type of activity can still be labeled an attack because the hackers are using the site for reasons other than its desired purpose. Additionally, their activities (even when benign) can have unintended consequences for the target site. This is, in part, why some view the term *ethical hacking* as a contradiction in terms.

## Hacktivism

Since its inception, the Internet has been considered a bastion of free speech and expression. Hacktivism is the electronic extrapolation of the right to free speech and expression coupled with modern-day activism. Certain individuals and groups take the ability to express ideals and beliefs a step further by taking direct action, which usually involves damaging or attacking sites with conflicting perspectives. This tactic is often deemed acceptable by the hacktivists due to the publicity such an attack can generate. Most hacktivists are of the opinion that the media attention generates public interest in their causes.

Current examples of hacktivism include the online disputes between Israeli and Arab hackers. The targeting of Israeli sites by an Arab alliance of hackers called Unity in a so-called "cyber jihad" has piqued the attention of the Israeli Internet Underground, who have in response attempted to raise the security awareness of Israeli sites. Hacktivism does not merely include the active promotion of political agendas, but it also encompasses human rights violations, green movements, worker dissatisfaction, and technology issues.

The controversy surrounding hacktivism centers not only on the ethics of such actions but also their effectiveness. Whether attacking a site is ever just, in any moral context, is an ideological tussle that well exceeds the scope of this book. What can be determined though, is their effectiveness to harm institutions, government bodies, and—most recently—businesses. The corporate world has to face up to the realization that hackers ideologically opposed to their pursuits can and will make them the unwelcome recipient of the hacktivism movement.

## Fifteen Minutes of Fame

In may be a gross generalization, but most people—no matter how modest—crave their 15 minutes of fame. To be the focus of attention can be particularly sweet for some individuals who predominantly act within the obscurity of the Internet. Launching a successful attack on a large e-commerce site is certainly a way of achieving fame, or perhaps more accurately, *notoriety.*

Naïve script-kiddies also view the idea of a successful attack as an opportunity to establish themselves in the hacking community. This usually backfires to some extent, because the more accomplished hackers do not subscribe to using prepackaged attacks of the point-and-click variety. Skilled hackers attempt to gain recognition not by using the garden-variety hacking tools, but with the use of innovative and original hacking techniques.

Accepting the plaudits for a well-orchestrated attack can be a double-edged sword for a hacker. It can provide a starting point for investigators, which allows them to attempt to track down the hacker using his or her online identity.

## Hell Hath No Fury Like a Hacker Scorned

Whole new unpleasant electronic avenues have opened up for the disenchanted in the business world. Acting from within the anonymity of the Internet they can act out their anger with an attack that may never be attributed directly to them.

However, like most people's anger, attempts at retribution through electronic means are usually fleeting. If an attacker cannot sate their desire for revenge in a relatively swift manner, then his momentum is usually blunted by the realization that a significant investment in time and planning is needed to damage a site. Those individuals who already have the skills or those who manage to maintain momentum that are particularly dangerous. The commitment shown to learn the correct skills and gather the necessary information usually implies that they may be short on forgiveness and not on resolve.

## Show Me the Money!

Many attacks are not driven by intellectual motives or anger, but rather the desire for financial gain. The Internet has opened up a plethora of ways to make money—and to lose money. A DDoS attack could quite easily be used to distract a company from any real hacking activity taking place. By focusing the businesses' attention on resuming normal operations, hackers can compromise the site via an alternate route and gain information such as credit card and bank account details. These details can then be resold on the Internet or used personally by the hacker.

Some hackers have attempted to manipulate stock prices by using electronic attacks as a means of driving stock prices higher or lower. These attacks could be directed at the company whose stock price they hope to manipulate (or at their competitors). In the last year, employees at companies such as Aastrom, PairGain, and Emulex manipulated stock prices through such tactics as issuing fake online news releases to investors, which resulted in a 30-percent stock price spike in one case, and a 60-percent drop in another.

Two other interesting slants on possible future motives behind DDoS attacks include blackmail and market dominance. The threat of an attack (such as a DDoS) could be used to blackmail companies all around the world with the intended message being either pay up or suffer the consequences.

The use of DDoS to affect the services of competitors could also be a future unsavory application of these tools. Some companies are not averse to using strong-arm tactics against competitors, and the use of DDoS programs could be the future electronic equivalent of these tactics. Consider the consequences to a major e-commerce firm if—on the launch day of a major product—their Web site becomes the victim of a successful DDoS attack. Losses could total in the millions, whereas profits on the sites of the competitors could soar.

## Malicious Intent

Every segment of society has its share of malcontents whose main aim is to sow disruption and pain as far as possible. Within the computing fraternity, this minority expresses their lack of intellect by indiscriminately attacking sites. Usually these attacks are accompanied by some form of publicly visible statement, often in the form of a defaced Web site.

Many have speculated that the anonymity provided by the Internet encourages hackers to project threatening personalities and indulge in extravagant and aggressive role-playing. It is impossible to determine the rationale behind attacks motivated purely through a will to deface or destroy; the best a business can do is to maintain best practices in defense and maintenance areas in an effort to stave off potential attacks.

# What Are Some of the Tools Attackers Use to Perform DDoS Attacks?

The number of DDoS programs that are freely available on the Internet is on the increase. Several of the more popular versions undergo modification and tweaking along similar development cycles to mainstream commercial software. The developers of the DDoS tools, however, are embracing a development technique that many commercial software houses are unable to—the open source model.

The idea behind the open source model is that the code used to develop a program is freely available for modification and redistribution. This provides a number of benefits for the attackers and a number of concerns for security professionals. Using the open source model allows a significant number of people to contribute to the development of new strains and versions of the DDoS tools. Contributions from hackers from a variety of backgrounds allow the code to develop organically and in surprising directions. Additionally, coding neophytes can pick at the source code used for a particular attack to hone and refine their own burgeoning skills.

DDoS software has matured beyond the point where it can only be used by the technically adept. The different programs are ready for the mass market, as the attacks in February 2000 so painfully illustrated. In the coming sections we examine some of the most popular tools used for DDoS attacks. Others are available out there, but trinoo, TFN2K, and Stacheldraht are the most popular.

One thing that these tools have in common is that hosts must be compromised in some form or other. Obviously this implies that securing your network resources is paramount. The details of how hosts could be compromised to install any of the software in the DDoS attacks described in the upcoming sections is not discussed, but later chapters cover the techniques and tools that can aide in DDoS protection and detection.

## Trinoo

Trinoo, one of the first publicly available DDoS programs, broke the ground for the other widely available distributed attack tools to come. Trinoo (also spelled "trin00") follows the three-tier design of most distributed attacks using an *Attacker* ➔ *Client* ➔ *Daemon* chain (see Figure 1.3). It rose to fame in August 1999 after it was used to successfully mount an attack on the University of Minnesota (mentioned earlier in the chapter). Scores of machines flooded the university's network with UDP packets, causing serious disruptions. Trinoo does not spoof the source address of the attack and the administrators were able to trace the attacks back to the daemons. The confounding factor for this attack was that just as the traced daemons were being shut down, the attackers brought more zombies into the attack!

In the early days, trinoo was found only on Linux and Solaris hosts, but a Windows-based version was soon developed. In comparison to more modern DDoS software, trinoo can be considered less dangerous due to the fact that it can only initiate one type of attack and is relatively easy to identify and trace.

### Understanding How Trinoo Works

Like most multi-tier DDoS attacks, the early stages of a trinoo attack involves the attacker compromising machines to become masters. The masters then receive copies of a number of utilities, tools, and—of course—the trinoo control and daemon programs. The master then compiles a list of machines with specific vulnerabilities (possibly involving buffer overflows in RPC services) targeted to act as zombies in the forthcoming attack. The trinoo daemon is then installed and configured to run on the compromised hosts.

Using telnet, the attacker connects to TCP port 27665 on the masters. A list of all the daemons that the master can contact is contained in a hidden file located on the master. Using this file, instructions can then be forwarded, unencrypted, onto the daemons running on the zombies over UDP port 27444. Communications from the zombies back to the master are conducted over UDP port 31335. When the attack commences, the victim is bombarded with UDP packets sent to random UDP ports. The UDP packets all have the same source port and contain four data bytes. The two main executable components of the trinoo DDoS program are *master* and *ns,* the client program and daemon program, respectively.

If an attacker is connected to a master (over TCP port 27665) and the master detects another incoming connection, the second connection's IP address is passed to the attacker. In other words, be careful when connecting to live masters, because this behavior could alert an attacker that his activities have been uncovered.

Not surprisingly, the Windows-based version of trinoo is called Wintrinoo. In combination with programs such as Cult of the Dead Cow's Back Orifice, a vast number of hosts can be compromised. The Windows daemon is installed by running the program service.exe, which after being executed copies itself to the windows\system directory. It then also inserts a registry entry, causing service.exe to run every time the machine is restarted. The Wintrinoo daemon then expects communication from the masters on UDP port 34555, while communication from daemon to master takes place over UDP port 35555. Table 2.1 provides the details of all the ports used by the trinoo attack hierarchy.

Table 2.1 Trinoo Communication Ports

| From | To | Uses Port | Comments |
|---|---|---|---|
| Attacker | Masters | 27665/TCP | Attacker usually connects via telnet. |
| Master | Zombies | 27444/UDP | A list of daemons that the master can contact is stored in the file ... (3 dots). |
| Zombies | Masters | 31335/UDP | Daemon usually compiles to a file called **ns**, but can be renamed as desired, or can be deleted from disk after execution to hide the footprint further. |

## TFN2K: The Portable Monster

Tribe FloodNet 2K (TFN2K) is the successor to TFN, developed by the hacker named Mixter. Many security professionals (and Mixter himself) perceived the development of TFN2K as an example of the growing complexity and sophistication of DDoS code. Although not a classic three-tier architecture, its design follows the basic multi-tier DDoS architecture that was illustrated earlier in Figure 2.3.

In accordance with the open source model, the code for TFN2K is freely available. The only legwork required on the part of the attacker is to compile the source on the desired platform of choice. TFN2K is portable to a number of platforms, opening up a plethora of opportunities for attackers. Even a relative novice can compile TFN2K on Linux, Solaris, or Windows NT.

### Understanding How TFN2K Works

The main components of TFN2K after compile time are two binaries, namely *tfn* and *td*. Using a well-defined syntax, the client program (tfn) sends commands to the TFN2K daemon (which can be unlimited in number) installed on compromised hosts. The daemon (td) then carries out the commands as directed by the client. At the most basic level, tfn instructs td to either commence or halt attacks.

The command syntax of TFN2K was designed in a manner that can accommodate much more complex attack instructions. Not only can the tfn client instruct multiple zombies to attack a target (using td), but it can also designate the attack method to use. The tfn client can instruct the td daemon to use the following attacks:

- **UDP flood** Deluges a target with a significant amount of UDP packets.
- **SYN flood** Manipulates the setup of the TCP three-way handshake by spoofing the source address of the packets sent to the target.
- **ICMP echo reply attack** Sends a significant number of ICMP echoes to a target host, to which the host then responds.

- **Smurf attack** An amplification attack that sends ICMP echoes to amplifier networks. The ICMP echoes are constructed so that they have the victim's IP address substituted as their source address. When the amplifier network receives the ICMP echoes, it responds by sending ICMP echo replies to the victim.
- **Mix attack** Attacks a victim with a combination of UDP, SYN, and ICMP packets in a 1:1:1 ratio.
- **Targa3 attack** Constructs specially tailored IP packets using invalid or unexpected header values, fragmentation, TCP segments, offsets, and packet sizes.

Additionally, the tfn client can instruct the daemon to execute programs on the target computer, or allow an incoming shell connection at a certain port. Communication between the client and the daemon is one way—no acknowledgement is returned to the client that commands have been received by a daemon, which makes detection more difficult.

The tfn client requires administrative (root) access on the master machine in order to run. On the master, the TFN2K client program (tfn) is nonintrusive and requires no system changes. The tfn client is then used on the master to issue attack commands to the compromised zombie hosts. When instructing zombies to commence or halt an attack, the tfn client encapsulates the attack commands within a number of packets destined for the zombie host, with the theory being that at least some of the packets will reach their final destination.

As noted earlier, communication is one-way—from master to zombie—and to further decrease the probability of detection, the client randomly sends the instructions over TCP, UDP, and ICMP. The message content is encrypted with the CAST-256 algorithm, using a key defined at compile time and then base64 encoded. Commands directed at zombies are interspersed with decoy traffic in an attempt to mask the sending of attack instructions.

TFN2K is quite versatile; it works on a number of platforms—even on Windows platforms using UNIX shells such as vmware and cygwin. Figure 1.4 illustrates a very basic summary of three different sets of attack packets directed at a Windows 2000 host. The attack was instigated using a compromised Linux master and a team of Linux zombies. The packet capture shows a subset of the packets sent to the victim during a TFN2K SYN flood attack, a mix attack, and an ICMP flood attack. An obvious detail that leaps out from the packet captures in Figure 2.4 is that all the source addresses are spoofed.

**Figure 2.4** A Packet Capture of an Attack Using TFN2K

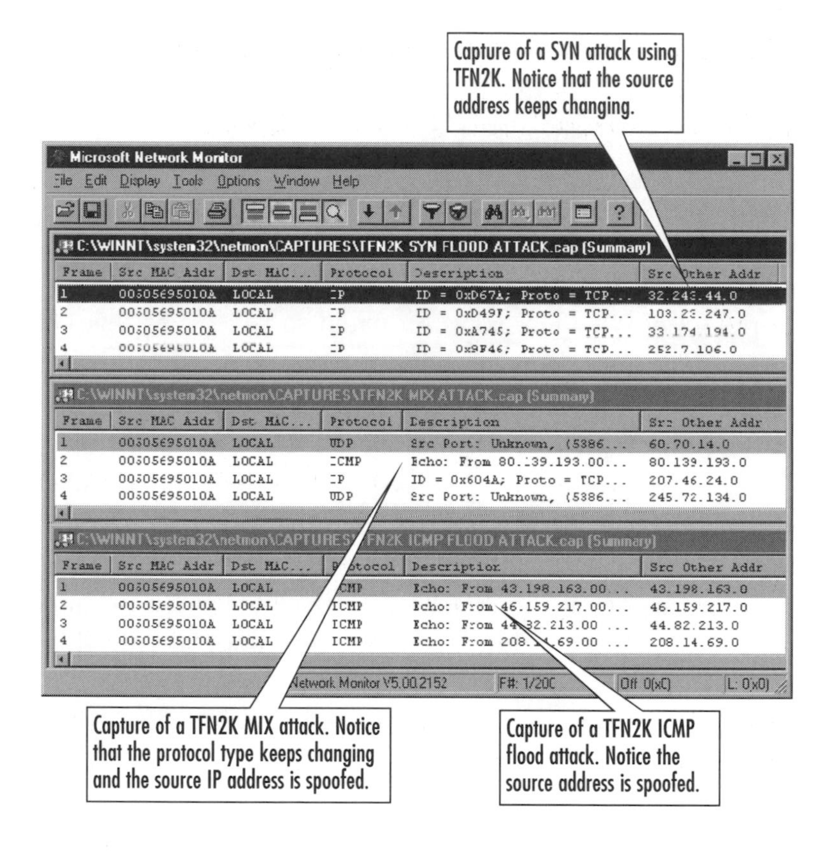


Figure 2.5 provides a view of the one-way communication stream from master to zombie. A particular characteristic visible in the diagram is that all commands sent from the tfn client to the td daemon contain a random number of As (0x41) at the end of packet.

**Figure 2.5** A Packet Capture of the Communication from Client to Zombie

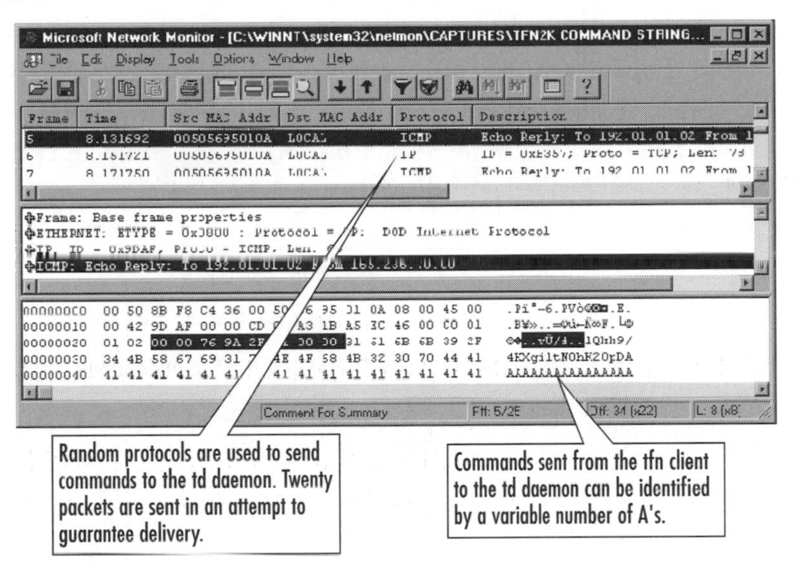

Random protocols are used to send commands to the td daemon. Twenty packets are sent in an attempt to guarantee delivery.
Commands sent from the tfn client to the td daemon can be identified by a variable number of A's.


# Stacheldraht—A Barbed-Wire Offensive

Towards the latter part of 1999, a new DDoS program called Stacheldraht (German for *barbed wire*) was discovered in use. Stacheldraht combines features found in other DDoS tools and also includes encryption between the client and masters. Stacheldraht is distributed in source code format and can be compiled on Solaris and Linux, although (obviously) the target of the attacks it generates is operating-system and network agnostic. An interesting feature of Stacheldraht is its ability to upgrade daemons installed in the field.

## Understanding How Stacheldraht Works

The compilation of the Stacheldraht source code results in the generation of three binaries. The three binaries are *client*, *mserv*, and *td* (sound familiar?), each of which is used in a separate tier in the attack model. When considering a classic DDoS attack tree, the methods that Stacheldraht employs can cause the terminology to be slightly confusing.

The client binary (which is just an executable file and should not be confused with the *client software*) is used to communicate with the master running mserv. The confusing part of the Stacheldraht terminology is that according to Figure 2.3, mserv is the *client software* because it runs on the master. Compromised hosts to be used as zombies are then configured to run the td binary, which contains the actual code to assemble attack packets and traffic streams. In other words, the software chain becomes

*client (on a compromised host)* ➔ *mserv (on master)* ➔ *td (on zombie)* ➔ *Victim*

Figure 2.6 illustrates this hierarchy.

**Figure 2.6** The Stacheldraht v1.1 Attack Hierarchy

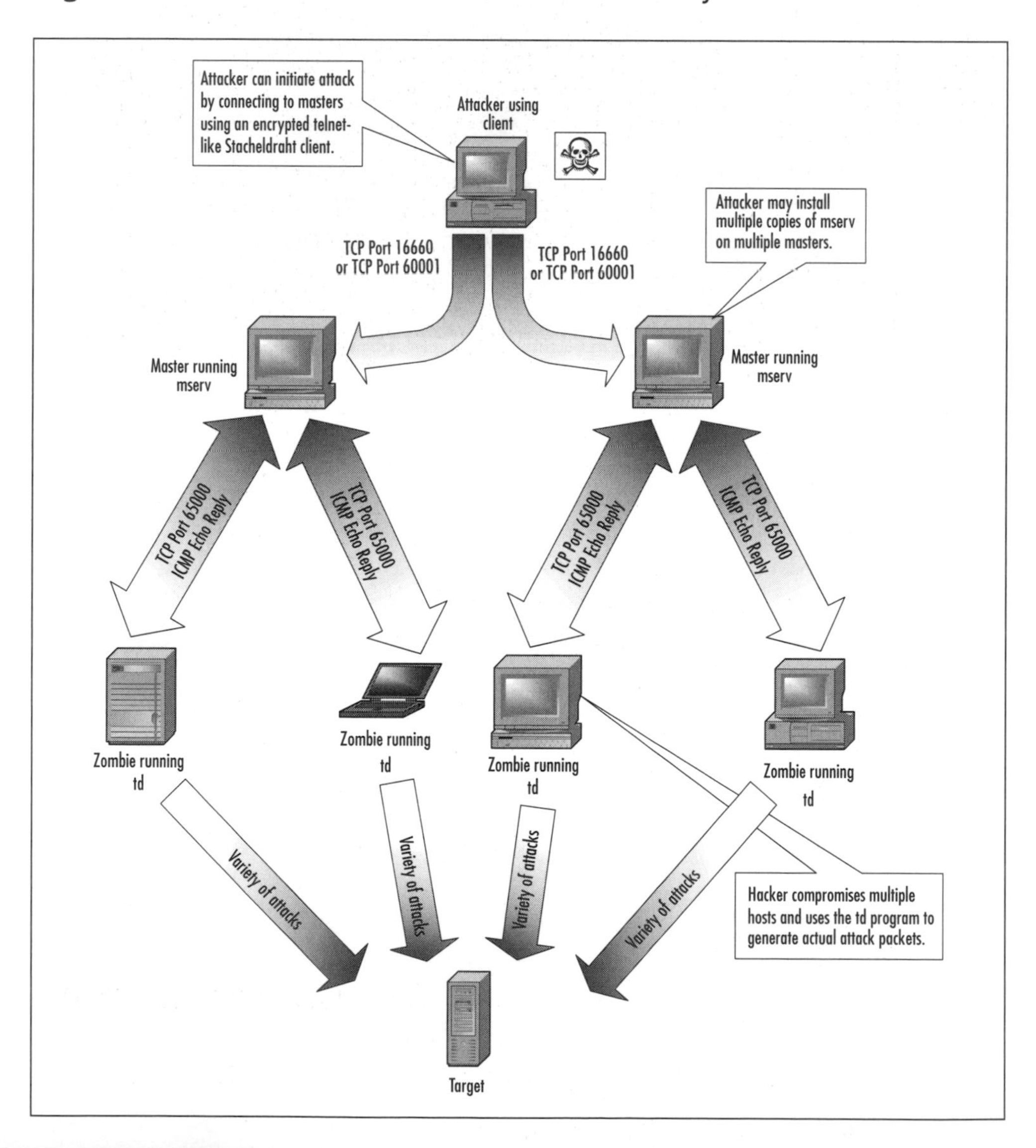

When the client binary is run, it establishes a telnet-like session with the master running the mserv program. A sample of this telnet-like session is shown in Figure 2.7.

**Figure 2.7** A View of the Telnet-Like Session Established with the Stacheldraht Client Executable

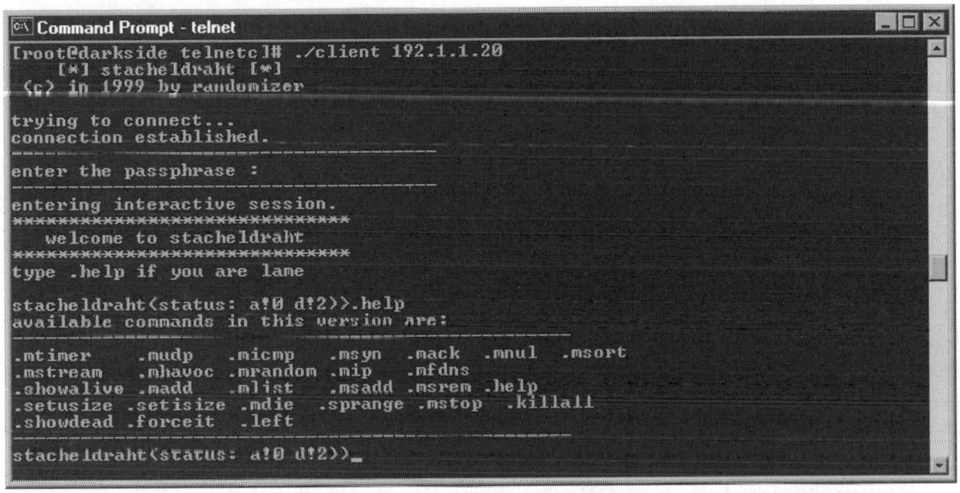

```
Command Prompt - telnet
[root@darkside telnetc]# ./client 192.1.1.20
    [*] stacheldraht [*]
 (c) in 1999 by randomizer

trying to connect...
connection established.
--------------------------------------
enter the passphrase :
--------------------------------------
entering interactive session.
******************************
   welcome to stacheldraht
******************************
type .help if you are lame

stacheldraht(status: a!0 d!2)>.help
available commands in this version are:
--------------------------------------------------
.mtimer    .mudp    .micmp    .msyn   .mack  .mnul  .msort
.mstream   .mhavoc  .mrandom  .mip    .mfdns
.showalive .madd    .mlist    .msadd  .msrem .help
.setusize  .setisize .mdie    .sprange .mstop  .killall
.showdead  .forceit  .left
--------------------------------------------------
stacheldraht(status: a!0 d!2)>_
```

At compile time, the mserv program requires a passphrase to be entered. Each time the attacker uses the client program to connect to the master running mserv, the passphrase is used to grant access (as seen in Figure 2.7) and symmetrically encrypts communications. Stacheldraht uses the freely available Blowfish encryption algorithm based on a 64-bit block cipher. The attacker then enters the relevant attack commands followed by the victim's IP address.

After connecting to the master, an attacker can instruct the daemons to use a variety of attacks, including ICMP floods, SYN floods, and UDP floods. A number of other attacks are available, such as:

- **Null flood** A SYN flood attack with TCP flags set to 0.
- **Stream attack** A flood of TCP ACK packets with random destination ports.
- **Havoc attack** A mixed attack of ICMP, UDP, SYN, and TCP packets with random flags and IP headers.

- **Random flood** Targets the victim with a TCP flood with random headers.

When executed on the master, the mserv program appears in the process list as (httpd) in an effort to escape detection. On the zombies, the daemon process hides itself behind the process name of lpsched.

When the td daemon is first compiled, it requires the IP address of the master(s) to be entered. The IP address is needed so that the daemon can contact the master when it is launched. The daemon's first communication with the master is to send out an ICMP echo reply that contains the characters "skillz." The master responds with an ICMP echo reply that contains the string "ficken."

The daemon then does something quite sneaky— it checks to see whether the network allows packets with forged source addresses to be routed out of the network. It achieves this by sending an ICMP echo with a source address of 3.3.3.3 and the IP address of the source daemon encapsulated within the data to the master. If the master receives the forged packet, it strips out the IP address encapsulated within the data and uses it to send an ICMP echo reply back to the agent with the string "spoofworks" in the data field. In this way, the daemon is informed whether attacks with spoofed addresses are allowed. See Figure 2.8 for a packet capture of the behavior of the td daemon and the mserv master at startup.

Different versions of Stacheldraht do not connect using the same port numbers, although Table 2.2 provides a list of port numbers for the more common strains.

**Table 2.2** Stacheldraht Communication Ports

| From | To | Stacheldraht v1.1 Uses Port | Stacheldraht v4 Uses Port | Comment |
|---|---|---|---|---|
| Attacker | Masters | 16660/TCP | 65512/TCP | Connects using the client binary. |
| Master | Zombies | 65000/TCP + ICMP Echo Reply | 65513/TCP + ICMP Echo Reply | A master can only control a maximum of 6000 zombies. |

**Continued**

**Table 2.2** Continued

| From | To | Stacheldraht v1.1 Uses Port | Stacheldraht v4 Uses Port | Comment |
|---|---|---|---|---|
| Zombies | Masters | 65000/TCP + ICMP Echo Reply | 65513/TCP + ICMP Echo Reply | Daemon examines an encrypted file for the IP addresses of masters. ELSE contacts default IP. |

**Figure 2.8** A Packet Capture of the Startup of the td Daemon and the Resultant Communication Streams

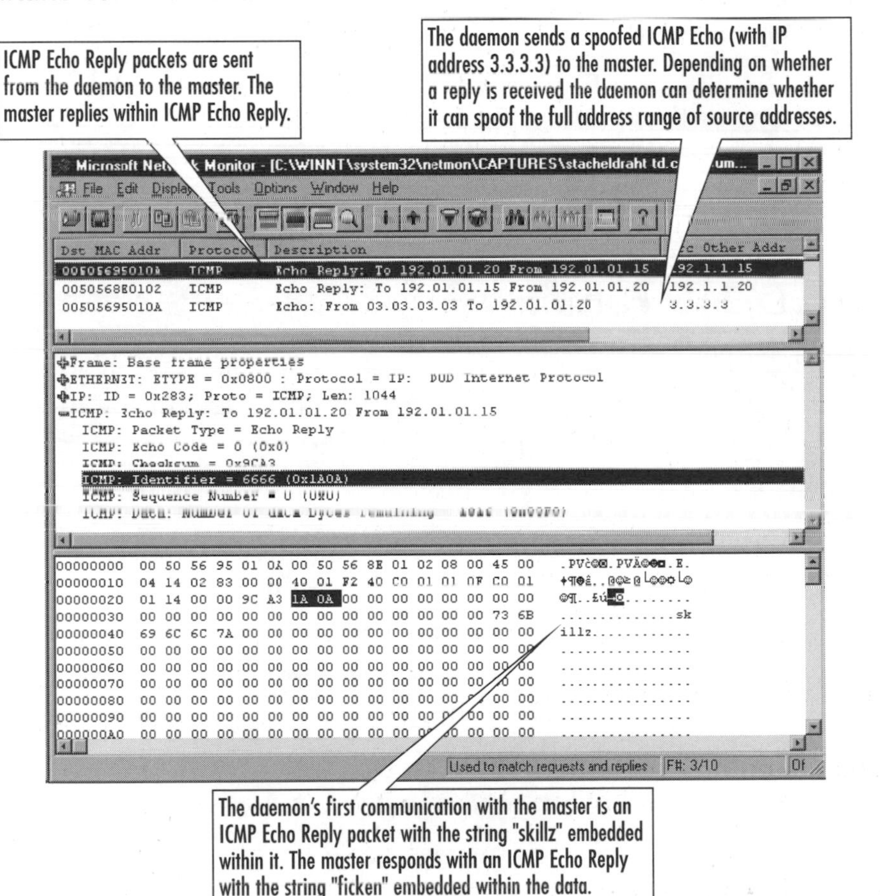

ICMP Echo Reply packets are sent from the daemon to the master. The master replies within ICMP Echo Reply.
The daemon sends a spoofed ICMP Echo (with IP address 3.3.3.3) to the master. Depending on whether a reply is received the daemon can determine whether it can spoof the full address range of source addresses.
The daemon's first communication with the master is an ICMP Echo Reply packet with the string "skillz" embedded within it. The master responds with an ICMP Echo Reply with the string "ficken" embedded within the data.

Keep in mind that most DDoS programs are works in progress and consequently different versions of the tools may have different capabilities and different configurations. For example, newer versions of Stacheldraht have included more attack types and better obfuscation techniques.

**SECURITY ALERT!**

A number of process names and port numbers have been detailed regarding the attacks discussed in this chapter. It is extremely important to note that because the source code is freely available, these parameters can be easily changed. For example, before compile time, the Stacheldraht config.h and td.c files can be modified to change process names, port numbers, and even the values that relate to the commands issued. Most attackers have the abilities to easily change many of the values used for the DDoS attack tools. Take none of these values for granted!

## More DDoS Families

A number of DDoS tools are under development in the Internet underground. Trinoo, TFN2K and Stacheldraht are just a few of the more popular in circulation. Other DDoS programs to be aware of include the following:

- **Mstream** This attack takes the stream2.c DoS attack and turns it into a three-tier distributed attack tool. The victims become the recipients of a flood of TCP packets that have a random source IP address and random destination TCP socket numbers. The first incarnations of this tool are not as advanced as other DDoS software, such as Stacheldraht and TFN2K.
- **Trinity** An attack tool that is controlled via IRC. When installed on a Linux host, trinity connects to an Undernet IRC

server on port 6667 when the executable daemon /usr/lib/idle.so is run. The daemon then awaits commands to be sent over an IRC channel. A number of attacks are available, such as UDP floods, SYN floods, and null floods.

- **Shaft** A DDoS program that can launch a variety of attacks supported by a multi-tier attack hierarchy. Shaft communicates from the client to the master via TCP port 20432, from the master to the daemons via UDP port 18753, and from the daemon back to the master via UDP port 20433.

Each of these DDoS tools has its own set of specific characteristics relating to configuration and operation. Just because they have not been covered in significant detail does not make them any less dangerous—remember that all of these have to some degree been found in the field.

# How Can I Protect My Site against These Types of Attacks?

No solution satisfactorily provides complete protection against the threat that DDoS attacks pose. In contrast to other security related incidents, such as the contagion of a new virus, no absolute antidote or cure exists for DDoS. As indicated earlier in the chapter, a successful DDoS attack may not be a result of a lack of preparation or foresight on the part of your business, but rather on the lack of security implemented in *other* sites.

Even taking this into account, you can still adopt a number of defensive practices to mitigate the effects of DDoS attacks. Additionally, you can use tools such as Zombie Zapper, Remote Intrusion Detection (RID), and nmap to afford your site a significant amount of "detect and protect" functionality.

Defending a site against DDoS requires security teams to adopt a consistent and focused approach. In particular, staying aware of current security issues and new attack methods is of particular importance. Ensuring a reasonable security profile is an ongoing and dynamic process requiring continual refinement and consideration. Most DDoS defensive measures fall into three camps that can be very loosely mapped onto the three maxims of security: *protect*, *detect*, and *respond*.

- **Reducing the effectiveness of possible DDoS attacks** This involves ensuring that strategies have been considered for traffic shaping, load balancing, application proxy, ingress filtering, prevention of network mapping, sacrificial hosts, split DNS, and incidence response.
- **Detecting DDoS attacks** Correctly identifying DDoS attacks can be part art and part science. It can involve understanding your site's baseline traffic patterns, the mechanics of the different DDoS families, and comprehensive log analysis (and having a suitably suspicious mind). The flexibility of modern DDoS tools ensures that you can't always accurately predict their behavior, softening the protection/detection ability of rule-based systems such as firewalls. Even taking this into account, IDSs and some firewalls do include pattern recognition for most communication streams between hosts in the DDoS attack hierarchy. For example, a network IDS can detect attack patterns, whereas host-based IDSs can detect the patterns and effects of the attacks.
- **Ensuring that hosts are not compromised and co-opted into the attack hierarchy** Egress filtering limits the ability of attackers to use compromised sites in coordinated attacks (this should be viewed as a preventative, not reactive, action). It is paramount to ensure that hosts and networks accessible from the Internet are adequately secured with the latest security releases. This should also include understanding what actions need to be taken if hosts are compromised, such as using tools like find_ddos, RID, and Zombie Zapper.

DDoS countermeasures also have to be viewed with a realistic understanding of risk versus expense. Risk is a matter of perspective and can only be fully qualified by understanding the trade-off between the cost of mitigating the risk and acceptable levels of exposure. Before constructing an effective plan to counter DDoS attacks and minimize their impact, consider a number of questions about the business and its infrastructure. Just a few of these questions to mull over would include the following:

- How does the business depend on the Internet? What non-technical actions can be taken to minimize the dependence?
- Are DDoS attacks and other security related issues covered under current corporate insurance policy?
- What level of exposure is deemed acceptable, and how far should we go to mitigate risk? Should this be incorporated into our disaster recovery plan?
- What staffing levels and technical abilities are required? For example, should technical staff understand how to gather forensic evidence?
- Is the current security profile of the site well known and current? If not, how is this obtained?
- Has the security policy been reviewed? What is the policy for log retention and other data available to forensic investigation?
- Have escalation procedures and supporting processes been defined? Has senior management endorsed them? Do technical staff understand and know how to follow the processes?

In the following sections we will cover useful strategies for protecting and deflecting DDoS attacks.

Damage & Defense…

### Crying Wolf

When a business suffers a denial of service, it is not always due to the involvement of malicious third parties. Denials of service are experienced more often as a consequence of legitimate events than as the result of the intervention of sinister black-hat hackers. Take for instance a Web site that receives high traffic volumes. If

Continued

volumes exceed certain thresholds, then other users will be denied access to the site through the simple laws of supply and demand. This is still a DoS, but not a DoS attack.

As an administrator, be very careful when alerting the business to what you perceive as a malicious targeted hack; a frightening number of legitimate DoS attacks occur, but so do a great number of cases of mistaken identity. Ensure that you have ample evidence and that the correct escalation procedures are followed.

Jumping to conclusions or raising false alarms on a frequent basis is an easy way for the business to lose faith in your ability to diagnose security threats. It may even cause the business to regard information security as a fad or a practice that should be conducted merely for due diligence purposes and not as an enabler for conducting e-business. In other words, if you neglect to follow each possible explanation down the right path, the business will begin to regard you as the boy who cried wolf one too many times.

## Basic Protection Methods

Awareness of DDoS attacks has grown considerably in recent years and its increased profile has ensured that there has been an investment in time and effort from vendors and businesses alike. The number of hosts required to mount a sizeable DDoS attack can be considerable, and consequently many attackers use automated procedures to sniff out hosts suitably configured to run the daemon process. Because the location of suitable hosts is usually automated, the scanning of sites can be a means of alerting administrators that something is afoot.

DDoS countermeasures usually include *egress filtering* of spoofed addresses and *ingress filtering* of broadcast packets. Egress filtering encompasses the filtering of outbound traffic, whereas ingress filtering relates to the filtering of inward-bound network traffic.

Nearly every modern IDS has some form of DDoS pattern-recognition mechanism. Other protection mechanisms include the strategic placement of firewalls and proxies.

Firewalls can have a hard time stopping a DDoS tool such as TFN2K because the tool does not communicate or attack over specific ports. The configuration of firewalls can be a complex and frustrating task. Without going into the mechanics of firewall configuration, the general method of establishing an effective rule base is to assume that all traffic is suspicious and opening up only those ports that are necessary. *Stateful inspection* of traffic elevates the ability of firewalls to manage connections, and many ship with the ability to detect malicious activity defined by the administrator.

A number of defensive actions can be taken proactively, some of which will not be suited to every environment. The following list provides a few of the options available to minimize DDoS exposure:

- **Keeping the security profile current** Implement a process whereby the latest patches and configurations are applied to hosts and network devices; this is important as a general security consideration, not only for DDoS. For example, operating systems should be configured to ignore directed broadcasts, to incorporate SYN flood resilience, to establish strong passwords, and have all unnecessary services turned off. *Remember, attackers can only create attack networks if there are weakly secured hosts or networks to compromise.*
- **Profiling traffic patterns** Trying to determine if an attack is taking place is difficult without understanding what the normal distribution and characteristics of incoming and outgoing traffic are. If, for example, a spike occurs in certain types of ICMP traffic, then without a baseline to compare this to, this information can be hard to interpret.
- **Splitting DNS infrastructure** Separating internal and external DNS infrastructures will make basic network footprinting more difficult. Consequently this makes proliferating zombies on the "clean" side of the firewall more difficult.
- **Load balancing** Providing a resilient and fault-tolerant site is key to the success of any e-commerce site. By using load balancing, not only does availability and speed improve but also

tolerance to DDoS attacks. A subtle variation on this theme is the use of distributed hosting services such as Akamai Technologies (www.akamai.com). Spreading sites across a distributed network by using DNS and other mechanisms improves the tolerance of sites to DDoS attacks.

- **Egress and ingress filtering** Ensuring that only well-defined traffic groups enter and exit the network decreases the possibility of the site being used as part of a zombie network and also decreases the chances of hosts being compromised. Your ISP should be required to implement ingress filtering, which can aid in identifying zombie networks. (Refer to the section "Using Egress Rules to Be a Better 'Net Neighbor'" for more detail.)
- **Tightening firewall configurations** By default, all Internet-accessible servers should be placed within DMZs. Implement strict change controls for rule base modifications and ensure that only the absolute minimum ports and protocols are allowed through the firewall. For example, consider filtering outbound ICMP echo replies by the firewall, along with Timestamp, Timestamp Reply, Information Request, Information Reply, and Time Exceeded packets. Usually most sites should start with making TCP port 80 available and then expand from there. Enable any defensive abilities native to the firewall itself, such as the ability to buffer the TCP connection process or detect malicious activity. Enable logging and shunt the data to syslogd (though this could prove to be resource intensive during an attack).
- **Securing perimeter devices and using traffic shaping** Some discretionary access control is required for traffic entering and leaving perimeter devices. The restriction of protocols and ports that are allowed through these devices needs to be developed in conjunction with firewall configurations. Enable protective mechanisms that are native to the device, such as TCP Intercept for Cisco routers and rate limiting. (Refer to later sections for more detail.)

- **Implementing an IDS** The implementation of a well-designed IDS can provide administrators with the ability to detect some client/master/agent conversations. Implement both a host-based and a network-based IDS.
- **Implementing a vulnerability scanner** A necessary companion to the IDS, the vulnerability scanner provides reports on existing vulnerabilities on hosts and network devices. It is imperative that the vulnerability scanner (and IDS) be updated with the most current list of vulnerabilities.
- **Implementing proxy servers** Configuring traffic leaving or entering the network to pass through a proxy can reduce exposure to DDoS attacks. The proxy servers can also prove to be a useful source of information after an attack has taken place.
- **Taking snapshots and conducting integrity checks of existing configurations** Because a change in configuration could result in a DoS, it is wise to ensure that as many configurations as possible can be backed up centrally. Additionally, run integrity checks on a scheduled basis against hosts. The purpose of an integrity check is to compare the current state of a host to the baseline for the host. By doing this, an administrator can verify file and directory integrity and highlight any changes made by attackers. An example of this type of tool for UNIX is Tripwire (www.tripwire.com).
- **Configuring sacrificial hosts** The creation of hosts with the purpose of misdirecting attacks or gleaning information about potential attackers is a controversial topic and many factors need to be considered before their implementation. For example, are there sufficient technical resources to analyze the data and is this configuration attracting unwelcome attention?
- **Increasing network and host management** By monitoring the resource utilization on networks and hosts, DDoS effects may be flagged when compared to normal operations. Many management programs can provide details on the software and services running on hosts.

- **Maintaining a response procedure** All the discussions needed to resolve a DDoS attack should take place before an attack happens. Attain a firm grasp of the capabilities of your ISP, routers, and firewalls as a matter of course. Understanding the depth of the ISPs ability to respond to DDoS attacks is critical. Determine where the ISP can add value:
  - How do they conduct ingress filtering?
  - How complete is their incident response procedure?
  - Have they disabled directed broadcasts?
  - Can they log and trace traffic effectively?

  A response procedure for the business incorporating this and other information should then be developed and maintained.
- **Deploying more secure technologies** A number of technologies have been developed that provide some protection against DDoS and associated exploits. Technologies such as IPv6, IP Security (IPSec), and Secure DNS provide greater protection than current implementations.

Even after investing a significant amount of time and money in defending a site against DDoS, the risk is still not eliminated. If an attack occurs, you should have a well-defined response procedure, dictating action plans, escalation procedures, and contact details. Some of the points to consider incorporating into the response procedure include:

- **Information gathering** How is information relevant to the attack gathered and interpreted? Does it answer basic questions such as what, when, where, and how? What devices and software can be interrogated?
- **Contacting the ISP** Request that the ISP instigate extraordinary procedures for your site and blacklist potential zombie networks.
- **Applying more aggressive filters** Change access control lists and filters on perimeter devices to drop packets to and from the attacking networks. Apply rate limiting rules to ensure that the

correct types of traffic receive the appropriate bandwidth. Ensure that only the minimum protocols and ports are entering and exiting the network. Even with more aggressive filtering in place, the effect of the attack may not be blunted because sufficient bandwidth headroom is necessary (above that used by the attacker) for legitimate traffic to reach the destination servers. Check the baseline configuration of perimeter devices.

- **Applying different routing options** Attempt to change the routing options available to incoming traffic.
- **Attempting to stop the attack** Using existing tools such as Zombie Zapper, it is possible to instruct zombies to halt the attack. (Refer to later sections for more detail.)
- **Changing the IP address of the target system** This may not be an appropriate tactic for many sites and is of dubious benefit. If addresses are changed, then you must be aware that DNS changes take time to replicate through the Internet. Be aware that this tactic may be totally useless if the daemons running on zombies are configured with host names, not IP addresses!
- **Commencing incidence investigation** In conjunction with the correct agencies—whether they are the ISP or a government investigation body—start gathering information. Do not rebuild hosts that have acted as zombies or masters—they may contain important information.

## Using Egress Rules to Be a Better "Net Neighbor"

In most cases, the damage sustained by the victim of a DDoS attack is not only a function of the victim's security, but also the lack of security of other networks. One of the ways of minimizing the spread of DDoS attacks is to become a better "net neighbor"—by this we mean understanding not only what you allow *into* your network, but also what you allow *out*. Being in control of the traffic that leaves your network is achieved through the use of egress rules.

Egress rules are a set of directives governing the flow of traffic out of a network, whereas ingress rules govern the flow of traffic into a network. Predominantly, most network administrators focus on protecting the network against incoming traffic, but an attacker can subvert these protective mechanisms in many ways and compromise a network or host, regardless. Assuming that an attacker gained access to a host, he could then (in the absence of egress rules) use the compromised hosts to take part in a spoofed packet attack. Because no laws govern the nature of packets exiting from that particular network, the spoofed packets are routed on to their designated target as if nothing were amiss.

An example of an attack that could take advantage of such a network configuration is a Smurf attack. To quickly review, a Smurf attack achieves its desired effect by sending ICMP echoes to amplification networks with a spoofed source address that has been changed to the victim's address. The amplification network then responds with a number of ICMP echo replies directed towards what it believes is the source of the original ICMP echo (which has been changed to the victim's address). This attack is based on the assumption that a spoofed ICMP echo would have to leave the original network on route to the amplification network with a source address that is not part of its legal network address space.

A similar story applies to the SYN flood attack. The initial TCP SYN is sent to the victim with a spoofed address or perhaps with a legitimate address that is not the attackers. This type of attack could only succeed if packets can leave the network with source addresses other than those within the legitimate address space of the originating network.

These scenarios could be easily prevented if the original network had rules in place allowing only packets to leave the network with a source IP addresses within its legal address space, or in other words, if it had used egress rules. By becoming a good net neighbor and using egress rules, you can reduce the possibility of your network being used in an attack. It is never too late to start implementing egress rules—prevention is better than cure.

Network *choke points* are usually an excellent place to apply egress rules or filters. Choke points requiring egress filtering include all internal interfaces on firewalls, routers, and dial-in servers.

## *Enabling Egress Rules and Hardening Cisco Routers to DDoS*

To paraphrase Request for Comments (RFC) 2827, "Best Current Practice for Network Ingress Filtering," generic router egress rules can basically be summarized by:

```
IF      outgoing packet has source address within the networks
        legitimate address space
THEN    route as appropriate
ELSE    deny route and do other (log, alert)
```

A number of vendors have provided papers detailing strategies to harden routers and networks against DDoS. For the sake of brevity, only a synopsis of some of the configuration changes recommended by Cisco have been included in this section, so check your vendor for the latest in-depth DDoS configuration countermeasures and egress rules.

The first task in hardening your Cisco edge routers to DDoS attacks is to issue the following interface command:

```
ip cef
interface xy
ip verify unicast reverse-path
```

This command ensures that only packets with a source that is consistent with the routing table are forwarded. This command is only valid on the input interface of routers at the upstream end of connections. Note that this command needs Cisco express forwarding (CEF) to be enabled.

The next task is to filter out all nonroutable addresses (see RFC1918) using access control lists. Earlier in the chapter, you learned that nonroutable addresses should not leave your network in the source address field of packets.

```
interface xy
access-list 101 deny ip host 0.0.0.0 any
access-list 101 deny ip 127.0.0.0    255.255.255.255 any
```

```
access-list 101 deny ip 10.0.0.0     0.255.255.255 any
access-list 101 deny ip 192.168.0.0  0.0.255.255 any
access-list 101 deny ip 172.16.0.0   0.15.255.255 any
access-list 101 permit ip any any
```

Establishing the ingress rules using access control lists follows this.

```
access-list 187 deny ip {network address} {netmask} any
access-list 187 permit ip any any
access-list 188 permit ip {network address} (netmask} any
access-list 188 deny ip any any
interface {egress interface} {interface #}
ip access-group 187 in
ip access-group 188 out
```

Another useful feature found in Cisco IOS is Committed Access Rate (CAR). This feature allows administrators to define bandwidth policies against access list. Consequently certain (potentially) undesirable traffic can be rate limited, such as ICMP described here:

```
interface xy
rate-limit output access-group 2020 3000000 512000 786000 conform-
    action
transmit exceed-action drop
access-list 2020 permit icmp any echo-reply
```

Rate limiting along with TCP Intercept should also be configured to ward off potential SYN floods. While on the subject of Cisco routers, it is relevant to note that IOS 12.0 or greater has disabled IP directed broadcast (protection against being used as an amplification network) by default, as per RFC2644.

**Security Alert!**

Beware of applying too many filters to a router, because forwarding performance may suffer as a result. Cisco, for example, recommends the use of TurboACLs and points out that access lists with more than 50 entries may impair performance.

## Defending against the SYN's of the Internet

Most operating systems and network devices now attempt to cater to the large number of connection attempts made during a SYN attack by increasing the connection queue and decreasing time-out values. Additionally, some operating systems implement a random early drop algorithm. A random early drop algorithm traverses the connection queue and randomly extracts unanswered SYNs.

### *The Linux Approach to SYN*

Linux takes a different tack on the SYN flood problem by employing a technique using SYN Cookies. To explain the benefits of SYN Cookies, let's play out the TCP three-way handshake again. The client host sends a SYN to the server with a copy of the client's ISN. The server then responds to the client with a SYN/ACK, but at this stage, instead of assigning a normal server ISN, one is calculated using a one-way MD5 hash that incorporates the source address, source port, source ISN, destination address, destination port, and a secret seed (phew). The server then relinquishes the state information for that connection—effectively freeing up the resources that a SYN flood tries to exhaust. If an ACK response is received (which probably wouldn't happen in a SYN flood attack) the server recalculates from the returned ISN – 1 whether it was in response to the earlier SYN/ACK. If it is, then the three-way handshake is complete and the server opens the connection. So, using SYN Cookies, connection queues cannot be exhausted.

To enable Linux SYN Cookies, enter:

```
echo 1 >  /proc/sys/net/ipv4/tcp_syncookies
```

## *The Microsoft Approach to SYN*

By default, Windows NT 4 retransmits SYN/ACK five times at intervals of 3, 6, 12, 24, and 48 seconds. A full 96 seconds must pass before the host closes the half-open connection (totaling 189 seconds). Windows NT 4 and Windows 2000 have a number of configuration parameters that protect against SYN attacks. For example, within HKEY_LOCAL_MACHINE\SYSTEM\CurrentControlSet\Services\Tcpip\Parameters they add or modify the following keys:

- **SynAttackProtect** This entry forces the connection queue to have a shorter time-out if it appears that a SYN flood is under way. Add an entry of type **REG_DWORD** and assign a value from 0–2. The default is 0: no protection. Setting the value to 1 provides SYN flood protection, whereas 2 provides the SYN flood protection and does not signal AFD (driver that supports Windows Sockets applications) until the TCP handshake is complete.
- **TcpMaxHalfOpen** After the value of this entry is exceeded by the number of half-opened connections, SynAttackProtect is enabled. Add an entry of type **REG_DWORD**.
- **TcpHalfOpenRetried** This value dictates the number of half-open connections for which there has been at least one retransmission of the SYN before SynAttackProtect commences. Add an entry of type **REG_DWORD**.
- **TCPMaxConnectResponseRetransmissions** This value controls the number of times the server responds with a SYN/ACK. The entry is of type **REG_DWORD** and the default value is 3. Setting the value to 3 retransmits SYN/ACKs after 3, 6, and 12 seconds with a cleanup after 24 seconds (total of 45 seconds). Setting the value to 1 causes a SYN/ACK to be

retransmitted after 3 seconds and performs a cleanup after 6 seconds (total of 9 seconds).

The *backlog* is the term used by Windows for the queue holding half-open connections. This backlog can be configured appropriately by modifying certain keys in HKEY_LOCAL_MACHINE\SYSTEM\CurrentControlSet\Services\AFD\Parameters.

- **EnableDynamicBacklog** This **REG DWORD** entry should be set to 1 if a server is under a SYN attack in order to allow the backlog to grow dynamically.

**SECURITY ALERT!**

Test any configuration changes carefully before using the Windows SYN protection facilities in a production environment—certain configurations can induce failures and other security risks!

### *The Cisco Approach to SYN*

Cisco provides a feature called TCP Intercept that protects a network from SYN floods. Using the intercept mode, the router captures SYN packets that match certain rules. The router then attempts to respond to the client's SYN with a SYN/ACK on behalf of the server behind it, effectively owning the server portion of the three-way TCP handshake. If the ACK from the client is received successfully by the router, then the original SYN is sent on to the server. The half-formed connections between the client and router and the router and the server are then joined to form a single legitimate connection between the client and server. But if the router's original SYN/ACK to the client is not successful, then the router drops the connection.

TCP Intercept can be configured to be less aggressive and merely monitor the handshakes in watch mode. If the connection attempt is not satisfactorily resolved within a given timeframe, then the router terminates the half-open connection. TCP intercept can be configured to work with all routed packets or those meeting certain source or destination criteria.

An example of the basic commands for enabling TCP Intercept are shown here, but for more complete documentation (on modes, timers, drops, and statistics) search for "TCP Intercept" on www.cisco.com.

```
ip tcp intercept list 101

!

access-list 101 deny ip 10.0.0.0   0.255.255.255
```

### How Other Devices Approach SYN

Other perimeter devices, such as firewalls, can provide some protection against SYN floods, for example Check Point Software's FireWall-1 SYNDefender. It provides two methods of SYN flood protection, namely SYNDefender Relay and SYNDefender Gateway. Much like TCP Intercept, SYNDefender Relay acts as a middleman in setting up a TCP connection until the three-way handshake is complete. The connection is sent on to the server behind the firewall only after a reply has been received to Firewall-1's SYN/ACK.

The SYNDefender Gateway solution takes a different approach by letting SYNs travel directly through the firewall to the server. When the server sends out the SYN/ACK, the SYNDefender Gateway responds with an ACK. This means that the server perceives that the handshake has been completed, and the connection is then moved out of the connection queue.

**Tools & Traps...**

**Are You a Smurf?**

To ensure that your network is not an unwilling participant in a Smurf attack, configure appropriate egress and ingress filters on edge devices. For Cisco devices, IOS version 12 and above disables

**Continued**

directed broadcast by default, but if you have not upgraded to the latest release, issue the following command:

```
no ip directed-broadcast
```

Also on Cisco devices remember to turn unicast reverse path forwarding on, using this command:

```
ip verify unicast reverse-path
```

For additional protection, most Linux distributions can be configured to enable source address verification using rp_filter:

```
for f in /proc/sys/net/ipv4/conf/*/rp_filter; do
     echo 1 > $f
done
```

Windows NT and Windows 2000 have the ability to filter TCP and UDP ports as well as specific IP addresses. They can be used to stop packets with a spoofed source address within the private address ranges.

In an effort to help eliminate IP directed broadcasts, the Web sites www.nestscan.org and www.powertech.no/smurf provide easy-to-use sites that simply require you to input the details of your Internet-visible IP network address. A script then determines the number of times that network broadcast and subnet address replies to a single ICMP ping. If either is greater than one, then your network is a potential amplifier.

# Methods for Locating and Removing Zombies

A profusion of tools are available to aid in the identification and recovery of networks involved in DDoS attacks. A few hardy souls have developed tools that can instruct daemons to stop attacking. Others have written programs that search for DDoS binaries on suspect hosts. Even more good news is that most of these tools are free.

The tools detailed in this section can quite easily be scripted so that they run proactively to maintain the security profile of the network during off-peak times. An aggressive version of the same scripts could be developed to help stave off a live DDoS incident.

A possible (and overly simple) combination of scripts could cause nmap to scan hosts within well-defined ranges for open ports signifying the presence of DDoS programs. On hosts with suspicious open ports tools, such as find_ddos or Tripwire, could then determine the presence (or lack thereof) of the DDoS programs.

## Using Nmap

*Nmap*—a multi-purpose scanning tool—is an essential part of any security officer's toolkit. By crafting scripts using nmap, an entire network can be scanned for the presence of zombies or masters listening on ports (UDP or TCP) known to the administrator. For example, during the TCP scan process, nmap can be instructed to send a SYN to the port at a specific address and report back a result depending on whether an ACK was received in reply.

A basic scan of a network with a subnet mask of 255.255.255.0 in order to identify Stacheldraht masters or zombies could look similar to this:

```
nmap -sS  -p 65000-65513 your.network.com/24
```

The output of nmap can be piped into a file and processed en masse at a later date. It would be quite easy to set up a script to mail an administrator with the IP address of hosts when open TCP ports 65000, 65512, or 65513 are discovered (realizing that these ports can change with modified or new versions). The number of applications for this tool is almost limitless and can, with a little ingenuity, automatically detect masters and zombies. You can download Nmap from www.insecure.org/nmap.

## Using Find_ddos

Developed by the National Infrastructure Protection Center (NIPC), *find_ddos* can determine if certain DDoS attack tools are present on a host. It can run on Linux and Solaris and is able to detect mstream,

TFN2K client, TFN2K daemon, trinoo daemon, trinoo master, TFN daemon, TFN client, Stacheldraht master, Stacheldraht client, Stacheldraht daemon, and Trinity v3.

The tool works by comparing files against the known characteristics of DDoS programs and can even detect if one is currently running. Like most software, it is not 100-percent foolproof and could produce false positives, but it is still a valuable and worthwhile tool. You can download Find_ddos from www.nipc.gov.

### Using Zombie Zapper

Developed by Bindview—a well-known security company—*Zombie Zapper* provides administrators with an easy way to instruct daemons in the throes of an attack to stop. Zombie Zapper comes in two versions—one for UNIX and the other for Windows.

As is usually the case, the UNIX version is command-line-driven, whereas the Windows version has a graphical front-end. Zombie Zapper can instruct trinoo, TFN, Stacheldraht, Wintrinoo, and Shaft daemons to stop attacking. There are a few caveats associated with using Zombie Zapper, namely:

- It assumes that the default passwords have been used to compile the relevant binaries.
- It stops the trinoo daemon totally, but for all other daemons it merely halts the attack currently in progress (which can help in locating the daemons).
- It does not work with TFN2K.
- If you are the recipient of an attack and you attempt to shut down daemons on a third-party network, keep in mind that you may be pointing Zombie Zapper at the wrong network as a result of packet spoofing, or the instructions issues by Zombie Zapper may be filtered by security devices such as routers and firewalls.
- It requires libnet 1.0 or higher. Libnet is a collection of routines and functions that ease the creation of network-aware applications and utilities.

Refer to Figure 2.9 for a view of the UNIX version of Zombie Zapper. The UNIX Zombie Zapper binary, called *zz*, has a number of parameters to fine-tune its operation. The Windows version provides a friendly interface, but the more experienced administrators may prefer to see the verbose information provided by using the **–vv** option. Using the UNIX version, you can even spoof the daemon kill packets generated by Zombie Zapper (very naughty!).

Download libnet from www.packetfactory.net/libnet and Zombie Zapper from the resourceful Bindview Razor team at razor.bindview .com/tools.

**Figure 2.9** The UNIX Version of Zombie Zapper

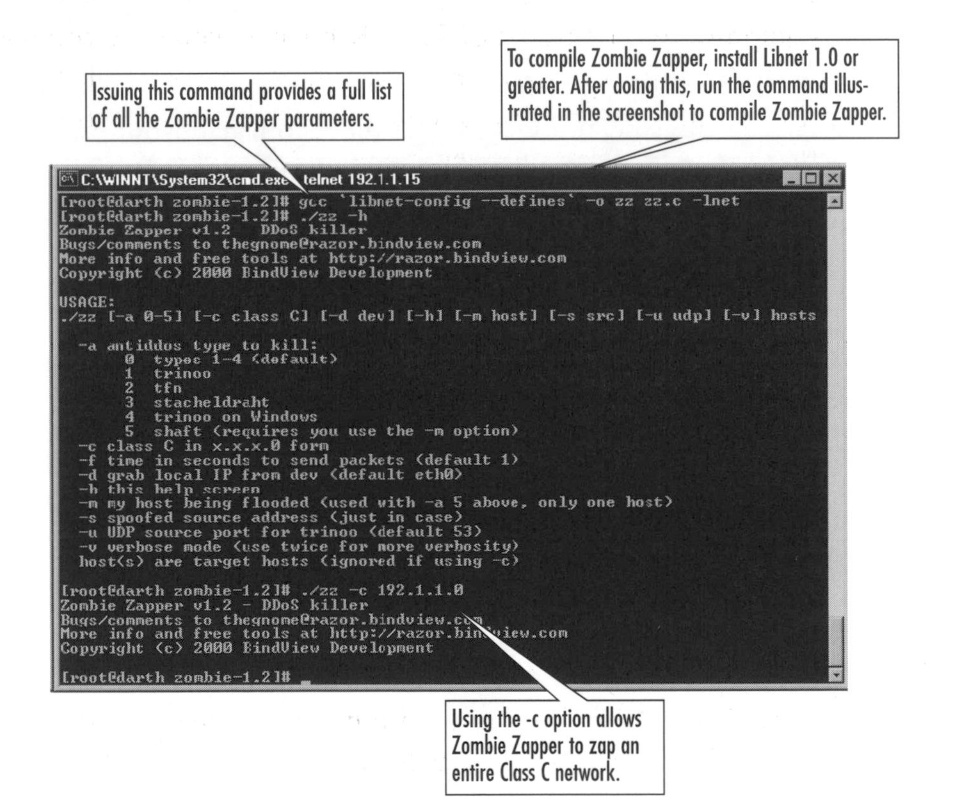

## Using tfn2kpass

An option at compile time for TFN2K makes it impervious to Zombie Zapper and its ilk. When compiling TFN2K it asks for a password to use for encryption, easily allowing TFN2K to navigate around the default password loophole used by Zombie Zapper. But never fear, help is at hand in the form of *tfn2kPass*.

Developed by Simple Nomad, tfn2kpass is distributed in source code format and can be compiled on Solaris, Linux, and FreeBSD. The compiled code can then be used to extract the password from the TFN2K binaries td or tfn. This is useful in a number of scenarios:

- If you have discovered that hosts on your network have been compromised, a new set of TFN2K binaries could be compiled with the recovered password. Using this freshly compiled version of tfn, an administrator could then command hosts running the daemon (td) to halt their attack.
- In the information gathering phase, the password could be used as evidence, or it could potentially be used on other password-protected code used by the attacker.

The source code for tfn2kpass can be downloaded at http://razor.bindview.com/tools. Compiling and running the source code is easily achieved by running the following commands:

```
gcc -o tfn2kpass tfn2kpass.c
./tfn2kpass tfn
```

## Other Tools

A number of other tools are available to mitigate or alleviate DDoS attacks. A few of them are briefly detailed in the following list:

- **RID** Developed by the Theory Group, RID can help administrators determine which hosts have been compromised by DDoS tools. RID issues packets that are defined in a configuration file; if these packets are replied to, RID knows that a host has been compromised. Example configurations exist for detecting Stacheldraht (v1.1 and v4), TFN, and Wintrinoo. You can download it from: www.theorygroup.com/software/RID, but it requires libpcap to run. You can download Libpcap from www.tcpdum.org.

- **DDosPing** A Windows-based utility that scans remote hosts for the presence of trinoo, TFN, and Stacheldraht. It can be run and configured via a graphical front-end. You can download it by selecting the **Scanner** option at www.foundstone.com/rdlabs/tools.php.
- **Ramenfind** Can be used to detect and remove the Ramen worm (which has been used to distribute DDoS tools). You can download it from www.ists.dartmouth.edu/IRIA/knowledge_base/tools/ramenfind.html.
- **DDS** Can be used to detect trinoo, TFN, and Stacheldraht. You can download it from http://staff.washington.edu/dittrich/misc/ddos.
- **GAG** Can be used to detect Stacheldraht agents. You can download it from http://staff.washington.edu/dittrich/misc/ddos.
- **Tripwire** A freely available tool that can check the file and directory integrity of a system and determine if modifications have been made, such as the installation of a rootkit or DDoS daemon. You can download it from www.tripwire.com.
- **Commercial third-party tools** A number of tools are available from reputable security companies that can detect DDoS programs. Vulnerability assessment tools can scan a host to determine whether the host is susceptible to a particular (DDoS) vulnerability and sometimes recommend actions. Mainstream examples of this type of software include ISS Internet Scanner (www.iss.net/securing_e-business/security_products/index.php) and Axent NetRecon (http://enterprisesecurity.symantec.com).

# Summary

DoS attacks are aimed at ensuring that the service a computing infrastructure delivers is negatively affected in some way. Though this type of attack does not involve the theft of electronic assets, the effect on the business can be significant. A number of DoS attack tools are available on the Internet; many of them have been designed with the premise that they should be simple to use. Consequently, the use of DDoS tools has extended beyond just those considered to be technically competent and into the hands of relative Internet neophytes.

DoS attacks primarily originate from remote systems, but they can also take place local to the host in question. The effects of a DoS attack are far-reaching and can be detrimental to both business and the corporate image.

Resource consumption attacks and malformed packet attacks are two categories of DoS attacks. A resource consumption attack involves the reduction of available resources by using a directed attack. These attacks can consume system resources such as memory, CPU, connection queues, or network resources such as bandwidth. Two common examples of resource consumption attacks are SYN flood and Smurf attacks.

A SYN flood achieves its desired impact by interfering with the mechanics of how a TCP connection is initiated. The basic steps involved in setting up a TCP connection involve the client sending a SYN packet to the server. The server then responds to the client's SYN with an ACK and its own SYN. The combination of the SYN/ACK is sent from the server to the client, which responds with the final part of three-way handshake—an ACK. A SYN flood attack tool leverages this handshake by sending the initial SYN to the server with a spoofed (forged) source address. The server receiving the SYN then responds with a SYN/ACK. Forging the source address has the consequent effect that the SYN/ACK with which the server responds is never answered.

The attacker sends a number of these SYNs in an effort to exhaust the number of allowable half-open connections. The number of SYNs that can be responded to is finite, and eventually the connection queue overflows and the server begins to reject connection requests from legitimate clients.

A Smurf attack leverages the undesirable ability of some networks to respond to directed broadcasts. The attacker sends directed broadcasts to these networks with a spoofed source address. The attacker substitutes the victim's address in the source of the directed broadcasts. All hosts on the amplifier network then respond to the broadcast with an ICMP echo reply directed at the victim. This can lead to bandwidth consumption and denial of service.

The second attack category—malformed packet attack—crafts a specifically tailored network packet that can result in unexpected behavior on the target systems. Examples include Teardrop and land attacks.

A DDoS attack is the next step in the evolution of DoS attacks, consisting of client software, master software, and daemon software. The attack hierarchy consists of compromised hosts running the DDoS software. After creating a distributed attack hierarchy, the attacker sends control commands to a master computer. This master computer, running the client software, then instructs zombies (running the daemon) to launch a coordinated attack directed at the victim.

Current advances in technology and Internet acceptance make e-commerce sites even more attractive targets for DDoS attacks. Unfortunately the sensationalism accompanying attacks feeds the cycle of Internet abuse. An attacker may target a site for a number of reasons, including financial gain, recognition, hacktivism, revenge, and the notion of ethical hacking.

There are a number of DDoS tools available in source code format including trinoo, TFN2K and Stacheldraht. One of the first DDoS tools, trinoo is technically not as advanced as its older cousins and is easier to detect. Trinoo follows the three-tier design of most distributed attacks using an *Attacker* ➔ *Client* ➔ *Daemon* chain.

TFN2K can be compiled on Linux, Solaris, and Windows NT and consists of two main binaries after compile time—tfn and td. The tfn program is the client program used by the attacker to instruct the daemon process (td) running on zombie machines to commence or halt attacks. Communication between the client and daemon software can be difficult to detect because it is one way, encrypted, and is interspersed with decoy packets.

When compiled, Stacheldraht consists of three binaries—client, mserv, and td. Each of the binaries are used in a separate tier in the attack model. Communication between the client and mserv is symmetrically encrypted with the Blowfish algorithm.

No solution can satisfactorily protect hosts and networks against DDoS attacks. All a business can do is aim to reduce the effectiveness of DDoS attacks, detect the attacks, and ensure that hosts are not compromised and forced to participate in the attacks. The cost of mitigating these attacks has to be realistically examined in relation to the cost of reducing the exposure.

# Solutions Fast Track

## What Is a DDoS Attack?

☑ A DoS attack attempts to reduce the ability of a site to service clients, be they physical users or logical entities such as other computer systems. This can be achieved by either overloading the ability of the target network or server to handle incoming traffic or by sending network packets that cause target systems and networks to behave unpredictably.

☑ Resource consumption attacks predominantly originate from outside the local network, but do not rule out the possibility that the attack is from within. These attacks usually take the form of a large number of packets directed at the victim, a technique commonly known as *flooding*. Other forms of resource consumption can include the reduction of connections available to legitimate users and the reduction of system resources available to the host operating system itself. A classic example of this scenario was the Melissa virus.

☑ A SYN flood usually involves a number of packets being directed at the target server, consequently overloading the connection buffer. Unfortunately the SYN flood attack can be quite effective, primarily because it can be launched by a hacker with limited resources and has the added advantage of obscuring the source of the attack in the first place.

☑ An *amplification attack* achieves its effectiveness by enlisting the aid of other networks that act as amplifiers for the attack. This allows hackers with limited resources to target victims with a considerable increase in resources. The networks used in the amplification attacks are usually oblivious to their part in the whole process. Two examples of amplification attacks are the whimsically named Smurf and Fraggle.

☑ A *malformed packet attack* usually consists of a small number of packets directed at a target server or device. The packets are constructed in such a fashion that on receipt of the packet, the target panics. A *panic* is considered to occur when the device or operating system enters an unstable state potentially resulting in a system crash. A classic DoS malformed packet attack is the Ping of Death.

☑ An often-neglected aspect of securing a site against DoS attacks is ensuring *physical* security. Not only must the physical security of the servers be considered, but also the cabling and power infrastructures.

☑ Indirect attacks could also become more relevant as DoS attacks attain greater subtlety. A savvy hacker could target the weakest link in your business chain instead of mounting a full frontal assault on the business itself.

☑ One of the significant differences in methodology of a DDoS attack is that it consists of two distinct phases. During the first phase, the perpetrator compromises computers scattered across the Internet and installs specialized software on these hosts to aid in the attack. In the second phase, the compromised hosts, referred to as zombies, are then instructed through intermediaries (called masters) to commence the attack. Microsoft became next in the line of bemused businesses subjected to successful DDoS attacks.

## Why Are E-Commerce Sites Prime Targets for DDoS?

☑ The more complex a site and the technologies it uses, the more difficult it is to maintain an aggressive security profile. The complexity of the site can reduce security coverage through human error, design fault, or immature technology implementations. Managing change control can be particularly troublesome for large sites, and each change has the potential to introduce vulnerability.

☑ The media continues to play a significant, though unintended, role. Attacks are intensely scrutinized not only by the IT press, but also by every conceivable TV station, newspaper, and magazine. Using the latest DDoS tools, even a fledgling hacker can bring down well-known international companies and get front-page coverage.

## What Motivates an Attacker to Damage Companies?

☑ Hacktivism is the electronic extrapolation of the right to free speech and expression coupled with modern-day activism. Certain individuals and groups take the ability to express ideals and beliefs a step further by taking direct action, which usually involves damaging or attacking sites with conflicting perspectives. This tactic is often deemed acceptable by the hacktivists due to the publicity such an attack can generate. Most hacktivists are of the opinion that the media attention generates public interest in their causes.

☑ A DDoS attack could force a business to focus attention on resuming normal operations, hackers can compromise the site via an alternate route and gain information such as credit card and bank account details. These details can then be resold on the Internet or used personally by the hacker.

- ☑ The anonymity provided by the Internet may encourage hackers to project threatening personalities and indulge in extravagant and aggressive role-playing or vandalism. It is impossible to determine the rationale behind attacks motivated purely through a will to deface or destroy.

## What Are Some of the Tools Attackers Use to Perform DDoS Attacks?

- ☑ Using the open source model allows a significant number of people to contribute to the development of new strains and versions of the DDoS tools. Contributions from hackers from a variety of backgrounds allow the code to develop organically and in surprising directions. Additionally, coding neophytes can pick at the source code used for a particular attack to hone and refine their own burgeoning skills.
- ☑ Trinoo, one of the first publicly available DDoS programs, rose to fame in August 1999 after it was used to successfully mount an attack on the University of Minnesota. Like most multi-tier DDoS attacks, the early stages of a trinoo attack involves the attacker compromising machines to become masters. The masters then receive copies of a number of utilities, tools, and—of course—the trinoo control and daemon programs. The master then compiles a list of machines with specific vulnerabilities (possibly involving buffer overflows in RPC services) targeted to act as zombies in the forthcoming attack. The trinoo daemon is then installed and configured to run on the compromised hosts.
- ☑ The main components of TFN2K after compile time are two binaries, namely *tfn* and *td*. Using a well-defined syntax, the client program (tfn) sends commands to the TFN2K daemon (which can be unlimited in number) installed on compromised hosts. The daemon (td) then carries out the commands as directed by the client. At the most basic level, tfn instructs td to

either commence or halt attacks. TFN2K is quite versatile; it works on a number of platforms—even on Windows platforms using UNIX shells such as vmware and cygwin.

☑ The compilation of the Stacheldraht source code results in the generation of three binaries. The three binaries are *client*, *mserv,* and *td*, each of which is used in a separate tier in the attack model. Mserv is the *client software* because it runs on the master. Compromised hosts to be used as zombies are then configured to run the td binary, which contains the actual code to assemble attack packets and traffic streams. When the client binary is run, it establishes a telnet-like session with the master running the mserv program. Stacheldraht uses the freely available Blowfish encryption algorithm based on a 64-bit block cipher.

## How Can I Protect My Site against These Types of Attacks?

☑ DDoS countermeasures include *egress filtering* of spoofed addresses and *ingress filtering* of broadcast packets. Egress filtering encompasses the filtering of outbound traffic, whereas ingress filtering relates to the filtering of inward-bound network traffic. Your ISP should be required to implement ingress filtering, which can aid in identifying zombie networks.

☑ Options available to minimize DDoS exposure include keeping the security profile current; profiling traffic patterns; splitting DNS infrastructure; using load balancing; tightening firewall configurations; securing perimeter devices and using traffic shaping; implementing an IDS, vulnerability scanner, and/or proxy server; taking snapshots and conducting integrity checks of existing configurations; configuring sacrificial hosts; increasing network and host management; maintaining a response procedure;, and deploying more secure technologies.

- ☑ Network *choke points* are usually an excellent place to apply egress rules or filters. Choke points requiring egress filtering include all internal interfaces on firewalls, routers, and dial-in servers.
- ☑ Operating systems should be configured to ignore directed broadcasts, to incorporate SYN flood resilience, to establish strong passwords, and have all unnecessary services turned off.
- ☑ A profusion of tools are available to aid in the identification and recovery of networks involved in DDoS attacks, including Nmap, Find_ddos, Zombie Zapper, tfn2kpass, RID, DDosPing, Ramenfind, DDS, GAG, and Tripwire.
- ☑ In case of attack, your response procedure should incorporate information gathering; contacting the ISP; applying more aggressive filters; applying different routing options; attempting to stop the attack; changing the IP address of the target system, and commencing incidence investigation.

# Frequently Asked Questions

The following Frequently Asked Questions, answered by the authors of this book, are designed to both measure your understanding of the concepts presented in this chapter and to assist you with real-life implementation of these concepts. To have your questions about this chapter answered by the author, browse to **www.syngress.com/solutions** and click on the **"Ask the Author"** form.

**Q:** What sites should I be examining for updated DDoS tools and security information?

**A:** A number of excellent sites provide a significant amount of information. Table 2.3 provides a rough sampling of just a few of the sites available.

**Table 2.3** Sources for DDoS Tools and Security Information

| Site name | Link |
|---|---|
| David Dittrich's DDoS site | www.washington.edu/people/dad |
| Security Focus | www.securityfocus.com |
| Bindview's Razor team | http://razor.bindview.com |
| Internet Security Systems X-Force | http://xforce.iss.net |
| National Infrastructure Protection Center | www.nipc.gov |
| Packet Storm | http://packetstorm.security.com |
| Hideaway.Net | www.hideaway.net |
| Attrition.org | www.attrition.org |
| Linux Security | www.linuxsecurity.com |
| Windows IT Security | www.ntsecurity.net |
| Technotronic.com | www.technotronic.com |
| Carnegie Mellon Software Institute | www.cert.org |

**Q:** I would like to configure my UNIX hosts not to respond to directed broadcasts. How do I do this?

**A:** Disabling directed broadcast is a good start to reduce the likelihood of being an amplifier network. If you are unsure whether edge devices have disabled directed broadcast, then they can be disabled at the operating system level. Be aware that using this method will take considerably more time than correctly configuring edge devices. Linux can be configured to ignore directed broadcasts by using this command:

```
echo 1 > /proc/sys/net/ipv4/icmp_echo_ignore_broadcasts
```

To disable directed broadcasts on Solaris, use the following command:

```
ndd -set /dev/ip ip_forward_directed_broadcasts 0
```

**Q:** My network has been compromised and Stacheldraht installed on several hosts. I have applied egress rules to my edge devices. Does this mean that spoofed packets cannot exit my network?

**A:** No. Even if the test Stacheldraht ICMP echo fails, the lowest eight bits of the address space is still spoofed.

**Q:** I have managed to track down the network addresses of hosts involved in a DDoS attack directed at my site. Why is Zombie Zapper not able to shut the clients down?

**A:** The networks infested with the Zombie hosts may not have sufficient bandwidth available for packets to make it back to the attacking hosts. Be very careful when using DDoS tools in this fashion; other administrators or monitoring agencies may mistake the intent of your directed packets.

Chapter 3

# Secure Web Site Design

Solutions in this chapter:

- Choosing a Web Server
- The Basics of Secure Site Design
- Guidelines for Java, JavaScript, and Active X
- Programming Secure Scripts
- Code Signing: Solution or More Problems?
- Should I Outsource the Design of My Site?

☑ Summary

☑ Solutions Fast Track

☑ Frequently Asked Questions

# Introduction

Securing your e-commerce site is more than planning and implementing a secure network architecture. Although these are great starts for a site, the most visible and often-attacked component is the site's server itself. In fact, in the last few years, Web hacking has become so common that some sites have begun to archive and hype Web site defacements. Attacks against Web servers are very common and in many cases they are among the most trivial of attacks to commit.

Protecting your site against Web-based attacks has to begin with the design of the site itself. Selection and proper installation of the Web server software, followed by the appropriate hardening techniques, must be applied to each and every site you design. Modifications, patches, and upgrades may also impact the security baselines, so they too must be considered. But with all the software choices and configuration options available, how do you choose what is right for your site?

The first step toward designing a secure Web site is choosing a server that suits the needs of your organization. This requires reviewing the features of a number of different Web servers, as well as the cost of the software. This chapter provides you with information on features included with numerous types of Web servers—and security features in particular. It will also take a closer look at two of the most popular servers: Apache Web Server and Internet Information Server (IIS).

After your server has been properly installed and configured, you must then ensure that your site uses secure scripts and applets. This involves following safe programming procedures and analyzing applets and scripts programmed by others to ensure they won't jeopardize the security of your site. To indicate to others that your programs are secure, you should consider code signing.

If you are unsure about your own abilities to design a secure site or perform certain tasks that will make your project successful, then you should consider outsourcing the work. Outsourcing is contracting out to professionals the entire project or jobs involved in the design of your site. Outsourcing will give you the comfort of knowing that the task is done correctly.

# Choosing a Web Server

The first step to having a good, secure Web site is choosing the right Web server. The type of Web server you choose will depend on an evaluation of criteria such as cost, the sensitivity of your data, the platform being used, who will need to access the data, and the security options you will require from the server system.

In choosing a Web server, remember this important point: Choosing a Web server that's right for your organization is subjective. What may be an excellent choice for one enterprise may not work as well in your company. You may find that your company doesn't require certain features; a particular Web server won't run on the operating system being used; or the price of a server is out of your price range. Determining what comparable companies and networks are using can be valuable in your decision-making; however, in the end, you will find that the server you choose will be an independent and individualized decision.

You should take time to identify what could be accessed through your Web server and identify what data is sensitive and must be protected. For example, you may want all users to access a default Web page that introduces your site and allow them to view products for sale by your company, but you wouldn't want them accessing a database of users or credit card numbers. You may want to allow users to access all content on the Web server itself, but you wouldn't want them to access any files off this machine, which are located on your internal network. In addition, your organization may have requirements that are set by outside groups (such as government agencies that require specific security settings). By identifying your security requirements, you will then be able to make a more informed decision as to what you're expecting out of your Web server.

## Web Server versus Web Service

In evaluating the needs of your organization, you may find that you do *not* require a Web server. Many organizations need a Web presence, but decide that no sensitive data will be available through the Web site. The site will have no secure or private areas, and no sales will be made through the site. Security isn't imperative, as any information available through the Web will be available to everyone. For example, a hotel or restaurant may want to advertise through a Web site and show what they offer. If they don't wish to take reservations, then they have no need for massive security efforts. If the site is hacked and content on the site is altered, it is merely a matter of uploading the HTML documents and graphics to the server or recovering it from a backup. In such cases, it may be wise to acquire space on an ISP's Web server. Because this server would be separate from the business's internal network, there is no chance that any sensitive data would be accessed through the Web server. This option also removes the need for heavy administration, because the webmaster's role would consist of generating and maintaining content.

The cost of having a private Web server is high and should be balanced against the benefits it will return. Although IT staff may find the prospect of having their own Web server exciting, and decision makers may like the prestige it implies, the cost will generally be more than it would to rent space on an ISP's server. Remember that renting such space removes the cost of purchasing servers, software, T1 lines to the Internet, and so forth. If problems arise with this equipment, it falls on the ISP to fix it, which saves you the responsibility of dealing with such issues.

Unfortunately, you will also lose a number of benefits by going through an ISP for hosting services. Any security, services, or extra software installed on the server will be decided by the third party. This is where it becomes vital that you choose a Web server that meets or exceeds the needs of your enterprise.

# Factoring in Web Servers' Cost and Supported Operating Systems

When looking at which Web server to use, you will be faced with a large number of choices. To narrow down your choices, you should first determine which ones are supported by operating systems already in use by your network or which your IT staff has some experience with. By using a platform your staff is already familiar with, there is less chance they will miss security holes they may already be aware of in other operating systems. Choosing an operating system that is already supported by the

IT staff will also lower training costs, because the webmaster and network staff won't need to learn a new system.

Cost is a major issue when preparing a budget for a project and deciding what will be needed for a project to be successful. In addition to having the necessary hardware, operating system, applications, and a connection to the Internet, you may find that you will need to pay for Web server software. In the case of most organizations, the purchases will need to be justified. Because the Internet is still relatively new and unfamiliar territory for many decision-makers, you will need to show why your choice may merit the added expense of paying for a particular Web server.

Remember that cost and operating systems that are supported are only two considerations for choosing a server. Table 3.1 shows a comparison of various Web servers, their approximate costs, and the platforms each supports. Security features are discussed separately, in the next section.

**Table 3.1** A Comparison of Web Servers

| Web Server | Web Site | Cost | Platforms Supported |
|---|---|---|---|
| America Online AOLServer 3.3 | www.aolserver.com | $0 | Windows 9x, Windows NT/2000, Digital UNIX, SCO, HPUX, Linux, FreeBSD, IRIX, Solaris |
| Apache Web Server 1.3.7 | www.apache.org | $0 | Windows 9x, Windows NT/2000, Novell NetWare 5, Solaris, OS/2, Macintosh, UnixWare, HP MPE/iX, IBM's Transaction Processing Facility (TPF), NetBSD, Digital UNIX, BSDI, AIX, SCO, HPUX, Be OS, Linux, FreeBSD, IRIX |

Continued

**Table 3.1** Continued

| Web Server | Web Site | Cost | Platforms Supported |
|---|---|---|---|
| IBM HTTP Server (two variations: one is based on Apache HTTP Server; the other is based on Lotus Domino Go Webserver) | www-4.ibm.com/software/webservers/httpservers | $0 (Bundled with WebSphere Application Server) | AIX, Linux, OS/390, OS/400, Sun Solaris, HP-UX, and Windows NT |
| Novell Enterprise Web Server | www.novell.com/products/netware | $0 (Included with Novell NetWare 5.1).$1295 for Novell NetWare 4.1x version | Novell NetWare |
| GoAhead WebServer 2.1 | www.goahead.com/webserver/webserver.htm | $0 | Windows 9x, Windows NT/2000, Windows CE, Embeded Linux, Linux, VxWorks, QNX, Lynx, eCOS |
| Hawkeye 1.3.6 | www.hawkeye.net | $0 (for private or educational use) | Linux |
| i-Planet Web Server | www.iplanet.com | $1495 | Windows NT (with SP4) / Windows 2000, HPUX, Solaris, IBM AIX, UNIX, IRIX |
| Microsoft Internet Information Server 4.0 | www.microsoft.com/ntserver/web/default.asp | $0 (included with NT 4.0 option pack) | Windows NT 4.0 |

Continued

**Table 3.1** Continued

| Web Server | Web Site | Cost | Platforms Supported |
|---|---|---|---|
| Microsoft Internet Information Services 5.0 | www.microsoft.com/windows2000/guide/server/overview/default.asp | $0 (included with Windows 2000 Server) | Windows 2000 Server |
| Netscape Enterprise Server 3.6 | http://home.netscape.com/enterprise | $1,295 | Windows NT/2000, Digital UNIX, AIX, HPUX, IRIX, Solaris, Reliant Unix |
| TinyWeb | www.ritlabs.com/tinyweb | $0 | Windows 9x, Windows NT |
| WebSTAR 4.3 | www.starnine.com | $599 | Macintosh |

You can see that the range of prices and operating systems supported vary, and not all of them may be useful in your organization. Many businesses are willing to spend a little extra if they have good reason to do so (like better security features). However, your IT staff may disallow certain operating systems to be used, if they feel they are less secure or stable. Because the Web server runs on top of the operating system like any other software, an operating system with better security features will thereby improve the security of your Web server.

For example, although Windows 95 can be used to run Apache Web server, it would be more secure to use Apache on Windows NT Server. Windows 95 has fewer security features and a less secure file system than NT. Therefore, a hacker would have an easier time accessing sensitive material by making his way through a Web server running on a Windows 95 system.

Remember that elements of your system will work together in providing security. A secure operating system, with restrictive policies set for users and a secure file system, will allow you to control what users are able to access when visiting your site. You can add a firewall to protect your internal network and control what information can be passed from the Internet to the user on your internal network. Antivirus software will protect your system from known viruses. Each of these will work with the Web server to make a secure Web site.

## Damage & Defense…

### Researching Web Servers

You can find a number of resources available for researching the features and advantages certain Web servers have over one another. Trade magazines, which provide significant information about different Web servers, are an established method of selecting a product. Newsgroups and chat rooms will allow you to discuss problems and successes other organizations have had with their server software. These will also allow you to pose questions to other IT professionals and get answers based on personal experiences. In addition to these resources, you may also find the following Web sites useful in your research:

- **Netcraft Web Server Survey** (www.netcraft.com/survey)
- **ServerWatch** (http://serverwatch.internet.com/webservers.html)
- **Web Server Compare** (http://webservercompare.internet.com)

After you've compared and narrowed down your choices, you should then visit the Web sites of the Web servers on your short list. On these sites, you will be able to see detailed features of the products and may also view information dealing with known security issues. This will allow you select one product from your short list and come to a final decision through an educated process of elimination.

# Comparing Web Servers' Security Features

Although firewalls, antivirus software, and a good operating system are important to designing a secure site, this in no way takes away from the importance of the security features of the Web server itself. The Web server is the foundation of an e-commerce site, which every Web application will work with, and through which most content will be viewed. This means that you will need to find the most secure Web server that will suit your needs.

After you've identified your security requirements, the amount you're willing to spend, and the platforms you're willing to run the Web server on, you're then in a position to compare the security features provided by different servers. However, cost and operating systems should not be the only (or even the primary) considerations. You should balance these against security and features.

You should be flexible in your decision making. If a Web server provides all the features you're looking for, then this will often be more important than the topics previously discussed. After all, there is no point in pinching pennies if the server will keep your site secure and avoid having to do damage control later. The outlying cost of a server is minimal compared to the price of lost data or having to rebuild a seriously damaged site.

In looking at the various servers, you should pay close attention to a number of features, specifically those that control authentication, use of the Secure Electronic Transaction (SET) protocol, the setting of rights and permissions, and the use of Common Gateway Interface (CGI) applications.

## Authentication

Authentication is vital to the security of your intranet and Internet sites, because it proves the validity of a user, service, or applications. In other words, you are verifying the identity of the user who is attempting to access content or resources, or you're verifying the integrity of a message or application that's being installed. Without secure methods of authentication, a user could manage to gain access to various parts of a system and make his or her way onto your local network. Authentication is generally provided through the operating system on which a Web server runs, but some authentication methods can be provided through the Web server or programs accessible through the site. A number of methods are available to perform authentication, including the following:

- Passwords
- Secure Sockets Layer (SSL)
- Windows Challenge/Response
- Digital signatures and certificates
- Smart cards
- Biometrics
- Cookies

In the paragraphs that follow, we discuss each of these methods and then look at various Web servers that may or may not support them.

## *Passwords*

Passwords are the most common form of authentication used on the Web and networks today. They involve entering a word, phrase, or code into a field. The password is compared to the one that was entered when the user account was initially set up. If the password matches, the user is allowed to continue. In most cases, the password is combined with a username, so that both the username and password must match before the user is authenticated.

There are a number of different types of authentication involving passwords, and the type available will generally depend on the Web server and operating system being used. These include:

- Anonymous
- Basic or clear text
- Basic with SSL Encryption
- Windows Challenge/Response

As you'll see in the paragraphs that follow, each of these methods may be used for different purposes and may not be useful depending on the operating system, Web server, or client browser being used.

*Anonymous users* work much like a guest account and allow any user to gain access. This is commonly used to allow visitors of your site to access public information, such as Web pages displaying products available for sale. Because everyone is allowed, there are no requirements for the type of client being used.

Although anonymous users don't require a user to enter a username or password, this doesn't mean that you should give them free reign. After setting up a Web server, you should set anonymous users with the most restrictive access possible and allow them to access only files in directories meant for public display. A number of servers, such as Microsoft IIS, allow full access to the server by default and need to be configured so that anonymous users can't access the data you don't want them to see.

*Basic or clear text* is an unencrypted method of authentication. Users are presented with a dialog box, requiring them to enter a valid username and password. This is sent to the server, which compares the information to that of a valid account. If the username and password match, the user is able to proceed. Because most clients support clear text, most browsers will be able to use this method when attempting to enter sites with minimal security. Membership sites that are semi-secure commonly use basic or clear text authentication. However, because user account information is sent unencrypted, others may be able to view the username and password, which may allow them to obtain valid user account information that they could then use to access your site. Therefore, this method should be used only for accounts that have a minimal or moderate level of access to Web server content or network resources.

*Basic authentication with SSL* encryption is similar to clear text, except that usernames and passwords are encrypted before they're sent to the server. This prevents hackers from obtaining valid account information and thereby accessing areas of your Web server or network that would be off-limits to anonymous users. SSL is the main protocol used for encrypting data over the Internet; developed by Netscape, SSL uses ciphers and keys to encrypt data and allows for 128-bit encryption to provide an extremely secure method of transmitting data. The SSL protocol is bundled in many different browsers on the market, allowing a wide variety of users to use this method of encryption. If a user is using a browser that supports SSL 2.0 or 3.0, an SSL session begins when the server sends a public key to the browser. The browser uses this key to send a randomly generated key back to the server, so that they can exchange data securely. It is commonly used on membership sites that require passwords to enter secure areas, or sites use it to send sensitive data (such as credit card numbers used in sales transactions).

*Windows Challenge/Response* is a method of authentication that can be used by Web servers running on Windows NT or Windows 2000, such as IIS 4.0 or Internet Information Services 5.0. In IIS 5.0, this method is also referred to as Integrated Windows Authentication. With this method, the user isn't initially presented with a dialog box in which to enter information. Instead, a hashing technology is used to establish the user's identity from information stored on the user's computer. The information is presented to the server when the user logs onto the domain. If the attempt to send this information fails, the user is then presented with a dialog box, which allows him or her to enter a username and password. If this fails, the user will be unable to gain access.

Because Windows Challenge/Response requires an NT Server or 2000 Server to be used, it will may not be useful for your particular Web server. For example, if you were using Novell NetWare on your server, then this method wouldn't be available for your uses. Also, only users running Internet Explorer 2.0 or later can use this method. Another drawback is that, unlike the other methods discussed, this method can't be used across proxy servers or firewalls. If a proxy server or firewall is used on a network, then they will use their own IP address in the hashing, and incorrect information will be passed to the Windows NT or 2000 operating system on which the Web server is running. If you are using Windows NT or 2000, with users running compatible versions of IE, then this method might be useful for a corporate intranet.

## Digital Signatures and Certificates

Digital signatures and certificates are another method of authentication. These methods are used to prove that documents, files, and messages are actually from the user or organization claiming to send them and to prove that it hasn't been altered. With a digital signature, encrypted information is used to protect what is being sent. The digital signature is actually an encrypted digest of the text being sent. When it is received, the digest is decrypted and compared to the received text. If the two match, then the message is proven to be authentic. If the document were altered after being sent, then the decrypted digest (i.e., the signature) wouldn't match. In addition, or instead of digital signatures, a digital certificate may be used.

Digital certificates are another method of identifying a sending party and proving that a file hasn't been tampered with. They are used to validate that a file you're receiving is actually the file that was distributed by its creator. A certificate authority (CA) issues the certificate, based upon information that the owner of the certificate supplies. The user is then issued a public key that is digitally signed by the CA. When a file is sent to a recipient, the certificate is sent with an encrypted message that verifies that the sender is actually the person or organization who owns the certificate. The recipient uses the CA's public key to decrypt the sender's public key, which is then used to decrypt the actual message.

Digital certificates can be issued by third-parties, which are widely used on the Internet, or using a certificate server run on your own Web server. This gives you the ability to generate your own certificates and validate files distributed through your server. As you'll see, a number of Web servers have integrated certificate servers, which allow you to provide this service. Digital certificates and code signing are discussed in greater depth later in this chapter.

## Smart Cards

A recent variation to digital certificates is the use of the Fortezza standard. With this method of authentication, a 56-bit public key and certificate is stored on a *smart card*. A smart card is a plastic card with an embedded chip that is used to hold various types of data. The card is inserted into a slot, which then reads this information. Unfortunately, the method has a number of drawbacks. The Fortezza standard can only be used on client computers that are compliant and have a smart card reader installed on it. Also, because both the certificate and public key are stored on the card, if the card is lost or stolen, then you will need to apply for another certificate. However, a PIN number is required to use the card, so if it is lost or stolen, others won't be able to use it without the PIN.

### Biometrics

Biometrics are another recent innovation in identifying users. It authenticates users on the basis of biological identification, such as fingerprints, handprints, voice, eyes, or handwritten signatures. Because these are so personal, it is almost impossible to circumvent security. Unlike with passwords or smart cards, malicious users can't steal this form of identification. However, this method requires extra hardware and can't be used by most users to access a network or server. Although this won't be useful in identifying users of your e-commerce site, this may be used to identify network users (including the administrator of your network or the webmaster).

### Cookies

Finally, cookies are another method of identifying users. Cookies are sent by the Web server and stored on the client's computer. When the browser visits the site again, this information is presented to the Web server. A common use for cookies is when forms are used to enter membership information. When you visit a site, you may need to enter your name, address, choose a username, password, and so forth. A cookie could be stored on the user's computer, and when he or she visits the site again, the cookie is presented to the Web server, so that the user doesn't need to continually enter this information with each visit. Another example would be when your e-commerce site needs to remember what a person has put in a shopping cart or how the user prefers items to be shipped.

Browsers generally have a feature that allow users to refuse cookies, so that they aren't stored on the computer. This is because cookies can be used for malicious purposes. It is possible for a hacker to access information in a cookie and obtain personal information about a user. It is also possible for a cookie to return more information than you actually want to be returned. For example, you may have noticed unsolicited mail (spam) being sent to your e-mail, even though you never signed up for e-zines or additional information from sites. This is often because a cookie was used to return information stored on your computer to a site you visited, and your e-mail address was then added to a mailing list. As you can see, cookies can be a security risk, as they may send more information than you actually want revealed. Unfortunately, many Web sites will not interact propertly with Web browsers that do not allow cookies.

## Using the SET Protocol

Secure Electronic Transaction (SET) is an open standard protocol that was developed by Microsoft, Netscape, Visa, and MasterCard. It was developed to address the problem of credit card fraud over the Internet, and is used in processing online credit card transactions. With SET, each party in the transaction (the customer, credit card issuer, merchant, and merchant's bank) is identified through certificates.

With SET, elements of the transaction are separated so that no single party (except the cardholder) is privy to all information about the purchase. The e-commerce merchant is given access to information about the item being purchased and whether the credit card payment has been approved but receives no information about the method of payment. The card issuer is given information about the price but nothing regarding the type of item being purchased.

SET does have drawbacks, however, because not all browsers support it or have the software to use it. Some e-commerce merchants may require the customer to have a SET certificate. Additionally, the browser must have a SET-compliant wallet, which is used to make the purchase. E-commerce sites using SET can make this available, or it can be acquired from the sites of various banks.

## Setting Permissions

Many of the servers we discuss also provide support for setting permissions, or they work with the operating systems they reside on, so that rights and permissions can be set on directories and/or files. This allows you to control what users are able to access and keep unauthorized users from accessing certain files and directories. You must set these properly and only give users the rights they need to do what you want them to do. For example, you will want anonymous users to be able to read an HTML document but not have the ability to write, which would allow a user to modify your Web pages, upload viruses, and so forth.

A number of Web servers will also provide the ability to hide certain parts of a document based on the security rules you set. This allows only part of a Web page to be displayed to a user so that critical information isn't made available to the public. This is useful when you have sensitive data that you don't want anonymous users to view.

## Using CGI Applications

Support of the CGI is another common feature for Web servers. CGI is used to pass requests to an application. Data can then be passed back to the user in the form of an HTML document. CGI applications are commonly used to process forms online. As you'll see later in this chapter, using CGI does have some drawbacks, as do many of the other features discussed so far.

## Security Features Side By Side

Now that we've looked at a number of features you'll see in Web servers, let's look at a number of Web servers that are on the market.

**Table 3.2** Comparison of Selected Security Features in Different Web Servers

**Features Key:**

A=Protocols Supported
B=Has ability to prohibit access by domain name, IP address, user and group
C=Access can be prohibited by directory or file
D=Configurable user groups, and the ability to change user access control lists without restarting server
E=Hierarchical permissions for directory-based documents
F=Ability to require password to acquire access
G=Security rules can be based on URLs
H=Has ability to hide part of a document based on security rules
I=Basic and digest access authentication
J=CGI Execution and built-in Tcl scripting language capabilities
K=Integrated certificate server
O=OTHER

| Web Server | Features and Comments |
|---|---|
| America Online's AOLServer 3.3 | A (S-HTTP and SSL); B; C; D; E; G; J |
| Apache Web Server 1.3.7 | A (SSL); B; F G; I; J (CGI execution only); K |
| IBM HTTP Server | A (SET, SSL, S-HTTP); B; C; D; E; F; G; H; J (CGI execution only); K |
| Novell's Enterprise Web Server | A (LDAP, SSL, RSA private key/public key encryption, Secure Authentication Services, smart cards and X.509v3 certificates).<br>O: Integration with NetWare Directory Services; Those who have purchased Novell NetWare 5.1 are allowed a free copy of IBM WebSphere Application Server 3.5 for NetWare (Standard Edition). |

Continued

**Table 3.2** Continued

| Web Server | Features and Comments |
|---|---|
| GoAhead WebServer 2.1 | A (SSL, S-HTTP); B; C; D; E; F; G; J (CGI execution only); K |
| Hawkeye 1.3.6 | B (user and group only); D; E; F; G; J (CGI execution only) |
| i-Planet Web Server | A (SSL, LDAP, SNMP, X.509 digital certificates). O: Users have the ability to set access themselves without administrator intervention; supports password policies, dynamic groups, and delegated administration. Similar features to Netscape Enterprise Server; ships with iPlanet Directory Server. |
| Microsoft Internet Information Server 4.0 | A (SET, SSL, S-HTTP); B; C; D; E; F; G; H; I (basic authentication only); J (CGI execution only); K |
| Microsoft Internet Information Services 5.0 | A (SET, SSL, S-HTTP); B; C; D; E; F; G; H; I; J (CGI execution only); K. O: Has wizards designed to make administration tasks involving security easier to manage. |
| Netscape Enterprise Server 3.6 | A (SET, SSL, S-HTTP); B; D; E; F; G; H; K |
| TinyWeb | A (SSL). O: Limited security features. |
| WebSTAR 4.3 | A (SSL); B; C; D (configurable user groups is n/a); F; G; H |

## *AOL Server*

AOLServer is a Web server created by America Online. It is designed for large scale Web sites. Because this is the Web server that AOL itself uses for its own Web site, it's proven to handle a significant number of hits without fail. It is extensible, allowing you to add features without rebuilding it, and provides a number of robust security features. It supports S-HTTP and SSL and allows you to set security rules based on

URLs. It also allows you to prohibit access by specifying the domain name, IP address, user, or group to be blocked. It allows you to configure user groups, rather than just user accounts, and provides the ability to change user access control lists without restarting the server. AOLServer allows you to protect sensitive data by prohibiting access by directory and file and allows you to set hierarchical permissions for directory-based documents.

### Apache Web Server

Apache has a long history of being a popular choice for Web servers. Since 1996, it has been the most popular Web server on the Internet. A large part of the reason for its popularity is its price: free. It is the result of an enterprise called the Apache Project, which is maintained by volunteer developers who make up the Apache Group. Contributors make suggestions on changes to the server, which are then voted on by a core group of members. However, given that large organizations that can afford any Web server still use Apache, its appeal obviously goes beyond the price.

The source code for Apache Web Server is freely available, allowing webmasters to analyze how it was built and how the functionality of the server can be extended. This information may be useful to programmers in your organization, who could use this low-level information when building Web applications and databases. The extensibility of Apache is most often done using the programming language Perl (a Perl interpreter is embedded in the server). Because Apache is open-source, those using the Web server can analyze the code and find security issues, from which patches can then be developed. By having the code distributed in this way, third-party developers have the ability to create modules that can be integrated with your Web server. However, the hackers also have access to the source code and can use it to find new vulnerabilities.

Another important factor in Apache's popularity is the number of systems it supports. As Table 3.1 shows, Version 1.3 can run on the following platforms: Novell NetWare 5, Solaris, OS/2, Macintosh, UnixWare, HP MPE/iX, IBM's TPF, NetBSD, Digital UNIX, BSDI, AIX, SCO, HPUX, Be OS, Linux, FreeBSD, IRIX, Windows 9*x*, Windows NT, and Windows 2000. Chances are you won't need to worry whether the server software will be incompatible with your existing network.

A major drawback to Apache is that it is one of the least user-friendly Web browsers, making it easier for someone who's unfamiliar with the server to make mistakes and compromise security. Apache doesn't offer browser-based or GUI administration, and setup and maintenance of this Web server are done through command-line scripting tools.

### IBM HTTP Server

IBM HTTP Server is available in two variations. One of these is based on Apache HTTP server, whereas the other is based on Lotus Domino Go Webserver. Although Apache is still on the market, with new versions being created and supported, Lotus has stopped making its Domino Go Webserver. The features of Lotus Domino Go Webserver have been incorporated into IBM HTTP Server, which is still available and supported.

IBM HTTP Server serves as the foundation on which other IBM Web products run from or work with. It includes an integrated certificate server, and supports SET, SSL, and S-HTTP. It allows you to set security rules based on URLs and prohibit access by domain name, IP address, user, and group. Using these rules, you can also hide part of a document so that only those authorized to view the content will see it. It has configurable user groups and the ability to change user access control list without restarting server. It also supports hierarchical permissions for directory-based documents and provides the ability to prohibit access by directory or file.

### NetWare Enterprise Web Server

NetWare Enterprise Web Server is for use on networks running Novell NetWare, so if you aren't using this network operating system, you'll have to look at another Web server for your organization. Many large companies use NetWare exclusively, or as part of a mixed network (working with servers like Windows NT and Windows 2000). As such, these enterprises may benefit from using Novell Enterprise Web Server, which integrates with Novell Netware. It also allows you to use a number of tools available or included with Novell NetWare, including IBM's Websphere

Web application server, Novell Firewall, Certificate Server, and so forth. As with Novell's other products, it is secure and robust.

Despite the limited platform, it provides a number of robust security features—features that will enhance your Web site dramatically. Enterprise Web Server is integrated with Novell Directory Services, allowing you to control access to files by setting security through NetWare Administrator. Someone running this network operating system would already be familiar with this tool, which makes site security easy to administer. Another important feature of this Web server is that it encrypts passwords over SSL. It also supports RSA private key/public key encryption, Secure Authentication Services, smart cards, and X.509v3 certificates to protect information on your server.

The integration of Enterprise Web Server with the NetWare network operating system is perhaps the greatest strength this Web server has in terms of security. Novell NetWare is designed with security in mind and is used on numerous security-critical networks. By building the Web server on this platform, you are thereby able to create a secure Web site. This means that the chances of unauthorized access are reduced.

Enterprise Web Server is included with NetWare 5.1. This version of NetWare also includes WebSphere Application Server 3.5 for NetWare (Standard Edition) and WebSphere Studio (Entry Edition). WebSphere is a Java-based application server produced by IBM, whereas WebSphere Studio is a collection of tools used to develop applications used for your site. In addition to these, there are also a number of NetWare products for allowing users to access content on your site. It includes NetWare FTP Server for creating an FTP site, from which users can download files. NetWare News Server allows you to create and maintain news groups, so that users can participate in threaded discussions using standard news readers. NetWare Search Server is used to index your site, so that users can search for content. As you can see, although it is limited to networks running NetWare, it has a number of robust features that can enhance your site.

### GoAhead WebServer

Like Apache, GoAhead WebServer is another product that is open-source and provides an impressive number of features. The GoAhead WebServer supports Microsoft's Active Server Pages (ASP), allowing you to display dynamic content based on user input. It also supports embedded JavaScript, in-process CGI forms, and standard CGI. It supports SSL, Digest Access Authentication, S-HTTP, and allows you to require a password to acquire access. For additional security, you can use the integrated certificate server to generate and maintain certificates. It allows you to prohibit access by domain name, IP address, users, and groups, and it allows you to set security rules based on URLs. It allows you to configure user groups and change user access control list without restarting the server. It also allows you to set hierarchical permissions for directory-based documents and provides the ability to prohibit access by directory or file.

### Hawkeye

Hawkeye is another Web server that is limited to a single platform. In this case, Hawkeye runs only on servers running the Linux operating system. Although you may need to switch operating systems to use it, Hawkeye does provide a number of features found in other more popular Web servers. It allows you to prohibit access by user and group and set security rules based on URLs. It has configurable user groups and provides the ability to change user access control list without restarting the server. It also supports hierarchical permissions for directory-based documents.

### Internet Information Server

Alongside Apache and Netscape, another major player in Web servers is IIS. IIS 4.0 was provided free for Windows NT 4.0 Servers by installing the NT Option Pack, which is available for download from Microsoft's Web site. Internet Information Server 5.0 is called Internet Information Services (also IIS) in Windows 2000 and is the Web server provided with Windows 2000 Server. This is an integrated Web service, used to provide Web and FTP support, as well as support for FrontPage, ASP, transactions, database connections, and receiving posts. By installing this software component, you will have a full Web server on your Windows 2000 Server.

One of the best features of IIS is that it has a GUI interface for installing and maintaining the Web server. This provides a user-friendly method of administrating your site. It also provides support for ASP, Open Database Connectivity (ODBC), and Microsoft Application Programming Interfaces (APIs). ASP provides a dynamic method of returning information through HTML documents. ODBC allows you to create pages that connect to various types of databases. A problem with this Web server is that it only supports Windows NT or Windows 2000; it isn't available for other platforms on the market.

While IIS 5.0 builds on many of the features found in IIS 4.0, a major difference is seen in new wizards that simplify common web-master tasks. The Permissions Wizard allows you to set up and maintain Web and NTFS security settings. The Web Server Certificate Wizard is used to obtain and install server certificates, and the Certificate Trust List Wizard is used to create and modify certificate trust lists.

IIS 5.0 also has expanded support for a number of standards including Fortezza, Transport Layer security using SSL 3.0, and Digest Authentication. Fortezza is a new security standard used by the U.S. government; digest authentication is a method of hashing authentication information.

### *Netscape Enterprise Server*

Netscape Enterprise Server is designed for large scale Web sites and is the Web server that Netscape uses for its own site. An interesting feature of this server is that it will convert Adobe PDF files to HTML. It also comes with an integrated certificate server, useful in providing enhanced security for your site. It provides a GUI for setting up the server, and maintaining it.

Netscape Enterprise Server has a strong emphasis on security. It has support for SSL, S-HTTP, and LDAP. It includes an integrated certificate server, and has features commonly seen in firewalls. You can prohibit access by domain name, IP address, or user account and group. You can even hide part of a document based on security rules that you set.

Although Netscape Enterprise Server is still available for download and use at the time of this writing, Netscape has become part of the development of i-Planet Web Server. This was launched by the

Sun–Netscape alliance and has features that are similar to Netscape Enterprise Server. As you might expect in a partnership with Sun, the i-Planet Web Server includes a number of Java-based tools and applications. i-Planet Web Server supports SSL, LDAP, SNMP, and X.509 digital certificates, and it allows users to set access themselves without administrator intervention. i-Planet Web Server also supports password policies, dynamic groups, and delegated administration. A benefit of i-Planet Web Server is that it ships with the runtime version of iPlanet Directory Server.

### TinyWeb

TinyWeb is only available for use on systems running Windows 9*x* and Windows NT, and is a useful tool for distributing information over a local intranet. It has limited features for security, and it is not advisable for corporations to use this software as an Internet server on the Web. Despite its limitations, it is free and fast. It is a small program and uses a limited amount of resources, making it a good choice for workstations that publish documents on a local network.

### WebSTAR

WebSTAR is a Web server for the Macintosh platform and isn't available for any other type of computer. If your Web server will be running on a Macintosh server, then you will benefit from its easy installation and administration capabilities. It provides integrated GUI-based and browser-based administration, making it a good choice if you're new to managing a Web server.

WebSTAR's security features are also impressive. It allows you to prohibit access by domain name, IP address, user and group, and set the Web server to require a password to obtain access. It allows you to set security rules based on URLs and hide part of a document based on these rules. If changes are made to the user control list, you don't need to restart the server to have these changes go into effect. WebSTAR also supports SSL, providing secure access to resources and content.

**NOTE**

In choosing a server, you may discover that you can't find a server that suits all your needs. Either it doesn't provide enough security, lacks certain features, or doesn't meet other needs. You should remember that although all servers have similar and special features, no one server does everything. If you find that certain necessities aren't met, but many are, then you have probably found the server for you. You can then use additional software such as firewalls, proxy servers, certificate servers, and so on to beef up your system. By adding such software, you will enhance the features and/or security provided and meet more of the requirements you outline for your site.

# The Basics of Secure Site Design

The basics of secure site design begin before the Web server is ever installed and configured. Establishing and maintaining security of an e-commerce site requires careful planning and forethought. All too often, deadlines can make you rush through the preliminary stages and cause you to spend even more time putting out fires and fixing problems that you could have previously avoided. In establishing a plan, you will need to consider protecting your site from a variety of problems and possible attacks.

## Creating a Security Plan

When developing a site, you should also create a security plan. This should include the following steps, which should be completed and revisited after the Web server is in place. As more data and services are added to the site, holes in security may develop, so you must reevaluate the security of your site as your needs change. The steps that follow will help in focusing your efforts so that important factors aren't missed:

- **Identify what needs to be secure** By identifying what data, software, services, and media will need to be protected, you will be able to implement proper security.
- **Identify the value of what's being protected** Some content on your site will require more protection than other files, due to its value. In the same way, you should determine the value of hardware used to keep your site operating. By determining the value of data, hardware, services, and software, you will be able to make an informed decision on how much money and effort should be spent on the implementation of security, insurance, and so forth.
- **Identify the risks involved with your site** Often, this will depend on your organization, system, and business. For example, if your Web server runs on a network server that others have access to (network administrators, programmers, and so on), you stand a greater chance of people intentionally or unintentionally modifying the site and its security.
- **Identify the exposure to risks** This requires analyzing the risks you've previously identified and determining how likely it is that different risks will become an actual problem. If a wave of hacking takes place on a certain server, and your company uses that server, then you are at greater risk of attack. If a hard disk fails, and you don't have a routine of backing up data, then you are at greater risk of losing data permanently if a hard disk fails. Risks that are likely to become actual problems should be given higher priority, and you should then take steps and make plans to deal with them.
- **Put the plan into action** Implement the security steps you've outlined in your plan. This should include making regular backups of data and storing copies off-site. It should also include regularly updating antivirus files and software and that insuring the latest patches and service packs are applied.
- **Establish a repeating timeline to update risk assessment** It's a continual process that needs to be repeated often enough to be effective.

Securing your Web server should also include hardware as well as software. You should keep your server in a secure room, where users won't be able to physically access it. Generally, this will require locking the server in a room or closet. You should also consider a backup power supply; a power outage will shut down your site as effectively as any hacking attempt. An Internet site experienced this problem a few years ago when a janitor's vacuum overloaded the electrical system and caused a power outage in the company's server room. This caused the site two be down for two-and-a-half hours. For some sites, this could result in a significant loss of profit.

## Protecting against Internal Threats

Damage to your site can not only come from hackers and viruses, but also from those from within your company. Common methods used to damage a site in this way include *data diddling* and *logic bombs.*

Data diddling can require very little knowledge of computers and programming, because it involves modifying data prior or during its input. A person with legitimate access to your Web server, and/or the files and databases residing on your site, could damage or tamper with information. For example, a data entry clerk could change the cost associated with an item, so that when the item is purchased online, the user is charged a lower price (or no price at all), thereby costing you money.

Data diddling can also be more sophisticated, requiring software or programming skills to carry out the crime. A number of programs on the Internet can alter data before it is entered, including one called a zapper. In 1997, some restaurant owners in Quebec used a zapper to modify their sales data. The zapper was used to skim up to 30 percent of the receipts, cheating the government out of an estimated millions of dollars in tax payments. As you can see, the results of modifying data can amount to a significant loss (in this case for Canadian taxpayers).

Data diddling can easily be overlooked as an existing problem or potential threat. When small amounts of money are subtly skimmed from the company, or sensitive data is modified irregularly over a period of time, a company may never be aware of it. However, the problem can easily be dealt with by performing regular audits and implementing policies that check the work performed by employees and the data being entered into systems.

Another common attack that can occur from within your company are logic bombs. Logic bombs are programs with code that runs at a specific date and/or time. The code can cause unwanted and/or unauthorized functions, such as altering or damaging data on a server. In many cases, a disgruntled employee (such as one who's received his or her termination notice) will create and/or install the software. In other cases, an unsuspecting user will install the program on a network computer or server, unaware that it has malicious code in it. When a specified time arrives, the bomb then goes off.

Logic bombs are often found after they are set to execute and after data has been altered or damaged. In cases where an internal user creates or installs the logic bomb, management may have the best of intentions in overlooking his dissatisfaction with the business or work environment or that he may have personal problems. In such cases, dealing with the person and restricting their access to the network and Web server will reduce the risk of a logic bomb attack. In cases where a user honestly believes that the program is harmless and installs it, the problem can be remedied by implementing policies forbidding the installation of unauthorized software. You can also reduce the threat of logic bombs by implementing security features and software. By using antivirus software, you can have logic bombs detected before they execute. You can also use firewalls to remove file attachments so that users of a network never receive a program containing a logic bomb.

# Adding Security Tiers beyond the Web Server

You should also be aware that a Web server shouldn't act as the main security measure. Other components in a multi-tier design can be used to secure the entire e-commerce operation, including application servers, database servers, and firewalls. When combined with a securely implemented Web server, these other tools can create a formidable defense against attackers.

When implementing security, you may think that a proxy server should be implemented for security reasons. Proxy servers aren't primarily meant to secure your network, but instead to help speed up Internet connections. They allow frequently visited Web pages to be cached so that the page is provided through the proxy server rather than over the Internet, which speeds up the browsing capabilities of users. However, proxy servers can generally provide additional security measures often not found or easily configured in the Web server application itself. Microsoft's Internet Security and Acceleration Server and its predecessor, Microsoft Proxy Server 2.0, are examples of this, providing inbound and outbound access control, packet filtering, and dial-in access controls.

**NOTE**

Proxy servers are commonly used on networks that allow users to connect to the Internet. It serves as an intermediary between a network user's workstation and the Internet, so that requests to access Internet resources (such as Web pages) are first passed through the proxy server. When the proxy server receives a request, it checks whether a site or Web page has been filtered. It will store previous requests in a cache, and looks in the cache to see whether that Web page is currently stored. If it is, it will return that stored page to the user, so that the request is never passed off the network and onto the Internet (thereby saving time). Although it may have some features that duplicate a firewall, it should never be considered a substitute.

For more information on proxy servers, visit the following Web sites:

- ServerWatch, located at http://serverwatch.internet.com/proxyservers.html
- Microsoft Internet Security and Acceleration Server, located at www.microsoft.com/isaserver
- Netscape Proxy Server, located at http://home.netscape.com/proxy/v3.5
- i-Planet Proxy Server, located at www.iplanet.com/products/infrastructure/dir_security/proxy_server

Port and packet filtering is an effective way of preventing unauthorized access to your network or for preventing internal network users from accessing the Internet or certain areas of the Internet. Packet filtering allows you to filter packets based on information contained in the IP header. This allows you to control access based on the source address, destination address, source port number and/or destination port number. Port filtering allows you to filter specific ports, so that specific protocols or applications are blocked. For example, if you wanted to filter Telnet traffic, you could set up a filter on port 23. This would block any Telnet requests. Table 3.3 shows a listing of port addresses that can be blocked with port filtering.

**Table 3.3** Well-Known Ports

| Protocol | TCP or UDP | Port(s) |
|---|---|---|
| DNS | TCP | 53 |
| FTP | TCP | 20 and 21 |
| HTTP | TCP | 80 |
| HTTPS over SSL | TCP | 443 |
| IdentID | TCP | 113 |
| IMAP v4 | TCP | 143 |
| LDAP | TCP | 389 |
| NNTP | TCP | 119 |
| POP3 | TCP | 110 |
| SMTP | TCP | 25 |
| Telnet | TCP | 23 |
| RIP | UDP | 520 |
| TFTP | UDP | 69 |
| Finger | TCP/UDP | 79 |

You should evaluate security policies that will be used for your Web site and keep them as restrictive as possible (see Chapter 4 for information on creating security policies). Remember that security is a trade-off. Users will need the access necessary to view content and work with the pages and programs provided but should be blocked from accessing anything beyond this. In checking what users can access, you should check the site by using the anonymous user account and also an account with the same access as other user accounts. This will allow you to see first-hand what users can and cannot get into.

One thing should have become obvious after discussing all these issues: a Web server will (and should) take considerable time to implement. It can act as a vital and valuable part of the network—or a challenging doorway for hackers. Make it a priority to properly plan and research its implementation before deploying it. After you've gone through the preliminary planning steps, you are ready to take the "first step" in having a Web server: installation.

**SECURITY ALERT!**

Be aware that no site design is completely secure. As time goes by, the tools hackers use will advance, and vulnerabilities in security will be revealed. Keeping security as a priority early in your design will minimize risk. After the site is made live, you must then keep on top of security by following suggestions offered throughout this chapter.

## Apache versus Internet Information Services

In the sections that follow, we will look at installing two of the most popular Web servers on the market: Apache Web Server and Microsoft Internet Information Services. According to most surveys, Apache is the world leader, being the Web server run on more sites than any other Web server. It is a free product that is secure and stable, with patches and bug fixes quickly released when problems are identified. Microsoft Internet Information Server (or Internet Information Services as its called as of version 5.0) has also made a significant impact and is run on millions of servers. Like Apache, it is free; it is included with Microsoft Windows 2000 Server, which is built on NT technology (well respected for stability and security features).

As mentioned earlier in this chapter, a benefit of Apache is that it is available for a wide variety of platforms. This is not the case with Internet Information Services, because it is a service that runs on Windows 2000 Server. It isn't available for any other platform.

Table 3.4 compares the features and functionality of these two servers, allowing you to make an informed decision as to which you'd like to use as your Web server. No recommendations between the two are offered; you should research these and other Web servers in depth before deciding which to deploy.

**Table 3.4** Comparison of Features in Apache and Internet Information Services

| Supported Feature | IIS | Apache |
|---|---|---|
| Ability for multiple hardware virtual servers to use separate IP addresses | Yes | Yes |
| Ability to manage multiple Web servers as a single server | Yes | Yes |
| Basic authentication (clear text) | Yes | Yes |
| Browser Administration | Yes | No |
| Built-in image-map handling | Yes | Yes |
| Content expiration | Yes | Yes |
| Custom error messages | Yes | Yes |
| Custom HTTP headers | Yes | Yes |
| Document footers | Yes | Yes |
| GUI administration | Yes | No |
| GUI setup | Yes | No |
| GUI wizards for common tasks | Yes | No |
| HTTP 1.1 standard | Yes | Yes |
| HTTP redirects | Yes | Yes |
| ISAPI | Yes | Yes (ISAPI modules written by third parties are available with the distribution. ISAPI extensions are supported, but ISAPI filters are not.) |

Continued

**Table 3.4** Continued

| Supported Feature | IIS | Apache |
|---|---|---|
| Logging (can write multiple logs) | Yes | Yes |
| Logging to ODBC database | Yes | Yes (required additional plug-in) |
| Restrict access by directory and/or file | Yes | Yes |
| Restrict access by domain name | Yes | Yes |
| Restrict access by group | Yes | Yes |
| Restrict access by IP address | Yes | Yes |
| Restrict access by user | Yes | Yes |
| SNMP (Simple Network Management Protocol) | Yes | Yes (commercial plug-in available for this functionality) |
| SSL 2.0 and 3.0 | Yes | Yes |
| Support for multiple software virtual servers using host headers | Yes | Yes |
| Platforms | Windows 2000 | Windows 9x, Windows NT/2000, Novell NetWare 5, Solaris, OS/2, Macintosh, UnixWare, HP MPE/iX, IBM's TPF, NetBSD, Digital UNIX, BSDI, AIX, SCO, HPUX, Be OS, Linux, FreeBSD, IRIX |
| WebDAV (Web Distributed Authoring and Versioning) | Yes | Yes |
| Web server administration using scripts for commonly performed functions | Yes | Yes |

# Installation: The First Step

When setting up a Web site, it is important that your server is properly installed and configured—and it's crucial that you carefully plan the configuration of your server *long before* it's installed. Many things can go wrong when you're performing the installation, or after installation is complete and you're fumbling through its actual configuration. Taking the time to read the manuals for your server will go a long way in this regard. Finally, you should give yourself ample time for installation, configuration, and testing.

It is important that you install only the services that are needed by your Web site. For example, if you don't want to use a News service that provides users with the ability to transfer files and exchange messages, then either don't install it, or disable or remove it after installation is complete. Remember that any extra services that are implemented on your system may serve as an avenue of entry or information for a prospective hacker. At the very least, it is one more thing that could possibly go wrong or cause conflicts with other services or applications that you *do* need and use on your site. Basically, the rule is: If you don't use it, lose it.

After installation, you should also remove any sample scripts or files that were installed with the Web server. These may also provide information for a hacker, including informing him or her of the type of Web server you're using, and scripting types accepted by your system. With modification, the hacker could even use these files to open areas of your system. Simply deleting or moving the scripts and files off the server will remove this from potentially happening.

Keeping these facts in mind, let's look at some specific factors involved in installing and configuring Apache Web Server and Microsoft Internet Information Services. These are two of the more popular Web servers, and they involve different methods of installation and configuration.

## Installing and Configuring Apache

Installing Apache consists of two or three major steps: acquiring the Web server software, compiling files, and actual installation. To acquire the installation files for Apache, you need to visit the Apache Web site (www.apache.org). At this site, you can download the files either in an uncompiled form or as binary executables. If you use the binary executables, you can skip the step of compiling them and move straight into the step of installing the software. Compiling these files yourself will allow you to choose which modules will be included in the server and allow you to set how the operating system will be configured during installation. After you've selected the modules to include and set the configuration information, you are ready to proceed with installation.

Selecting the modules to include in your installation is done through the Configuration script included with the uncompiled files. This file is located in the SRC directory of Apache's distribution and can be opened and edited with a text editor. In this file, there is a listing of modules that are to be included by default with the installation, and optional modules that are commented out with number symbols ("##"). Optional modules are located at the bottom of this file, where there are lines stating AddModule. Descriptions of the purpose of each module appear above it. To add any of these modules, remove the comment at the beginning of the line. To keep default modules from being installed, simply add a comment to the line showing the module you don't want installed. However, because many of these modules are necessary for Apache to run properly, you will need to check Apache's site to ensure that Apache can run without the module effectively.

The script also allows you to configure Apache for your operating system. Such configuration will occur during installation. Generally, you wouldn't alter the file for this reason, unless you were adding modules that required additional library files to run. When the script runs, it will create a MAKEFILE. Typing **MAKE** will then compile the source files, and a binary file called HTTPD will appear in the SRC directory.

The HTTPD file is included with the binary distribution of Apache. If you want to avoid compiling Apache yourself, you can download the binary distribution from Apache's Web site. This allows a simpler method of installing Apache. Installation of Apache depends on the operating system being used; here we discuss installing Apache server on the Windows platform.

### Installing Apache Web Server on Windows 2000

Like the source code files on Apache's Web site, binary executables are also available for download. After downloading these files, you begin the installation process by double-clicking on the executable. This will unpack the installation files and start the Setup Wizard.

1. The first screen of the wizard welcomes you to the setup process. It warns that you should exit any other applications. To quit the installation, you can click the **Cancel** button from this or any other screen in the wizard. Click the **Next** button to continue.
2. The screen that follows provides a licensing agreement, which you must agree with to continue through the installation process. If you click the **No** button, the installation process stops here, and the Setup Wizard shuts down. Clicking the **Yes** button allows you to continue.
3. The next screen is the Choose Destination Location screen, which allows you to specify where the Web server will be installed. You can accept the default location and click **Next** to continue, or you can use the **Browse** button to specify another location. If you click the **Browse** button, a window appears allowing you to browse your hard disk and select a folder in which to install Apache. Clicking **OK** returns you to the previous screen, where you can click **Next** to move to the next screen.
4. The Setup Type screen follows, allowing you to select how Apache is to be installed. You have three options on this screen: **Typical**, **Compact**, and **Custom**. **Typical** installs Apache Web server with the most common components, and should be used by most users of the software. **Compact** installs the minimum components required by Apache Web server to run. This should be used if you have limited hard disk space. Finally, **Custom** allows you to choose what options will be installed. You select which **Setup Type** to use by clicking on the radio button beside the option. Clicking **Next** begins this method of installation.
5. If you choose **Custom** and click **Next**, then a screen appears allowing you to select which components will be installed (see Figure 3.1). There are five components that can be installed:
   - **Web Server Application Files**, which are the basic files needed to run Apache Web server.

- **Web Server Source Code**, which are source code files for the Apache Web server and its support tools. If you don't require these for development purposes, you can deselect this component.
- **Web Server Manual**, which is documentation for the Apache Web server. This is useful for administration of the server.
- **Web Server Additional Modules**, which are additional modules that can be used to extend the server's functionality.
- **Web Server Icons**, which are icons used for Web server directory indexes.

After you've selected the components you want installed, click Next to proceed to the next screen.

**Figure 3.1** Select Components Screen for the Apache Web Server Installation Wizard

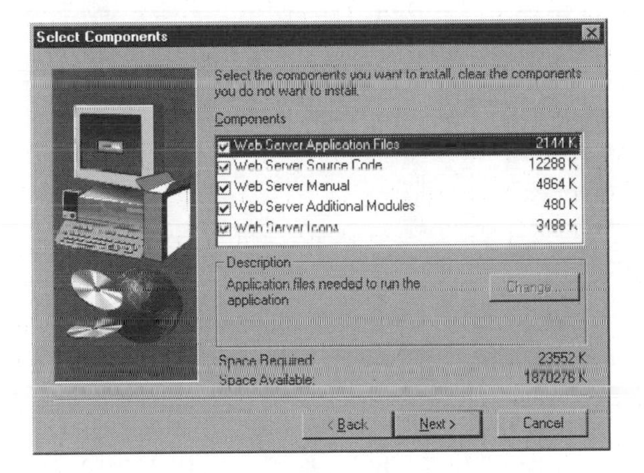


6. The Select Program Folder screen is what you see next. This allows you to select the folder in which the icons will be placed, which will be used to launch Apache Web server and other utilities. By default, this is named Apache, but you can enter a different name for the folder if you prefer. Click **Next** to begin installing the selected components and for the wizard to perform basic configuration of your system.

7. After the configuration is completed, you see the Setup Complete screen. This screen has a checkbox offering the chance to view a Readme file. If you don't want to read this file, click on the checkbox to uncheck it and then click **Finish**. After you've completed the installation, a new folder appears under the Programs folder of your Start menu. This folder is called Apache Web Server, and it contains folders and icons for using Apache.

8. After installation is complete, you then need to configure Apache Web Server for use. Configuration files for this are found in the CONF directory of where the server was installed. Here there is a file called **httpd.conf**, where you configure directives used by the server. The **http.conf** file is the main configuration file for Apache server, and it contains directives that instruct Apache how to perform. The directives in this file are broken into three sections:

   - **Global Environment**, which controls the Apache's environment and determines how it will run.
   - **'Main' Server Configuration**, which sets the parameters for the default server and provides default values for virtual servers.
   - **Virtual Hosts**, which determines the setting for virtual servers.

   These directives are shown in Table 3.5 and are used to configure Apache Server.

**Table 3.5** Listing of Directives Used to Configure Apache Web Server

| Directive | Section of HTTP.CONF | Description |
|---|---|---|
| ServerType | Global Environment | Determines whether the server is standalone or inetd. The Inetd mode is only available for servers running on a UNIX platform. |

Continued

**Table 3.5** Continued

| Directive | Section of HTTP.CONF | Description |
|---|---|---|
| ServerRoot "*<pathname>*" | Global Environment | This is the root of the directory tree. Under this root directory, the configuration, error and log files are kept. By default, it is the directory in which Apache was installed. |
| PidFile | Global Environment | Used to specify the file in which Apache records its process identification number at startup. |
| ScoreBoardFile | Global Environment | Used to specify the file used to store internal process information. |
| ResourceConfig | Global Environment | Used to specify the processing of the resource configuration file. By default, this option is commented out and has the value of conf/srm.conf. |
| AccessConfig | Global Environment | Used to specify the processing of the access configuration file. By default, this option is commented out and has the value of conf/access.conf. |
| Timeout | Global Environment | Specifies the number of seconds before a request times out. By default, it is set to 300. |
| KeepAlive | Global Environment | Specifies whether more than one request per connection is allowed. By default, it is set as "On." |

Continued

**Table 3.5** Continued

| Directive | Section of HTTP.CONF | Description |
|---|---|---|
| MaxKeepAliveRequests | Global Environment | Specifies the maximum number of requests to allow in a persistent connection. By default, it is set to 100. To allow unlimited requests, it should be set to 0. |
| KeepAliveTimeout | Global Environment | Specifies the number of seconds to wait for a client to send the next request. By default, it is set to 15. |
| MaxRequestsPerChild | Global Environment | This specifies the number of requests a child process can process before it dies. By default, it is set to 0 for unlimited. |
| ThreadsPerChild | Global Environment | Specifies the number of concurrent requests the server will allow. By default, it is set to 50. |
| Listen | Global Environment | Used to bind Apache to other IP addresses and/or ports. By default, this option is commented out. |
| BindAddress | Global Environment | Used to specify the IP address to listen to. By default, this option is commented out. |
| ExtendedStatus | Global Environment | Specifies whether full or basic status information will be generated. By default, it is set to OFF to generate basic information. |

**Continued**

**Table 3.5** Continued

| Directive | Section of HTTP.CONF | Description |
|---|---|---|
| Port | 'Main' server configuration | Specifies the port that a standalone server will listen to. By default, it is set to 80. |
| ServerAdmin | 'Main' server configuration | Specifies the e-mail address that will appear on error documents and other server-generated pages. |
| ServerName | 'Main' server configuration | Specifies the registered DNS name that will be returned to clients (such as www.microsolved.com). |
| DocumentRoot *<pathname>* | 'Main' server configuration | Specifies the directory that will store documents provided to users of your server. |
| AllowOverride | 'Main' server configuration | Specifies options the .htaccess files in Apache can override. This can be set to NONE, ALL, or a combination of different options. By default, it is set that none of the options can be overridden. |
| Order allow,deny Allow from all </Directory> | 'Main' server configuration | Specifies who can access the server. |
| UserDir | 'Main' server configuration | Specifies the directory that is appended to a user's home directory. This option is applied only if a ~user request is received by Apache. By default, it is set to the USERS directory in which Apache was installed. |

**Continued**

**Table 3.5** Continued

| Directive | Section of HTTP.CONF | Description |
|---|---|---|
| DirectoryIndex | 'Main' server configuration | Specifies the default HTML document that is served when a user accesses a directory on the site. By default, it is set to index.html. |
| AccessFileName | 'Main' server configuration | Specifies the file used by Apache to retrieve access control information for each directory. By default, it is .htaccess. |
| CacheNegotiatedDocs | 'Main' server configuration | Specifies whether Apache will request documents to be cached by proxy servers. By default, documents are not cached. |
| UseCanonicalName | 'Main' server configuration | Specifies whether Apache will use a client-supplied port or a URL that refers back to the server that a response came from. By default, it is set to use the ServerName and Port to form the canonical name. |
| TypesConfig | 'Main' server configuration | Specifies where the mime.types file resides on the server. By default, it is set to the mime.types file located in the CONF directory in which Apache was installed. |

Continued

**Table 3.5** Continued

| Directive | Section of HTTP.CONF | Description |
|---|---|---|
| DefaultType | 'Main' server configuration | Specifies the default MIME type used for documents. By default, it is set to text/plain (for textual or HTML documents). If applications or images are commonly sent, then set this to application/octet-stream. |
| MIMEMagicFile | 'Main' server configuration | Specifies the file that Apache uses to gather information on file types. By default, it is located in the magic file in the CONF directory in which Apache was installed. |
| HostnameLookups | 'Main' server configuration | Specifies whether the names of clients or just their IP addresses are logged. By default, it is set to OFF to specify that only IP addresses are logged. |
| ErrorLog | 'Main' server configuration | Specifies the location of the error log file. By default, errors will be logged to the error.log file located in the LOGS directory in which Apache was installed. |
| LogLevel | 'Main' server configuration | Specifies the number of messages that will be logged to the error.log file. |

Continued

**Table 3.5** Continued

| Directive | Section of HTTP.CONF | Description |
|---|---|---|
| CustomLog | 'Main' server configuration | Specifies the location and format of the access log. By default, it is the access.log found in the LOGS directory in which Apache was installed. |
| ServerSignature | 'Main' server configuration | Specifies whether the version of the server and name of the virtual host should be added to any server-generated pages. By default, it is set to ON. Other options can be OFF or EMAIL (to also add the e-mail address specified in the ServerAdmin directive). |
| ScriptInterpreterSource | 'Main' server configuration | Enables Windows-specific behavior. By default, it is commented out to have Unix-specific behavior enabled. |
| Alias | 'Main' server configuration | Specifies aliases. |
| ScriptAlias | 'Main' server configuration | Specifies the directories containing scripts. |
| ScriptAliases | 'Main' server configuration | Specifies aliases of items to be treated as applications. |
| DefaultIcon | 'Main' server configuration | Specifies the icon to display when a file doesn't have an icon explicitly set for it. |
| AddDescription | 'Main' server configuration | Specifies a short description after a file in server-generated indexes. |

Continued

**Table 3.5** Continued

| Directive | Section of HTTP.CONF | Description |
|---|---|---|
| IndexIgnore | 'Main' server configuration | Specifies filenames that directory indexing should ignore and not include in a listing. |
| AddEncoding | 'Main' server configuration | Used to allow browsers to uncompress information automatically. |
| AddLanguage | 'Main' server configuration | Specifies the language of a document. |
| LanguagePriority | 'Main' server configuration | Used to set priorities of some languages over others. |
| Action | 'Main' server configuration | Specifies the media type that will execute a script when a matching file is called. |
| MetaDir | 'Main' server configuration | Specifies the directory containing meta information files. |
| MetaSuffix | 'Main' server configuration | Specifies the name suffix for files containing meta information. |
| VirtualHost | Virtual Hosts | Specifies VirtualHost containers for sites containing multiple domains or hostnames. |

For example, search for the ServerAdmin directive and change the value beside it to the e-mail address that belongs to the administrator of the Web server. Search for the ServerName directive and change the value beside it to the registered DNS name for your Web site. Search for the HostNameLookups directive and change the value beside it to ON. This enables logging of client names as well as their IP addresses. Search for the ServerSignature directive and change the value beside it to EMAIL. This adds the e-mail address you specified in ServerAdmin to server-generated pages.

9. Save the **httpd.conf** file and exit the text editor.

## Installing and Configuring Internet Information Server 5.0

If you've performed a clean install of Windows 2000 on your server, then chances are that IIS was already installed on your server by default. If, however, you have upgraded from a previous version of Windows, then it may or may not have been installed during the upgrade. If you had Internet Information Server installed on your previous Windows NT installation, then it will be upgraded to IIS 5.0 during the Windows 2000 upgrade. If IIS was not installed on the previous system, then you will have to install it manually.

### *Installing IIS on Windows 2000 and Running the Internet Services Manager*

1. Insert your Windows 2000 installation CD into the CD-ROM drive of your server. From the Start menu, select the **Settings** folder and then click on the **Control Panel** icon.
2. Double-click on the **Add/Remove Programs** icon. By opening this applet, you see a dialog box offering different options for installing new programs. Selecting the **Add/ Remove Windows Components** is what is used to install IIS—this launches the Windows Components Wizard. By selecting this item, your server will be checked, and a listing of components appears. This wizard is shown in Figure 3.2. Installed components have a checkmark in the checkbox beside it.
3. Scroll through the listing of components until you see Internet Information Services (IIS).

**Figure 3.2** Windows Components Wizard

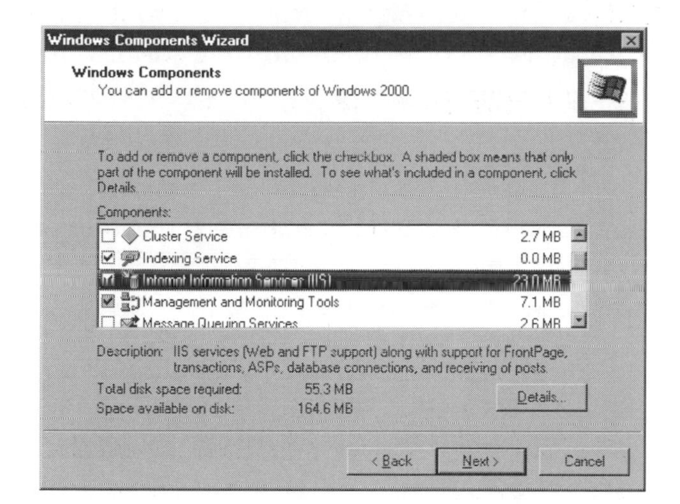


4. If there is no checkmark in the checkbox beside this item, it means that it isn't installed. In such a case, click on the checkbox and then click the **Next** button. The wizard begins installing the necessary files and configuring your system.
5. After the configuration is completed, click the **Finish** button to complete installation.

   You can also launch the installation of IIS through the Windows 2000 Configure Your Server, which is found in the **Programs | Administrative Tools** folder of the Start menu. When Configure Your Server starts, select the **Web/Media Server** item on the left side of the dialog box. This expands to show two items: **Streaming Media Server** and **Web Server**. By clicking on the Web Server item, you are offered two choices in the main pane of the Window. One of these allows you to learn more about IIS, and the other starts the Windows Components Wizard. If you use the **Configure Your Server**, you can return to this tool after installation is complete and then click the **Next** button to launch the Microsoft Management Console (MMC) and manage IIS.

6. Configuring IIS is done through MMC with the Internet Service Manager snap-in. MMC is a tool that is used to manage a Windows 2000 Server by loading various snap-ins that perform different tasks. To start MMC, click on the **Run** command from the Windows Start menu and then type **MMC**. Click **OK** and the MMC opens.
7. Now it is just a matter of loading the appropriate snap-in. From the Console menu of MMC, click on the item called **Add/Remove Snap-in**. This shows the Add/Remove Snap-in dialog box.
8. On this screen, click the button labeled **Add**. Doing so displays a listing of available snap-ins. In the listing, select the item called **Internet Information Services** and click the **Add** button. This adds the item to the snap-ins you want installed, but you need to click the **Close** button to exit out of the dialog box.
9. Check that Internet Information Services appears in the listing of snap-ins to be added to MMC. If it does not, repeat the previous step.
10. To fully install the snap-in and begin managing IIS, you must finish by clicking **OK**.

As shown in Figure 3.3, MMC shows a listing of elements making up your site. Through this console, you can modify default directories and set various properties. By right-clicking on elements, you can select properties to configure a particular element and thereby configure your site. Of importance to configuring your Web site, you will need to set the default properties of your Web server. Right-clicking on the **Default Web Server** folder in the left pane of MMC and selecting **Properties** will bring up the property sheet to do this. The dialog box that appears contains a variety of tabs allowing you to change the default directory for resources, IP Address of the site, connection timeouts, TCP port, and more. For further information on configuring IIS, you will need to check the Help documentation included with the Internet Information Services.

**Figure 3.3** Microsoft Management Console with the Internet Service Manager Snap-In

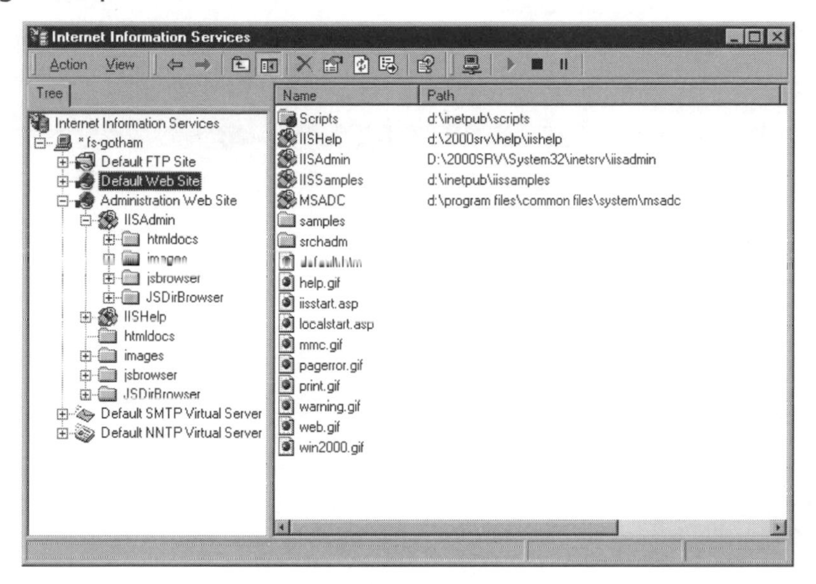


IIS also allows you to administer your Web site remotely over HTTP or HTTPS connections. As shown in Figure 3.4, IIS provides an HTML version of the Internet Services Manager. This allows you to perform administration tasks through a Web browser such as Internet Explorer or Netscape Navigator. The HTML version can be accessed in one of two ways. First, you can select the **Administration Web Site** node in MMC with the Internet Service Manager snap-in and then select **Browse** from the Action menu. Second, you can access this administration tool directly by specifying the server name, TCP port number assigned to the site, and the administration Web site address in the Address field of your Internet browser. This will display the IIS Web page that will enable you to perform administration tasks.

**Figure 3.4** HTML Version of Internet Services Manager Accessed through an Internet Browser

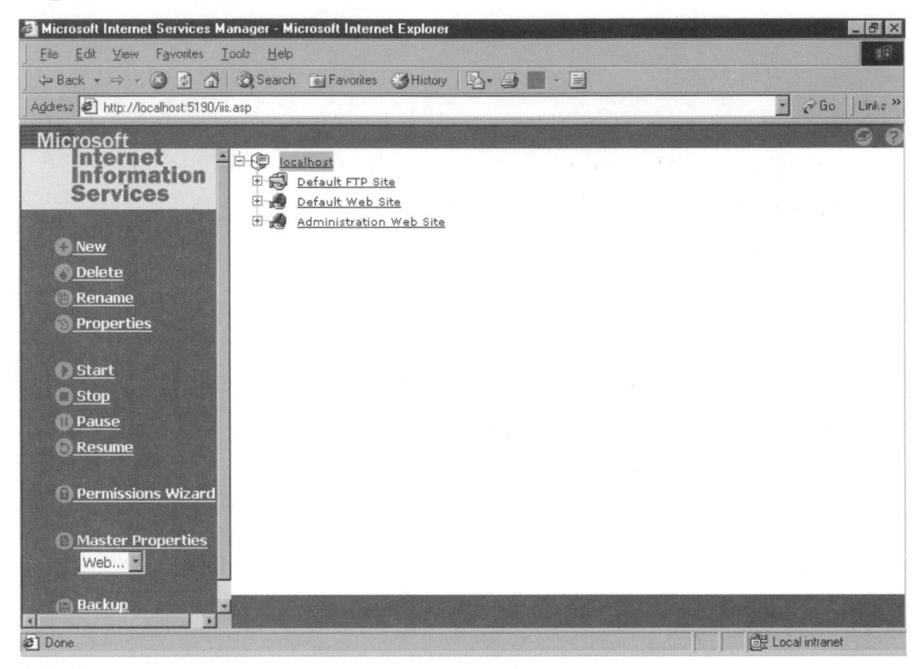


## Windows 2000 Server and Internet Information Server 5.0 Security

In setting up IIS, you will need to remember that certain configurations should be made to both IIS and to the Windows 2000 Server used to host your site. You should look at the account used for anonymous connects and ensure that it is properly configured to your needs. You should also determine whether other configurations to the server, its groups, and accounts are necessary.

Active Directory Users and Computers (another MMC snap-in) must be used to configure accounts on a Windows 2000 Server. When IIS is installed, an account called IUSR_*computername* is automatically created (where *computername* stands for the name of your server). This is the account used by anonymous users of the Web server and is automatically added when IIS is installed. You will want to modify this account and limit the access it has to resources on your network.

1. To modify the IUSR_*computername* account, you will need to open Active Directory Users and Computers. You can open this tool by starting MMC. Click on **Run** on the Windows Start menu, type **MMC**, and then click **OK**.
2. From the Console menu of MMC, click on the item called **Add/Remove Snap-in** to display a new dialog box. Click **Add** to display a list of available snap-ins and then select the item called **Active Directory Users and Computers**.
3. Click **Add** to add this snap-in, click **Close** to return to the previous dialog box, and then click **OK** to confirm. Active Directory Users and Computers now appears in the MMC console.
4. In the left pane of the console, you need to open the folder identifying your server to view another folder called **USERS**. This is the folder in which the IUSR_*computername* account has been created. By selecting the users folder, a list of user accounts appears in the right pane of the console.
5. Double-clicking on the IUSR_*computername* account displays its properties, which you can then configure.
6. As shown in Figure 3.5, this dialog box provides a number of tabs that allow you to modify the account, including the account's ability to access resources. The **Account** tab is particularly important because it allows you to set whether Kerberos preauthentication is required, set password settings, disable the account, set hours the account can log onto the server, and so forth. The **Member Of** tab is another important area of configuration, as this allows you to set what groups this user account is a member of. By adding permissions to groups, and then adding the user accounts to groups, it is easier to manage large groups of members.

Regardless of the operating system or Web server software being used, a secure server will have strict policies for user rights and permissions. You should never give a user the ability to access more than what they need, because doing so will create a hole in your security measures.

**Figure 3.5** IUSR_*computername* Account Properties

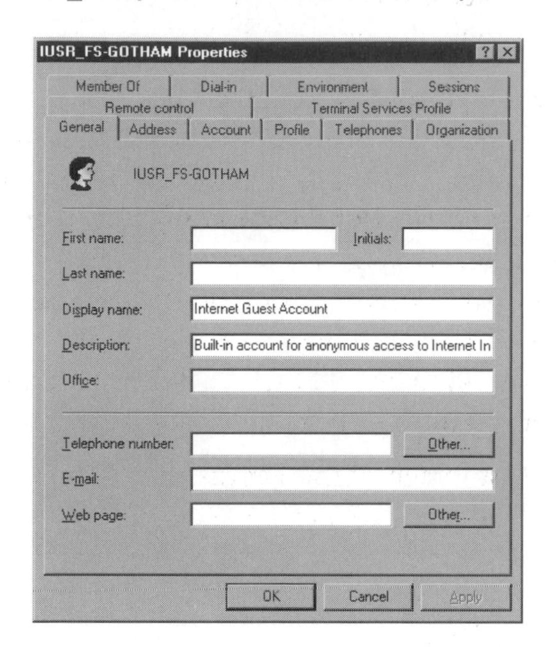


This means removing the ability for the anonymous user (and many other user accounts) to write to files in the directory containing scripts, applets, and HTML documents. If users are able to modify these files, they can vandalize Web pages or hack your Web server. When assigning permissions, you should also use the strongest file system possible. In terms of Windows NT and Windows 2000, you should use NTFS as your file system. This will allow you to control access to individual files and folders on your server.

In addition to tools used to manage Windows 2000 Server, Internet Information Server 5.0 provides a number of wizards that walk you through the process of setting and maintaining security. These wizards include the Permissions Wizard, Web Server Certificate Wizard, and the Certificate Trust Lists Wizard. Although tasks performed by using these wizards can also be done manually, the wizards simplify securing your site.

The Permissions Wizard allows you to configure permissions and authentication used on your Web server. This wizard is used to set what users are able to access in folders on your server, but it is limited to controlling permissions for folders used to publish information to the Internet or intranet. This keeps users from accessing data that is meant to be restricted and should not be published to anonymous users of your site.

1. Start the Permissions Wizard through MMC with the Internet Information Services snap-in. You can do this by selecting your Web or FTP site in the right pane of the console and then clicking on the **Permissions Wizard** item found in the **All Tasks** folder on the Action menu. You can also start it through the HTML version of Internet Information Services Manager. To start the wizard here, select the Web or FTP site in the browser window, and then click the **Permissions Wizard** hyperlink in the left frame of the Web page.
2. The first screen of the Permissions Wizard welcomes you to using the wizard. Clicking **Next** displays the Security Settings screen (Figure 3.6). The first option on this screen allows you to set permissions to be inherited from a parent site or virtual directory. The second option allows you to select new security settings from a template. If you select the first option and click **Next**, you are informed as to what security settings will be applied and can then click **Next** again to reach the final screen of the wizard. If you select the second option and click **Next**, you are asked questions to describe your site.

**Figure 3.6** Security Settings Screen of the Permissions Wizard

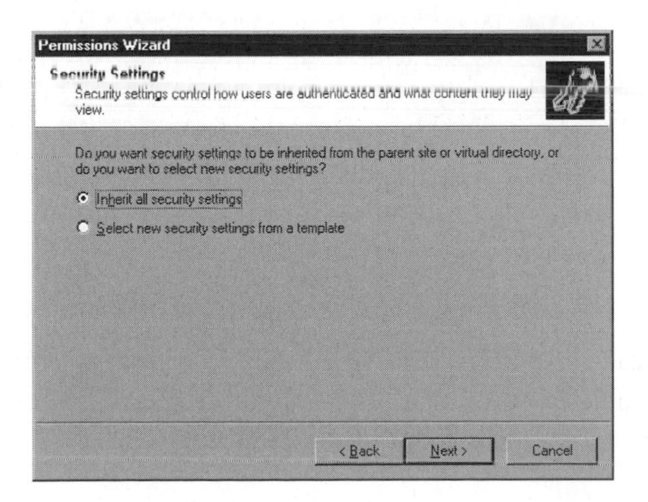

3. Upon selecting the **Select new security settings from a template** option and clicking **Next**, you see the Site Scenario screen. This allows you to pick a scenario that best suits your site. If you choose **Public Web Site** as a scenario, users will be able to browse content on your site. This applies security settings that are cross-browser compatible. Regardless of the browser being used or whether the user has an account on the site, any user will be able to use your Web site. If you choose **Secure Web Site** is chosen, then only users with a valid Windows 2000 account will be able to access the site.
4. After choosing the desired selection and clicking **Next**, you reach the final screen. Click **Finish** to apply your settings and exit the wizard.

The Web Server Certificate Wizard is used to set up and manage certificates used on your site. (Although we discuss certificates in greater detail later in this chapter, you should know that certificates are used for authentication.) This wizard identifies where the information originated and allows you to exchange data securely. It allows you to set up an SSL-enabled site so that you can use SSL encryption and client certification authentication. By using this wizard, you can create and administer certificates used by your Web server when transferring information between the server and client.

1. Start the Web Server Certificate Wizard through MMC with the Internet Information Services snap-in. By clicking the **Server Certificate** button on the **Directory Security** tab of your Web site's Properties sheet, the wizard is launched, showing an initial welcome screen. Clicking **Next** displays the Server Certificate screen shown in Figure 3.7.
2. Clicking the first option on this screen allows you to create a new certificate, which users of your intranet or Internet site can use. If you have an existing certificate, then you should select the second option. If you wish to import a certificate from a backup file, select the third option.

**Figure 3.7** Server Certificate Screen of the Web Server Certificate Wizard

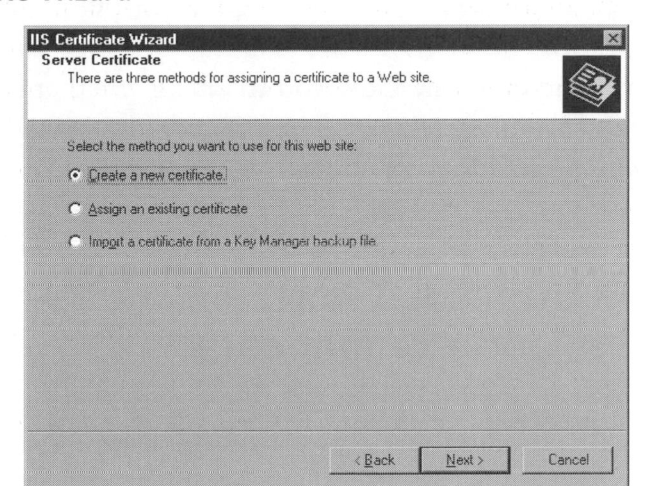


3. Upon selecting your option, follow through the wizard and then click **Finish** to apply the settings.

The Certificate Trust Lists Wizard is the third IIS wizard we mention here. This wizard is used to configure certificate trust lists (CTLs) that identify trusted CAs. A CA is a vendor that manages certificates, associating public keys with those applying for the certificate. The CTL allows you to specify which of these vendors is trusted by a site, and it is especially useful for ISPs that have several sites running on a single server. In these cases, different sites may trust different CAs.

## Hardening the Server Software

After installation is complete, you should *harden* the Web server. Basically, what this refers to is that after initially being installed, the Web server may be "soft" in regards to security and reliability. After its initial release, certain bugs or security holes may have been found in the software. By simply installing the Web server and throwing it online, these issues will continue to exist and may cause problems for you later. Hardening the server software isn't difficult, but it is necessary if the server is to meet your expectations.

## Install Patches

Immediately after installing the Web server, you should determine any patches exist for the server software. Visiting the Web site of the Web server's manufacturer will allow you to check whether any service packs or bug fixes have been released. The site may also provide security reports, which provide suggestions as to how you can enhance the security of your server by making certain modifications.

## Disable Unneeded Ports, Services, and Components

Earlier in this chapter, we mentioned how port and packet filtering can be useful in controlling access to your Web server. We also saw that your Web server uses a number of well-known ports to "listen" for requests from client computers. If you aren't offering certain services, then you should turn the ports associated with those services off. For example, if an FTP service isn't going to be used, then ports 20 and 21 should be turned off. Because these are unneeded, they won't affect the usability of your site, but turning them off will improve your site's security. Each server will have different methods of turning off unneeded ports, so you should check your server documentation on how to do this. You can use Table 3.2 as a reference in determining which you won't need.

Services that you don't want to offer on your site should be removed or disabled. For example, if you don't offer FTP services on your site, then you should disable or remove FTP features. The same should apply to TFTP, Gopher, finger, systat, and any other services that may have been installed. This will involve checking Web server documentation to see what is installed by default but should also include checking the Web server itself. If the Web server provides an administrative interface, determine what services are showing as active. You may also use a browser, FTP program, or other software to attempt to access these features to determine whether they are available on your site.

When removing or disabling services, you shouldn't merely stop the service and leave it at that. If the service is set to start automatically, then these services will become available again the next time the system is rebooted. Merely setting the service to be started manually is a less than favorable alternative. If the service remains on the system, then a hacker could potentially start it remotely by using commands to activate it. The unused services should either be completely uninstalled or disabled.

Deleting unnecessary components is another important step in creating a secure e-commerce site. As we saw with Apache, a number of modules can be used to enhance the functionality of this Web server. Other types of Web servers may offer similar components or plug-ins so that different features are thereby installed. By allowing unnecessary components to remain on your hard-disk, the possibility exists that a hacker could access your system and load them. If these components aren't needed, but are running on the Web server, then they could be used to acquire various abilities over your system. Any security holes in the components could be used to perform various unauthorized and unwanted functions.

## Delete Unneeded Scripts and Files

When Web servers are installed, they commonly install a collection of sample scripts, which you can use to configure your system or perform common tasks associated with the server. If these are left on the server, hackers may be able to access, modify, and/or run them. This allows the hacker to perform unauthorized and unwanted events, which may include shutting down the server (or worse). Sample scripts may be located in different directories of the Web server, and it is important to check the Web server's documentation to determine where these scripts are located. After you've found the location of these files, use the documentation (or review the scripts) to determine their functionality. If you don't need particular scripts, you should delete them or move them to a separate directory, with permissions that allow only the webmaster/network administrator access. It is important that users don't have the Write permission to this directory, because they will then have the ability to upload dangerous scripts and files to the server and run them.

In addition to scripts, any other executable files should be moved to a separate directory that will prevent unauthorized users from modifying them. You should ensure that permissions will deny unauthorized users from executing the program or script, and you should deny all users the ability to modify files and upload to the directory. This will make it easier to set permissions on who can execute scripts and programs in that directory and also make it easier when setting up auditing. Shells and interpreters should also be removed from your system, because these present a possible security problem, which hackers can use to access your system. Scripts require interpreters to run and process the various commands contained within them. For example, to run Perl-based CGI scripts, a Perl interpreter is used. Therefore, if you don't use Perl for CGI scripts on your Web site, you should remove the interpreter.

# Hardening the Overall System

In addition to hardening the Web server, you will also need to harden the overall system. As with Web server software, bugs and security holes may be found in the operating system and other software running on your server. To deal with these issues, service packs, patches, and bug fixes may be released after the installation CD was put on the market. You should check the Web site of the operating system's manufacturer, as well as the sites belonging to any other software running on your system. Installing the fixes to these problems will make your system more secure and reliable.

As with components used by the Web server, you should removed unneeded components and software on your server. Each unnecessary item should be viewed as a potential threat. By leaving software that serves no valuable purpose on the system, security holes in that software could be used to access parts of your system.

If you haven't done so already, you should ensure that the server is using the available security features. The file system being used should be one that provides as much security as possible. If you are using Windows NT or Windows 2000, you should use NTFS, which is more secure than FAT or FAT32. Therefore, if your NT Server is using FAT or your Windows 2000 Server uses FAT or FAT32, then you should convert your hard disk's file system to NTFS. If NTFS is being used, then you should review NTFS permissions on network drives. By default, Windows assigns Full Control permissions to the Everyone group to new shared resources, including new folders. You will want to ensure that anonymous users have limited access to these resources.

Permissions are an important issue for secure site design. The location of where HTML documents are stored (such as the document root), and where log and configuration files are stored (such as the server root) should be kept confidential. In other words, don't let anyone know the location of these directories. The server root should have permissions set up so that only the webmaster can write to configuration directories, log directories, and their contents. No one except the webmaster or members of an administration group should have read permissions on these, or it is possible that others may be able to view information contained in them.

The document root will have different permissions from the server root, because visitors to your Web site will need to be able to read files from this directory. If they don't have the read permission, then they will be unable to load the document into their browser and view your Web pages. Only the webmaster and members of the administration group should have the ability to write to this directory, because this will be needed to upload new content to the site.

CGI programs are commonly stored in a directory called CGI-BIN, and different permissions should be associated with it. Because users may run scripts contained within them, this directory will need to be readable and executable by all users or users whom you want to be able to run CGI programs. Under no circumstances should you allow permission to anyone other than the webmaster or members of the administration group to write to this directory.

You should also ensure that any passwords used by the Administrator user or members of an Administrator group are difficult to guess. Although this is often stressed to users, members of IT staff may forget or get sloppy with their own passwords. You should remember to change passwords regularly, especially after a member of your IT staff leaves your organization. If you are unsure whether the Admin password has been changed since the server was installed, or for any significant period of time, then you should take this as a cue to change the password.

In terms of physical security, you should ensure your server is stored in a secure place. This can be a room or server closet that is locked. After taking so many steps to secure your system, you don't want to leave the server in a place to be modified. Problems could easily occur if a user mistook the server for a workstation, got curious, or decided to be malicious and began making changes to it.

**SECURITY ALERT!**

It is fairly common for administrators to fail to regularly upgrade Web server and system software with service packs, patches, and bug fixes—Egghead.com, the online electronics superstore, admitted that they had not installed the latest fixes at the time they were broken into before Christmas 2000. Administrators may upgrade to the latest version of software as often as they can, but may fail in hardening the software between versions. If a hacker comes across a site that didn't apply the manufacturer's patch to fix a problem, he can then use the vulnerability to attack your system.

# Password Hacking and Analysis Tools

Passwords seemingly are a fairly basic issue, but accessing a site or network through another's user account and password is the most common method of hacking. In setting password policies and protecting your account and site from password hacking, you should remember the following:

- Set policies on what types of passwords are good passwords.
- Set time limits on passwords and change passwords frequently.
- Keep passwords secret.
- Don't leave terminals unattended or servers unprotected.
- Maintain account policies and review user accounts often.
- Limit membership to an administrator group and limit knowledge of administrator passwords.
- Inform users to report suspected problems.

Inform users about how to choose passwords that are difficult to hack. All too often, a user will use the name of a spouse, child, or pet, or other obvious person, place, or thing associated with her life. In many cases, you can crack someone's password by looking at items on her desk or in her office, such as photographs or items that are obviously of value to them. An optimal password will include upper- and lowercase letters (A–Z, a–z), numbers (0–9) and special characters (-=[]\;',./`~!@#$% ^&*()_+{}|:"<>?). The worst thing you could possibly do is replace one password with another easy-to-guess password.

Time limits should be placed on passwords. The longer a user has a password, the greater the risk that someone has knowledge of it. You should also remember to change administrator passwords frequently, especially when an employee leaves.

Another common issue is when users share passwords. Rather than waiting to acquire the proper permissions, they will get another user to provide his password. In some occasions, this may even occur between members of an IT staff, providing an administrator password to those who shouldn't have it.

Computers being left unattended are another problem and may affect your site if a user within your company sit at your workstation when you or other members of administration are logged in. She can sit at your computer, add a new account with high access, or modify her own to set the needed permissions to do damage or investigate the hidden areas of your site. The same can apply to servers that aren't stored in secure areas, don't have password-protected screen savers, or aren't locked down. Due to the threat of users having unauthorized access to an administrator account or the account of a user who's a member of an administrator group, you should limit who is a member of this group and also limit who has access to the administrator account.

By reviewing user accounts on a regular basis, you can determine whether any users should no longer be allowed access to certain directories or files. You should review the rights and permissions given to users (especially the anonymous account), because new directories may have been created that give these users full access. To monitor user accounts in this way, you should have auditing turned on and should monitor when security policies have changed (and who has changed them).

Finally, you should make it clear that you appreciate the reporting of suspected abuse of accounts or observations of security problems. Many times, users may find out—before you do—that a hacking attempt has occurred, that data has been tampered with, or that holes in security have opened. Because they are worried that they'll be blamed for the problem, they won't inform the webmaster. For example, a user may be visiting your site, find a backdoor, and stumble across a directory containing sensitive data. In accessing this, they may worry that they'll be blamed for hacking the site. By letting users know that you appreciate such information being passed along, you can then fix the security hole before it is hacked by a malicious user.

In addition to dealing with password issues with users, remember to modify administrator accounts that were set up by default when the server was installed. When a Web server is installed, there may be an account setup that will allow unlimited or high access to your site. Such an account may be used to modify access for other users or allow access to certain files on the server. If such an account exists, it will have a default password associated with it. This should be changed immediately, so that anyone who's familiar with the default password can't hack your system with it.

To determine whether your site and network are vulnerable to problems with passwords (and other issues), a number of tools are available on the Internet. One such tool is called L0phtCrack. This tool, shown in Figure 3.8, will crack a large number of passwords on Windows NT and 2000 servers. It determines NT/2000 user passwords from cryptographic hashes stored on the operating system by using a variety of methods.

L0phtCrack is available for download from a number of Internet sites, including Security Software Technologies (www.securitysoftwaretech.com/l0phtcrack/download.html). This is a 15-day evaluation version, but you can also purchase an unlimited version. Using this tool, you can acquire usernames and passwords in a variety of ways:

- **Dump Passwords from Registry** (Tools menu), which dumps password hashes from the Windows Registry.
- **Import SAM File** (File menu), which allows you to import a SAM file that stores password hashes. Because this can't be read

**Figure 3.8** LOphtCrack Is a Tool Used to Reveal Passwords

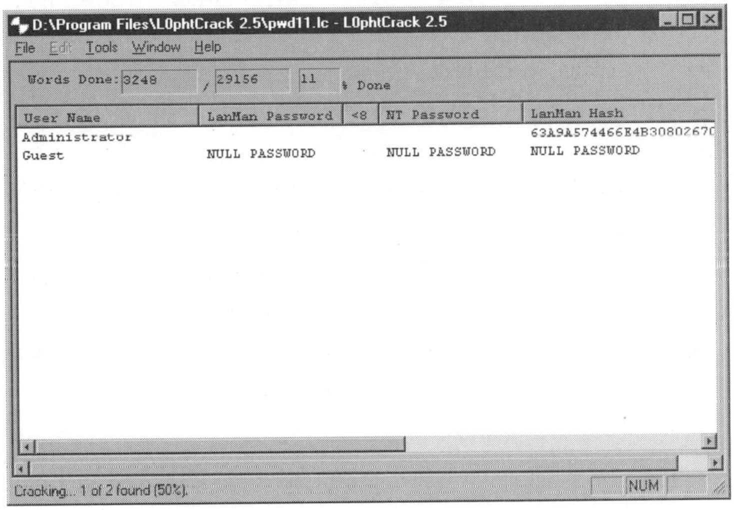

from the file when the operating system is running, you could access the SAM file from a backup, Emergency Repair Disk, or from the repair directory on the system hard disk.

- **SMB Packet Capture** (Tools menu), which allows you to capture packets containing password hashes over the network.

After this is acquired, you then select Options from the Tools menu and determine the level of attack used to crack the passwords. After you've set this, you can press F4 or select Run Crack from the Tools menu. This will begin the process of auditing passwords.

Another tool that can be used to gather information on users and passwords (and more) is the Cerberus Internet Scanner (CIS), which is developed by Cerberus Information Security, Ltd. This tool is available for download from www.cerberus-infosec.co.uk/cis.shtml. It will run approximately 300 tests on your system, including the Web site, FTP, SMTP, POP3, Windows NT, NetBIOS, and MS-SQL. After it has completed the tests, it will provide detailed information in the form of an HTML document, as shown in Figure 3.9.

As you can see by the results of a scan on a Web server, CIS provides a comprehensive listing of information. As Figure 3.9 shows, this may also include revealing Administrator passwords. Other information provided by CIS can show the groups on your system (and the users who are members of these groups), Registry settings, services running on your operating system, various Web service security issues, and whether anonymous logons are permitted by FTP.

**Figure 3.9** Cerberus Internet Scanner Results, as Displayed through a Web Browser

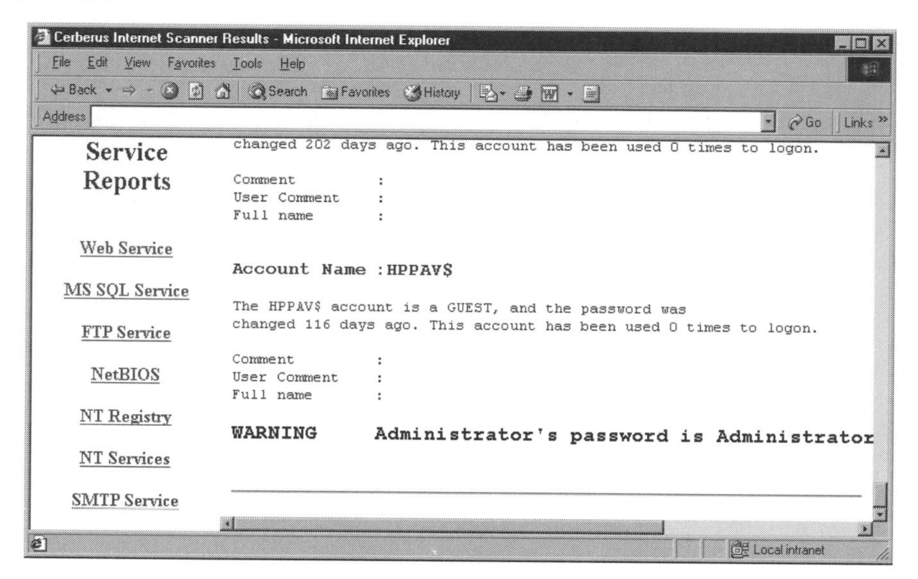


To obtain information about your system using CIS, complete the following steps:

1. After CIS is running, click **Select Host** from the File menu.
2. When the dialog box appears, enter the name or IP address of the server you want to test and then click **OK**.
3. Click **Select Modules** on the File menu.
4. When the dialog box appears, select what you would like to test (such as **Web** or **FTP**), and then click **OK**.
5. Click **Start Scan** on the File menu.
6. When all checks are complete, click **View Reports** to analyze the results, which are then displayed in the default Web browser on your computer.

As with any of these and other tools, they can be used for analyzing your own site for security vulnerabilities or used by others to obtain information that can be used to acquire unauthorized access. As such, you need to properly analyze your system using such tools, so that you can determine problems before others take advantage of them.

## Web Design Issues Dealing with HTML Code

Given that most of your site will consist of HTML documents, it should come as no surprise that HTML can be used by hackers, and it should be included as part of your security plan. The HTML used to create Web pages may contain significant information that reveals services available on your site, pathnames to files, and various other bits of data that a hacker may benefit from. As we show in the sections that follow, Web design issues dealing with HTML code will require you to do the following:

1. Review HTML code in all Web pages posted to your site.
2. Remove or revise sensitive information contained in HTML code.
3. Ensure that directories on the site have proper permissions.
4. Determine whether Server Side Includes (SSI)are a potential threat to your site.
5. Determine whether certain Server Side Includes should be disabled or if Server Side Includes shouldn't be allowed on your site.

### Information in HTML Code

In World War II, a common line of propaganda was: "loose lips sink ships." This was a warning not to reveal information that could be used by an enemy for an attack. Although this wisdom was decades ahead of the Internet, the warning is as valuable today as it was then. The less an enemy knows about you, the lower the chance they could cause harm. Because of this, you shouldn't reveal more than you want to through your Web pages.

Hackers will view a site's HTML code, looking for vulnerabilities and information. Such source code can be viewed by selecting Source from the Internet Explorer's View menu, or by selecting Page Source in Netscape Navigator. Hackers may go page-by-page through a Web site, viewing each page's source in search of clues on how to break the site's security. Information in the HTML may include comments for developers and Web page authors. Such comments may provide insight into who created the site (such as her name and contact information), server information, and how scripts work or what their purpose is. Vulnerabilities in code may also be seen and used against the site. Other information readily acquired through the HTML code may reveal IP addresses, directory structure, e-mail addresses, domain names, and so on. To illustrate, let's look at a simple Web Page:

```
<!— Note to developers, please use the following directory
structure
/inet/html
/inet/cgi-bin
/inet/dev
 —>
<HTML>
<HEAD>
<META HTTP-EQUIV="Content-Type" CONTENT="text/html; charset=windows
    -1252">
<META NAME="GENERATOR" CONTENT="Microsoft FrontPage 4.0">
<META NAME="ProgId" CONTENT="FrontPage.Editor.Document">
<TITLE>Welcome</TITLE>
</HEAD>
<BODY>
<P>Welcome to our Web site</P>
<P><IMG BORDER="0" SRC="file:///C:/inet/brick.jpg"></P>
</BODY>
```

```
</HTML>
<!— further information can be acquired from the Administrator at
(555)555-5555, ext. 1234 or via email at mcross@microsolved.com—>
```

In looking at this source code, you can find considerable information. The location of a JPG image and comments in the code show the directory structure. It shows that the Web site is located in C:\inet, with CGI scripts located in C:\inet\cgi-bin and HTML documents located in C:\inet\html. The directory for developers is C:\inet\dev. The comments also show that the administrator has an account called mcross in the microsolved.com domain. This person's business phone number is (555) 555-5555, and his extension is 1234. In addition to this, the meta tags show that the page was created using Microsoft FrontPage 4.0 and suggests that FrontPage extensions may be used on the server.

**Note from the Underground...**

### Hacking a Site Using Information Provided By the Web Pages

Considerable information may be found in Web pages displayed to the general public. You should analyze the source code of pages, because they may contain information that will make your site vulnerable. Pay particular attention to pages with forms, or those that access Web-based applications or secure sites, and determine if any of these contain usernames and passwords. Although this sounds strange, a large number of sites contain just this, providing hackers with information they need to burrow into the depths of your server. More often, you may find commented text that provides more information than necessary about your site, how it's structured, or the names of various accounts. You're better off to be a little paranoid and avoid making such information public.

You should also limit or avoid hidden tags to store information used by your site. Hidden tags are used to store hidden values, such as the prices of items sold on a Web page. Each hidden tag can be used with forms on your site and includes a name and a value. When the form is submitted, the name and value in the hidden field is included with the results. For example, the following line of code shows an input value of $100.00 associated with a variable called "cost."

```
<input type=hidden name="cost" value="100.00">
```

Using a text editor or HTML editing program, a hacker could alter the value so that the value is changed to a lower amount. For example, the $100.00 could be changed to $1.00. This would allow buyers to purchase products at a significantly reduced amount.

## Using Server Side Includes (SSI) in HTML Code

Server Side Includes (SSI) are another security issue dealing with HTML code. These are server directives that are embedded into HTML documents, which can provide Web page authors with a quick way to obtain the system date/time or even execute system commands and CGI scripts. Common examples of SSI are Web pages that show the last date a particular Web page was modified, or hit counters showing the number of visitors to a page. Another example of an SSI could be e-mail addresses that are included on Web pages. You may have such an e-mail address used on each page, so that users can report problems with the page. With SSI, you could put a tag in the HTML code that has the server parse the document before it is passed to the browser. In this example, it could include the text in another file that has the e-mail address of the webmaster. If the e-mail address changes, you simply edit the text file instead of each of the Web pages.

A common attack with SSI is done through guest books, where users can post their comments on a Web page with that of other users. When the hacker writes the comment, he or she includes an SSI program in the comment. Typically, a CGI program will take these comments and append them to the guest book. When the next person views the guest book contents, the SSI is parsed by the server, and the SSI runs. If your site doesn't have a guest book, you may want to keep it that way.

In looking at the most used SSI commands for hacking, three of them stand out. These are **echo**, **include**, and **exec**. Whereas other SSI commands can also be used for hacking a site, these are often used to attack a site.

The **echo** command, which instructs the server to print some information into the Web page that's returned to the client's browser, is commonly used with SSI,. To see a common effect, let's look at the following HTML tag:

```
The current date is <!—#echo var="DATE_LOCAL" —>
```

When the server reads this code, it will see a pound sign (#), which indicates that an SSI command follows. It will see that a variable, defined by the code var=, is to be returned. In this case, the variable is DATE_LOCAL, which tells the server to return the current date and time.

Using the echo command, a hacker could modify this variable to return other information from your server. For example, by merely changing the variable from DATE_LOCAL to DOCUMENT_NAME (another common variable used by SSI), a hacker can return the path and filename of the current document, thereby revealing part of your directory structure.

Another common SSI command used in hacking is **include**. As shown in the following HTML document, it is used to add information from another file to your Web page. The file to include in your page is specified using the file= parameter.

```
<html>
<head>
<title>Demo Page</title>
</head>
 <body>
 <h1>Our Home Page</h1>
If you have any comments or suggestions, contact the webmaster.
```

```
<!—#include file="email.htm"—>
See you later!
</body>
</html>
```

As you can see by this example, a file called email.htm is added to the document, which is then displayed to the user. The problem with this code is that—if proper permissions aren't set, and the Web browser allows you to specify any path you want—a hacker could change the path of the specified file and pull up any file that's accessible on your network. This could include sensitive documents, password lists, and so forth.

The third SSI command we discuss is **exec**, which allows you to perform various tasks, similar to an executable. With this command, you can open files, return output, run batch files called shell scripts, or execute various other programs on your system. An example of code using the **exec** command is as follows:

```
<!—#exec cgi="/cgi-bin/test.pl"—>
```

A number of Web servers require an SSI executable to have the file extension .CGI for the specified file to be executed. However, you should check your server documentation to see if this is indeed the case. As is the case with other commands, much of the functionality a hacker could acquire through this command depends on whether permissions have been properly set up on the server. If you don't require SSI or this command, iyou should disable it.

If permissions are improperly configured, then SSI can be a major problem. For example, if all users had read privileges to all files or full access to programs on the server, then SSI could be used to read these files or execute various programs. As stated earlier, you will need to evaluate permissions given to users and determine what default permissions are given to newly created directories.

On many Web servers, SSI must be turned on before you can use its functionality, and you should check your Web server to determine whether it is enabled by default. If SSI isn't used on your site, you should turn it off. Some Web servers, such as Apache, provide the ability to disable the types of SSI that can be passed to the server. If your Web server doesn't provide this functionality, then you could use a firewall to block SSI, or you could use pre-parser scripts that will remove unauthorized SSI before they are passed to the server.

# Guidelines for Java, JavaScript, and Active X

Java, JavaScript, and ActiveX components are often overlooked as potential threats to a Web site. These are client-side scripts and components, which run on the computer of a visitor to your site. Because they run on a user's computer, any problems will generally affect them rather than the Web site itself. However, the effect of an erroneous or malicious script, applet, or component can be just as devastating to your site. If a client's computer locks up when one of these loads on their computer—every time she visits your site—it ultimately will have the same effect as your Web server going down: No one will be able to use your site.

As we show in the sections that follow, a number of problems may result from Java applets, ActiveX components, or client side scripts such as JavaScript. Not all of these problems affect the client, and they may provide a means of attacking your site. Ultimately, however, the way to avoid such problems involves controlling which programs are made available on your site and being careful about what is included in the content.

## Understanding Java, JavaScript, and ActiveX—and the Problems They May Cause

Web designers will use public domain applets and scripts for their Web pages, even though they don't fully understand what the applet or script may be doing. Java applets are generally digitally signed or of a standalone format, but when embedded in a Web page, it is possible skirt around this requirement. Hackers can program an applet to execute code on a machine, so that information is retrieved or files are destroyed or modified. Remember that an applet is a program and has the capability of performing malicious activities on your system.

Java is a programming language, developed by Sun Microsystems, which is used to make applications (applets) for the Internet as well as standalone programs. Applets are embedded into the Web page and are run when the user's browser loads the HTML document into memory. In programming such applets, Java provides a number of features related to security. At the time the applet is compiled, the compiler provides type and bytecode verification to check whether any errors exist in the code. In this way, Java keeps certain areas of memory from being accessed by the code. When the code is loaded, the Java Virtual Machine (JVM) is used in executing it. The JVM uses a built-in Security Manager, which controls access by way of policies. In Netscape's JVM, however, a problem was discovered where certain conditions caused the JVM not to check code that was being loaded. Because all of the code wasn't being checked, this allowed code to be run that circumvented Java's type verification. Shortly after this problem was identified in Netscape Communicator, a similar problem was identified in Internet Explorer.

In looking at this identified problem, you may recognize that any problems would affect the user's computer and not the Web server itself. As is the case with other Internet programming methods discussed in this section, Java runs on the client side. Generally, this means that the client, rather than the Web server, will experience any problems or security threats. However, if the applet is designed to extract information from the client machine, usernames and passwords may be obtained and used to hack your site. Also, if the client machine is damaged in any way by a malicious applet, then the user will only know that he or she visited your site and experienced a problem. This will have an impact on the public perception of your site's reliability and the image of your company.

ActiveX is Microsoft's implementation of applets, which are embedded in HTML documents using the <OBJECT> tag. ActiveX controls can provide a variety of functions, such as allowing users to view multimedia on the Web page. If a user accesses an HTML document with an ActiveX control, it will check whether the control is already on the user's computer. If it isn't, it will be downloaded, the Web page will be displayed, and the ActiveX code will be loaded into memory and executed.

Because ActiveX, Java, and JavaScript run on the client side, many of the issues you'll find with them deal with your user's machine and not the server. An issue with ActiveX was revealed in 1999 when the "Safe for Scripting" security hole was revealed. Programmers could set the Safe for Scripting flag so that their ActiveX controls weren't checked for an Authenticode signature before being run. Microsoft's Authenticode is used to authenticate the control through code signing, which we discuss later. When Authenticode is used, the ActiveX code is signed and authenticated by a third-party. This ensures that the code hasn't been modified since the time it was created. When the Safe for Scripting flag was enabled, the code checking was bypassed, and the control could be run without the user being aware of a problem. Two controls shipped with IE4 that had this problem were Scriptlet.typelib (which had the ability to create, edit, and overwrite files on the user's hard disk) and Eyedog.ocx (which had the ability to gather information from the registry). This was a major security issue, because hackers could benefit from this weakness. To deal with this, a patch was made available through Microsoft's Web site, which fixed the problem.

JavaScript is different from ActiveX and Java in that it isn't compiled into a program. Despite this, JavaScript uses some of the same syntax and functions as Java. When a user accesses an HTML document with JavaScript in it, it is run through an interpreter. This is slower than if the program were already compiled into a language that the machine can understand. For this reason, JavaScript is slower than Java applets.

Although JavaScript is different from ActiveX and Java in regard to it being a scripting language, it is still possible that a hacker may use a script to acquire information about your site or use code to attack a site or client computer.

# Preventing Problems with Java, JavaScript, and ActiveX

Preventing problems with scripts, applets, and other components that are included on your site isn't impossible to avoid, if precautions are made beforehand. First, don't include components that you don't fully understand or trust. If you aren't certain what a particular script is doing in a line of code, then don't add it to a page. Similarly, you should use applets and ActiveX components that make their source code available. If you have a particular applet or component that you want to use, but don't have the code available, then ensure that it was created by a trusted source. For example, you can find commercially available recordable CDs (CD-Rs) that are filled with various applets, scripts, and components. Well-known companies, who don't want to tarnish their corporate image of selling products with dangerous code, create many of these. Also, a number of companies such as Microsoft provide code samples on their site, which can be used safely and successfully on a site.

Make sure that you check your code for any flaws, because you don't want the end user to be the first to identify them. A common method is to upload the Web page and component to the site, but don't link the page to any other pages. This will keep users who aren't aware of the page from accessing it. Another method is to use a test server, which is a computer that's configured the same as your Web server but separated from the rest of your network. With a test server, if damage is done to your site, then the real site will be unaffected. After this is done, it is wise to access a site using the user account that will be used to view the applet, component, or script. For example, if it was going to be used by everyone, then view your site using the anonymous user account. This will allow you to effectively test for problems.

A common problem that hackers will use to their advantage regards scripts and programs that trust user input. This was an issue that was mentioned when we discussed how a guest book could be used to have an SSI command run and possibly damage your site. In this, we saw that CGI programs written in Perl can be used to run batch files. Scripting languages can also be used to run shell functions. With a properly written and executed script, the cmd.exe could be used to run other programs on a Windows NT or 2000 system.

In addition to user input, you will need to write programs and scripts so that input passed from a client is not trusted. Tools such as Telnet or other programs available on the Internet can be used to simulate requests from Web browsers. If input is trusted, then a hacker could pass various commands to the server through the applet or component.

As we discussed in a previous section, considerable information may be found in Web pages. Because scripts can be embedded directly into the Web page, the script can be displayed with the HTML by viewing the source code. This option is available through most browsers and may be used to reveal information that you didn't want to be made public. In looking at the code in an HTML document, you may even find passwords and usernames. Scripts in Web pages may be used to pass usernames and passwords to Access or SQL databases. Windows NT requires such scripts to include the usernames and passwords to connect to such databases, and it is possible that you may also show the hierarchy in such code. By displaying this information, it is possible to make yourself open to attack.

To protect yourself, you should ensure that permissions are correctly set and use other security methods available through the operating system on which your Web server is running. For example, the NTFS file system on Windows NT and 2000 supports Access Control Lists (ACLs), which can be configured to control who is allowed to execute a script. By controlling access to pages using scripts, you are better protected from hackers accessing this information.

**Damage & Defense...**

### Limit Access and Backup Your Site

Hackers may attack a site for different reasons. Some may simply poke around, look at what's there, and leave, whereas others may modify or destroy data on the site. Even malicious hackers may modify a site so that sensitive material isn't destroyed, but the effects are more akin to graffiti. This was the case when the Web site of the Royal Canadian Mounted Police (RCMP) had data modified. Cartoon images appeared on the site showing RCMP officers riding pigs rather than horses. Although the images were quickly fixed by simply uploading the original content, this case does illustrate the need for proper permissions on directories and regularly backing up your site.

Continued

Generally, you will create content on one computer, then transfer it to the actual Web site. In many cases, you may feel this is enough, but you should still back up your site so that if a problem occurs, the proper content can be uploaded to the site. By backing up content, you are insuring that if a script, applet, or component is misused, the site can be restored and repaired quickly.

Before a problem occurs (and especially after one happens), you should review permissions to determine if anonymous or low-level users have more access than they should. If they can write to a directory or execute files, then you may find that this is too much access (depending on the directory in question). In any case, you shouldn't give a user any more access to a directory than they could possibly need, and you should ensure that directories lower than this in the hierarchy have excessive permissions due to their location. In other words, if a directory is lower in the hierarchy, it may have the same permissions as its parent directory, even though you don't want this high a level of access.

Because of the possible damage a Java applet, JavaScript, or ActiveX component can do to a network, in terms of threatening security or attacking machines, many companies filter out applets. Firewalls can be configured to filter out applets, scripts, and components so that they are removed from an HTML document. By removing such elements from ever being displayed, the Web page will appear different from the way its author intended, but any content that is passed through the firewall will be secure.

On the client side, many browsers can also be configured to filter content. By changing the settings on a Web browser, you can prevent such programs from being loaded into memory on a client computer. The user accessing the Internet from your network is provided with the HTML content, but isn't presented with any of these programmed features. Although JavaScripts aren't compiled programs, they can also be used to attack a user's machine. Because JavaScript provides similar functionality to Java, it can be used to gather information or perform unwanted actions on a user's machine. For this reason, you should take care in the scripts used on your site.

In creating applets, components, and scripts, you should keep in mind that not all browsers support these components. Also, some scripts will run on Internet Explorer or Netscape Navigator, but will not run on both or other browsers. You should provide a secondary set of Web pages that don't use them, or you should add code that determines the type and version of browser a user is using and allows execution based on this type and version information. If the script or applet isn't supported, then you can set up your HTML code to allow it to be skipped over. To show this, let's look at the following functions:

```
navigator.appName()

navigator.appVersion()
```

The first line is used to retrieve the name of the browser being used; the second line is used to retrieve the version of the browser. By using these functions, you can determine whether a script or applet should run. This is done as follows:

```
if (navigator.appName = = "Netscape") {
     Insert code here;
} else if (navigator.appName = = "Microsoft Internet Explorer") {
     Insert code here;
} else {
     document.write ("Internet Explorer or Netscape is required to
          view this page");
}
```

Another method of keeping errors from occurring in your JavaScript is to use comments, which will prevent errors in browsers that don't support a scripting language. To illustrate how to do this, let's look at the following piece of HTML code:

```
<SCRIPT LANGUAGE="JavaScript 1.1">
<!–
     insert JavaScript here
// – >
</SCRIPT>
```

Looking at this line by line, you will notice that the first line specifies the language being used in the script. If an older browser is being used that doesn't understand the script tag, then it will ignore it. If it does support the language, then this tag will inform the browser's interpreter what language is to be interpreted. The next line shows an opening comment. If an older browser that doesn't understand JavaScript reads this line, then any JavaScript between the opening and closing comments will be ignored. If JavaScript is supported, then it will then begin to process your script.

Although the best course of action is to only use applets and scripts created by you alone, this may not be feasible. You may not know how to create Java applets, JavaScripts, or ActiveX components, or need ones that perform tasks that are beyond your abilities to program. Although it is a good idea to avoid applets and scripts created by untrustworthy or unknown individuals, you may feel forced to do otherwise. Try to find programmers in your own company who have the skills you need to script or program, or purchase or acquire existing scripts and applets from an established source. If the source code is available, or if you are using scripts, then look over how it was created and determine what it actually does. This will save you considerable problems in the long run.

# Programming Secure Scripts

In the previous section, we looked at client-side programs and scripts, which run on the user's machine. In this section, we look at server-side programs and scripts, which run on the Web server rather than on the machine being used to browse your site. Server-side programs and scripts provide a variety of functions, including working with databases, searching your site for documents based on keywords, and providing other methods of exchanging information with users.

A benefit of server-side scripts is that any source code is hidden from the user. With JavaScript, any scripts are visible to the user by viewing the source code through the browser. Although this isn't an issue with some scripts, server-side scripts may be used to access confidential information. The last thing you want to do is reveal how information in a corporate database may be accessed.

The CGI allows communication links between Internet applications and your Web server, allowing users to access programs over the Web. The process begins when a user requests a CGI script or program using his browser. For example, the user might fill out a form on a Web page and then submit it. The request for the processing of the form is made to the Web server, which executes the script or application on the server. After the application has processed the input, the Web server then returns output from the script or application to the browser.

CGI uses the HTTP protocol in the TCP/IP protocol suite. The Web server knows to pass this to an application because the application is specified in the URL of a hyperlink or in the form's tags. An example of such a tag is shown in the following code:

```
<FORM METHOD=POST ACTION=http://www.microsolved.com/
    cgi-bin/myprog.pl>
```

In this tag, the form's data is sent to the Web server at www .microsolved.com, which passes it to a CGI program that's written in PERL.

PERL is another scripting language that uses an interpreter to execute various functions and commands. It is similar to the C programming language in its syntax. It is popular for Web-based applications, and is widely supported. Apache Web Server is a good example of this support, as it has plug-ins that will load PERL permanently into memory. By loading it into memory, the PERL scripts are executed faster.

Microsoft has offered an alternative to CGI and PERL in ASP—HTML documents with scripts embedded into them. These scripts can be written in a number of languages, including JScript and VBScript, and may also include ActiveX Data Object program statements. A benefit of using ASP is that it can return output through HTML documents extremely fast. It can provide a return of information that is quicker than using CGI and PERL.

Unfortunately, using ASP can cause problems that are similar to those seen in client-side scripting. Embedding the scripts into the Web pages allows curious and malicious users to view ASP code. Depending on what's included in the page, a hacker may be able to acquire usernames and passwords and identify vulnerabilities in the code.

Common to all of these methods is that scripts and programs run on the server—attacks using these will often affect the server rather than the end-user. Weaknesses and flaws can be used to exploit the script or program and access private information or damage the server. An example of this is the PHF script that came with early versions of NCSA HTTPD server (version 1.5a-export or earlier) and Apache Web Server 1.0.3. The problem with this script was that it didn't properly parse and validate input. The PHF script is a phone book script. Whenever a newline character (%0a) was used in the script, any additional commands were also performed with the privileges of the user account running the Web server. To deal with this problem, the script should be removed from your Web server.

ITesting and auditing programs before going live with them is very important. In doing so, you may reveal a number of vulnerabilities or find problems, such as buffer overflows, which may have been missed if the code had been made available on your site. In testing, using a test server is best. This server should have the same applications and configurations as your actual Web server.

**NOTE**

---

Any programs and scripts available on your site should be thoroughly tested before they are made available for use on the Web. Determine whether the script or program works properly by using it numerous times. If you are using a database, enter and retrieve multiple records. You should also consider having one or more members of your IT staff try the script or program themselves, because this will analyze the effectiveness of the program with fresh eyes. They may enter data in a different order or try a task differently, causing unwanted results.

---

# Code Signing: Solution or More Problems?

Code signing addresses the need for users to trust the code they download and then load into their computer's memory. After all, without knowing who provided the software, or whether it was altered after being distributed, malicious code could be added to a component and attack a user's computer.

Digital certificates can be used to sign the code and to authenticate that code hasn't been tampered with—and that it is indeed the file distributed by its creator. The digital certificate consists of a set of credentials for verifying identity. The certificate is issued by a certification authority and contains a name, serial number, expiration date, copy of the certificate holder's public key, and a digital signature belonging to the certificate authority. The elements of the certificate are used to guarantee that the file is valid.

As with any process reliant on trust, code signing has its positive and negative aspects. In the sections that follow, we discuss these issues and show how the process of code signing works.

## Understanding Code Signing

Digital certificates are assigned through certificate authorities (CAs). A certificate authority is a vendor that associates a public key with the person applying for the certificate. One of the largest organizations to provide such certificates is VeriSign (www.verisign.com), which provides Authenticode certificates. An Authenticode certificate is used for software publishing and timestamp services. It can be attached to the file a programmer is distributing and allows users to identify that it is a valid, unadulterated file.

Digital certificates can be applied to a number of different file types. For example, using VeriSign Authenticode, developers can sign such files as the following:

- .EXE, which is an executable program.
- .CAB, which are cabinet files commonly used for the installation and setup of applications. These contain numerous files that are compressed in the cabinet file.
- .CAT, which contain digital thumbprints used to guarantee the integrity of files.
- .OCX, which are ActiveX controls.
- .DLL, which are dynamic link library files, containing executable functions.
- .STL, which contain a certificate trust list.

When a person downloads a file with a digital certificate, the status of that certificate is checked through the certificate authority. If the certificate isn't valid, the user will be warned. If it is found to be valid, a message will appear stating that it has a valid certificate. The message will contain additional information and show who the certificate belongs to. When the user agrees to install the software, it will then begin the installation.

## The Strengths of Code Signing

Digital signatures can be used to guarantee the integrity of files and that the package being installed is authentic and unmodified. This signature is attached to the file being downloaded, and it identifies who is distributing the files and shows that they were unmodified since being created. The certificate helps to keep malicious users from impersonating someone else.

This is the primary benefit of code signing. It provides users with the identity of the software's creator. It allows you to know who manufactured the program and provides you with the option of deciding whether to trust that person or company. When the browser is about to download the component, a warning message is displayed, allowing you to choose whether it is to be installed or loaded into memory. This puts the option of running it in the user's hands.

## Problems with the Code Signing Process

A major problem with code signing is that you must rely on a third-party for checking authenticity. If a programmer provided fake information to a CA or stole the identity of another individual or company, then it would be possible to effectively distribute a malicious program over the Internet. The deciding factor here would be the certificate authority's abilities to check the information provided to them when the certificate was applied for.

Another problem is if valid information is provided to the CA, but the certificate is attached to software with bad or malicious code. An example of problems with code signing is seen in the example of Internet Exploder, an ActiveX control that was programmed by Fred McLain. This programmer obtained an Authenticode certificate through VeriSign. When users running Windows 95 with Advanced Power Management ran the code for Internet Exploder, it would perform a clean shutdown of their system. The certificate for this control was revoked.

Certificate Revocation Lists (CRLs), which store a listing of revoked certificates, may also be considered problematic. Web browsers and Internet applications rarely check certificate revocation lists, so it is possible for a program to be used even though its certificate was revoked. If a certificate was revoked, but its status wasn't checked, then the software could appear to be okay even though it has been compromised.

In talking about problems with code signing, it is important to realize that this doesn't necessarily apply to any given CA. Certificates can also be used over your intranet using software such as Microsoft Certificate Server. Using this server software, you can create your own digital certificates for use on a network. This allows someone to self-sign their code with their own CA and give the appearance that the code is valid and secure. You should therefore verify the validity of the CA before accepting any files. By ensuring that the CA is a valid and reputable one, you can avoid installing a hacker's code onto your system.

An additional drawback to code signing for applications distributed over the Internet is that users must guess and choose who they trust and who they do not. The browser will display a message informing who the creator is, a brief message about the dangers of downloading any kind of data, and then leave it up to the user whether to install it or not. The browser is unable to verify code.

Tools & Traps...

### Problems with Code Signing

The possibility exists that code may have a valid certificate or use self-signed code that is malicious. Such code may have names similar to valid certificate authorities, but are in no way affiliated with that CA. For example, you may see code signed with the vendor name of VerySign, and misreading it as VeriSign allow it to be installed. It can be easy to quickly glance at a warning and allow a certificate, so you should remember to read the certificate information carefully before allowing its installation.

# Should I Outsource the Design of My Site?

Outsourcing is the hiring of third-parties to perform work that may exceed the skills of people already employed by a company. It is a major decision, even when there is a full-time webmaster on staff. After all, the person doing your Web site may be a genius at creating content, but she may lack the necessary skills to install and effectively configure a Web server and firewall.

Deciding to outsource work is generally a controversial topic in a company. To even consider outsourcing is to realize that your own staff lacks the technical skills and experience to do the job. It can bruise egos and will cost additional money. On the other side of the coin is the knowledge that the work will (probably, hopefully) be done right. Your final choice will generally be someone who does the work regularly and has years of experience behind them. Outsourcing may save money in the short term, but be sure that security responsibilities are clearly delineated in the event of a security breach.

**NOTE**

Take the time to plan what you want and need to in order to determine whether outsourcing is a viable solution. This requires analyzing the individual needs of your company, and gathering input from various departments and individuals. If you determine that outsourcing isn't an option, then you can apply this information to the project and formulate a plan of how you can do the work with existing staff members.

## Understanding the Required Skills

The skills required by whomever you outsource work to depend on what you expect and desire from your Web site. You may need Web server software provided or may already have purchased the software. You may feel comfortable installing the Web server, but need them to configure it and install and set up the firewall. You will need to spend time determining exactly what you want done and write this out in a point-by-point format.

If you are hiring someone to create content for your site, you should decide what elements you want on your site and find what skills are required to create them. Begin by looking at the type of site being created. For example, you may be creating an online banking service that requires SSL and transaction code in the database that's being accessed. Such a site would require greater programming skills than would be required for an online news agency, which may require heavy graphics and hyperlinks, or for a retail vendor that might require secure connections to a credit card company's site for online purchases. After you've looked at the type of site, you will then narrow your focus and look at the content going onto those sites. Web pages with custom graphics would require someone with the graphic art and HTML skills, whereas a search engine would require knowledge of CGI, PERL, or ASP. You may also want to implement specialized programs, which will require Internet programming skills to create ActiveX components.

The content of a site would dictate the type of tools and server software used to create it. Databases on your site would require tools such as Microsoft Access or SQL Server, whereas a graphic-intensive site would require Adobe Illustrator, Corel Draw, or similar tools. You may wish to include graphics that combine images with programming and implement features such as Flash or Shockwave. This would not only require someone who knows how to create HTML documents but also has graphic design talents and programming abilities.

If you're uncomfortable or unfamiliar with determining the required skills for the project, use the Internet. By visiting the Web sites of your competition or similar organizations, you may find bids or job postings that reveal this information. This can be used as a template for determining what you want, because you can remove items that don't apply and add elements that adhere to your specialized needs.

In determining the skills, you should establish a basic level of experience that the contractor should have—and the level you'll feel comfortable with. If you don't set this level and ask how much experience a contractor has doing the work, you could wind up with someone who's doing the work for the first time. In such a case, you would have been better off having a member of your staff trained and having your team do the work themselves.

## Pros and Cons of Outsourcing Design Work

In deciding whether to outsource design work, you will need to weigh the pros and cons. Any project involves risks, and outsourcing adds another risk factor to that project's success. Although many of the factors in this decision will vary from company to company, most businesses that outsource work face several common issues.

### Workload

Outsourcing your design work to an established individual or company means that you will have someone with the experience and skills necessary to get the job done right. By giving these responsibilities to another person, you are freeing your IT staff to perform other duties. In the end, the end product will be more professional.

In many cases, however, outsourcing work is like having temporary staff added to your team. You will need to work closely with the contractor, taking the time and effort to manage them so they finish the job correctly.

## Security

Another drawback in outsourcing design work is the possible compromise of security. Additional security issues must be considered when bringing even one additional person onto the project. You should determine what information the contractor will need to do her job without compromising the security of your network. You should also determine what security policies will be used for the Web server to keep the contractor from accessing unauthorized data (and whether these policies will impact existing policies).

A very real complication in outsourcing is that who you hire may not be who does the work. A number of companies may bid on the job and may offer everything you hope for—but when the time comes to actually do the work, they may subcontract it to another individual or company. When determining whom to hire, you should inquire as to whether they will do the job themselves or use outside contractors.

**Damage & Defense…**

### Checking References

You should check the references of any contractor. Like any other job, people may fudge a little on their resume and say that they have more experience or knowledge than they do. They may also have experience but have done the work so incompetently that it caused major problems. Ask what other contracts an individual or company may have performed, and then call them and ask what they thought of the contractor. Recently, one of the authors was asked about a person who stated that he maintained a Web site

**Continued**

that the author is webmaster of. This person had never worked on the organization's site nor worked for the organization. No one had heard of him, but this person was applying for jobs and taking credit for other people's work.

It is also important that you treat anyone applying for outsourced work like you would any other contractor. You may have heard horror stories of a handyman taking the money for a job, but not doing the work. This also happens with Internet-related work, in which a "professional" is doing a scam. Checking previous customers will help to reveal such con artists.

In some cases, security may be such a concern that you may not be able to outsource work. This may not only revolve around data on the network but the nature of the industry. For example, certain government intelligence and law enforcement agencies may require high levels of clearance. If you were considering outsourcing work to set up a Web server, policies may disallow these people from accessing the server room or entering certain areas of the building. Even in cases where this was allowed, a member of the IT staff may need to supervise the person while they're working. The loss of such a member being able to perform his regular duties would need to be considered in the cost and requirements of outsourcing.

## Contracts and Cost

Other reasons why outsourcing may be an issue could revolve around contracts and cost. Union contracts may prohibit or inhibit hiring individuals from outside the organization. In other cases, the cost of the outsourced work may be considerably higher than the cost of training a member of the staff. If there is enough time to have a member of the IT staff trained, and that individual has the transferable computer skills to learn, then it may be wiser to send the person to school part-time. Although you'll lose the experience of someone who does such outsourced work on a regular basis, your company will gain an onsite expert on how to install, maintain, and administer the Web server.

# No Matter Who Designs It, Double-Check before You Implement It

Regardless of whether you outsource work or do it yourself, it is important that the work is double-checked and tested before it is implemented. Accepting another person's design without checking to see if there are any existing security vulnerabilities or problems is foolish. Although you may not be an accomplished hacker, checking the work will show whether users may stumble into areas they don't belong.

Checking this work is monotonous but necessary. You will need to go through each page of the site. As you open each page, view the source code and look at what it contains. Determine what information is being displayed and whether that information represents a security threat.

As mentioned previously, you can check the source code of HTML documents by selecting Source from Internet Explorer's View menu or by selecting Page Source in Netscape Navigator. This will not only display the HTML, but also any JavaScript (or other scripts) that have been added to the page. If you see any code that you don't understand, you may want to either discuss it with the author of the code or check with a secondary source. This may involve asking another member of your company's IT staff, checking with other developers in a news group or chat room, or hiring a secondary party to look over the content that's been created for your site.

In reviewing the content, pay close attention to the information provided through the Web page. This may include comments for developers and Web page authors, explanations of what purpose the code serves, server information, directory hierarchies, and so forth. You will want to ensure than no more information than is necessary is being posted publicly.

Go through each Web page and check it from a user's perspective. This involves looking over the page and clicking every hyperlink. If forms or Web applications are used, you should enter data and test whether it works. Check the information on the page for spelling mistakes and clarity. Even though a program may function, instructions on how to use it may be confusing.

When testing a site, you should use the same account that a typical user will to access a particular document, file, or program. For example, if a page running a particular applet was meant for everyone to use, then you should access this content using the anonymous user account. By using the webmaster/administrator account, you may not experience the site in the same way that your end-user will.

Before making the site public, you should view content and run scripts, applets, components, and other programs on a test server. This is a computer running the same software and configured the same way as your Web server. The difference is that it will not be connected to your local network or the Internet. If a problem results from certain code, then it will only affect that computer.

You should also use more than one type of browser when checking your site for problems. Some scripts or programs may run fine on Internet Explorer 5, but won't run properly (if at all) on other browsers, such as Netscape. By checking with different browsers, you will be able to see that all users will be able to take advantage of the functionality provided by different Web pages.

You should ensure that any software on the machine has the latest patches and security packs applied to them. If vulnerabilities have been found and solved after the software's release, adding these patches will fix them. Although it is simple enough to do, this may have been overlooked when the software was initially installed.

In checking content, you should also remember that the Web site is a reflection of your corporate image. Errors in scripts, graphics that don't display properly, and other issues will impact how users of the site view your business. Consider outsourcing your testing: Indepenent Verification and Validation (IVV) testing can be very effective in finding problems before your customers do.

# Summary

Secure site design covers a wide variety of issues, starting from the time you decide to use your own Web server, as opposed to using one provided through an ISP. It requires exact planning and giving yourself enough time to complete the project within a reasonable time so that it isn't rushed and doesn't jeopardize security. The Web server can act as a gateway from the Internet onto your internal network, so you should either separate it from your internal network or take other measures to ensure a secure site.

Choosing a Web server is based primarily upon the needs of your company, and these needs are then compared to the features and functionality of the Web server software. The features provided by the Web server for your e-commerce site should attempt to match up with your business needs and the security needs of your company. Often, this will also require looking at operating systems, firewalls, and other software that will enhance the existing benefits of the Web server itself. You should look at the cost of a server, whether your company can afford it, whether it can be expanded, and whether the features offered meet what your company requires and desires. Primary to your decision should be security features offered by the Web server and also the operating system on which the server software will run.

Once installed, you must then begin the process of configuring and implementing elements that will make your site unique and secure. You should implement the strongest file system possible and assign only the minimum of permissions that users will require to access the data they need. You will need to determine whether client-side or server-side scripting will be used, and ensure that these aren't used as methods to hack your site. To authenticate software accessed through your site or downloaded from the Internet by network users, code signing may be useful. If the design and implementation of server software and content is beyond your skills or time constraints, you may want to consider outsourcing.

# Solutions Fast Track

## Choosing a Web Server

☑ The expense of having a private Web server will generally be more costly than it would be to rent space on an ISP's server. Remember that renting such space removes the cost of purchasing servers, software, and T1 lines to the Internet. If problems arise with the equipment, the ISP is responsible for fixing them. However, any choices regarding security, services, or extra software installed on the server will be decided by the third party.

☑ By using a platform your staff is already familiar with, there is less chance they will miss security holes because they may already be aware of them in other operating systems.

☑ Because the Web server runs on top of the operating system like any other software, an operating system with better security features will improve the security of your Web server. For example, although Windows 95 can be used to run Apache Web server, it would be more secure to use Apache on Windows NT Server. Windows 95 has fewer security features and a less secure file system than NT.

☑ In looking at the various servers, pay close attention to certain features, specifically those that control authentication, use of the SET protocol, the setting of rights and permissions, and the use of CGI applications.

## The Basics of Secure Site Design

☑ When developing a site, you should create a security plan that includes the following steps: Identify what needs to be secure; identify the value of what's being protected; identify the risks involved with your site; identify the exposure to those risks; put the plan into action.

☑ Proxy servers can provide additional security measures often not found or easily configured in the Web server application itself, for example, providing inbound and outbound access control, packet filtering, and dial-in access controls. Port and packet filtering is an effective way of preventing unauthorized access to your network.

☑ A number of Web servers require an SSI executable to have the file extension .CGI for the specified file to be executed. However, you should check your server documentation to see if this is indeed the case. Much of the functionality a hacker could acquire through this command depends on whether permissions have been properly set up on the server. For example, if all users had the read privileges to all files or full access to programs on the server, then SSI could be used to read these files or execute various programs. Evaluate permissions given to users and determine what default permissions are given to newly created directories.

☑ Web design issues dealing with HTML code will require you to: review HTML code in all Web pages posted to your site, remove or revise sensitive information contained in HTML code; ensure that directories on the site have proper permissions; determine whether Server Side Includes are a potential threat to your site; determine whether certain Server Side Includes should be disabled or if Server Side Includes shouldn't be allowed on your site.

## Guidelines for Java, JavaScript, and Active X

☑ Java applets are generally digitally signed or of a standalone format, but when embedded in a Web page, it is possible to skirt around this requirement. Hackers can program an applet to execute code on a machine so that information is retrieved or files are destroyed or modified. Remember that an applet is a program, and it has the capability of performing malicious activities on your system.

- ☑ A common problem that hackers will use to their advantage regards scripts and programs that trust user input. Scripting languages can also be used to run shell functions. With a properly written and executed script, the cmd.exe could be used to run other programs on a Windows NT or 2000 system. In addition to user input, you will need to write programs and scripts so that no input is trusted that is passed from a client.
- ☑ Because of the possible damage a Java applet, JavaScript, or ActiveX component can do to a network, in terms of threatening security or attacking machines, many companies filter out applets. Firewalls can be configured to filter out applets, scripts, and components so that they are removed from an HTML document. By removing such elements from ever being displayed, the Web page will appear different from the way its author intended, but any content that is passed through the firewall will be secure. On the client side, many browsers can also be configured to filter content. By changing the settings on a Web browser, you can prevent such programs from being loaded into memory on a client computer. The user accessing the Internet from your network is provided with the HTML content but isn't presented with any of these programmed features.

## Programming Secure Scripts

- ☑ Active Server Pages have problems that are similar to those seen in client-side scripting. By embedding the scripts into the Web pages, this allows curious and malicious users to view ASP code. A hacker may be able to acquire usernames, passwords, and identify vulnerabilities in the code.
- ☑ Any programs and scripts available on your site should be thoroughly tested before they are made available for use on the Web. Determine whether the script or program works properly by using it numerous times. If you are using a database, enter and retrieve multiple records. Have members of your IT staff try the script or program themselves, because they may enter data in a different order or try a task differently.

## Code Signing: Solution or More Problems?

- ☑ Digital signatures can be used to guarantee the integrity of files and that the package being installed is authentic and unmodified. This signature is attached to the file being downloaded. The signature identifies who is distributing the files and shows that they were unmodified since being created. The certificate helps to keep malicious users from impersonating someone else.
- ☑ A major problem with code signing is that you must rely on a third-party for checking authenticity. If a programmer provided fake information to a CA or stole the identity of another individual or company, then it would be possible to effectively distribute a malicious program over the Internet. Another problem is if valid information is provided to the CA, but the certificate is attached to software with bad or malicious code.
- ☑ Using software such as Microsoft Certificate Server, you can create your own digital certificates for use on a network. This allows someone to self-sign their code with their own CA, and make it appear that the code is valid and secure. You should verify the validity of the CA before accepting any files to avoid installing a hacker's code onto your system.

## Should I Outsource the Design of My Site?

- ☑ You should determine what information will need to be provided for the contractor to do her job right without compromising the security of your network, and you should also determine what security policies will be used for the Web server to keep the contractor from accessing unauthorized data (and whether these policies will impact existing policies).
- ☑ A very real complication in outsourcing is that who you hire may not be who does the work. When determining whom to hire, you should inquire as to whether they will do the job themselves or use outside contractors.

- ☑ Accept another person's design without checking to see if there are any existing security vulnerabilities or problems is foolish. You will need to go through each page of the site to view the source code and determine whether that information represents a security threat.
- ☑ Before making the site public, you should view content, run scripts, applets, components, and other programs on a test server. You should also use more than one type of browser when checking your site for problems. Last, you should ensure that any software on the machine has the latest patches and security packs applied to them.

# Frequently Asked Questions

The following Frequently Asked Questions, answered by the authors of this book, are designed to both measure your understanding of the concepts presented in this chapter and to assist you with real-life implementation of these concepts. To have your questions about this chapter answered by the author, browse to **www.syngress.com/solutions** and click on the **"Ask the Author"** form.

**Q:** I've heard that Server Side Includes are always a security risk and should never be included in a Web page. Is this true?

**A:** Server Side Includes can be used for hacking, as can many of the other features that may be offered on a Web site. Ensure that permissions to various directories are set correctly, disable certain SSI commands, and prevent users from providing input (such as through a guest book)—after performing each of these steps you can use Server Side Includes safely with minimal threat from hackers.

**Q:** I want to create a members-only area to my Web site for business customers with special needs. I plan to have a dialog box appear asking for a username and password. Is there a secure method of controlling access?

**A:** Use authentication methods that use encryption, such as SSL. If clear-text is used for authentication, then a hacker can possibly access this information during transmission of the username and password.

**Q:** I am responsible for creating an intranet site and later this year becoming the webmaster of a new e-commerce Web site. I have never installed and configured a Web server. I'm familiar with several operating systems and have no problem maintaining security on them. Which Web server should I choose?

**A:** Although you can choose among numerous Web servers, unfamiliarity with installing and configuring a Web server may create security holes. You may find Web servers that provide GUI interfaces—user-friendly functionality will be easier to use. However, if a Web server that doesn't provide these features is better suited to your security needs, then ensure that permissions are properly set on the intranet server and use this as a testing ground to learn from. Although security on an intranet site is vital, there is less chance that you'll experience malicious hacking and viruses than you will when administering the Internet site. You may also want to seriously consider outsourcing the installation and configuration of the Web servers for your intranet and e-commerce site and focus on creating content.

**Q:** My company wants to implement its own Web server, and I'm responsible for choosing the server that we'll use. What should my choices be based on?

**A:** Choosing a Web server is based on any number of issues. You should begin by strategizing what your company's needs and wants are and gauging how much they're willing to spend. You should also consider the platform that the Web server will reside on. Remember that a Web server potentially may not support the operating system you were planning to use. After you've identified your needs, compare these to what each server offers. Above everything, you should make security a priority. Different Web servers provide different security features, and not all of them may be suitable to your needs. Also, if a different operating system provides better security, then you should run your Web server on it instead. Finally, you should consider complementing your site with other tools mentioned in previous chapters, such as firewalls, virus-scanners, and so forth, because many Web servers provide limited security features when compared to these tools.

**Q:** I have heard that Java is 100 percent secure. If this is true, then why should I worry about which Java applets are used on my site or accessed by my network users who are on the Internet?

**A:** No program or programming language is 100 percent secure. Java is a highly secure method of providing programs to users of your site, but like any program, it can be used to harm or help users. Since Java implements a virtual sandbox and severely limits file system access, it is more secure than alternatives like PERL.

**Q:** What is the difference between CGI, PERL, and Active Server Pages?

**A:** CGI is an interface that acts as a middleman between the Web server and a Web application. It isn't an actual scripting language but uses scripting languages such as PERL. Active Server Pages are an alternative to CGI that was developed by Microsoft. With ASP, code is embedded into the page.

**Q:** I've outsourced my design work to another company. Is there anything I should do before my site goes live?

**A:** Double-check any work that was done. You should inspect the code and try to locate any vulnerabilities in the code, security policies, or software used on the server.

**Q:** Where can I find commonly exploited Web server vulnerabilities?

**A:** Investigate the Web site of the manufacturer of your Web server software. These sites often show where vulnerabilities may exist and how you can keep them from becoming a problem. You should also research trade magazines offering information on Web servers and technical material such as Microsoft TechNet. In addition to this, several vulnerability databases on the Internet provide significant information on known vulnerabilities. One such database is found on Security Focus's site (www.securityfocus.com).

**Q:** Are there automated tools that can check the security of my site, and should I use them?

**A:** A number of tools that can automate security and administrative tasks are available on the Web. However, you should download only tools from sites you trust. Some scripts or programs may offer detailed analysis or automation of tasks but are designed to transmit information about your system to an e-mail address or Web site. Download such tools from either established sites and/or the Web site belonging to the manufacturer of your Web site. For example, Microsoft's Web site provides a number of tools, as does several security sites mentioned in this chapter. Other sites that provide a large number of tools for download include @Stake (www.atstake.com), ZDNet (www.zdnet.com), and Packet Storm (http://packetstorm.securify.com/).

**Q:** How can I keep up with fixes and patches, and how can I know when new fixes and patches are released?

**A:** Visit the Web site of the Web server's manufacturer. You should also remember to visit the sites of the manufacturer of your server hardware, operating system, and other software on the Web server. Such sites will have an accessible download area where fixes and patches can be downloaded. Some sites, such as Microsoft's, provides the ability to be automatically notified. When you go on the Internet, your system or browser can automatically check or access a site that will check your system and decide whether certain patches should be applied. Many of these sites also offer you the chance to be notified via e-mail or added to a newsletter that will include information on the latest service packs, versions, fixes, and patches.

**Q:** If I keep up with applying the latest patches and fixes, do I really need to upgrade to newer versions of the Web server software?

**A:** You may be able to avoid immediately upgrading to the latest version, but you should upgrade to newer versions regularly. By keeping older versions of Web server software, you will miss out on benefiting from improved security, tools, and other features. Also, remember that older versions of software will be supported only for a limited time. After that, you must either upgrade or risk running a system that may be considered vulnerable to improved hacking tools and methods.

Chapter 4

# Designing and Implementing Security Policies

## Solutions in this chapter:

- Why Are Security Policies Important to an E Commerce Site?
- What Elements Should My Security Policy Address?
- Are Any Prewritten Security Policies Available on the Internet?
- How Do I Use My Security Policy to Implement Technical Solutions?
- How Do I Inform My Clients of My Security Policies?

☑ Summary

☑ Solutions Fast Track

☑ Frequently Asked Questions

# Introduction

The primary and most basic security tool of any organization is its security policy. The security policy is the backbone of the entire operation because it defines the rules by which business is conducted. These rules create the expected protocols to be followed by systems, applications, employees, and even clients.

Creation of the security policy is a large undertaking, but with careful attention to detail and some forethought into possible situations that could arise, it is a manageable and rewarding task. The security policy should be considered a "living document" in that it will be constantly revised and amended as new lessons are learned and as the organization evolves.

The security policy should also be used as a tool to assist with the creation, implementation, and configuration of technical tools such as firewalls, Intrusion Detection Systems (IDSs), and the like. These technological solutions should all reflect the security policy in their operation. They should be simply enforcing the rules set forth by the policy as acceptable and disallowing behaviors deemed by the policy as inappropriate.

# Why Are Security Policies Important to an E-Commerce Site?

Hopefully, the reason you're reading this book is to understand how to protect your e-commerce Web site so that your organization can profit from operating it. If there is no profit, then it's unrealistic to venture into the world of Internet commerce in the first place. This chapter focuses on creating the business policies that lead to profit by implementing security solutions for your site that are cost effective, increase sales, and reduce loss of revenue.

Failing to implement cost-effective security solutions affects the profitability of your site from several perspectives. Insufficient security can lead to expenses from downtime, lawsuit, or data loss; security that is too extreme can inhibit productivity, constrict customer interaction, or require too much in the way of administration costs. Profitability lies somewhere in the middle, and that somewhere is different for every e-commerce venture.

Unfortunately, e-business tends toward the extreme end of security to even be able to operate, so it's important to understand upfront how the decisions you make about security can affect the overall money-making potential of your site. As a site architect, you don't make these decisions alone; it takes many developers, system administrators, network engineers, marketers, managers, and policy makers to create a secure e-commerce Web site. Making good decisions about security, then, means communicating the requirements for it among many people, so that each individual fully understands the security goals they are expected to reach. Your organization's security policy creates the common language for this understanding by clearly stating requirements that others need to know when making technical implementation decisions. For those not involved in decision making, the security policy sets forth an expectation of behavior by employees when using company equipment and services, to ensure that security and availability is maintained as the decision makers intended it to be.

# What Is a Security Policy?

Request for Comments (RFC) number 2196 defines security policy as: "... a formal statement of the rules by which people who are given access to an organization's technology and information assets must abide." This is a succinct although stiff description. It implies that companies know exactly how they want you to use their technology and what can happen if you use it in different ways. However, that's not always the case. Instead of considering security policy to be a strict list of things you're not allowed to do, it's better to consider it as a business tool, a way of creating secure processes that work, an aid for people to work more efficiently together, and an enabler for achieving profit.

Security policies should exist to help others make good decisions, not to get in the way of productivity. The surest way to kill your efforts at creating a security policy is to make them too extreme. An effective security policy strikes a balance between *cost of risk* when you don't have security versus *cost of productivity loss* when you do. Many a security manager with lofty ideals has been rendered ineffective by not understanding the need to limit his goals, at least in the short term, to what is realistic to be achieved under the circumstances. The political machine is a slow moving one.

E-commerce security means protecting information, but information security is more than just computer security. Setting your own site's security goals will require examining several trade-offs and striking the balance between corporate-culture, business requirements, risk abatement, cost realization, and worker productivity. The balance is seldom achieved the first time, and it isn't held for long. The policy is always evolving and requiring modification based on the direction of the e-business at the moment.

## Value versus Risk

The optimal level of security for any sales organization, whether e-commerce or brick-and-mortar, is determined by the value of the assets being protected and the tolerance the organization has for loss of those assets. Cost-effective security doesn't spend more to protect an asset than it's worth to the business, although its value to a particular business may be more or less than the actual market or street value. Some traditional brick-and-mortar business managers also may not fully comprehend the value of intangible assets such as source code or customer data. Yet understanding exactly what is to be protected—from what threats and at what cost to the business—has to precede the implementation of any protective measures. Otherwise, you can't know whether a security software or hardware solution will meet your needs. A substantial part of the security policy is simply the result of analyzing and writing down what assets the company wants to protect, what threats to those assets it considers cost effective to protect against, and what the definitions are of acceptable uses of those assets.

## Security versus Services Provided

Virtually every service that is run on a computer system brings with it inherent flaws with possible compromise risks associated with them. Each additional user on a computer system using a given service increases the opportunity for mistakes that could result in a compromise. Limiting the services offered and the users allowed to access the service reduces the number of situations that can lead to compromise. However, limiting the services provided to users also affects the kinds and amounts of work the users can do, which lowers productivity. Security improvements generally have an inverse relationship with productivity, but both end up costing money if taken to the extreme. When making even small improvements to security have large affects on ease of use, there is a large hidden cost in productivity loss even if the cost of the security improvement is relatively small.

This isn't permission to neglect security in favor of productivity, although some people might view it that way. Rather, this demonstrates the need to minimize the impact security measures have on users' ability to get work done. If a user can't get his work done because security is so tight he can't access a piece of information he needs to do his job, then he will find a way around your security measures so that he can do his work. When he does, the effectiveness of your security measures is reduced to zero. If you could achieve 100 percent security for every single system for every single user against every single bug, this wouldn't be a problem. But 100 percent security isn't possible. If you want to prevent users from circumnavigating security, ensure that they have a secure way to do their work. Examining this trade off will no doubt result in several additions to your security policy.

As an example, consider the company that discontinued remote access services for its employees due to cost of the phone lines and equipment. Several managers needed their employees to work remotely. The managers requested modems to be installed for their employees, but the IT department refused, citing the new security policy. The managers bought the modems out of their own department's budget and let the users install them, which was done so insecurely that a compromise resulted, costing the company much more than running a secure remote access service would have.

## Cost of Security versus Cost of Not Having Security

It may seem obvious that the cost of having versus not having security is a trade-off, but distinguishing between the kinds of costs that may be involved is important. They are not always visibly monetary. For instance, the dollar cost of a software package that provides fast encryption may seem high until the impact of slow encryption on the Web site's performance is discovered to be costing much more in lost sales. The cost of one-time password authentication may seem high until nonrepudiation of transactions becomes a legal issue for your company. Loss of privacy is a cost to customers and your site that must be weighed against the need to sell or publish their information.

Sometimes security also just doesn't cost anything. Making small changes in business processes can make great strides in reducing the risks of e-commerce. For instance, turning on password enforcement mechanisms that already exist in software to ensure that passwords get changed every 90 days doesn't cost much beyond the time spent changing passwords, but preventing a compromised weak password could save big money on lost data.

### *Perception Is Everything*

Because the Internet is still in its infancy, many e-commerce sites still resemble street vendors more than giant commercial concerns. Some smaller sites are really just that: street vendors. But if your site is a business-to-business concern, if your end users are major corporations, or if the products you sell are critical components of other e-commerce products, then you have a lot more at risk by hanging your shingle on the Internet than the guy down the street who's selling herbal remedies from his home computer. Increasingly, legislation and world policy are stepping in to govern commerce on the Internet the way it is governed everywhere else. The corporate lawyers look at the security policy as much more than a quality assurance tool. They view it as a contract between the employer and the employee, an agreement between producer and consumer, a deterrent between network and cracker, and evidence to be cited in court.

An old cyber legend tells of a computer intruder that could not be prosecuted because the system had no logon banner stating who could use it, and the logon message said "Welcome." The defendant successfully argued that he was invited to log onto the system and therefore could not be considered an unauthorized user. The company had no security policy that required a logon banner, and so they lost the case. The company immediately added logon banners to all their systems that told unauthorized users to stay out. But if one were accidentally left out and later was compromised, the company could use its security policy (which now states the banner requirement) as evidence that the intruder was not welcome.

Publishing your security policy, or at least a summary of it, on your Web site can also be a useful tool to discourage amateur intrusion attempts and to increase customer awareness of your efforts to protect their data. Ironically, your site doesn't have to actually be 100 percent secure to ward off some intrusions, but it does have to look that way to make an amateur decide to go somewhere else for some fun. Of course, sounding threatening could have the opposite affect and act as a dare to an intruder, so statements should be firm but matter of fact.

## Where Do I Begin?

If your organization is a traditional company that is testing the waters of the Internet for the first time, you should investigate if there is already a security policy in place that may be applicable or may need adapted for the rigors of e-commerce. If there is no policy, you will need to begin from scratch and create one. Regardless, it will be crucial to solicit the input of managers, technical support staff, human resources, and legal, to ensure that the policy specifies a set of guidelines that are appropriate, workable and that the company supports as a whole. If the whole company isn't behind the policy, it won't be enforceable.

Starting with a template or advice you can find on the Internet, develop policies customized to suit your business by soliciting several rounds of input from key managers and staff. As you create the policy, try to be brief. The longer it is, the less likely users will read it. However, all the relevant topics need to be covered, so it needs to be long *enough*. The policies need to be clear, doable in your environment, and enforceable.

After a draft basic policy has been created, let the legal department review and edit as necessary until it is ready to pass around for managerial approval. After management has given it the thumbs-up, educate users about the policy by having a high-level manager endorse it publicly in a pamphlet, broadcast email, or article on your intranet Web site. The endorsement will let everyone know the importance of taking the policy seriously and operating within its guidelines. Figure 4.1 shows a sample process flow diagram for producing a security policy.

**Figure 4.1** Policy Creation Work Flow

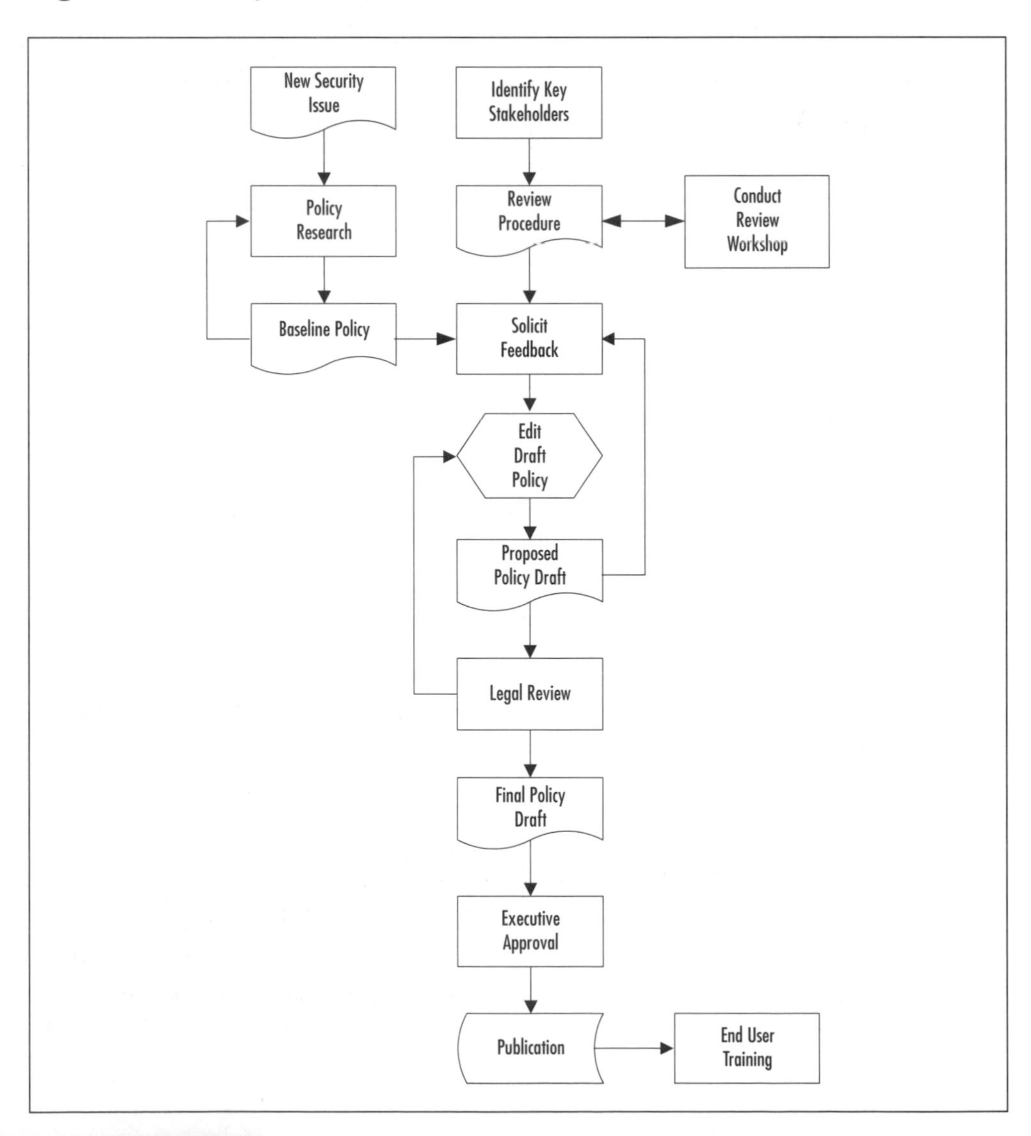

## Damage & Defense...

### Get Legal Advice

Your legal counsel may seem like your ally or your foe, depending upon the attorney. Some attorneys seem to understand the need to spell out the specifics, as in a contract. Others seem to want lots of gray area as leeway to argue in court. It is possible to word your policy so that it does its job either way, but do make sure that everything gets approved through your legal department or outside legal counsel, who knows the ramifications of the provisions in the policy.

Note that so far we have discussed the concept of the policy as *what* must be done, not *how* to do it—this is intentional. Generally, if the policy specifies *what* without specifying *how,* supporting departments are granted greater leeway to develop innovative solutions to problems and still stick to the overall security goals. For instance, your security policy may say, "The network must be monitored for intrusions on a 7x24 basis." This is *what* must be done. If the policy states that "The network must be monitored for intrusions on a 7x24 basis using the console-based product *X*," then this defines *how* and could be eliminating other innovative and potentially less costly solutions that your intrusion detection specialist may know about. Of course, if product *X* is the only software made that integrates into your environment, then it is appropriate to specify its use as "what" must be done, at least for now. But someday, it may have competition, and you'll have to revamp your policy accordingly.

Establishing a few ground rules early in the process of writing the policy is useful. It's best not to specify solutions if possible, only specify what they must accomplish. For instance, if the policy says, "State-full packet filtering firewalls must be used," then the networking group responsible for implementing firewalls is locked into a particular set of vendors. At Internet speeds, vendors topple each other every day for market share, and today's technology won't always be the best solution. It would be better to say, "Unauthorized traffic will be prevented from entering the network," and include provisions that the network engineer can use in deciding what kinds of traffic are authorized. Defining words in simple terms before they are used prevents differing interpretations later on. If you need to provide essential context for a policy, follow a simply stated policy with a more verbose commentary that explains the policy's intention to those who are implementing it. Using our firewall example, you could follow up the firewall requirement with a commentary that explains the kinds of traffic it is expected to disallow or intentions you may have for integrating with intrusion detection systems.

Ideally, the security policy should be established, approved by management, and communicated to all the people developing your site before development even begins. This way, security can be built into the site product at the beginning, as functional requirements for it are first being identified. As the product is being developed, the security policy will offer guidance during software selection, coding, and network build-out as people ask questions like "What type of encryption should we use?" and "How should this data file be stored?" After the site is fully developed, quality assurance testing will automatically include security testing, because test suites are typically created from the functional requirements. As new challenges are addressed after roll out, the policy's specification for a disaster recovery plan (see Chapter 8) will direct any recovery efforts that may become necessary. The following sections look at some of the characteristics of a good security policy.

# What Elements Should My Security Policy Address?

A comprehensive security policy is actually made up of several individual policies, each of which targets unique aspects of the site's business processes. These aspects must be considered individually across each tier of security provided for the site, such as perimeter security, network security, and host application security, because each policy applies differently at each tier.

- **Definition of security terms** This includes such terms as "confidential" data versus "normal" data.
- **Accountability statement** This defines roles and procedural ownership. This policy defines the scope of the security committee or team and sets the enforcement expectation for various departments within the organization.
- **Acceptable use policy** This sets expectations for access controls, warning banners, and responsibilities of use. It defines acceptable protocols, authentication mechanisms, traffic flows, and what constitutes an intrusion.
- **Privacy policy** This defines expectations for privacy, including what kinds of data are collected, who will have access to the information, and how violations should be disclosed.
- **Administration policy** This describes system hardening procedures and change control. This policy specifies how remote administration should happen and how outsourced IT tasks are handled.
- **Auditing policy** This describes enforcement requirements to ensure that the policy requirements are being met, including logging, monitoring, and intrusion detection.
- **Availability policy** This defines the requirements for resource availability, maintenance windows, incident response, and disaster recovery, as well as requirements for tape backups and spare parts inventories covered.
- **Purchasing policy** This states the security features required for software and hardware purchases. The level and kind of encryption software must support, procedures for acquisition of nonsanctioned software, and specifications for maintenance software are included here.

We will discuss these individual policies by examining how they work together to achieve three vertical assurances for each security tier for your site. These assurances are the ultimate goal of your policy within limits set by the trade-offs we discussed earlier. If they can't be provided cost effectively through direct implementation, they may be able to be supplemented with insurance, which is discussed in a later chapter as a mechanism for distributing the cost of providing this assurance over time. The three assurances for each security tier are:

- The confidentiality of information assets.
- The integrity of information assets.
- The availability of information assets.

## Confidentiality and Personal Privacy Policies

In the context of e-commerce, the term "assets" includes intangibles such as customer data, authentication mechanisms, software source code, and the like. Your policy needs first and foremost to define what is meant by "data that require special handling," and then provide requirements for handling different kinds of data. It's impossible to enumerate all the types of data that may be encountered, such as "credit card numbers" or "phone numbers"; attempting to be this specific inevitably omits something important. Instead, define categories of data with general characteristics so that developers and administrators can classify data themselves, while being specific enough to distinguish between the different categories.

For example, a typical e-commerce Web site may collect private information, such as social security numbers, along with information that may not need to be held in confidence, such as a log entry indicating the time a particular Web page was requested. Generally speaking, if private data becomes public, someone is harmed, particularly if the data clearly identifies the person with whom it is associated. Therefore, one possible definition of data might distinguish between "normal" data, which cannot in any way be associated with its creator or be identified as characterizing a particular owner or as harming the owner if made public, versus "confidential" data, which can. Apply the "reasonable man" test to decide if the average person would consider the data confidential or not.

Confidential data in this context would clearly include customer medical information, diagnoses, prescription numbers, purchasing history, and financial forms, and this may be stated in commentary following the simple policy statement. Confidential information is something held on behalf of another or which provides access to something held on behalf of another. Confidentiality brings with it an ethical obligation to protect the data from theft or destruction. It's important that employees view confidential business data as an asset belonging to the business that has been entrusted to their care. Normal data does not have this requirement; the average person would not be terminated from their employment for making normal data public to a nonemployee.

Now that we have a definition of the data we need to protect, let's investigate some of the policies we need to protect it.

## Requirements for Authentication

Traditionally, authenticating a user to an application was a matter of creating an account and password. Applications would run on a mainframe connected to terminals. The password was entered across a secure network and didn't need to be protected from outside interception or cracking. Today, the needs for authenticating users are much different. Client-server applications such as those that are being deployed on the Web have brought with them the need to protect the session between client and server end to end. Web sites may even have several applications that require a customer to authenticate before using. Sending a clear text password for any one of them across the Internet risks interception and intrusion.

In many Web-enabled applications today, the client side is a Web browser and the server side includes an off the shelf software that provides for customizations to suit the e-commerce site. The software may have various mechanisms for managing user authentication that should be investigated for adequacy in your particular environment as your site is being developed. Developers will need to review security policy as they make decisions about which software security features are required for your site. Obviously, it's impossible for the security policy to address all possible features of all possible software packages. But the policy can provide guidelines that must be met to provide adequate authentication for both client and server.

For example, Web developers use Secure Sockets Layer (SSL) encryption as the standard means of protecting user logon screens by encrypting the session between a client browser and a Web server. If you need more information about SSL, a good source is a certificate provider such as VeriSign (www.verisign.com). The important thing to know about SSL for this discussion is that "server" certificates are installed on the server, they authenticate the server to the client, and they establish a secure session between them. If your site is going to accept credit cards from customers, the customer probably wants to know for certain that he's not sending his credit card number to a site that is impersonating yours, so your site needs to provide that assurance by use of a server certificate issued by a trusted certification authority (CA), such as VeriSign. Any Web pages you provide that involve the customer entering their private information should be secured using SSL. Your security policy should stipulate a method for determining which pages should require SSL for server authentication and periodically auditing to ensure they still do. Typically, if the page allows a customer to enter or review her confidential information, it should use SSL.

### Client Authentication

If your site requires a user to log on so that you can maintain information about him, such as a pharmacy site, medical services site, or financial site where users can obtain financial information from you, the standard logon method has traditionally been to create a Web page where the customer enters his username and password over the SSL session generated by the server using the site certificate. Many security policies specify that log on screens must be protected with a site SSL certificate, but this alone is not sufficient for some sites and some kinds of data. A site certificate doesn't tell the server anything about the client, which could be impersonating your real customer.

Server-side SSL ensures only that the session has not been intercepted, not that the identity of the client is known. One way to authenticate your customer is to use access control mechanisms that are built into the Web server software. However, these rely on reusable passwords and are plagued with the problems that reusable passwords bring. How does your site know whether a password is being used by your customer or by an imposter? If your site requires only a single reusable password and doesn't enforce strong password policies for the user, then the password is vulnerable to guessing, viewing over someone's shoulder, or other recovery methods that don't involve session interception. SSL server authentication alone does not prevent someone from establishing a secure channel in which to brute-force attack the logon page. It does not prevent the use of the Back button at a Web café or Internet kiosk to view the session of the customer who used the system just previously.

To be certain that your site is not handing out confidential information to impersonators, you should strongly authenticate customers as well as assuring your site's identity to them. Currently, this involves the use of a client digital certificate as a digital ID to identify the customer. Most e-commerce Web sites are not yet requiring the use of client digital IDs, because they require action on the part of customers that is difficult to explain to them, ("You mean my password typed into that window is bad, but typed into this one it's good?"). Yet the future of fully featured e-commerce will depend on being able to establish a two-way trust between the customer and the application, so building this capability into your site now will facilitate that transition.

Your security policy should stipulate that the correct SSL implementation be used for the type of business your site engages in. This is particularly true if your e-commerce site is a business-to-business site or extranet where your site's data requires protection from your customers' data. Your site will need to provide access controls that differ for business partners based on their identity. Because of this, Gartner (www.gartner.com) recommends that application service providers use two-factor authentication.

Two factor authentication involves examining something the client knows, such as a password, along with something they possess, such as a client certificate or one-time password token device. Deciding whether to require single- or dual-factor authentication in your security policy depends on the type of services your e-commerce business provides. VeriSign has an informative white paper describing specifics on implementing client authentication at its Web site (www.verisign.com/repository/clientauth/ent_ig.htm#clientauth) if you are interested in learning more about implementing personal certificates.

## *Password Requirements*

For those applications where use of a standard reusable password can't be avoided, the security policy should state the requirements for ensuring that those passwords are robust and securely managed. For instance, your password policy should state a minimum length of password that is allowable, and whether it should contain numeric or special characters in addition to alphabetical characters. A good practice is to require a minimum of eight-character passwords with at least one numeric or punctuation character and at least one upper case character. CERN, the European Organization for Nuclear Research, has a Web page describing how to choose a good password at wwwinfo.cern.ch/pdp/ose/security/cern/documentation/password.html. MIT also has one at http://web.mit.edu/answers/accounts/accounts_choose_password.html.

If nonalphabetic characters are allowed in passwords, they should be restricted to just a few characters such as 0–9, "_", and "-" to prevent the potential for misinterpretation by some applications. UNIX systems, for example, assign meaning to "!", "|", and ";" characters that start a process and should be disallowed any time your site interprets text input into a table, URL, or Web page field by an end user. Assume that the user is going to type in something like "mypass|/bin/cat /etc/passwd" as her password. If your Web page passes the password to a UNIX application that mishandles it, the password file could be displayed back to the browser. Perhaps it won't work with your application, but perhaps there's a bug and it will. It's easy enough to prevent with proper input validation. Your security policy needs to specify the mechanics of input validation in terms of what characters are allowed, rather than enumerating the disallowed characters. This way, nothing is accidentally omitted.

Password aging is another topic the policy should visit. Customers need to change their passwords through an easy to use mechanism and need to be reminded when it's time to do this. Forcing passwords to be disabled if not changed after a period of time is good security, although it tends to ire end users. Mediating this problem can be addressed with adequate warnings far enough in advance that users are not caught by surprise.

Managing passwords on external systems residing in a DMZ pose a different kind of problem than managing passwords on an intranet or on internal systems. It's important to use different passwords internally than externally for administrators and developers who do their work in both locations. This way, if an administrator's password on an external system becomes compromised, access to internal systems such as a database is not provided by default. In fact, use of different account names externally that can't be matched up with internal accounts is an extra measure that can help protect internal data.

This concept applies to account passwords, default system passwords, application passwords, and so on, which should be changed from their default setting at installation time. Simple Network Management Protocol (SNMP) passwords are commonly overlooked in this regard and often remain set at "public" for read-only access and "private" for write access. Those familiar with SNMP who find it running may try these default passwords first in an intrusion attempt, because SNMP is very useful for providing information about a system in preparation for a targeted attack later on. Many system administrators don't use SNMP, though, and may not realize the impact of leaving it set to the default password. Requiring by policy that default passwords be changed for all systems at install time will help ensure that this is not overlooked, whether the system is a router, a computer, an application, or a card-key access badge.

Some password management methods are inherently too insecure for use on an external DMZ and should be disallowed by policy. Allowing an internal NIS or NT domain to span externally is not a good idea. Keeping password management as standalone as possible while still maintaining scalable maintainability is the goal to strive for. One way to do this on UNIX systems is to use password files that are copied to the Web server over an encrypted session but managed internally on an administrative server. Because the session is encrypted, the files are not in danger of interception in transit. Because they are managed internally, password maintenance tools such as /bin/passwd can be deleted entirely from the external systems, which can help foil attempts to install backdoors if the external system later becomes compromised. A good policy would be to require an encrypted password update procedure for external systems, and let administrators provide input on how it can best be implemented.

## Requirements for Protecting Customer Information

The first consideration for protecting information stored at your site is to be well informed of government regulations that affect your business. If your site is in any way involved in medical or health-related services, you probably are required to comply with the Health Insurance Portability and Accountability Act (HIPAA). HIPAA imposes penalties on doctors, hospitals, and insurance companies that do not adequately protect medical information for services rendered on the Web. You can find out more about the privacy requirements for HIPAA at http://aspe.os.dhhs.gov/admnsimp.

Other regulations in your state may affect whether your site can collect customer email addresses without opt-in permission from them. By most definitions of spam, if you collect and retain your customer's email address without first asking them to click a button that give you permission to do so, you will be spamming the customer with Unsolicited Commercial Email (UCE) later when you send them product literature. Some states in the U.S. also limit the amount and format of commercial marketing email your business can send out before it becomes defined as "spam." Nevada prohibits unsolicited commercial email unless it is readily identifiable as such by inserting the letters "ADV" into the subject line, for instance. Your policy needs to address the legal requirements for controlling emails sent to customers doing business with your site.

After confidential customer data has been passed to your site, the site has an obligation to protect it. Unfortunately, some Web sites use SSL to encrypt data between the client Web browser and server, but then do not provide adequate protection for the data as it traverses the site's external network segments. Most theft of data from Web sites occurs because the data is not properly encrypted or stored after the Web server has received it. After a Web server decrypts an SSL session, data is often stored in the clear in an internal database or sent to an application server for further processing. If the Web application is not properly written, a malicious user can exploit a weakness in it, causing the Web server to expose the data to the client browser.

Attacks of this kind might involve exploiting a poorly written cgi script or an asp application, or by simply crafting a URL carefully. Your policy should provide guidelines for examining the kinds of data stored on behalf of your site's customers and by examining state requirements for encrypting confidential data at various stages of processing within the site. For instance, it might state that SSL is required between client and server, application encryption between Web server and application server, and database encryption after the data is written to a database. It should provide for security zones enforced by a firewall, and that databases must always reside behind the firewall for added protection.

**Tools & Traps...**

### A Word about Session Management

A sometimes overlooked exposure of customer information results from the way client sessions are managed. Most e-commerce Web sites want to provide a customer with the ability to begin a session, leave, and then come back later to finish the session. Keeping track of where the customer is in this process is tricky, and many different methods have evolved to address the issue. One way is to use a cookie or session identifier in the URL to tell the server what page the client is accessing at the moment, so that finishing the session is independent of time. The cookie typically contains information about what Web pages are accessible with it, so anyone who can obtain a cookie may be able to view another person's information.

Continued

When session identifiers are used in URLs, it may be possible to guess another user's identifier and view pages that are valid for that session. Alternatively, the back button on shared systems can expose customer data by displaying it to subsequent browser users. A better way to manage session state is to track it for each user in a database, but this relies on the ability to properly identify the end users. Authentication policies work hand-in-hand with session management to provide the best protection for customer information.

### *Sharing Customer Information with Partners*

The most common cause of theft of data occurs by a trusted person with internal access to the data. If your e-commerce site is an extranet or other business-to-business venture, employees of your business partners may be just as big a threat to your data as your own company's employees are. Protecting every partner's data from each other can be a daunting (or impossible) task unless data is properly segmented, such that access controls can be implemented separately for each segment and user. An example of data segmentation is database tables within a single application that is shared among several partners. Unless access to the tables is correctly controlled, a savvy user might be able to access a table full of data that "belongs" to another business partner by utilizing some feature of the shared application. Designing data storage controls with this in mind from the beginning can help prevent the possibility that partners access or overwrite each other's data later on. Your policy should stipulate that partners in a shared application must not be able to access each other's data.

A practical example of this idea would be if your e-commerce site provided inventory processing for several businesses with e-commerce sites of their own. Your site might be virtually connected to theirs via the Internet for handling orders as they are placed. Without proper data controls, one business might be able to access another's customer information through their mutual connections with your site's application. Security policy needs to consider the potential for accessing of data between partners, and it needs to stipulate the controls necessary to deal with any potential found to exist. In this particular case, your policy might require that data from separate partners must be stored in separate databases or at least in separate tables with access controls applied independently.

Another consideration when sharing data between partners is the transport mechanism. Today, many corporations integrate information collected by a third party into their internal applications or those they provide to their customers on the Internet. One well-known credit card company partners with application vendors and client corporations to provide data feeds for employee expense reporting. A transport method they support is batch data files sent over the Internet using Secure (encrypted) File Transfer Protocol (SFTP). SFTP is equivalent to running regular, unencrypted FTP over Secure Shell (SSH). Alternatively, regular FTP might be used over a point-to-point VPN. Security policy needs to state that confidential data must use some kind of secure transport when leaving the confines of the internal network destined for a partner location.

## Privacy Policies

Privacy policy is perhaps the best illustration of how a company's position may be different based on whether a customer or internal staff is involved. Most companies reserve the right to examine employee computer systems and email for evidence of wrongdoing, for example. To protect this right, security policy must state that employees are offered no guarantee of privacy of data stored on company-owned computers. The company needs to reserve the right to monitor and inspect the computing resources and data stored on them at any time.

This isn't just pandering to paranoia on the part of the company. Regulations are coming into existence that require companies to be prepared to report on their employees' and customers' activities on the Internet. The controversial International Cybercrime Treaty, for all countries that adopt it, would require individuals and companies to disclose encryption keys and provide access for data collection at the request of law enforcement officials. For more information on how the International Cybercrime Treaty may affect your e-business, check the Web site http://conventions.coe.int/treaty/en/projets/cybercrime.htm.

This lack of a privacy guarantee is in direct contrast with what a customer of an e-commerce Web site expects for protecting private information. The privacy policy that customers want to see describes the measures taken by your site to ensure that their information is not sold or freely distributed. Posting your site's privacy policy informs customers of their rights when doing business with your company but brings with it legal obligations to the customers. If your privacy policy states that customer information will never be sold and later it is, lawsuits will inevitably ensue. Be realistic about privacy policies but balance the needs of the customer and the organization if you want to keep customers around long enough to be profitable.

## Information Integrity Policies

Assuring information integrity means assuring that information maintained on your site has not been altered. There are many aspects to assuring data integrity at various tiers of your organization's security model, which we can view from the perspective of nonrepudiation. Nonrepudiation provides proof that data is received exactly as it was sent, that the sender is known and cannot deny having sent it, and that the recipient is known and cannot deny having received it.

Using SSL to send data from the server to the client browser assures that the data sent by the server is the same as the data received by the client and provides nonrepudiation of the transport mechanism. From an operating system perspective, tracking checksums of critical configuration files and system binaries ensures that they have not been replaced with a Trojan horse during an intrusion and demonstrates proper handling of the data while in control of the operating system. Client authentication using strong cryptographic methods provides nonrepudiation of the originator of a transaction. The customer cannot dispute having entered into a transaction when presenting a strongly authenticated digital signature to the site and engaging in the transaction using a secure transport. However, depending upon the authentication used, identities can still be stolen and 100 percent nonrepudiation is still only a possibility today; not a certainty. Biometrics holds promise, but no system is 100 percent free from potential compromise.

Protecting information while it is stored on your site means protecting the servers themselves by defining specifically what a secure server, or bastion host, should look like. A bastion host is a computer system with special modifications that fortify its ability to withstand a targeted attack. When operating systems are first installed, they require modification to install special security features and to remove unnecessary capabilities that facilitate compromise. A system-hardening document specifies the steps to take to produce a bastion host from an initially installed operating system. For any given operating system, administrators will have wildly differing ideas about exactly what steps to take to produce one. The expectations need to be set by the security policy.

Describing all the details of how to do system hardening is beyond the scope of this chapter, but many sources on the Internet can be used as a guideline for writing down the requirements for your site's server security policy.

- **Microsoft (Windows NT)** www.microsoft.com/ntserver/security
- **Microsoft (IIS)** www.microsoft.com/technet/security/iischk.asp
- **IBM (Securing AIX 3)** www.alphaworks.ibm.com
- **Securityportal (Securing Sun Solaris)** www.securityportal.com

# Quality Assurance Policies

Although some security policies are procedural, such as requiring a firewall to protect internal systems from the Internet, the purpose of other policies is to provide for enforcement of the overall security model. Enforcement policies provide assurance of the quality your security implementation has achieved, and they also provide mechanisms for detecting areas where security is lacking. We can view quality assurance policies as specifying how to keep a site secure after it has been built that way.

The requirement for a firewall on your network is actually a means for enforcing the business security policy. The policy specifies allowed protocols, transports, and traffic flows, and the firewall enforces the policy.

Likewise, the security policy states requirements for authentication and behavior for users to be allowed remote access into the network, but the policy is enforced via the controls placed on the remote access server.

One of the most easily neglected quality enforcement policies involves managing updates, maintenance, and configuration changes for your site after it is up and running. Your security policy should require a change control system to ensure that maintenance and upgrades to production systems are tested, verified, and controlled prior to deployment. This is easier said than done and may require lots of cooperation between business divisions, which is why it is sometimes neglected.

Changes to production systems need to be approved, or at least acknowledged, by affected parties ahead of time, and the correctness of the change needs to be verified by some kind of audit mechanism after it is made. Without configuration and change controls, administrators may make mistakes that can result in a compromise that leads to lost data or downtime. Configuration management reduces this possibility and makes an effective enforcement mechanism for your service availability policy. Your policy might specify, for example, that operating system patches be tested in an environment that mimics your production site prior to deployment. It might also specify that for every one administrator that does the work, another comes along behind to verify that the work is complete and correct. Keeping copies of files altered or moved during the work is also necessary in case the change has to be backed out.

## Auditing and Intrusion Detection

Another quality assurance policy specifies audit controls for your site. What processes or objects within your site should be logged when they are accessed? What files should be noted if they change? Where are the logs going to be stored? If log files are not handled securely, an intruder can edit them and remove any evidence of the intrusion. Dynamically monitoring CPU utilization, network utilization, disk status, and so on, can often flag intermittently failing hardware before it fails completely, increasing overall uptime.

Windows NT provides the ability to audit access to any and all files you specify along with logon attempts, application errors, and other system events. UNIX systems can audit processes and log system and application events to any log file you specify on this or another server. It's a good idea to store copies of audit and log files on an internal system, where they are inaccessible (hopefully!) to an intruder. If this isn't possible, store audit logs on write-once CD media and arrange to have the media changed out frequently.

Log generation, storage, and analysis is just one part of an overall intrusion detection policy. IDSs should span all tiers of security at your site. On the host side, an IDS collects logs and issues alerts when critical system or access events occur. On the network side, IDS network sensors monitor network traffic for common patterns that match known intrusion signatures. In the middle, log analysis provides trending data about uptime and critical events. Your IDS may also need to provide for scanning of Web or email traffic to detect and quarantine malicious content. Virus scanning plays a role in IDS as well.

The goal of an IDS is to detect intrusions more quickly than log analysis alone can provide. If an intruder can be detected while he is still gathering information necessary to implement a targeted attack, you may be able to take steps to prevent the damaging part of the attack before it occurs. Configuring an IDS to issue alerts when critical events happen and then responding appropriately to those alerts is part of the overall incident response policy. An IDS can even be tied to your site's firewall to close sessions that involve traffic matching an intrusion signature.

If your site maintains a Network Operations Center (NOC), the policy should specify that alerts from IDSs be sent to the NOC for immediate examination. An IDS doesn't do any good if no one examines the alerts it produces. IDSs aren't foolproof, however, and are fraught with false positives that must be tracked down and integrated with the configuration. Security procedures should provide for handling false positives in such a way that the "cry wolf" syndrome is avoided. After awhile, the tendency is to ignore the flurry of alerts produced by IDS, so keeping the false positive rate to minimum helps recognize the real events that are happening.

## Assuring Information Integrity through Technology

All the topics we've discussed so far in this chapter can be brought together with software that helps manage the whole environment according to the company's security policy. Policy managers are special software that allow administrators to state the security policy at a high level. The policy manager turns the company's high level policy into low level configurations for various enforcement mechanisms such as VPN hardware, routers, and firewalls.

For instance, configuring the policy manager to allow only TCP/IP on the network would result in intrusion signatures on the IDS system that don't bother looking for intrusions involving IPX, optimizing the IDS for your environment more quickly than sifting through all the rules yourself. If the policy manager ties into your firewall, the firewall rule sets would be generated to follow the policies configured in the policy manager. Usually, a policy manager is proprietary and works only with the equipment or software from the same vendor, so you may wish to consider policy manager features as part of purchasing the solutions for enforcing the policy.

Policy manager software can help maintain host-based intrusion detection software too. One example is software to produce checksums of critical application files. A checksum is a digital signature that is unique for each file, and it is produced by a cryptographically strong mechanism such as the MD5 message digest program. Tripwire (www.tripwire.com) is commercially available software that provides this service. If a file is altered in any way, Tripwire produces an alert with relevant information about the change. If your site has 50 servers, all of which need similar configurations for managing checksum logs, the Tripwire policy manager can make the task much simpler by specifying one policy that applies to all of them.

## Availability of Service Policies

Requirements for service availability are typically based on some kind of service level agreement between the provider and consumer of the service. In the case of e-commerce, the customer expectation of uptime versus the uptime the company can afford to provide determine the service level agreement for the customer. Tolerable downtime limits are specified in the security policy to set the expectation for support services necessary to implement the overall policy within those limits.

The service availability policy addresses the hours/days that internal staff can expect various services to be available for doing their work. It includes guidelines for when and how users may expect certain services to be made available. Some companies, for instance, don't allow internal employees to surf the Web except on their lunch hour, and they expect all workstations to be turned off when they leave for the day. The service availability policy would stipulate that the Web is available only during the lunch hour, in that case. The requirement that workstations be turned off might be covered by the acceptable use policy or the service availability policy, either one. Provisions for enforcing service availability requirements are included in the administration and audit policies.

If your e-commerce site should eventually become the target of an intrusion, success or failure in prosecuting the culprit may depend on how well trained your staff are in forensics methods to investigate and preserve evidence for later examination in court. Security policy should address the creation of an incident response team, procedures for notifying managers and administrators, policy for handling the media, and recovery procedures after the fact. Establishing an effective disaster recovery policy before you need one will improve the quality of your site's service by reducing downtime and lost revenue recovering from the event.

The disaster recovery plan typically also covers tape backup procedures to ensure data recovery can happen properly, as well as needs for hardware and software redundancy to ensure uptime requirements are met. Offsite storage requirements, acceptable backup media, and contact numbers for restoring data in an emergency should be included. Disaster recovery is covered in much greater detail in Chapter 8.

# Are Prewritten Security Policies Available on the Net?

Of course, you can find many prewritten security policies on the Net—the bad news is, they aren't prewritten for *you*. However, lots of other resources on the Internet can help create a security policy that's appropriate for your business.

If you need a security policy but don't have time to write one yourself, you have a lot of options. On the more expensive side, you can hire a security company to do the legwork for you. Starting with an outline of items that should be covered, the consultants can arrange the manager meetings, inventory processes, data gathering, and policy building that's the most time-consuming part of the process. Most will be happy to sell you some vulnerability testing for your site right along with it and maybe even some insurance.

On the less expensive side, some security companies provide consulting services to help you better understand the implications certain policies might have in your particular business environment. An example of this is if you aren't quite sure if your site's design has inherent vulnerabilities that should be addressed early on. Auditing a design before it is built can save the money that would be lost if it were later found to require a significant change, and sometimes the quickest way to find that out is by an external design audit.

## All Organizations Are Different—and So Are Their Policies

The companies that are most successful at implementing security policies are those that avoid the "do it and forget it" mentality and somehow convince all the employees that security belongs to each of them, that it is an ongoing function of doing business, and that success of the company depends on it. Beyond that, the content of the security policies will vary as greatly as businesses themselves do.

A successful policy implementation will be a partnership between the technical staff who understand the issues "in the pits" and the high-level managers with authority to require that certain processes be followed. That last part is important. Without backing at a high level within the company, the policy won't be successful. Grassroots efforts don't work when it comes to creating a security policy, no matter how well the "underlings" understand the issues and how right they are. Management has to like it, want it, and endorse it. It may seem counter-intuitive, but it's better to implement a poor policy all the way than to have a really good one that no one uses because management doesn't agree with it 100 percent. At least you'll be able to understand where your weaknesses are and plan for them.

# Example Policies and Frameworks

If you are determined to do the work in-house, start with an outline of items that must be covered somewhere in the policy and begin fleshing it out after obtaining the necessary input from others. Here are a few Web locations that provide excellent guidelines and outlines to get you going.

The System Administrators Guild (www.usenix.org/sage) is a special technical group of Usenix (www.usenix.org), the Advanced Computing Systems Association devoted to "presentation and discussion of the most advanced information on the developments of all aspects of computing systems." SAGE has an excellent security policy template describing the essential, recommended, and optional elements of a security policy at www.usenix.org/sage/publications/policies/fr_template.html. This template is a recommended starting point for developing your own policies.

The SANS Web site (www.sans.org) has a link to a set of Model Security Policies that are prewritten and ready for you to substitute your company name into them. The policies include:

- Computer Usage Guidelines
- Acceptable Use Statement
- Special Access Policy and Agreement
- Network Connection Policy
- Escalation Procedures for Security Incidents
- Incident Handling Procedure
- Partner Connection Policy

**NOTE**

The Web site www.faqs.org/rfcs/rfc2196.html is an RFC known as the Site Security Handbook. It is the bible for anyone embarking on creating a security policy for the first time.

### A Word about the Outsourcing of Policy Development

If a security consultant tries to sell you a canned security policy without spending considerable time investigating your business culture, management goals, and unique business aspects, run away fast, because you'd be wasting your money. The people who run your company know it better than anyone else. What management at one company would approve, management at another company may not. What works in one business culture may not work in another. But that doesn't mean you have to do all the work yourself.

Creating a security policy is a lot of work. Wouldn't it be a shame to let all that work go to waste? What happens if other department managers don't agree with the policies? Success of your policies depends on support departments endorsing them. To improve acceptance, allow consultants or other outsourced services to use a template as a guideline, but require them to spend enough time getting input from various support departments about the policies being developed. You're only going to have one shot at making a policy that works, so make it count.

## How Do I Use My Security Policy to Implement Technical Solutions?

How do you know when your security policy is finished? After you have finished developing the policy, it should represent the complete vision of the business in terms of security goals (and their costs) moving forward. Every tier of security implementation within your network needs to be brought into compliance with the policy, or the policy needs to be adjusted where that turns out not to be possible. The task of enforcing the policy begins by implementing technical solutions to perform that enforcement at every tier of security within the company.

What do I mean by "tier of security?" Let me explain by referring to Figure 4.2, which shows how an external attack on one of your e-commerce systems might proceed. From an external viewpoint, an intruder performs a large amount of reconnaissance work at first, sending a lot of traffic to your site in preparation for a targeted attack. The perimeter security solution enforces security policy by allowing through only permitted traffic, whether through a firewall, access list, or routing tables.

**Figure 4.2** Technical Solutions Emerge Naturally from Security Policies

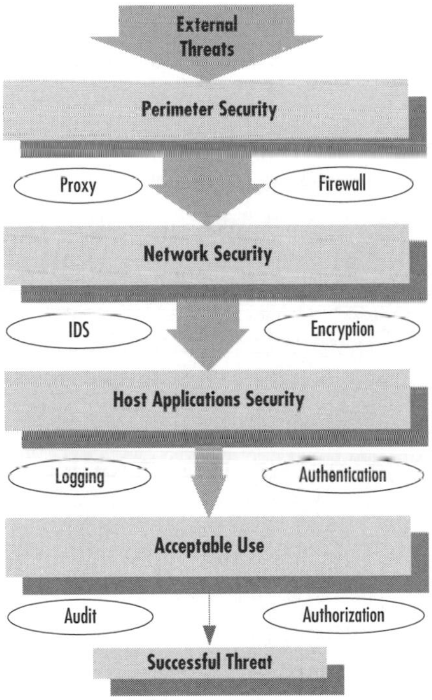

The traffic that makes it through perimeter security is then subject to network monitoring, network-based intrusion detection, and other segmentation or internal access controls, which further reduce the probability

of a successful penetration. If the intruder is able to reach a host's operating system, he may still be thwarted by host-based intrusion detection, host-based access controls, and application level security.

By a successive failure at every step, or tier, of the implementation, an intruder may violate the company's acceptable use policy and thereby succeed in the targeted attack. But that assumes that every tier is implemented perfectly and contains no unknown security vulnerabilities, which is not possible. Thus security at any tier depends on the success of security at every tier, in succession.

Perimeter security primarily concerns itself with lower protocol layers where policy can be enforced by limiting traffic flows at those layers. Host and applications security represents the upper protocol layers, where session controls and application security can be used for enforcement. Network security mechanisms fill in any gaps between the two and perform logging and auditing enforcement functions.

Let's look at a specific policy, one that defines the kind of traffic allowed on the internal network. This security policy specifies *that* certain kinds of traffic will be restricted, it specifies *what* traffic the enforcement mechanism should restrict, *where* (in general terms) it needs to restrict it, and *who* is expected to implement the enforcement mechanism. In the case of data networking, the *how* for enforcing this policy might be a firewall, VPN, or remote access solution. For internal network security, *how* might be router access lists, domain-based access controls, and network traffic monitors. For host and application security, *how* might be NT domain security, TCP wrappers to log port connections, and host-based intrusion detection. The social aspect is even covered by educating users and training recovery staff for handling incidents. Every tier implements the same policy, just in a different way.

We talked about policy managers earlier, and now is a good time to revisit the idea in terms of our diagram. A policy manager can integrate with the technical solutions deployed at every tier, depending on the vendor and the solution. By changing or creating one policy, administrators can produce configuration changes across multiple tiers or multiple systems within a single tier. Pushing multiple changes at once reduces the possibility that something is missed if manual changes were to occur one at a time.

Damage & Defense...

### When You Can't Afford Enforcement Technologies

There's a difference between have no policy and having one that is not enforced with technology. It's very possible your e-business won't be able to afford everything it takes to enforce the ideal security policy. Some things aren't negotiable, of course, such as using a firewall or doing tape backups. But some things may be beyond the financial ability of the company just now, such as client authentication. If your company's management examines the risk and decides it's worth taking, insurance may be a more cost effective option than enforcing particularly expensive policy provisions. The goal of security policy is to use it as a tool for assuring security at your site. Assurance can be met by implementing security directly or by insuring against the risk of not enforcing it. Many security companies today are beginning to offer insurance against intrusions for this reason.

## How Do I Inform My Clients of My Security Policies?

As a customer of a bank, you expect the bank to keep your money safe. As a customer of a hotel, you expect your possessions to still be in your room when you return at the end of the day. As a customer of an e-commerce transaction, you expect your credit card and personal information to be kept as private as you consider it. So does every other e-commerce customer. Many people still won't do business on the Internet now, in 2001, until they can be assured that their data is safe.

Businesses have traditionally looked at security as a necessary evil, something that stands in the way of the desired goal. Brick and mortar shops don't usually invest in security infrastructure because their customers demand it, the purchase is to protect their own assets. When they do, they certainly don't use it as a selling feature: "Buy your sofa here, we'll keep you from getting mugged on the way out!" Talking about security implies a lack of it, which turns people away because they're probably not thinking of physical safety as they shop. But homebuilders can sell homes by touting built-in alarm features in gated communities because they *are* selling peace of mind—so when online theft is front-page news, why wouldn't a Web site sell more products by calming buyers' fears over loss of credit card data?

# Building Customer Confidence through Disclosure

Electronic selling is still selling, just the same. Customers still respond favorably to a kind face, an honest explanation of the product, a fair price, and a convenient location in which to buy the product. E-commerce lends itself wonderfully to everything except the first thing customers expect to see when they walk in the door. Somehow, your site has to put a face on itself, one that's worthy of remembering. Disclosure of security policy is a way to build customer confidence by putting a kinder, gentler face on at least a portion of your site.

A good example of security disclosure in this regard is Amazon.com (www.amazon.com). They have devoted several Web pages to addressing customer fears over making a purchase. They state in very certain terms in their "Safe Shopping Guarantee" that the customer experience is safe. Their privacy statement describes exactly what information the site will gather about the customer, what will be done with the information, and what the customer stands to risk from third parties. Amazon.com takes a definite risk by posting information about the security of e-commerce transactions. If it turns out not to be true, they'll get hit with lawsuits. They must be pretty confident about their security implementation to make a guarantee like that, and customers know it.

Usually, too much of a good thing isn't good, so Amazon has a small link at the bottom of their main page that takes you to a bigger information store about privacy, acceptable use, and information safety. You have to be concerned enough to look for it, but it's there to reassure you when you find it. Disclosing security information shouldn't be "in your face" to be effective. Overdoing it might actually have the opposite effect and entice an intruder to find out what all the boasting about security at your site is really about. On the other hand, subtlety has the effect of a whisper in the ear, "We know you're concerned, but you don't have to be, and here's why." In an industry where you can't see the face of your customer, you have to anticipate what must be going through her mind and provide the answer to the questions before they are even asked.

## Security as a Selling Point

Smart shoppers are becoming security-savvy about e-commerce in the same way they became savvy about carbon copies of credit card slips in the 1970s. Convincing them to do business with your site means you don't just take a stab at securing your Web site, but you must do it extremely well—and then tell everyone about how well you do it. Raise the bar for the competition and sell more products than *they* do because you can do it more securely. Advertise your success at securing customer transactions on your own site, and use it as a tool to create an image of your company as empathetic with what the customer needs and wants.

When faced with two equal methods of doing business, customers will choose the one they are most comfortable with, not because of what is done or how it works, but because of who stands behind it. People generally like the convenience of doing business on the Internet, but they are still very unsure about it, and rightfully so. It's hard to put a face on e-business, and most sites don't have it quite right.

Time and again, customers choose to do business with companies that are successful in projecting an image of being the helping hand that guides them, the one that's in their corner, the one that can meet their need and be trusted. In the end, the successful e-commerce ventures will be the ones that sell this same image to their customers as hard and fast as the physical products those customers are buying. That's how today's successful brick-and-mortar companies became that way.

# Summary

Security policies are important to an e-commerce site because it takes so many different people working together and making decisions independently to produce the site. People who make decisions about purchasing hardware may never even get to talk to a site developer, if the project is large and distributed across several locations. Security policies ensure that people are always working toward the same goals and are implementing technical solutions that will achieve the expected results for the site.

A security policy needs to address a fairly well-defined list of topics, although the specifics need to be tailored to your own business by considering its culture, business requirements, inventory of probable risks, and so on. At a minimum, your policy should clearly define the term "confidential data," identify acceptable uses of your site's hardware and software, describe minimum privacy standards, and provide for effective enforcement. Ideally, your policies should work together to provide an assurance to your customers and your business that information confidentiality, integrity, and availability are maintained.

Building and enforcing a security policy is an effective tool for ensuring that your site is profitable. Your security policy can help reduce expenses from downtime, of course, but it can also be a means for increasing sales. Customers who are edgy about doing business on the Internet need some assurance that they aren't going to regret trying something new. Disclosing information about what they can expect regarding protection of their information can build customer confidence in having chosen a good company to do business with. In the end, your site's success will depend on building a helpful, friendly image that customers will remember—using security as a marketing tool can help move your site one more step in that direction.

# Solutions Fast Track

## Why Are Security Policies Important to an E-Commerce Site?

☑ Failing to implement cost-effective security solutions affects the profitability of your site from several perspectives. Insufficient security can lead to expenses from downtime, lawsuit, or data loss; security that is too extreme can inhibit productivity, constrict customer interaction, or require too much in the way of administration costs. Profitability lies somewhere in the middle, and that somewhere is different for every e-commerce venture.

☑ Security policies should exist to help others make good decisions, not to get in the way of productivity. Cost effective security doesn't spend more to protect an asset than it's worth to the business, although its value to a particular business may be more or less than the actual market or street value. Security improvements generally have an inverse relationship with productivity, but both end up costing money if taken to the extreme.

☑ As you develop the policy, try to be brief. The longer the policy, the less likely that users will read it. The policies need to be clear, doable in your environment, and enforceable. Generally, if the policy specifies the "what" without specifying the "how," supporting departments are granted greater leeway to develop innovative solutions to problems and still stick to the overall security goals. Defining words in simple terms before they are used prevents differing interpretations later on.

## What Elements Should My Security Policy Address?

☑ A comprehensive security policy is actually made up of several individual policies, each of which targets unique lateral aspects of the site's business processes. The individual policies work together to provide three basic assurances for the site: confidentiality, integrity, and availability of data.

- ☑ To be certain that your site is not handing out confidential information to impersonators, you should authenticate customers as well as assuring your site's identity to them. A site SSL certificate doesn't tell the server anything about the client's identity, which could be impersonating your real customer. The security policy defines client authentication requirements for your site.
- ☑ Most external theft of data from Web sites occurs because the data is not properly encrypted or stored after the Web server has received it. Security policy should be clear about requirements for encryption at every stage of processing, from client browser to Web server, to application server, to database. The policy needs to require session management that prevents others from viewing pages that are part of another users session.
- ☑ Protecting information while it is stored on your site means protecting the servers themselves by defining specifically what a secure server, or bastion host, should look like. A bastion host is a computer system with special modifications that fortify its ability to withstand a targeted attack. The security policy specifies the steps to take to produce a bastion host from an initially installed operating system.
- ☑ Quality assurance policies specify enforcement mechanisms that include change control, auditing, reporting, and intrusion detection. Availability of service policies specify uptime requirements, acceptable use guidelines, and disaster recovery procedures.

## Are Any Prewritten Security Policies Available on the Net?

- ☑ The companies that are most successful at implementing security policies are those that avoid the "do it and forget it" mentality and somehow convince all the employees that security belongs to each of them, that it is an ongoing function of doing business, and that success of the company depends on it. Beyond that, the content of the security policies will vary as greatly as businesses themselves do.

☑ If you are determined to do the work in-house, start with an outline of items that must be covered somewhere in the policy and begin fleshing it out after obtaining the necessary input from others. The Internet is a good resource for locating templates to begin the process. If you don't have time to write one yourself, you can hire a security company to do the legwork for you. If a security consultant tries to sell you a canned policy without spending considerable time investigating your business culture, management goals, and unique business aspects, run away fast, because you'd be wasting your money.

## How Do I Use My Security Policy to Implement Technical Solutions?

☑ The task of enforcing the policy begins by implementing tech nical solutions to perform that enforcement at every tier of security within the company. Perimeter security primarily concerns itself with lower protocol layers where policy can be enforced by limiting traffic flows at those layers. Host and applications security represents the upper protocol layers, where session controls and application security can be used for enforcement. Network security mechanisms fill in any gaps between the two and perform logging and auditing enforcement functions.

☑ If a policy requires a certain network transport, enforcement mechanisms include a firewall at the perimeter, access lists on network routers internally, and session-based controls on the host or application.

## How Do I Inform My Clients of My Security Policies?

- ☑ Electronic selling is still selling, just the same. E-commerce lends itself wonderfully to everything about selling except the first thing customers expect to see when they walk in the door. Disclosure of security policy is a way to build customer confidence by putting a kinder, gentler face on at least a portion of your site.
- ☑ Disclose the components of your site's security policy that will assure customers of the safety of their transactions, but don't do it with great fanfare. A small link that takes customers to a page detailing what they want to know meets the need without over doing it.
- ☑ Customers choose to do business with companies that are successful in projecting an image of being the helping hand that guides them, the one that's in their corner, the one that can meet their need and be trusted. In the end, the successful e-commerce ventures will be the ones that sell this same image to their customers as hard and fast as the physical products or services those customers are buying.

# Frequently Asked Questions

The following Frequently Asked Questions, answered by the authors of this book, are designed to both measure your understanding of the concepts presented in this chapter and to assist you with real-life implementation of these concepts. To have your questions about this chapter answered by the author, browse to **www.syngress.com/solutions** and click on the **"Ask the Author"** form.

**Q:** My customers need to download files about their account activity that are too large to transfer efficiently over http. I'd like to use FTP to save money, because there's an FTP server on our DMZ already. Would this pose a problem from a security standpoint?

**A:** If the data is confidential, then yes it would. FTP transfers cross the Internet in cleartext. When users access your FTP server, their passwords are also sent across the Internet in the clear and are easily intercepted. Another issue is that FTP servers have been plagued with vulnerabilities over time and so are a frequent target for intruders. A better solution would be to transfer files across an SSH session using SCP or SFTP. At least the data would be encrypted, and the session could use a stronger public/private key authentication mechanism than is provided with regular FTP.

**Q:** Our system administrators want to install a tape backup system that will use a dedicated network to back up servers in our DMZ. The external servers will be multi-homed, with one interface on this dedicated backup network. We thought we'd save money by using the same server to back up internal hosts, too. Is this a good idea?

**A:** No. The backup network would introduce a way to circumvent the firewall if one of the external servers were compromised.

**Q:** What is a reverse proxy, and why would I need one?

**A:** A reverse proxy makes connections to internal systems on behalf of external clients. It's the opposite of a normal proxy, which makes connections to external Internet systems on behalf of internal clients. The idea behind a reverse proxy is that a client browser connects to your reverse proxy, and the reverse proxy makes a call to an application or database server on the inside, receives the data, encrypts it, and then forwards it back to the client browser. Because the browser never directly connects to the application server or the database server, it's more difficult to compromise the internal system. Reverse proxies are particularly useful if you want to use an application that needs the server and database to reside on the same system, but the data is too sensitive to allow the server to reside in a DMZ. Because the server is on the inside of the firewall, you would have had to open up a hole in the firewall to allow Internet users to access it, unless the reverse proxy were used.

**Q:** I know that my business needs a formal security policy, but I can't seem to sell my non-technical boss on the idea. Any advice?

**A:** Start small, and put the concept into financial terms. Nontechnical managers don't always understand how security can save them money unless you spell it out. Sometimes, you have to work hard just to get one or two policies put into place and let the rest go for now. But the important part is to make progress for the company. Try to put a dollar cost on the worst security risk affecting your site and describe exactly how implementing the policy you want would alleviate the expense. Focus on just repairing that one risk first and try to build credibility with your success. If nothing you do will work, document your concerns and don't lose sleep over it. Some people just have to learn things the hard way.

# Chapter 5

# Implementing a Secure E-Commerce Web Site

## Solutions in this chapter:

- Implementing Security Zones
- Understanding Firewalls
- How Do I Know Where to Place My Components?
- Implementing Intrusion Detection
- Managing and Monitoring the Systems
- Should I Do It Myself or Outsource My Site?

☑ Summary

☑ Solutions Fast Track

☑ Frequently Asked Questions

# Introduction

By now you have learned how to design an e-commerce Web presence and what policies you will need to protect it. You also should have an understanding of what managing an e-commerce site will entail and what are the basic roles of your security staff.

This chapter explains how to create the actual infrastructure to build, manage, and maintain your site. Depending on your business idea and the logistics involved, your actual implementation may vary slightly from the designs included here, but the basic concepts remain the same. Whether your site is a basic implementation or a more advanced system with all the bells and whistles, maintaining the security of your clients and your business should be a basic principle.

We explore the process of grouping your systems together in common areas as defined by their requirements for security. These groupings or *security zones* will be regulated by the control systems (such as firewalls and routers) that you deploy in your site. They will also be monitored against attack by intrusion detection systems (IDSs) and other tools deployed within your environment.

Constant management and monitoring of any site is essential. There are no plug-and-forget solutions or magic silver bullets. In e-commerce, staying alert and keeping knowledgeable about events happening around you will help to ensure your success.

Lastly, this chapter covers some options and considerations for outsourcing your site to a partner at this stage of the project. We will examine how to select the right partner and the right type of outsourcing solution to meet your requirements as well as explore the various types of solutions available to you.

# Introduction to E-Commerce Site Components

An e-commerce site is usually made up of several integral components, including the normal network components such as routers, hubs, and switches. But you may not be as well-acquainted with some other components: firewalls, IDSs, Web servers, load balancers, database servers, and financial processing servers.

- **Firewall** A firewall is a device used to provide access controls for a network or segment. Think of this system as a network traffic cop, allowing or disallowing traffic into a network based on who the requestor is and the type of connection they are asking for.
- **Intrusion Detection Systems** An IDS can be network-based or hot-based, or both. These tools are very flexible; they can monitor an manage data and make content filtering decisions.
- **Web servers** This is the most common server in an e-commerce site. This system's job is to serve up the Web pages or content that the consumers using your site request.
- **Load balancers** These specialized devices are used to regulate the traffic flow to the Web servers, ensuring that the work load is balanced between the multiple systems that perform the work of your site.
- **Database servers** These systems are used to store the information your site depends on for business, including catalogs, product descriptions, consumer data, and all the other bits of information that you need to do business. If these servers have consumer information on them, they must be protected even more carefully than systems just serving your site's data to the Web.
- **Financial processing servers** These servers are used to store and process customer and vendor financial information. They are often the end-line goal of most attackers, so they must be given the most care of any of the systems on your network. Losing the information in these servers could spell the doom of your business, so treat these systems with the utmost of respect.

Your site may have additional components, or redundant sets of these types of devices, but these are the basic commonalities across the board. In this chapter, we use these components to detail the basic understanding of e-commerce site layouts and security measures.

As your site grows in functionality and profit margin, you may find yourself adding more and more bells and whistles to the site implementation. You may create redundant sets of these systems or devise new methods of performing your business functions with better speed and accuracy. All of these changes can impact the security of your site, so revisit Chapter 1 often, and stay in tune with the security auditing processes described in Chapter 7 to ensure that you don't accidentally introduce weaknesses into your design. Remember to keep your security zones clear of one another and not to mix and match functionality and access requirements as your site grows. Use this chapter as a guideline to make sure that your new designs still meet your initial security requirements.

# Implementing Security Zones

The easiest way to think of security zones is to imagine them as discrete network segments holding systems that share common requirements, such as the types of information they handle, who uses them, and what levels of security they require to protect their data. They may be the same type of operating system or different operating systems altogether. They may be PCs, or servers, or even a mainframe.

In the early days of business Internet connectivity, the first security zones were developed to separate systems available to the public Internet from private systems in use by an organization. They were separated by a device that acted as a firewall. A firewall is a computer or hardware device that filters traffic based upon rules established by the firewall administrator. It acts as a sort of traffic cop, allowing some systems on the Internet to talk to some of the systems on the inside of the organization, but only if the conversations meet the pre-defined rules. This protects the computers on the inside from being accessible to the general population of the Internet, but still allows the users inside the organization to access the Internet for resources. See Figure 5.1 for a visual representation of the firewall concept.

Modern firewalls are feature-rich and complex devices, but as a minimum most provide the ability to:

- Block traffic based upon certain rules. The rules can block unwanted, unsolicited, spurious, or malicious traffic.

- Mask the presence of networks or hosts to the outside world. The firewall can also ensure that unnecessary information about the makeup of the internal network is not available to the outside world.
- Log and maintain audit trails of incoming and outgoing traffic.
- Provide additional authentication methods.

**Figure 5.1** A Basic Firewall Installation

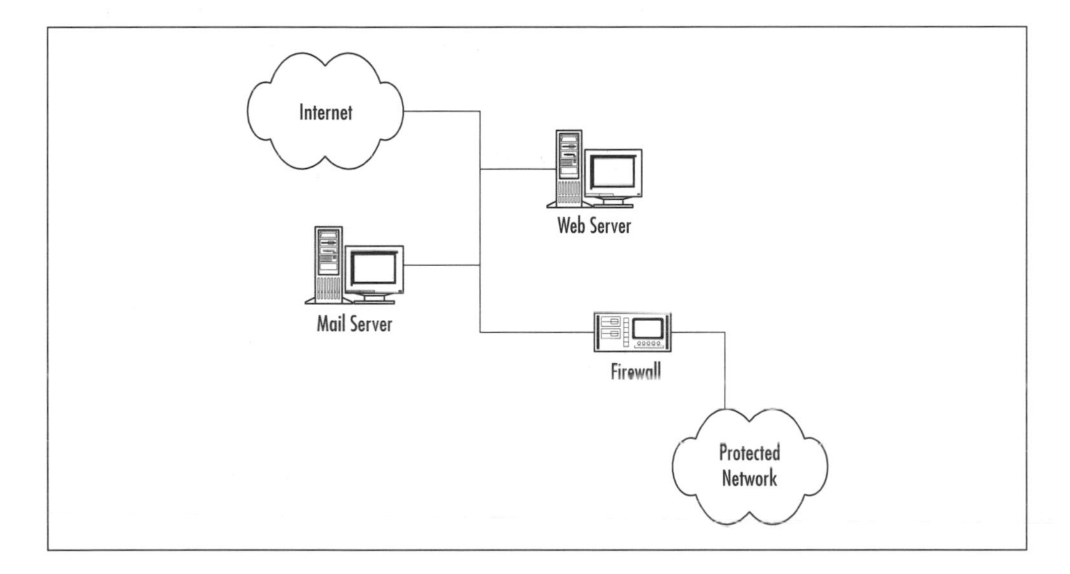


Some newer firewalls include more advanced features such as integrated virtual private networking (VPN) applications that allow remote users to access your local systems through a more secure, encrypted tunnel. Some firewalls are now "adaptive" in that they have integrated IDSs into their product and can make firewall rule changes based upon the detection of suspicious events happening at the network gateway. (More on IDS products and their use is covered later in this chapter.) These new technologies have much promise and make great choices for creating a "defense in depth" strategy, but remember that the more work the firewall is doing to support these other functions, the more chance these additional tools may impact the throughput of the firewall device. In addition, these new features, when implemented on any single device (especially a firewall), create a wide opportunity for a successful attacker if that device is ever compromised. If you choose one of these new hybrid information security devices, make sure to stay extra vigilant about applying patches and remember to include in your risk mitigation planning how to deal with a situation in which this device falls under the control of an attacker.

Although this installation protects the internal systems of the organization, it does nothing to protect the systems that were made available to the public Internet. A different type of implementation is needed to add basic protection for those systems that are offered for public use. Thus enters the concept of the Demilitarized Zone (DMZ).

## Introducing the Demilitarized Zone

A DMZ is a military term used to signify an area between two countries where no troops or war-making activities are allowed. In computer security, the DMZ is a network segment where systems accessible to the public Internet are housed and which offers some basic levels of protection against attacks.

The creation of these DMZ segments is usually done in one of two ways. In many cases, the systems are placed between two firewall devices that have different rule sets, which allows systems on the Internet to connect to the offered services on the DMZ systems but not to the computers on the internal segments of the organization (often called the *protected network*). Figure 5.2 shows a common installation using this layered approach.

The other way DMZ segments are implemented is to actually add a third interface to the firewall and place the DMZ systems on that network segment. See Figure 5.3 for a picture of this installation method. This allows the same firewall to manage the traffic between the Internet, the DMZ, and the protected network. Using one firewall instead of two lowers the costs of the hardware and centralizes the rule sets for the network, making it easier to manage and troubleshoot problems. Currently, this multiple interface design is the primary method for creating a DMZ segment.

**Figure 5.2** A Layered DMZ Implementation

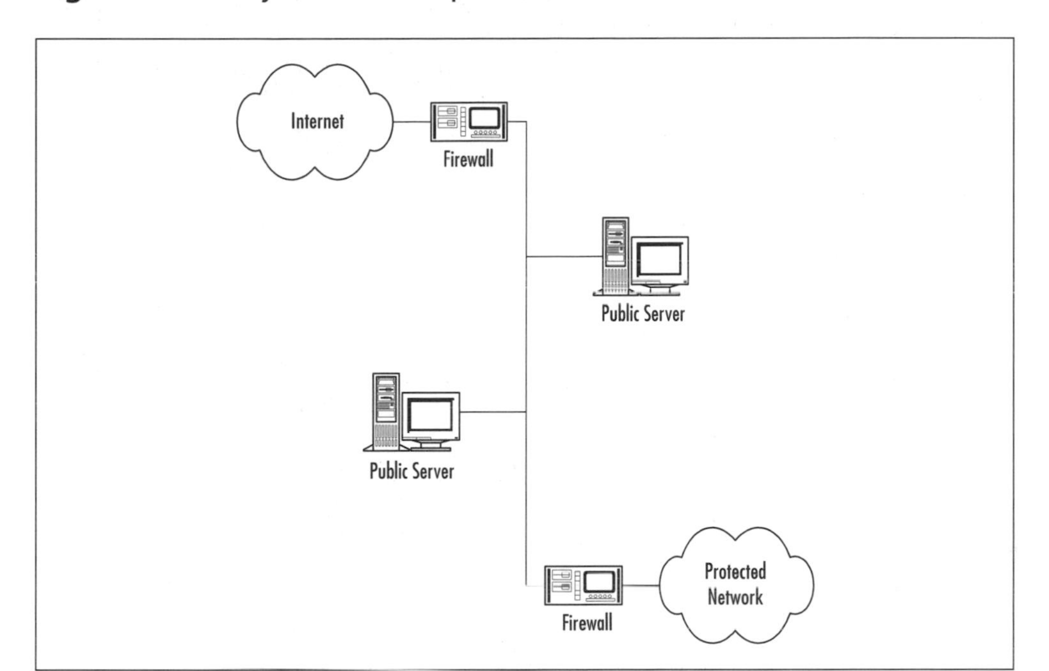


In either case, the DMZ systems are offered some level of protection from the public Internet while they remain accessible for the specific services they provide. In addition, the internal network is protected by firewall and from the systems in the DMZ. Because the DMZ systems still offer public access, they are more prone to compromise and thus they are untrusted by the systems in the protected network. This scenario allows for public services while still maintaining a degree of protection against attack.

The role of the firewall in all of these scenarios is to simply manage the traffic between the network segments. The basic idea is that other systems on the Internet are allowed to access only the services of the DMZ systems that have been made public. If an Internet system attempts to connect to a service not made public, then the firewall will drop the traffic and log the information about the attempt. Systems on the protected network are allowed to access the Internet as they require, and they may also have access to the DMZ systems for managing the computers, gathering data, or updating content. In this way, systems are exposed only to attacks against the services that they offer and not to underlying processes that may be running on them.

**Figure 5.3** A Multiple Interface Firewall DMZ Implementation

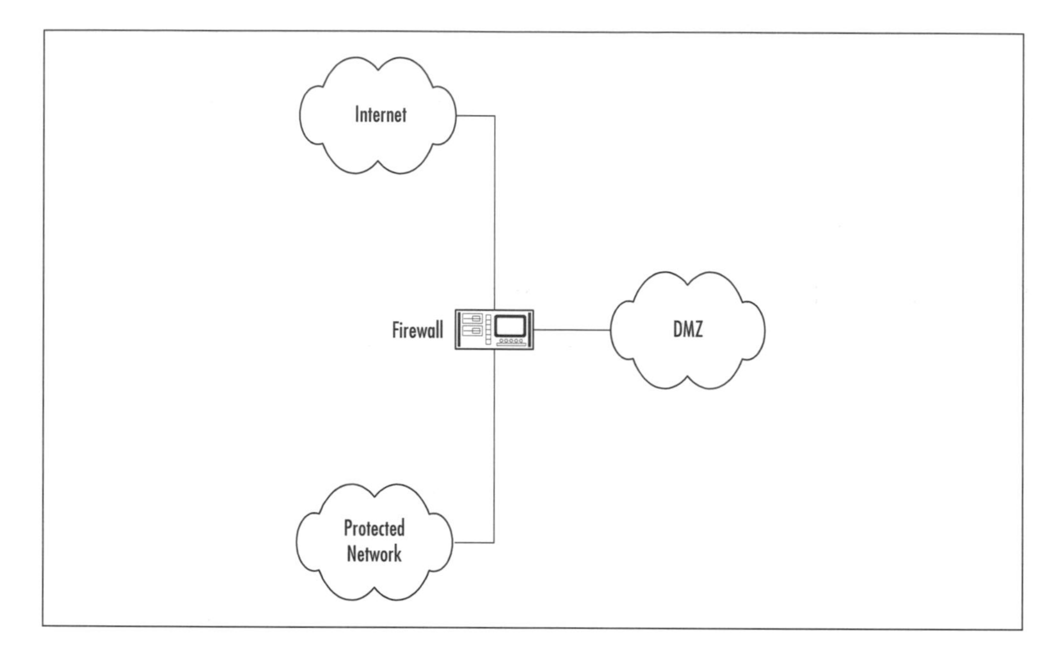


In any event, the systems in the DMZ could offer e-mail, ftp, gopher, and eventually World Wide Web access to the Internet as well as a host of other services. Demand for business applications has swelled, and these basic implementations have gotten more complex. With the advent of e-commerce, more attention must be paid to securing the transaction information that flows between consumers and the sites they use, as well as between e-commerce businesses themselves. Customer names, addresses, order information, and especially financial data needs greater care and handling to prevent unauthorized access. We accomplish this greater care through the creation of specialized segments similar to the DMZ called *security zones.*

## Multiple Needs Equals Multiple Zones

Requirements for storing customer information and financial data are different from the normal information that businesses are accustomed to handling. Because this data requires processing, however, and much of that processing is done over the Internet, more complicated network structures need to be created. Many sites choose to implement a multiple segment structure to better manage and secure their business information.

New segments with specific purposes and security requirements can be easily added to the model. In general, two additional segments have become accepted. The addition of a segment dedicated to information storage is the first, and a segment specifically for the processing of business information is the second. This changes the network structure to look like the drawing in Figure 5.4.

**Figure 5.4** A Modern E-Commerce Implementation

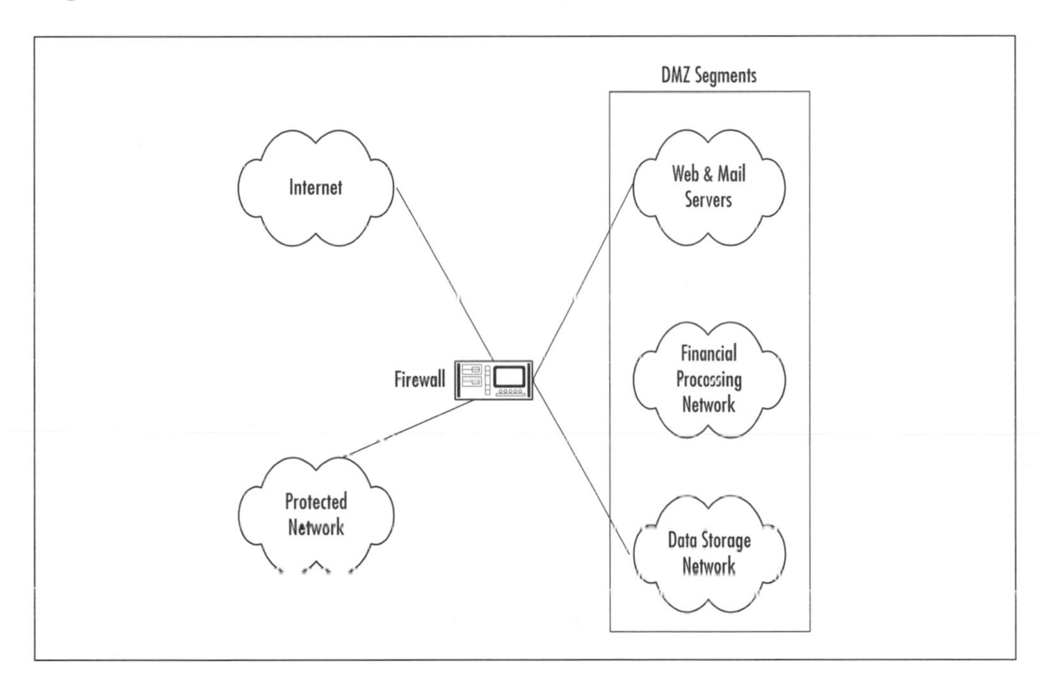


The diagram shown in Figure 5.4 includes the two new zones: the data storage network and the financial processing network. The data storage zone is used to hold information that the e-commerce application requires, such as inventory databases, pricing information, ordering details, and other non-financial data. The Web server devices in the DMZ segment are the interface to the customers, and they access these systems to gather the information and to process the users' requests.

When an order is placed, the business information in these databases is updated to reflect the real-time sales and orders of the public. These business-sensitive database systems are protected from the Internet by the firewall, and they're even restricted from general access by most of the systems in the protected network. This helps to protect the database information from unauthorized access by an insider or from accidental modification by an inexperienced user.

The financial information from an order is transferred to the financial processing segment. Here the systems perform the tasks of validating the customer's information, and the systems process the payment requests to the credit card company, a bank, or a transaction clearinghouse. After the information has been processed, it is stored in the database for batch transfer into the protected network, or it is transferred in real time, depending on the setup. The financial segment is also protected from the Internet by the firewall, as well as from all other segments in the setup. This system of processing the data away from the user interface creates another layer that an attacker must penetrate to gather financial information about your customers. In addition, the firewall also protects the financial systems from access by all but specifically authorized users inside the company.

Access controls also regulate the way in which network conversations are initiated. For example, if the financial network systems can process their credit information in a store-and-forward mode, they can batch those details for retrieval by a system from the protected network. To manage this situation, the firewall permits only systems from the protected network to initiate connections with the financial segment. This prevents an attacker from being able to directly access the protected network in the event of a compromise. On the other hand, if the financial system must use real-time transmissions or data from the computers on the protected network, then the financial systems have to be able to initiate those conversations. In this event, if a compromise occurs, the attacker can use the financial systems to attack the protected network through those same channels. It is always preferable that DMZ systems do not initiate connections into more secure areas, but that systems with higher security requirements initiate those network conversations. Keep this in mind as you design your network segments and the processes that drive your site.

In large installations, you may find that these segments vary in placement, number, and/or implementation, but this serves to generally illustrate the ideas behind the process. Your actual implementation may vary from this design. For example, you may wish to place all the financial processing systems on your protected network. This is acceptable so long as the requisite security tools are in place to adequately secure the information. I have also seen implementation of the business information off an extension of the DMZ as well as discrete DMZ segments for development and testing. Your technical requirements will impact your actual deployment, so deviate from the diagrams shown earlier as you require.

# Problems with Multi-Zone Networks

Some common problems do exist with these multiple-zone networks. By their very nature, they are complex to implement, protect, and manage. The firewall rule sets are often large, dynamic, and confusing, and the implementation can be arduous and resource intensive.

Creating and managing the security controls such as firewall rules, IDS signatures, and user access regulations is a large task. Keep these processes as simple as possible without compromising security or usability. Start with deny-all strategies and permit only the services and network transactions that are required to make the site function. Carefully manage the site's performance and make small changes to the access controls to more easily manage the rule sets. Using these guidelines, you should quickly be able to get the site up and running without creating obvious security holes in the systems.

As your site grows and offers new features, new zones may have to be created. Repeat the process above for creating the rule sets governing these new segments and you should not encounter too much trouble. As always, be sure to audit and inspect any changes and keep backups of the old rule sets handy in case you have to revert back to them in a hurry.

# Understanding Firewalls

Hundreds of firewall products are available on the market today. There are commercial products that are loaded on top of commercial operating systems such as Windows NT or Solaris. There are even open source products that are included with Linux and Free BSD. Even more easily managed are the newer breed of appliance firewalls that have become popular in the last few years.

No matter which firewall you consider, almost all firewalls on the market fall into two distinct categories: packet filters or proxy-based firewalls. These two technologies are the basic platforms that power these devices. There are many schools of thought as to the type of firewall that is the most secure, so I suggest learning a bit about each type and deciding which best fits your need. As a platform for your decision, reflect on the following considerations:

- Packet filters can act only on a combination of source addresses, destination addresses, and port numbers. The rules defined for these devices can be based only on the contents of the IP header.
- If an attacker breaches a packet filter firewall, then the entire network is often open to abuse.
- Logging on packet filtering firewalls can be confusing.
- Proxy firewalls tend to be slower than packet filters and often can not keep up with today's faster network bandwidth demands.
- Proxy firewalls can be very confusing to set up and to maintain their rule sets, which can sometimes lead to misconfigurations and security holes.
- Prices may vary widely from vendor to vendor and platform to platform, and may not reflect the overall security of a solution or the feature set that the product possesses.

## Exploring Your Firewall Options

Packet filtering firewalls make decisions about whether or not to pass network traffic based upon the source and destination information in the headers of the packets being transmitted. If the source address of the packet is allowed by the rule set to talk to the host at the destination of the address in the packet, and the ports used for the conversation are allowed, then the firewall will pass that packet and allow the conversation. If the source address, the destination address, or the ports used for the conversation are denied by the rule set of the firewall, then the firewall will drop that packet and log the information about the attempt. Some packet filtering firewalls also track the state information about a network conversation, and parse the packets against that information as well, to prevent illicit packets from being accepted which do not fit the conversation. These devices are called *stateful packet filters* or *active state filters,* meaning that they maintain a record of the state in which conversations are being conducted.

Proxy-based firewalls also make decisions based upon the source and destination addresses of packets, as well as the ports used for the conversation. Just like a packet filter, if any of these are denied by the rule set, the firewall will drop the packets and log the attempt. The additional work done by a proxy firewall is that it inspects the data load portion of a packet and attempts to decide if the data fits the proxies requirements for such a conversation. The requirements may include the type of application in use, the commands contained in the packet, or even some rules about what the data load may contain. Although this brings an extra level of testing to the conversation, it is not without its tradeoffs. The largest tradeoff is that proxies can't handle the high network throughput that packet filters can due to the additional processing.

Hybrids between the two technologies have also emerged and may be a good fit for your organization if you desire the proxy level of control and the speed of a packet filter. These firewall devices integrate both the proxy and packet-filtering technologies to create solutions that monitor data load and achieve high throughput speeds. These hybrid devices allow you to implement proxy validation on services where the security requirements are of a higher priority than the throughput speed. In addition, they are flexible enough to allow packet filtering rules as the protection method where high speeds are required. A few of these hybrid products have even created service specific proxies (such as for SQL*Net) that only allow certain commands to be issued through the firewall protection. Some of these products have become very popular, and vendors of existing packet filtering systems have begun to integrate proxy tools into their devices to fit into this new category. To choose a hybrid firewall for your organization, look for a system that integrates the services you need into their proxy mechanisms. Read more about these technologies and firewall products on the Web. You will probably find a product that exactly fits your site's needs.

Tools & Traps...

### Some of the Most Common Firewalls and Their Sites

Here is a list of some of the most common firewall products and their respective sites. Use such sites as these to compare the features of available firewall products to decide which best fits your needs. Remember to compare based upon your security requirements, throughput speeds your site requires, and, of course, cost of purchase and maintenance. You may find that some of the less commonly-known firewalls better fit your needs and your budget.

- **CheckPoint FW-1** (www.checkpoint.com/products/firewall-1) The market leader in firewalls as of this publication.
- **Cisco Pix Firewall** (www.cisco.com/warp/public/cc/pd/fw/sqfw500) Cisco's Firewall solutions.
- **Gauntlet Firewall** (www.pgp.com/products/gauntlet) A popular proxy-based solution.
- **Symantec Raptor Firewall** (enterprisesecurity.symantec.com/products/products.cfm?ProductID=47&PID=3505192) Another popular proxy-based solution.

Continued

- **Secure Computing's Sidewinder Firewall** (www.securecomputing.com/index.cfm?skey=232) A highly touted firewall solution based on the trusted OS and proxy concepts.
- **WatchGuard Appliance Firewalls** (www.watchguard.com) A Linux-based firewall appliance.

Several magazines—such as Network Computing, PC Week, and Information Security Magazine—also perform periodic firewall reviews and comparisons. Just remember not to base your decision on these reviews only; "management by magazine" can create bad decisions very quickly. Test the firewalls yourself, or get an independent lab or consultant to give input as well.

After you have selected the proper firewall product for your site, you can proceed to planning for the implementation of the firewall system into your site's network. If you have chosen a firewall that requires additional systems for consoles and/or log management, you need to carefully consider where those devices will be placed and how communications between the firewall and these components will be secured. Work with your firewall vendor to ensure that placement of these systems in the desired locations will not impact the performance or the security of the firewall and your network. After you have planned for the firewall systems and the security zones your site is going to utilize, then you must move forward to planning a rule set for the firewall.

## Designing Your Firewall Rule Set

The actual process and syntax for your firewall rule set will vary from product to product. Some firewalls must receive their rule-set configurations via a fancy graphical user interface (GUI), whereas others may be configured using a simple flat-text file typed or imported from a command line. Other firewalls products may also have default rule sets which must be used as a starting point and tweaked from there for your site-specific needs. Whatever the case, the basic process of designing your rule set is the same.

## It Starts with a "Deny All" Attitude

The process of designing the rule set for any firewall should always start with a "deny all" attitude, which means that you begin by making the firewall deny any connections that you do not specifically allow. Thus, starting with nothing, you can add in the connections required between each of the security zones to allow the systems on those segments to perform their work and to be administered, but nothing else. This helps to prevent the possibility of allowing unneeded services and additional gateways for an attacker to compromise your servers.

So, this being said, how do you go about adding the services needed for each of your components? The answer is analysis, of course! Each system and each segment must be completely analyzed for the services and connections it requires to perform its functions. Although this process is often difficult, it is the best way to create the security your customers expect if your company is going to stay in the e-commerce business.

## Common Ports for Common Communications

To determine what ports and protocols each of your servers and network segments require, you should return to the planning documents and diagrams you made in Chapter 1. If you can't locate them, begin the process anew by examining each system and detailing the functions it performs. Then, use these functions to determine what ports and protocols each of the functions requires to operate. Use the port and protocol information to create a pseudo-code rule set for planning and implementation documents. Below is an example pseudo-code rule set for a very basic e-commerce setup. Keep in mind that your firewall may have other options that can be used to handle packets that match rules other than allow or deny. Some of these options might be redirection, reject, forward, or encapsulate. Refer to your documentation for specific information on these rule settings.

Remember as you design these pseudo-code rules that the order matters. Most firewalls read from the top down and the first matching rule is how the packet is handled. Read your firewall manual or contact your vendor for specific information about how your firewall processes its rule set.

```
#Pseudo-Code Ruleset for E-Commerce Network Firewall
#Format is as below:
#Allow or Deny, Src Address, Src Port, Dest Address, Dest Port
#Pound signs (#) indicate comments
#DMZ Network is 10.1.0.0/24
#Database Network is 10.2.0.0/24
#Financial Processing Network is 10.3.0.0/24
#Internal Company Network (Protected Network) is 10.4.0.0/24
#Allow Internal Network Traffic To All Except Dbase and
    Financial Nets
deny 10.4.0.0/24 all 10.2.0.0/24 all
deny 10.4.0.0/24 all 10.3.0.0/24 all
allow 10.4.0.0/24 all all all
#Allow the world to talk to the web servers on ports 80 (http)
    and 443 (https)
#You should also lock this down to specific hosts if possible.
allow any any 10.1.0.0/24 80
allow any any 10.1.0.0/24 443
#Allow the master web server to talk to the Dbase server via
    a defined port
allow 10.1.0.100/32 10092 10.2.0.10/32 10092
#Allow the dbase server to talk to the Financial Server through
    an SSH Tunnel
allow 10.2.0.10/32 any 10.3.0.15/32 22
#Allow SMTP and Pop3 into the DMZ for Mail
allow any any 10.1.0.15/32 25
allow any any 10.1.0.15/32 110
```

```
#Deny all else "Clean Up Rule"
deny any any any any
```

Obviously, this is a *very* basic rule set but it serves as an example of the pseudo-code method. The most common question about this part of the process is how to discover which ports a specific process uses for communication. You can do this in several ways. One of the easiest is to ask the vendor or technical support for the product in question. You may also find an answer using the Internet Assigned Numbers Authority (IANA) list of registered ports. This list defines the ports that vendors have registered with the IANA group and though the list is not complete, it often holds the answers to most common ports and products. The list can be found at www.iana.org/numbers.htm, and older versions are available by using any search engine to search for Request for Comments (RFC) 1700. Other ways to locate a port for a specific product, or the product that corresponds to a specific port, is by using a search engine to search for the specific port number or product name. Most UNIX systems also contain a list of the commonly utilized ports in the location /etc/services.

## Converting Pseudo-Code to Firewall Rules

The next step in the process is to convert your pseudo-code into the real firewall rule set your firewall product requires. As mentioned earlier, this may be through a GUI or by typing line by line into a command prompt or visual editor. Some firewall products can even import this pseudo-code rule set and convert it to the syntax the product requires. See your manual for specific methods and requirements.

After the rule set is complete, the testing process can begin. Bring the systems online in a test environment and monitor to see if you missed any processes or communications ports that are used. Make changes to the rule set as required—just be sure that you know why each and every port and protocol is required for operation. After you have the systems stable, you might want to begin an assessment process to test the firewall rules and the impact your settings have made upon the overall security of your site. Follow the processes laid out in Chapters 1 and 7 to perform these tests.

Don't sweat it if you missed something or made a mistake. That is why you are testing before moving into production. Take your time, assess, make changes, and re-assess the rules and configurations until you are comfortable with the process and your site. Use policies, IDSs, and other tools to mitigate the risks that your business requirements force you to accept.

## Protocols and Risks: Making Good Decisions

After you have come to terms with the rule sets for your site operation, you need to ensure that you allowed only the required protocols, and only to the servers or segments where they are needed. For example, if you opened up a rule to allow Secure Shell (SSH) connections to your servers, that rule should allow only the Transmission Control Protocol (TCP). User Datagram Protocol (UDP) is not supported in current versions of SSH, so they should be denied by the firewall. Following this example, check each rule to ensure that you have restricted the proper protocols and allowed the ones you need to work.

The most commonly debated protocol for firewall rule sets is the Internet Control Message Protocol (ICMP). This is the protocol used by the ping program and most implementations of traceroute (some use UDP). Although this protocol is very handy for administrators and general Internet monitoring, attackers use the protocol for a myriad of activities ranging from network mapping to denial of service (DoS) attacks. In some cases, communications with Trojan horse programs and hacker malware have even been hidden in ICMP packets to escape detection and circumvent firewall systems. Usually, the site administrators determine what risks they are willing to accept and which ICMP packet types they will allow into their networks. At a minimum, all host information requests via ICMP from the public Internet should be denied at the firewall or border routers. Never allow ICMP packets that enumerate a host system's netmask or timing settings to be passed into your networks from the Internet. Remember that what an attacker knows can hurt you!

If your systems or the administration staff requires ICMP protocols, just be sure to again follow the basic *deny all* pattern and allow only the types of ICMP required into your networks and restrict the systems to which these connections may be made to the specific hosts required. Note that no ICMP should ever be allowed into your database segments or your financial networks from the public Internet. Allowing attackers access to these hosts in *any way* always spells trouble down the road!

To read more about the dangers of each protocol and port, check with your IDS vendor and ask them about what attacks are used over those protocols. A good site at which to research this yourself is the advice section of www.networkice.com or the vulnerability databases and forums at www.securityfocus.com.

# How Do I Know Where to Place My Components?

After you have created a general idea of what segments your implementation is going to require, the next step is figuring out how to group the systems you are using and determine the segment in which to place them. This is best done by building a profile of the systems, based upon the risks associated with common criteria such as user groups, the sensitivity of the information they will be processing, what applications they will be hosting, and the levels of risk that exist in your setup for the particular systems involved.

After you have profiled the systems, pick out the commonalities and create groups of systems that have like characteristics. Then map groups into the appropriate network segments to determine your security zones. You control access to each of the systems and segments through a combination of local user controls and firewall rules.

## Profiling Systems by Risk

It all begins with risk. The first step in the process is to create a spreadsheet with the following common criteria:

- Users
- Sensitivity of data

- External visibility
- Internal access controls required
- Encryption requirements

You may have additional criteria depending on the specific needs of your site, but these are good starting points.

The first criterion is users. Who will be the primary users of this system? Will it be the general public via the Internet, or will it be your financial staff? Are the primary users external to your organization, or is the system to be accessed only by your staff? If the system is to be used externally, is it primarily for customers, partners, or vendors? The answers to these questions will let you create a baseline of who will be interacting with the systems on a regular basis.

Next, define the sensitivity of the information the system will process or store. Is the data for public use? Is it business sensitive? Is it financial information that must be protected all costs? Create three or more levels such as these and then rank the data into these categories.

The external visibility of a system is the next thing to evaluate. Here the simple question is: does the system need to be accessible from the public Internet? If the system must remain visible, then it will need to be placed into a segment with public access. Never place a system that requires public access initiated from the Internet in segments where high security requirements are in place. If possible, always ensure that any system requiring a higher level of security is placed into a zone where only members of that segment can initiate transactions with other systems. This helps prevent attackers from directly interacting with those systems.

Evaluate the internal controls the system will require next. The criteria here is the type of access controls the operating system or applications you are using have built into them. Add on to this factor the controls established by any host-based security tools you plan to use on the system. The more granular the access controls of a system, the more security those controls generally add if configured properly.

Encryption requirements are also a criterion. If the primary means of interaction with a system is going to be via an encrypted session such as Secure Sockets Layer (SSL) or the like, this will greatly limit the effectiveness of a network-based IDS, and thus must be compensated for using a different approach. Again, here a simple yes or no will do.

Lastly, define any other risks that you may not have had criteria for. For example, if you know that a specific application must be run on a specific version of an operating system and is unsupported on any other versions (a horrible situation indeed, but I have seen it), then you know that the system in question may already have known vulnerabilities or may experience them in the future without any chance of a patch or upgrade. In this case, you would note this and you would be forced to locate this system in a very tightly guarded segment of your site or change your implementation to replace this component.

## Establishing Risk Control Requirements

Now that you have created the criteria and evaluated each system by them, the next step is to begin to establish control mechanisms to enforce their separation. In cases where the systems will be offering public access, this may be as simple as defining specific user accounts for administrators and using firewall rules to manage the connectivity to only specific services for the public. It is highly recommended that you disable all unneeded services on your systems to narrow the gateway for compromise should an attacker circumvent your primary protection methods.

Using your criteria, you should now be able to decide what systems will be primarily protected by the firewall, what systems will be dependant on internal authentication methods, and what systems will require additional tools for protecting them from unauthorized access.

Begin by creating a rough diagram showing what services (and using what ports) will need to communicate with other systems and users. Keep in mind the rules discussed earlier for initiating conversations. This rough diagram will become the template for creating your firewall rules. It will also be used to tune your IDSs and log monitoring tools to better manage and control your level of risk.

## Creating Security Zones through Requirement Grouping

After you have created the diagram of conversations, the time has come to group the systems together and assign them to network segments. To do this, look for the commonalities and place those systems together. As you define each system's location, make any necessary changes to the conversation diagram that is required.

Many times you will find that you have systems that seem very similar in requirements, but have some small difference that makes you feel uncomfortable about placing them with their peers. If this is the case, consider using host-based tools such as IDS, log monitoring, or a customized configuration to resolve the issues. If the problems are large enough that they can't be rectified by this step, then it may be necessary to create another network segment specifically for that system and other systems like it. The cost of implementing such a segment is often significantly lower than the risks of exposing that system to undesired threats.

Now that you have your systems placed, use your conversation diagram to create your firewall rule set. Refer to your manual for specific instructions for your firewall. Generally, start with a basic principle that *everything that is not specifically allowed is denied* and then add in the conversations that you believe need to be allowed. You will probably miss some that may be required for your site to operate, but your firewall will log these attempts and after you ensure that they are required, you can add them into the rules. Fine tuning is always required, and should be an important part of testing your site's operation before launch.

# Implementing Intrusion Detection

It is no doubt that intrusion detection is a hot button in today's security world. In fact, next to firewalls, IDSs are often the most commonly used security product. Vendors have been hyping the wonders of IDSs for years now, and although the products have improved over time, in general they have failed to meet many of the expectations they had promised.

The commercial world is not the only source for IDS products. The open source community has come up with solutions that rival, and in some ways exceed, the commercial offerings. Open source tools such as Snort!, Shadow, and PortSentry have brought IDS to market as well. Some of the freeware security tools have complete documentation, online support, and a plethora of add-ons, plug-ins, and extensions. For example, to complement the Snort IDS, users have written new rule sets, reporting engines, management interfaces, and many other tools to make using Snort easier and more user-friendly.

Whether you choose a commercial IDS, an open source product, or a combination of both, keep in mind that intrusion detection is a tool. Like a firewall or antivirus software, it is a not a magic bullet or a guarantee that your site won't get compromised. It is simply another piece in the security puzzle. Used correctly, it can spot a multitude of problems. Used incorrectly, it is little more than a false sense of security.

Tools & Traps...

### IDS Products

Choices in IDS products include the following commercial, open source, and freeware solutions:

- **Snort!** is a network-based IDS written by Martin Roesch and is available from www.snort.org.
- **Shadow** is a network-based IDS sponsored by The US Government and the System Administration, Networking, and Security (SANS) Institute and is available from www.nswc.navy.mil/ISSEC/CID
- **PortSentry** is a host-based IDS written by Psionic Software and is available from www.psionic.com.

Continued

- **Tripwire** is a commercial tool that is free for use on Linux. It is owned by the company Tripwire and is available from www.tripwire.com.

Other sources for IDS information around the Web are plentiful. General information about the technologies involved can be found online or in many books on the market today. Searching Amazon.com will reveal many titles with varying levels of detail about these exciting tools. Popular online references include:

- www.whitehats.com
- www.networkintrusion.co.uk
- www.networkice.com
- www.sans.org/newlook/resources/IDFAQ/ID_FAQ.htm

The last entry above, the SANS IDS Frequently Asked Questions list, is a fantastic resource for answering most basic—and many advanced—questions about IDS products and technologies.

## What Is Intrusion Detection?

Intrusion detection is the name given to a family of products that are deployed to look for suspicious events that occur on a network or system. When the tool notices an event that matches its definition of "suspicious," it will perform some action such as logging the details, alerting an administrator, killing the traffic or process, and/or updating other devices such as firewalls to prevent the problem from happening again.

IDS systems that respond to events by simply logging the details and/or alerting someone that an event has occurred are called *passive* intrusion detection systems. These tools are used primarily to gather forensic information or details of an attack. Because they do not impede the attack itself, the attacker may actually still compromise the target system.

Although this is certainly not a wonderful solution, it is better than not knowing you have been compromised at all. Last year in the United

States, a home or business was broken into every 11 minutes. Based on information from various response teams within the same time frame, computer attacks and break-ins occurred more than once a second.

IDS systems that respond in ways to interrupt the attack or prevent further damage from an attacker are called *active* intrusion detection systems. When they see an event, they usually log and alert in addition to doing things like resetting the attacker's connection or notifying the firewall to deny packets from the suspicious host.

Although some IDS tools are very versatile, others may be very difficult to configure and may not be able to recognize patterns outside of those programmed into it by its creators. Most IDS systems compare traffic or user patterns against databases of known attack fingerprints or signatures. When selecting your IDS, one of the primary questions you should ask is how easy it is to have signatures added to the database. In some cases, you can simply edit a file. In others, you may have to use a specific tool or write the signature in a specific language or format. Least desirable are the systems that require you to request signature additions from the vendor. That situation may expose your systems to threats for a period of time that may be unacceptable to you. The bottom line for selecting an IDS is the same as any other product: Buyer beware!

## Your Choices in Intrusion Detection

Over the years, methods of performing intrusion detection have evolved greatly. New ideas and methods to determine what constitutes a suspicious event have brought about great discussions and a myriad of tools and processes. Today, there are generally two flavors of IDS: network-based tools and host-based tools.

In this area, as with firewalls, there are schools of thought that believe that each of these types of solutions are better than the other. Some people believe that network-based systems outweigh the need for a host-based tool. Others feel that because most network-based products are blind to the encrypted traffic that has come into such wide use today, host-based tools are the only way to achieve peace of mind. The truth probably lies somewhere in the middle of both extremes.

I have found that deploying a combination of network-based IDS and host-based tools achieves a balance that makes me more comfortable. Network-based systems can monitor and manage the visible network traffic, and once tuned to their environment can be a dependable source of information for a security administrator. In addition, host-based tools provide controls for systems that speak only encrypted protocols, or where additional, more finite access rules are needed to manage users and system behaviors.

Remember to be sure that your IDS installation is a reflection of your defined security policy. Make sure that it enforces the rules that your policy sets. However, refrain from using the IDS as a network spy or employee monitoring device; this is an easy way for the system to get misconfigured or to pollute the security information you are collecting. If you must use these types of tools, deploy a separate system for that purpose. Also remember that in the event your IDS detects a security incident, always refer to your incident response policy or your incident handling process.

Whatever the type or combination you choose for your site, become familiar with your IDS products and spend the time to fine-tune them to your environment. A well-managed and well-configured IDS can be a big help if and when trouble arrives.

Damage & Defense...

### Realistic Expectations of an IDS Tool

Many people have begun to see IDS tools as a panacea for network security and the associated risk problems of e-commerce. The same was thought of firewalls when they began to appear on the scene. The truth of the matter is that there really are no magic bullets or panacea solutions to the security problem.

IDS tools are just that: *tools*. They are a part of a total solution, but not a solution in and of themselves. They are a part of a deployed program of "defense in depth." In the defense-in-depth

Continued

scenario, many tools such as firewalls, antivirus programs, policies, routers, IDSs and other items work together to create a mesh of security checkpoints and choke points to regulate and inspect all aspects of network transactions. Only by using this combined approach can you ever hope to maintain real security. Even using this strategy can be complex and difficult, but it yields the most results over time.

Be sure that your expectations for your IDS tools are realistic. For example, it is very realistic to expect your IDS tools to help you make more sense of your network traffic data or to assist you in detecting malicious assaults against your site. But, if you expect your IDS to compensate for a weak site design or low authentication requirements, you will more than likely be disappointed when attackers succeed in compromising your systems. Remember that IDS systems are not perfect; they are getting better, but they still have thresholds of behavior, they often miss traffic in congested networks, and they may have other shortcomings that vary from product to product and design to design.

Use your IDS as a tool and implement it as a part of a comprehensive solution and you will fare very well. But, depend on it to the magic shield against attackers and you may find yourself gravely disappointed.

## Network-Based IDS

Network-based IDS products monitor the network traffic streams for suspicious traffic patterns. As before, those patterns may be user-defined or a set of signatures programmed in by the product's creators. The system acts as a sensor reading the data flow off of the wire and parsing it against the database of patterns.

When a pattern match is found, the system will perform the actions defined in its configuration. These actions may include logging, alerting, killing the connection, updating firewall or router rule sets, or other actions determined by the administrator. Many IDS products even allow you to define your own responses by shelling out to a program or script that you write. Just remember to be careful with these options and take only actions that are safe in your environment—and take care not to create a new DoS attack for yourself.

Several problems exist with the network-based IDS platform. Most network IDS tools are blind to encrypted traffic because they can't decrypt the data on the fly. Packet fragmentation issues also affect some network-based systems. In such a situation, the tool is unable to reassemble packets that have been fragmented by other network systems and compare the total information of the stream against the database of signatures. Instead, the tool compares only the unfragmented packets, which may not match any signatures because the patterns are incomplete and thus may miss attacks hidden in this manner.

Another issue with network-based IDS tools is that they have problems operating in switched network environments. In this case, because the switch only propagates the network traffic onto specific ports, the IDS can only see traffic on its own port. Administrators have overcome this difficulty by creating a span or mirror port that shows all or more of the traffic on the switch. The drawback to this is that if the traffic levels get too high for the IDS to keep with them, the tool begins to miss packets in the stream, which could cause it to miss an attack.

Placement of sensors for a network-based IDS tool are critical for its success. The common areas for placement are behind the firewall, in the various DMZ segments, and on the highly sensitive areas of the protected network. See Figure 5.5 for placement ideas. The sensor behind the firewall is in place to detect any illicit activity that may have made it through the firewall defenses. It also alerts you to hostile traffic that originates on your own protected network, thus preventing your staff from being bad netizens. The DMZ-placed segments watch for traffic that is outside your normal patterns of use.

Some sites choose to place an additional IDS sensor outside of the firewall for continual monitoring of their threat level or to gather forensic information. I suggest that if you choose to do this, use that sensor for information only and do not respond to the events that it alerts on. The external IDS will generate a much larger amount of alerts than the systems deployed elsewhere if your firewall is doing its job correctly. However, many sites find this sensor informative, and I mention it here in the event that you should desire such data.

**Figure 5.5** Typical Deployment of Network-Based IDS Sensors

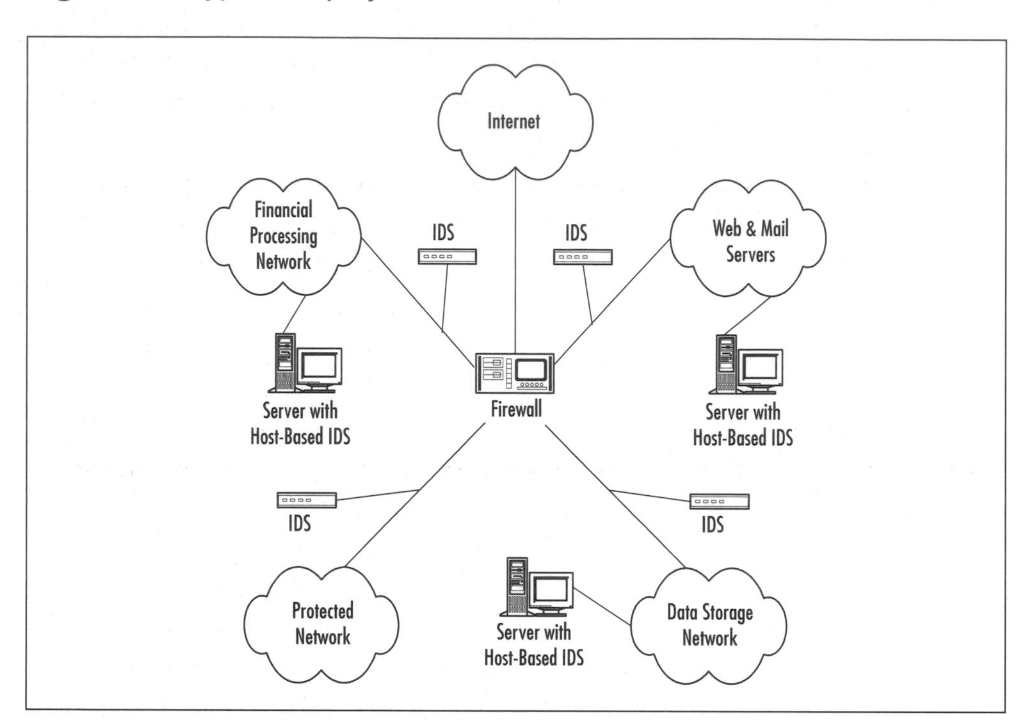


Overall, even with the issues surrounding it, network-based IDSs continue to be a major tool in the administrator's toolkit. Properly placed, managed, and configured, a network IDS is a great help.

## Host-Based IDS

Host-based IDS tools range widely in their options and their abilities. The basic principle is that these tools reside on the host and that they watch events from the view of the computer's operating system. As events occur, they compare those events against their rules base, and if they find a match, they alert and/or take action.

Some host-based tools watch the file system. They take periodic snapshots of the file system layout, its critical files, and/or the contents of those files. They use a technique called a checksum to validate that changes have not occurred. A *checksum* is a mathematical algorithm that totals mathematical values assigned to each character in a file. If a single character or any other part of a file is modified, the checksum will be different for that file after the change. The IDS program runs the first time and creates a database of the files and their associated checksums. After that, the IDS program is run periodically and rechecks its findings against the database. If any checksums don't match, the system alerts the administrator or responds as it is configured to.

Other host-based tools operate by watching network traffic that is destined for them. They open various ports on the system and wait for connections to them. Because these connections are to ports that are not really in use on the system, they are by definition suspicious. A common strategy for using these tools is to open ports that are commonly attacked, such as remote procedure call, or RPC (111), NetBIOS (135-139), and common Trojan horse ports such as 37337 and 12345. Other ports that are useful are the ports zero (0) and one (1), which can be used to detect port scans. After the program notices the illicit connections, it can respond or alert just like the other tools.

There are also tools that monitor user activity and look for suspicious events, such as attempts to gain access to files they do not have access to, attempts to load software onto the system, and hundreds of other signatures considered to be suspicious. Other products profile users by the times and days they normally access the system and alert if their accounts are used outside of this pattern. IDS tools are available that even profile the typing speed of users and their typical errors, and alert when these patterns change or differ.

The eventual goals of host-based IDS tools are to become so familiar with your users' normal patterns of behavior that they will detect even slight changes that might mean that someone else is using their account. The effectiveness of these tools continues to improve but have a long way to go to reach their full promise.

Carefully evaluate your needs for host-based tools and apply them liberally to your systems. They can be used to provide very granular controls when paired with a properly tuned operating system. Again, take the time to fine tune them and they will become indispensable tools in your toolkit.

# Example of a Network-Based IDS

RealSecure is a network-based IDS made by Internet Security Systems (ISS) (www.iss.net).

The system is broken down into two components: a network sensor (RealSecure Network Sensor) and a management console (RealSecure Manager). The network sensor is loaded as an application on a Windows NT or Solaris system and is also available as a plug-and-play appliance from Nokia. The management console is also available for either Windows NT or Solaris.

The network engine is deployed on the network segment that you wish to monitor. It then watches the network traffic and parses it against the database searching for known signatures. The engine can be remotely managed from the console and reports its finding back there as well. Events are represented graphically by the management console and the technical details are written to a database. Figure 5.6 shows the management console event monitoring screen.

**Figure 5.6** The RealSecure Event Management Console

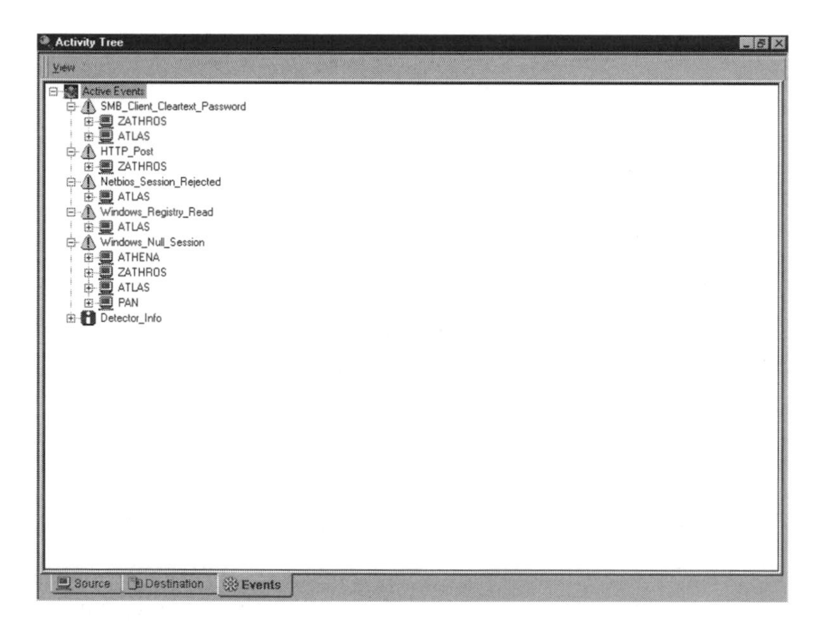

RealSecure supports users creating their own signatures through the management console and a graphic interface. The sensor also supports reassembling fragmented network traffic prior to comparing it against the signatures database. ISS support issues regular updates to the signature file, and technical support is available to the users for building their own signatures.

RealSecure also features a wide range of responses when it sees an event. The IDS can alert and log the details as well as interrupt and reset the network conversation. It can communicate with CheckPoint firewalls to block additional traffic from the offending host. It also supports executing user-written programs or scripts to vary the responses if desired.

The network sensor can send the alerts to more than one manager or to other tools such as Tivoli or HP OpenView. It can also send Simple Network Management Protocol (SNMP) traps to any system or program with support for SNMP notification. These options make RealSecure a very enterprise-friendly solution. The product works well in large corporate environments and small companies alike. It has a low learning curve and is manageable with a minimum of training.

## Example of a Host-Based IDS

ISS also makes a version of RealSecure that is a host-based product. It is available in two different configurations, called RealSecure OS Sensor and RealSecure Server Sensor. The products support the Windows NT, Solaris, AIX, and HP UX operating systems. These host-based IDS tools can even share the same management console with the network sensors, making for an easily monitored solution.

The OS Sensor is a traditional host-based IDS product. It monitors the operating system's log files and performs checksum monitoring of the file system. It also opens listening ports on the system and waits for connections to those ports, as explained earlier. OS Sensor even goes one step farther and reports false banner information back the connection's originator. If an event occurs or a system file changes, it alerts the management console and logs the details to the database. It can also respond in a more active manner, taking actions such as terminating the user's connection and even suspending the account from further use.

The Server Sensor product is a newer tool to the IDS market. It is essentially an upgrade to the capabilities of the OS Sensor. The Server Sensor product does all the things the OS Sensor does, plus adds additional tools that monitor the kernel level processes to detect Trojan horses and logic to make detection of distributed scanning easier. The new product also includes a new response function that adds the offending address of the attacker to a database that denies all further traffic from that host to the protected system.

All of the ISS sensors report their data back to the central management console and from there, all events may be monitored and reports generated. The sensors are also configured from the same console (see Figure 5.7) giving the ability to control many sensors, either host- or network-based, from a single location.

**Figure 5.7** A RealSecure Server Sensor Configuration Screen

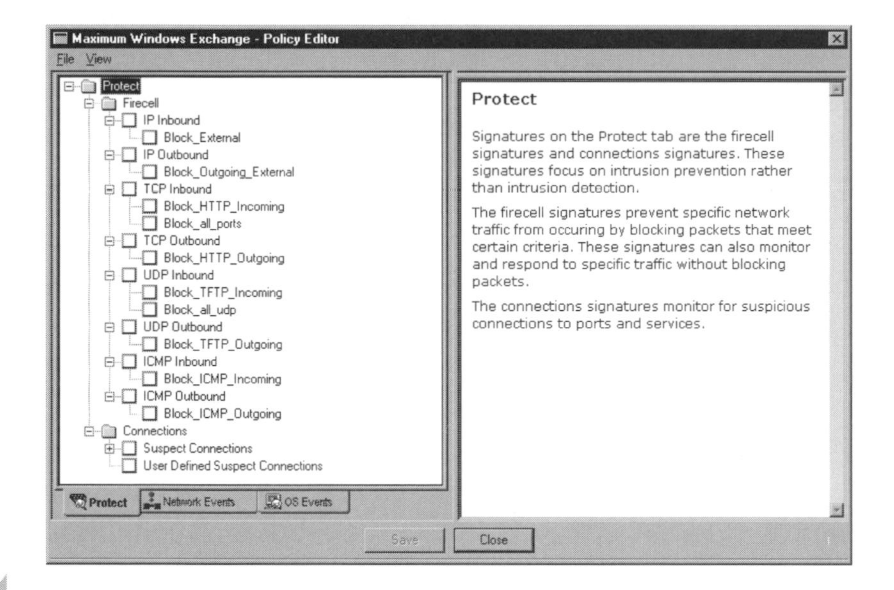


## NOTE

More information on the RealSecure product line is available at www.iss.net/securing_e-business/security_products/index.php.

# Managing and Monitoring the Systems

One of the largest jobs of operating your e-commerce Web site will be managing and maintaining its systems and network components. The tasks of a system administrator can be very diverse and often very in-depth. All aspects of the computer systems must be monitored on a regular basis so that any issues can be resolved with the utmost of speed.

In addition, new patches, fixes, and upgrades are often issued at a rapid pace, tying up even more of your time and resources. Each of these modifications has to be tested, researched, authenticated, and finally installed. System administration can be an exhaustive task. Automating the various day-to-day tasks will help you over time, but be ready for a crunch in the beginning.

## What Kind of Management Tasks Can I Expect to Perform?

The day-to-day tasks required to manage a Web site vary from site to site in their specifics, but they do share many commonalities. Every Web site administrator must spend time reviewing the system and application logs each day. They must search through these logs for error messages that indicate a problem with the system. Some of these problems may be related to security issues, but the majority will be messages that indicate common problems such as a log file or database that is nearing its maximum size or a message indicating that the tape backup system encountered an error during its last attempt to back up a network drive. Each of these messages must be examined and the problems they describe must be addressed and resolved.

Administering system backups is another task common to site managers. Although devices exist to change tapes or other media, and the software handles scheduling and other requirements of the backup process, they are not without problems. Media ages and goes bad over time, network errors occur, and other problems interfere with the backup process. Although these issues are not daily in their occurrence, guarding against them is. You can expect to spend a large amount of time dealing with backup issues, no matter what hardware or software devices you choose for your site.

As explained earlier, time must also be spent each day ensuring that your systems are running the current versions of your operating systems and applications. Patches, hot fixes, and workarounds have to be applied as new security issues and other problems are discovered and repaired. Each of these revisions has to be authenticated, tested, and will require re-verification of the security posture of your site. This process is very time-consuming and often frustrating as changes arrive in a rapid fashion.

Changes to the content and features of your site will also be a continuing concern for you. Successful sites on the Internet must be changed on a very frequent basis to keep them fresh and new and to keep customers interested. New features are added to sites to increase their usability and assist customers in new ways. Each of these changes and features has the possibility of bringing new problems to your site. For example, even slight modifications to a site's Common Gateway Interface (CGI) scripting can bring a multitude of performance and security issues. Placement of a command interpreter such as perl.exe in a wrong location can cause complete compromise of a server and possibly an entire network. With the stakes this high, much of your time will have to be spent reviewing these changes and carefully evaluating the possible effects they could have on your site.

Many other problems and duties will crop up to consume your time, but these are the most common and basic ideas. Issues arrive and depart on a regular basis as they are either resolved, accepted, or mitigated. Just keep alert and remember the basic duties each and every day.

# What Kinds of Monitoring Should I Be Performing?

Monitoring is a majority of the work of managing a site. Handling these duties can be done in many ways. If you run a small e-commerce site, you may be able to manually perform the system monitoring either by physically accessing each of the systems directly, or by performing the processes remotely over a network connection. However, in large sites this is usually impossible because resources are often not available to manually observe each system. In these situations, automated monitoring tools and network management systems are frequently used.

Automated tools (or agents) reside on the host computer being monitored and communicate with a management console via a network connection. The agent watches usage patterns, processor workload, log files, disk space, and other items for signs of a problem. If a problem occurs, the agent sends a message to the management console with the appropriate details. The management console often assigns a follow-up task to the appropriate administrator and alerts them to the condition. Some management systems also track the problem through its resolution and log the collected information for trend analysis and other types of reporting.

## Tools & Traps...

### Monitoring Packages Resources

More information about commercial system monitoring packages can be found on vendor Web sites. Below are the URLs of some of these products:

- **Symantec Enterprise Security Manager (ESM)** http://enterprisesecurity.symantec.com/products/products.cfm?ProductID=45
- **E-Security Open e-Security Platform** www.esecurityinc.com/products/
- **Tivoli NetView** www.tivoli.com/products/index/netview/
- **BB4 Technologies Big Brother Network Monitor** (Free for most uses) www.bb4.com

Many of these tools are geared towards monitoring and managing more than security problems. They also provide assistance with general operation problems, user issues, and many other data points. Sites of all sizes often find these tools indispensable. Even small sites can gain from the deployment of open source or freeware solutions that perform similar functions to their commercial counterparts. A multitude of solutions are available with a variety of features and functions.

No matter if you choose to perform the monitoring processes manually or rely on automated tools to assist in the job, monitoring will become a daily task of the administrator. With careful observation, you can often prevent minor issues from becoming major problems.

## Basic System Monitoring

Monitoring the basic activities and needs of a system involves observing such things as usage levels, available resources and the overall health of a given system. Depending on which operating systems you have chosen, you may find that tools are built into them to provide this information to you easily. Monitoring these system status indicators is often done in the process of managing the security of a system, because these resources affect the overall operation of the device and could be symptoms of security-related problems.

For example, a system undergoing a SYN flood attack may exhibit high processor loads and a drain of memory and other system resources. By monitoring these changes, the administrator may be alerted before the system crashes or stops responding. This allows the administrator more flexibility in dealing with the attack and mitigating the risks of it reoccurring.

Manually performing these operations can often be done using various tools built into the operating system. For example, in Windows systems, the Task Manager displays much of this data, whereas in UNIX systems it is observed by using tools such as "uptime" or "top." Other add-on products may consolidate the data collection into one window or interface. A myriad of tools are available both commercially and in the open-source arena for these tasks.

Each of the commercial products mentioned in the preceding section's sidebar contains automated programs for performing these functions as well. Again, open-source tools are also available to make these monitoring tasks automatic as well.

## Monitoring Your Security Devices

Monitoring your security devices will probably require a bit more attention than monitoring your servers and network components. Because these systems serve as gatekeepers and guards, you need to pay careful attention to their logs and alerts.

Manually monitoring these log files can be a huge undertaking. Each of your tools will probably have its own log file format, which makes matters even worse. Scripts and processing tools are available for performing some basic functions on most security log files, though more advanced data analysis often requires a commercial application and a dedicated system for storage of the information long term.

In the simplest case, these log files must be inspected at least daily and used to determine if security events have taken place that require intervention or response. (This is where your security policy comes into play again!) If an event has occurred, more information must be gathered to create the data needed to respond to the incident. If not, the data can simply be discarded or logged for overall analysis. The thing to keep in mind here is that the more data you have to analyze over time, the bigger your picture will be, and the more likely you are to catch slow scans and long term probes.

Automating these processes is usually a good idea as long as a *human* is involved somewhere in the process to evaluate the automated alerts and output and to periodically check for missing events. In addition, if you do choose to automate the security log inspection process, make sure that you have multiple levels of security devices observing your traffic. For example, make sure that you have an IDS sitting behind your firewall, so that if one system gets compromised, your entire alerting process does not fail you in your time of need.

## Log File Management

The most common problems of dealing with log files are the logging of too much information and knowing how many generations of the files should be kept for data analysis. These problems exist across the board, whether the system is a server, a network component, or a security device. Obviously, the answers depend on your environment.

The magic solution is to find the level of logging that allows you to capture the picture of your risks and the operation of your site. The proper amount of logging is just enough to get the information you need without generating false positives and without missing anything in the process. The number of generations to keep depends on what you need to create your big picture. Too granular an approach may cause you to miss probes, whereas too wide an approach may cause you to spend too much time chasing ghosts.

To determine what level of logging your site needs to perform, establish clear goals for each of the types of systems you are monitoring. Do you need to know every time someone browses your Web page? The answer is "probably" if you want to create usage statistics. Log that data on your Web server and make sure that your IDS is not logging every Web browser as well. Do you really need to log every time your Web server gets pinged or do you really want to be notified only if a ping flood is occurring? If you care only about the ping flood, then depend on your IDS for that notification and don't log that data on your server. These are simple examples but they define the concept of ensuring that you are using the right system for generating the right logs, which can help eliminate excessive logging.

Determining the generations of your log files to retain is not so easy. It depends mainly on the resources you have at your disposal and the processes you are using to parse the retained data over time. For many sites that lack the resources to perform analysis of long-term data, they retain the log files in compressed formats for about ninety days. Of these ninety-day log file sets, only about two weeks worth are kept live for analysis, the rest are archived for access if needed, or in the event that an incident is discovered. Sites that have the storage and processing power to perform analysis of log files over a wide span of time may keep logs for twelve to thirty-six months before archiving them off to long-term storage media! This mainly applies to systems that deal with highly confidential information or the largest of e-commerce businesses such as banks and other major institutions of finance. These log files are parsed against new log files to create threat baselines and risk analysis information that is probably overkill for most e-commerce sites. The bottom line is to retain enough data to feel comfortable and archive the rest in the event that you need to refer to it later. Logs are handy to have around in an incident, so keep them available in case you need them.

For more information on intrusion management or incident response, refer to Chapter 10 of this book, which deals with these topics and the processes entailed in managing a security incident.

# Should I Do It Myself or Outsource My Site?

As discussed in previous chapters of this book, when deploying your e-commerce Web site you may be faced with the option of outsourcing the deployment or management of your site. You may also decide that creating the infrastructure to run the site yourself may be more than your budget will support, and you want to look at the option of outsourcing your site's operation to an Application Service Provider (ASP). In either case, the same rules of outsourcing apply here as with all of the other junctions in the project. You have to consider the feasibility of training a staff member or members to perform the functions against the costs of hiring someone who already has those skills to perform it for you. You also have to look at the security requirements for your site and determine if your policy and processes allow for outsourcing to hired personnel. In many events, however, you may find yourself requiring assistance with the setup of the security systems, and you may want an external opinion of your plans and implementation. In these situations, outsourcing may be a great fit for your organization.

ASP companies have become popular solutions in the past few years and their business numbers and features continue to grow. With most ASP companies, the entire site implementation and management are performed wholly by the ASP. Often, the ASP also works with the client to do the majority of the planning for the site as well. For a fee, the day-to-day operation and monitoring of the site is performed by the ASP's staff, whereas the e-commerce company mainly provides content and the support needed by the e-commerce company's customers. Although the ASP assumes the responsibility of providing and maintaining the security of your site, if you choose to do this type of outsourcing be sure to maintain the rights to audit and inspect the security processes of the ASP you work with. Performing regular vulnerability assessments against your site and the ASP itself will ensure that your policies are being enforced.

## Pros and Cons of Outsourcing Your Site

Certainly there are advantages and disadvantages to outsourcing the deployment and management of your site. On the negative side, you have the loss of control over the day-to-day operations, the need to trust the security of the vendors involved, and the reliance on their staff to perform quality work. On the positive side, you free up your resources to stay focused on the regular business requirements without worrying about the administration issues of the site; you have the contracts and reputation of the vendors to protect you against problems with their performance; and you can offset the costs of building the skills or infrastructure yourself.

With careful management of the project and by clearly establishing and communicating the goals and policies of your site with your vendors, you will probably find that most negatives can be mitigated. To make this process work best, ensure that your contracts clearly establish the security expectations of the vendor with regards to your site. Also ensure that the contracts provide you with the right to audit, inspect, and make changes to the security practices and policies of your site at any time. Using these contract guidelines and actually performing the audits and inspections, you can establish that your rules are being followed and that your processes are being maintained as you require.

## Co-Location: One Possible Solution

If outsourcing the whole installation and management of your site seems too scary or costly for you, then you may want to look at another possible solution called *co-location*. Co-location is a service provided by many vendors to allow companies to share the costs of establishing bandwidth and other infrastructure components (such as credit processing systems and the like) while still providing them with the freedom of owning their own servers and support systems.

Co-location is a popular solution for companies who want control over the day-to-day management and operation of their site, but who may not be able to afford or manage the entire e-commerce network on their own. These companies often rent, sell, or lease servers to companies wishing to take advantage of their existing e-commerce support systems. Some simply allow companies to provide their own servers and plug into their frameworks for power, bandwidth, and other needs. The co-location company then charges a fee for the use of their support systems and resources, while the site owner is responsible for all support, monitoring, and management of their own systems or those rented or leased from the provider.

Co-location can be a great way to lower your investment and resource requirements while still making e-commerce viable for your company. As in all other outsourcing situations, however, it is "buyer beware." Make sure that your contracts are clear and your expectations have been communicated and documented. Audit, inspect, and pay attention to the co-location service regularly to ensure that operations in their environment still meet your requirements.

## Selecting an Outsource Partner or ASP

Price is all too often the deciding factor when choosing an outsourcing partner. The fact that companies decide based upon price—and not quality—is a shame. This often leads them to vendors who cut too many corners and may leave their sites exposed to risks that they would not be comfortable with if they ran the sites themselves. Although I am not against bargain shopping for services, I simply believe that you usually get what you pay for.

The single greatest tool in making a wise selection of an outsourcing partner is references. Always ask vendors for specific references and the services that they have performed for those companies. The next step is a simple one; check the references. Contact the people the vendor referred you to and ask about their satisfaction with the vendor and the work that was performed. Use the Internet to search for reviews of their services, security, and reputation. Post to appropriate mailing lists and Usenet news groups asking about the particular vendor in question. Do this for each vendor you consider and then evaluate the responses to pick your partner.

Beyond references, be sure to have all outsourcing contracts and agreements reviewed by your attorney. Be sure that the contracts include a process for terminating the vendor relationship if their services do not meet your defined requirements after a period of notification. This process of terminating the contract is your insurance that the vendor will have to perform to your standards or fix any problems that you discover, or risk losing your business. Attorneys are required in this process, and because this is your business you are putting on the line, be sure to use them and protect yourself.

Outsourcing does not have to be risky or uncomfortable. With proper care in selecting a partner and proper attention to detail when creating the agreements, you will find that outsourcing can be a big help for your site. Choose your partners carefully and then let them work for you to create the best site on the Internet!

# Summary

This chapter deals with deploying the systems and network components needed to make your e-commerce site operate. By carefully examining your systems and their usage requirements you can create groups of components with common requirements and place them together in security zones. Using firewalls, IDSs, and other security measures, you can enforce the rules required for each of these security zones independently of each other to create an overall process to perform e-commerce securely.

We also learned about the types of firewall systems and IDS tools that are available on the market today. These tools add the controls and monitoring capabilities that are so important in the e-commerce world. By combining the strengths of the various types of these tools, we create an overall strategy of defense in depth.

Monitoring the firewalls, systems, and other security tools can be a big job but automation and centralized process can make these tasks easier for large-scale environments. Tools built into the operating systems and common add-on products also make this manageable for smaller sites and individuals creating their own e-commerce presence.

Lastly, we talked about the decisions involved with outsourcing your site in the deployment phase or for total management by an ASP. Many options are available to organizations to help lower costs and resource requirements for e-commerce. Some of these solutions, such as using an ASP or co-location, may prove to be good fits in certain situations. In addition, this chapter covered what to look for in an outsourcing partner and how to select between vendors based upon quality and experience—and not primarily on cost.

# Solutions Fast Track

## Implementing Security Zones

☑ Security zones are discrete network segments holding systems that share common requirements, such as the types of information they handle, who uses them, and what levels of security they require to protect their data. They may be the same type of operating system or different operating systems altogether. They may be PCs, or servers, or even a mainframe.

- ☑ DMZ systems are offered some level of protection from the public Internet while they remain accessible for the specific services they provide. In addition, the internal network is protected by firewall and from the systems in the DMZ. Because the DMZ systems still offer public access, they are more prone to compromise and thus they are untrusted by the systems in the protected network. This scenario allows for public services while still maintaining a degree of protection against attack.
- ☑ Customer names, addresses, order information, and especially financial data are protected from unauthorized access through the creation of specialized segments similar to the DMZ called *security zones.* Many sites choose to implement a multiple segment structure to better manage and secure their business information.
- ☑ Access controls also regulate the way in which network conversations are initiated. It is always preferable that DMZ systems do not initiate connections into more secure areas, but that systems with higher security requirements initiate those network conversations.
- ☑ Creating and managing the security controls such as firewall rules, IDS signatures, and user access regulations is a large task. Start with deny-all strategies and permit only the services and network transactions that are required to make the site function. Carefully manage the site's performance and make small changes to the access controls to more easily manage the rule sets.

## Understanding Firewalls

- ☑ Packet filtering firewalls make decisions about whether or not to pass network traffic based upon the source and destination information in the headers of the packets being transmitted.

☑ Proxy-based firewalls also make decisions based upon the source and destination addresses of packets, as well as the ports used for the conversation. The additional work done by a proxy firewall is that it is inspects the data load portion of a packet and attempts to decide if the data fits the proxies' requirements for such a conversation.

☑ Hybrids between the two technologies have also emerged and may be a good fit for your organization if you desire the proxy level of control and the speed of a packet filter. These firewall devices integrate both the proxy and packet-filtering technologies to create solutions that monitor data load and achieve high throughput speeds.

☑ The process of designing the rule set for any firewall should always start with a "deny all" attitude. That means that you begin by making the firewall deny any connections that you do not specifically allow. Thus, starting with nothing, you can add in the connections required between each of the security zones to allow the systems on those segments to perform their work and to be administered, but nothing else. This helps to prevent the possibility of allowing unneeded services and additional gateways for an attacker to compromise your servers.

☑ After you have come to terms with the rule sets for your site operation, you need to ensure that you allowed only the required protocols, and only to the servers or segments where they are needed.

## How Do I Know Where to Place My Components?

☑ Evaluate your systems using such criteria as users, sensitivity of data, external visibility, internal access controls required, and encryption requirements.

- ☑ Using those criteria, decide what systems will be primarily protected by the firewall, what systems will be dependant on internal authentication methods, and what systems will require additional tools for protecting them from unauthorized access.
- ☑ Group the systems together and assign them to network segments by looking for the commonalities and placing those systems together. Consider also using host-based tools such as IDS, log monitoring, or a customized configuration when for some reason a system should not be placed with its similar peers, or create another network segment specifically for that system.
- ☑ When you have your systems placed, create your firewall rule set. Generally, start with a basic principle that *everything that is not specifically allowed is denied* and then add in the conversations that you want to allow.

## Implementing Intrusion Detection

- ☑ Intrusion detection is the name given to a family of products that are deployed to look for suspicious events that occur on a network or system. When the tool notices an event that matches its definition of "suspicious," it will perform some action such as logging the details, alerting an administrator, killing the traffic or process, and/or updating other devices such as firewalls to prevent the problem from happening again.
- ☑ *Host-based* IDS tools reside on the host and watch events from the view of the computer's operating system. As events occur, they compare those events against their rules base, and if they find a match, they alert and/or take action. *Network-base*d IDS products monitor the network traffic streams for suspicious traffic patterns. The system acts as a sensor reading the data flow off of the wire and parsing it against a database of patterns.
- ☑ Although some IDS tools are very versatile, others may be very difficult to configure and may not be able to recognize patterns

outside of those programmed into it by its creators. Most IDS systems compare traffic or user patterns against databases of known attack fingerprints or signatures. When selecting your IDS, one of the primary questions you should ask is how easy it is to have signatures added to the database.

☑ Open source tools such as Snort!, Shadow, and PortSentry have brought IDS to market as well. Some of the freeware security tools have complete documentation, online support, and a plethora of add-ons, plug-ins, and extensions.

## Managing and Monitoring the Systems

☑ Patches, hot fixes, and workarounds have to be applied as new security issues and other problems are discovered and repaired. Each of these revisions has to be authenticated, tested, and will require re-verification of the security posture of your site. Changes to the content and features of your site will also require ongoing evaluation.

☑ Use automated tools (or agents) that reside on the host computer being monitored and communicate with a management console via a network connection. The agent watches usage patterns, processor workload, log files, disk space, and other items for signs of a problem. If a problem occurs, the agent sends a message to the management console with the appropriate details. The management console often assigns a follow-up task to the appropriate administrator and alerts them to the condition. Some management systems also track the problem through its resolution and log the collected information for trend analysis and other types of reporting.

☑ Automating monitoring processes is usually a good idea as long as a *human* is involved somewhere in the process to evaluate the automated alerts and output and to periodically check for missing events. In addition, if you do choose to automate the security log inspection process, make sure that you have multiple levels of security devices observing your traffic.

## Should I Do It Myself or Outsource My Site?

- ☑ Consider the feasibility of training a staff member or members to perform the functions against the costs of hiring someone who already has those skills to perform it for you. Look also at the security requirements for your site and determine if your policy and processes allow for outsourcing to hired personnel.
- ☑ If an ASP assumes the responsibility of providing and maintaining the security of your site, be sure to maintain the rights to audit and inspect the security processes of the ASP you work with. Performing regular vulnerability assessments against your site and the ASP itself will ensure that your policies are being enforced.
- ☑ Co-location is a service provided by many vendors to allow companies to share the costs of establishing bandwidth and other infrastructure components (such as credit processing systems and the like) while still providing them with the freedom of owning their own servers and support systems; this a popular solution for companies who want control over the day-to-day management and operation of their site, but who may not be able to afford or manage the entire e-commerce network on their own.

# Frequently Asked Questions

The following Frequently Asked Questions, answered by the authors of this book, are designed to both measure your understanding of the concepts presented in this chapter and to assist you with real-life implementation of these concepts. To have your questions about this chapter answered by the author, browse to **www.syngress.com/solutions** and click on the **"Ask the Author"** form.

**Q:** When we defined our security zones we ended up with more or less segments than in your examples. Did we do something wrong?

**A:** Probably not. The examples we used in the book are to explain the concepts of security zones. In real life applications you may find that your network differs from our examples. This is OK as long as you followed the process and created the zones you need for your site. Remember to use host-based security tools to meet granular differences in otherwise grouped systems within a single zone.

**Q:** How should we go about deciding which type of firewall or intrusion detection system meets our needs?

**A:** This can be a confusing task and with so many possibilities and products it is not an easy question to answer. Use the resources the vendors provide, but beware of hype and sales jargon. Use the Internet to search for references and case studies. As with service partners, ask the vendor for references and check them. Also ask online about the products you are considering and get feedback from the security community.

**Q:** How do I know if I am logging too much or too little information on my systems?

**A:** Log the information you feel that you need to make good decisions. If you have problems sifting through the logs to locate issues and you have had proper training, then you need to eliminate the log entries that you do not use to make decisions or keep those log entries and use an automated tool to select only the entries you are interested in. You are logging too little information if you do not have a picture of your systems' operations and your users' behaviors.

**Q:** I don't have the skills or resources to create my e-commerce site myself and the outsourcing options you detailed seem too expensive for my budget. What are my alternatives?

**A:** Other alternatives do exist. For example, you should investigate partnering with existing e-commerce sites and offering your products through their sites as a distributor. You could also arrange for selling your products or services on a consignment basis through these and other sites. Co-ops are also available in the online world where—for fees that are lower than outsourcing a full site—you can set up an offering area on one these systems. In any case, just be sure to read and understand the contract language and have it reviewed by an attorney before signing anything.

Chapter 6

# Securing Financial Transactions

## Solutions in this chapter:

- Understanding Internet-Based Payment Card Systems
- Options in Commercial Payment Solutions
- Secure Payment Processing Environments
- Understanding Cryptography
- Examining E-Commerce Cryptography
- A Virtual POS Implementation
- Alternative Payment Systems

☑ Summary

☑ Solutions Fast Track

☑ Frequently Asked Questions

# Introduction

Consumer confidence in the security and trustworthiness of business conducted over the Internet is the single most important issue facing electronic commerce today. Internet-based credit card fraud is reaching epidemic proportions and is driving hundreds of online businesses to the brink of extinction when their merchant banking relationships are terminated due to excessive fraud and chargeback costs. According to the Gartner Group (www.gartner.com), fraud is 12 times higher on the Internet than in the physical world of face-to-face or Mail Order/Phone Order (MOTO) sales. Cybersource (www.cybersource.com) reports that 83 percent of online merchants complain of the problems they experience with fraudulent charges on credit cards.

The Internet is fundamentally changing the way we do business. The traditional ideas of the marketplace and the consumer have morphed into previously unheard of models as technology evolves. The Internet is also changing our concept of money. New online forms of payment come forth regularly. Some of these nontraditional currencies are bringing about new challenges and new rewards to businesses and consumers alike. But, as the saying goes, the more things change, the more they stay the same—criminals exist online just as they do in the physical world, and many of them are working feverishly to beat the system.

Security and trust issues loom even larger when you look at projected volumes of business via the Internet over the next few years. Industry experts such as International Data Corporation estimate that $220 billion will be spent worldwide via the Internet in 2002, up from $2.6 billion in 1997. The sales records over the last two Christmas shopping seasons speak for themselves—according to the Census Bureau of the Department of Commerce, online holiday spending in 2000 increased 67 percent in the United States, with fourth-quarter Internet sales at $8.6 billion.

Securing payment information on the Internet is challenging work, but it *is possible*. With proper care, attention to detail, and selection and use of the right tools, e-commerce site administrators can indeed ensure privacy and integrity of data for both their employers and customers alike. Remember that any security solution requires constant attention or it risks becoming a problem in and of itself.

Because of the nature of Internet sales, it's impossible to ignore traditional credit cards and their cousins, debit cards and charge cards, wherever e-commerce is conducted. Before looking at ways to bring about an improved online environment of trust and security with payment card data, it's important to understand some fundamental operating principles and common operating practices to help better define where to focus security efforts.

# Understanding Internet-Based Payment Card Systems

With today's technology of intelligent Point of Sale (POS) devices, high-speed communication networks, and hidden back-end host systems, charge processing can appear simple, transparent, and intuitive to the uninitiated, but, in fact, the participant involvement and the steps of processing are far from trivial when you examine the sheer number of systems involved and the high volume of charges. The technical complexities stem from the foundation of the equally complex concept of *trust*.

Credit cards, charge cards, bank cards, payment cards, no matter what you call them, all relate to a family of payment options that involve relationships rooted in trust and good faith. You trust that the financial institution that issued you a card will pay the merchant for the goods and services you purchase. Merchants trust that the card issuers will pay them reasonably quickly, and the card issuers trust that you'll pay your bill on time each month to reimburse the money they're advancing on your behalf.

## Credit, Charge, or Debit Cards: What Are the Differences?

Although they're often thought by most people to be the same, credit and charge cards differ in how they work and in the agreements associated with each. Many of these payment cards are considerably different from one another in several ways.

In general, a credit card represents an account that carries a preset spending limit established by the card issuer, based on a line of credit obtained at the time of issue. Some are *signature* lines of credit, while others are *secured* lines of credit, where funds on deposit limit charges and serve as *collateral* for the credit card in the event of nonpayment of charges.

In addition, their balances against that line of credit may be paid in full or financed over time. As such, finance charges apply to unpaid balances left at the end of the month, at fixed Annual Percentage Rates (APR) that are set at the time of issue and that may or may not change over time. Visa and MasterCard are the most prevalent examples of credit cards issued by specific banks or other financial institutions that license the use of Visa and MasterCard trademarks from the brand associations.

Charge cards, like the American Express Personal (Green), Gold, and Platinum Cards, are not tied to revolving lines of credit—they carry no preset spending limits, are due in full at the end of the month, and do not accumulate interest or finance charges under normal uses. Diners Club and Carte Blanche are two other examples of charge card products.

Debit cards, on the other hand, are tied to a checking account and may be used in place of a check for payment. Once the balance of the underlying checking account is exhausted, requests for payments using the associated debit card will be declined, unless there are other arrangements in place (e.g., overdraft line of credit loans, savings account fund transfers, etc.). These arrangements are usually made before the debit card is issued or may be added anytime while the account is in good standing. Another distinctive feature of debit cards is the presence of a Personal Identification Number (PIN) to use the card at Automated Teller Machines (ATMs). The card and PIN together form what's called *two-factor authentication*, where the card is the token (first factor, what you have) and the PIN is the secret (second factor, what you know) to access the account. Thus far, e-commerce systems don't attempt to emulate the work of ATMs, so payments using a debit card are treated the same as charge card payments, as far as merchants are concerned.

Without considering where the Internet comes into play for charge processing, for now, let's follow a credit card charge from its origins on a typical POS terminal at a merchant brick-and-mortar storefront to its final resting place as a debit to the buyer and a credit to the merchant.

# Point-of-Sale Processing

Imagine you are shopping at the Apollo Marketplace, have finished making your selections, and have taken your goods to the register for checkout. You've elected to use your MasterCard that was issued from Bacchus Bank (an *issuer bank*). Apollo Marketplace has signed up for MasterCard Merchant Processing Services from the National Bank (an *acquirer bank*) and is happy to accept your card as payment for your purchase. While the National Bank provides merchant services for any merchants that sign up, they're too small to operate the expensive systems needed to process charges; they commission the work to a *third-party processor.* Let's say Delphi's Card Processing Service handles that work on behalf of the National Bank. Delphi's Card Processing Service was also the vendor that set up the equipment at the Marketplace.

The cashier at Apollo Marketplace swipes your MasterCard on the POS terminal, keys in the amount of the sale, and hits the Send button. This kicks off the first step of an *authorization request.* Based on the data contained on the card (such as the account number), the POS terminal knows where the request needs to be routed. Because they're somewhat intelligent (that is, programmable), POS terminals will typically support a feature known as split-dial to process multiple card brands. With routing information in hand, the terminal initiates a phone call to Delphi's Card Processing Service that finds the records for your account at Bacchus Bank via the *Bank Interchange Network.* The *open-to-buy amount* on your account is reviewed, and if it's sufficient for the sale amount you're requesting, an *authorization code* is provided to allow the sale's completion. This authorization step creates a temporary debit to your account under the assumption that the charge will be *settled* at some point in the near future. These debits prevent you from exceeding your credit limit with any subsequent charges. They'll remain on your account until one of two events occur: either a settlement of the charge is sent in, or the debit expires, freeing and returning the requested amount to your open-to-buy availability.

The POS terminal then prints out a sale receipt as a *record of charge* (ROC). The cashier tears it off, has you sign it, checks your signature for a match on the back of your card, and hands you the customer copy, a register receipt, your card, and your goods. While you'll never actually see what happens to place your charges on your bill, you trust that they get there.

As these charge authorizations occur, the merchant's terminal collects what are called *capture records* that uniquely identify the transactions. These records make up what will be called a *Batch Settlement File*. This settlement file may contain dozens, hundreds, or thousands of unique capture records, waiting to be processed through the banks that have issued cards on those accounts represented within the batch. When the batch is deemed sufficiently large (in terms of counts or total dollars), the *submission*, *capture*, and *settlement processes* begin.

## Differences That Charge Cards Bring into the Picture

The processing steps for charge cards and debit cards are identical to those for credit cards, with the exception of the mechanics involved in the authorization request and settlement processing. Because charge cards are not based on preset spending limits, the notion of an open-to-buy is irrelevant. Rather, charge card systems use other means to authorize or decline a charge request. Some companies use risk models, heuristics, patterns of spending, or manual review.

The sophistication in current systems also permits card companies to detect acts of fraud during POS transaction authorization processing. Because consumer buying habits can be modeled as patterns, any out-of-pattern spending may be deemed suspicious. If the card is suspicious (by the bank's criteria), and if it goes into what's called a *referral status*, the POS software simply turns this into a decline with a message for the card member to contact his or her bank offline. Often, merchants are asked to call an authorizer (a human being) who asks the merchant some questions or requests to speak to the cardholder. On the Internet, this is next to impossible to do. Cookies can't be used to weed out fraud charges.

Another important concept in the payment card world is the *open-loop* and *closed-loop* systems. When a financial institution serves as a broker between the user of its cards and the merchants that accept its card via transaction processing, it is called closed-loop systems. In other words, the same company owns both the cardholder and merchant relationship and steps in as an intermediary for all uses of the cards. American Express, Discover, and Diners Club are examples of closed loops. There is *one* American Express franchise, *one* Diners Club franchise (now owned by CitiBank), and *one* Discover Card company.

When a cardholder with a bank card from Bank A uses the card to transact with a merchant whose account is at Bank B and the transaction is processed through a different third party, it's called an open-loop system. Bank card systems using Visa and MasterCard are examples of open loops. In reality, neither the Visa nor MasterCard companies issue cards directly to consumers. Rather, they rely on their *member banks* to establish the lines and set the terms for consumer credit and debit within their own portfolios. They also rely on the banks to offer the Merchant Services to enable retailers to accept their cards as forms of payment. Typically a merchant's bank will provide such services in addition to the other banking services retailers need.

Visa and MasterCard serve as *Brand Association* authorities that establish and maintain the by-laws that frame the uses of their logos and the accompanying agreements between their member banks. Both Visa and MasterCard claim they each have over 20,000 member banks throughout the world to form their franchises.

In a closed-loop system, the cardholder and merchant accounts are typically operated on the same systems. Settlement (see the next section) then becomes a matter of debiting one side of the system and crediting the other side without any need to access the banking network, except to collect charges from any other acquirers who may process charges from the closed-loop system brand.

## Capture and Settlement

In *settling* a batch, the card processor must first receive it. The software in Apollo Marketplace's terminal initiates a file transfer that sends it via the private line to Delphi's Card Processing Service. At Delphi's, the batch is sorted by the Bank Identification Number (or BIN, a piece of information contained in the account numbers) in preparation for capture processing. Each set of transactions with the same BIN is sent to the bank identified by the code where the bank will turn those earlier temporary debits into permanent debits. Each bank sums up the total charges on its accounts and performs a wire transfer to the account indicated for Apollo Marketplace at the National Bank. This work is performed using *Automated Clearing Houses* (ACHs) that enable wire-transfer operations. At this point, your account at Bacchus Bank reflects your charge and awaits the cycle cut that prepares your billing statement. Once an entire batch is settled, Apollo Marketplace's account at the National Bank reflects the total batch's credits (less returns and voided transactions, and less processing and discount rate fees). With the next batch, the process begins anew.

As you see, at every step of the process, someone has a hand out looking for fees. Merchants are expected to pay these fees for the convenience of accepting payment cards and generally consider them a cost of doing business. It's also the merchant that pays when a customer discovers and reports that a charge is made using a lost or stolen card. In these cases, the bank issues the merchant what's called a *chargeback* to its merchant account, reversing the original credit to the account. On top of the chargeback, the merchant bank will charge a fee for handling and sometimes add additional nuisance fees to encourage the merchant to be more careful in what cards he or she is accepting. This situation is similar to the hefty fees levied when a checking account customer bounces a check. Force enough chargebacks or bounce enough checks, and your bank will begin to reevaluate its relationship with you and may terminate it altogether.

In the Point of Sale world, it's easy enough to take adequate precautions to prevent chargebacks (by checking a signature or a picture ID, for example), but in today's online world, the task is much more difficult, and thus far, banks are doing little to help merchants gain confidence when accepting payment cards online.

As you'll see later in this chapter, various methods and alternative payment systems for Internet uses are being developed to reverse the trends of increased fraud and chargebacks and to foster an atmosphere of mutual trust.

# Steps in an Internet-Based Payment Card Transaction

Let's revisit the Apollo Marketplace, but this time we'll bring the Internet into the picture to see what's different about the transaction. Along the way, we'll also point out some of the riskier pieces of the puzzle that attract hackers.

Over the months, the Apollo Marketplace's business had exploded. Customers, tired of the frequently long lines at the register, began demanding that the Marketplace offer shop-at-home services with rapid delivery.

A few months earlier, Delphi's Card Processing Service started offering Internet payment acceptance to those merchants that it services. It built *virtual POS* software that merchants can access via the Internet to process card authorization requests and settlement steps. The Marketplace decides to implement the online service.

Before any transactions can take place, merchant e-commerce Web sites need special software on their own servers to interact with the virtual POS. Let's assume that merchant systems are ready for such payment processing—we'll call that Phase 0. The subsequent phases outline the progression of the marketplace's online processes.

- **Phase 0: All merchant e-commerce software and requisite systems are in place.** The Apollo Marketplace web site at www.Apollo-market.com is up and running. The Marketplace offers a full line of products for sale through the simple click of a few buttons and local delivery within two hours. The site is a model of customer service. Traffic is on the increase, as are sales. Just last week the business took in over $95,000 from Web site sales alone!
- **Phase 1: The shopping experience.** At the Apollo's "Marketplace on the Web," customers are also helped out to prepare for checkout. The Marketplace has hypertext and content on its home page to attract people into using *their plastic* for shopping there. They have linked in privacy policies, visible assurances of security and trust, and even links to bank Web sites

that offer credit cards. With a single click on Apollo Marketplace's Home Page "Shop Now" button, shoppers can browse through the vast catalog of items, examine product details, and decide what they want to purchase.

- **Phase 2: Item selections.** As shoppers select their goods, they add them with the *shopping cart software* that Apollo Marketplace's Merchant Server uses, which dynamically tallies up the sale. Each item is added through a link directly below the product photograph and price.
- **Phase 3: Checkout.** Just as a shopper pushes his or her shopping cart to the cash register, the Merchant Server responds in kind when the consumer clicks the "Check Out" icon found on every page he or she sees. The shopping cart software adds up the items in it, adds sales tax and delivery and handling fees, and presents a list of the items and the totals to the customer. If the customer is satisfied with the order, he or she proceeds to the payment selection phase.
- **Phase 4: Form of payment selection and entry—RISK AREA 1.** With order totals still displayed on the screen, the consumer is given a choice of payment options. The customer may select from MasterCard, Visa, American Express, and Discover Card. The customer also has the option of paying cash-on-delivery (COD) or paying with a check-by-phone prior to order delivery. For our purposes, let's choose MasterCard as the form of payment. Customers are presented with a form in which to enter their payment card number or, if they prefer, a phone number to call it in.
    - **Risk Description.** Nonprotected form data is transported over the Internet as Hypertext Transfer Protocol (HTTP) plaintext—visible by any device (router, gateway, packet sniffer, etc.) on the network that touches the packets as they make their way from source to destination. This is the same problem that makes using email to transport sensitive or confidential data a poor choice. See the section later in this

chapter on the Secure Sockets Layer (SSL) protocol to mitigate this risk.

- **Phase 5: Payment Initiation Processing—RISK AREA 2.** When the form with the payment and purchase information is received back at Apollo Marketplace's Merchant Server, software then begins preparing an electronic message intended for the virtual POS at Delphi's Card Processing Service that operates the system on behalf of the National Bank merchant services. This message includes information about the merchant's identification, the payment card number, card holder name, expiration date, amount of charge, and other identifying information. Banks also offer additional services (at a fee, of course) to help reduce fraud and chargebacks. One of these services is called the Address Verification Service (AVS) to verify that the billing address provided matches the one in the records the bank keeps. To help differentiate themselves in a crowded market, other card processors offer a variety of value-added services to help reduce fraud and chargebacks.
    - **Risk Description.** On receipt of the HTTP Post operation, Apollo Marketplace's Web server holds sensitive and confidential information that's at risk for theft if the Web server is compromised. Depending on what the Web server does with the data (whether it stores it in its own file system or calls a back-office server for storage and processing), the risk model changes. In general, it's a poor idea to store any data on a Web server that's needed by mission-critical applications.
- **Phase 6: Payment Authorization Request and Response—RISK AREA 3.** Delphi's Card Processing Service uses the details about the amount of sale, the merchant account requesting it, and the payment card information to decide where to send the request. On Delphi's system, software is used to create a bank standard authorization request (using ISO8583 as the guide) and place it on the bank's Interchange Network that locates your account at Bacchus Bank. With an approval code from Bacchus Bank to proceed with the sale, software at

the National Bank sends back a message to the virtual POS on Delphi's system that authorizes Apollo Marketplace's merchant software to complete the sale. The Marketplace's system responds with a confirmation of the sale, produces an electronic version of a receipt or record of charge, and stores the record for eventual capture and settlement processing.

- **Risk Description.** The database containing payment card numbers, expiration dates, cardholder's names, and billing addresses is an irresistible target for both outside hackers and insider malcontents, so you must take precautions to prevent attacks on this data from all corners.

- **Phase 7: Delivery of Goods.** An hour and half goes by, and the customer hears a knock on the door. As a premier customer, Apollo Marketplace always gives this customer its best service. The customer accepts the box of goods with a signature on the delivery form, and the Marketplace is assured that the customer is satisfied and the sale is final.
- **Phase 8: Capture and Settlement—RISK AREA 4.** With the successful authorization code from Phase 6, Apollo Marketplace's merchant software received and stored a capture record. With the sale completed and the goods delivered, the Marketplace's merchant software can initiate a *Capture Request* to finalize the sale with Delphi's Card Processing system. With each *Capture Response*, the Settlement File builds up, awaiting the Marketplace's decision to deposit these receipts into the merchant account at the National Bank in exchange for funds transfer. Unless you're selling goods that can be delivered immediately over the Internet (software, images, etc.), you're left with no other choice but to wait until you ship your goods to the customer before you settle the charge. Bank card association rules often *forbid* authorization, settlement, and capture to occur together for Mail Order/Phone Order (MOTO) merchants, and almost all E-commerce sites are treated as MOTO merchants.

- **Risk Description.** Databases of settlement records are at risk while they're stored (see Risk Area 3 above), and they are at risk while in transport to and from the processor. As batch files, you may consider using standard File Transfer Protocol (FTP) to send and receive, but FTP cannot protect the contents during transport. Consequently, you'll need another channel to share this data or protect the Internet channel through cryptography.

While the actual processing work is identical to the work initiated via a POS terminal operating on a private network, virtual POS terminals make it possible to use the Internet for communicating between the parties needed for charge processing. To protect this information from prying eyes or outright theft, these systems rely on applied cryptography and other defense-in-depth mechanisms.

## Toxic Data Lives Everywhere!

As you can readily see, payment card data flows through a number of disparate systems as a charge traverses its way through the Internet and through private networks. Sometimes the data winds up in the wrong hands.

Wherever the data is stored (in the clear) or placed on the network (in the clear), it becomes at risk for theft. Hackers love credit card data for a number of reasons: It's easy to steal, it's easy to resell, and it's hard to get caught.

The best targets are those that are loosely protected, contain large volumes of payment card data, and are easy to access over the Internet. Merchant e-commerce servers should come to mind right about now. Protect yourself from becoming a target for payment card theft, and you protect the very nature of e-commerce itself! If you think about e-commerce data as a form of hazardous materials, you'll begin to get the right ideas about how to treat it with utmost care.

Understanding the phases of the Internet shopping experience and their related risk factors will help you instinctively determine what safeguards to employ, and where.

Damage & Defense...

### FBI Warns of Organized Credit Card Theft Ring

The FBI's National Infrastructure Protection Center (NIPC) issued a warning in March 2001 of credit card thieves from Eastern Europe who are targeting vulnerable U.S. e-commerce sites, and who have already stolen more than a million credit card numbers.

Groups of hackers from Russia and the Ukraine are targeting Microsoft NT systems that aren't up to the latest patch levels that close down the vulnerabilities they're able to exploit. The hackers attempt to extort the merchants for ransom on the data, and if their demands aren't met, they publish the card numbers on public Web sites.

After the NIPC warning surfaced, the Center for Internet Security published Steve Gibson's PatchWork Tool as a free tool for merchants to help them determine if their systems have all the patches that the FBI lists as necessary to repel the attacks. PatchWork can also audit the merchant systems to see if any telltale signs of a previous compromise are present. Go to www.cisecurity.org/patchwork.html to download the PatchWork Tool.

## Approaches to Payments via the Internet

Consumers on the Internet have it easy. All the banking laws revolving around payment cards favor the consumer, and no change to this policy is likely to happen anytime soon. Merchant chargeback rates are skyrocketing at the same time that the stakes are getting higher. Within the last year, Visa and MasterCard have tightened up their rules about how many chargebacks their merchant accounts can process before they start incurring fines from the merchant bank. Merchants can even lose their merchant accounts altogether.

Chargebacks are usually measured as a percentage of volume. If $100,000 goes through your merchant account in one month, and $1,000 gets charged back against your account, you've got a 1 percent chargeback rate. The magic number of 1 percent is the target that the banks would like to see. In the world of the Web, however, where fraud is by far the biggest problem, bank card associations are reporting that fraud has created an untenable situation that calls for immediate solutions. Although only 2 percent of Visa International Inc.'s credit-card transactions are acquired via the Internet, 50 percent of its disputes and discovered frauds are in that area, claimed Mark Cullimore, director of emerging technology at Visa International Asia-Pacific.

"This has become a significant issue for our industry over the past six months," he said. "It is all down to the problem of authentication, which has become the most important issue in the financial industry."

With the experience that's been gained to date with Internet payment card processing, new solutions to the fraud and chargeback problems appear on the market almost daily. Many of these systems rely on advanced uses of technology for risk management, including predictive models, scoring of confidence, etc.

In the next section, we'll look at what's being done to help merchants gain some confidence that the payment cards they accept are legitimate and in the hands of legitimate users.

# Options in Commercial Payment Solutions

If customers truly want the goods or services your online store offers, but they find bugs in the implementation of your product catalog or when using your shopping cart software, or they find your site less-than-easy to navigate, they're likely to forgive you and continue with their purchases. If they find bugs or problems with your payment processing, you can be sure you'll never see them again. Imagine that a happy customer will tell 4 or 5 friends, but an unhappy one will tell 10 or more. Your duty is to assure your customers that your site is reliable and that their private and confidential information is kept safe and sound.

Payment systems are viewed as two major categories—one where you operate the system on equipment you own or control (as in Phases 4, 5, 6, and 8 described earlier) and ones that are operated on your behalf by third-party providers. The next sections will explore these systems and their subcategories. First, it's essential to decide the route you want to choose.

Consider your overall business objectives first before you choose a route. If you can afford it, running your own operation may be your best choice. If you are more inclined to first "test the waters" and gain experience in online selling, or if you maintain a small catalog or have low sales volumes, you may not be able to justify the investment or security rigor that's required for an in-house system.

## Commerce Server Providers

A breed of Internet Service Providers (ISPs) that are tailored to the needs of the small to mid-sized online sales community is cropping up all over the globe. These *Commerce Server Providers* (CSPs) will lease you access to the system, allocate disk space for you to maintain your products, may offer multiple payment processing options, and may even provide robust site reporting and easy Web-browser-based interfaces for maintenance. Many of them are operated under secure and trustworthy environments and may even offer Web design service. Be careful, though—not all CSPs provide the same levels of service or the same payment processing fee structures. If your CSP is also a local ISP, customers may find your site too slow to tolerate because you're sharing resources with dial-up PPP users and other locally hosted content or transactional sites. As you pore through lists of CSPs, decide if you're willing to use all the services the CSP provides or if you can "bring your own service." You may find a better bargain in payment processing if your options are greater. You may also want to offer your customers a mix of payment types to increase your odds of a sale by those who can't or won't use credit cards online. For example, you may want CyberCash to process your credit card charges, your bank to process online checks, and Qpass to handle micropayments (for small dollar purchases like news articles, clip art, and shareware).

CSPs are also more likely to pay close attention to known security problems in Internet sales environments. To protect an electronic mall, CSP operators make huge investments in network and personnel infrastructures to satisfy security requirements and to keep a careful watch on how their hosted sites are being used.

When you're out shopping for a suitable CSP, make sure you ask the *tough questions* before you commit to their services. Areas to explore include these:

- Downtime schedules and frequency
- Service level agreements for performance and security
- Relationships with external payment acquirers and processors
- Fee structures
- Merchant server software and compatibility with your back-office systems and databases
- Store administrator functions and features
- Reputation
- Other customers you can contact for their opinions and experiences with the CSP

## Braving In-house Resources

Readers of this book are more likely to fall in the category of operators who use in-house systems and have far more decisions to make about operations and security. You can choose an outside payment processor service with whom your commerce server communicates, or you can operate your own POS processing software using secure architectures for e-commerce services. The choices you make here may lead you into further branches where still more decisions may need to be made, such as whether your merchant bank's processors are compatible with your POS software, which types of cards you're prepared to accept, and any special processing that may be required (such as fraud checks). Obviously, the more work you're willing to take on in building your own payment infrastructure, the fewer middlemen you'll need to involve, and the more revenue you'll be able to keep by avoiding certain middleman fees. But this processing work comes at a cost in added security requirements, added responsibilities, and greater strains on your computer equipment and staff.

To further complicate matters, all those choices mentioned are not necessarily mutually exclusive. You can mix and match them to maximize your customer's choices and optimize your profits. Be careful, though—hidden support costs increase as site complexity increases.

Some of the systems found in the category of in-house payment processors move the real-world POS technology to the virtual world by performing in software what would otherwise be accomplished with physical devices and cards. A small sampling of some commercially available systems include these:

- **Cybercash's ICVERIFY** (www.cybercash.com)
- **Verifone vPOS** (www.verifone.com)
- **Authorize.net** (www.authorize.net)
- **Verisign Payflow** (www.verisign.com)

In the next section you'll see how POS servers fit into e-commerce server architectures. In later sections we'll peek under the hood of Cybercash's ICVERIFY system to see how it supports payment processing requirements.

One common theme that's central to any payment processing environment is the security of the environment in which payments are made. Hack-proofing a payment-card handling system requires both secure architectures to ensure network and server-based security and the uses of complex cryptography protocols running atop the network layer—primarily at the application layer. Most of today's payment protocols incorporate multiple forms of applied cryptography for its functions.

In Chapter 5 you learned about Security Zones for discrete application processing of network segments (data storage, Web server farms, etc.) and learned how to group functions by their security requirements. A payment processing system necessarily requires a secure zone that's far away from the Internet connection. The best approach for creating these zones uses what are called *three-tier* or *n-tier* architectures.

When you're ready to expand your information-only Web site into an e-commerce capable site and have decided to bring all processing in-house, you'll want to start out with a secure processing environment rather than try to add security later (it never works out right!). Aside from all the other issues related to operating a data-center (regardless of size), the choices for your network architecture could spell the differences between success and doom. To help reduce many of the threats to e-commerce, the three-tier network implementation comes to the rescue. Three-tier or n-tier architectures separate processing into abstract layers, typically by separating work across Web servers, application servers, and database servers.

Security experts embrace three-tier systems for Internet, intranet, and extranet applications. When they're present, these three tiers—Web server(s), application server(s), and database server(s)—greatly reduce many of the threats to production back-office systems and networks and empower you to perform an excellent job of "border protection." These concepts arise from industry best practices and recommendations from security experts around the world. Because, by definition, your e-commerce site must be "security conscious," you're advised to utilize these principles as much as possible in your own designs. Figure 6.1 illustrates one example of n-tier network architecture that's well suited for e-commerce and payment processing applications.

# Secure Payment Processing Environments

Three-tier systems benefit everyone in the organization, especially people in IT departments. The three-tier model is appealing for enterprise-wide distributed transaction-processing applications in that it offers these advantages:

- **Centralization** permits IT to control and secure programs and servers using an already accepted, mainframe-like environment that's scalable, predictable, and easily monitored.

- **Reliability** is enhanced because equipment resides in a controlled environment that can be easily replicated or moved onto fault-tolerant systems.
- **Scalability** is easier because servers or processors can be added to achieve acceptable levels of performance. Centralized database services tend to be optimal because constant monitoring leads to prevention and quick detection of server or network problems.
- **Flexible**, well-defined software layers permit the highest degrees of IT responsiveness to changing business needs. With lightweight and inexpensive client desktop requirements, wholesale changes to desktop systems can be made at any time without any effect on the program layer or the database layer, allowing companies to quickly adopt improvements in technology. Additionally, non-PC clients (e.g. POS devices, voice-response units, handheld devices, etc.) can be used at any time because the interfaces to the application are based on open industry standards and are well-defined to the developer.
- Existing mainframe services can be reused through the virtue of a **flexible data layer**. Mainframe services can be made to look just like any other data service layer, thus preserving the transaction processing capabilities of the mainframe. This is significant because mainframes tend to be optimal environments for high-volume transaction processing.
- Systems based on **open industry standards** allow companies to rapidly incorporate new technologies into the operation, without the concern of interoperability problems that exist in products based on proprietary approaches.

Figure 6.1 shows you how it's possible to add security as traffic moves beyond the Web servers into deeper tiers. As you move through the inner firewalls, you can turn off protocols that don't belong there. You can also enforce the uses of *trusted hosts* to help prevent unwanted requests from processing.

**Figure 6.1** A "Security Conscious" Payment Processing Environment

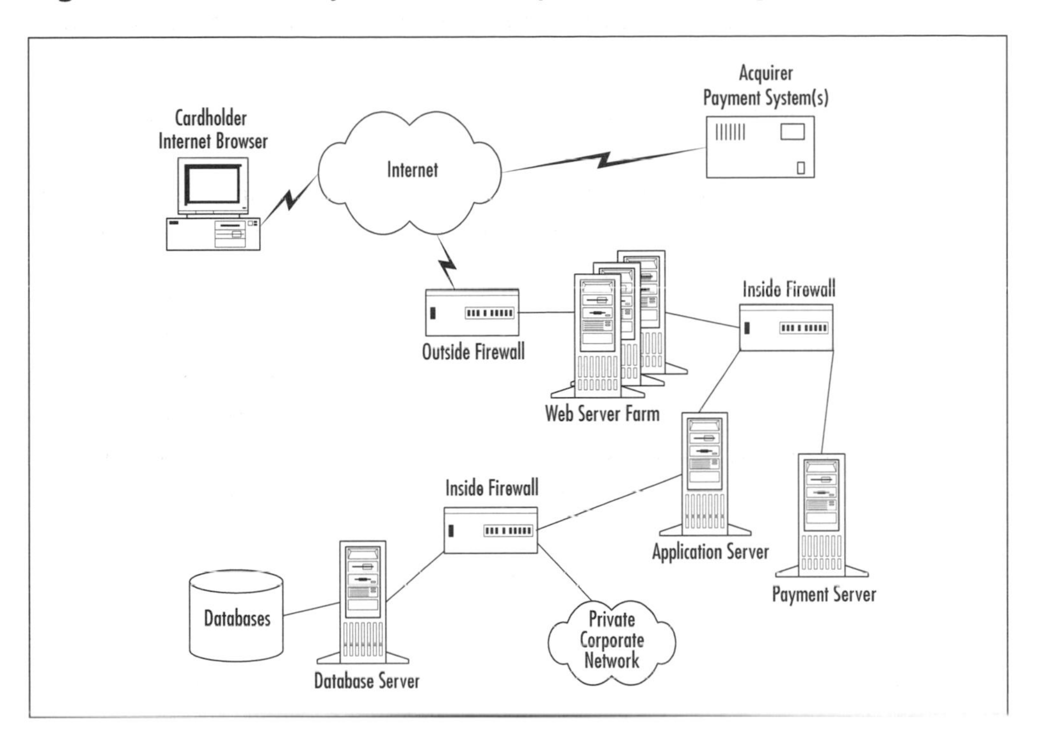


For performance reasons and the lack of any need for specific protection, you might opt to keep your materials "intended for the public" directly within the file systems of the Web servers themselves. Normally, this will include only information that people could otherwise locate via your other advertising channels (catalogs, images, marketing brochures, etc.). Any dynamically generated data (stored billing and shipping information, etc.) should be kept as far out of reach from the Internet as possible. Furthermore, any data that your customers supply via Web-based forms should immediately be removed from the Web server through as many firewalls as needed to safely secure it. It's this data that thieves want, so you must be extra careful with its handling. This is the *most* fundamental security precaution that you can take. Never store anything on the Web server itself because you can *never* really be sure the server will remain constantly in your control. Should a man-in-the-middle attack occur, perhaps a few Web pages will be spoofed, but your important assets will remain secure. Never operate your CGI or ASP scripts on the Web server that's handling public HTTP traffic. Rather, move them to the application zone or tier to make it harder for hackers who take over the Web server to learn useful information about back-office operations and databases. The idea here is to limit the damage from a successful attack on the Web tier by not permitting any peeking into other network zones that contain valuable company assets.

Control over the Web server zone using these principles mitigates most of the risks identified in Risk Areas 2, 3, and 4 of the shopping experience described earlier in this chapter.

Another sound measure you can take is to switch the protocols your network supports as you move backward. Because of inherent HTTP protocol vulnerabilities, you don't want it running past the outer firewall. Permitting HTTP routing into the back office places you at risk of hackers tunneling through HTTP to try to take over another server. Cut them off at the knees! Consider using protocols like CORBA/IIOP, RMI, socket connections via TCP, or DCOM on Microsoft NT to gain access to services residing on the Application tier. From the Application tier to the Database tier, switch the protocols on the firewalls again, only allowing Open Database Connectivity (OBDC) for SQL Server, native database clients (e.g., Sybase's OpenClient, Oracle's SQL*Net, etc.), and message queuing protocols, like Microsoft's MSMQ and IBM's MQSeries.

With the three-tier approach you can begin to see how to add still more layers of security both between and within each tier. Before the outer firewall, consider using intrusion detection systems to scan for known attack signatures and to automatically alert those in charge of the network—in real time (see Chapter 5). The uses of cryptography for security both at the transport layer and the application layer are also possible without rewriting programs. Later you'll see how the Secure Sockets Layer (SSL) protocol for encrypted communications of information and the Secure Electronic Transaction (SET) protocol for credit card information—running atop the architecture described—can help turn your e-commerce site into a genuine citadel.

*Trusted hosts* are another security measure that you may elect to use. Using Access Control Lists (ACLs) on your application servers helps to thwart attempts at running or installing programs without the authority to do so. If your application software can somehow be identified as legitimate and trusted, you add still another layer of protection to your resources. Yet another approach might use server-to-server authentication with digital certificates to provide two-way assurances that application requests and responses are legitimate.

Fixed (static) access control information (database log-in IDs and passwords stored as parameters and database connection strings) that you store on your servers should be kept in the most obscure forms possible. Never leave this type of information *in the clear* anywhere on the file systems. Move them to registries on the operating system in encrypted forms, or encrypt the configuration files themselves. Even if the server is hijacked, the attacker will still have a hard time accessing other systems or doing anything destructive.

On the Database tier, consider encrypting the contents—at the field level, the row level, the table level, or at the entire database level. Different data elements call for different situations, so analyze your needs carefully. Where audit trails of activity are crucial, turn on database auditing to help in monitoring activity or for prosecution purposes. Implementing security controls on the Application tiers and the Database tiers helps to mitigate many of the other risks identified in Risk Areas 2, 3, and 4 of the shopping experience.

## Additional Server Controls

We've looked at switching protocols and closing ports on firewalls, but there's still more to do at the server level:

- Make certain that your e-commerce servers and any payment system processors are running on separate servers that are insulated from both the Internet and from other domains within your organization. Remove all unnecessary server software that's not specifically for operational purposes. This may include language compilers, Perl/CGI/PHP libraries, administrative utilities, and factory-supplied logons and passwords.

- Firewalls should disallow FTP, telnet, or requests on any open ports.
- Don't operate software such as FTP, telnet, or email systems on any e-commerce server or Web server hardware. Instead use a separate server for these functions.
- Whenever remote operations (telnet, xterm, etc.) are needed, make sure the Secured Socket Handler (SSH) and Secure Copy (SCP) are used. These protocols secure the data in transmission using encryption.
- Make sure httpd and merchant server software (catalog and shopping cart software) is protected against hostile browsers by keeping your Web servers patched with all the latest patches, and monitor the security advisories for newly discovered vulnerabilities and patches on common Web server software implementations.

As much as possible, set up your servers to provide unique functions and capitalize on the distributed nature of the network.

## Controls at the Application Layer

Through the logical access control mechanisms afforded by intelligent distributed designs rooted in the principles described previously, you'll foil many of the attacks on your site launched at the network itself. Application layer security addresses the aspects of *data security* not specifically covered at the network or on the server. In some instances, an application may duplicate some security measures that are also performed at the network by other services. Think of application layer security as the final door in a series of multiple locked doors that you must pass through to reach the programs and systems you need.

Often, these application layer controls rely on industry standards for data content, context, and security. Most of the industry standard methods to secure data at the application layer require robust uses of digital cryptography. POS processing, for example, needs cryptographic processing for securing data while it's in transit and while it's stored and processed within your stewardship. Let's take a look at some fundamental principles of applied cryptography; then we can examine some of the common mechanisms used to protect e-commerce systems.

# Understanding Cryptography

*Cryptography* is the science (or art) of using and building cryptosystems. A *cryptosystem* disguises messages so that only intended people can see through the mask. Messages that are directly readable by humans are called *plaintext. Encryption* is the act of passing a plaintext message through a mathematical formula to create *ciphertext. Decryption* turns ciphertext messages back into plaintext messages. Cryptosystems can be simple or robust, but each one relies on a protocol or a set of well-defined rules that enable it to operate.

## Methodology

Although you don't need to become a cryptographer to take advantage of using cryptographic protocols for e-commerce systems, you'll benefit by understanding basic cryptography to add layers of trust back into a system. The next sections will take a look at the two basic methods that have evolved into secure mechanisms that modern e-commerce application programs rely on—the substitution and transposition methods.

### Substitution Method

The substitution method exchanges each letter of each word with a different letter using a scheme that's only known between the sender and the receiver(s). The most common example of the substitution method is known as Rotate or ROT "n" system. Julius Caesar, who had little trust in his messengers, used the Rotate system to communicate his marching orders to his generals in the field during battles.

Caesar's Rotate system relies on substituting one letter of the alphabet for another using a shared value (secret) that's known only between sender and receiver. If Rotate 3 is used, "A" becomes "D," "C" becomes "F," and so forth. If Rotate 26 is used, then no substitution occurs at all, leaving the message as plaintext. The shared secret (rotation value) must be in the hands of the receiver before the first encrypted message arrives and must be kept consistent until instructed to use a different secret. As you'll see later on, the sharing of secrets is one of the most significant challenges of cryptography.

With today's modern computer systems, a message encrypted using the Rotate cryptosystem could be cracked rather quickly simply by trying all possible rotation values and inspecting the results. This technique—called a *brute-force* attack—succeeds more often than you'd like to think. Almost no one uses the original Rotate system on its own today because, frankly, it's not very secure.

## Transposition Method

Transposition methods for cryptography are used to "scramble" the contents of a message using a shared secret between the sender and receiver(s). Let's look at the method to see how it's an improvement over the substitution method. Suppose you want to send me the secret message: "COMMENCE BOMBING RUN AT MIDNITE: TARGET ALPHA TANGO."

Here's the approach:

- **Stage 0: Select, agree on, and share a secret or *key* value we'll use for further communications.** In this phase, we'll choose a word that's six letters or more, preferably one without any letters that repeat. Next, we need to share the secret between us, but we also need assurances that no one can eavesdrop on our communications. If we're within arm's reach, I can write down the secret on a piece of paper, hand it to you, ask that you memorize it, and destroy the paper afterward. If handing you the secret is not practical, we've got a larger problem to solve. If we're not extra careful with the process of sharing secret keys, there's little point in proceeding. If I intend to use the Internet for further communication, I'd opt to share the secret with you using a channel *other than* the Internet to mitigate the threats of eavesdropping. Most likely, I'd choose to send you the secret in a sealed envelope using a trusted courier who can check your ID and obtain a signature, proving that you received it securely.

Alternatively, I might use a different secret that I share with you over the telephone that I'll use to encrypt the *real* secret that I'll send you via the Internet. Cryptographers call this a Key Encrypting Key, or KEK. The point is that you can never be too careful when moving key materials about. Wherever the activities of key generation, key sharing, or key replacement are needed, you'll want to ensure that the tightest security measures ride beside them.

- **Stage 1: Encrypting the message.** Here the sender encodes the message using the protocol along with the keyword already selected and shared.
- **Stage 2: Sending the message.** With the message disguised, the sender uses any communication channel to share the ciphertext.
- **Stage 3: Decrypting the message.** Once the encoded message is received, the receiver performs the steps of decryption (the mirror image of encryption) turning the ciphertext back into plaintext.

## Transposition Example

In this example, let's imagine we've found an impervious way to share our secret and we've selected the keyword **SECURITY**. In the Internet world, software developers usually rely on known industry standard *key-exchange* processes that are generally regarded as impervious to eavesdropping attacks.

1. Write down the shared secret as column headings along the top of a piece of paper:

```
S    E    C    U    R    I    T    Y
```

2. Write down the order of the letter's appearance in the alphabet directly underneath the letter. "C" is first, "E" is second, and so forth):

| S | E | C | U | R | I | T | Y |
|---|---|---|---|---|---|---|---|
| 5 | 2 | 1 | 7 | 4 | 3 | 6 | 8 |

3. Write down the message below the column headings, wrapping around to the next line once you reach the end of the row and eliminating the spaces and punctuation between words:

| S | E | C | U | R | I | T | Y |
|---|---|---|---|---|---|---|---|
| 5 | 2 | 1 | 7 | 4 | 3 | 6 | 8 |
| C | O | M | M | E | N | C | E |
| B | O | M | B | I | N | G | R |
| U | N | A | T | D | A | W | N |
| T | A | R | G | E | T | A | L |
| P | H | A | T | A | N | G | O |

4. Read down along each column in the order previously assigned and write down the letters you find (The column for letter "C" is first, "E" is second, and so forth):

```
MMARA  OONAH  NNATN  EIDEA  CBUTP  CGWAG  MBTGT  ERNLO
```

5. Send the ciphertext message using any channel you want. Because you've kept the shared secret secure, there's little fear the message will be deciphered immediately unless the secret appears along with it *and* an attacker knows what we're up to.

## *Transposition Example Decryption*

Once I receive the message, I follow the same steps you used to encrypt it because I already know the secret.

1. Write down the shared secret as column headings along the top of a piece of paper.

| S | E | C | U | R | I | T | Y |
|---|---|---|---|---|---|---|---|

2. Write down the order of the letter's appearance in the alphabet directly underneath the letter.

| S | E | C | U | R | I | T | Y |
|---|---|---|---|---|---|---|---|
| 5 | 2 | 1 | 7 | 4 | 3 | 6 | 8 |

3. Write the groups of letters vertically underneath the ordered set of numbers. The first group goes under "C-1," the next under "E-2," and so forth.

| S | E | C | U | R | I | T | Y |
|---|---|---|---|---|---|---|---|
| 5 | 2 | 1 | 7 | 4 | 3 | 6 | 8 |
| C | O | M | M | E | N | C | E |
| B | O | M | B | I | N | G | R |
| U | N | A | T | D | A | W | N |
| T | A | R | G | E | T | A | L |
| P | H | A | T | A | N | G | O |

4. Read across each row, skipping to the next when the end is reached, revealing the original message:

```
COMMENCE BOMBING RUN AT MIDNITE: TARGET ALPHA TANGO
```

With subsequent messages, you repeat the activity beginning with Step 4 for encryption. Even with this simple example, you can see how a protocol is formed:

- The steps are well-defined.
- They must be performed in order.
- They cannot be altered.
- None of the steps can be skipped.

If you can accomplish this by hand with only pencil and paper, imagine what you could do with a computer! In fact, cryptographers rely on these same methods, but they use far longer secrets with far more robust techniques.

# The Role of Keys in Cryptosystems

Keys (secrets) used for encryption and decryption come in two basic forms—symmetric and asymmetric—simply meaning either the same key is used to both encrypt and decrypt, or a pair of keys is needed.

## Symmetric Keys

When you use the same key to both encrypt and decrypt a message, it's called *symmetric key cryptography*, and it is the method we used in the example. The most common form of symmetric key cryptography is the Data Encryption Standard (DES). It was developed by IBM at the request of the U.S. government. DES was adopted as a Federal Information Processing Standard (FIPS) in 1976 for use with unclassified government communications between agencies. It uses 64 bits of data (8 bytes) with a 56-bit (7 byte) key within it. Triple DES (3DES) is identical, but it uses a double-length key (128 bits) that encrypts, then encrypts, then encrypts again (called *folding* in cryptospeak). DES is commonly used by banks to protect your PIN number when you enter it on an ATM or POS keypad. Your PIN is never stored by the bank as you know it—it's always stored in encrypted forms to prevent its use in the event of theft. If the ATM enciphers your PIN exactly as your bank stores it, then access is granted.

As mentioned earlier, one of the most significant challenges with symmetric key cryptography lies in sharing keys prior to needing them. To help out in that task, we turn to asymmetric key cryptography.

## Asymmetric Keys

With *asymmetric key cryptography*, a pair of keys is needed. A message encrypted using one key can be decrypted only by using the other and vice versa. One of the keys is called a *public key*, and the other is called a *private key*. Fundamental to operating properly, we must ensure that the private key *always* remains private and is never shared or copied from where it was generated.

Using asymmetric key cryptography, I share my public key with everyone I want to communicate with privately, but I keep my private key far away from everyone else. My private key essentially IS my identity so that when you can successfully decrypt a message I send you with my public key, you know that it could ONLY have come from me. Conversely, you can rest assured that any message you send to me that's encrypted using my public key can only be read by me. That's the basis of asymmetric key or Public-Private Key (PPK) cryptography.

The two keys that compose a key pair are mathematically related, but neither can be derived from the other. Typically, the key lengths that are used with *strong* asymmetric key cryptography are 1024 bits long (128 bytes) and are meant to foil a brute-force attack on messages that are signed and encrypted using standard PPK applications.

PPK cryptography enables you to communicate over any open channel with high degrees of confidence and permit you to trust in these ways:

- **Authentication** Messages you receive are from their advertised source.
- **Privacy** Messages you send can be read only by their intended receiver(s).
- **Message Integrity** All messages sent and received arrive intact.

# Principles of Cryptography

Cryptosystems are considered either weak or strong with the main difference being the length of the keys used by the system. U.S. export controls are showing signs of loosening, but they continue to discourage the export of strong cryptography because of fears that government enemies will use the systems to thwart eavesdropping on illegal or anti-government activities. DES was originally designed so that the supercomputers owned by the National Security Agency (NSA) could be used for cracking purposes, working under the premise that no other supercomputers of their sort are in the public hands or control.

Strong cryptography always produces ciphertext that appears random to standard statistical tests. Because keys are generated for uniqueness using robust random number generators, the likelihood of their discovery approaches zero. Rather than trying to guess a key's value, it's far easier for would-be attackers to *steal* the key from where it's stored, so extra precautions must be taken to guard against such thefts.

Cryptosystems are similar to currency—people use them because they have faith in them. You can never *prove* that a cryptosystem is unbreakable (it's like trying to prove a negative), but you can demonstrate that the cryptosystem is *resistant* to attacks. In other words, there are no perfect cryptosystems in use today, but with each failed attempt at breaking one, the strength of the faith grows. The moment a cryptosystem is broken (and knowledge of that is shared), the system collapses and no one will use it anymore. The strongest systems resist all attacks on them and have been thoroughly tested for assurances of their integrity. Strength of a cryptosystem is described in the size and the secrecy of the keys that are used, rather than keeping the algorithm itself a secret. In fact, when a new cryptosystem is released, the algorithms are also released to allow people to examine and try to create an attack strategy to break it (called cryptanalysis). Any cryptosystem that hasn't been subjected to brutal attacks should be considered suspect. The recent announcement by the National Institute of Standards and Technology (NIST) of the new Advanced Encryption System to replace the aging DES system (described earlier) underscores the lengths to which cryptographers will go to build confidence in their cryptosystems.

For those of you with a keener thirst for knowledge in the field of cryptography, I strongly recommend that you obtain a copy of the book that's considered the bible for cryptographers, *Applied Cryptography: Protocols, Algorithms, and Source Code in C, 2nd Edition* by Bruce Schneier (John Wiley & Sons, ISBN: 0471117099). There's also a terrific tutorial about it on the Web called "Cryptography: a summary of the field for engineers" by Bennett Todd. You can find it at: http://people.oven.com/bet/crypto/crypto-summary.html.

## Understanding Hashing

Now that you've begun to understand the principles of public and private key pairs, it's time to examine how PPK systems are used for authentication, privacy, and message integrity. To start, you need to be familiar with a computer programming technique called *hashing*. A hash is a transformation of data into distilled forms that are unique to the data. You run a document through a one-way hashing formula to produce a small *fingerprint* that's unique but repeatable for that exact stream of data. This process is also called digesting data or creating a message digest. The Unix operating system employs this principle for storing passwords in the /etc/passwd file.

## Digesting Data

Several well-known digest-creation techniques, including the Secure Hashing Algorithm (SHA-1) and the Message Digest 5 (MD5) algorithm, are common with e-commerce systems. Using SHA-1, unique message digests (fingerprints) are computed such that the chances of two different messages computing to the same digest values are 1 in 1 X $10^{48}$. After computing the message digest for your message, you'll encrypt it using your *private* key and append (attach) the encrypted message digest to your original message. This process is called creating a *digital signature* or *digitally signing* a message, and it is illustrated in Figure 6.2. At this point, if you send your message to your recipient (who already holds a copy of your public key), he can "test" your signature to see if the message really came from you and arrived unaltered.

**Figure 6.2** A Digitally Signed Message

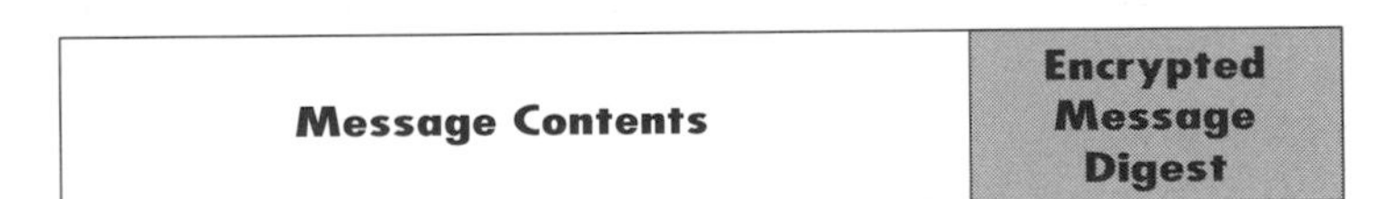


This is how it works: Because the digital signature can be decrypted only by using your public key, your recipient knows that you created the digest because you *never share* your private key with anyone else. Your recipient's software also uses the same hashing algorithm that you used to compute message digests, so he or she runs the message received through it. He or she (his or her software) then compares the newly calculated message digest to the one that he or she successfully decrypted from you. If they match, the recipient is now also assured that the message received is the same message that you sent without any alteration.

Think of digital signatures in a similar vein as Notary Public services. If you receive a notarized document, you have a high degree of assurance that the person who signed it is the person he or she claims. As a society we *trust* notaries. Digital signatures actually enhance the process and add security to communications. If I were to send you a nine-page document bearing a Notary seal, you'd know it came from me, but you wouldn't know if the document was altered after the notary attested to my signature. With a digital signature if even a single byte of data were changed, the message digest computes to a completely different value. If your recipient's comparison of the two digests doesn't match, the software will indicate that the message should not be trusted and recommend that it be discarded.

With a single process, we can add both sender authentication and message integrity to the otherwise untrusted communication channel we call the Internet. But we still need to take care of privacy, too.

In practice, you would never send a digitally signed message out on its own. Because the digest is appended to the plaintext message, the message itself could still be read by anyone who intercepted it en route. Rather, you'll need to put the message and its digest into a safe and secure envelope before you send it on its way. To accomplish this, you'll use your *recipient's public key* (of which you already have a copy or know where to find it) to encrypt both the message and digest, creating what's called a *digital envelope*. Because no one else has the private key from your recipient's key pair, you're assured that no one else can "open" the envelope. Now you have all the elements you want—sender authentication, privacy, and message integrity. A graphical look at the digital signing process is found in Figure 6.3. A look at the process to create digital envelopes is found in Figure 6.4.

**Figure 6.3** Using Public-Private Key Pairs to Create a Digital Signature

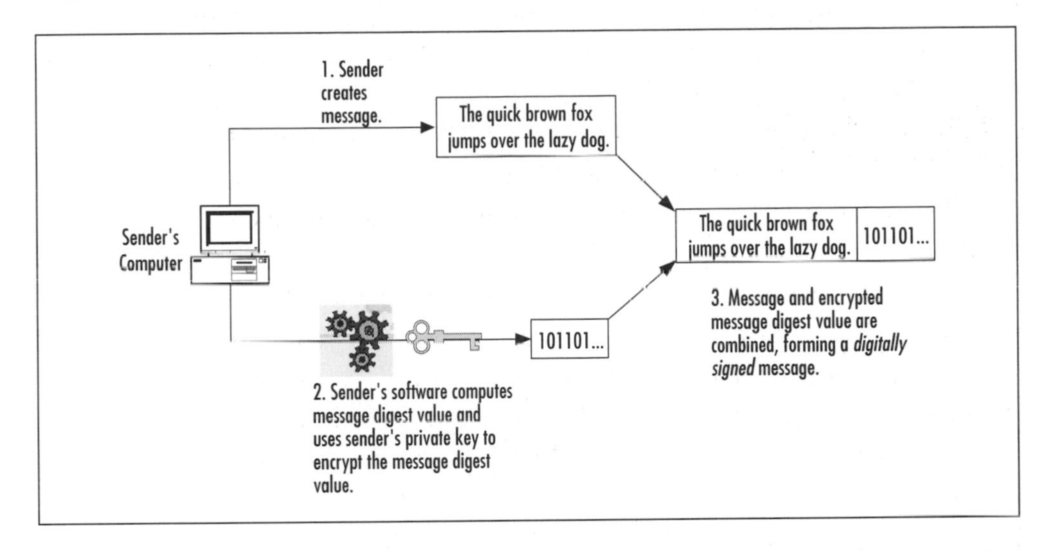


**Figure 6.4** Using Public-Private Key Pairs to Create a Digital Envelope

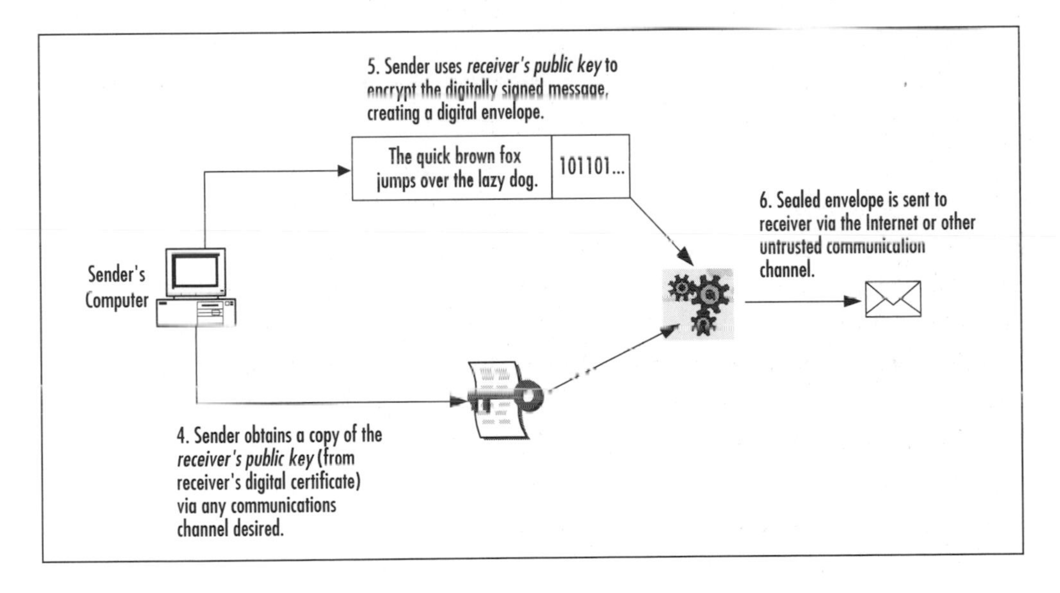

In summary, Table 6.1 shows the purposes and uses of public and private keys to secure electronic communications.

**Table 6.1** Public/Private Key Uses

| | Create Digital Signature | Verify Digital Signature | Create Digital Envelope | Open Digital Envelope |
|---|---|---|---|---|
| Sender's private key | X | | | |
| Sender's public key | | X | | |
| Receiver's public key | | | X | |
| Receiver's private key | | | | X |

You can't rely on the users of your e-commerce systems to manage their own cryptographic keys and provide the amount of trust that's needed for success. Because of these needs for high levels of trust, businesses require a predictable infrastructure under which key management is the only theme. As an environment of trusted relationships, e-commerce requires a Public Key Infrastructure (PKI) that you'll need to build for establishing and maintaining trusted *Digital Certificates*.

## Digital Certificates

Digital certificates behave in the online world the same way driver's licenses, passports, and other trusted documents behave outside of the online world. Using the basic public-private key (PPK) cryptography principles, digital certificates offer the security that people demand for private communications and electronic commerce. The digital certificate standard, X.509, governs how certificates are constructed and used between communicating parties.

When used for signing electronic messages (creating digital signatures), the private key associated with the public key that's contained in the digital certificate creates the unforgeable fingerprint (digest) for the message.

For PPK's successful operation, the principles dictate that public-private key pairs are obtained in a manner that's impervious to attack.

The primary assumption is that a person's private key will always remain private. Digital certificates help to implement this principle.

## CCITT X.509

In 1988, X.509 became an International Telecommunications Union (ITU) recommended standard and has since become a de facto industry standard for user authentication on open systems, such as the Internet. X.509 certificates are similar to notary seals in that they bind a person's identity to a pair (or pairs) of cryptographic keys.

Digital certificates are issued by a trusted party, called a *Certificate Authority* or CA. These CAs operate on behalf of those who wish to operate a Public Key Infrastructure (PKI) using X.509 recommended standards. Figure 6.5 illustrates the structure and contents of a typical X.509 public key certificate.

**Figure 6.5** An X.509 Public Key Certificate's Structure

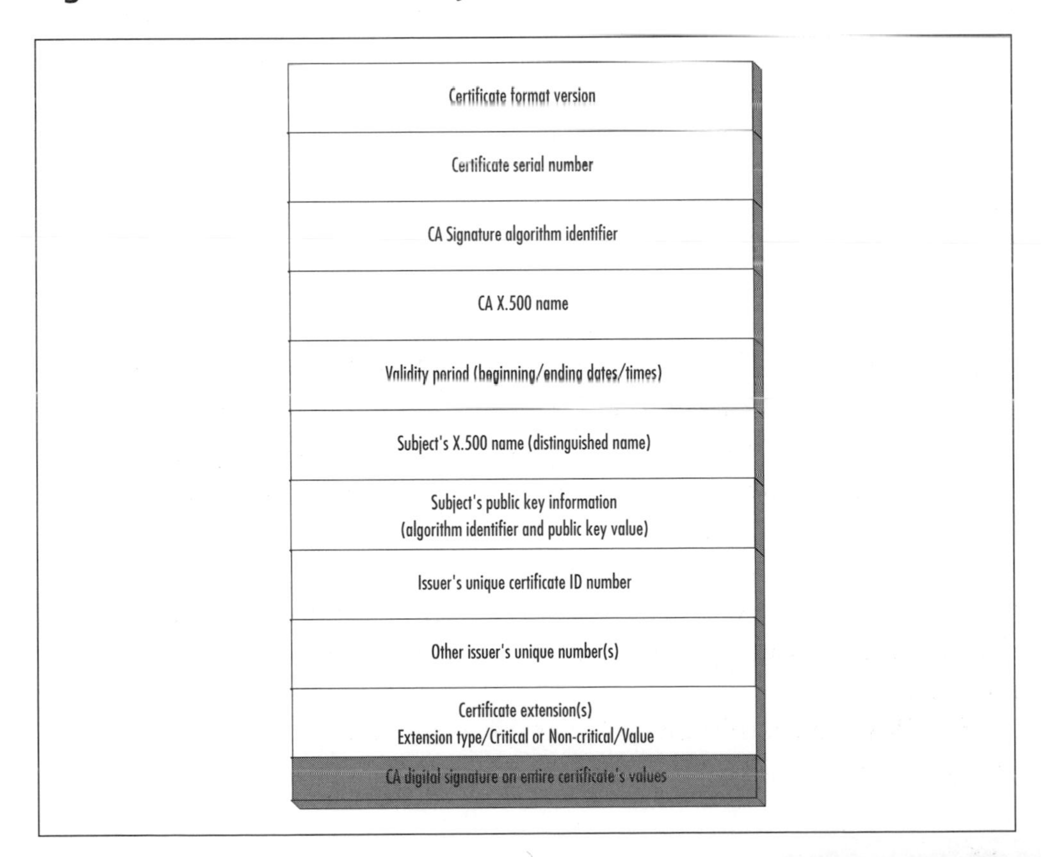

Certificates often contain extensions (shown at the bottom of Figure 6.5) that describe how the certificate may be used and under which conditions. In other words, a certificate that's used to access network resources cannot be used to access bank accounts. Each certificate is issued under specific uses and guidelines, as described within the certificate's extensions.

CAs maintain a "Tree of Trust" that's checked each time a certificate is presented as proof of one's identity. Once the tree of trust is successfully traversed, proof of identity and proof of a person's right to use the key can be ascertained by the recipient.

Many of the higher-order e-commerce protocols, such as Secure Electronic Transactions (SET), use a robust set of digital certificates to authenticate people and resources for assurance that all parties possess the rights needed to transact. A corporation may issue digital certificates to its employees as an alternative to IDs and passwords for access to network services, mainframe applications, etc. These certificates will normally be stored in software that resides on the user's PC within a Web browser. Certificates may also be stored on Smart cards to permit access.

Using digital certificates, system users are offered high degrees of security along several dimensions of communications. Through their cryptography, anyone receiving a signed message, along with the public key in the sender's digital certificate, can be confident that the message came from the specific person (user authentication) and that the message itself arrived intact (integrity).

PKIs are often rather challenging to develop. Not only do they require extremely tight security measures to protect CA private keys, they're also difficult to transition from electronic forms to the real world.

Armed with a basic understanding of the principles of modern cryptography, we'll tour through some common implementations that are mixed and matched to produce useful work in securing e-commerce resources and data.

# Examining E-Commerce Cryptography

Let's take a look at a few cryptosystems that have come into e-commerce vogue over the years. Some of the categories we'll examine are these:

- Hashing functions (SHA-1 and MD5)
- Block ciphers (DES, 3DES, and AES)
- Implementations of RSA Public-Private Key (PPK)

## Hashing Functions

We looked at the more common hashing functions to create the message digest for digitally signed messages. Hashing-type functions can also be used with symmetric key cryptography, and the result of the operation is called a Message Authentication Code or MAC. When you hear the term *hash*, think of digital signatures, and when you hear the term *MAC*, think of shared secret cryptography operations.

Hashing is a powerful mechanism to protect user passwords on e-commerce sites. Should your site require IDs and passwords for personalization reasons, you'll want to store the passwords that people create in the form of a hash value. That way, even if a hacker steals your security database records, the hacker won't be able to use the data to impersonate your customers directly. Instead he or she will need to use additional resources (and time) to attempt to find out what passwords are associated with which user IDs. Unix operating systems have implemented this technique right from the start. Microsoft Windows NT implementations are similar, but they are considered weaker because of backward-compatibility issues with older versions of Microsoft operating systems.

The Secure Hashing Algorithm 1 (SHA-1) and Message Digest 5 (MD5) are the two most common variants of hashing functions that you'll encounter with e-commerce software. You'll also find these functions readily available in any cryptographic function toolkits that you purchase for use with software that you develop internally (Microsoft CryptoAPI, RSA Toolkit, etc.).

## Block Ciphers

Earlier we looked at the Data Encryption Standard (DES) and Triple-DES as the most common forms of symmetric key block cipher cryptosystems. DES uses a 56-bit (7 bytes + checksum byte) key (considered weak today), and Triple-DES uses a 112-bit (14 bytes + 2 checksum bytes) key (adequate for today).

Block ciphers are important for encrypting/decrypting data in bulk, such as files or batches of data. They're also useful for encrypting data in storage systems to prevent unauthorized access. Block ciphers may be used to encrypt data fields (attributes) in records and tables, entire records (except the keys), or entire files or tables. You might also consider using block-cipher cryptosystems to encrypt batch settlement data prior to FTP-ing it to your payment processor service bureau.

Besides DES and 3DES there are plenty of other block cipher algorithms out there, and many of them have already been subjected to brutal cryptanalysis attacks. In early October 2000, the National Institute of Standards and Technology (NIST) announced the end of a four-year search for a successor to the aging Data Encryption Standard (DES), used to protect nonclassified government information and systems. The Advanced Encryption Standard (AES) will be based on the Rijndael algorithm that takes its name from its Belgian co-creators, Vincent Rijmen and Joan Daemon. NIST expects that AES will be adopted by the U.S. Department of Commerce as a Federal Information Processing Standard (FIPS) sometime in 2001. AES will likely also be adopted by the private sector as well (just as DES was) and will find its way into encrypting sensitive corporate, e-commerce, and banking data.

## Implementations of PPK Cryptography

Public Private Key cryptography has found its way into numerous implementations intended to better secure Internet communications and prove identities. We'll take a quick look at these systems:

- Secure Sockets Layer (SSL)
- Transport Layer Security (TLS)

- Pretty Good Privacy (PGP)
- Secure Multipurpose Internet Mail Extensions (S/MIME)
- Secure Electronic Transactions (SET)
- XML Digital Signatures

# The SSL Protocol

SSL is the most popular form of PPK and has become the de facto standard for transporting private information across the Internet. It's intended to mitigate some of the risk identified in Risk Area 1 of the shopping experience. People have not only grown more comfortable in entering their payment card information into Secure Socket Layer (SSL)-protected sessions—they demand it and have grown to expect it. Unless you can offer them this minimal assurance of security for transporting private information, you're likely to end up with an empty virtual cash register. Most everyone who uses the Web recognizes the ubiquity of SSL. Figure 6.6 shows how Netscape Navigator browsers indicate that SSL is "active."

**Figure 6.6** An SSL-Enabled Web Browsing Session

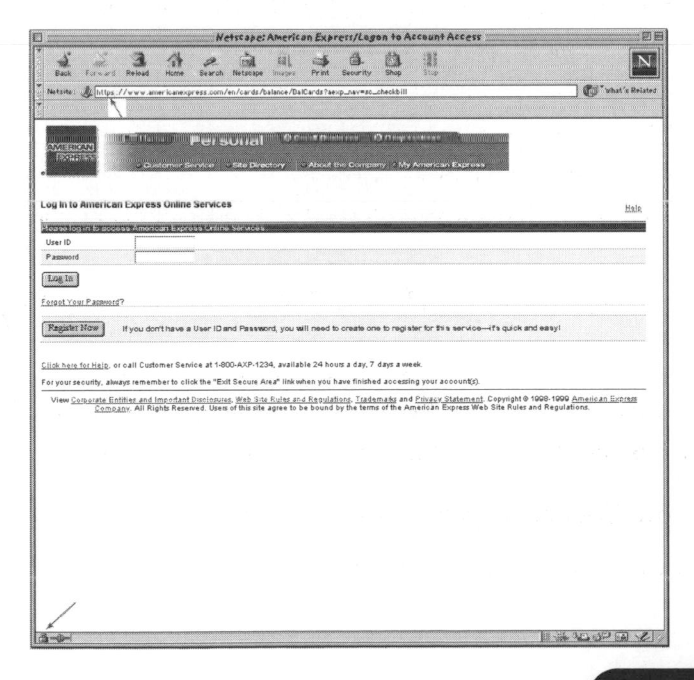

SSL addresses some of the concerns of transporting confidential data via the Internet. SSL's goals are to ensure the privacy of the connection, to authenticate a peer's identity, and to establish a reliable transport mechanism for the message using integrity checks and hashing functions. It does not go far enough, though, for E-commerce security in the eyes of most security analysts.

SSL was designed for client/server applications, preventing the unwanted tampering of data transmission, whether it be eavesdropping, data alteration, or message forgery. It's intended to ensure the privacy and reliability of communications between two applications. See Figure 6.7 for an illustration of the "handshake" between the various layers of protocol in SSL.

**Figure 6.7** The SSL "Handshake"

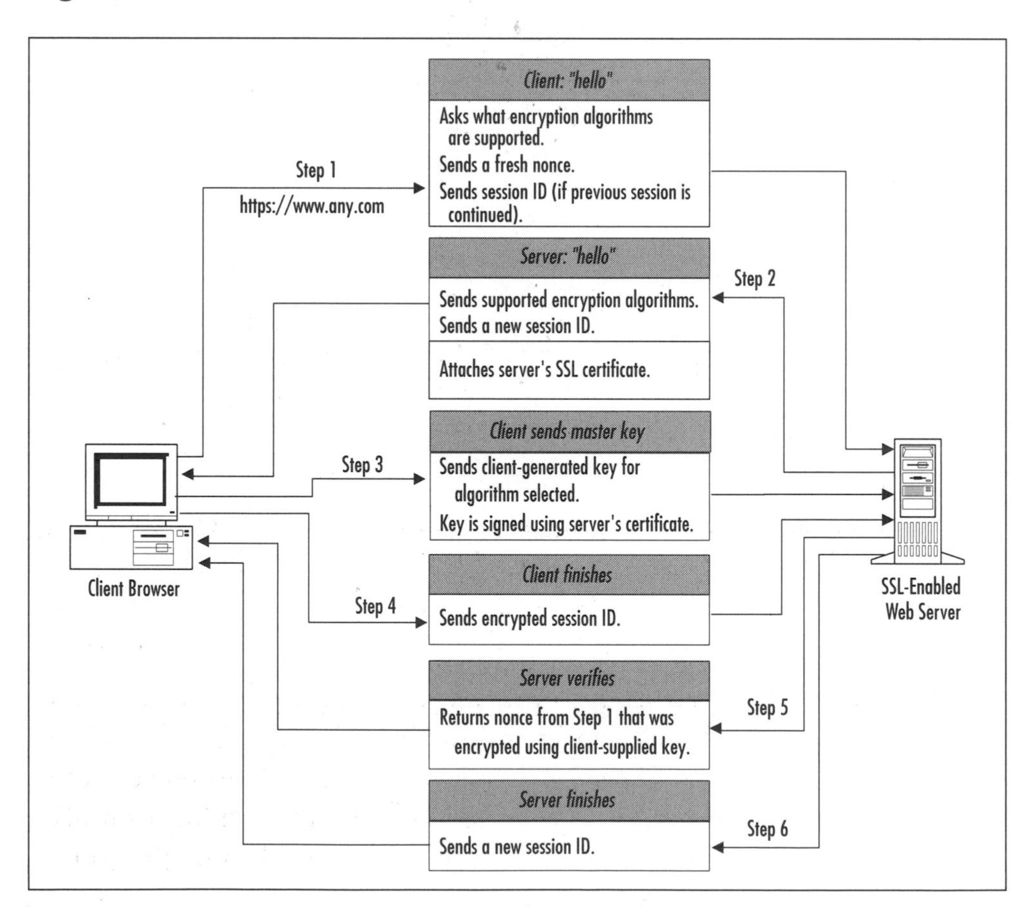

The handshake is used between clients and servers to agree on and share a session key that's needed for message passing as long as client and server remain engaged in conversation (as in a purchase transaction). Client computers can examine the server's SSL certificate and make certain trust decisions about it, but the merchant server does not share that luxury, leading to SSL's first criticism—mutual authentication is *not normally possible* because clients aren't electronically identifiable since they're seldom issued digital certificates for the credit cards by the issuing bank.

The second criticism of SSL lies in *how* the client authenticates the server. Recall the earlier discussion on the CA Tree of Trust where a digital certificate's signature can be *tested* all the way up to the root of the tree. With most of today's SSL implementations, merchant digital certificates are often treated as *root certificates* where no further authenticity checks are performed. Sometimes these trusted certificates are issued to fraud operators or are simply stolen from a legitimate owner who failed to protect the associated private keys.

# Transport Layer Security (TLS)

The TLS protocol is designed to provide communications privacy over the Internet. The protocol allows client/server applications to communicate in ways that are designed to prevent eavesdropping, tampering, or message forgery. The goals of TLS Protocol are to provide the following:

1. Cryptographic security. TLS should be used to establish a secure connection between two parties.
2. Interoperability. Independent programmers should be able to develop applications utilizing TLS that will then be able to successfully exchange cryptographic parameters without knowledge of one another's code.
3. Extensibility. TLS seeks to provide a framework into which new public key and bulk encryption methods can be incorporated as necessary. This will also accomplish two subgoals: to prevent the need to create a new protocol (and risking the introduction of possible new weaknesses) and to avoid the need to implement an entire new security library.

4. Relative efficiency. Cryptographic operations tend to be highly CPU intensive, particularly public key operations. For this reason, the TLS protocol has incorporated an optional session caching scheme to reduce the number of connections that need to be established from scratch. Additionally, care has been taken to reduce network activity.

TLS is slowly working its way into the mainstream of secure Internet communications. Developers are continuing to work out interoperability problems between TLS and SSL, and progress is occurring.

## Pretty Good Privacy (PGP)

PGP is a distributed key management approach that does not rely on Certificate Authorities. Users can sign one another's public keys, adding *some degree* of confidence to a key's validity. Someone who signs someone else's public key acts as an introducer for that person to someone else, with the idea that if they trust the introducer, they should also trust the person who's being introduced.

PGP was written by Phil Zimmerman in the mid 1980s, and it remains popular because of its ability primarily to encrypt electronic mail. Zimmerman distributed his first version of PGP over the Internet as freeware, then ran into legal problems because he didn't realize he had given away the rights to public key cryptography patents (most notably the RSA patent). Legal matters were eventually straightened out in 1993 when ViaCrypt, a company with a valid license for the patent, worked out a deal with Zimmerman to distribute a commercial version of PGP. Today, NAI (www.nai.com) is the predominant player in the PGP world.

One of the main criticisms of PGP is its reliance on what is known as an informal *Web of Trust* rather than the more structured hierarchy (tree of trust). With a Web of Trust multiple people may certify the authenticity of another person's public key. Critics of PGP claim that you can't, for example, get a user's public PGP key from the Internet and feel secure in the belief that the public key really belongs to whom you think it does. Limitations on the Web of Trust make PGP's uses impractical for conducting electronic commerce on the Internet. Instead, banks and credit card companies use structured hierarchical networks because of sophisticated risk models that a Web of Trust can't satisfy.

## S/MIME

Based on technology from RSA Data Security, the Secure/Multipurpose Internet Mail Extensions (S/MIME) offers another standard for electronic-mail encryption and digital signatures. S/MIME, along with a version of PGP called "Open PGP," are implemented in Netscape Communications Corp. Web browsers. Unfortunately, the dual electronic-mail encryption standards are creating problems for users while vendors continue to clash over whose standard should dominate.

S/MIME and Open PGP use proprietary encryption techniques and handle digital signatures differently. Simply put, if Person A uses a Web browser that supports S/MIME and tries to communicate with Person B who uses a different browser supported by PGP, the two individuals most likely will not be able to communicate successfully.

## Secure Electronic Transactions (SET)

Secure Electronic Transaction (SET) addresses most of the consumer demands for privacy when using a credit card to shop online. SET's uses are specific to the payment acceptance phases of the shopping experience. It covers the steps from the point a particular payment card is selected for use through the point the merchant completes the transaction and settles the batch with its acquirer bank or processor.

SET was released to developers in draft form on June 24, 1996. SET is embodied in three separate documents, containing sufficient specifications for developers to build components that would *bolt on* to existing Web browsers, merchant commerce servers, and financial institution credit authorization systems. SET appears as the following:

- **Book 1.** The business description containing background information and processing flows. It was intended as a primer on software that interfaces with payment systems and employs public-key cryptography.

- **Book 2.** The programmer's guide containing the technical specifications for the protocol intended for use by software developers who wish to build cardholder and merchant software components.
- **Book 3.** The formal protocol definition, intended for use by cryptographers analyzing SET's security aspects, writers producing programming guides for toolkits or components, and system programmers developing cryptographic and messaging primitives.

On May 31, 1997, SET Version 1.0 was released to the public. SET addresses seven major business requirements:

- Provide confidentiality of payment information and enable confidentiality of order information that is transmitted along with the payment information.
- Ensure the integrity of all transmitted data.
- Provide authentication that a cardholder is a legitimate user of a branded payment card account.
- Provide authentication that a merchant can accept payment card transactions through its relationship with an acquiring financial institution.
- Ensure the use of the best security practices and system design techniques to protect all legitimate parties in an electronic commerce transaction.
- Create a protocol that neither depends on transport security mechanisms nor prevents their use.
- Facilitate and encourage interoperability among software and network providers.

SET uses a robust set of strictly controlled digital certificates to identify cardholders, merchants, and acquiring payment gateways to ensure the security of messages passing through open channels like the Internet. It also uses multiple forms of symmetric key cryptography (like DES) to provide confidentiality of payment card and transaction data.

Giants in the industry offer software that meets the needs of each of SET's constituents. Suites of SET-compliant software are available from IBM, VeriFone, CyberCash, and a few others. To date, SET still longs for mainstream acceptance, and pilot testing of it around the world continues as merchant banks begin mandating it in riskier credit card fraud areas. For more detailed information about SET and its implementation, pick up a copy of *Building SET Applications for Secure Transactions* by Merkow, Breithaupt, and Wheeler (Wiley Computer Publishing, 1998).

# XML Digital Signatures

XML has exploded as an effective solution to many of the stickiest Internet communications problems but suffers from a lack of security mechanisms to protect XML documents and messages. IBM has implemented one potential solution to these problems with its XML Security Suite.

At the heart of the suite you'll find DOMHASH as a reference implementation for computing digital signatures on XML documents. IBM is offering the XML Security Suite as the basis for the digital signature discussions occurring at both the Internet Engineering Task Force (IETF) and the World Wide Web Consortium (W3C). IBM provides support for element-wise encryption on XML data, digital signatures on entire XML documents, and access control features that aren't possible under SSL transport layer security.

DOMHASH is intended as a canonicalizer (reduces to canonical forms) for XML digital signatures. A sample implementation is provided with the tool. You can download a copy of the XML Security Suite (for free) from IBM's alphaWorks site within the Resources:Tools area at: www.alphaWorks.ibm.com/av.nsf/xmltechnology.

Another XML security solution comes out of the banking industry. The Signed Document Markup Language (SDML) is also working its way through the IETF process. Its intent is fourfold:

- Tag individual text items within a document.
- Group the text items into document parts that can have business meaning and can be signed individually or together.

- Allow document parts to be added and deleted without invalidating previous signatures.
- Allow signing, cosigning, endorsing, co-endorsing, and witnessing operations on documents and document parts.

SDML is a part of the Electronic Check Project from the Financial Services Technology Consortium (FSTC). Another initiative from FSTC is called the Bank Internet Payment System, or BIPS. It includes a protocol for sending payment instructions to banks via the Internet, along with a payment server architecture for processing those payment instructions. Appendix G of the specification includes the XML structures and DTDs for BIPS.

Characteristics of Network Payment Protocol (NPP)-specific messages include the following:

- All messages are in XML.
- All messages begin with a BIPS XML header.
- All fields are self-identifying.
- All messages are signed.
- All messages include the originator's certificate.
- All request messages include a user-supplied transaction number.
- All message responses include the signature of the user on the original request.
- All response messages include a bank-supplied transaction number and the user-supplied transaction number.

As you see, there's more than one way to skin a cat, and cryptography implementations underscore that point. They're useful to e-commerce systems in a number of ways and under a number of different conditions. Unfortunately, there's no universal recipe that will cover all situations.

In spite of all the progress that's been made since the Internet became commercialized, SSL remains the baseline protection for transporting payment card data, and many merchants contend that it's *good enough* for e-commerce applications.

But SSL is *not* good enough on its own. E-commerce still requires careful controls over data after it's delivered via SSL, and failing to provide such controls is begging for disaster. Remember CD Universe? (See the sidebar, "CD Universe Succumbs to Credit Card Theft.")

Any of the in-house virtual POS software that you'll select to implement can't guarantee security unless you deliberately set out to install it securely on secure network resources. While much of the system's documentation offers advice on secure implementation, it can't provide it automatically.

In practical terms, this means hardening your application servers, setting up ACLs carefully, and subnetting the POS processing to zones where you can keep a close watch for intruders or unexpected behavior.

Tools & Traps...

## CD Universe Succumbs to Credit Card Theft

In December 2000, an 18-year-old Russian cracker, who goes by the nickname Maxus, sent an email message to InternetNews.com claiming to have breached the security of CD Universe.com, a now-defunct online music store. Maxus said he had defeated a popular credit card processing application and obtained a database containing more than 300,000 customer records from CD Universe.

He then posted these stolen card numbers to visitors of his Web site, titled The Maxus Credit Cards Datapipe. Included with the numbers were card expiration dates and cardholder names and addresses. With the click of a button, visitors could launch a script that purportedly obtained a valid credit card "directly from the biggest online shop database," according to a message at the site. Before the rogue site was taken down, it had handed out more than 25,000 card numbers to site visitors.

Maxus said that he set up the site after company officials at CD Universe failed to pay him $100,000 to keep silent about the

Continued

security hole. Maxus announced his new site on December 25 in an Internet Relay Chat group devoted to stolen credit cards. A guest book at the Maxus site contained dozens of entries from visitors, many of them in Russian.

Elias Levy of SecurityFocus.com explained to MSNBC, "He claimed that he was able to use the software to take a charge from one account and credit it to a different credit card—basically doing a money transfer. But this is not the same thing as a hole being used to steal the credit cards in the first place." It's unclear whether ICVerify was the source of the vulnerability, but it's almost certain Maxus found access to years' worth of plaintext database log files, saved and unencrypted by CD Universe.

# Virtual POS Implementation

Armed with a basic understanding of how application software and cryptographic functions are combined to produce useful and secure work, we can turn our attention to what you might find in the marketplace when shopping for merchant commerce solutions and POS processing software. Let's take a closer look at one merchant POS implementation: ICVERIFY from CyberCash.

## ICVERIFY

ICVERIFY is designed to handle in-store, mail, telephone, and Internet-based transactions. Multiple merchant support capability allows more than one merchant ID on a single copy of the software to support multiple e-stores running in a single environment (cybermalls).

ICVERIFY's features include the following:

- Importing credit card transaction data from other PC applications, such as spreadsheets or databases.
- Offline group mode to submit a batch of transactions at one time for authorization.

- Support for Address Verification Systems (AVSs), Retail AVSs, CVV2s, and CVC2s to help reduce fraud due to stolen or fraudulent cards.
- Data import analysis of files for errors before import.

Figure 6.8 shows some of the options in the ICVERIFY interface for manually processing a charge request.

**Figure 6.8** ICVERIFY Real-Time Processing Entry Screen

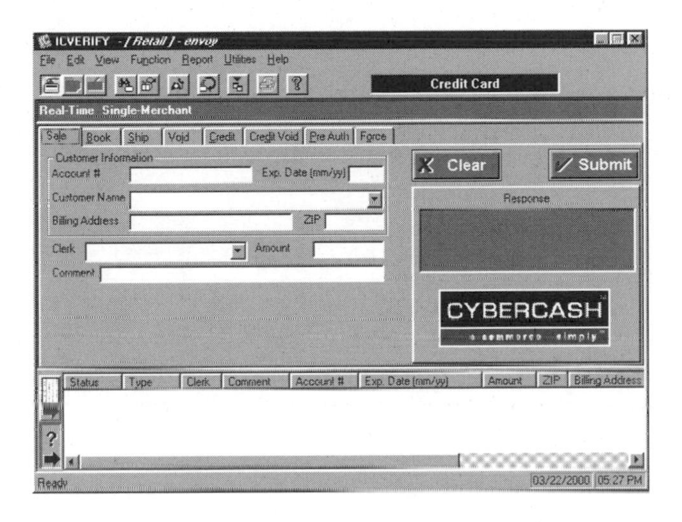


Most of the commercial implementations of merchant POS software should provide you with a similar set of features and functions as ICVERIFY does. It's left up to the merchant system administrators, however, as to which methods to select for implementing the system and protecting the data. Using the suggestions offered in this chapter and throughout the book will help you to determine what forms of security you require and where they're required. As mentioned earlier, the more work you decide to perform in-house, the wider the field of risk you choose.

For more information about ICVERIFY, visit the CyberCash Web site at www.cybercash.com. There's a wide variety of other options for merchant POS systems; check with your merchant bank or third-party processor for a list of the systems that they support.

**Damage & Defense...**

### Shopping Carts Fall under Media Attacks, Too

Everyone knows that e-commerce is under attack—and not only by its critics! Media critics, however, have a field day whenever they can report on Net-based credit card problems, and they usually place the blame on the software instead of the poor implementation of the software. ICVERIFY is no exception and came under media attacks in the spring of 2001.

The important point here is that *no* software on the planet can protect itself from threats to the environment it runs in or from misconfiguration problems due to a lack of proper care in securing computing resources. Defense in depth works successfully only if all layers in place are operating as intended—firewalls can do you no good if you're leaving ports open for database server access from the Internet!

## Alternative Payment Systems

This chapter primarily focuses on the traditional and most common uses of payment cards on the Internet today, but it will cover some other payment possibilities that are slowly finding their way into the mainstream. Alternative payment systems are designed to answer a variety of concerns and problems that plague E-commerce, such as these:

- Fraud
- Chargebacks
- Lack of user authentication
- Unwillingness to transact
- Escalating processing fees

Solutions to these problems vary, depending on which problem is being addressed. Categories of solutions that have emerged include the following:

- Smart card (chipcard) systems
- Proxy services
- Point and loyalty rewards

## Smart-Card-Based Solutions

Smart cards are credit-card-sized devices that are distinguished from ordinary credit cards by the presence of a microchip on the front or reverse side of the card. The chip turns a static data source into a rich and dynamic environment where all kinds of possibilities exist. Banks and other issuers are putting these cards in the marketplace to gain acceptance—but more important, to fight fraud.

The most notable application this far is the Europay, Mastercard, and Visa (EMV) specification for credit, debit, and charge card data storage and processing using integrated circuit cards (ICCs).

### EMV

EMV is a joint working group of the Europay International, Mastercard International, and Visa International card associations. Europay, MasterCard, and Visa have been working jointly to develop the EMV specifications that define a broad set of requirements to ensure interoperability between chip cards and terminals on a global basis, regardless of the manufacturer, the financial institution, or where the card is used. EMV represents the joint specifications for ICCs and point of sale (POS) and ATM terminals used by the payment systems. The latest version of the specifications, EMV 96 version 3.1.1, was published in May 1998 and is currently in use by the chip card and terminal manufacturers as a basis for their development efforts today. A new draft version of EMV, called EMV 2000, is out for comment and is working its way through the standardization processes.

EMV is designed to help reduce or eliminate two types of credit card fraud that continue to dog banks and merchants: skimming and counterfeiting.

## Reducing Skimming

Skimming is the problem where the image of the data on the magnetic stripe (on the back of the card) is obtained and stored for later uses when the card is no longer present. This skimmed data is often copied onto a different card's magnetic stripe or simply "played back" from the recording device and used for fraudulent purposes. EMV helps to prevent this problem by cryptographically protecting the card number and associated authentication data so that it cannot be forged or misused through merchant-initiated fraud or through stolen cards.

## Reducing Counterfeiting

Counterfeit credit cards look and feel just like any legitimate credit card, but the data embossed on the front of the card does not match the data encoded on the magnetic stripe on the back of the card. The magnetic stripe images may be obtained through skimming (see above) or may be absent or damaged entirely, causing the merchant to use a manual imprint process instead of network authorization. EMV is also designed to prevent this problem through strong cryptography that authenticates the chip to the terminal (and vice versa), as well as using cryptograms to authenticate the card to the host system (when a transaction goes "online").

EMV was established to help reduce the dependence on the inter-banking network and European dial-up connections to the network by providing the ability to conduct transactions offline from the bank. Depending on the card issuer's risk management policy, EMV can be configured to authorize some number of transactions between the card and terminal without going online to the bank for every transaction. EMV provides for a Lower Consecutive Offline Limit (LCOL) and an Upper Consecutive Offline Limit (UCOL) to manage risk and simplify transaction processing. Once the limits established by the bank are reached, the next transaction is forced online, where the bank can then execute issuer-scripts to update the EMV application and collect the offline transaction data. This advantage is very appealing where phone access charges are high or the reliability of the phone system is questionable.

The EMV specification cannot be implemented on its own. There are multiple choices and options within EMV that are specified separately by each card association wishing to support EMV. The Visa ICC Specifications, or VIS for short, define a subset of choices and options that Visa International is willing to support for its member banks. These specifications, along with issuer bank or national banking body (such as APACS in the United Kingdom or Carte Bancaire in France) option choices, are then used to develop applets that are compliant with EMV for use on issuer-specific and brand-specific smart cards.

EMV is prevalent throughout Europe and is working its way to the United States as well. As EMV is integrated into Internet-based e-commerce, you'll begin to see expanded uses of smart cards from issuer banks and a drive to help build the desktop-based infrastructure for using smart cards online. The Chip Electronic Commerce (CEC) specification is intended to help these efforts along.

Further details on EMV are available from the Visa Chip Card Specifications Page (www.visa.com/cgi-bin/vee/nt/chip/circuit.html) maintained at the VISA International Web site.

Another class of solutions that rely on chip cards is called electronic purses (e-purses), which permit a user to transfer value to the chip from reload points of interaction (such as ATMs) and use the card as though it were cash.

## MONDEX

MONDEX is one of these smart-card-based electronic purse applications, built for the MULTOS smart card operating system for chip cards. E-purses eliminate the requirement to share payment account information with a merchant, eliminating many of the threats to large databases full of "toxic data."

MONDEX uses strong cryptography to transfer value between participants in the scheme. Because it's a noncleared (nonsettled) system, transfers of value occur in real time and costs to processes are dramatically reduced.

Because it's electronic, MONDEX is useful in person, over a phone line, or via the Internet. The chip maintains the last 10 transactions and locks the application with a user-selected personal identification number (PIN). Private payments between individuals are also possible.

The MONDEX purse is divided into five separate "pockets" that permit five different currencies on the same chip to add convenience to international travelers.

## Visa Cash

Visa Cash, like MONDEX, is a smart-card-based e-purse that's implemented on both proprietary cards and Java-based Open Platform cards. There are two main types of Visa Cash cards:

- Disposable
- Reloadable

Disposable cards are loaded with a predefined value. These cards come in denominations of local currency, such as US $10. The disposable card version uses low-cost memory cards to store VISA cash money. When the value of the card is used, the card is disposed of and a new card may be purchased.

Reloadable cards come without a predefined value. These cards can have value added to them in specially configured devices such as ATMs, EFT POS terminals, or other load devices. When the value is used up, you can reload the card again.

Visa Cash is a Secure Application Module (SAM)-based system and requires merchant terminals to contain a card reader for the customer card as well as for a SAM smart card to receive transferred cash value. This merchant card is retained within the unit at all times. To process a transaction the customer's card is inserted in the merchant's device and the transaction amount is entered.

The merchant SAM effectively controls the flow of the transaction. The terminal application alerts the SAM when a card is inserted into the reader, and the SAM instructs the terminal how to process the transaction request. In the VISA Cash system all transactions are stored in the terminal's memory and stored in the SAM in case the terminal fails. The SAM manages the security details to ensure that a transaction log cannot be fraudulently modified either while it is stored in the terminal or while it is being transmitted to the acquirer.

Visa Cash cards are sold at face value (if disposable) or in whatever denominations the user chooses for the reloadable cards. Merchants pay a setup fee through their acquiring merchant bank to accept Visa Cash, similar to setting up credit card acceptance services, with the additional costs of the requisite smart card readers.

## The Common Electronic Purse Specification (CEPS)

The increased uses of Visa Cash and other electronic purse programs around the world have resulted in the need for global standards to ensure interoperability. In 1999, a set of standards was created to govern electronic purse programs—the Common Electronic Purse Specifications (CEPS). CEPS defines requirements for all components needed by an organization to implement a globally interoperable electronic purse program. Visa Cash is intending to migrate to the CEPS standard once it been finalized and accepted. As of spring 2001, CEPS is still under review.

# Proxy Card Payments

With a proxy payment service, a consumer opens an account with the service and provides information about his or her credit cards or checking accounts. When the consumer wishes to make a payment, he or she logs on to the Web site of the provider and enters information about the sale (amount, account to use, merchant to pay, etc.). The service then provides the interface to the merchant without revealing the personal account information of the buyer, also eliminating the need to store credit card numbers and details.

## PayPal

The most ubiquitous example of a proxy payer is PayPal (the payment method used in many eBay auctions), found at www.paypal.com. Paypal accepts payment arrangements from anyone with a working email address. Payments may be made via credit card, via personal check, or from an electronic funds transfer from the buyer's bank. PayPal also sets a credit limit initially at $500 to help limit any potential misuse.

PayPal is a money transfer system; it was originally launched for customer-to-customer transactions and now offers business-to-customer transactions. PayPal can accept money from the purchaser by charging the purchaser's credit card, debiting a checking account, or debiting a PayPal account.

In terms of fees, business and premier sellers are charged a 1.9 percent discount rate on transactions. If account holders want the money moved into their checking account daily, Paypal charges an addition 0.6 percent of each transaction.

## Amazon Payments

Amazon Payments is a service made available to Amazon Marketplace, Amazon Auctions, and zShops. Amazon deposits the buyer's money directly in the merchant's bank account and notifies the merchant via e-mail. Funds in the account are deposited every two weeks.

Amazon.com Payments offers resources for refunding the buyer, tracking sales, and downloading account information. The Amazon Payments fee structure is as follows:

- Amazon Marketplace sellers are not charged for using via Amazon.com Payments.
- Amazon zShops and Amazon auction sellers pay 25 cents per item purchased using Amazon.com Payments, plus 2.5 percent of the transaction amount.

More information about Amazon Payments can be found on its Web site at http://payments.amazon.com.

## Funny Money

The area of *funny money* relates to payment mechanisms that are generally thought of as points and rewards programs. Points, which are backed by cash (typically a penny or so), may be earned in any number of ways, including Web browsing, reading sales offers, purchasing merchandise, or given away as incentives for employees or customers. Two popular programs are Beenz and Flooz.

### Beenz

Beenz is one way to attract and reward consumers on a Web site: You pay them to shop and buy with beenz points that are usable at other places on the Internet. Employers can recruit, reward, and retain e-workers with beenz.

For every beenz you pay to your e-workers and Web visitors, beenz charges you one cent and does not charge any other setup or integration fees. Online stores can accept payments in beenz just like any other currency. They pay businesses half of one cent (US) for every beenz spent by a consumer on their web site, and they provide the software to carry out the transactions.

Beenz.com operates as an Application Service Provider (ASP) to enable remote access for business functions.

### Flooz

Flooz is another alternative payment that's backed by prepaid credit card charges or prepaid corporate accounts. Flooz is intended for gift-giving of Flooz points to anyone with an email address. Points may be given through online offerings and incentives or through codes that the recipient enters on the Flooz Web site at www.flooz.com.

# Summary

Payment card systems are complicated enough for an e-commerce merchant without security concerns about Internet fraud and theft, but researching both areas is a bare necessity for entering e-business.

Mitigating or reducing these risks takes vigilance on your part, vigilance through well-thought-out and well-implemented secure architectures to protect the network, and applied cryptographic controls to protect the application and data layers. Choosing partners as solution providers or going it on your own are decisions that you must make early in your journey toward an electronic sales presence. If you're new to the technology or unprepared for the mental and capital investments needed not only to do e-commerce *well*, but also *secure*, your best bet may be to partner with the experts in electronic commerce, get some experience under your belt, and decide later if you're truly ready to go it alone.

Once you've made the decision to bring processing in-house and you're prepared for taking on sole responsibility for operations and security, you'll need to design your systems and purchase software that can best fit your unique requirements for the day-to-day secure operations deemed essential for success. Aside from what you can buy in the marketplace, you'll need to provide a safe environment where your customers can trust you and where you'll need to maintain their trust. By understanding the features—and limitations—of today's computer systems and application software, you can design your systems to offer the best protections you can provide. Anything short of prudent measures for securing e-commerce is the guaranteed fast path to imminent catastrophe when your systems are compromised.

Protection begins at the core of your systems and extends all the way to your Internet connection, where any possibilities for trust simply fade off into the sunset.

This chapter has introduced you to many of the advantages—and disadvantages—of accepting payment cards and systems (both traditional and alternative) via the Internet, and you should be able to clearly understand your roles and obligations in keeping transaction and order data secure. E-commerce security is challenging work but still possible.

# Solutions Fast Track

## Understanding Internet-Based Payment Card Systems

- ☑ Hackers love credit card data for a number of reasons: It's easy to steal, it's easy to resell, and it's hard to get caught. The best targets are those that are loosely protected, contain large volumes of payment card data, and are easy to access over the Internet.
- ☑ Credit cards, charge cards, bank cards, and payment cards all relate to a family of payment options that involve relationships rooted in trust and good faith. You trust that the financial institution that issued you a card will pay the merchant for the goods and services you purchase. Merchants trust that the card issuers will pay them reasonably quickly, and the card issuers trust that you'll pay your bill on time each month.
- ☑ The processing steps for charge cards and debit cards are identical to those for credit cards, with the exception of the mechanics involved in the authorization request and settlement processing. Because charge cards are not based on preset spending limits, the notion of an open-to-buy is irrelevant. Rather, charge card systems use other means to authorize or decline a charge request. Some companies use risk models, heuristics, patterns of spending, or manual review.
- ☑ Internet sales can be viewed as seven distinct phases where unique security requirements come into play as data collects and processing commences.
- ☑ POS processing adds complexity to already vulnerable Internet-attached networks and heightens the need for strict security controls.

## Options in Commercial Payment Solutions

- ☑ Commercial payment systems appear in three basic forms: outside turnkey solutions, in-house solutions, and combinations of the two.
- ☑ Commerce Server Providers (CSPs) will lease you access to the system, allocate disk space for you to maintain your products, may offer multiple payment processing options, and may even provide robust site reporting and easy Web-browser-based interfaces for maintenance. Many of them are operated under secure and trustworthy environments and may even offer Web design service. Be careful, though—not all CSPs provide the same levels of service or the same payment processing fee structures.
- ☑ Hack-proofing a payment-card handling system requires secure architectures to ensure network and server-based security, and they require the uses of complex cryptography protocols running atop the network layer—primarily at the application layer. Most of today's payment protocols incorporate multiple forms of applied cryptography for its functions.

## Secure Payment Processing Environments

- ☑ Security experts embrace three-tier systems for Internet, intranet, and extranet applications. When they're present, these three tiers—Web server(s), application server(s), and database server(s)—greatly reduce many of the threats to production back-office systems and networks. Add still more layers of security both between and within each tier.
- ☑ Secure payment processing environments rely on careful separation of activities where a "defense in depth" approach can help to shield you from threats coming from the Internet.
- ☑ Diligent and knowledgeable system administrators are essential to maintaining the controls needed for e-commerce success.

- ☑ Any dynamically generated data (stored billing and shipping information, etc.) should be kept as far out of reach from the Internet as possible. Furthermore, any data that your customers supply via Web-based forms should immediately be removed from the Web server through as many firewalls as needed to safely secure it.
- ☑ Permitting HTTP routing into the back office places you at risk of hackers tunneling through HTTP to try to take over another server. Consider using protocols like CORBA/IIOP, RMI, socket connections via TCP, or DCOM on Microsoft NT to gain access to services residing on the Application tier.
- ☑ On the Database tier, consider encrypting the contents at the field level, the row level, the table level, or the entire database level.

## Understanding Cryptography

- ☑ Most of the industry standard methods to secure data at the application layer require robust uses of digital cryptography. POS processing, for example, needs cryptographic processing for securing data while it's in transit and while it's stored and processed within your stewardship.
- ☑ Strong cryptography always produces ciphertext that appears random to standard statistical tests. Because keys are generated for uniqueness using robust random number generators, the likelihood of their discovery approaches zero. Rather than trying to guess a key's value, it's far easier for would-be attackers to *steal* the key from where it's stored, so extra precautions must be taken to guard against such thefts.
- ☑ Using cryptography effectively on a well-designed and well-implemented secure network builds up the layers of defense on the application software layer where merchant operators tend to have the greatest degree of control over processing.

- ☑ Multiple solutions relying on cryptography are needed to address specific needs for security and data integrity on all points of sales processing, from end to end.
- ☑ Any cryptosystem that hasn't been subjected to brutal attacks should be considered suspect.
- ☑ The Secure Hashing Algorithm (SHA-1) and the Message Digest 5 (MD5) algorithm are common with e-commerce systems. SHA-1 is used in the process for creating a digital signature, which is authenticated with a public and private key system. You can't rely on your e-commerce customers to manage their own cryptographic keys—e-commerce requires a Public Key Infrastructure (PKI) for establishing and maintaining trusted digital certificates.
- ☑ Many of the higher-order e-commerce protocols, such as Secure Electronic Transactions (SET), use a robust set of digital certificates to authenticate people and resources for assurance that all parties possess the rights needed to transact.

## Examining E-Commerce Cryptography

- ☑ The three goals of secure messaging—sender authentication, message integrity, and confidentiality—require complex cryptography if they're to succeed.
- ☑ Hashing is a powerful mechanism to protect user passwords on e-commerce sites. Should your site require IDs and passwords for personalization reasons, you'll want to store the passwords that people create in the form of a hash value. That way, even if a hacker steals your security database records, the hacker won't be able to use the data to impersonate your customers directly.
- ☑ Secure Sockets Layer (SSL) has emerged as the de facto standard for today's private communications on the Internet, but it does not go far enough to meet e-commerce security demands.

- ☑ PGP is a distributed key management approach that does not rely on Certificate Authorities. Users can sign one another's public keys, adding some degree of confidence to a key's validity. Limitations on the informal Web of Trust that PGP relies on makes it impractical for conducting electronic commerce on the Internet.
- ☑ Secure Electronic Transaction (SET) addresses most of the consumer demands for privacy when using a credit card to shop online. SET's uses are specific to the payment acceptance phases of the shopping experience. It covers the steps from the point a particular payment card is selected for use through the point the merchant completes the transaction and settles the batch with its acquirer bank or processor.

## A Virtual POS Implementation

- ☑ POS products available on the market today have become more and more sophisticated in their features and flexibility.
- ☑ Any of the in-house virtual POS software that you'll select to implement can't guarantee security unless you deliberately set out to install it securely on secure network resources. While much of the systems' documentation offers advice on secure implementation, it can't provide security automatically. Regardless of the system you choose, it's left up to you to install it, operate it, and maintain its security.
- ☑ ICVERIFY, one merchant POS software option, is designed to handle in-store, mail, telephone, and Internet-based transactions. Multiple merchant support capability allows more than one merchant ID on a single copy of the software to support multiple e-stores running in a single environment (cybermalls). Most of the commercial implementations of merchant POS software should provide you with a similar set of features and functions as ICVERIFY does.

## Alternative Payment Systems

- ☑ Alternative payment systems are designed to answer a variety of concerns and problems that plague e-commerce, such as fraud, chargebacks, lack of user authentication, an unwillingness to transact, and escalating processing fees.
- ☑ Smart cards are credit-card-sized devices that are distinguished from ordinary credit cards by the presence of a microchip on the front or reverse side of the card. EMV specifications define a broad set of requirements to ensure interoperability between chip cards and terminals on a global basis, regardless of the manufacturer, the financial institution, or where the card is used.
- ☑ MONDEX is one smart-card-based electronic purse applications. E-purses eliminate the requirement to share payment account information with a merchant, eliminating many of the threats to large databases full of "toxic data." MONDEX uses strong cryptography to transfer value between participants in the scheme. Transfers of value occur in real –time, and the costs to processes are dramatically reduced.
- ☑ The Common Electronic Purse Specifications (CEPS) defines requirements for all components needed by an organization to implement a globally interoperable electronic purse program.
- ☑ With a proxy payment service, like PayPal and Amazon Payments, a consumer opens an account with the service and provides information about his or her credit cards or checking accounts. When the consumer wishes to make a payment, he or she logs on to the Web site of the provider and enters information about the sale. The service then provides the interface to the merchant without revealing the personal account information of the buyer.
- ☑ Funny money, like beenz and Flooz points, relates to payment mechanisms that are generally thought of as points and rewards programs backed by prepaid credit card charges or prepaid corporate accounts. Points may be given through online offerings and incentives.

# Frequently Asked Questions

The following Frequently Asked Questions, answered by the authors of this book, are designed to both measure your understanding of the concepts presented in this chapter and to assist you with real-life implementation of these concepts. To have your questions about this chapter answered by the author, browse to **www.syngress.com/solutions** and click on the **"Ask the Author"** form.

**Q:** Where can I find a current list of Commerce Service Providers and Payment Solutions that I can use for comparison shopping?

**A:** Visit the E-commerce Guide (ECG) Web site Reviews Section at http://ecommerce.internet.com/reviews for an updated list of commercial products.

**Q:** What information on my e-commerce site needs to be protected with cryptography?

**A:** Wherever customer personal or confidential information is collected, processed, or stored, cryptography is needed for trusted security measures. Any toxic data, such as credit card numbers, checking account numbers, billing addresses, and some customer preference choices, should be encrypted on databases and encrypted wherever its movement requires Internet-based communications.

**Q:** Where can I find out more about the uses of cryptography for electronic commerce?

**A:** Pick up a free copy of the RSA Laboratories' Frequently Asked Questions About Today's Cryptography. It's in Version 4.1 with new updates since the 1998 version 4.0. Some new questions have been added, some obsolete questions have been removed, and an appendix with some mathematical concepts has been added. You can obtain a copy of the FAQs at www.rsasecurity.com/rsalabs/faq.

**Q:** What is the banking industry offering in the way of technology to address the problems of escalating fraud and chargebacks?

**A:** You can find out the details about new products, services, and standards for security and technology at the following two Web sites: Visa New Technologies: www.visa.com/nt/main.htm and Mastercard Merchant Systems: www.mastercard.com/business/merchant.

**Q:** If I use SSL to encrypt my client's information when it is in transmission and I store it in encrypted databases on nonpublic accessible servers, then is my site secure?

**A:** These two countermeasures are effective as the beginning of a secure site, but a number of other factors are also needed, such as effective controls over cryptographic keys, application software, and secure architectures that implement "defense in depth" principles for computer security.

**Q:** Where can I learn more about smart cards for credit card security?

**A:** Visit the About.com Smart Card Technology section at: ecommerce.about.com/smallbusiness/ecommerce/cs/smartcards.

Chapter 7

# Hacking Your Own Site

## Solutions in this chapter:

- Anticipating Various Types of Attacks
- Performing a Risk Analysis on Your Site
- Testing Your Own Site for Vulnerabilities
- Hiring a Penetration Testing Team

☑ Summary

☑ Solutions Fast Track

☑ Frequently Asked Questions

# Introduction

What would a book about "hack proofing" your own e-commerce site be without a section on hacking? This chapter explains what types of attacks you can expect against your site and how to simulate them to test the security on your own.

Although there is no such thing as a totally secure system, performing your own evaluation will probably bring your site much closer to your expectations. Many times, in the rush and excitement of building a new site, a few steps or pieces get missed along the way. These accidental omissions may open the door to an attacker down the road, so if they are found early by your team you can avoid having them be used against you.

What can you expect from testing your security? You can expect that your team will find some holes. You can expect that they will be fixed. You can expect that more will be found, and that the cycle will continue forever. You can also expect that after your site is open to the public, other people will test it for you. That's the whole purpose of this chapter: to put you one step ahead.

# Anticipating Various Types of Attacks

In order to begin planning an attack against your site, you should know what the various types of attack are, and how they work. Any attack will attempt to subvert some combination of confidentiality, integrity, and availability, as outlined in Chapter 2. It's your job to maintain confidentiality, integrity, and availability, and it's the attacker's "job" to compromise them with the attacks we describe in this chapter: denial of service attacks, information leakage attacks, file access attacks, misinformation attacks, special file/database attacks, and elevation of privilege attacks.

## Denial of Service Attacks

The easiest kind of attack to understand is the Denial of Service (DoS) attack. It's also potentially the hardest to defend against. A DoS attack is an attack against availability, and it generally doesn't affect integrity or confidentiality. (In some cases, however, if the DoS attack causes a crash, some files may become corrupted. However, any corruption generally isn't under direct control of the attacker, so this is usually just considered collateral damage.)

The two main categories of DoS attack are *flood* and *targeted*. A flood attack works by burying the victim in pure volume, whether it's data or network traffic. A targeted attack seeks to exploit some particular bug or condition to cause a machine or site to become unavailable.

Let's cover flood attacks briefly, though Chapter 1 of this book has already described one of the most devastating examples of such an attack. One way to accomplish such an attack on a network level is to simply have a bigger pipe. If I have a T3 (45Mbps) and you're on a home digital subscriber line (DSL) connection, then you lose. You can eventually mitigate the problem by getting your Internet service provider (ISP) to block my traffic or by getting me kicked off the Net or thrown in jail, but those solutions take time, and meanwhile you can't function. If I want to be really nasty about it, I'll spoof my source addresses so that you can't easily track me down to complain to my provider; or I'll make the traffic look as much like your normal traffic as I can, so that your provider can't tell what to filter and what not to; or I may even use multiple machines or sites to do the flooding, so it takes much longer to track me down. The latter characteristics are what a Distributed Denial of Service (DDoS) brings to the table.

Flood attacks are not limited to networks. It's entirely possible to flood a disk (that is, use up the space), or use things like fork bombs (A program that recursively copies itself by calling on the fork function to eatup resources on the host machine causing the host machine to slow down and ultimately crash.) to use up CPU, memory or process slots. This type of flood attack can sometimes be used in conjunction with a more specific attack. Imagine if an attacker were to fill up the logging disk with garbage before launching the real attack, in order to prevent the logging of the attack.

A targeted DoS attack has similar results to a flood attack, in that something becomes unavailable when the attack is successful. The difference is that a targeted attack doesn't need to use brute force and volume to accomplish its task. Instead, it takes advantage of some weakness or hole in a system. In many respects, a targeted attack may be very similar to a regular exploit, except that the damage is limited to availability.

The simplest example of a targeted attack is when some service running on a machine can be made to crash by simply connecting to it and sending malformed data. This could be a Web server, Domain Name System (DNS) server, mail daemon, and so forth. These bugs sometimes occur on an OS level as well. In a few cases in the past, Windows boxes could be rebooted by sending the right few packets.

Naturally, a type of DoS attack exists that falls somewhere between a flood and a targeted attack, such as a SYN flood attack. This involves repeatedly sending SYN packets from spoofed Internet Protocol (IP) addresses, which will fill up all of the buffers set aside for new connections on older operating systems. Each new connection is usually attached to a several-minute timer, so it will eventually recover, unless the stream of packets is kept up. So, a constant stream of packets is required, but not at an extremely high rate (the pipe isn't full of SYN packets).

## Information Leakage Attacks

The next class of attack is *information leakage.* An information leakage attack is an attack against confidentiality. Information leakage occurs when an attacker is able to obtain some information that you'd rather he or she didn't. The leakage does not give enough information to allow immediate access to your systems, but rather information that might give an intelligent attacker an idea of how to proceed, or perhaps information he could combine with other information that would then lead to a penetration.

All systems leak some information about themselves—this is unavoidable. Operating systems have so many differences between them, for example, that an attacker can use even subtle clues to determine what OS you're running. An attacker's job is to collect as much information about his target in order to plan an attack. If the defender has done his job well, minimal information will leak out, and it will be of little assistance to the attacker. If the defender has done a poor job, they may find that someone can piece together enough information to lead directly to a compromise.

A classic example of an information leakage problem is the *finger service*. Way back when, most UNIX machines ran a service called *finger*. When used, a matching finger client command would provide information about a particular user on a particular machine. It would look something like this:

```
# finger -l ryan@localhost
[localhost]
Login name: ryan                    In real life: Ryan Russell
Directory: /home/ryan               Shell: /bin/sh
On since Feb 10 20:24:09 on pts/0 from adsl-xx-xxx-xxx-
    xx.dsl.xxxxxx.xxxxxxx.net
Mail last read Sun Feb 11 00:59:17 2001
No Plan.
```

This reveals all kinds of useful information. Another variant of the finger command will reveal either all users on that box or all currently logged-in users, depending on the finger daemon.

Again, this type of information does not lead directly to compromise, but it's rather disheartening how often a user's password matches their username—finger is a quick way to collect some usernames.

Some of the pieces of information an attacker typically does want to have are the operating systems being used and the available services. We take a look at how to find that out later in this chapter in the section on scanning tools.

# File Access Attacks

A *file access* attack is, as the name implies, an attack that gives an attacker access to files on a system. This is an attack against confidentiality *and* integrity. There are any number of subcategories under file access, such as read access, write access, and delete permissions. Read access directly affects only confidentiality, whereas others permit modifications, which affects integrity. However, if an attacker is able to read arbitrary files on a target, then further compromise is almost assured.

An attacker might be able to access files the defender might not want him to in a number of ways. Usually, these means exist due to misconfiguration or a hole. Most services exist to give people access to files in one form or another, so the fact that holes and misconfigurations occurs so frequently isn't surprising.

Most file-based services, such as File Transfer Protocol (FTP) and Hypertext Transfer Protocol (HTTP) servers, attempt to limit which files the user can access. An application root directory is declared, and users aren't supposed to be able to access files outside of that directory structure. However, mistakes are sometimes made. Take for example the often-seen "dot dot" ("**..**") bug. Both UNIX- and DOS/Windows-based operating systems use **..** to represent the parent of the current directory, so that entering **cd ..** will take you up one directory level. Some server software fails to take this into account and will allow **..** to be used in the file request, allowing an attacker to step out of boundaries.

# Misinformation Attacks

A *misinformation* attack is designed to confuse the defender. It's an attack against integrity—not the integrity of the systems themselves, but rather the defender's information *about* the systems. It's an attack against the integrity of meta-information, if you will.

The difference between an attack that, say, modifies or removes a log file, and a misinformation attack is that with a misinformation attack, the original information is still there. However, it's been *added* to.

An easy example to understand involves the log file. Imagine that you have a log file containing entries for failed login attempts. An unsubtle attack that is trying to guess the password of user *ewinter* will write a script to try that account over and over again. In your logs, you'll see hundreds of failed attempts to log in as ewinter, which will make pretty clear to you what is going on, and you'll know which account to keep an eye on. You can go talk to the user that the ewinter account belongs to to see what they know about it. You can look at the last entry in the log and perhaps assume that either the attacker finally made a good guess or that they gave up.

Now imagine that you see hundreds of log entries for each of your users, thousands of lines in all. You obviously know that someone is guessing passwords, but if the log entries keep up in a consistent manner, you don't know who or if some individual is being targeted, you don't know when the attacker has made a successful guess, and you don't know which of your users to talk to in order to see if someone had any "shoulder-surfers" or weird phone calls recently.

Another example of a misinformation attack is an nmap scan that will generate extra traffic aimed at your host alongside the real packets doing the scanning. The real information is there, but you have to separate it out.

## Special File/Database Access Attacks

A *special file/database access* type of attack is nearly identical to a file access attack. The only difference is that it's against something that is not a traditional file system, though all the same concepts apply. The concept involves a structured collection of information, usually with some sort of permission controls attached to it. Like a file access attack, the attacks may be against confidentiality and integrity, depending on the level of access obtained.

Examples of the types of special files in question are any sort of database with its own access method, such as Oracle, Sybase, or MySQL, and similar concepts like the Windows registry.

Ultimately, such special files usually live on top of a regular file system, though the entire collection of information may be contained in only one regular file. Thus, if access to the underlying file system is obtained, compromise of the special files may also be possible. Note, however, that directly accessing the underlying file of a database or similar file may result in corruption of the file, especially if the file is "live." Database programs and Windows (for the registry) keep track of indexes of the information that must be kept in sync with the information, and they may also try to write to the file at the same time as you. Caching is also taking place, so that even if you manage to successfully write to the file correctly, the working copy may be in memory, rendering your version irrelevant. If that's the case, your copy will probably also be overwritten when the cache is flushed.

Read access, however, is often very practical, if you are able to properly interpret the file format. So although you might have a great deal of difficulty trying to write a new password to a database file by modifying the underlying file directly, reading a copy (if you have that level of file system access) could definitely be useful.

Increasingly, a lot of the interesting stuff at a site lives in a database. This is especially true for e-commerce sites. Also, one extremely common programming mistake developers make when developing a Web site is to improperly escape or filter user-supplied data, giving an attacker a way to send SQL commands to a database. Often, an attacker can get a remote shell by feeding the right set of commands to a SQL server.

## Elevation of Privileges Attacks

Ultimately, what any attacker usually wants is higher privileges on the victim machine. If an attacker can gain root on a standard UNIX box, then they can accomplish anything on that box that they want to. More subtle attacks exist, or some that accomplish just the goal of the attacker, but if root can be obtained in an earlier step, then all the other security mechanisms on that machine are essentially turned off.

An *elevation of privilege* attack is an attack against the integrity of the security structure, though it often leads directly to other compromises. If an attacker can gain further capabilities beyond what they were supposed to have, then a security mechanism somewhere has been broken. Such a mechanism may be broken due to a bad design, a bug, or just because the administrator implemented the mechanism improperly.

The file access and special file access attacks fall under the category of elevation of privilege as well. If an attacker finds a combination of characters that allows him to roam the server's hard drive at will, then clearly he's gone from the intended restriction (remaining within the capabilities of the CGI script's designer) to having a higher level of access.

Some attacks are purely elevation of privileges, though. A classic example is a setuid root UNIX binary with a buffer overflow. An attacker is able to divert the program flow and launch a copy of the shell as the root user. At that point, nothing else has taken place except that the attacker is now the equivalent of root and can continue from there.

Another example of a privilege escalation is any service with a hole that yields a remote shell. This kind of hole allows an attacker to go from a position of being able to perform only the functions that the services provide (which is what the administrator wanted) to being able to run arbitrary commands and poke around the file system. She may be doing so as a user with no special privileges, but it's much easier for an attacker to gain root access after they have a shell.

# Performing a Risk Analysis on Your Site

Risk is a quantity. It's a percentage, a probability, a number between 0 and 1. The percentage that represents the likelihood that you'll be compromised is a function of three things: vulnerability, threat, and assets. In fact, it's a product:

risk = vulnerability X threat X assets

If you are extremely vulnerable (you have lots of holes in your software) or an extreme threat exists (such as when a government agency has declared information warfare on your site) then your risk approaches 1 or 100 percent risk, meaning that you will get nailed. If your assets are 0, your risk drops to 0 as well, which means you have no business—plus, if your assets are 0, you don't have a site to begin with.

Even if your assets are low (you run a Web site with a picture of your dog), if you are very vulnerable, then you are still at high risk. A worm that automatically exploits common security holes doesn't know or care that your Web site is just a picture of your dog, it breaks in anyway.

You may have a situation where vulnerability is *relatively* low (you have all the known holes patched away, and you've used good judgment when picking products) but may be faced with a dangerous attacker. One example of such an attacker is someone who is capable of finding new holes in software and writing exploits for them, and he isn't worried about being caught. He might not be worried because he just doesn't think they will be caught, or perhaps it's not even illegal to break into computers where they live. If an attacker of this sort targets your site, risk becomes high.

You'll never be able to assign an accurate percentage to your risk. You have vulnerabilities you don't know about. You have attackers you don't know about or have limited information about. Many companies don't have a good handle on their assets. Even if your company can assign exact values to your assets, you'll never get an exact figure for vulnerabilities or threats.

But all is not lost. You can make a best estimate of vulnerabilities and threats, and along with information about your assets, you can make a judgment about your risk. As new information becomes available, you adjust your risk value. For example, if a new remote root vulnerability is announced in a software package you run, until the time you can get the patch in place, your risk is high.

Let's take a look at some possible ways to measure each of these factors.

## Determining Your Assets

Your company or project has assets, things that have value to you—they either have value to you because they are present, or because you would be damaged in some way if they were lost or disclosed (an asset either makes you money, or you lose money if you lose the asset). As you'll see, an asset need not be money, literally.

Here are some examples of assets:

- Money and financial information
- Customer information
- Products
- Intellectual property
- Employees
- Reputation

Someone within the company ought to be concerned with all of these assets. Most information security professionals are only concerned with a subset of these. From the above list, this may include financial information, customer information, products (if your company sells things on the Web), intellectual property, and reputation.

Did you know that you kept your reputation on the Web server? If you're an e-tailer, and you suffer a Web defacement or credit card database theft, then your attacker just removed your customer confidence from your Web server.

Your job within the security team is to try to reduce the number of exposed assets as much as possible—weighed against business needs, of course. Ideally, you won't have a reason to have any of your private financial information out on your demilitarized zone (DMZ). However, some companies have a need to share that sort of thing with partners via a private section of their Web site.

One type of information that nearly all e-commerce Web sites must maintain is customer information, things such as names, addresses, order history, and credit card numbers. The credit card number data is one of the more worrisome pieces. We've all heard horror stories about hundreds of thousands of credit card numbers being stolen from e-commerce databases. Perhaps you've even had to get a new card or experienced some fraud due to such an intrusion.

If you have some sort of for-pay downloadable product on your Web site, you will want to protect that as much as possible. You may have some intellectual property on your Web servers. Perhaps you have some code to issue license keys that is proprietary. Perhaps your business logic in embedded in your database.

The rule of thumb for minimizing assets is this: Don't have anything exposed that doesn't absolutely need to be. It's obvious but often overlooked. Chapter 5 discusses secure site design, and Chapter 6 has information on ways to deal with credit card information. Refer to these chapters for more help in these areas.

# Why Attackers Might Threaten Your Site and How to Find Them

We know an attacker is one type of threat; others include power outages, loss of connectivity, or anything that will impede your ability to do business securely. Chapter 9 discusses availability issues, so in this chapter we focus on attackers.

Two main types of threats you might receive are an attack of convenience and a targeted attack. An attack of convenience occurs when the attacker has some new exploit that they want to try on every machine in the world, which includes yours. So, although they are scanning the whole Internet looking for vulnerable machines, they scan yours on the way through. The vast majority of the time, these types of scans are for older, known holes. If you keep any kind of minimal vigilance about your patches, you should be pretty safe from this type of attack.

A targeted attack is one aimed specifically at you. Usually, such an attacker will take a little time to research your site before blindly firing attacks at you.

An attacker that is specifically targeting you is more dangerous. They will be more persistent, they will generally be more intelligent about which attacks they try, and they may even spend the time to do some original research about problems with the software you use to run your site.

Your job is to watch for these attackers and to determine what kinds you have coming after you, which is not an easy task. You have very limited information, and you're trying to determine the intentions of an attacker who may be thousands of miles away, whom you've never met. As hopeless as it sounds, you still have a little bit of information to go on.

An attack of convenience is usually looking for a limited set of vulnerabilities. Worms are a good example of this. At the time of this writing, the Ramen worm is making the rounds. The Ramen worm scans hosts for ports 111 (portmapper), 21 (ftp), and 515 (lpd/lprng). It has rpc.statd and wuftpd exploits that work on Red Hat 6.2, and a lprng exploit that works on Red Hat 7.0. You might have slightly different versions of the same software, and it may even have the same vulnerabilities, however the automated exploit won't necessarily work as offsets may be different in your situation.

An attacker (or a worm) with an exploit of this type will try it out on you, and if it doesn't work, she'll typically just move along to the next IP address. She isn't interested in *you* per se, just any machine that will fall for this exact exploit—or perhaps 100 machines.

An attacker targeting you would likely try some variations on the same theme, trying to break into your server. He may make adjustments to the exploit, or just move on, having already determined that it doesn't apply to you.

An attacker targeting your site will also usually do some reconnaissance, usually involving port scanning, OS fingerprinting, and perhaps some simple exploit attempts in order to gauge your level of defense and perhaps grabbing some file samples.

By carefully watching firewall and IDS logs—you will begin to understand the difference between someone who has tried their trick and moved on and someone who is sticking around for a little while. You may manage to spot an attacker that looks like he is taking some care to stay below the radar, perhaps by doing a slow scan. Hopefully, the attacker will come from a consistent set of IP addresses, but that may not always be the case. Many times, however, you will often have multiple attackers at a time, which complicates matters further.

As a general rule of thumb, you will need to stay informed about the commonly scanned ports for new exploits. You can learn this type of information by reading the Bugtraq and Incidents mailing lists, among others. After you've developed a list of things you commonly get scanned for—the noise, essentially—you can focus on the other attacks you receive.

Tools & Traps...

## Gauge Your Threat Level with a Honeypot

A honeypot (in an information security context) is a system that is designed to be broken into. Setting up a honeypot will give you an opportunity to study tactics of attackers and possibly pick up a new attack or two along the way. Naturally, the attacker shouldn't be aware that he has broken into a honeypot, and he should think that he's gotten into an ordinary machine with no special monitoring. In fact, a honeypot machine typically has extensive monitoring in place around it, either on the machine itself or via the network. In order for the honeypot to be effective, as much information as possible must be collected about the attacker.

It's also important that the honeypot machine not be able to act as a client on the Internet in general. You don't want to have to explain your honeypot project to law enforcement when they show up wanting to know why your machine was breaking into other people's machines. To avoid this, honeypots are usually placed behind an inverse firewall of sorts; connections get in, but they don't get out. This may tip off an attacker somewhat, but it's better than the alternative. It's also part of your signaling mechanism that something interesting has happened on your honeypot. When your honeypot machine, which normally does nothing on the network, suddenly starts trying to get out to the Internet, then chances are good that someone got in. Even if the attacker figures out that he's been duped, you have already collected some information.

Note that some people decide that a particular machine is a honeypot *after* it's already been broken into, that is, after they detected the intrusion on their regular machine, they decided to keep the attacker around to keep an eye on him. I don't recommend this, as it's never much fun trying to track an attacker without being prepared ahead of time, but it's an option. For some entertaining examples of people who have decided to take

Continued

this route, take a look at the book "Cuckoo's Egg: Tracking a Spy Through the Maze of Computer Espionage" by Clifford Stoll (Pocket Books), and "An Evening with Berferd" by Bill Cheswick, Steve Bellovin, Diana D'Angelo, and Paul Glick at www.all.net/books/berferd/berferd.html.

Honeypots can be a part of your mechanism for determining your threat level. Some folks are of the opinion that trapping an attacker to study his techniques will give you some advance notice. It's true that an attacker that is targeting your site will often spend some time on the first machine he can break into (your honeypot should be the easiest machine to penetrate on your network.) My opinion is that little has been formalized in terms of using honeypots in order to gauge attackers. However, little in the world of trying to determine your threat level has been formalized, so it may very well be a valid technique. One has to have some familiarity with forensic techniques, log analysis, and protocol analysis to make a honeypot useful, but help is available in those areas if you're a beginner.

Honeypots serve other useful functions besides determining threat levels. A community of people running honeypots can often provide each other with information about new exploits and worms. For one of the best examples of a community of honeypot operators, check out the Honeynet project (http://project.honeynet.org/).

# Testing Your Own Site for Vulnerabilities

After you've made your best effort to determine what your assets are and have tried to determine what your current threat level is, it's time to actively audit and assess your vulnerabilities.

Before we get to the technical items, let's discuss a bit some of the factors that affect your decisions on exactly how to perform your vulnerability audit (also called a penetration test). The most obvious factor is budget. Can you hire people for this purpose? Can you train people you have? Can you afford the time, the tools, and equipment? As with most IT functions, you can trade man-hours for capital (or vice versa) when testing for vulnerabilities.

Another factor that affects cost is how often you conduct your audit. A penetration test isn't something you can have done just once. Things change over time, whether the state-of-the-art tools in security and penetration have changed, or whether new systems have been added to your site, upgrades to software or configuration changes have been made. Even an experienced security administrator will make mistakes, perhaps forgetting to turn off a change intended to be only temporary.

For all of these reasons, you need to recheck your level of vulnerability every so often. How often you do is again probably a matter of resources, though checking too often may be disruptive depending on what type of IDS setup you have. If you have the luxury of dedicated staff to do the security assessment, you might check as often as once a month. Limited resources may dictate that you only do a full test once per year, though the idea of going a year without some level of security confidence is a bit frightening.

A good change control process can help with minimizing the risks in between full scans. Each time some change is made, make a best effort to determine exactly what will be affected and recheck just those things that are affected. This is harder than it sounds, because it requires a fair amount of discipline on the part of the people making changes to accurately record and assess any changes they make and to report the changes to the people who will need to recheck. Some host-based IDS systems will help enforce this, because they will catch some of the changes, but they will never be as effective as accurate records from the people actually making the changes in the first place. You can think of these as incremental penetration tests, similar to doing incremental backups in between full backups.

## Determining the Test Technique

You might briefly consider what type of attacker you want to play against your own site, whether opportunistic or targeted. You could take all the exploit code you can download, compile it up, and throw it at your site. As discussed before, though, not all exploits will work as-is. This could easily result in false negatives, reporting that a service isn't vulnerable when it is. Of course, any tool or testing method could potentially result in false negatives, but blindly running exploits will result in a much higher false negative rate. Frankly, the vast majority of attacks of convenience attempt to take advantage of well-known holes, for which patches have been available for some time. If you're getting caught by attacks of convenience, then you need to take a hard look at your procedures for tracking new vulnerabilities and applying vendor patches.

In almost every case, you should be performing the most intelligent attack possible. You should take advantage of your special knowledge of your site setup, short of actual secrets such as password and crypto keys. The types of knowledge you should take advantage of include the following:

- Trust relationships
- IP addresses on all network segments
- Brands and versions of all your software
- The type of network gear you use
- Source code for all the software if available (especially custom software)

The reason that all of this leverage should be used is that you have to assume that an outside attacker will eventually be able to determine or infer the same information. In most cases, tools are available to probe for this sort of thing. The free program nmap, for example, will allow an attacker to pretty effectively determine OS versions (welook at how to use nmap in the next section).

The attitude behind the assumption that an attacker can determine the above types of knowledge is embodied in the phrase "security through obscurity doesn't work." Ultimately, all security relies on some sort of "obscurity." However, you want your security to be reliant on something *really* obscure, such as a good password or a 128-bit crypto key—not the fact that you're running a Web server on port 81 (which will be determined rather quickly.)

So, it makes sense to give your invited attackers, whomever they may be, as much information is as useful to them. Yet again, there is a resource issue, so you may not be able to get as far as a full source code review, but plan on making the source available in case it becomes useful. It's always possible that your penetration team may determine quickly that things appear to be locked down pretty tightly, and that they will be focusing on individual application holes or perhaps CGI script holes. If that situation arises, then having the source for as many of those applications as possible will accelerate that process.

Your administrators and developer would have ideally been performing these checks all along, but they have a different goal. They generally are trying to get things to function, not be secure. They also may not have the same level of security expertise as your penetration test team. For all these reasons, having a separate security audit makes sense.

Let's discuss the issue of stealth for a moment. In real life, an attacker may try to use some stealth techniques to evade detection. This may include doing certain types of stealth portscans (these are of limited use, because just about any network IDS will pick these up. Some host-based measures such as TCP wrappers may not.) Other techniques are slow scans (doing a port scan slowly over time so as not to set off an IDS threshold and make the red port-scan light go off), packet fragmenting (effective against a number of IDS systems), and various types of misinformation attacks.

The question is, does having stealth techniques used against your site during a penetration test have any value? The answer is, of course, it depends—if you want to test strictly for vulnerabilities, then no, trying to be stealthy probably doesn't have a lot of value. (Note that some stealth techniques such as packet fragmenting may also function as a way to bypass security measures. Use appropriate judgment in what to leave out.) However, if you want to test your IDS systems, and possibly your response procedures, then using stealth techniques may have some value. It's not unheard of for someone in another part of an organization to spring a surprise penetration test on a particular set of systems to determine in part whether it's detected and how it's reacted to. If you need to also test your mechanisms for determining current threat level, then go ahead and do this. After (or if) your defense team has made the determination that an attacker is out there, go ahead and share the information about the penetration test taking place and turn off the stealth techniques to avoid spending unnecessary cycles.

# Researching Your Vulnerabilities

Your first step is to do some research. This is a big step, and when done properly, may yield all the information needed to complete a break-in. The types of information that are most important to you are the following:

- IP addresses
- Names
- Open ports
- OS versions
- Software versions
- Network structure
- Firewall configuration(s)

These pieces of information are needed for targeting known holes—having all of this information allows you to often just look up the combination of software you've found and download an existing exploit. It may require customization, but it's a quicker route than writing from scratch. (Note that the bullet list above, and indeed most of this book, is very Internet-oriented—that is, we say "IP address," and give examples for TCP/IP—however, the concepts apply to any type of networking or OS.)

One of the best tools for gathering a couple of these items of information is nmap, a free tool created by Fyodor. (You can find it at www.insecure.org/nmap.) It has two main features of interest to us: It's a great port scanner, with just about all the port scanner options you'd want, and it has an OS fingerprinting feature. Nmap takes note of the subtle differences contained within the packets that it gets back when scanning a host and consults a database of OS types for matches.

Probably the easiest way to illustrate this is to show an example (an explanation of the options follows the code example):

```
[root@ns1 rc3.d]# nmap -vv -sU -sT -O -P0 -e eth0 66.38.151.2


Starting nmap V. 2.53 by fyodor@insecure.org
     ( www.insecure.org/nmap/ )
Initiating TCP connect() scan against ns2.securityfocus.com
     (66.38.151.2)
Adding TCP port 22 (state open).
The TCP connect scan took 855 seconds to scan 1541 ports.
Initiating FIN,NULL, UDP, or Xmas stealth scan against
     ns2.securityfocus.com (66.38.151.2)
Too many drops ... increasing senddelay to 50000
Too many drops ... increasing senddelay to 100000
Too many drops ... increasing senddelay to 200000
Too many drops ... increasing senddelay to 400000
Too many drops ... increasing senddelay to 800000
adjust_timeout: packet supposedly had rtt of 8100232 microseconds.
Ignoring time.
adjust_timeout: packet supposedly had rtt of 8100259 microseconds.
Ignoring time.
The UDP or stealth FIN/NULL/XMAS scan took 2501 seconds to scan
     1541 ports.
For OSScan assuming that port 22 is open and port 53 is closed
     and neither are firewalled
Interesting ports on ns2.securityfocus.com (66.38.151.2):
(The 3078 ports scanned but not shown below are in state: filtered)
Port         State        Service
22/tcp       open         ssh
53/tcp       closed       domain
53/udp       open         domain
```

```
113/tcp    closed      auth

TCP Sequence Prediction: Class=random positive increments
                         Difficulty=42998 (Worthy challenge)

Sequence numbers: 76B1034E 76B8D898 76BEE1B2 76C50F02 76CC2ED6
    76D2E0FF
Remote operating system guess: Sun Solaris 8 early acces beta
    through actual release
OS Fingerprint:
TSeq(Class=RI%gcd=1%SI=A7F6)
T1(Resp=Y%DF=Y%W=60DA%ACK=S++%Flags=AS%Ops=NNTNWM)
T2(Resp=N)
T3(Resp=N)
T4(Resp=Y%DF=Y%W=0%ACK=O%Flags=R%Ops=)
T5(Resp=Y%DF=Y%W=0%ACK=S++%Flags=AR%Ops=)
T6(Resp=Y%DF=Y%W=0%ACK=O%Flags=R%Ops=)
T7(Resp=Y%DF=Y%W=0%ACK=S%Flags=AR%Ops=)
PU(Resp=N)

Nmap run completed — 1 IP address (1 host up) scanned in 3411
    seconds
```

Without trying to repeat all of the instructions for nmap, let's go over the options we used in this case briefly. The **-vv** is for extra verbose, which shows some of the steps that nmap performs while working; **-sU** tells it to do a UDP scan; **-sT** tells it to do a full connect TCP scan; **-O** tells it to do OS fingerprinting; **-P0** tells it not to ping to check for whether the host is up; **-e eth 0** tells it which interface to use to scan; followed finally by the target IP address. The full list of options can be found in the man page or simply run **nmap** with no arguments, and it will produce a short list of what the options are.

You can see that this scan took some time to complete (it was done across the Internet). It has determined that the OS is "Sun Solaris 8 early acces beta through actual release"; it is in fact Solaris x86 version 8 release. Nmap is unable to determine which processor architecture it's looking at in this case, so you'd have to use another method to determine that. That information is often critical if you're trying a buffer overflow. It also reports on the TCP sequence predictability, which is important to know if you're going to try TCP spoofing.

Assume for the moment that the port list nmap returned is accurate. (This is not always a safe assumption, because port scanners aren't always perfect, and other circumstances may affect your scan, such as dropped packets.) In this case, the machine in question doesn't seem to be running much, or some firewalling is going on, or both. It looks like we have access to 22/TCP and 53/UDP.

To complete this machine, let's try to figure out the version numbers of the software we can reach. Here's one way to do it for SSH (port 22):

```
[root@ns1 /root]# telnet 66.38.151.2 22
Trying 66.38.151.2...
Connected to 66.38.151.2.
Escape character is '^]'.
SSH-1.99-OpenSSH_2.3.0p1
^]
telnet> quit
Connection closed.
```

Most SSH daemons will volunteer what type and version they are (they have to at least advise the client which protocol version they speak). In this case, it appears to be OpenSSH 2.3.0p1. Port 53 is DNS. If the remote DNS server is BIND, you can often get it to tell you what version it is with the following command:

```
[root@ns1 /root]# nslookup -q=txt -class=CHAOS version.bind.
    66.38.151.2
*** Can't find server name for address 66.38.151.2: No response
    from server
```

```
*** Default servers are not available
```

In this case, we didn't get an answer, so this is no help. Here's what it looks like when it works correctly:

```
[root@ns1 /root]# nslookup -q=txt -class=CHAOS version.bind.
    207.126.127.66
Server:  www1.securityfocus.com
Address:  207.126.127.66


VERSION.BIND    text = "8.2.3-REL"
```

In this case, it looks like it's BIND 8.2.3-REL (release). In general, this method of trying to determine what software is running by seeing what kinds of information it will volunteer is called *banner scanning.* Banner scanning is somewhat equivalent to connecting to a given port and seeing what kind of output you get. This works fine for TCP, but UDP is a bit harder. Many UDP services are organized around the concept of a *datagram,* a single packet (though possibly fragmented) in a particular format. So although one can use a simple tool like a Telnet client to connect to many TCP services and get back some output, this often does not work with UDP. (Specifically, a Telnet client doesn't work with UDP at all, but the concept could be done with something like netcat in UDP mode. The point is, most UDP services won't volunteer output immediately.) For UDP, you have to issue the right kind of request and see what kind of output, if any, you get. However, if you're trying to figure out what the service is, you won't know what kind of request to send—it's an obstacle of a chicken-and-egg nature, so you'll usually have to make some intelligent guesses or correlate other information.

So, in this case we can't easily determine which DNS software is being run (if, in fact, that's what is listening there). We might guess it's not BIND, because it doesn't respond to the query that works on most BIND servers. (If you're curious, in this case it's tinydns from the djbdns package.) If it were really important to your test, you could probably develop some profiles of how various DNS servers answer queries and compare the response that you get from this one. This is the same idea that nmap uses to determine OS. Or, if you happened to search through the djbdns mailing list archives, you might notice that I made a number of posts asking questions about implementing djbdns in the not too distant past and make inferences from that.

In either case, for this machine you're left with pretty limited information about what might be attackable. Because SSH is open, you always have the option of trying to brute-force guess usernames and passwords. However, if the site in question has done a decent job at all with their password policies, this should prove pretty fruitless. You could also try some BIND exploits. If you're not trying to be stealthy, you have nothing to lose.

At the time of this writing, djbdns has no known holes, nor does that version of OpenSSH. That leaves you with the option of moving on to a different box (if there are any others) or searching the source of OpenSSH and djbdns for new holes so as to write an original exploit. The developers for both OpenSSH and djbdns are pretty security conscious, so I'd put that last on my list.

Let's take a look at a box that would be a bit easier to deal with:

```
Starting nmap V. 2.53 by fyodor@insecure.org
    ( www.insecure.org/nmap/ )
Interesting ports on  (x.x.x.x):
(The 1512 ports scanned but not shown below are in state: closed)
Port        State       Service
21/tcp      open        ftp
23/tcp      open        telnet
79/tcp      open        finger
80/tcp      open        http
98/tcp      open        linuxconf
113/tcp     open        auth
513/tcp     open        login
514/tcp     open        shell
1024/tcp    open        kdm
5680/tcp    open        canna
```

```
6667/tcp    open        irc

TCP Sequence Prediction: Class=random positive increments
                         Difficulty=3267068 (Good luck!)
Remote operating system guess: Linux 2.1.122 - 2.2.14

Nmap run completed — 1 IP address (1 host up) scanned in 20
    seconds
```

I've hidden the address in this case to protect the victim. Not my victim, mind you—this is a box that set off my IDS by scanning me for port 111 (portmapper). It seems strange that some random Linux box would be running an IRC server (or so nmap says, 6667/tcp.) However, the banner presented when Telnetting to that port is this:

```
SSH-1.5-1.2.27
```

It's an SSH server. Any number of rootkits for Linux will install an SSH or telnetd equivalent on some high port number and leave it for an attacker to get back in with later. This Linux machine has almost certainly been broken into, which is why it was scanning me. It's probably scanning most of the Internet. Let's take a look at some of the other banners on the open ports.

```
21/tcp
220 looks FTP server (Version wu-2.6.0(1) Fri Jun 23 09:17:44 EDT
    2000) ready.

23/tcp
Red Hat Linux release 6.2 (Zoot)
Kernel 2.2.14-5.0 on an i686
login:

79/tcp
```

```
No one logged on.


80/tcp
(HTTP servers don't send data automatically; I typed "HEAD /
    HTTP/1.0[cr][cr]")
HTTP/1.1 302 Found
Date: Tue, 20 Feb 2001 03:34:24 GMT
Server: Apache/1.3.12 (Unix) ApacheJServ/1.1
Location: http://x.x.x.x/servlet/st?rw=
Connection: close
Content-Type: text/html; charset=iso-8859-1
```

The others simply produce an error when you press Enter or disconnect you without any output. Obviously, knowing the proper protocol will allow you to probe those further.

So, it seems apparent that we have a Red Hat 6.2 box that has been broken into, probably by a worm, and had a rootkit installed. And it's proceeding to look for other victims. Interestingly enough, because this looks like an otherwise totally default Red Hat 6.2 install, you'd expect to find portmapper, lpr, and BIND running. We didn't show a UDP scan here, but a quick check for those particular ports shows them not listening. A number of known remote root vulnerabilities in stock Red Hat 6.2 would be exploitable if those services were listening. It looks like after the attacker moved in, they cleaned up. Some of the Red Hat worms are known to do this.

But in any case, back to the issue of breaking into machines. A quick check on the SecurityFocus.com vulnerability database shows that version of wuftpd to be vulnerable. One of the attacks (the one used by the Ramen worm, for example) requires a login to function, usually anonymous is enabled. It wasn't in this case, yet more evidence that Ramen has moved in and closed the holes behind it. However, at least one other hole in that version of wuftpd looks like it's still viable. (So is the first if you can guess a login, but then you could probably just Telnet to it in that case, though the wuftpd hole gives root directly. You can use many local holes after you have a shell.)

I'm not going to break into this machine, I don't have explicit permission. Port scanning is considered rude and may be against some ISPs' acceptable use policy, but it's not illegal where I'm located. Actually breaking in would be, even though I'd just be joining the party. Plus, you never know when it's a honeypot or when law enforcement is leaving it up waiting for the attacker to come back.

## Mapping Out a Web Server

Having touched briefly on some general methods for determining what is running on a box, let's take a more detailed look at what might be available via a specific service, HTTP. Web servers are particularly interesting, because on a full-featured site one may be able to interact with several full applications via HTTP. The more functionality, the more opportunity there is for something to be wrong and for you to get in.

We already touched on a tiny bit of research for Web servers. Most Web servers will volunteer several items of information about themselves when asked. For example:

```
[root@ns1 /root]# telnet slashdot.org 80
Trying 64.28.67.150...
Connected to slashdot.org.
Escape character is '^]'.
HEAD / HTTP/1.0

HTTP/1.1 200 OK
Date: Tue, 20 Feb 2001 04:52:35 GMT
Server: Apache/1.3.12 (Unix) mod_perl/1.24
Connection: close
Content-Type: text/html

Connection closed by foreign host.
```

The Web server at slashdot.org has volunteered that it's running Apache 1.3.12 on UNIX, and that it has the (optional) mod_perl loaded, version 1.24. None of this is news if you're familiar with Slashdot, but it illustrates the point. The command used is HEAD / HTTP/1.0, followed by two carriage returns (press Enter twice). If you're doing this manually with the Telnet client, you can't make any typos, and you can't backspace. If you screw up, disconnect and try again.

This is no more than banner scanning, though. To really dig into a Web server, you'll need a way to get a list of as many files on that server as possible. More specifically, you want ones that do some sort of server-side processing or contain sensitive information. However, because you probably won't have a good way to get just those, you'll probably go after all of them, and sort them out later.

One way to essentially grab a whole Web site is to use **wget** (available from your local GNU archive.) This will by no means be stealthy. Depending on the size of the Web site you're trying to grab, it may take an extremely long time, and it's possible it may swamp the Web server you're hitting as well, especially if it manages to step into a portion of the Web site that contains a lot of dynamic content. But, if you're willing to deal with those problems, it is a rather complete way to grab what you need for later searching and inspection.

We won't go into great detail here on how to compromise server-side processes, as a big portion of the previous book in this series, "Hack Proofing Your Network: Internet Tradecraft" spends quite a bit of time on this subject. But briefly, what you will be looking for are Web "pages" ending in extensions that indicate server processing, such as .pl, .asp, .shtml, .php, and so on. You'll also want to keep an eye out for directories with names containing cgi or cgi-bin. Next, use the **grep** command to search through the files you've grabbed looking for submit tags, links with a **?** in them, or anything that indicates dynamic processing. You'll want to look for pages that seem to have errors or SQL code leaked onto them, which will give you clues as to what effect your attempts are having. Keep an eye out for hidden variable tags because they could possibly indicate sloppy programming.

Unfortunately, I can't give you a set formula for finding these types of problems, because they may often be site specific. You'll need to have an understanding of how Web servers work, the various scripting languages, and probably SQL as well. The process is creative, so it's more art than science.

Beyond the clue that the Web server hands you outright, you can get links to explore from other places. One of my favorites is the Web search engines. You can go into http://altavista.com, for example, and enter the search phrase: **+host:www.example.com +url:cgi**. It will give you all of the URLs on the host www.example.com that contain "cgi." Some of these may not be linked from the site itself anymore, so the **wget** method might not reveal them, but the search engine archives can go back for some time, and the actual file may still be there even if it isn't linked. This method is also particularly nice because it doesn't directly touch the target Web server.

Finally, there may be files on the site that you can attack that are linked from nowhere, so you'll never know they are there except through intelligent guessing. The most common of these are the default files that come with any Web server. They often aren't removed, and in many cases, they have had vulnerabilities. For example, all copies of IIS 4.0 Web server contained a sample file called showcode.asp, whose purpose in life is to show the source code for an .asp file rather than running it, a feature any attacker would love to have. To make matters worse, it has a **..** bug that lets you walk around the Web server file system with it. The Web site will likely not have a link to this file anywhere in its pages, but it may well be there.

The way to discover files like these is to consult vulnerability databases for the version of the Web server you're looking at or to duplicate the setup in question as much as possible. If there are standard sample files, when you install the same software on your machine, you'll have the same files. Finally, one other way to find these files is to use an automated tool that has them programmed in.

## Using Automated Scanning Tools

We've been waiting until this point in the chapter to cover automated scanning tools because they are of little use if you can't take advantage of the information produced by them. The automated tools can only take you so far, and then you'll have to have to skills to back up what you find out. Even if the automated tools were 100 percent accurate, the majority of them will not actually carry out a penetration, they will only try to determine if a site is vulnerable or not. It will be up to you to actually exercise the vulnerability.

Automated scanning tools play an important part in a penetration test, though. They help ensure that you don't forget something, or skip over something simple, thinking that "the target couldn't possibly be vulnerable to *that*..." As a systems or security administrator, it's very easy to forget to check services that you believe aren't running or to assume that your coworkers won't pick really bad passwords that are easily guessed.

Damage & Defense...

## Automated Scanner as Time Saver

At one point in my career, I received a phone call from a person I used to work with, who had since moved onto another job. She had inherited the job of security management, but didn't feel that she knew as much about the job as she would like. They were planning to fire a contractor that day, and they were a little concerned that he might try to retaliate by trying to break into their site from home after he'd been escorted out. I offered to check their site for them, secured the appropriate permission, and explained that I'd be doing my scan over the Internet.

I didn't need to be stealthy about it, so I figured I'd fire off Internet Scanner from ISS at them, just as a quick way to figure out what services were running and to possibly grab some usernames. That process normally takes some time, so I swiveled my chair back to another machine to check my e-mail. About 60 seconds later, I glanced at the scanning machine, and was shocked to see that it had found an administrator password!

Sure enough, the password it had guessed (username *support*, and password *support*) was in the domain administrators

Continued

group. After some quick checking, it also looked to me like I had control of a machine all the way on the *inside* of their network.

I immediately phoned my ex-coworker to report what I had found. Every machine I had scanned had every port listening that I would expect for a non-firewalled machine, and I could reach them from the Internet. I told them they needed a firewall, badly. They told me that they *had* a firewall. I explained that I saw no sign at all of a firewall, and that I was reaching everything. It turned out that their network was bigger than I thought, and what was happening was that they were doing NAT on their firewall. They did indeed have a firewall (at least they had a box with the word firewall painted on the side) but what they had done was to take an outside address and translate it to an inside address and *open every port to that box*. They had no DMZ whatsoever.

I was a bit stunned. I told them that I hoped their contractor didn't get too disgruntled, because they weren't going to be fixing their problems before he left.

Eventually, they fixed their setup. The point of the story is not to discount really stupid stuff that you think people would never do in a million years. An automated scanning tool is one way to help make sure you don't, because you can let it try the dumb stuff.

Automated scanning tools run the entire spectrum of features, complexity, and cost. A particular tool may target one specific area, such as Web server holes, or it may try to find as many different types of bugs as possible. Complexity may range from a very terse "service X is vulnerable to attack Y," all the way up to multiple levels of reporting, histories, and trends. Cost ranges from free to very expensive.

Some of the most popular scanners are Nessus, Internet Scanner by Internet Security Systems, CyberCop Scanner by Network Associates, NetRecon by Axent, HackerShield by BindView, Cisco Secure Scanner, and various descendents of Security Administrator Tool for Analyzing Networks (SATAN), such as Security Administrator's Research Assistant (SARA) and System Analyst Integrated Network Tool (SAINT). If you're curious about some of the differences, there's one recent review at www.networkcomputing.com/1201/1201f1b1.html.

(Incidentally, that review favors Nessus, which is one of the free scanners. This evaluation was based on letting each scanner loose on a number of systems with known holes and counting how many were spotted by each scanner.) Out of the above list, Nessus, SATAN, SARA, and SAINT are free. You can get demo versions from most of the commercial vendors.

Let's go ahead and take a look at Nessus as an example. The scanner portion runs on UNIX, whereas the GUI can run on UNIX, Windows, or Java (presumably meaning any OS with a full Java implementation.) The example screens shown here are from the Windows GUI.

Figure 7.1 shows what Nessus looks like during the scanning process, after you've installed everything, logged into your scanning server, and have chosen a range of IPs or names to scan. The portscan is done by nmap as an external process, so currently the Portscan bar shows 0 done until the entire portscan is complete, then jumps to 100 percent. The Attack bar will advance with each attack, and the current attack in progress is shown next to "Security check." This example took a couple of hours to complete.

**Figure 7.1** Status Screen during Scanning

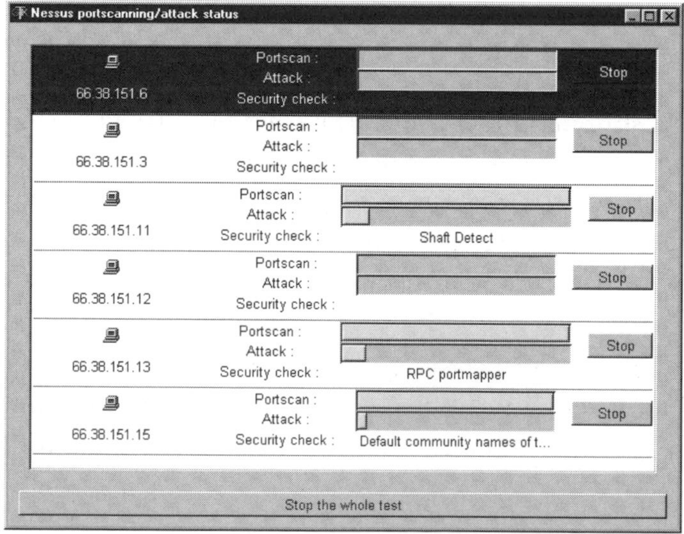

After the scan is complete, a screen is displayed showing the IP addresses scanned, and any vulnerabilities or warnings found (see Figure 7.2).

**Figure 7.2** Nessus Report Screen

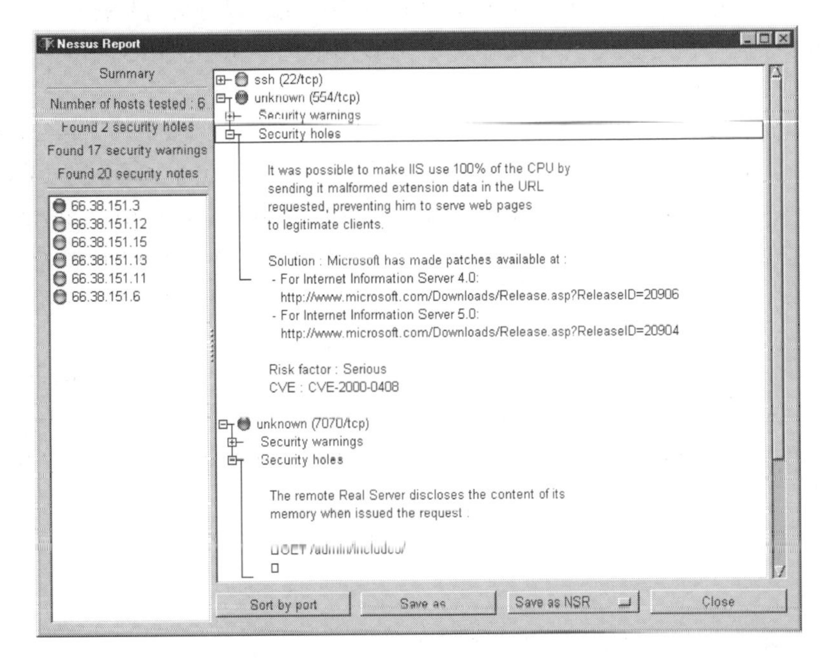


This Nessus interface is somewhat typical of vulnerability scanners. They often have a red/yellow/green rating system (red and orange, in this case.) Here, 66.38.151.3 is flagged with a red ball. If we select that IP address, a short list at the right is presented. I've clicked on the plus signs to expand a couple of the items marked as "holes." It doesn't appear that Nessus has figured out that this is a Real Server, but it did find one "hole" that is Real Server–specific. Of course, the IIS hole doesn't apply at all. It also turns out that the GET admin/includes hole has been patched on this server. Still, it's better to have false positives than false negatives. You can manually dismiss false positives, but if you're getting a lot of false negatives, then the tool isn't helping much. This particular network is a production network, so there are no holes there that we know of.

The rest of the items that it flagged are innocuous. There is an example shown in Figure 7.3.

**Figure 7.3** Nessus "Orange" Warnings

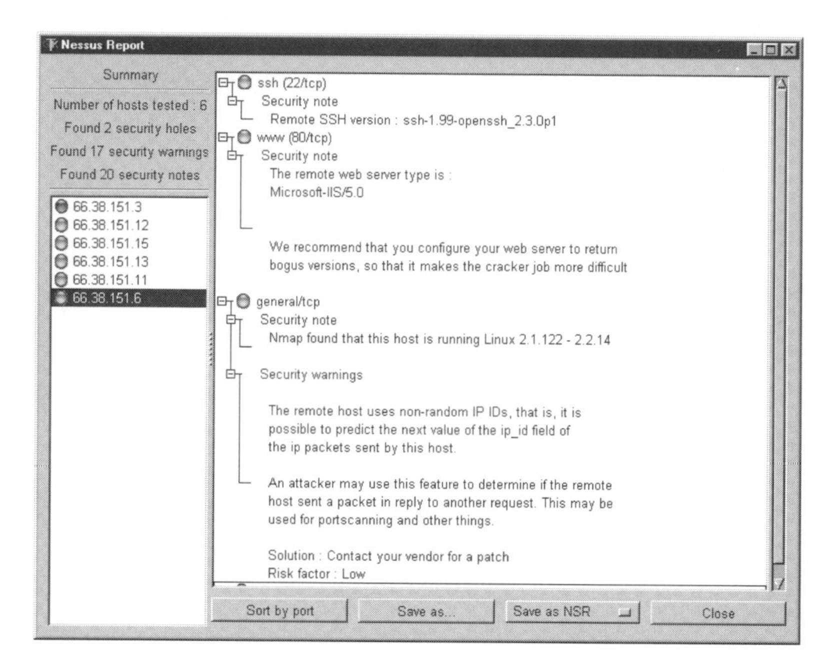


Here Nessus has recommended that you configure your Web server to lie about what software it is (this one already does, as you might infer from the fact that it's identified as Linux.) It also reports what OS nmap detected. It also notes that the IP IDs are predictable, which is not of great concern to us, though interesting to know. This is not the same class of problem as having predictable TCP sequence numbers. Nessus can also produce reports in other formats, such as HTML, and include some simple graphs.

# Hiring a Penetration Testing Team

Should you have an internal team or an external team doing your penetration test? As usual, the answer depends a great deal on your resources.

You can hire any number of individuals or teams to perform a penetration test of whatever scope you like. In an ideal world, you would have both internal and external teams performing the audit at regularly scheduled intervals. However, few of us can afford that, or even if we can, justifying the expense is difficult.

Let's assume for the moment that we have the resources to have a single team perform a penetration test. Should it be an internal team or an external team? Here are some of the reasons you would want an internal team to do the test:

- You won't have to share sensitive info with any external parties.
- Your employees will learn from the work done, and you will retain the expertise within your organization.
- Your employees are already on your payroll.
- Your team knows the intricacies of your site better than anyone.

Here are the main reasons you'd want an external team:

- Lack of penetration testing skillset in-house.
- Contractual obligation to have audit done by third party.
- You want an evaluation by someone else other than the team that implemented the security in the first place.
- Your staff doesn't have the time.
- The process will be more formalized if you pay someone else to do it.

Some of the items will determine right away that you'll need an external team, for example having a requirement that a 3rd party audit you or lacking the skillset in-house. The default choice tends to be to do it internally, because it is often perceived as being "free." There's nothing wrong with doing it internally per se, but it should be taken seriously and formalized. This means that you should expect the same kinds of results you would get if you went outside.

Let's go over what you can expect from an external audit. You should expect references and resumes of the individuals that will be performing your audit. You should expect to sign an agreement indemnifying them of any repercussions from a successful penetration. You should expect to outline in detail what you want done and what you do not want done. You should expect an estimate for the work asked for and an agreement that you will be contacted for approval if extra time is needed. You should expect a report of findings, both what was tried and failed, as well as what was successful.

There is no reason why your internal people couldn't conduct the same kind of audit if they have the skillset. There is also no reason why you shouldn't require the same documentation that you would get from an external audit.

Back to the question of having multiple audit teams or perhaps different audit teams for different scheduled audits. If the teams are comparable in terms of skills, then having different perspectives can be helpful.

You'll have to decide at some point about network positioning for the audit. This has to do with where the auditor will audit from. Many auditors might prefer to do their work across the Internet, allowing them to work from home base and not spend a lot of time traveling. The only real problem with this is that there's always a chance that some third party will be monitoring your traffic and will learn of a new vulnerability in your site as a result of the audit. My personal opinion is that if you have someone monitoring your traffic like that, you have worse problems. However, some folks are not so quick to dismiss this issue. For them, there are VPN-like solutions that should allow the auditor to conduct his business across the Internet without being monitored, at least not until the last bit of network. And you can always fly the auditor out to your location and plant them at a desk in your facility. Obviously, this may increase costs somewhat.

In addition to where the audit sits is the question of what locations in your security structure he is allowed to test from. The first obvious place is from the outside—from the equivalent of the Internet. But perhaps you'd like to know what could be done from one of your DMZ segments to find out what happens when your firewall is breached. Your security design ideally ought to be failsafe in layers. Even if the firewall wasn't there, or was misconfigured, would you still be safe? If an attacker somehow managed to get control of a machine on your financials DMZ segment, what would that buy him in terms of getting onto other machines? This type of testing can be done by coordinating with the auditor(s) and plugging their auditing machines into the appropriate network segments for each phase of the test. This assumes that they don't get in from the Internet side in the first place. If they actually manage to get control of a machine on a DMZ segment, then the repatching issue is irrelevant. For internal auditors, they can place themselves in the appropriate spots as needed.

Note that if you're going to do both an internal and external audit, it might be smart to do the internal audit first. The ideal is to get rid of any easy problems first, so that you get the most for your money from the external auditing team. If they can't spot any easy problems right off, they will have to work a bit harder and be more thorough.

# Summary

The goal in attacking your site is to assess how good your security design is and how well it has been implemented. In order to be an effective attacker, you need to understand what kinds of attacks can be launched against you. These include Denial of Service, information leakage, file access, misinformation, special file access, and elevation of privilege. Ultimately the attacker wants a higher level of privileges on your system.

In order to effectively protect your site, you have to know what your risks are. The three components of risk are vulnerabilities, threats, and assets. If you have assets to protect and vulnerabilities or threats are high, then your risk is high. Assets are typically fixed, so your goal is to minimize vulnerabilities and threats.

Measuring threats can be challenging, because you're trying to assess the intentions of remote attackers that you have probably never met. Your best tools for figuring out what kinds of attackers you have coming against you is the logs about what kinds of attacks they are trying. Typically, attacks of convenience will be targeting specific services rather than scanning for wide ranges or port numbers. IDS systems can be of assistance in weeding out the common attacks from the more persistent ones, because some of them can spot scanning patterns. You will also need to watch the various mailing lists for information about the latest worms and script kiddie tools.

Assessing your level of vulnerability is a bit easier. It's a technical problem, requiring technical expertise. The chief way that vulnerability (other than day-to-day administration) is assessed is through a penetration test. A penetration test is a test to see if your site can be broken into. You can use either an internal or external penetration team to do your testing. In either case, you should expect a report of what work was done and what attacks, if any, were successful.

One of the aids to penetration testers is an automated scanning tool. These can often perform tedious tests that a human might miss or might not have time to do. Automated scanning tools come in all shapes, sizes, and prices. Most are available for evaluation purposes (some are free) to help you decide which one is right for you.

# Solutions Fast Track

## Anticipating Various Types of Attacks

☑ An information leakage attack is an attack against confidentiality. A classic example of an information leakage problem is the *finger service.* Way back when, most UNIX machines ran a service called *finger.* There was a matching finger client command that would provide information about a particular user on a particular machine. This type of information does not lead directly to compromise, but it's rather disheartening how often a user's password matches their username—finger is a quick way to collect some usernames.

☑ A *file access* attack is an attack against confidentiality *and* integrity. There are any number of subcategories under file access, such as read access, write access, and delete permissions. Read access directly affects only confidentiality, whereas others permit modifications, which affect integrity. For example, UNIX- and DOS/Windows-based operating systems use **..** to represent the parent of the current directory, so that entering **cd ..** will take you up one directory level—some server software fails to take this into account and will allow **..** to be used in the file request, allowing an attacker to step out of boundaries.

☑ A *misinformation* attack is designed to confuse the defender. It's an attack against integrity—not the integrity of the systems themselves, but rather the defender's information *about* the systems. An example of a misinformation attack is an nmap scan that will generate extra traffic aimed at your host alongside the real packets doing the scanning.

☑ A lot of the interesting stuff at a site lives in a database. This is especially true for e-commerce sites. One extremely common programming mistake developers make when developing a Web site is to improperly escape or filter user-supplied data, giving an attacker a way to send SQL commands to a database.

- ☑ An *elevation of privilege* attack is an attack against the integrity of the security structure, though it often leads directly to other compromises. If an attacker can gain further capabilities beyond what they were supposed to have, then a security mechanism somewhere has been broken. Such a mechanism may be broken due to bad design, a bug, or just because the administrator implemented the mechanism improperly.

## Performing a Risk Analysis on Your Site

- ☑ Assets at risk can include money and financial information, customer information, products, intellectual property, employees, and reputation.
- ☑ By carefully watching firewall and IDS logs, you will begin to understand the difference between someone who has tried his trick and moved on, and someone who is sticking around for a little while. You may manage to spot an attacker that looks like he is taking some care to stay below the radar, perhaps by doing a slow scan.
- ☑ A honeypot is a system that is designed to be broken into. Setting up a honeypot will give you an opportunity to study the tactics of attackers. Your honeypot should be the easiest machine to penetrate on your network. One has to have some familiarity with forensic techniques, log analysis, and protocol analysis to make a honeypot useful.

## Testing Your Own Site for Vulnerabilities

- ☑ A good change control process can help with minimizing the risks in between full scans. Each time some change is made, make a best effort to determine exactly what will be affected and recheck just those things that are affected. Accurately record and assess any changes made and report the changes to the people who will need to recheck. Some host-based IDS systems will catch some of the changes, but they will never be as effective as accurate records from the people actually making the changes in the first place. Think of these as incremental penetration tests, similar to doing incremental backups in between full backups.

☑ Any tool or testing method could potentially result in false negatives but blindly running exploits will result in a much higher false negative rate. If you're getting caught by attacks of convenience, then you need to take a hard look at your procedures for tracking new vulnerabilities and applying vendor patches.

☑ Types of knowledge you should take advantage of include the following: Trust relationships, IP addresses on all network segments, brands and versions of all your software, what type of network gear you use, and source code for all the software if available (especially custom software).

☑ An attacker may try to use some stealth techniques to evade detection. This may include doing certain types of stealth portscans (these are of limited use, because just about any network IDS will pick these up. Some host-based measures like TCP wrappers may not.) Other techniques are slow scans (doing a port scan slowly over time so as not to set off an IDS threshold and make the red port-scan light go off), packet fragmenting (effective against a number of IDS systems), and finally, various types of misinformation attacks.

☑ The pieces of information needed for targeting known holes and downloading an existing exploit include IP Addresses, names, open ports, OS versions, software versions, network structure, and firewall configuration(s).

☑ Banner scanning is the method of trying to determine what software is running by seeing what kinds of information it will volunteer, somewhat equivalent to connecting to a given port and seeing what kind of output you get. This works fine for TCP, but UDP is a bit harder. Although one can use a simple tool like a Telnet client to connect to many TCP services and get back some output, for UDP you have to issue the right kind of request and see what kind of output, if any, you get.

☑ The default files that come with any Web server often aren't removed, and in many cases, they have had vulnerabilities. For example, all copies of IIS 4.0 Web server contained a sample file called showcode.asp—its purpose is to show the source code for an .asp file rather than running it, a feature any attacker would love to have.

☑ Even if automated scanning tools were 100 percent accurate, the majority of them will not actually carry out a penetration, they will only try to determine if a site is vulnerable or not. It will be up to you to actually exercise the vulnerability.

## Hiring a Penetration Testing Team

☑ Running an external audit, you should expect references and resumes of the individuals that will be performing your audit. You should expect to sign an agreement indemnifying them of any repercussions from a successful penetration. You should expect to outline in detail what you want done, and what you do not want done. You should expect an estimate for the work asked for, and an agreement that you will be contacted for approval if extra time is needed. You should expect a report of findings, both what was tried and failed, as well as what was successful.

☑ There is no reason why your internal people couldn't conduct the same kind of audit as an external team if they have the skillset. There is also no reason why you shouldn't require the same documentation that you would get from an external audit.

☑ If you're going to do both an internal and external audit, it might be smart to do the internal audit first. The ideal is to get rid of any easy problems first so that you get the most for your money from the external auditing team.

# Frequently Asked Questions

The following Frequently Asked Questions, answered by the authors of this book, are designed to both measure your understanding of the concepts presented in this chapter and to assist you with real-life implementation of these concepts. To have your questions about this chapter answered by the author, browse to **www.syngress.com/solutions** and click on the **"Ask the Author"** form.

**Q:** What advantages do commercial scanners have over the free ones?

**A:** What you are paying for is support, tools that work cleanly (are easy to install and run), often more functional reporting systems, and for your vendor to maintain and update the tests for you. Nothing can guarantee your vendor will be around forever, but many people feel comfortable that vendors will continue to maintain and enhance their products if they have a financial obligation to. Ultimately, what matters is if you are able to use the product to meet your needs. If the free products (usually a desirable choice due to cost) don't meet your needs, is the cost of the commercial product worth it to you? Also of note is that many commercial products tie into other products from that vendor, possibly giving you a more complete solution.

**Q:** What about hiring some guy with a mysterious hacker name? He was able to break into NASA.

**A:** Questions of trustworthiness aside, you have to realize that being able to break into some high profile site doesn't necessarily translate into the right skillset to perform a professional penetration test. It's really not that difficult to take a recently discovered exploit and try it against 1,000 high profile sites, and be successful some small percentage of the time. That does not indicate that the attacker even understands how the particular exploit works. Also, a big part of what you want out of a penetration test is a decent report and probably some advice on how to clean up your security, which a hit-and-run attacker isn't usually accustomed to doing. If you really want an auditor with a cool name, try hiring one of the companies that has hired some of these people and ask them what their standards are for determining skill level. You also shouldn't assume that someone is the type to break into NASA just because he *does* have a handle.

**Q:** Where can I find some of the free scanning tools?

**A:** Check out the following locations:

| | |
|---|---|
| Nessus | www.nessus.org/ |
| SAINT | www.wwdsi.com/saint/ |
| SARA | www-arc.com/sara/ |
| SATAN | www.fish.com/satan/ |
| Whisker | www.wiretrip.net/rfp/ |

# Chapter 8

# Disaster Recovery Planning: The Best Defense

**Solutions in this chapter:**

- What Is Disaster Recovery Planning?
- Ensuring Secure Information Backup and Restoration
- Planning for Hardware Failure or Loss of Services
- How Do I Protect against Natural Disasters?
- Understanding Your Insurance Options

☑ Summary

☑ Solutions Fast Track

☑ Frequently Asked Questions

# Introduction

You've written appropriate, solid security policy, your e-commerce servers are patched, your software is well written, and you monitor your Web servers routinely for intrusions. But one of your servers is down anyway. Now what do you do? Whether caused by act of nature, system failure, security breach, or administrative accident, avoiding downed services is impossible. Disasters that cause downtime don't have to come as a complete surprise though. Thinking through what to do before a crisis happens is a necessary part of business known as disaster recovery planning.

This chapter assists you in creating a disaster recovery plan, so that you can identify key areas where prevention may avert the disaster—or at least minimize the risk of downtime—and you will know how to proceed in the event of any type of loss. Ensuring that your backup and restore systems are optimized is essential. Adding fault tolerance to your Web site eliminates single points of failure in your configurations that can be the cause of downtime; this chapter discusses various methods of increasing redundancy. Another form of redundancy, protection, and recovery this chapter covers is choosing a remote hot site location and services in the case of a natural disaster such as flooding. Last, we explore the relatively new field of insurance as it relates to e-commerce liabilities.

# What Is Disaster Recovery Planning?

The Disaster Recovery Journal (www.drj.com), an electronic journal dedicated to business continuity during emergencies, defines a *disaster* as "Any event that creates an inability on an organization's part to provide critical business functions for some predetermined period of time." Likewise, *disaster recovery planning* is defined as "The advance planning and preparation that is necessary to minimize loss and ensure continuity of the critical business functions of an organization in the event of disaster." Anything that causes your e-commerce business to be offline for a period of time is a disaster if it affects your company's bottom line. Whereas with brick-and-mortar companies a disaster recovery plan (DRP) typically involves what to do during the period of time that a business must be closed, tolerance for downtime in an e-commerce business approaches zero. Disaster recovery planning for e-business more closely resembles disaster *prevention* planning if the business is successful. In this chapter, we investigate aspects of both, and observe how spending a little time, effort, and money upfront could save you from spending a lot more later on.

Many business managers never consider the potential effect that even major service outages could have on operations. Consider the flood in downtown Chicago on April 13, 1992. Water overflowed the banks of the Chicago River and flooded the basements of buildings in the city's financial district. Electricity was cut off. Basement computer rooms became flooded. The Chicago Board of Trade was forced to close, causing losses in the billions on world trade markets. Better-prepared managers might plan to locate data centers above ground level in high-flood-risk areas. In January of 1990, an AT&T phone switch suffered an intermittent failure, causing a major service outage across the national US phone network. The failure was later identified as a programming error. Today, backup wireless phone networks can maintain critical business communications in the event of a similar outage, although many businesses are not yet equipped to use wireless technologies effectively to keep in touch with customers should their primary phone services become unavailable.

The major goal of a disaster recovery plan is to prevent support personnel from wasting critical time evaluating an emergency and deciding how to proceed. Formulating a recovery plan as you go takes time that could otherwise be spent actually doing the recovery work. The DRP should spell out the details of how to proceed before the recovery is needed. In an emergency, staff members may not have access to all the information necessary to make the best decisions, so the DRP must gather critical recovery information into one location. In case of a catastrophic event such as a fire, unavailable communications systems may prevent staff members from being able to communicate about the recovery, so the DRP must specify alternate methods of communicating in these situations. If a security breach occurs, support personnel may inadvertently taint evidence necessary for successful prosecution of the perpetrator unless they are prepared ahead of time in forensic methods.

The DRP must specify how investigations should be handled to protect the company's ability to prosecute criminal activity.

A disaster recovery plan in its simplest form can be little more than a spreadsheet with relevant phone numbers and information passed around to staff members. Or, it can be as complex as a published business continuity plan that provides for fully equipped backup data centers running in continual standby mode, ready to deploy on a moment's notice. Obviously, there is quite a difference in cost and practicality between these two extremes, and most e-commerce ventures will fall somewhere in the middle. But just as the business grows, so does the need to adjust and rethink the disaster recovery plan. Because it is always evolving, it doesn't have to be perfect the first time around. The most important thing is to get started, put something down on paper, plan to practice, and then practice the plan.

## Structuring a Disaster Recovery Plan

Most disasters related to e-commerce are characterized by one of three common elements. A good disaster recovery plan addresses all three of these areas:

- Loss of trade secrets or critical data
- Loss of access to hardware and software systems
- Loss of personnel or critical skill sets

Common to all three situations is the need to identify key staff members responsible for responding to emergencies, how they should be contacted, what their authority levels should be, and under what circumstances they will be called upon. To prevent misunderstanding, the DRP should specify one individual as primary and one as the backup person in charge, and it should also specify how to maintain communication with upper management during an emergency. To demonstrate why this is important, let's consider what would happen if your e-commerce site became compromised and credit card numbers were stolen. First, it would be imperative for an incident response team with the proper skills in investigative forensics to preserve evidence while bringing the systems back online. Keeping communications to a minimum with parties not involved in the investigation would be important, because the intruder might actually be an employee. But it would also be essential to quickly and securely communicate the extent of the damage to members of the business management, who are in a better position to address expense control, public relations concerns, and notification of shareholders about what has occurred. The DRP should list whom to call with different types of information about a disaster or intrusion. The DRP should specify that post-event communications specifically about security breaches should not involve e-mail, which might be intercepted and read by the intruder (which would be disastrous!). You may also wish to insert provisions for an incident response team for investigating and recovering from intrusions and then train the team members in forensic methods as a preventive measure. More information about creating incident response teams is included in Chapter 10 of this book. Lastly, if the intruder is identified and prosecution is sought, the DRP will need to provide procedures and clear roles and responsibilities for contacting legal entities, handling subpoenas, and notifying company attorneys, because these roles may not necessarily follow normal reporting lines under unusual circumstances.

## Loss of Data or Trade Secrets

Loss of data or trade secrets might happen as the result of theft by an intruder, accidental deletion by an internal staff member, deliberate destruction by a disgruntled employee, or inadvertent access by a trusted third party. Intellectual property data can be a very expensive business asset to lose. Software source code is a prize targeted by intruders wanting to learn how to crack the licensing mechanisms or find weaknesses that can be used to escalate user privileges. Believe it or not though, the vast majority of data loss is actually the result of damage by trusted employees, where proper checks and balances on their activities are not in place. According to an Internet crime survey conducted in March 2000 by the FBI and Computer Security Institute (www.gocsi.com), there is a greater than 60 percent chance of system threat from someone on the inside. Sometimes, system administrators just make mistakes. The only way to prevent internal data mishaps is to have the controls in place that challenge the authority of all staff members to make changes, and then check and double check any changes they make. When accidents happen despite controls, you better be ready with good, quality backups of your data. The DRP should provide information about how to restore software and data, prioritize critical systems to be restored first, and centralize recovery information about backup tape locations and staff members available for performing the tasks. More information about specific procedures for data backups is included later in this chapter.

When lack of proper security controls results in data lost to an external intruder, the DRP can help ensure that it never happens again. Western Union learned about recovering from external data loss the hard way when over 15,000 credit card numbers were stolen from its Web site in September 2000. During performance testing of their newly expanded e-commerce site, a file was left in place with insecure permissions, resulting in the ability of an intruder to access unauthorized information. Western Union acted quickly, took down the site, and began notifying customers about the problem. They did everything right from a recovery standpoint...*except prevent the intrusion from occurring in the first place.*

The job of the Disaster Recovery Plan in cases like this one would be to provide the right feedback to site developers, testing managers, and IT staff that are authorized to make changes to production systems. Armed with information about how the attack occurred, these teams can then implement better controls on procedures, build or improve testing labs, and develop other internal strategies to prevent reoccurrences of the event. The goal of recovery efforts is not to hide what has happened or to point fingers, but to maximize learning from it to better the business. Toward that end, the DRP specifies an information-sharing process after the fact. It should provide a template for a disaster analysis report to be performed after recovery is complete. The template might touch on the important elements to be included in the analysis, such as evidence collected, essential causal information (without being accusatory of employees who may have made mistakes), how recovery was achieved, any temporary fixes that will have to be repaired later, and a timeline of events. A routing list of managers who should see the analysis might also be included. The security team responsible for maintaining the company security policy should no doubt be included on the routing list, so site policy can be adjusted for any deficits that might have led to the intrusion. The HR team will no doubt want to review the matter if an internal employee is involved, so provisions for HR involvement might also be included in the DRP.

## Loss of Access to Physical Systems

Loss of access to physical systems can happen during a natural disaster such as fire or flood, from network unavailability of your Internet Service Provider (ISP), from a denial of service or other attack on your site, or simply through hardware or software failure. The best way to plan ahead for this type of loss is by building fault tolerance into your systems as a preventive measure. One way to improve fault tolerance is by implementing High Availability (HA) features of hardware and software. In a HA configuration, multiple hardware is installed with special software configurations capable of detecting if one or more of the devices is unavailable. The software eliminates the dependency of the system as a whole on any one device. The redundancy concept can be extended to multiple systems, multiple data centers, and multiple ISPs. More information about system and site redundancy is included later in this chapter.

### *Physical Security*

In the event of a large disaster, you'll need to know whether power, air conditioning, and fire suppression systems within your data center are sufficient to accommodate additional servers and personnel during the recovery process. Documenting the capacity limitations of your physical facilities and providing for alternate facilities in recovery situations that require them are all functions of the DRP.

Another consideration is the physical security system and whether it logs physical access by staff members. For instance, if a system were turned off, how would you identify the last person to access the computer room? If the power went out, could the system administrators get into the computer room to shut down critical systems gracefully before the UPS runs out of power? If the recovery effort involves replacing hardware, the DRP can provide for quick acquisition of replacement hardware and software by collecting up information about support providers, service agreements, key contacts, critical installation procedures, documentation, and spare parts inventories. Copies of the DRP should be stored offsite, because in the event of a physical disaster this will be your main starting point for rebuilding your systems.

### *Denial of Service Attacks*

You will also want to document how you plan to deal with a denial of service (DoS) attack if your site becomes the unfortunate victim of one. As we saw earlier in the book, a DoS attack sends large amounts of unwanted traffic to overload your systems and prevent them from being accessed by legitimate users. But you can take steps to deal with the traffic. For instance, if the attack fills up your Internet connection with traffic using the ICMP protocol—and because ICMP is not a critical component of Web services—you can request that your ISP temporarily stop routing ICMP to your site, relieving the load on your primary router and firewall. You wouldn't want things to remain in this state after the attack is over, but quick action by you and your ISP can make this particular kind of attack more transparent to your customers. As we shall see in a later chapter, your ISP may also be able to help you temporarily increase the bandwidth on your Internet connection to help you get through an attack, depending on the type of telecom equipment and connection you have. Your ISP can also help prevent attacks by managing spoofed IP addresses within their networks. If your site is the victim of a DoS attack, the post-event report should make note of steps that could be taken to prevent it from occurring again in the future.

If the DoS is against your Web site directly, you may be able to play some tricks with routing, Web redirection, and Domain Name Service (DNS) updates to route attack traffic away from a main Web server. If your site involves a Web redirector, your main site hostname (www.yoursite.com) will match up to the IP address of the redirector, which in turn balances Web traffic loads to several Web servers clustered together for redundancy and load sharing. If the main site's IP address is suddenly overloaded with some kind of traffic your network connection can handle but your servers can't, and if you can act quickly to identify the type of traffic used in the attack, you can adjust network routes, DNS records, and/or local redirector configurations to send that traffic to just one server in the cluster and send the remaining good traffic to the other systems. If you can't segregate the DoS traffic by protocol or destination, but you can identify the source IP or source port of the attacker's software, you can then block the traffic before it enters your site. All of these actions require quick investigation of the attack followed by action to contact the ISP or block the traffic at your site, but these actions don't necessarily have to be done by you. Your company may already have an intrusion analyst on staff that analyzes intrusion traffic routinely and may have a networking department that manages your firewalls and routers. As part of recovery planning, you will want to think about how you will handle external attacks and lay the foundation for fast recovery ahead of time by making advance arrangements with your ISP and any other departments that manage your network. The DRP should then document the procedures and contact information for later reference.

Damage & Defense...

### Creating a Cost-Effective Disaster Recovery Plan

The first step in creating a Disaster Recovery Plan is to understand your vulnerabilities. Determine the most likely risks, estimate the effect on the e-business, and then formulate recovery measures to protect against the most business-critical situations. In the era of global e-business, where the entire public image of a company may depend on its presence on the Internet, and where e-commerce may represent a company's entire revenue stream, it may take only a few minutes of downtime to have a devastating effect.

- What would happen if your e-commerce site went down for an hour? A day? A week?
- What would be the impact if customers were unable to obtain technical support for products you sell?

Continued

- How much revenue would be lost per day or hour from lost sales during an outage?
- What would be the impact if data you keep about your customers or products were stolen?
- How will shareholders or business owners react to system downtime? How will the media react?
- Under what circumstances could the business no longer recover?

The second step is to prioritize the risks to the e-business. Prepare an inventory of the communications and equipment involved in your e-commerce site, along with the quantity of each type of equipment or service, and a brief summary of the support agreement you have with vendors and service providers. Enlist the input of the company's management in determining the ability of the business to tolerate different kinds of failures or outages. Assign a priority to each system and support function—keeping in mind that in the event of a catastrophic loss such as a flood, not all systems or functions can be restored to full capacity immediately. Ask yourself questions about the people, facilities, and systems that support your e-commerce site.

- Do hardware vendors provide on-site service within a few hours, or is there a delayed shipping time for spare parts?
- Is the data center located in a vulnerable area? Is it physically secure?
- Does the facility have sufficient power and air conditioning to accommodate additional servers?
- Are backup tapes available from which to restore critical data?
- How long does it take to rebuild the hardware and software your e-commerce site depends on?

**Continued**

- Is your site dependent on a single ISP?
- Does key support staff have backup help to do restoration work?

Armed with a prioritized list of system and human dependencies, you can now formulate recovery measures that are cost-effective for your e-business. Some examples of recovery measures that can be critical but not costly:

- Create an incident response team, or decide how one will be created for each new emergency, and provide copies of the team plan to the employees responsible for performing recovery.
- Provide the incident response team members with business and home phone numbers, vendor contact information, and owners or locations of critical documents.
- Write down the physical locations of critical hardware, software, parts, and tape backup media.
- Practice procedures for restoring software and critical data from backup tape.
- Develop forensics procedures that must be followed in the event of a security breach.
- Assign a primary and a backup person responsible for each recovery activity.
- Practice emergency situations such as fictitious security breaches and discuss where improvements should be made.

More costly recovery measures may include keeping spare hardware parts in inventory, expanding vendor service agreements, and creating redundant servers, disk mirrors, or backup data centers. Enlist the input of upper management in quantifying the value to the business of taking further, more costly steps to ensure the availability of the e-commerce site.

## Loss of Personnel or Critical Skill Sets

Loss of personnel results in loss of intellectual property and key administrative or development skills through layoff, voluntary termination, or physical disaster. To minimize the effects of employee turnover, your DRP will need to identify a primary and a backup person responsible for each recovery process. Periodically review your site's processes, such as applying software patches, performing database maintenance, or installing configuration management software, to ensure that multiple people are available for each task. In the event of a regional disaster such as an earthquake, key administrative staff may be unable to travel, and their functions in the recovery process will need to be replaced, at least temporarily. Having multiple people available to perform each recovery task will mitigate this risk. From a prevention perspective, you should never to allow any single individual to know, or have access to, every portion your e-commerce Web site. Doing so is just inviting that person to tamper with the site by installing backdoors or performing other destructive acts when he or she leaves the company. If it's unavoidable to have a single person accessing every part of your site, then your disaster planning should ensure adequate logging and monitoring capability when that person leaves the company. It's also a good idea to require all changes to be reviewed by another person for accuracy. A fresh set of eyes can often catch a mistake before it becomes critical.

# Practicing Compliance with Quality Standards

If your e-commerce business plans to pursue compliance with quality standards set by the International Standards Organization (ISO), preparing a Disaster Recovery Plan will be an essential component of the ISO certification process. ISO is a standards group begun in 1947 in Sweden that helps address international quality and compatibility issues across many different aspects of doing business. To date, ISO includes standards bodies in 120 different countries. ISO standards apply to all types of business processes, because they allow the business to define its own standard of quality, document the processes that create that standard, and then demonstrate through periodic external audits that the quality standards are being maintained. The ISO certification process for an e-commerce venture can assist your company in writing down what its own Web service standard will be, which should include such concerns as site security, privacy of customer data, maximizing uptime, and so on. Developing a workable and documented Disaster Recovery Plan that includes such details as how and when data backups are performed is a required step in the ISO 9000 certification process. If your e-commerce site is a business-to-business site, you may find that ISO certification is even required for doing business with foreign organizations, especially those in Europe. However, even if your e-commerce venture is small or you just don't wish to pursue ISO certification right now, it's still good business to self-audit your e-commerce quality standards, think ahead about what might happen tomorrow, and formulate steps you can take today to prevent and plan for emergency situations.

What does all this talk about quality assurance have to do with disaster recovery planning? Simple. The easiest disaster to recover from is the one that doesn't happen, because quality is kept to the highest standard possible. Identifying what standard of quality will be maintained must precede allocation of budget and staff to maintain it. The more emphasis put on quality upfront, the less emphasis must be put on recovery at the back end. You can pay for quality assurance or you can pay for disaster recovery, except that disaster recovery can cost substantially more, especially if lawsuits are involved. Thus, disaster recovery planning is a spiraling arm of the quality control process, building on the company security policy as early as requirements for your e-commerce site are being drafted and continuing throughout software code review, hardware implementation, and intrusion analysis. Your final recovery plan should have to cover only those risks and vulnerabilities remaining even after copious amounts of testing, review, testing, and yet more testing of your e-commerce site.

# Ensuring Secure Information Backup and Restoration

When a computer hard drive fails, a database becomes corrupt, or a security breach brings into doubt the integrity of your online data, your last line of recovery is to start over from known-good backup copies of the data stored offline. Establishing an effective data backup procedure is perhaps the most important step in an overall disaster recovery plan for an e-commerce site. Without quality backup copies of your data, a system failure may result in permanent loss of critical information about customers or products. Many hours or days could be required to rebuild software and systems one at a time through the same process by which they were initially created. Data input to the e-commerce site by customers since the last backup may simply be irrecoverable. The more frequently the data is backed up, the less data will be lost if the system crashes.

Documenting the process for performing data backups and restores is an essential part of disaster planning, because backup and restore procedures may vary slightly from system to system. For example, it is important to know which software must be stopped before a backup occurs. If a file is backed up while a software program is writing to that file, the backup image may become corrupted. For this reason, taking a critical system off the network during backup procedures is advisable, especially if the disk is mounted remotely to another computer system or if users frequently write to files on the disk being backed up. Most database software has to be stopped prior to backing up the database, or the backup image can be corrupt. The last thing you need at recovery time is corrupt backup media, so you should plan ahead for that possibility.

Noting the type and size of hard disk partitions being backed up is also useful at recovery time. If an entire disk must be restored in the future, having documentation on-hand about the size of the disk partitions that existed on the system at the time the backup image was taken can prevent wasted time restoring to a hard drive that is too small to accommodate the data on the backup media. In the event a large number of systems must be rebuilt, the task of restoring data from backup may need to be outsourced or handed off to staff that are not normally involved with the task, in which case documentation will be crucial to the success of recovery.

## The Need for Backups and Verification

Assuring the integrity of your data backup is not as simple as making a copy and forgetting about it. For instance, an application that writes data to a database may need to save its state and complete a transaction before backups begin, otherwise the last transaction can be lost without getting backed up. Restoring a database that was backed up mid-transaction may cause the restored image to become corrupt and unusable. Certain operating systems are unable to read files for backup until the files are closed, so software writing to those files must be stopped before backups can begin. Certain other operating systems may not sync data from memory to disk unless a manual synchronization is performed prior to doing the backup. Tapes can also become old after awhile and no longer retain their data without becoming corrupted. Raid disk mirrors may become corrupted after losing a hard drive, making the backup copy unrestorable. Any backup media can be destroyed by fire or flood.

The worst time to learn that your backup data is no good is the moment it is needed for restoration. The most effective way of assuring the quality of your data backups at restore time is to perform a routine verification of the data as it is backed up, typically by restoring all or a portion of the data back to disk and comparing it to the original. Most backup software provides an automated mechanism for verifying the data that was written to the backup media is an exact copy of the data on disk, but it may be up to the backup operator to make sure that feature is turned on. It takes longer to do backups using the verification procedure, but it's well worth the extra time.

After you are certain you have a good backup copy, you must protect it to ensure that it stays good. Different backup media have different environmental storage requirements for optimum life span of the media, so be sure to read the label. If the backup media is another disk, it can be stored in another physical location by performing the backup across a network. Periodically, backup tapes should be sent to a different physical location to ensure that they won't be destroyed in the same disaster that causes them to be needed in the first place. If your backup tapes get waterlogged or smoke damaged in a flood or fire, companies that offer data recovery services may be able to salvage the media and retrieve the data, but these services can be expensive. If possible, prevent the damage in the first place by rotating the media offsite. The procedures used to rotate media in and out of an off-site storage location is known as a backup rotation process.

## An Example Backup Rotation Process

You can choose among many different procedures to store backup data for sending offsite. The simplest is to take a complete image of the data once a day and store it on some medium, whether hard disk, optical disk, DLT 4mm or 8mm tape, or CD-ROM. When the need arises to perform a restore operation, you need only go back to yesterday's media to obtain a full image of the data to be restored. Each day, as today's image is backed up, yesterday's media is sent to an offsite storage facility, ensuring that only one day's worth of data is ever at risk of permanent loss in a fire or flood. Each Friday, as the Friday tape is sent offsite, the Monday through Thursday tapes are brought back and reused next week, so only the Friday tape is kept offsite permanently. This is an excellent strategy when you have a large amount of data that changes almost entirely from one day to the next. When you don't, however, much of the same data may be copied onto different media day after day, potentially inflating media expenses. Figure 8.1 is a diagram showing that each day's backup contains all the data changes since last week's backup on the same day of the week.

**Figure 8.1** Daily Full Backup

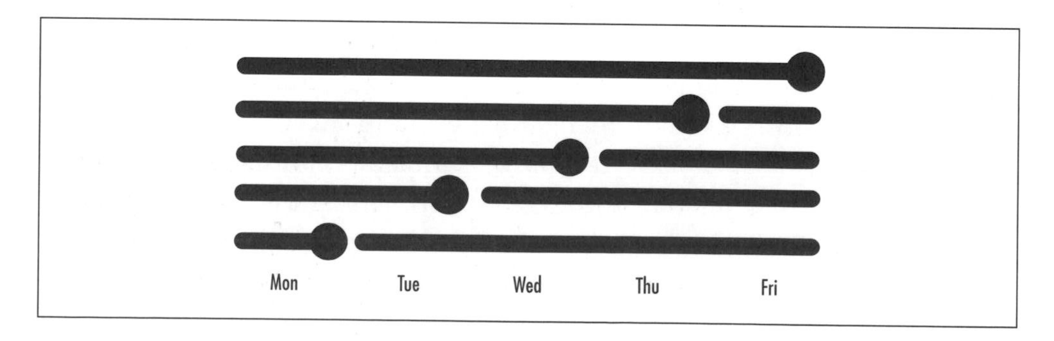

One strategy to minimize wasting media where data does not change often is to use a media rotation that takes a full image only once per week, with a partial image on the days in-between (see Figure 8.2). On the days in-between full backups, the only data that is backed up is that which has changed since the last full backup was taken. The images taken in between full backups are known as incremental backups. To do a restore in a rotation scheme such as this, you'll need the last full backup media, which is potentially up to one week old, plus yesterday's incremental media, which has all the data that changed since the last full backup was done. Each time a full backup is performed, the previous week's backup media can be sent to an offsite storage facility, ensuring that only the current week's data is ever at risk in a catastrophic loss situation. The incremental media from last week is reused this week, if it is still in good physical condition.

**Figure 8.2** Friday Full with Daily Incremental Since Last Full Backup

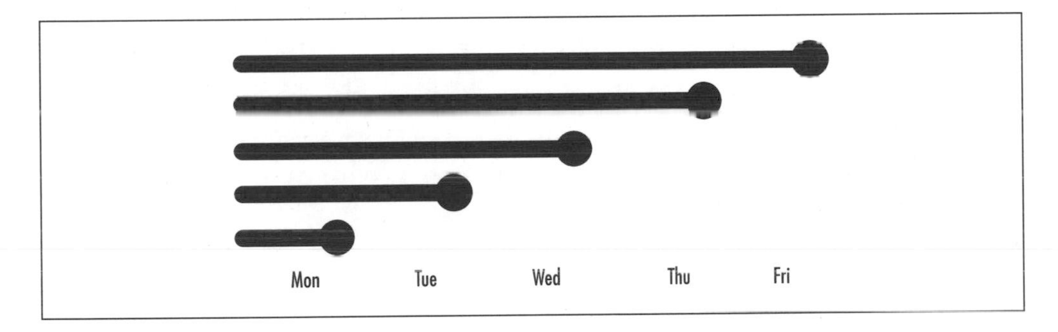


Another way to utilize incremental backups is to take an incremental each day of only the previous day's changes in data and take a full backup image once per week to send offsite (see Figure 8.3). In this rotation scheme, only the Friday tape is sent offsite, and the Monday through Thursday tapes are reused each week. When a restore is done on Thursday, you will need to restore last Friday's tape first, followed by this week's Monday through Wednesday tapes in date order.

As a practical example, let's consider a company with a large product database that is served as dynamic content to a Web server. The application that serves the dynamic content sits on a second server and the database resides on a third. In this example, if the first backup scheme

**Figure 8.3** Friday Full with Daily Incremental Since Last Incremental Backup

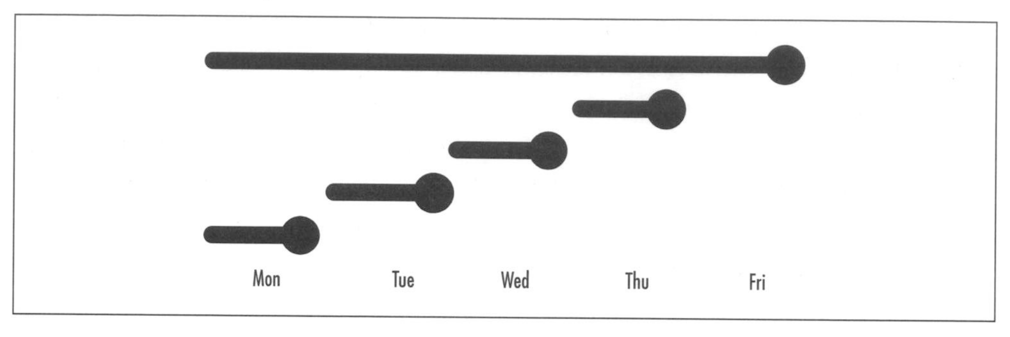


were used, a full backup would be taken daily of all three servers. Because the Web server has no static content, it doesn't contain anything that changes, so the image of the software and operating system are fairly stable. Taking a full image of that system day after day would be wasteful of media (refer back to Figure 8.1). On the other hand, the database is very dynamic, because it has product updates frequently or has customer updates with every order. Taking a full image of the database makes more sense especially because sensitive customer data is involved (refer back to Figure 8.2). In fact, large customer databases may even need to be backed up incrementally several times a day, with a full backup once per day (refer back to Figure 8.3).

## Storage Area Networks

Because the application server writes to the database, it is possible that the image of the application must be taken at precisely the same time as the image of the database in order to ensure that the transactional state is properly preserved. In situations like this one, a Storage Area Network (SAN) might provide the best results. A SAN consists of a series of large data storage devices connected by a high-speed network. The disks can be striped together to look like one big disk, or two sets half as big each. One set can be the primary disk storage partition and the other can be a mirror of the first. Mirroring means that data is written twice for redundancy. The computer systems writing to the SAN copy the data to the mirror with each write operation to the primary. Once a day, the mirror can be broken long enough to stream the data to a tape device, which can be part of the same SAN. After the data is streamed to tape, the mirror is restored and repopulated with data until the next backup operation. Alternatively, there can be two mirrors, one for the active mirror and one for the backup mirror streaming to tape. For that matter, the tape device and the backup mirror don't have to be onsite, they can be housed at a remote data storage facility. The proliferation of cheap and large disk arrays points the way to SANs as the future of data backups, although the technology for offsite SANs is still relatively immature and holds the potential for problems. Your mileage may vary.

# Protecting Backups of Sensitive Information

We've spent a lot of time in this chapter discussing disaster recovery and methods to recover data lost during a disaster. One such disaster is theft or destruction of data by an intruder during a security breach. But security breaches don't just happen over the network. If I were determined to steal your data, I might covertly examine your operations from every angle and consider all the alternatives, including stealing your backup tapes. Why should I spend time cracking a login password when I can lift a backup tape off someone's desk and just read the data right off it? If a contractor has access to your internal network, and you have your backup tapes neatly stacked in an online tape library that he can access them from the network, he can just copy the data right from tape (a good reason never to share a tape device over the network). If he's an external data thief, it might be cheaper in both time and money to engage in a little social engineering and convince the offsite storage facility that he's a contractor working for your company and needs a tape to do a restore. How might he find out who your offsite storage facility is? By going through your trash. For that matter, if he's going to these lengths to do something illegal, it might be less time consuming to bribe the offsite courier to let him borrow a tape or two for a few hours. If he wants the data badly enough, he will get it. Don't assume that your backups are protected just because you pay an offsite storage facility to come pick them up every Friday.

Easy enough to fix, you say: just encrypt the data as it is backed up. Good idea, but how? You have 6 administrators maintaining 72 servers for your site in various locations, and each administrator is responsible for doing their own backups. Let's say they all use the same software package that streams data to a remote backup server, which then encrypts the data before storing it on tape. The data is protected on tape but not while traversing the network. The guy in the corner can sniff it off the network because it is sent across in the clear. You need a software package that encrypts before sending the data across the network, not after. Let's walk through the steps an administrator might take in deciding what kind of backup software best protects sensitive data on an e-commerce Web site.

## User Authentication

Starting off, we buy a nice software package that says it does encryption and we install on every NT server so it can only be run by the privileged administrator account. The administrator logs in every day and kicks off a backup of the critical data. This gets old and tedious after awhile so the administrator sets up the software to do this task automatically every day. When a restore is needed, the administrator logs in and clicks on a set of files, and the software decrypts the files as it streams them from the remote tape library.

Now think about what has to happen in this scenario. Either no additional password other than the NT login password is required for the administrator to use the backup software, or the password is stored on disk somewhere and retrieved from that location during the automated backup. If no additional password is required to run the software, then how does the remote backup server know that it's not okay for the guy in the corner to write to its tapes? If anyone can write files there, then anyone can fill up the tape with garbage, preventing your legitimate backup from happening correctly overnight. Or, perhaps someone can overwrite one of your good backups or delete a backed-up file, before you make it in to work the next morning. You think you're sending a good tape offsite the next day, but in reality it's full of nothing useful. We need a software package that requires users to authenticate so that only authorized users can write to the tape library.

If the software already requires a separate run-time password and is stored on disk in human readable form, perhaps I can remotely mount the disk where the file is stored and read it (Fix: Never share your C: drive to everyone) or take it from the registry (Fix: Configure your systems to not allow remote registry reads by anyone but the administrator). If the password is scrambled, it has to be stored in a way so that the backup software can retrieve it when you're not around, which means a one-way hash isn't being used. If the password is encrypted, then it has to be decrypted at some point, so the secret key used to encrypt the password must also be stored on disk somewhere, perhaps in the registry or perhaps in a configuration file associated with the software (Fix: Don't buy that software). To prevent storing keys and passwords on disk at all, we need a software package that uses a different password for each user and checks it using a secure authentication method.

## Data Encryption and Controls

We pitch that software and go find a new software package that authenticates each user separately. We're impressed with the strength of the authentication and encryption algorithms it uses. We can choose 3DES or Blowfish to encrypt files, so it must be good, right? The software generates a strong encryption key at install time that is copied to each server to encrypt data before it is sent across the network. What's wrong with this software package? Unless each user's files are encrypted using a different key, all authenticated users can still decrypt and read the other users' files. Breaking one user's passphrase or obtaining the one private key is sufficient to grant access to data for potentially all the servers (although it might be necessary to spoof a server's IP address to get the backup data off the network). This problem is best illustrated if you consider that the hosts being backed up sit on a DMZ, and the tape server is inside the firewall. If the Web server became compromised, accessing the application server's database from backup tape shouldn't be possible, yet this is precisely possible unless each server backs up using different keys. Obviously, each backup user needs to be uniquely authenticated *and* each server's data needs to be uniquely encrypted before being sent across the network. Our software also needs to allow us to prevent restores to a DMZ in the event it becomes compromised. If a system becomes sufficiently broken to need a restore, it should be taken offline, brought inside, repaired, and then returned to the DMZ. Allowing restores to go out through the firewall is asking for trouble. One way to prevent this is to purchase software that performs backups on one port and restores on another and then block the restore port at the firewall.

## Key Management

Now we've decided to eliminate automation in the backup process, we have software that authenticates each user and encrypts data using different keys for each server, and our firewall blocks restores to the DMZ. But we're still not out of the woods. All six administrators use passwords and/or passphrases that only they know. One leaves the company without telling anyone the passphrase to restore the data that was backed up with his private encryption key. The data that was encrypted using the lost key is now useless without the ability to decrypt it at restore time. If the remote backup software stores copies of the private keys, are they stored in a secure database? Is that database backed up? Do you have the ability to retrieve the private keys without the associated password or passphrase?

If there is an administrative account that has access to all the secret keys, it is a vulnerability point that might be easy to exploit. If there isn't, you may be out of luck to restore a file if a passphrase is later forgotten or unrecoverable. Even if you are able to retrieve the private key, managing many private keys can be difficult, especially if you maintain good security and change them frequently. We either need a key management infrastructure or we need to minimize the difficulty of managing keys manually. It's probably more cost effective to do the latter if your business is small, so we decide to have only two people do backups full time instead of six doing it part time. Their manager now generates new keys for them every 90 days and retains the old keys with their dates of use for later restores, if needed. Copies of keys are stored on a secure server inside the firewall that is backed up frequently to a different backup server, to prevent a single point of failure. If we had only implemented this solution from the beginning, it would have saved us the price of two software packages.

Protecting extremely sensitive data means investigating the kind of backup processes and software your enterprise is using, who is involved with it, how secure the keys are, how authentication and encryption are performed, where the data is stored, how it is transported, and so on. Keeping the number of people doing backups to a minimum may help with the problems of physical access, key management and frequent key changes. Relying on software that encrypts only on the remote end isn't sufficient, but encrypting on both ends using different keys might be even better than encrypting only locally. Remote storage companies offer emote data storage services that allow you to encrypt your data and stream it offsite to their servers, where it is encrypted again in case their servers are compromised and your passphrase is weak. Of course, the safety of your data depends on the safety of your link with the remote data storage site, but then again, you don't have to worry about how your data gets physically transported either. Another strategy is to separate the authentication function from the encryption function when doing backups and restores. If you have two backup operators, where one knows the authentication password, the other knows the encryption passphrase, and it takes both people to do a backup or restore, the risk of either being able to damage backup data alone is diminished.

# Planning for Hardware Failure or Loss of Services

No computer system is built without inherent imperfections that can (and will!) manifest themselves at the worst of times. Most e-commerce Web sites are comprised of a complex array of servers, redirectors, application software, databases, firewalls, and network and telecommunications equipment, often in physically disparate locations. A failure in any one component has the potential to bring to a halt the end-user customer's experience with your Web site. Planning ahead for equipment failures means minimizing the opportunity to fall victim to single points of failure by introducing as much fault tolerance into your site as possible.

Most businesses have local phone lines that can be utilized for dial-backup solutions when normal network services become unavailable. If you have a leased line as your network connection, chances are the data service unit (DSU) that connects it to your internal network can do dial backup too. Dial backup doesn't have to rely on wired phone services, either. You can implement backup wireless networks or wireless modems to automatically dial out when your normal network provider takes a hit.

## The Single Point of Failure Problem

A company one of the authors did some work for had a field office that was connected to headquarters via a wide area network (WAN) link. Another field office in a nearby suburb was also connected to headquarters via a second WAN link leased from a different network provider. The use of different network providers was deliberate to avoid a single point of failure. The network engineer knew that each WAN line was a single point of failure for the office it served, so he established a redundant link between the two offices such that if one WAN line went down, the other would handle traffic for both offices. He even got a third local provider for the office-to-office link to add additional redundancy. What he didn't realize, though, was that both WAN link providers handed their traffic to the same long haul carrier as it left the city. When that carrier went down one day due to cut fiber lines near a construction site, both offices were unable to send traffic to HQ despite all the built-in redundancy.

This example illustrates the problems a single point of failure can introduce into the most carefully planned High Availability configurations. Every point end-to-end between every component of your e-commerce site must be examined for single points of failure if you are implementing a High Availability configuration. Let's look at some common types of High Availability solutions and how they can solve the single point of failure problem for different parts of your site.

Damage & Defense…

### Number of Nines

If your site has a service level agreement with your customers, it probably includes an explanation of the amount of uptime they can expect from your site. Often, the amount of uptime is expressed as "Number of Nines" of availability in marketing literature or contract explanations, but what does this term mean?

As Table 8.1 shows, if your site achieves two nines of availability, then it will be unavailable due to planned or unplanned outages less than 87 hours in a year's time. If your site achieves three nines, the downtime drops to less than eight hours per year. For ISPs and major data centers, the number of nines requirement may be six or more. A single nine can make a big difference in your ISP's guaranteed service level.

**Table 8.1** Availability Expectations ("Number of Nines")

| Percentage Availability (%) | Allowed Downtime per Year |
|---|---|
| 99.9999 | 32 seconds |
| 99.999 | 5.3 minutes |
| 99.99 | 53 minutes |
| 99.9 | 8.7 hours |
| 99.0 | 87 hours |

## ISP Redundancy

If your line to one ISP goes down one day, you'll want a second redundant ISP ready to cut over immediately to take its place. You might contract with this second ISP to advertise a low priority route to your site while the first advertises a high priority route. If the first goes down, the other will then automatically pick up the traffic. If your site can't afford two network service providers, the next best thing would be to install either two separate physical lines going to the same service provider or two service providers routing traffic to the same local loop.

To illustrate this idea, let's say your business contracts with Gee Whiz ISP as your network service provider. Gee Whiz places an order with the local phone company to have a leased line wired into your building. After installation is complete, your new ISP routes traffic from your customers to your site via the phone company, which is known as the local loop provider. If traffic couldn't get from your customer to Gee Whiz for some reason, the possibility still exists that your customer could get to your site if it could get to another service provider with routes to your local loop. Let's say you also contract with Golly Gee ISP as a redundant provider. In this example, when Gee Whiz can no longer route traffic to you, Golly Gee gets to work and the customer never has to know one of your Internet links is down. The local phone company is a single point of failure in this example, but the ISP's aren't as long as they don't share any common lines upstream. Having redundant ISPs in this situation would provide redundancy for your customers everywhere as long as the local loop is capable of sending traffic to the ISP.

Let's say for a moment that Gee Whiz and Golly Gee are both small service providers that send all their traffic to the same backbone provider company such as WorldCom or Sprint as it leaves your city. An example of how this might happen is if only one network access point exists for the backbone provider in your city. The only way either ISP can connect into that provider is by sending traffic to the single network access point. Having two ISPs in this case would provide redundancy only to customers within your city in the event the backbone carrier couldn't receive traffic from either ISP. This can happen if a fiber line gets cut near the network access point. If most of your customers are outside your city, it probably wouldn't benefit you much to have redundant ISPs in this situation. A better solution would be to investigate how your ISP accesses the Internet backbone and select a redundant ISP that uses a different backbone provider. If one uses Sprint and the other uses WorldCom for example, the likelihood of both being down at once is much lower than either one alone.

## Network Hardware Redundancy

Networking equipment also has High Availability features you can implement. An example HA router configuration might be two identical Cisco (www.cisco.com) routers running Cisco's Hot Standby Routing Protocol (HSRP). HSRP is the means by which both routers detect that the other is either up or down. HSRP advertises a virtual router address as the gateway to the network. The two physical routers have different addresses and negotiate for which will be the active router that actually routes traffic for the virtual address. The inactive router periodically checks in to make sure that the other is still up. If not, it begins handling the traffic for the virtual address. Because network clients send their traffic to the virtual router, they never know that a different physical router is now handling their traffic. The first router can be taken completely off the network, repaired, and reinstalled while the second handles the traffic seamlessly.

Firewalls have similar features that allow you to cluster several together for load balancing and for high availability. Nokia (www.nokia.com), for example, uses Virtual Router Redundancy Protocol (VRRP) that performs a similar function as HSRP does for Cisco routers. Up to 256 Nokia boxes can be connected in serial fashion using VRRP to appear as a single common firewall. This many routers might be overkill for High Availability but could come in handy if you want to load balance a lot of traffic across them.

## System Hardware Redundancy

From the standpoint of CPU, the Sun (www.sun.com) Enterprise 10000 is an example of High Availability concepts designed into hardware from the beginning. This system has multiple CPU boards that can be configured to look like several different computer systems. The boards are hot swappable, meaning they can be pulled out and replaced without bringing the whole system offline. Different CPUs can be assigned for different tasks, so that load associated with one application doesn't have to affect another application.

Even if your budget doesn't allow for a premier solution like the E10000, you can purchase servers with multiple CPUs and assign them to perform different tasks. For example, if you have a database server that stores the data used by your content application, you can configure the database software to use one CPU and the application software to use another. All other operating system tasks could use a third, if you have three CPUs on board. Many different software based-clustering solutions are also available. These typically allow you to configure several servers to appear as a single virtual server to the network.

Redundant Arrays of Inexpensive Disks (RAID) provides several redundancy options for people needing to eliminate single points of failure from disk storage solutions. RAID specifies several methods of writing data to several hard drives at once, also known as "striping." Different levels of striping provide different RAID redundancy options:

- **RAID 0** Data is striped across multiple disks, but no copies are provided. Improves data throughput but does not prevent data loss when a disk fails. Fastest, but provides no fault tolerance if a disk becomes corrupted or fails.
- **RAID 1** Data is written to two or more different drives or drive sets. Commonly referred to as mirroring, the data on one set of drives is always exactly the same as on the other set so redundancy is provided by keeping a backup copy of your data at all times.
- **RAID 2** Data is handled like RAID 1 except error correction codes are provided for drives that don't have built-in error detection. Not useful for SCSI drives, which already have error-correction.
- **RAID 3** Data is striped by byte across several drives, with one drive held in reserve to contain the parity bits for each byte written to the other disks. Because parity can be determined, failure of any one disk results in the loss of only one bit, which can be calculated using the other bits and parity bit. Failure of two or more drives is not recoverable. Byte-level striping needs special hardware to be efficient, but this level of RAID is optimal for large data reads, such as a database.

- **RAID 4** Data is striped similar to RAID 3 except by block instead of byte. Efficiency in reads is similar to RAID 0, although writes are slower because parity has to be updated each time, so the parity drive is a bottleneck. Redundancy is assured if one drive is lost but not two or more.
- **RAID 5** Data is striped like RAID 4 except parity is also striped across all the disks. This prevents the slowdown from having a parity drive. Small writes are speeded up, but this doesn't provide speed improvements where large contiguous blocks of data are written. Again, redundancy is only assured if one drive fails.

Server redundancy options for Web servers typically allow you to implement High Availability and Load Balancing as part of the same solution. Loading cluster software on the servers, or placing the servers behind a network device that redirects traffic to the server with the least load, allow you to use multiple servers to mimic the actions of a single server to provide redundancy. Windows 2000 has network clustering capability built in, for example, to manage multiple physical servers as one virtual IP address. If you have one Web server with one nine of uptime on average, it will be down 10 percent of the time. If you add a second server, the odds of having both down at once drop to 1 percent. Adding a third can bring your site to five nines availability.

## Expanding the Scope of Your Solutions

If your site is required to provide five nines of availability, and you implement this requirement by installing three redundant servers with 90 percent uptime for each on average, consider what happens when one goes down. During the time it takes to repair the server and bring it back online, your site is running with only two systems with a 10 percent chance that one will fail at any given moment, and a 1 percent chance that both will fail simultaneously (.1 x .1 = .01). That's considerably less than five nines of availability; it's two (99 percent). If you must guarantee five nines at all times, you should plan for maintaining five nines with at least one of your systems down. This way, your guarantee is met even during instances of routine hardware failures or planned upgrades.

So far our discussion has been about hot standby systems that automatically take over for one another during a failure. If this option is too pricey for your budget, another alternative is to implement warm or cold standby systems. An example of a warm standby would be a system that is kept constantly identical to the currently active system, but doesn't automatically fail over when the active system goes offline. Perhaps it is mounted in a rack, turned on, and continually gets its disk mirrored with copies of live data, but it would take manual intervention to convert to the warm standby, such as changing its IP address to be that of the failed system. An example of a cold standby is a spare hardware unit sitting on a shelf, ready to be installed with whatever software is necessary for it to replace a failed system. Obviously, the amount of recovery time increases the colder (further away from a duplicate live system) the standby becomes. On the other hand, a cold standby can potentially be loaded up with different kinds of software that turn it into a replacement for five different kinds of servers, whereas with hot standby solutions you must purchase five equivalent standby systems. Cold standbys can be much less expensive and still provide you a fairly fast recovery choice. By combining your redundant hardware solution hot standbys with warm or cold standby replacement hardware, you can reduce the amount of time your availability figure is below the desired number of nines.

# How Do I Protect against Natural Disasters?

At some point or another, every part of the country will be hit with a natural disaster such as flood, earthquake, or tornado. As we discussed earlier in this chapter, your disaster recovery plan will need to detail how this kind of disaster will be handled. But let's examine how we can prevent a natural disaster from being a total disaster to your business. Just as hardware and network redundancy helps to build fault tolerance into your site, data center redundancy can add fault tolerance to your whole business' operations. If your business can't afford to have a backup copy of it's whole data center, you can still take steps to plan ahead for needing additional data center space in which to perform recovery efforts. Whether you decide just to lease extra space, equip that space with just environmental provisions, or also equip it with computers and systems, the steps you take now can save you time and effort if they are ever needed.

## Hot Sites: The Alternate Path to Recovery

A hot standby data center that can fully function as your main site is known as a hot site. In the event of a total unavailability of critical business functions, the hot site is ready to turn up replacement services with very little downtime, say, 48 hours. Hot sites may need to provide computing facilities, equipment, services, security, and living quarters for critical support personnel depending on the recovery function you need it to perform. It can be a second complete data center in a building owned by your company, it can be a small cage space in a co-location facility operated by your ISP, or it can be disk space and applications residing on hardware owned by a vendor performing hot site services on your behalf. Some hot site service companies will bring satellite dishes and mobile data center trailers to your location when needed. In any event, it's a good idea to locate it away from your main data center, perhaps in another city or state, so it isn't affected by the same event that caused your primary site to be unavailable.

In contrast to a hot site is a warm site. Whereas a hot site might contain a fully functional set of hardware, software, and data, a warm site would need a little work to get it up and running. Warm sites might provide a fairly hospitable place to which you can relocate but not necessarily all the equipment or facilities to get running immediately. A good warm site would provide adequate space, air conditioning, UPS, and power, but computing equipment would not necessarily be installed there yet. A further extreme of this idea is the cold site, which might be simply warehouse space in which personnel can gather to begin recovery efforts or in which spare hardware is stored to be used in the event of emergency.

## How Do I Choose a Hot Site?

The first step in choosing a hot site is to determine what services you want it to perform. Will the site provide a fully redundant data center that includes all payroll and support services, or will it simply be a redundant Web site for sales? How many servers do you need to locate there to provide that service, and how much space, air conditioning, and power is required to run them? Is your call center a critical component of your Web site? The critical server inventory you prepared for your Disaster Recovery Plan will come in handy for answering these questions.

After you have an idea of what size and capacity you're looking for, first examine locations within your company that might be able to provide it. Remote offices of the same company make ideal hot sites, because capital has already been invested in those locations. Often, a remote office will have an empty conference room or office that can easily be turned into a computer room with the addition of better air handling and a portable UPS. If your company is small and doesn't have remote offices, many ISPs offer co-location services. These are buildings where you can house computing equipment in locked cages, with the ISP providing network access, power, and environmental controls. The ISP may or may not provide system administration, parking, and workspace for employees in an emergency, however, so consider your needs for this when looking at co-location sites. If you decide to go the co-location route, choose a provider that has facilities in an area that is remote to your main location but isn't prone to natural disasters like tornados or floods. However, consider your staffing needs accordingly, because they may not be able to travel if your operations have to be relocated. When doing it yourself is cost-prohibitive, several companies can assist with disaster recovery service if you need more specialized help. Creating backup call centers and contracting for portable floor space brought to your door are examples of services these companies can provide.

## Testing the Process

After your hot site is selected and equipment is installed, it's time to test if it works. A yearly practice disaster drill should be performed to ensure that your DRP is up to date and everyone knows the part they need to play recovering systems and software. It isn't essential to actually cut services over to your hot site, but you'll want to practice the cut-over as if it were really happening. Or, if you want to fully test the abilities of your hot site, you can set up its Web servers with a fictitious name and assign several people to be fictitious customers visiting it after the cutover. If you've chosen an alternate site where personnel should meet in event of fire, you can instruct them to act as if a fire just occurred and they must now recover the business. It may be melodramatic, but disaster drills force people to think about questions they don't normally have to ask.

# Understanding Your Insurance Options

Even the best-prepared companies buy insurance to protect themselves from events outside their control, but until a couple of years ago most business liability policies didn't provide adequately for hazards related to e-commerce. Historically, brick-and-mortar businesses have maintained a general liability policy that protects against damage to tangible property. This kind of policy covers damage claims for bodily harm that happen by accident on company property or as the result of the company's business operations and typically include claims of libel, slander, or defamation in the context of business advertising. However, the Internet has introduced new definitions of property, damage, and lost revenue that simply don't fit well with the provisions of traditional general liability policies. The result? Companies expecting their loss was covered found themselves incurring large legal expenses to force their insurance companies to pay, and in many cases the insurance companies won. To address deficiencies in coverage by these traditional policies, new insurance products have emerged over the past two to three years targeting the needs of various types of e-commerce businesses.

Some of the new insurance product offerings are hybrids of security and insurance that aim to reduce risk prior to underwriting insurance. For example, Lloyd's of London (www.lloyds.com) and SafeOnline (www.safeonline.com) are e-business insurance underwriters that have partnered with Counterpane systems to perform ongoing security monitoring of their customers. These underwriters require a security audit and installation of Counterpane's security monitoring service before selling insurance to cover the remaining risk. Lloyd's has also partnered with Tripwire (www.tripwire.com) to offer a 10 percent discount on its two-year-old product E-Comprehensive if the insured installs Tripwire's intrusion detection software. INSUREtrust (www.insuretrust.com) offers assessment services and insurance products aimed at e-commerce risk management. IBM has teamed with large insurance broker Sedgwick to provide data protection insurance to e-businesses, with IBM performing security audits as part of the qualification for insurance. Marsh and McLennan Company (www.mmc.com) provide risk assessment and insurance services for all aspects of the enterprise including e-commerce. Many other insurance companies also require a one-time security assessment as part of the qualification process.

The new era of e-commerce insurance products can be classified into several major categories, although product lines are continuing to evolve with developments in intellectual property and e-commerce law. Most e-business insurers have products covering three major areas:

- Professional liability, also known as professional services errors and omissions coverage.
- Liability coverage related to publishing, such as trademark and copyright infringement.
- E-commerce property and income protection for the company and/or for third parties.

## Errors and Omissions Coverage

Professional liability insurance (E&O) protects against damage done by professionals such as doctors, lawyers, engineers, and design consultants as they do business with their clients. These policies cover negligent acts and errors of omission as defined by the courts. Many doctors or lawyers dispensing services over the Web find that their traditional malpractice insurance doesn't cover their services anymore when they are delivered over the Web. Software development companies that hire consultants also want protection against claims resulting from deficiencies in the work they perform. However, damage claims caused directly by software, or by failure of software to perform properly, are not covered by general liability policies because software isn't considered a tangible property and can't by itself cause bodily injury. As a result, many software companies today require contractors and consultants to provide certificates of E&O coverage to protect themselves.

As an example of a professional liability, consider what would happen if a Web designer created an e-commerce site for a client company and in the process made a recommendation that the company purchase a particular software to run the site, but at delivery the software turned out to be incompatible with the company's hardware. If the consultant has made a specification error, his E&O policy would cover the cost of replacement software for the company. If the hardware or software vendor has improperly advertised the capability of their product on their own Web sites, then the vendor's policy would cover the cost. Even if the error is not your fault, E&O policies typically cover legal expenses incurred during your defense. This type of coverage is indispensable for smaller companies and individual contractors that can't afford large legal expenses yet find themselves forced to defend against a frivolous or groundless lawsuit. Bear in mind, E&O coverage doesn't include bankruptcy or poor market conditions resulting in business failure, and it won't cover expenses found to be the result of making poor business decisions.

## Intellectual Property Liability

E-business Web sites that merely advertise a brick-and-mortar company's products have the least risk of all e-commerce ventures, but their risks are still not necessarily covered by traditional insurance products. Prior to the Internet, companies infringing on a trademark in a printed brochure were limited in damages by the circulation of the brochure. Today, a trademark violation on a Web site might incur damages worldwide. The Internet has also created e-mail risks for traditional companies. An employee that sends e-mail discussing a customer could become the target of a lawsuit if the e-mail contains private details that get posted to a newsgroup or otherwise made public. Because e-mail is not considered advertising or marketing by general liability policies, the damages are not covered without special provisions and endorsements addressing e-business.

## First Party E-Commerce Protection

E-commerce protection typically includes coverage for hazards caused by hackers, DoS attacks, computer viruses, malicious acts by employees, loss of intellectual property, and damage to third-party systems. Typically, comprehensive insurance products targeted directly at e-commerce businesses also include professional errors and omissions provisions directly or by endorsement, and they cover copyright and trademark issues as well. If your site resells its Web services to other companies, E&O provisions of a comprehensive e-commerce package will be an important consideration to protect your business if the services you sell don't meet customer expectations. Specialty e-commerce policies may cover damage to the insured, damage to third parties, or both, and exact provisions vary widely from one underwriter to the next.

The need for specialized e-commerce insurance can be illustrated by examining how a traditional commercial insurance product would cover a disaster resulting in lost revenue for the insured company. Disasters traditionally have meant earthquakes, fires, and floods that prevent the business from opening its doors for days or weeks at a time and may have waiting periods of several days before income continuance coverage takes affect. Delays in coverage can mean no coverage at all if an e-commerce site suffers a DoS attack for a few hours, yet even a few hours can mean large revenue losses if the site is the company's main source of doing business. Lean and tightly financed dot-coms suffering a service outage may have to depend on coverage by the insurance company for sudden expenses to deal with the public relations and recovery fallout and can't wait for the coverage delay.

Perhaps the greatest reason for considering e-commerce coverage is provisions for theft or loss of intellectual property. High-tech companies are becoming increasingly aware that the data stored on their computer systems is far more valuable than the systems themselves. Yet traditional commercial property products don't view data as tangible property and won't cover the expense of theft or damage by a disgruntled employee or intruder. Intentional destructive acts by an employee, such as inserting a backdoor into software or deliberately disabling the software product during coding, is illegal; neither kind of insurance product covers legal expenses for the person committing the act. However, the company employing the individual may be covered under e-commerce insurance if the company is named in a lawsuit and can demonstrate that it did not know about or participate in the illegal activity.

Data theft is not the only type of loss you may need coverage for. Legal expenses arising from a patent or copyright infringement suit can put you out of business before the case is even settled. Domain names are often trademarked but you may not know this when you register. Unless you can demonstrate good faith, damages the court can award for cyber-piracy (meaning, intentionally registering a domain name to which someone else believes they own the rights) range from $1,000 to $100,000 (source: American Intellectual Property Law Association, 1999; www.aipla.com). Web crime endorsements can also cover losses you may incur reimbursing, investigating, and prosecuting if an intruder uses your Web site to perform a criminal financial transaction.

## Determining the Coverage You Need

The first step in deciding what coverage is needed is to examine the venture to be covered and write down in detail what the e-commerce operations include. Most underwriters will ask for this detailed e-business description when you apply for a policy. You will also need to provide financial statements for the business. If the company has only been in existence a short while, the underwriter may also request leadership or resume information about the owners or upper management.

Examine carefully the set of risks you want to insure and make a list so you can examine suggested policies for coverage of items you consider critical. To date, there is wide disparity between product offerings among different insurers, so you should inspect the policy carefully to see if it meets your needs. For instance, if your Web site is a brochure-only type site that advertises but does not engage in selling products online, you will need to focus on risks associated with publishing such as trademark infringement, copyright protection, and defamation. However, some e-commerce policies exclude advertisement sites if they are covered by your general liability insurance. If your site also collects customer data and advertises products, general liability policies won't cover damages to or loss of that data. You may need to request an optional endorsement if you want to ensure you have this coverage.

If your site is part of an extranet where different business partners share data or cross-develop products, the risk of spreading a virus or Trojan horse between companies may pose a significant financial risk to the partners. Reality Research (www.realityresearch.com) reports that the cost incurred by U.S. companies in lost productivity and downtime related to computer viruses and security intrusions are $266 billion (U.S.$). This represents 2.5 percent of the gross national product and total downtime of 3.2 percent (source: PricewaterhouseCoopers). Some policies exclude damage to third-party systems caused by a virus originating from your site, so you should examine the policy or purchase an optional endorsement to ensure that you are covered.

Another consideration is whether or not your company hires consultants and contractors. Insurance policies may distinguish between employees, consultants, and temporary workers in terms of coverage. Even if your company requires E&O coverage by consultants, those policies may not cover the company's expenses if it is named in a lawsuit along with a consultant. Consider the provisions of the policy carefully and purchase an option endorsement to provide coverage for consultants if necessary.

If you purchase E&O coverage and are later sued, the policy may provide that the insurance company chooses legal counsel for you to defend the case. If you wish to retain the right to choose your own counsel, you may need to request this as an optional endorsement, depending on the insurer. Likewise, if the insurance company determines that a settlement is in order but you wish to continue defending the suit to clear your name, you may need to request this separately. Some companies simply don't offer the choice, and others offer it with the insurer subject to the famous "hammer clause." This clause requires you to pay the difference between what the insurance company could have settled for and the actual damages resulting from the court decision. Another consideration is that general liability insurance typically covers legal expenses in addition to the limit of liability dollar amount specified in the policy, but newer electronic errors and omissions policies may lump defense costs in with other covered expenses when applying the limit. Make sure you purchase an adequate amount of insurance to cover your need.

So-called "Hacker Insurance," which covers damage done during a security breach, is not included in e-commerce liability insurance by some insurers but is included as an automatic provision by others. According to Betterley Risk Consultants (www.betterley.com) some companies such as AIG (www.aig.com) don't exclude security breaches at all, whereas others such as Chubb, Evanston, and Kemper exclude security breaches unless a breach resulted from broken security software being used to protect against the unauthorized access. St. Paul excludes security breaches as part of the standard policy but offers optional endorsements to provide the coverage.

## Financial Requirements

Most underwriters will require a security audit before selling e-commerce insurance but may offer a discount on the insurance that covers the entire cost of the audit if results are within expectations. A security audit can cost as much as $20,000 or higher depending on the provider, if not. Minimum annual premiums for e-commerce policies start at $1,000 to $3,000 with liability limits of $1 million ranging upward from $25 to $50 million, depending on the insurer. Deductibles range from $2,500 to $10,000, depending on the insurer and the policy. These policies are suitable for small- to mid-size businesses with less than $25 million annual revenue and less than 500 employees entering into business on the Internet for the first time. Betterley Risk Consultants estimates a $10 million NetAdvantage policy from AIG at between $100,000 to $300,000 per year.

If you are a consultant or contractor building e-commerce sites for other client companies, you likely will be asked to provide a Professional Liability Certificate to the company hiring you. Typical E&O policies for consultants have a $1 million minimum limit of liability and premiums begin at about $1,000 per year. InsureNewMedia (www.insurenewmedia .com) provides some sample professional liability premium quotes on its Web site for various business sizes, as shown in Table 8.2. If your e-business is adult-oriented, maintains online medical records, involves downloadable music, or sells health-negative products such as tobacco, you may have trouble obtaining insurance at all from certain providers with "No, Thank You" customer preferences.

**Table 8.2** Sample E&O Quotes from InsureNewMedia.com

| Size | Employees | Revenue (Millions) | Premium (Yearly) |
|---|---|---|---|
| Small | 1 | Up to $.5 | $1,750 |
| Medium | 10 | $.5–$2 | $2,250 |
| Large | 25+ | $3+ | $4,000–$15,000 |

## The Delicate Balance: Insurance and the Bottom Line

Insurance should only be considered when the risk of not insuring is more than the business can tolerate. Risk of incurring expenses from a disaster means evaluating the uncertainty of a high-cost event against the certainty of a lower cost event. Deciding which is better must be viewed in the context of the business, so each decision is different. One way to view insurance expense is to accept the cost of the insured event as given and spread that cost out over a period of time. Quantifying the value to the business of absorbing the cost gradually as opposed to suddenly determines how much can be spent on the cost of insurance. Small companies that are sufficiently well capitalized may decide to self-insure against e-commerce threats, whereas larger companies without spare cash may decide that the predictable expense is better for its business model.

## Coverage That May Not Be Needed

The best way to keep insurance costs to a minimum is to shop around for policies that most precisely fit your need. If your Web site does not accept credit cards, you may not want policy provisions for merchant fraud insurance that protect against customers using fraudulent credit card numbers on your site. If you are a Web designer, a comprehensive e-commerce product is probably overkill when you are primarily interested in protecting against errors and omissions claims by client companies, but you might be interested in an additional trademark infringement endorsement to protect you against accidents.

Many insurers offer a comprehensive package of insurance comprised of several smaller products you can choose individually. Individual products can usually be tailored to suit your needs with optional endorsements. To obtain a specific endorsement you may have to consider several insurers' products to find one that's suitable. Some policies include provisions for worldwide coverage that you may be able to exclude, for example, if your only customer base is in the US.

One consideration in purchasing an umbrella policy intended to cover several business locations is whether standard provisions covering punitive damages would even apply in all states in which you are conducting business. Some states exclude punitive damages as coverable by statute, so you should try to exclude those from the policy.

Another consideration is how the policy covers indirect injury. Some policies include coverage if your business unknowingly provides a defective product that causes injury when used by a third party. An example of this might be if your company were to provide a financial calculator on its Web site that another company used for calculating payroll expenses, and due to an unknown bug in your calculator, the other company understated payroll for several employees. The employees would have suffered an indirect injury caused by your calculator software. If your policy covers this type of injury but your Web site is not involved in any activities that could result in this type of claim, it would be wasteful not to exclude the provision.

You can also purchase coverage against events that may result in a liability claim, but it does not cover income continuance in the event your site goes down. The first is an example of a third-party coverage, and the latter is first-party coverage. Your business may not need the first-party coverage provisions of the policy. If this is the case, you can save money by purchasing a policy that only covers third-party claims.

## Summary

In this chapter we've covered the basics of disaster recovery from the perspective of e-commerce. We looked at the various components of a good disaster recovery plan and how some companies fare without one. Some of the components of disaster recovery involve planning for how to deal with losing trade secrets or data, losing access to critical systems, and losing key personnel. Planning can help identify key areas where prevention may avert the disaster before it happens. Events that can't be prevented can still be examined for ways to minimize the risk of downtime. Certain quality assurance programs can assist businesses in the process of creating a disaster recovery plan. The importance of quality can't be stressed enough, because maximum uptime is quality of service to your customers. Involving upper management early on in the planning process is also essential to provide direction for downtime and budgetary tolerances.

When disaster strikes and data must be recovered, quality backups are critical. In this chapter we examined the importance of storing backup media offsite and discussed several offsite rotation schemes. Feel free to implement a hybrid scheme that fits best with your business, but do remember to retain your offsite tapes long enough to restore everything that may be required. Some companies have agreements to retain data for a number of years, which should be factored into the retention schedule. Backups of data classified as sensitive by your security policy need to be encrypted to prevent data theft. We discussed several key features of backup software that provides encryption, how they are used, and why these features are important.

Adding fault tolerance to your Web site eliminates single points of failure in your hardware and software configurations that can be the cause of downtime. We discussed several ways to add redundant hardware, software, network services, and even data center hot sites to act as standbys in case of catastrophic failure of one or more systems. Warm and cold standby hardware and data centers also offer benefits if budgets are too small to implement full hot-standby options. After you select a hot site, you should plan one or two practice drills per year to test fail over capabilities to it.

After all the planning has been done, there will still be disasters that happen for which you failed to plan. The last thing your e-business needs is for an unforeseen situation to cause bankruptcy, so purchasing insurance may be the best option to cover the risk. Insurance can be viewed as a way to spread the cost of a catastrophic event across a long period of time, so the events you should consider insuring are the ones that are likely to happen. Insurance also provides an element of assurance to your customers by demonstrating that the business will not fail in the event of a disaster.

# Solutions Fast Track

## What Is Disaster Recovery Planning?

☑ A disaster recovery plan in its simplest form can be little more than a spreadsheet with relevant phone numbers and information passed around to staff members. Alternatively, it can be as complex as a published business continuity plan that provides for fully equipped backup data centers running in continual standby mode, ready to deploy on a moment's notice.

☑ A good e-commerce disaster recovery plan addresses these three areas: loss of trade secrets or critical data; loss of access to hardware and software systems; loss of personnel or critical skill sets. Common to all three is the need to identify key staff members responsible for responding to emergencies, how they should be contacted, what their authority levels should be, and under what circumstances they will be called upon.

☑ If your e-commerce site is a business-to-business site, you may find that ISO certification is required for doing business with foreign organizations, especially those in Europe. However, even if your e-commerce venture is small or you just don't wish to pursue ISO certification right now, it's still good business to self-audit your e-commerce quality standards, think ahead about what might happen tomorrow, and formulate steps you can take today to prevent and plan for emergency situations.

## Ensuring Secure Information Backup and Restoration

- ☑ The most effective way of assuring the quality of your data backups at restore time is to perform a routine verification of the data as it is backed up, typically by restoring all or a portion of the data back to disk and comparing it to the original. Most backup software provides an automated mechanism for verifying that the data written to the backup media is an exact copy of the data on disk, but it may be up to the backup operator to make sure that feature is turned on. It takes longer to do backups using the verification procedure, but it's well worth the extra time.
- ☑ Documenting the process for performing data backups and restores is an essential part of disaster planning, because backup and restore procedures may vary slightly from system to system. For example, it is important to know which software must be stopped before a backup occurs. Most database software has to be stopped prior to backing up the database, or the backup image can be corrupt. The last thing you need at recovery time is corrupt backup media, so you should plan ahead for that possibility.
- ☑ Your software also needs to allow you to prevent restores to a DMZ in the event it becomes compromised. If a system becomes sufficiently broken to need a restore, it should be taken offline, brought inside, repaired, and then returned to the DMZ. Allowing restores to go out through the firewall is asking for trouble. One way to prevent this is to purchase software that performs backups on one port and restores on another and then block the restore port at the firewall

- ☑ If you have two backup operators, where one knows the authentication password, the other knows the encryption passphrase, and it takes both people to do a backup or restore, the risk of either being able to damage backup data alone is diminished.

## Planning for Hardware Failure or Loss of Services

- ☑ Most businesses have local phone lines that can be utilized for dial-backup solutions when normal network services become unavailable. If you have a leased line as your network connection, chances are the DSU that connects it to your internal network can do dial backup too. Dial backup doesn't have to rely on wired phone services, either. You can implement backup wireless networks or wireless modems to automatically dial out when your normal network provider takes a hit.
- ☑ Every point end-to-end between every component of your e-commerce site must be examined for single points of failure if you are implementing a High Availability configuration.
- ☑ If your line to one ISP goes down one day, you'll want a second redundant ISP ready to cut over immediately to take its place. You might contract with this second ISP to advertise a low priority route to your site while the first advertises a high priority route. If the first goes down, the other will then automatically pick up the traffic. If your site can't afford two network service providers, the next best thing would be to install either two separate physical lines going to the same service provider or two service providers routing traffic to the same local loop.
- ☑ Redundant Arrays of Inexpensive Disks (RAID) provides several redundancy options for people needing to eliminate single points of failure from disk storage solutions. RAID specifies several methods of writing data to several hard drives at once, also

known as "striping." Different levels of striping provide different RAID redundancy options.

## How Do I Protect against Natural Disasters?

☑ Just as hardware and network redundancy helps to build fault tolerance into your site, data center redundancy adds fault tolerance to your whole business' operations. In the event of a total unavailability of critical business functions, hot standby data center (hot site) is ready to turn up replacement services with very little downtime, providing computing facilities, equipment, services, security, and living quarters for critical support personnel. Locate it away from your main data center, so it isn't affected by the same event that caused your primary site to be unavailable.

☑ A yearly practice disaster drill should be performed to ensure that your DRP is up to date and everyone knows the part they need to play recovering systems and software. Disaster drills force people to think about questions they don't normally have to ask.

## Understanding Your Insurance Options

☑ The Internet has introduced new definitions of property, damage, and lost revenue that simply don't fit well with the provisions of traditional general liability policies. To address deficiencies in coverage by these traditional policies, new insurance products have emerged that target the needs of various types of e-commerce businesses. Some of the new insurance product offerings are hybrids of security and insurance that aim to reduce risk prior to underwriting insurance.

☑ If your site resells its Web services to other companies, errors and omissions (E&O) provisions of a comprehensive e-commerce package will be an important consideration to protect your business if the services you sell don't meet customer expectation. Specialty e-commerce policies may cover damage to the insured, damage to third parties, or both, and exact provisions vary widely from one underwriter to the next.

- ☑ Perhaps the greatest reason for considering e-commerce coverage is provisions for theft or loss of intellectual property. High-tech companies are becoming increasingly aware that the data stored on their computer systems is far more valuable than the systems themselves.
- ☑ Some policies exclude damage to third-party systems caused by a virus originating from your site, so you should examine the policy or purchase an optional endorsement to ensure that you are covered.
- ☑ So-called "Hacker Insurance," which covers damage done during a security breach, is not included in e-commerce liability insurance by some insurers but is included as an automatic provision by others.
- ☑ Most underwriters will require a security audit before selling e-commerce insurance, but may offer a discount on the insurance that covers the entire cost of the audit if results are within expectations. A security audit can cost as much as $20,000 or higher depending on the provider, if not. If you are a consultant or contractor building e-commerce sites for other client companies, you likely will be asked to provide a Professional Liability Certificate to the company hiring you.
- ☑ Many insurers offer a comprehensive package of insurance comprised of several smaller products you can choose individually. Individual products can usually be tailored to suit your needs with optional endorsements.

# Frequently Asked Questions

The following Frequently Asked Questions, answered by the authors of this book, are designed to both measure your understanding of the concepts presented in this chapter and to assist you with real-life implementation of these concepts. To have your questions about this chapter answered by the author, browse to **www.syngress.com/solutions** and click on the **"Ask the Author"** form.

**Q:** Are there free resources online to help with creating a disaster recovery plan?

**A:** Check out www.fema.gov/library/bizindex.htm, which is the FEMA Web site with guidelines to help businesses of all kinds create a disaster recovery plan. MIT also has a sample DRP template at http://Web.mit.edu/security/www/pubplan.htm. The Disaster Recovery Journal (www.drj.com) also has sample plans you can read and modify for your own use, but you may need to become a member to download them.

**Q:** How does e-commerce insurance pay out benefits when I incur a loss?

**A:** Types of insurance payout provisions are "Pay on Behalf" vs. "Indemnification." Pay on Behalf takes care of expenses as they are incurred by the insured and works a bit like homeowner's insurance. If the policy covers your defense in a lawsuit, the legal fees will be paid as they are incurred. Indemnification reimburses the insured for covered expenses already incurred and works a bit like traditional health insurance. You pay for the covered expense and then apply for reimbursement from the insurer. Most insurance offerings for e-commerce are of the "Pay on Behalf" variety.

**Q:** What's the difference between a password and a passphrase?

**A:** A passphrase has spaces in it and is made up of multiple words. "ex&mpl3" is a password and "4 sc0re & s3v3n ye4r5 @go" is a passphrase.

**Q:** Which is better for backups, Digital Linear Tape (DLT) or Digital Audio Tape (DAT)?

**A:** DAT tapes are 4mm tapes that are recorded using a helical scan technology, which is exactly the same thing used in most video tape recorders. DLT tapes are half-inch tapes recorded linearly on multiple tracks. DAT drives are slower than DLT because DLT can write multiple tracks at once. DLT tapes are also more reliable for backups, because there is less risk for de-alignment. Data transfer rates for DLT tapes range up to 6MB per second, compared to 4.8MB for DAT, so backup and recovery speed is also better with DLT.

# Chapter 9

# Handling Large Volumes of Network Traffic

**Solutions in this chapter:**

- What If My Site's Popularity Exceeds My Expectations?
- How Do I Manage My Bandwidth Needs?
- Introduction to Load Balancing
- Strategies for Load Balancing

☑ Summary

☑ Solutions Fast Track

☑ Frequently Asked Questions

# Introduction

Every e-commerce business person has the same dream: You put your site up on the Internet, you do some advertising, and the customers browse your site. The orders begin to arrive and the business is booming. That's usually when the nightmare begins. What if so many people come to your site that you can't handle all the business? Your site can only handle so many customers and browsers at one time. If others try to connect and the system is full, they will either get such a slow response that they will give up or they may get outright rejected at the start. Either way, capacity problems can do damage to your reputation and your bottom line.

The other side of this coin is also true. Building your site with too much bandwidth and too high of an investment in capacity can spell doom another way—through the slow death of financial drain. It's a fine line to walk and almost an art form to perfect. The correct mix of bandwidth and capacity to match your business flow is difficult to achieve, but it is also the Holy Grail of e-commerce businesses. This chapter discusses how to achieve this arcane balance.

In this chapter you will learn what it means to have an overloaded site, how to measure that, and how to track down which components are the cause. You will learn what load is and how to measure it on a variety of servers and devices. You will learn how to estimate your bandwidth needs and what your options are for obtaining it. You will learn what the tradeoffs are between a co-location facility and having bandwidth delivered to your premises. You will learn what a load balancer is, what the pros and cons of using one are, and what methods they employ to perform their function.

# What If My Sites Popularity Exceeds My Expectations?

What will the symptoms be if your site exceeds capacity? Depending on which components are "maxed out," you may see slow response times, browser errors, error messages from the Web servers or database (DB), or connection resets. Worse, if it's a connectivity problem, the site may look fine to you, but your customers may have problems.

A typical e-commerce infrastructure includes Web servers, database servers, e-mail servers, Domain Name System (DNS) servers, network equipment, and possibly some other specialized servers, such as media servers or financial transaction servers. If any one of these components is at capacity, then your overall site is not working properly. For most sites, a core set of components make up the most critical part of your site. It might not be a huge problem if your e-mail is being delayed 30 minutes. Perhaps you can tolerate customer credit cards not being charged for an hour or two. You probably can't tolerate customers not being able to place orders for half a day.

For most sites, the critical core will be the Web servers, some portion of the database servers, and the network equipment. Your Web servers may depend on a central file server as well. If any one of those pieces is down, then the whole site is down. One of the pieces of documentation you should develop is a list of which pieces are required to run which features of your site. It may be a list as simples as "Real Media Server—requires Real Server to be up, and Internet connection to be up." It may be an extensive list of which Web servers, database servers, routers, switches, and load balancers need to be functioning.

A device being completely down is one thing, but a device being overloaded is something different. It is different in that the symptom isn't necessarily an unreachable Web site. It may be that it's really slow, or that some of the items on the page load, and others don't. Perhaps it works one moment and then not the next.

An overloaded device is often harder to troubleshoot than a device that is down all the way—some of your tests might pass on an overloaded device, whereas they will fail for a down device. For example, if you have a script that pings all of your boxes to make sure they are "up," the ping may work just fine on a box on which the Web server process has nearly pegged the CPU, but it won't on a box on which the power supply has failed. In this case, ping is a relatively poor test, but that's the point. You have to have a set of tests or procedures to cover the conditions you are actually interested in. For a Web server, you don't really care that the box is "up" per se, what you are interested in is whether it can serve a Web page in *n* number of seconds. Having a bad test may cause you to skip the problem device in your testing procedure.

So what is *load,* how much do you have when your site is working acceptably? How do you measure it? How much is too much?

## Determining the Load on Your Site

Your job, in terms of load and performance, is to chase bottlenecks. Your site will always have a bottleneck—that is, some component that is the limiting factor. By definition, you can't handle an infinite load, and some piece will always max out first. You can simply upgrade and rearrange the current bottleneck so that some other piece is now the limiting factor, but at an overall higher load. (Strictly speaking, the same component may still be the bottleneck, but you have done something to make it faster.)

In order to discuss load, let's look at an example diagram (Figure 9.1) of a generic site, or rather a portion of it: the components needed to serve the main Web pages.

**Figure 9.1** A Simple Web Site Component Diagram

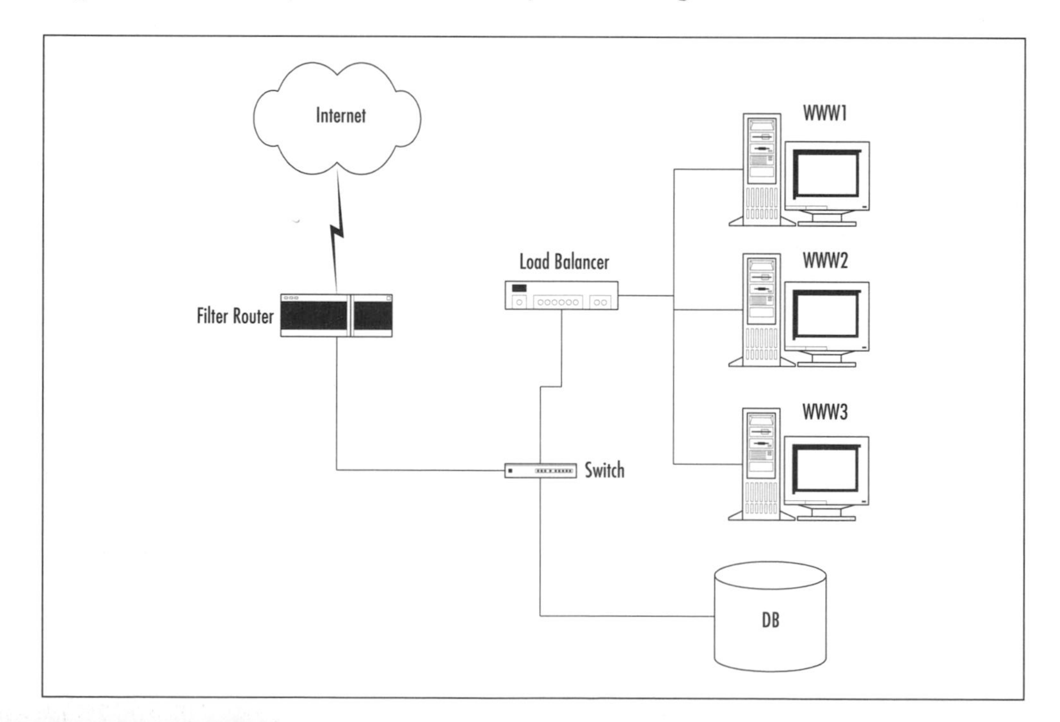

The pieces are an Internet connection, an access/filter router, a load balancer, a switch, a group of Web servers, and a database server. Smaller sites with very light traffic requirements may have just one Web server, and no load balancer, but this setup is pretty typical.

The term *load* collectively refers mostly to a combination of network throughput, CPU utilization, and I/O (input/output, usually to disk or memory. Network throughput is technically a form of I/O as well, but it deserves its own category in this context.) If any one of these items becomes maxed out, then the rest really don't matter much, because the box isn't going to go any faster. This is a tiny bit of an overgeneralization, because a box can be I/O bound and still serve some requests that depend only on the CPU and what is in RAM, but the box as a whole will be at capacity.

The external symptom is that the box is "slow." Naturally, after you've determined which box is slow, you have to quantify things a bit more than that, because you have to fix it. Fixing it may range from reconfiguration to upgrading hardware.

As mentioned before, if any one of the components shown in Figure 9.1 becomes overloaded, then the result is that the entire Web site is slow. So how do you determine which component is the current bottleneck? This isn't always simple, but it can be accomplished.

## Determining Router Load

Let's start determining what the bottleneck is by looking at some of the simpler components. How do you know if you're at capacity for your Internet connection? Most routers provide a throughput average, input, and output for a particular interface. Figure 9.2 is an example from a Cisco router, using the show interface command:

**Figure 9.2** The Output of the **show interface** Command on a Cisco Router

```
FastEthernet0/0 is up, line protocol is up
  Hardware is AmdFE, address is 0002.b95e.eb70 (bia 0002.b95e.eb70)
      Internet address is 192.168.0.1/24
```

**Continued**

**Figure 9.2** Continued

```
MTU 1500 bytes, BW 100000 Kbit, DLY 100 usec,
   reliability 255/255, txload 2/255, rxload 1/255
Encapsulation ARPA, loopback not set
Keepalive set (10 sec)
Full-duplex, 100Mb/s, 100BaseTX/FX
ARP type: ARPA, ARP Timeout 04:00:00
Last input 00:00:00, output 00:00:00, output hang never
Last clearing of "show interface" counters 5w0d
Queueing strategy: fifo
Output queue 0/80, 0 drops; input queue 0/100, 8608 drops
5 minute input rate 143000 bits/sec, 145 packets/sec
5 minute output rate 838000 bits/sec, 176 packets/sec
   969832132 packets input, 4282579182 bytes
   Received 0 broadcasts, 0 runts, 0 giants, 0 throttles
   1 input errors, 1 CRC, 0 frame, 0 overrun, 0 ignored
   0 watchdog
   0 input packets with dribble condition detected
   1124479790 packets output, 1554763051 bytes, 0
       underruns(0/0/0)
   0 output errors, 0 collisions, 0 interface resets
   0 babbles, 0 late collision, 0 deferred
   0 lost carrier, 0 no carrier
   0 output buffer failures, 0 output buffers swapped out
```

You have to know what your arrangement is with your service provider in order for these numbers to be meaningful. For example, in the above output, it shows an interface running at 100Mbps, full-duplex Fast Ethernet. However, this interface is plugged into a switch, and attached to the same switch is the handoff from the provider, which is

10Mbps full-duplex Ethernet. In either case, the input and output rates are well below maximum, and the error counts are nearly nonexistent.

This sample was done at a rather off-peak time, though. For more proactive monitoring, you will want to use a network management package of some sort that keeps statistics over time and perhaps offers utilization graphs. Still, when troubleshooting, this method is adequate to determine current traffic at the router.

While we're here, let's take a look at CPU utilization, using the show process command (see Figure 9.3).

**Figure 9.3** Output of the **show process** Command on a Cisco Router

```
CPU utilization for five seconds:2%/2%; one minute:1%; five
    minutes:2%
PID  QTy       PC Runtime (ms)   Invoked   uSecs   Stacks   TTY   Process
 1  Csp 603A1CB8  44         626627    0      2600/3000   0    Load Meter
 2  M*          0  1304       36          36222 3536/6000  226   SSH Process
 3  Lst 60388D30  1315420   345780    3804  5636/6000  0    Check heaps
 4  Cwe 60380530  0          1         0        5568/6000   0   Chunk Manager
 5  Cwe 6038EEE8  76         269       282      5592/6000   0   Pool Manager
 6  Mst 602FB590  0          2         0        5564/6000   0   Timers
```

This is just a brief sample; the listing of IOS processes and stats about each goes on for pages. The item we're interested in is on the first line—the CPU utilization. In this case, we can see we're pretty low. This item can also be monitored by a network management package. Things that can affect router CPU utilization are features like NAT, access lists, routing multiple protocols, huge route tables, and just plain high traffic levels. Keep in mind that each bit of monitoring you do also uses a small amount of resources on the router, so don't go nuts grabbing every bit of information the router offers.

This router is primarily a filtering router, so the bulk of its time is spent processing access lists, both static and reflexive. I was able to significantly improve performance by careful reordering and rewriting of the access lists. One obvious change you can make is to place more frequently matched rules higher in the list. I was also able to put in a number of static matches that prevented falling through to the reflexive access lists, thereby keeping them to a manageable size.

If you're not familiar with the different types of access lists, it's worth taking a moment to explain them. Routers were one of the earliest types of firewall. On most routers, you could write what was called an access list: a list of what kind of traffic was and wasn't allowed. The rules you could use were pretty simple. You could either pass a packet through or not; the criteria you had available to program this decision making process included IP addresses, protocol type (Transmission Control Protocol or TCP, User Datagram Protocol or UDP, Internet Control Message Protocol or ICMP) and port numbers, if applicable.

These types of access lists, called *static* access lists, worked well for some things, but not others. For protocols like the File Transfer Protocol (FTP), which had a back connection component, you would end up having to open gaping holes in the access lists to get it to work. As security concerns increased, people realized that static access lists weren't adequate for many security purposes. Meanwhile, dedicated firewall programs were able to do what was referred to as *stateful* packet filtering. In essence, this allowed them to avoid the gaping holes that protocols like FTP caused.

Cisco at least has added some new access list types. One is the *reflexive* access list, which allows reciprocal connections in. For example, if a DNS server makes a request out from port 1024 to port 53 on some outside server, the reflexive access list will only allow in the reply from port 53 to port 1024. Previously, the static access list would require that you allow in any UDP packet from port 53, leaving a large hole. The reflexive access list removed this hole.

Finally, there are *dynamic* access lists, which are very much like stateful packet filtering, on par with low-end firewalls. Cisco refers to this capability as their firewall feature set for routers. Dynamic access lists are much like reflexive access lists, only a bit smarter. They can monitor application-layer information and react to that. This finally solves the FTP problem, for example.

All of these capabilities are not without a performance impact, however. The more capable the access list you use, the slower the router can process it. What is called for is judicious mixing of the access list types. You will want to write your access lists so that the static access lists handle as much of your traffic as possible, and that you only call the reflexive access list as needed. Reflexive access lists grow as needed and can become large very quickly. This can result in a router crash, due to the router running out of memory. As a general rule, you can use static access lists for inbound (that is, to your demilitarized zone, or DMZ) TCP and UDP connections. You can allow arbitrary traffic to the ports you want open and allow arbitrary traffic (replies) out. If your DMZ machines need to act as clients to the Internet (say, to deliver mail or make DNS requests), then you'll have to account for that. For TCP, you could allow in packets that are marked established, with minimal risk. Allowing in packets marked established will allow for some types of TCP port scans to take place, but the attacker won't be able to start any connections.

For UDP (commonly DNS), you'll probably have to start using reflexive access lists. Because UDP is stateless, there is no "established" indicator to check for. What you do in this situation is allow the connection out via a reflexive access list, and the reply will be allowed back in.

## Determining Switch Load

The next item in the chain will be a switch (or in some cases, a hub). In general, there isn't a whole lot to go wrong with a switch. Most modern switches will have no trouble maintaining wire-speed communications, unless you have a lot of features turned on or are doing a lot of filtering or something similar. Some switches will display similar information to what was shown above for the Cisco router interface. The Cisco 2900 family of switches uses the same show interface command, and displays nearly identical information, for example.

In addition to making sure that none of your interface on your switch are overloaded or having an unusual number of errors, you can get a quick idea about which interfaces are carrying the most traffic, possibly indicating where to look for problems.

If you have a non-manageable switch or hub, you'll have a bit more difficulty measuring your network traffic. You can go to each machine attached to your network, pull similar statistics of off each interface, and do some totals. If, for example, you have a 10Mbps Ethernet hub, and the total of all the traffic on all the interfaces of the machines plugged into that hub are approaching 6 or 7Mbps, then you've reached the limit of shared, half-duplex 10Mbps Ethernet. If you're using one of the less expensive switches, and you're hitting some performance limits, you may not have an easy way to tell because you don't have a way to determine what kind of load the switch is under. As quickly as possible, you'll want to move to manageable network gear, but the obvious trade-off is cost.

If you have a manageable switch with 100Mbps ports, and you've reached the throughput limit on one or more of the interfaces, then obviously you have little choice but to upgrade to a switch with Asynchronous Transfer Mode (ATM) interfaces, or Gigabit Ethernet. Of course, if you have the kind of servers it takes to consistently fill 100Mbps pipes, then you've probably got a significant cash investment in your servers, and hopefully the expense of the high-end network switches won't be too much of a burden.

## Determining Load Balancer Load

Without discussing in too much detail what a load balancer is (because we do this later in the chapter), let's briefly cover checking load on a load balancer.

It's somewhat difficult to be very specific about how to check a load balancer without talking about an actual product. Many different load balancers are on the market, and most of them work in different ways. Some load balancers work via software agents that live on each Web server. Some load balancers act like Layer 2 switches. Others work via a form of Network Address Translation (NAT).

In any case, checking load is generally straightforward. Like a router or switch, you can usually check CPU load, traffic through interfaces, and so forth. In addition, the load balancer will usually tell you what its opinion of the response time of your Web servers is. This is helpful not only because it may save you some troubleshooting steps, but also because the load balancer's measurement of Web server response time controls which Web servers get chosen to handle the most traffic. Most load balancers shouldn't be a bottleneck, but it's a possibility.

The Web servers are one of the pieces most prone to overload (in addition to the database server.) They are also the most flexible in terms of configuration options and the most complex to measure. As the Web servers are almost always general-purpose servers, you can configure them in a nearly infinite number of ways. And that's before you even touch the Web server software, any Web applications, and your own code.

In the next section, we take a look at some basic techniques for determining which component of a Web server is causing the slowdown.

# Determining Web Server Load

Let's go over some of the basics for identifying bottlenecks within your Web server. First, any modern OS offers a way to get a rough measurement of overall load of a system, without getting into specifics as to what exactly is causing it. For UNIX-style operating systems, you can use commands such as uptime and top (see Figure 9.4):

**Figure 9.4** Output of the **Uptime** and **Top** Commands on a UNIX System

```
$ uptime
 10:01pm  up 41 day(s), 11:26,  3 users,  load average: 0.02,
    0.13, 0.27

# top
last pid: 14176; load averages: 0.07,  0.12,  0.25        22:02:57
50 processes:  48 sleeping, 1 zombie, 1 on cpu
CPU states: 99.5% idle, 0.0% user, 0.5% kernel,  0.0% iowait,
    0.0% swap
Memory: 512M real, 33M free, 44M swap in use, 470M swap free
```

**Continued**

**Figure 9.4** Continued

```
  PID USERNAME THR PRI NICE SIZE   RES STATE   TIME   CPU COMMAND
14164 root       1  48  0  1788K 1076K cpu0     0:00  0.41% top
 6845 dnscache 1  58  0    25M   24M sleep 220:45  0.07% dnscache
  164 qmails     1  58  0   992K  312K sleep 373:24  0.04% qmail-send
  166 qmaill     1  58  0  1360K  304K sleep 155:38  0.02% splogger
  157 root       7  31  0  1704K  496K sleep 302:57  0.02% syslog-ng
  192 dnslog     1  58  0   752K  212K sleep  61:06  0.02% multilog
  168 root       1  44  0   764K  204K sleep  40:44  0.02% qmail-lspawn
14147 root       1  48  0   236K  232K sleep   0:00  0.02% sh
  160 qmaild     1  58  0  1364K  200K sleep  36:53  0.01% tcpserver
  169 qmailr     1  58  0   768K  240K sleep  21:16  0.01% qmail-rspawn
  170 qmailq     1  58  0   744K  184K sleep  72:32  0.01% qmail-clean
 5339 root       1  58  0  2480K  360K sleep   0:01  0.01% sshd
  159 root       1  58  0  1352K  296K sleep  64:57  0.00% splogger
    1 root       1  58  0  1864K  100K sleep   3:43  0.00% init
22923 root       1  58  0  2160K  600K sleep   3:37  0.00% sshd
```

**NOTE**

It is not clear in Figure 9.4, but the **top** command runs full-screen and updates itself every 5 seconds until you stop it. The **top** command doesn't always come with the UNIX you might be using, but you can obtain it at www.groupsys.com/top/.

The uptime command gives a very rough idea about what load is. Basically, if you use it frequently, you'll have an idea what it is when things are working correctly. When it goes up beyond "normal" by a factor of 2 or more, you know that something is wrong. For example, on one MySQL server we used to administer, normal load was about 0.5.

When things got bad, it would go to 3, or even as high as 50. It didn't tell me what specifically was wrong, but it confirmed very quickly that something was. The top program, on the other hand, goes a lot farther. Briefly, it tells you (for that 5-second snapshot) what percentage of the CPU time was idle, user and kernel. It tells you what percentage of the time it was waiting on I/O and swapping. It also ranks the processes from most to least busy. So, at a glance, if the machine is busy you can figure out which process is sucking up your CPU time, and if it's I/O bound, or wants more memory (that is, swapping.) That's not 100 percent accurate, of course, but it gives a really big clue as to where to look.

Windows users have Performance Monitor (perfmon) to provide this kind of information and the Task Manager to give a quick CPU utilization amount. The task manager is shown in Figure 9.5, and perfmon is shown in Figure 9.6.

**Figure 9.5** CPU Utilization in Task Manager

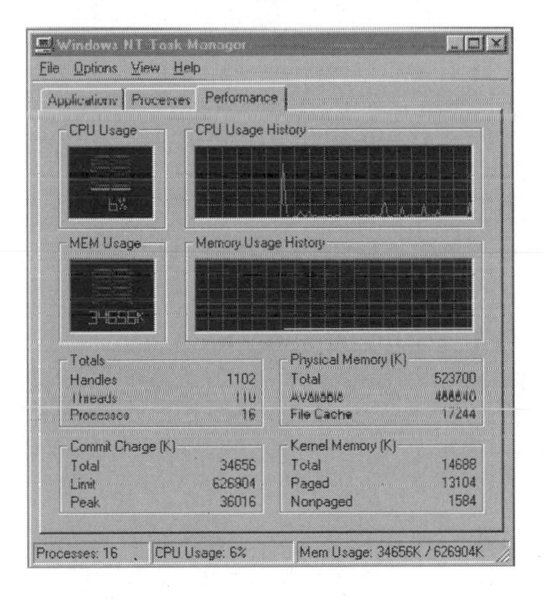


The Performance tab on Task Manager gives us a quick glance at how the machine is doing in terms of CPU load and memory. At the moment, this machine isn't doing much and has plenty of memory available.

**Figure 9.6** Resource Monitoring in Performance Monitor

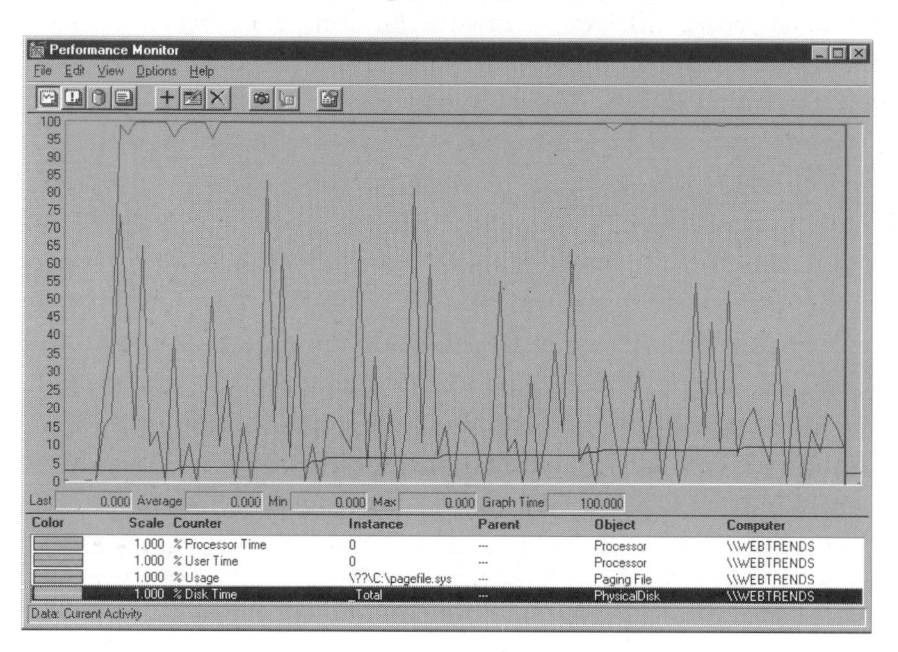


For the perfmon example, we've taken the same machine and started a log analysis process running. You can monitor a large number of parameters with perfmon. Here, we've chosen to monitor Processor Time, User Time, Pagefile Usage, and Disk Time. Overall, the processor is at maximum nearly the entire time, and the pagefile is slowly becoming more and more used. (The program in question takes gigabytes of logs and reads them into memory for processing, so these results aren't terribly surprising.)

You can find a brief explanation of each counter at www.microsoft .com/technet/winnt/perform.asp.

## Performance Tuning the Web Server

After you've determined that your Web server is at or approaching capacity, you have to decide what to do about it. Unfortunately, Web server software is not simple, and it tends to be infinitely extendible by the Webmaster. In general, what you will be looking for are the parts of the Web server that are slow in responding. If you have an extremely simple site that consists of just static pages (no server-side processing, no database, just serving files off the disk) and Web server software that does caching of files, then there is really nowhere to go except a faster Web server, more RAM, or more Web servers.

That type of Web site is pretty rare, though, and you obviously can't take any orders that way, so it's not much of an e-commerce scenario, either. As mentioned before, most e-commerce Web sites have at least one database server, so there's one dependency, and they may also have a file server. Other pieces may exist , such as media servers, authentication servers, and other special-purpose servers. They might have a performance impact, and you would troubleshoot most of them in a similar manner to the rest of the devices that we've talked about.

Taking input from the customer and inserting records into the database requires what is called server-side processing on the Web server. This means that the Web site takes some action based on user input, which is so common in Web sites now that the mechanics of what takes place behind the scenes aren't given much thought. However, this is where the majority of performance problems crop up. A typical Web server package does a decent job of running itself and serving files off of the disk, but the performance of server-side processes (usually written by the customer or a third party, not the Web server software developer) are totally out of the control of the Web server.

A few well-known procedures exist for improving performance of a server-side process, such as algorithmic tuning, caching techniques, precompilation, using modules such as modperl for Apache instead of doing a full fork to an external process, and persistent state maintenance mechanisms. These procedures are specific to the Web server software you will be using and what language you will be programming in.

For example, in IIS for Windows NT, you have a number of choices for how to handle server-side processing. One is to write a standalone .exe program, and have the Web server run that each time the appropriate Web page is selected. It will work as desired, but the Web server has to launch this program each time. This takes time. If you were able to write the equivalent program as an .asp file, the IIS Web server would be able to handle the execution as part of its own process and not have to take the time to run a separate program. Under the right circumstances, this can be an order of magnitude faster.

Assuming that you've gone through the process of tuning your server-side processing, and you're not stalling out waiting on external bottlenecks, such as a database server (we talk about database server performance in a moment), then your only real choice is to upgrade your hardware. As mentioned before, this upgrade might be getting a faster individual machine, or it might mean that you add an additional separate physical machine to help take on some of the work.

Let's talk about what it means to have more than one Web server machine, because that opens up a can of worms. With one Web server, all your files live on disk. If your Web server maintains some sort of state about visitors to your site, that information is sitting there in memory waiting to be requested. So, with the second Web server, how do you keep the files the same on both machines? Your only choices really are to have some sort of mechanism for keeping the same files on both machines, which is problematic, or having one or both of them mount the files from an external file system, which is also problematic. Either mechanism can break or cause additional performance problems. Either one will likely introduce yet another single point of failure. The short answer is that most sites opt for the remote mount choice. The second Web server will mount the content off of the first Web server, or the files are placed on a third box (perhaps a dedicated file server appliance) and they both mount that system's shared disks.

Are there any solutions to the problem of the file server being a single point of failure? Some experiments in distributed file systems have taken place that could theoretically help with this problem, but they haven't really reached prime time yet. Most sites end up putting the files on a server dedicated to that purpose, either a general-purpose computer or a dedicated appliance. The appliance route is attractive because many of them have some hardware redundancy features built in, such as redundant power supplies and hot-swappable RAID drive arrays. Some high-end appliances will have features such as redundant processors and multiple fiber data paths. These features can be set up on a general-purpose computer as well, but you have to do it yourself. It's still a single point of failure, but it's one that will (hopefully) not go down if you maintain it properly.

Next, how do the Web servers maintain state when there is more than one Web server? Some Web server software includes built-in features to track state of a visitor across the stateless Hypertext Transfer Protocol (HTTP). This may be done via cookies, hidden form variables, or specials URLs. In general, these built-in mechanisms will keep some small bit of information in memory or perhaps on a local disk. So what happens if, due to your load balancing mechanism, a visitor pulls one page off of Web server 1 (with state information embedded) and tries to pull the next one off of Web server 2? Web server 2 wouldn't know anything about the state information contained on Web server 1.

There are a few solutions to this problem. One, if your load balancing solution supports it, have it make sure that the same visitor goes to the same Web server for the duration of their visit. The downside to this is that they might get stuck with a slow Web server, or their server might go down in the middle. Another choice is to redirect the visitor to another Web server name when they first connect, (that is, they hit www.example.com and are randomly redirected to www5.example.com). This is how Hotmail works. It has the same problems as causing the same user to go to the same Web server each time. Another choice is to keep the state information on the shared mount point. The only downside to this is that it might be slightly worse in performance that other solutions, and prevents you from making the mount read-only to the Web servers.

Finally, there's the option to keep the state information in the database. This is conceptually similar to keeping it on a shared drive, and has the same downsides. On the other hand, it will probably perform better (compared to writing files to the drive), and all of the potential file-locking problems are already solved for you using a database. Databases tend to perform better because they are built for this sort of thing and have caching built-in. You also have indexing features that will make lookups of the state information quicker as well. If there is state information to be maintained, most sites will opt for this database method.

There is another choice of sorts, which is to not require the server to maintain any sort of state information. However, if you require authentication of any type, you really can't avoid having the systems keep state data. The point is, after you move to a second Web server, you'll probably have to recheck your design for this sort of dependency and the security implications that these redundancy issues have upon your site.

Tools & Traps…

### Measuring Your Performance from the Outside

We mentioned that if you're getting at your Web site via a local area network (LAN) connection of some sort, you often get significantly better performance to your site than your customers will. How do you find out how your site performs from someone else? (Other than waiting for complaints, of course.)

You can subscribe to commercial services for this sort of monitoring. Keynote (www.keynote.com) is one of the better-known companies that offer this service. Basically, after the service has been contracted for, the company in question will retrieve the page you've given them every so often, say once an hour, from several key places around the Internet. How many places, how often, and how many pages are monitored, are all dependent on how much you're paying. After the data has been collected, it can be graphed and manipulated for viewing and analysis. Some of the services will allow you to watch key competitors alongside your site or compare yourself against an amalgamation of sites similar to yours.

These businesses place computers at various Internet locations around the world and set them to remotely collect the statistics needed. As you might imagine, the services can be somewhat pricey, ranging from a couple of hundred to over a thousand dollars per month, again depending on services required.

You can find a review of some of these services here: www.informationweek.com/784/metrics.htm.

# How Do I Manage My Bandwidth Needs?

Earlier in the chapter, we stated that one place to look for bottlenecks was in your Internet connection. What type of connection you have, or more specifically how much throughput it provides, is colloquially referred to as "bandwidth." Communications engineers may object to the misuse of the term, but the connotation has stuck. For most people, bandwidth is how fast your connection is.

But the real questions remain: How much do you need, how do you get more when you need it, and what about cost and reliability?

## Contracting for Bandwidth

Almost every company (except for perhaps the carriers themselves) has to buy its Internet connection from some sort of Internet service provider (ISP). As covered earlier in the book, this bandwidth can either be delivered to your premises, or it might be in the form of a handoff at a co-location facility. The major differences between the two are cost and convenience. The co-location option tends to be cheaper, and it's less convenient. Having the bandwidth delivered to your location is very convenient, it's where your staff is, but it can also be fairly expensive, especially if you need a large amount of it. You also would probably want the air and power conditioning and battery and generator backup you would normally get at the co-location as well, so you'd have to provide that yourself.

In what forms can you get your bandwidth? Ignoring typical home Internet access option such as dialup modems, cable modems, and low-end digital subscriber line (DSL), options for businesses include leased line, business DSL, and for co-location solutions, Ethernet and ATM handoffs. A leased line is a dedicated communications line provided by a telephone carrier to your premise. The other end of the line goes to your ISP, or to another type of carrier, typically a frame relay provider. Leased line capacities range from 56K all the way up through OC-12 and beyond. A 56Kbps is typically too small to run a Web site off of, though they can be useful for some backup purposes or out-of-band management. It is possible to multiplex multiple 56K lines to make something larger, but most places will start with a T1 or business DSL. A T1 is essentially a 1.544Mbps digital line. They have been around for years, and usually come with a particular level of Service Level Agreement (SLA) that dictates how the carrier will respond to problems should they arise (you get pretty good response from your local phone company when your T1 goes down).

Many markets now offer business DSL service. DSL is a way of using standard single-pair telephone lines at frequencies beyond the normal voice channels, yielding a much higher throughput. Most business DSL providers can offer up to T1 (1.5Mbps) speed, if the phone lines to your location meet the criteria (DSL is sensitive to the distance between your location and the central office.) Many DSL users report that response to outages on DSL lines is much poorer than with T1 lines. It isn't clear exactly why this should be, whether it's due to the fact that DSL is newer, and technicians aren't as well trained, or whether it's because the carriers don't treat them as "seriously" as T1 lines. In any case, many people feel that DSL isn't up to "bet the business" quality, though even these problems can be addressed via redundancy (discussed later in this chapter.)

A huge difference typically exists in price between T1 and DSL service. DSL prices usually start at around $150 per month for low-speed business DSL, and range up to around $500 depending on such variables as speed, guarantees, equipment, and number of Internet Protocol (IP) addresses. T1 lines typically cost $1,000 or more per month for just the line (not counting Internet service.) T1 lines are priced on distance, so it might be higher than that at a given location, and T1 prices have been dropping lately, presumably due to competition from DSL and cable modems. A common total cost for T1 Internet access is around $2,000 per month. Like 56K lines, either T1s or DSL lines can be multiplexed together, though the carriers who have T1 service are much more accustomed to doing multiplexed arrangements. In Europe, they use E1s instead of T1s, which are 2Mbps, but all the other information is the same, though prices may vary wildly from those given for the United States.

Beyond T1 speeds, the next option is usually only T3. A T3 line (properly, a DS3 line) is a digital telecommunications line capable of carrying up to 45Mbps. This size line is about the minimum most serious e-commerce sites should consider. Unfortunately, they can be very expensive. In the U.S., T3 lines often cost between $8,000–$15,000 per month for the line alone, with no Internet service. Internet service on top of that can be thousands of dollars per month as well, depending on the services provided. The break-even for multiple T1s and a T3 is usually around 6–8 T1s, cost-wise. That is, you can implement around 6–8 T1 lines for the cost of a single T3.

Beyond T3 speeds, some carriers can offer OC-3 or OC-12 speeds. OC-3 is ATM running at 155Mbps. The OC stands for optical carrier (fiber optic) and the 3 refers to the T3 carrying capacity. In other words, OC-3 can carry 3 T3s, plus overhead. OC-3 and above almost always must be delivered via fiber, so installation costs may be significant. OC-12 is 622Mbps. Faster speeds, such as OC-48 do exist, but so far they are used almost exclusively by carriers and huge ISPs to carry all their aggregate customer traffic. At the time of this writing, I don't believe that any sections of the Internet are faster than OC48, and only a handful of those exist. Some telephone carriers have OC192 lines for all of their traffic combined (voice, data, and video.) OC-3 and above are all customer-priced services, and depend a great deal on where you want the lines.

So what do co-location costs look like in comparison? Pretty good, usually. Many co-location facilities will provide you with rack space, a private cage, air conditioning, battery backed-up power (with generator for longer outages) and a Fast Ethernet handoff with a couple of megabits worth of service for a few thousand dollars per month. Compared to the costs of pulling in your own lines and building an equivalent environment, the costs are *very* attractive. Because of the economies of scale (the co-location has lots of customers in one place), it's not clear that there is ever a break-even point for when you would bring it in-house with, say, a T3, based purely on cost. A co-location facility may just be able to do it cheaper than you can.

Which means that there are other reasons why people do their sites in-house. These include the aforementioned staff problem (if your site usually takes several hands-on visits per day, how do you do that if the co-location is 100 miles away? Some of your staff will be the unhappy campers assigned to sit at the co-location that day.) Other reasons are security concerns, frequent equipment turnover rates, backups, and the need to have a quicker response time to problems. Some co-locations will provide some of these services, if that addresses your needs. One of the biggest issues with co-location is the need for what would normally be DMZ machines to speak to machines inside your network.

## Estimating Required Service Levels

One of the questions you need an answer to in order to shop for service is how much bandwidth you will need. This isn't always easy to estimate, especially if the primary protocol in use is HTTP. You don't want to be stuck not having enough bandwidth to serve your customers, and you don't want to pay for more than you need.

How do you plan for bandwidth for a new site? Some services, such as media serving, have fairly fixed bandwidth needs. For example, if you want to run a RealAudio server and be able to handle 100 simultaneous users at 56Kbps, then you need somewhere in the neighborhood of 5.6Mbps of bandwidth to handle the peaks. If you want to run an FTP server to support up to 100 users at 100Kbps each, then you need 10Mbps to handle the peaks.

HTTP traffic isn't quite as smooth to calculate. It tends to be lots of small, burst transfers, rather than a small number of large, long transfers. TCP, which HTTP uses for a transport, has a "slow start" feature where it starts out using a small amount of bandwidth and uses more and more as it goes, if the connection is working well. If you observe an FTP transfer of a large file, you will see the transfer rate increase and usually level out at some point. HTTP transfers are often short enough that they never get out of the slow part of the transfer. By the time TCP is starting to speed up, the transfer is over. This has two effects: One, 10 50K files sent over HTTP will go much slower than one 500K file sent over HTTP, and two, if any packet loss occurs (due perhaps to not having enough bandwidth), then the short HTTP transfers will tend to stall out longer than a larger transfer.

So it's not quite as simple a matter as measuring the total number of bytes of all the files that make up a Hypertext Markup Language

(HTML) page, and multiplying it out by the number of simultaneous users. First of all, because the files are sent in smaller, separate chunks, there is more protocol overhead. Second, you will need to have extra bandwidth available to handle the bursts so that packets aren't lost. A good rule of thumb is to take the simple product of byte totals per page times number of simultaneous users you need to support and double it. Note that the number of users is *not* the same as the number of orders you can handle at a given moment, because you need to accommodate people who are just looking as well!

# How Do I Know When I Need More Bandwidth?

There's one sure way to see how much bandwidth you need, and that's to throw your site up and see how much you use. You might be surprised by how many sites get done this way. And actually, it's not always such a terrible thing, if the situation is right. Assuming for the moment that you've decided to go that route, how do you know when you need more bandwidth?

You measure it. Any number of network management packages can measure line utilization for you. In addition, you can use packet monitoring tools to look for things like excessive retransmits, though in an Internet environment, the problem causing this type of behavior might not always be on your end.

Most networking technologies can just about run up to the full wire speed before they start to have problems. One notable exception is half-duplex Ethernet. Half-duplex Ethernet starts to have trouble at about 70 to 80 percent utilization, so if for example you're using 10Mbps half-duplex, use 7 or 8Mbps for your maximum.

So you pick some percentage of maximum as your threshold for when to upgrade and wait to hit that threshold. In fact, you may find that your ISP offers bandwidth measurement tools that you can use. Some make these available for customers, because they are already doing the measurements anyway.

So when you hit your threshold, what do you do? Or, more to the point, how *quickly* can you do something?

## Obtaining Bandwidth on Demand

Bandwidth is sold in two ways: one, with a cap at a particular speed, and two, with an agreement for a particular speed and charges for going over that. Even if your bandwidth is "unlimited," the cap is the maximum speed of the pipe, and that's intentional.

The amount of bandwidth you contract for usually comes into play with larger pipes, such as a 10Mbps Ethernet co-location handoff or a T3 line. The ISP doesn't expect you to just use all you can consume, unless you pay for it. For example, you might have a T3 line, but contract for a 6Mbps average. When you contact for an "average" utilization, most ISPs will have a particular sampling rate and will check at something like the 95th percentile of those samples. For an averaging scheme, you will also have a cost for exceeding your average. If you go over your average, you usually find out via a larger bill at the end of the month, unless you have been tracking your traffic levels as well.

The other choice is to have a bandwidth cap. This is the same as having a pipe of that size. Attempts to use more bandwidth than that will usually result in dropped packets. The advantage to a hard cap is that your costs are also fixed.

So what's the point of having a T3 if you're going to cap it at 6Mbps? Why waste the money? Wouldn't 4 T1s do the same thing? The difference is how quickly you can make changes, and this is a critical point. If you have a T3 capped at 6Mbps, you can change it relatively quickly to something higher if you require it, at a higher cost of course. But, if you had 4 T1s, and were at capacity, you'd have to bring in additional lines, or upgrade to a T3. Typical lead time to get new circuits in often ranges from weeks to months. If you have a capped T3, then your provider can change that for you without intervention from the carrier. The change will be on the order of days, depending on what paperwork your provider requires and what their procedures are. If you're thinking about opting for a capped bandwidth solution, be sure to get an answer as to how long it will take to make changes. With many providers, these change times are often detailed in their contracts. Check with your ISP, or prospective ISP, on their lead times and contractual obligations.

If you're paying on an average, then going beyond your normal level is not a problem, it will just use the extra bandwidth, and you'll be billed extra. You still need to watch your usage levels though, because letting it go past your agreed-upon level automatically is more expensive than if you had set your threshold higher. For example, if you're paying for a 6Mbps average at $6,000, and you end up using 8Mbps that month, you might pay an extra $1.50/Kbps over the 6Mbps mark. You'd end up paying around $9,000 for the month. However, the contract rate for a pre-agreed upon 8Mbps might only be $8,000. This is similar to how the cell phone companies work. You pay for a certain number of minutes per month, but if you go over, you pay at a much higher per minute rate. If you buy more minutes, the bill will be cheaper overall. Your goal is to hit the "sweet spot" to minimize expense. The goal of the providers is to get you to pay for more upfront. This helps them plan for their overall bandwidth needs better, and they come out ahead if you don't use everything you paid for that month.

It should be obvious that you can only take advantage of any sort of bandwidth-on-demand arrangement if you have extra capacity in your connection. The flexibility makes it worthwhile for many companies. Could you live for a month without enough bandwidth while you wait for your new line?

Getting more bandwidth at a co-location facility generally isn't a problem either. You can usually go to a bigger pipe by just changing your billing, up to the size of their feeds, of course. Again, check with your co-location provider about their policies on changes and use this as a comparison point for selecting a co-location provider.

# Introduction to Load Balancing

So far, we've mentioned load balancing numerous times in this book. Load balancers are worth covering in detail because they are usually an integral part of an e-commerce site. In this section, we take a detailed look at load balancers, including how they work and what they can do for you.

## What Is Load Balancing?

We've already discussed the need for multiple Web server machines. We even discussed one method that can be used for a type of load balancing, the one Hotmail uses, which is dynamically redirecting clients to different DNS names. Another method many companies attempt before going to the expense of buying or building a load balancer is round robin DNS.

Round robin DNS is simple in concept. Normally, you have a DNS name, like www.example.com, pointing at a single IP address, say 192.168.1.1. With round robin DNS, you have the same name point at more than one IP address, such as 192.168.1.1 and 192.168.1.2. Your DNS server will return both answers when queried for that name, in a random order. So, one time it will return 192.168.1.1, 192.168.1.2, and another time it returns 192.168.1.2, 192.168.1.1. The machine that originally asked for the address decides how to handle the multiple addresses. Often, it will just use the first one on the list (which is why they are returned in random order.) The idea is that you want a way to have clients on the Internet use both of your Web servers. This way, some clients will use .1 part of the time, and others will use .2 part of the time.

So what's wrong with this scheme? Several things, the biggest one being maintenance. DNS records have cache times associated with them. To avoid having to look up a DNS address every single time you make a request, intermediate DNS servers, as well as the clients themselves, will cache name lookups. How long should they cache them for? It is built into the DNS protocol that there is both a maximum amount of time that a name should be cached, as well as an amount of time after which the DNS server should be asked again. This is controlled by the DNS server that has the original answer. For example, it may say to cache names for no more than 5 days but ask again after 2 days.

So what does that mean for maintenance? It means that when one of the two Web servers goes down for maintenance, whether planned or unplanned, half of the clients will still want to talk to the down server, due to DNS caching.

In addition, round robin DNS does not reflect the relative load of each Web server. One Web server may be responding twice as fast, either because the slower one is busy handling resource-intensive requests, or perhaps just because it has slower hardware. Round robin DNS will still distribute the load more or less evenly, leaving the slower Web server to struggle, whereas the faster one is spending some of it's time idling.

So, round robin DNS helps with distributing load, but it does nothing to dynamically remove non-working machines from rotation and can't dynamically distribute load based on response time of the servers.

This is where an *external load balancer* comes in.

Generically speaking, a load balancer will allow you to configure a virtual IP address that represents all of your Web servers, and that's the address you put in for your www DNS name. Most load balancers measure response time of the various Web servers, relative to each other (that is, it has measured that Web server 1 is responding 50 percent faster than Web server 2 at the moment). When the load balancer receives a connection request to the virtual IP address, it determines which Web server should service the request. It then "passes" the connection to the Web server it has picked.

How the connection is passed to a Web server can be fairly involved and is one of the major points of difference among all the load balancer vendors. Some of them work by modifying Media Access Control (MAC) addresses, some of them work by modifying IP addresses, some work by proxying, and some work via custom software on the Web servers or clustering.

## Changing the Destination MAC Address

One of the simpler (for the load balancer) mechanisms is to keep a table of HTTP clients as they come in, and simply change the destination MAC address as the frames pass through the load balancer. For this to work, each Web server has to have the virtual IP address configured as an interface alias. You also have to prevent the Web servers from answering Address Resolution Protocol (ARP) requests for the virtual IP address, because the load balancer has to have the MAC address for the virtual IP address as far as the other pieces of equipment are concerned.

For example, a client, say 10.0.0.1, makes a request to your virtual IP address (named www.example.com). The load balancer takes note of the 10.0.0.1 address and puts it into its table with the MAC address of the Web server that it has picked to serve the request, as well as probably some TCP header data from the packet. It then changes the destination MAC address of the frame to the Web server in question, and puts the frame onto the wire. The Web server gets the packet just as if it had received any normal request, and replies appropriately.

Configuration in this arrangement is fairly minimal. You have to configure the virtual IP on each Web server, and configure them not to respond to the ARP; this can be accomplished on NT for example, by installing the loopback adapter, binding the virtual IP address to that adapter, and modifying the route tables. Your load balancer vendor will have instructions for each OS if their product works this way. You have to configure the IP address of each Web server on the load balancer so that it can pick up their MAC addresses via ARP, and so that the load balancer can make its own HTTP requests to measure performance.

## Modifying the IP Addresses

Another method for getting the requests to the right Web server is to modify the IP addresses. Most load balancers that work this way will look like a LAN switch or router to the rest of the network components. These types of load balancers work by changing the destination IP address as the packets pass through it. This is in essence Network Address Translation. However, the NAT that most people are accustomed to translates source addresses (at least on the way out). You might think of this as reverse NAT, but the internal software is essentially the same.

If the 10.0.0.1 client makes a request to the virtual IP 192.168.0.1, the load balancer adds an entry to its table for that TCP connection, translates the destination IP to, say, 192.168.0.5, and forwards it to the right MAC address for 192.168.0.5. When the reply comes back from 192.168.0.5 for 10.0.0.1, it changes the (now) source address to 192.168.0.1 and forwards it back onto the Internet.

One of the advantages of this type of load balancing is that it's transparent to the Web servers, and no special configuration on the Web servers is required. The load balancer has to be told what virtual IP to use, what the IP addresses of the Web servers are, and what balancing metrics to use.

## Using a Proxy Server

Similar to how a Web proxy server works to handle outgoing HTTP requests from your network, you can get some kinds of proxies that will distribute requests among multiple Web servers. You might think of this as inverse proxying.

When a request comes in from client 10.0.0.1, it is sent to the IP address of the proxy 192.168.0.1 (which is equivalent in concept to the virtual IP address of other load balancers). The proxy then decides which Web server should handle the request and requests the file itself. The Web server, say 192.168.0.5, replies, and after the proxy has collected the file (or some portion—proxies can start replying to the original requester before they get the complete file), it replies to 10.0.0.1 from its 192.168.0.1 address.

This requires no special configuration on the Web servers. However, the Web logs now indicate that all HTTP requests come from 192.168.0.1, rather than the original client (10.0.0.1 in our example.) Many sites use their Web logs to measure visitor data. These logs now essentially live on the proxy server instead of the Web servers. This might even be a bonus, because Webmasters would have previously had to put together all the logs from the various Web servers to get the whole picture. Now they are in one spot.

Proxying will tend to be a bit slower on equivalent hardware than solutions that work primarily on changing frame and packet addresses. This is because they simply do more work. However, if your hardware is sufficient to handle your requirements, it's really not a major factor. If the proxy server is also able to do some caching, it may help speed up some requests.

## Finding a Custom Software/Clustering Solution

As a catch-all for the remaining solutions, various custom software solutions and OS features allow for load balancing, or something with similar results (uptime, load distribution, and easy maintenance).

For example, it's possible to write custom Web server software to run on multiple machines that will listen on the wire in promiscuous mode and communicate among all the Web servers to decide which will handle particular requests. When a request hits the shared Web server segment, Web server 192.168.0.5 is elected to respond to the current request from 10.0.0.1, all the while writing the packets so that the headers say the replies are from 192.168.0.1.

Some operating systems have clustering capabilities that allow them to appear as a single IP address but share the processing load. This type of solution may or may not require special Web server software.

## Determining Load

Regardless of the method used to distribute requests, the load balancer has to have some mechanism to determine the load of the Web servers and spot when they go down. The main methods are by measuring request response time, inference, and software agents.

Measuring request response time is conceptually simple. The load balancer starts a timer, asks for a Web page, or graphic file or something from the Web server, and checks how long the server took to respond. The longer it takes, the slower the Web server must be at that moment, and the fewer requests the load balancer will send it. The URL you tell the load balancer to monitor determines how much functionality it checks. If you give it a simple static file, it checks that much. If you give it a page that depends on the database server, then that essentially gets checked too.

The inference method works by measuring responses that normal clients make, perhaps in conjunction with some method to determine that a given server is up at all. A request comes in from the Internet, and as the load balancer passes it along, it starts a timer. One of the problems with this method is that the request may be for a really long page or a really short graphic. An absolute time isn't useful in this case, but a ratio of size/time might be.

The software agent method involves loading a software agent onto each Web server, which will often measure many of the items you would normally look at when troubleshooting performance of a Web server yourself. Ultimately, it will come up with a metric to indicate how busy the server is, and communicate that back to the load balancer. These agents are normally proprietary and may limit what operating systems you can use for your Web server if your load balancer requires these.

# The Pros and Cons of Load Balancing

To summarize, the pros and cons of load balancing are fairly straightforward. The benefits include the following:

- Allows distribution of load among a group of Web servers
- Can measure relative load, and act accordingly
- Can automatically take failed Web servers out of rotation
- Allows for maintenance to be performed

The drawbacks of load balancing are:

- Single point of failure
- May introduce some delays
- May require extra configuration work to be done
- Potential bottleneck
- May introduce security issues

# Load Balancing and Security

Note that the last item listed in the previous section as a drawback mentions security. For the most part, load balancers don't change security much, and in fact some can enhance it by acting as limited firewalls. However, in a few cases, security may be impacted.

Obviously the load balancer itself may have security problems—most products do. Attacks against the management interface or address of the load balancer may occur. In this sense, it's much like any system on your network, which might be compromised and give an attacker better leverage for other attacks. If an attacker manages to gain administrative control over your load balancer, they might be able to cause a "virtual defacement" by redirecting your Web traffic to a page of their choosing.

Some load balancers may be vulnerable to the kinds of tricks that IDS systems and firewalls sometimes are, such as difficulties dealing with special customer-crafted packets. It may be possible to exhaust the memory for state tables in types of load balancers, causing a denial of service attack. It's possible that some may be vulnerable to remote overflows. Like any product on your network, you should investigate these possibilities when choosing a product and then remain vigilant about watching for upgrades, patches, and new holes.

In a few rare cases, the load balancer may make it *easier* to attack your site. Recently, it was announced that the Cisco routers had an extremely predictable Initial Sequence Number (ISN). This makes it really easy to blindly spoof TCP connections to Cisco routers. However, it turns out that devices behind Cisco routers that can be reached via address translation inherit the weak ISN at the outside address. Although the Cisco load balancer products don't appear to have this problem, this is an example of the kind of thing that can go wrong.

Tools & Traps...

### Commercial and Build-Your-Own Load Balancing Solutions

What are some of the products that are out there, and which methods do they use? Are there any free solutions? Let's take a look at a few options.

Cisco formerly offered a product called LocalDirector, but recently purchased the company Arrowpoint, which produces competing products. Cisco has adopted the Arrowpoint load balancers as their load balancing solution, now called the Content Services Switch (CSS) line. (Appendix B of this book outlines in detail a load balancing solution using LocalDirector, DistributedDirector, and CSS). The CSS products look like a Fast Ethernet switch (some with Gigabit Ethernet ports). However, once configured, they will translate destination IP addresses of incoming HTTP requests to the appropriate Web server. The Web servers must be attached to the CSS switch, meaning that all packets go through it, for this to work. To determine load, the CSS will request an administrator-defined Web page (or make a HEAD request) to the Web servers. It also has the capability to take actions based on the URL being requested, such as redirect to a different one or have a particular set of pages living only on a subset of the Web servers. You can find more information at www.cisco.com/univercd/cc/td/doc/pcat/11000.htm.

IBM offers a software product called WebSphere Edge Server, which grew out of an earlier product called the WebSphere Performance pack. The software is a custom Web server software package, with additional software components to handle load balancing and caching. As such, it only supports certain operating systems and hardware platforms. The IBM software is extensive, and it includes many other capabilities outside the scope of what we are discussing here. One interesting feature is that it can distribute load across multiple locations, whereas many load

Continued

balancing solutions require LAN connections. You can find more information at www.ibm.com/software/webservers/edgeserver/about.html.

If you're running Windows NT services, you might take a look at Microsoft Windows NT Load Balancing Service (WLBS). It's free if you already have Windows NT Enterprise Edition licenses. You can obtain it at www.microsoft.com/ntserver/nts/downloads/winfeatures/WLBS/default.asp. This is a clustering solution, and Microsoft claims this will also provide redundancy and load sharing for other service beyond HTTP, such as FTP and the Database server.

If you'd like to try to build your own, you can use the Linux Virtual Server (LVS) software, which is available at www.linuxvirtualserver.org/. The LVS has a couple of different modes, including one that looks like NAT load balancing and another that looks like MAC address translation load balancing.

You can find a fairly complete, if somewhat dated, review of a number of load balancers at www.nwfusion.com/reviews/0614rev.html.

# Summary

One of the problems that any successful e-commerce site must face is having sufficient capacity. If some component in the chain is faltering, the result is usually that the customer sees a slow, unreachable, or not fully functional Web site. For an e-commerce site, this can be deadly.

Most e-commerce sites have an interdependent chain of components, such that any one of them failing will result in the Web site as a whole being unusable. These components are usually some combinations of Web servers, databases, load balances, switches, routers, hubs, and Internet connections.

Any one of those components may become overloaded, and you'll be called upon to determine which one is having trouble and how to alleviate the problem. One of the main tasks for running an e-commerce site is chasing bottlenecks. Some component will always be the slowest one in the chain, and you need to make sure that it has sufficient capability to keep up with demand.

Nearly all the components have a similar set of resource that can be measured to determine load. These include memory, CPU load, I/O, and bandwidth. Like the chain of components, if any of them is maxed out, that component will likely not be able to perform any faster than the overloaded resource will allow. All of the components offer a way to measure the utilization of these resources to see which ones are at capacity.

One of the big pieces that must be carefully maintained is the bandwidth of your Internet connection. You want enough to be able to function properly, even at peak times, and yet not be paying for more than you need. A large number of bandwidth delivery mechanisms exist, but the major decision is whether to bring a connection to your location or whether to co-locate. Each has its plusses and minuses, but the major factors are cost and convenience. The co-location option is often cheaper, but less convenient. The line to your premise is more expensive, but more convenient.

Another key component of most e-commerce sites is some sort of load balancing solution. A load balancer allows you two make a collection of Web (or other) servers appear as a single IP address. This allows the work to be shared among the servers, and allows you the greatest flexibility for adding and removing servers to the pool. Load balancers work via several mechanisms and range all over the board in price. Some load balancers require software to be loaded on the Web servers. Others work as a network device and are transparent to the Web servers.

# Solutions Fast Track

## What If My Site's Popularity Exceeds My Expectations?

☑ A typical e-commerce infrastructure includes Web servers, database servers, e-mail servers, DNS servers, network equipment, and possibly some other specialized servers, such as media servers or financial transaction servers. If any one of these components is at capacity, then your site overall is not working properly.

☑ An overloaded device is often harder to troubleshoot than a device that is down all the way—some of your tests might pass on an overloaded device, whereas they will fail for a down device.

☑ By definition, you can't handle an infinite load, and some piece will always max out first. The term "load" collectively refers mostly to a combination of network throughput, CPU utilization, and I/O.

☑ Determine which component is the current bottleneck. The Web servers are one of the pieces most prone to overload (in addition to the database server.) They are also the most flexible in terms of configuration options and the most complex to measure. Determine current traffic at the router—for proactive monitoring, you will want to use a network management package of some sort that keeps statistics over time and perhaps offers utilization graphs. In general, switches don't have a whole lot to go wrong.

- ☑ Assuming that you've gone through the process of tuning your server-side processing, and you're not stalling out waiting on external bottlenecks, such as a database server, then your only real choice is to upgrade your hardware, whether getting a faster individual machine, or adding an additional separate physical machine to help take on some of the work.

## How Do I Manage My Bandwidth Needs?

- ☑ Bandwidth can either be delivered to your premises, or it might be in the form of a handoff at a co-location facility. The co-location option tends to be cheaper, and it's less convenient. Having the bandwidth delivered to your location is very convenient, but it can also be fairly expensive, especially if you need a large amount of it.
- ☑ Try to estimate ahead of time as best you can what your bandwidth requirements will be. Some services, such as media serving, have fairly fixed bandwidth needs. HTTP traffic isn't quite as smooth to calculate; a good rule of thumb is to take the simple product of byte totals per HTML page times number of simultaneous users you need to support, and double it. Also, a number of network management packages will measure line utilization for you.
- ☑ Leave yourself room to grow into your pipe and try to pick a solution that will allow for expansion with a minimum of notice.

## Introduction to Load Balancing

- ☑ Load balancing permits you to use one virtual IP address for multiple servers. How the connection request is passed to a Web server is one of the major points of difference among all the load balancer vendors. Some of them work by modifying MAC addresses, some of them work by modifying IP addresses, some work by proxying, and some work via custom software on the Web servers or clustering.

- ☑ Load balancers allow for relatively seamless on-the-fly addition and removal of servers.
- ☑ Drawbacks of load balancers are that they introduce one more single point of failure or bottleneck, and they are as open to compromise by an attacker as any other system on your network.

## Frequently Asked Questions

The following Frequently Asked Questions, answered by the authors of this book, are designed to both measure your understanding of the concepts presented in this chapter and to assist you with real-life implementation of these concepts. To have your questions about this chapter answered by the author, browse to **www.syngress.com/solutions** and click on the **"Ask the Author"** form.

**Q:** What freeware packages are available for monitoring my bandwidth usage?

**A:** One of the most popular packages is MRTG (go to http://ee-staff.ethz.ch/~oetiker/webtools/mrtg). MRTG will collect and store statistical data from routers via SNMP and build graphs to display on Web pages. It pretty much automatically does everything that you'd want to do to monitor your bandwidth usage.

**Q:** Which pieces in my infrastructure are most likely to break?

**A:** My personal experience has been that more general-purpose devices (such as a full operating system running on standard PC hardware) fail more often than special purpose hardware and software (that is, "appliances"). This is more an indictment of the software than the hardware. The more software is loaded and the more it tries to do, the more bugs there are and the more often it fails. The appliance hardware is often designed to a better set of specifications than generic PC hardware and often has features such as a reduced number of moving parts and redundant power supplies. So, having a little more redundancy on the general purpose machines (such as your Web servers) makes sense.

**Q:** How do I set up redundant database servers?

**A:** This problem is harder than most of the others discussed so far, and it is very vendor-specific. Each database vendor has different ways to do this, ranging from dual commits for each transaction to having some sort of warm standby that must be manually cut over. There's no good short answer, but if you want this feature, you'll have to be particularly picky up front when choosing your database software. Here are some links to the popular Database vendors, and their replication/ high availability options:

**Oracle** http://technet.oracle.com/products/oracle7/htdocs/rep/section.htm

**Sybase** www.sybase.com/products/eaimiddleware/replicationserver

**Informix** www.informix.com/informix/products/technologies/extensibility/replication/index.html

**MySQL** www.mysql.com/doc/R/e/Replication.html

**Q:** How do I set up redundant Internet connections?

**A:** This is fairly common for large sites. The idea is to protect you from such events as circuit outages and ISP problems. Essentially, you have to have a portable set of addresses (not tied to your ISP) and connections to more than one ISP. The connections each have to be able to carry the full load of traffic if you're actually going to be redundant, but you can often use all of them during normal operations to achieve better performance. In order to have dynamic failover to another provider, you will have to run a routing protocol with your ISP, likely BGP.

Chapter 10

# Incident Response, Forensics, and the Law

## Solutions in this chapter:

- Why Is an Incident Response Policy Important?
- Establishing an Incident Response Team (IRT)
- Setting the Prosecution Boundaries
- Establishing an Incident Response Process
- Introduction to Forensic Computing
- Tracking Incidents
- Resources

☑ Summary

☑ Solutions Fast Track

☑ Frequently Asked Questions

# Introduction

If you build it, they will come—attacks, that is. Expect your site to be probed, poked, prodded, tested, and scanned several times a day at a minimum. If you are a popular site, expect to be attacked several times an hour in some respect or another. Sounds like a lot, doesn't it?

The whole point of the incident response process is to separate the noise from the signal, so to speak. With all these events, how do you know which ones are actually threats and which ones your defense systems are handling? Well, with the proper application of incident tracking and incident policies, you can ensure that you will respond when needed, and will cut out most of the extraneous issues.

Incident response also depends on personnel. People require training, communication channels, and a proper process to follow. This chapter explains how to create a team to handle security events, and how to build policies to ensure that events are tracked and handled correctly. Finally, this chapter explains how to interface with law enforcement officials, should you ever require their assistance.

# Why Is an Incident Response Policy Important?

An Incident Response Policy (IRP) is important for the same reasons that a security policy is important; namely, that it dictates how you react when the situation arises. By way of illustration, let's look at some example scenarios.

## Panic or Be Calm: You Decide

Imagine you're one of the network engineers for an e-commerce site. At your company, the network group is responsible for security. You're at home on Saturday evening when your pager goes off. It's the private number for your company help desk. You're the one on call this weekend, so you're obliged to answer the call. You call the help desk, assuming that there is some network problem, and hoping you won't have to drive in.

The person at the help desk reports that she received a call that your Web site has been "defaced," and when she checked, it certainly wasn't the normal page. The person at the help desk asks you, "Did we get hacked?" You reply that you'll take a look, and call her right back.

Breaking out into a sweat, you fire up your computer, and load your Web browser. Sure enough, right there on your start page is a message saying that maybe your company ought to fix its security—followed by "greetz" to a bunch of names you've never heard of.

You're supposed to call the help desk back and tell them how to proceed. What are you going to tell them to do? If you've made the mistake of waiting until a major incident has occurred before giving any thought to how to handle it (the same mistake most companies make), then you've got to decide *right now* what to do.

You can immediately think of a number of decisions that have to be made. Do you need to contact management or legal? Maybe contact the PR department to handle any inquiries about the intrusion? What if they also got into the database! What do we need to do to get the Web site back? Should we shut it off so that people can't see the defacement? What should I tell the help desk to say? Are you going to be able to find a system administrator and database administrator to help you clean up?

## How Not to Handle an Incident

You call the help desk back, and ask them to do several things for you. You ask them to power off the Web server, and leave it alone until you get there. You tell them to make up some story about unexpected maintenance for any other callers, and deny any security problems for now. You also ask them to see if they can contact anyone from Legal at home. You tell them you'll be there in half an hour.

On the way in, you page the on-call system administrator, and ask him to meet you there. Upon arrival, the help desk tells you that they had a call from a reporter asking about the Web site being hacked, and they denied it. They say the reporter says that someone called Attrition.org had a mirror that he has looked at. You don't have time to worry about the reporter right now; that will be management's or PR's decision. The help desk hasn't been able to find anyone from Legal yet.

Shortly thereafter, the system administrator arrives, and you explain what you saw on the Web site. The two of you head for the computer room. You find the Web server off as requested. After disconnecting the network cable and attaching a terminal directly to the console port, the system administrator powers it back up. The system reports a few disk errors, which the SA tells the *fsck* programs to go ahead and fix. After the SA logs in, he finds that the original index.html file has been renamed to index.bak and replaced. He also sees a new entry in the password file that shouldn't be there, which he deletes. You ask him to copy off any logs on the box so you can look at them later, and to put the original index.html file back. You have him do a **netstat –an** command to see if there are any strange ports open. You don't see anything obvious.

You still don't have any input from management or Legal. You make the call to put the Web site back up, and plug the network cable back in. You hop on a PC, and connect to the Web site. Everything looks normal.

What mistakes were made in this hypothetical situation, and why? Read on for how the incident should have been handled.

# Proper Policy Pays Off

Let's look at the same hypothetical situation again, but this time with an incident handling policy in place. Assume that along the way you already know what the steps are, probably because you helped write the policy, or because you've got a copy accessible to you as the on-call engineer. We start over again with you at home just having finished your initial call with the help desk, and having confirmed that your Web site has in fact been defaced.

You call the help desk back and tell them that anyone who calls asking about the Web site will be told that the site is down for maintenance at the moment, and to apologize for the inconvenience. If they ask specifically about security issues, the help desk staff are to say that they have no comment at this time, but offer to take their name, title, and telephone number. You know that outright denying it will be worse when later it's confirmed that there was an intrusion, but there's no sense commenting until you've had an opportunity to make a full assessment of the damages and contact PR.

You also tell the help desk to unplug the network cable of the Web server but to not power it off. You're aware that there may be important evidence in RAM that would be lost when the power is cut, as well as normal disk corruption that can occur any time a system isn't properly shut down. You tell the help desk to assign an individual to stand physical guard over the machine. You tell them to do so right now while you're on the telephone, and you record the name of the individual. You speak to him for a moment and inform him that he is not to leave the machine until you get there, and not to permit anyone to touch the machine or access the console in any way, on authority of the incident handling team. You know that maintaining the chain of custody is important, and that if it is not properly handled, any evidence collected may not be admissible.

You tell the help desk that you'll be there in half an hour. You also tell them that in a moment, the rest of the machines on the DMZ will begin to report as unreachable, because you're going to intentionally isolate the DMZ network segment. Before you leave, you connect to the home office, and shut off the firewall interface that connects the DMZ segment to the rest of the network. You know that if the Web server was compromised, then the attacker had better leverage to attack the rest of the machines on the DMZ. Since the attacker announced himself with a Web page defacement, it seems unlikely that he would do any more damage, but you can't be sure. There's always the possibility that he has been in your systems for weeks, and that the defacement was the final act, rather than the first. There's no sense in taking chances.

On your way into the office, you phone the on-call system administrator. You tell him to meet you there as soon as possible, and apologize in advance for ruining his weekend. You tell him to be prepared to get a spare machine out of stock, and to do a complete restore from the last Web server backup onto it.

Arriving at work, you first retrieve your incident handling kit, and head for the server room. From your incident handling kit, you produce your chain of custody form, and have the help desk employee sign that he is the only one who has been in possession of the machine since the incident was discovered, and that no one has operated it during that time. You thank the help desk employee, and excuse him to go back to his regular duties.

Next, from your kit you get out your portable evidence collection computer. You attach directly to the network port of the Web server with a cross-over cable. After reconfiguring the portable to appear to be on the same subnet as the Web server, you log on to the Web server, and issue a series of commands that will do a sector-by-sector copy of each disk partition on the Web server to the portable. The portable has a second network interface on it in case you are forced to store images on a remote computer, due to the copies being too large to fit on the portable itself. You know that a sector-by-sector copy is important, in case there are deleted files or portions of files to be recovered, as well as the possibility of hidden files if a rootkit of some sort has been applied.

After the copy is complete, you force a crash, which writes the contents of RAM to the portion of disk specified for that purpose. This will allow you to comb through the RAM contents afterward if necessary. The process also synchronizes the disks, preventing corruption due to a mismatch of the file tables on disk versus the ones in memory. Following this, you power down the Web server, and remove both the Web server and portable to an office with a lockable door. You place the equipment inside, and place a sign on the door that says "Investigation in progress—Do Not Enter," and lock the door behind you as you leave the office.

You visit the help desk, and point out to them that they are responsible for tracking down Legal, PR, and management for you. (Obviously, you're going to be too busy for a while to be trying to track people down.) Your next task, according to the procedure, is to try to make an assessment of how the attack was accomplished, when, and whether it is likely that any other machines were compromised as well.

You sit down at your desk, and prepare to begin your investigation. Your first place to check is the secure logging machine. This machine was put in place to receive logs live from the other DMZ machines, in case of a compromise. The attacker could erase any local logs, but not the ones on the log machine, not without breaking into it as well, which should be much harder. You procedure calls for checking firewall logs eventually as well, but that should be less useful. Your firewall only allows particular ports in, and it doesn't log URLs. At best, you might see some unusual connection attempts out from the Web server.

After combing through the logs, about all you see that is obviously unusual is a restart of the Web server software about four hours ago. You make a note of the time, which so far marks your earliest piece of evidence to indicate when the attack occurred. It was sometime before four hours ago (assuming that was the reason for the restart, which seems extremely likely).

Conspicuously absent from the logs is any indication that the other DMZ machines were poked at. No failed login attempts (no logins today at all, actually), no application errors, no restarted daemons, and so forth. According to your written procedure, this indicates that no other machines are likely to have been penetrated. As a sanity check, you log in to each, and run a command to look for files modified in the last two days. There are none, aside from those that should be (the database files are updated constantly, for example) plus the ones you just caused to be changed by logging in. The list of recent logins indicates nothing unusual.

You declare the other machines to be safe, and proceed to reenable the DMZ by turning the firewall interface back on (you had to attach a machine directly to the DMZ temporarily to accomplish your logins). The Web site isn't back yet, but other auxiliary functions can be restored in the meantime, such as e-mail and DNS. This part of your day is going well at least. Had there been evidence that the other machines had been penetrated, then you would have had to repeat the same procedure that you did for the Web server for each machine compromised.

According to procedure, before the replacement machine can be put into production, you have to determine the time the penetration took place and what hole was used, if possible. Since the log server had no definitive evidence, you'll have to examine the information available on the Web server itself.

You return to the evidence room to see what evidence you can find. You still need a copy of the RAM dump, as well as backup copies of the disk partition dumps. To accomplish this, you partially disassemble the Web server machine. You open the case, and disconnect the hard drive cables from the disk controller. Since this server uses SCSI disks, you are able to leave the drives mounted in the server, and rearrange the cables a bit. You attach a terminator to the end of the cable that was attached to the controller, and connect your evidence computer to the external SCSI connector of the Web server, via a SCSI cable. This allows you to mount the drives on the Web server on your evidence computer, and take a copy of the RAM dump file, taking care to mount the drives read-only, so as not to damage any evidence such as file access times.

Now that you have a complete set of raw evidence files from the hard drive, you proceed to make two tape backups of the files with the tape drive in your incidence response kit. These tapes are labeled and set aside (within the evidence room).

You now need to examine the partition dumps. This means that you'll have to have a means to mount them on a machine so you can examine the files (read-only, of course). Fortunately for you, the files systems are of a type that you can mount the partition backups directly on your evidence machine. Were they not, you would have had to go to the trouble of restoring them onto a spare drive, and possibly installing the appropriate operating system to read them.

Since the firewall only allowed ports 80 and 443 from the outside, it seems reasonable to take a look at the Web logs. So you grep through the Web logs for index.bak, and sure enough, you find several entries from the same client IP. You grep a second time for all requests from that IP address. It looks like, after some initial poking around on the part of the attacker, that all of the requests were for a particular CGI script, which must be vulnerable. The script is intended to allow e-mail to be sent from a Web form. It appears that the attacker is able to pass a vertical bar (pipe) character in one of the variables, and have the Web server execute the command following the pipe.

You grep through the logs yet another time looking for all cases where that CGI script was requested. The requests with the pipe characters started about six hours ago. The last one was an echo command to place the new Web page in index.html. You now have what looks like a workable start time, and you know what the hole is. It doesn't look like the attacker was trying to hide his actions in your logs.

In order to be safe, you log on to the machine with the archived Web logs. (The logs are moved off once a week in order to be processed for usage statistics.) On that machine, you grep for the CGI script and pipe character together. You find one entry from about six weeks ago. The command issued in that case was just a directory listing command. Either someone else knew you were vulnerable back then and decided not to do anything about it, or it was your same attacker doing reconnaissance work. The IP addresses in the two instances don't seem to be related.

So, it seems reasonable to assume that you were not compromised before earlier today, which means that last night's backups should be clean, and hopefully you can get back into production relatively quickly. Speaking of which, the system administrator poked his head in a few hours ago to let you know he was there, and that he would begin the restore. You had told him to wait for your approval before putting the machine into place, in case the original had been compromised before today. If it had, then the image on last night's backup would have been tainted as well. Plus, you needed to figure out what the hole was before you could go back into production. Even if the backups were clean, the same hole would still be there. Clearly, there was at least one attacker out there who knew about the hole, and was willing to use it. Putting a replacement machine back out there with the same hole would have been a waste of time.

You track down the system administrator, who says that the restore has about another hour to go. You give him permission to put the replacement system into production, minus the offending CGI script. You make a point of stating that the CGI script must be gone *before* it goes onto the DMZ. The Web people can worry about replacing the script with a fixed version when they come in on Monday.

Before you leave the system administrator, you ask him how much time he has spent so far, and how much more he expects to spend before he gets to go home. You make note of the numbers, and ask him to e-mail you a final number when he's done. You ask the help desk personnel the same, and tell their supervisor that you'll need copies of the call logs that indicate how many calls were taken asking about the Web site outage. You'll need all these figures to help figure a damages amount. This will include your own time, of course, which you are recording.

You return to your desk to begin your preliminary report. You mark pages for initial indication of the incident (defaced Web page), a timeline of events, relevant log sections, cause, a tracking number, law enforcement case numbers (when and if those are obtained), time spent by all personnel, and a final damages amount (which will be updated as you go).

Even though the technical stuff is all but done, you know that there will be much more to come. Management and possibly PR will want to meet with you to find out what happened. You might need to contact the appropriate law enforcement agency (that decision is up to the Legal department, according to your procedure). If you open a case with law enforcement, you'll have to give an official statement. There's even a remote possibility that the case could go to court, and that you'd have to testify.

And one of these days, you'll have to decide when to put the hardware for the old Web server back into the pool.

# Incident Response Policy Recap

Obviously, if you have a well thought-out incident response policy that calls for you to do all the "right things," then when you have an incident, you'll be doing a lot more work. That shouldn't be a big surprise; doing things the right way usually takes more work.

As you were reading the two extremes discussed earlier, you might have been thinking to yourself, "Any security person who knows what he or she is doing wouldn't make those mistakes." That might be true for some of the technical points, but it can't be assumed for any of the political ones; for example, whom you are allowed to pull in to help, or who must be contacted for decisions. A policy is not there because you don't know what you are doing; it's there because not everyone will agree with your way of doing things. If you handle something "wrong," especially if management is in shock because they were laboring under the delusion that something like this could never happen to them, then you may get in quite a bit of trouble. However, if you've gotten signoff from all concerned parties ahead of time, and you follow the procedure outlined, then it will be much more difficult to hold you at fault. A well-written policy will tell you what your responsibilities are, and what other people are on the hook for. In some cases, it will tell you when you're done and can go home (at least until the people who didn't read all of the report have finally clued into what is going on and call you up to ask questions).

Incidentally, what originally went wrong in this scenario? Why was it possible to deface the Web site? In this instance, it's because a CGI script had a hole. If this had been caught anywhere ahead of time, it would have been during a change control process. Had the script been reviewed by a knowledgeable person ahead of time, it's entirely possible that the problem would have been spotted. However, with large closed-source programs being used in similar capacities, that isn't always possible. For most sites, keeping an accurate inventory of software, and watching for bug announcements, is about all you can do.

# Establishing an Incident Response Team

The key to handling an incident properly is a well-prepared Incident Response Team (IRT). You could have the best policy in the world, but without people to back it up, it won't do you much good. It should be noted that while the term *team* is used, obviously we're not always talking about a large group of people dedicated to this purpose. What kind of team you can build will almost always be resource constrained. Your "team" may consist of one person, or perhaps an agreement with an outside firm that can provide expertise when an emergency arises.

Even so, let's take a look at what might be considered a full-size inhouse IRT. As evidenced by our hypothetical stories earlier in the chapter, you need people who can write and maintain policy, manage routers and firewalls, perform system administration tasks, perform computer forensics investigation, interface with other departments, and interface with law enforcement. That's a lot to ask of an individual or small team, and expect them to do all of those tasks well. If you're like most companies, you won't have an IRT with those dedicated capabilities; rather, you will pull them in from other parts of the organization as needed. You'll have a virtual team.

Even companies with small IT departments will usually have a network person and a systems administrator, if not more than one of each. You'll likely need to involve them. You'll probably need a representative from your Legal department or attorney's office. A system administrator or a dedicated security engineer can handle the forensics work. Finally, you'll need a dedicated security function that will form the core of the team, and tie it together. This may be a dedicated person, or perhaps a portion of a person's time, but the responsibility must belong to one or more individuals.

The core person's responsibility will be to call meetings, make sure representation is present from all concerned organizations, coordinate writing policy and getting agreement on policy, arrange for training as needed, and drive actual incident response when the occasion arises.

It may be obvious, but it's worth mentioning: Someone will need to be on call at all times to handle any incidents that arise. Hopefully, you will have enough team members that this duty can be rotated. This also implies that there is some mechanism to detect an incident, whether it's an IDS or an e-mail address that people can use to report issues as they arise.

# Setting the Prosecution Boundaries

At some point during an incident, a decision must be made as to whether you wish to pursue legal or civil action, or even just report the incident to a provider or third-party organization. This is not a trivial decision. Pursuing legal action is expensive, and you must consider what you will get out of it.

## Attackers Crossing the Line

The first line you have to draw is the line between attempt and incident. It doesn't matter who you are, whether you're tiny or huge, you will get attempts to penetrate your site. Some of these attempts will be downright useless or idiotic—in fact, most of them will be. This includes things like trying NT exploits against a Unix Web server, or trying to *rsh* to a Windows NT database server. At one large software company where

I managed the firewalls, there were over 1000 attempts to Telnet to the main Web server, per day—all day, every day. Every single attempt was stopped at the firewall and logged. One has to wonder what they would have tried to do if they were able to connect, try logging in as *guest*?

Unfortunately, the reason that the stupid stuff is attempted is that many hosts are vulnerable to it. An attacker may figure that 5 percent of the hosts that he tries have some stupid misconfiguration or hole, so what does he have to lose by trying?

So, all day long, you will receive probes and scans. These are people trying out new tools, or potential attackers gathering intelligence information, or even automated worms. You may get somewhere between dozens and thousands of these per day. You can't possibly treat them all as full incidents, because no one has that kind of time to spend.

You need a set of criteria for deciding how a particular event will be handled. Your possible response ranges from ignoring them, to taking legal action. There are a handful of options in between, such as notifying the attacker's ISP or company. Your incident response team, or whoever writes policy for that team, has to decide where the boundaries are for each response.

One fairly common response for relatively benign attempts (besides ignoring it, of course) is to report the attempts to the appropriate ISP, company, or their provider. This can be time consuming, and you may not get much response from the organizations to which you are reporting. Some IDS software includes a reporting mechanism to help generate reports and locate the proper e-mail addresses to contact. There are also services, such as the ARIS service offered by SecurityFocus.com (note that this author works on the ARIS project), which allows users to submit their IDS logs, and assists them in producing incident reports, and mailing them in. The reports can be done in a number of languages, appropriate to the address where the report is being sent. This service is free.

Another recourse is posting the incidents to a community mailing list, such as the Incidents list, also hosted by SecurityFocus.com. Many subscribers to the Incidents list have been able to confirm that others are seeing the same new scan, or to get answers as to what an attacker is looking for. In the past, much of the traffic to such a list has consisted of "I'm seeing this scan..." followed by a number of lines from an IDS or firewall log. It seems likely that services such as ARIS will eventually take over the mechanical function of correlating attacks among multiple users, and the mailing lists will remain an advice and discussion forum.

What remains to decide is when to go into full-blown incident response mode. Clearly, that would almost always qualify in the event of an actual *intrusion*. An intrusion would consist of an attacker gaining a higher level of privilege that you intended for him or her to have. You would probably also want to treat a significant denial-of-service (DoS) attack in a similar manner. Will there be any cases where you would want to treat *unsuccessful* attempts the same way you would an actual intrusion? Possibly, if the attacker was persistent enough. For example, if you have an attacker who is doing password grinding—that is, trying usernames and passwords repeatedly—you might want to go to the trouble of tracking him or her down. For most people, this would probably have to be an especially persistent attacker—for example, if every time you blocked the IP address or range that the attacker is coming from, he or she started again from a different one. An attacker who is coming at you from obviously compromised machines elsewhere on the Internet would probably be another case that you'd want to track down. (Note that for the latter, you would need to take care that the traffic seemed to have some human intelligence behind it. There are many worms in the wild that will come at you from compromised machines, but they have so far been very single-minded.)

You should take into consideration all of the types of attacks and risks that are discussed in this book, and for each one, decide how you should respond to it. This would necessarily include different levels of severity as well. For example, you might find yourself the recipient of a bunch of traffic coming from a Smurf amplifier, but it may not even be impacting your service.

How to calculate damages needs to be discussed. What is fair to include in damages? Most of the time, it's only going to be the time spent dealing with the incident. This includes investigation, meetings, preparing documentation, and so forth. Businesses that have a documented daily revenue amount, and those revenues wouldn't be mostly recovered when service was restored, may be able to include that lost amount in the damages. For example, an online brokerage that does a certain dollar amount in trades per trading day might be able to claim that very amount in damages if they lose an entire trading day to a DDoS attack. However, they likely wouldn't be able to if it occurred over a weekend when the markets were closed.

# Understanding the Chain of Custody

The chain of custody defines, quite simply, who has access to the evidence during the entire investigation process. The basic reason for this concerns tampering (it also makes sure that the evidence doesn't show up missing). Starting from when it's clear that evidence is present, a log needs to be kept of who has had access to it.

If at all possible, you should also go back as far as when the evidence first became present (usually back to when the penetration took place). This will not always be possible; for example, some evidence may be months old. In our hypothetical scenario earlier in the chapter, careful record was kept when the investigation was being conducted according to a policy. However, one of the minor items of evidence that was collected was about six weeks old. For that one evidence item, it would probably not be possible to determine all the people who had access to the old Web logs. It would include all the people who have a login to that machine, as well as whoever has access to the room in which the physical machine resides. The chain of evidence is one of the many reasons why it's important to conduct a careful investigation as soon after the incident occurs as possible.

Maintaining a chain of custody list isn't difficult; you just have to record several items:

- Who was in custody (possession) of the evidence?
- Where was the evidence?
- What security measures are in place at that location?
- What items of evidence existed at that time?

You must write down a new entry each time one of these things changes, such as turning the evidence over to a new person, adding a piece of evidence, or moving it.

Where you maintain the evidence is obviously important, as it affects whether someone would have had an opportunity to tamper with it. You might wonder who would have access to your premises that you would have to worry about, but a significant portion of incidents are caused by insiders or someone in cooperation with an insider. Police property or evidence rooms are secured, which illustrates nicely the point about having a secured storage area, and the idea that you can't always trust the other folks in the building with you. Police evidence security is in part to guard against tampering by other officers.

The ideal place to maintain evidence is in a safe. That can be problematic due to the size of the evidence to be maintained. The next-best option would be a locked room, with a limited number of folks who hold a key. If janitorial services has a key, then the room isn't very secure. Surveillance of some sort would be ideal.

You maintain a chain of evidence in case you have to use it. This could be for internal action, such as putting someone on report or firing an employee, or to turn over to law enforcement or enter into court evidence. Once the evidence has been turned over to law enforcement or a court, they are responsible for maintaining the chain of custody.

Even if something goes wrong with the chain of custody, all is not lost. The evidence may still be perfectly usable, but if you're in a situation where the evidence is already in question, it won't help if the chain of custody hasn't been maintained. A court is much more likely to accept evidence that has had a proper chain of custody recorded.

# Establishing an Incident Response Process

Once you have a policy in place that dictates how you will respond when an incident occurs, you need to build a set of processes to support your responses. This covers the range from really minor attempts, all the way up to full intrusions. Among the items you need to set up are your forensics toolkit and skills, and your incident tracking system, which we'll cover in the following sections.

The most technical part of the whole incident handling process is the forensics aspect. For many security engineers, it's also the most interesting. However, like most jobs, incident handling is 20 percent interesting work, and 80 percent grunt work.

Probably one of the reasons that the forensics part of an investigation is so interesting is because it's challenging. Computer forensics requires a deep understanding of how the operating system you're investigating works. You will need to understand how the files are stored on disk, how the processes interact, how all the software is configured, and what log information is available to you. And you have to know this for each operating system you need to investigate.

There is a practically infinite combination of operating systems, applications, and configurations. Each new application provides a new opportunity for forensic information to be collected. This section attempts to provide an introduction to computer forensics as a basis for further learning.

Once you have your incident response procedures written down, and have your tools, inventories, and some training in place, you'll need a system for tracking incidents that occur. This goes beyond actual intrusions and cases that you investigate, and should include things like attempts, and interesting traffic patterns that your IDS picks up.

# Introduction to Forensic Computing

The first step in any forensic investigation is to make a backup of all the information available to you, if possible. Unfortunately, this doesn't just mean backing up the drives. Before you even get to that point, you have to decide how to examine what might be in memory when you arrive. There may be some evidence in memory that you want to get at, and not all operating systems have a provision for dumping RAM to disk. Even for those that do, you normally have to configure that ahead of time.

There is a basic problem that you will face as an investigator; you need to do something with a machine that is under the control of an attacker. The vast majority of the time, everything will be straightforward, and you will have no worries. There will be nothing special in memory, and you will be able to shut down without losing anything or causing damage. However, there is always the possibility that your system will get broken into by a very special attacker, one who cares a lot about what evidence he or she leaves behind.

In such a situation, doing investigation of the machine is extremely tricky. You will probably be able to log on and poke around; however, the attacker controls your view of reality. A sophisticated attacker can go as far as to replace parts of the operating system, live, in memory. Such an attacker can hide processes, files, or anything he or she wants. As long as you are dependent on the running OS to provide you with information, the attacker can provide you with lies.

Depending on which tricks were used, the tricks can be partially countered. For example, some rootkits will install a module that will allow modified executables to go undetected. When you run your MD5 hash calculation tool, the original file is presented, and it checks out. However, when you run the file, the replacement version is run.

Dominique Brezinski gave a presentation on these topics at the Black Hat Briefings in 1999. This presentation has been provided for public viewing online, and can be found at www.blackhat.com/html/bh-multi-media-archives.html. Search the page for "Building a Forensic Toolkit that Will Protect You from Evil Influences." This situation can be a damned-if-you-do, damned-if-you-don't situation. One choice is to shut the system down, and boot your own OS to do your investigation, thereby removing the possibility that the victimized operating system will be altering your view of reality. However, what if the attacker designed in a booby trap to erase everything if you try to shut down? Alternately, you can keep the machine up, and try to do an interactive investigation, but you're at the mercy of the running OS, and run the risk of destroying date and timestamps with each command you type, with no backup.

Even disconnecting from the network might possibly set off a booby trap. What if the attacker designed his or her compromise software to erase everything if it stops receiving a certain signal from the outside? That's possibly a signal that you can't replicate, because it's encrypted.

You could monitor traffic to and from the machine, but that will be time consuming.

There is no single right answer. Based on how most of the existing forensics tools work, current best practice is to just pull the plug on the machine. This allows for later backup, and doesn't give any shutdown code an opportunity to execute. This is based solely on how often a really clever attack occurs (or more specifically, doesn't occur). This opinion could easily change as time goes on, and will mostly be dependent on the state-of-the-art in rootkits. There have been viruses in the past that encrypt the FAT table of a hard drive, making it difficult to examine the hard drive without the virus running. A rootkit could act in a similar manner, but so far, none of them do.

Tools & Traps...

## Rootkits

Briefly, a rootkit is a piece of software designed to be installed on a victimized machine that permits the attacker to burrow in and hide. Rootkits will allow for things such as hiding files, modifying the output of commands such as ps or netstat, and install various backdoors to let the attacker back in. The idea behind a rootkit is for the break-in to go undiscovered as long as possible.

Rootkits are operating-system specific, as they need to hook into very specific OS functions, replace the exact proper binaries, and so on. Here's a sample of several popular rootkits:

- Rootkit for Windows NT www.rootkit.com
- An analysis of t0rn www.securityfocus.com/focus/ids articles/t0rn.html
- A large collection of Unix rootkits http://packetstorm .securify.com/UNIX/penetration/rootkits
- A Linux rootkit detector www.chkrootkit.org (there's a good set of links for more rootkit reading there, too)

It bears repeating that backup is critical. You should back up first, investigate second. Unfortunately, this isn't a terribly easy problem to solve. Well, let's qualify that: It isn't easy to solve if you want to grab a backup before shutting the compromised system down, especially on Windows. It's generally quite easy to do a sector-by-sector backup of a hard drive if you can boot the machine to your own operating system, or if you can remove the drives and attach them to another system you control.

The general problem with backing up a compromised system before you shut it down is that any use of the compromised system damages the evidence to some degree. Obviously, if you feel you need to do a backup prior to initial shutdown, you'll have to do your best to minimize damage. You also need to not rely on the installed support libraries as much as possible, in case one of them has been replaced with a modified version. For most operating systems, this means statically compiled binaries (no dynamic libraries). You'll probably want to run off a CD-ROM, or similar read-only removable media.

For Unix systems, the backup could be accomplished with minimal damage if you prepare the static binaries ahead of time. You can use a combination of *dd* and *netcat* to grab copies of entire partitions, including the "unused" sectors that the file system indicates don't have any data on them. As shown in this section's sidebar, this method was used by The Honeynet Project in their Forensic Challenge. The tradeoffs associated with this method are nicely summarized in the answer given in the sidebar; in particular, chain of custody is a little bit fuzzier here, because of the fact that the drive will keep changing. You can't step into the same stream twice, and if the original computer is collected for evidence, and law enforcement does its own forensic analysis, there may be some question as to why there are differences. The Forensic Challenge wasn't concerned with this, as prosecution wasn't their goal. This is not to say that your evidence will be invalidated, but it's another variable.

Getting a backup of a running Windows system may be even more difficult. At present, all the prepackaged backup tools that I have found for Windows require an install step, and they are file based, meaning that they won't get the "empty" drive space. They will also not take any care to not modify the file system being backed up, and will do things such as modify the last accessed times and archive bits. There have been scattered reports of using a port of *dd* for Windows to do similar backups to the one illustrated in our Honeypot sidebar, but no one has written a clear procedure for its use, and it appears that *dd* can't support all drive types on Windows, at least for the current ports.

## Note from the Underground...

### The Honeynet Project Unix Backup Method

As stated in this section, you can use a combination of *dd* and *netcat* to grab copies of entire partitions, including the "unused" sectors that the file system indicates don't have any data on them. This method was used to prepare a backup of a compromised system for The Forensic Challenge, put on by The Honeynet Project (http://project.honeynet.org). The method they used is addressed in their FAQ, as shown in the following excerpt:

**Q:** How did you make images of the compromised system?

**A:** The file images.tar is an archive containing 6 GNU zip compressed files, taken from each of the systems' active partitions at the time of compromise. It was created 08 November, 2000, at 21:00 CST. The following process was used to take the images, with minimum data pollution as a primary goal. We did not take the system down during the process. The following actions were taken while the system was still live.

1. Mounted cdrom containing forensic analysis tools (all statically compiled).
2. Used static binaries of dd(1M) and netcat(1M) from the cdrom to dd images of the hard drive to a trusted forensic system over the network. This is done by the following:

Continued

**Trusted System:** Initiate a listening daemon on port 10000 of the trusted system using netcat:

```
nc -l -p 10000 > honeypot.hda8.dd
```

**Compromised System:** Copied the each partition of the hard drive using dd(1), then piped the dd images of the drive over the network to the trusted system (192.168.1.1) listening on port 10000:

```
/cdrom/dd bs=1024 < /dev/hda8 | /cdrom/
    nc 192.168.1.1 10000 -w 3
```

This process was repeated for every partition on the hard drive, including swap. We now had an image of every partition on the trusted forensic system. MD5 checksums were produced at this time to compare against subsequent copies. These images were then combined into a single for ease of transmission, which was also checksummed for the same reason.

Note that using this method does not allow a direct comparison against the original partition contents on the hard drive, since the system (continuing to run) would constantly change bits in the file system as programs are run, buffers flushed, etc. If you are imaging a system for possible prosecution, you may wish to use a different procedure that supports a more clear chain of custody for the bits on the drive. The Honeynet Project chose this method as it allowed the blackhat to return in the future and we could continue our surveillance and information gathering."

The FAQ for The Forensic Challenge can be found at http://project.honeynet.org/challenge/faq.html. Lance Spitzner of the Honeynet Project invites readers of this book to read their paper "Know Your Enemy: Honeynets," which details some of their setup, similar to the question quoted here. It is found at http://project.honeynet.org/papers/honeynet.

So, it seems that for Windows, the current best practice is to abruptly halt the system (possibly through judicious plug pulling), and perform the backup afterward. The good news is that there is a ton of options on PC hardware for performing backup and analysis once you can boot your own OS, or remove the drives.

There are tools that are intended to "image" systems to restore them to a particular state. These may be used in a classroom environment, for example, to restore the systems to a known state at the beginning of each week when new students come in. These tools can also be used to create an image of the drives of a compromised system. The advantage is that many of them are designed to boot from DOS, and to send the images across a network. This includes products such as Ghost from Symantec, CodeBlue from Innovative Technologies, and Replica from Stac (Replica is reported to do sector-by-sector images). Remote Recover from Winternals Software is designed to permit access to remote drives by booting the remote machine from a floppy disk and accessing it across a network. This could be used in conjunction with backup software to create images.

Finally, there are the professional forensics backup programs. These include SafeBack from NTI, Byte Back from Tech Assist, SMART from ASR DATA, EnCase from Guidance Software, and ForensiX from Fred Cohen & Associates. This last set of tools, marketed specifically for forensics purposes, tends to be much more expensive, but also much more capable. Most of them include features to do MD5 checksums to verify data integrity, for example. Some of them are entire forensics toolkits, and go well beyond just taking an image of a disk. Some of them even include full scripting languages to help automate the use of their features. If you're going to need to use other features that these programs provide, then you might consider getting a whole package rather than just the piece that performs the backups.

And, of course, don't forget that you always have the option to boot a Linux distribution of some sort, and use the *dd* and *netcat* option mentioned earlier. Actually, Linux can be a powerful analysis platform, due to its ability to mount a wide variety of disk partition types. You can even directly mount the image files created with *dd*, which could be a huge timesaver. If you mount a *dd* image, you don't have to find another disk on which to restore your backup to investigate. Obviously, you need to have enough space to hold the image file, but you won't have to do any partitioning or formatting.

If you want to learn more about using Linux as an investigative platform, Dave Dittrich has written a paper titled "Basic Steps in Forensic Analysis of UNIX Systems." While it is about doing forensic work for Unix systems, it offers some great information about mounting other file systems under Linux. It can be found at http://staff.washington.edu/dittrich/misc/forensics.

Before we finish this short introduction to forensics, I want to reemphasize one key point: *preparation*. During an actual investigation, you won't have time to try to download the tools you need, build static versions of them, figure out which operating systems you need them for, and put them on CD-ROMs. If you wait until you need them to build them, the only possible outcomes will be sloppy investigation, or taking too much time. This means that you need an inventory of your systems, such as what OS they are running, whether they've all got CD-ROM drives, and probably the root/administrator password.

Furthermore, you need to practice your techniques ahead of time. The last thing you need during an investigation is to not have something go as expected.

# Tracking Incidents

While much of this chapter has had to do with investigating actual intrusions, the work doesn't begin there; the work begins as you are being probed. Even if you don't do anything with them, your IDS and/or firewall logs form an extremely crude incident tracking system (ITS). An ITS is a collection of programs designed to help an IRT manage the incidents that occur in their environment. These programs range from simple port scans that you do nothing about, all the way up to full-blown legal cases with appropriate legal documentation.

The variety of products and programs that make up incident tracking systems fall into three main categories:

- Software to assist security incident tracking
- Software to assist with a help desk function
- Software to tracks bugs in a software development environment

There's a reason they are all considered ITSs, and that is that they all perform somewhat similar functions, especially the security incident tracking and help desk variations. In fact, many companies use the Remedy Corporation product, which is primarily a help desk application, as an ITS.

Let's take a look at the key elements of an ITS:

- **Request tracking** This is how a new case is created and assigned a case number.
- **Message coordination** The ITS needs to be able to manage the communications around each case, often in the form of e-mail.
- **Status update** Appropriate parties need to be able to check the status of a given case at any time.
- **Aging** The ITS needs to be able to send reminders about items that require attention or are taking too long, according to an agreed-upon amount of time in which cases should be resolved.
- **Evidence tracking** For cases that require investigation, the ITS needs to track where the evidence is.

These are the functions that an ITS must provide. To accomplish these functions, there are a number of information items that must be tracked, including the following:

- System affected
- IP address of affected system
- IP address of offender (if known)
- Ports/services scanned
- Software installed
- OS version

- System administrator of affected system
- Location
- Criticality to normal operations
- Security zone (DMZ, inside, etc.)
- Currently assigned IRT member (if applicable)
- Case priority (low, medium, etc.)
- Messages/notes about the case
- Evidence type
- Evidence location
- Chain of custody
- Court/LE case numbers
- Notification status (Management, Legal, HR, etc.)

There are probably custom fields you would want to add. Let's talk for a moment about how you might organize this information. Obviously, some of the fields lend themselves well to being inside a traditional database. Others do not. (For example, you wouldn't want to cram an 8GB disk image file into most databases.) You might find it useful to maintain a traditional database for the items that fit easily into one, and a second database that is more free-form, to contain electronic evidence.

Like most IT problems, how you acquire an ITS boils down to "buy versus build." Much of that decision will have to do with what other ticketing or tracking systems you might have in place, or will need in the future. For example, if there is already an existing help desk ticketing system, or relational database that contains information about your computers, then you will want to integrate them.

Interestingly (although not surprisingly), it seems that universities have done a fair amount of work in the area of ITSs. There are a few ITSs available from universities, or at least information on how to build them. There's a set of slides located on Ohio State's Web server that describes the process they went through to choose an ITS (they decided to build their own). Their slides can be found at www.net.ohio-state.edu/security/talks/2000-04-26_building_an_incident_tracking_system/SecWOG-000426.htm.

If that URL is too lengthy for your tastes, then go to www.net.ohio-state.edu/security/talks.shtml and scroll down to April 26, 2000. While you're there, check out the other presentations as well, some of which are highly pertinent to the topic of this chapter. For pointers on where to find free and commercial ITSs, please check the *Resources* section at the end of this chapter.

Once you've figured out how you're going to get an ITS, you need to figure out how to put it to use. For cases where you are entering data manually, this is fairly self-evident; you'd use whatever interface the ITS has, and input the data. However, the vast majority of your incidents will be really minor things that you will probably not end up doing too much with. There will also be a large number of these, and you won't want to input them by hand. These are the items you get from your firewall and IDS logs, and you need to figure out a way to script them so that they are automatically entered into your ITS.

This piece will likely be custom software for you, as there won't be anyone else out there who has the exact set of DIS and/or firewall you do, your ITS, and your idea of what constitutes an incident worth tracking. Many of the things your IDS will report will be false alarms, but this is totally dependent on your particular environment. You will need to spend some quality time with your IDS, tuning the rules to reduce these as much as possible, and then documenting the ones you can't eliminate entirely. Later, when the few false alarms end up in your tracking system, you can recognize them and close them quickly.

The SecurityFocus ARIS project was mentioned earlier. This won't be suitable for use as a primary ITS, mostly because the data is eventually archived off. However, if you decide that you're going to report your less serious incidents to the appropriate organizations and ISPs, then ARIS is an excellent tool for that purpose. It's also a great way to learn more about what the individual IDS signatures mean, how common they are, and how prone they are to false positives.

# Resources

Listed here are some resources available on the Internet for topics discussed in this chapter. We recommend that you take the time to go through these, and take note of the ones that best meet your needs to later referral.

## Legal/Government/Law Enforcement

The site www.cybercrime.gov is a great resource for the legal aspects of computer intrusion. They maintain one of the best lists of cases I've seen (under the section "Cases"). In addition to computer crime, they have similar resources for intellectual property crimes. The site is maintained by the Computer Criminal and Intellectual Property Section (CCIPS) of the United States Department of Justice (DOJ).

The National Infrastructure Protection Center (NIPC) of the U.S. (www.nipc.gov) has information about current issues, links to relevant laws, and original publications and advisories. This is one of the places you can file incident reports with the U.S. government.

CERT is a federally funded R&D center that operates out of Carnegie Mellon University (www.cert.org). They publish advisories on widespread security incidents, and collect incident reports from companies. The also publish papers, and offer training.

## Backup/Forensics

SafeBack (www.forensics-intl.com/safeback.html) is one of the programs designed specifically for forensic backup purposes. NTI (whose Web site is referenced here) supplies a number of forensics tools, and the site is worth exploring. They also have some free tools found at www.forensics-intl.com/download.html.

ForensiX (www.all.net/ForensiX/index.html) is a forensics tool designed to facilitate backup and examination of a compromised machine.

The backup tool CodeBlue can be found at www.tapedisk.com/codeblu2.html.

Guidance Software (www.guidancesoftware.com) is the home of the EnCase forensics product. They also offer training and assistance.

Snapback (www.snapback.co.uk) is another forensic backup vendor, creator of the SnapBack package. They offer a demo for evaluation on their Web site.

You'll find a collection of free forensic tools and information at www.incident-response.org. If you're assembling your own toolkit, this site is worth checking out.

I include the URL (www.htcia.org/_disc1/0000003d.htm) as a way of addressing an issue I've run across with forensic backup software. It seems there's a general assumption that only "official" forensic software will be accepted in court. This post states that SafeBack and EnCase have "made it through the court system." You might want to consult with your Legal department or an attorney on the admissibility status of your method if there is a question.

*Information Security Magazine* published an article on forensic investigation, and included brief reviews of several forensic toolsets, found at www.infosecuritymag.com/articles/march00/cover.shtml. This is definitely worth checking out if you're considering purchasing a commercial tool.

# Incident Tracking Systems

The following are Web resources for incident tracking systems:

- **http://security.uchicago.edu/tools/fits** Freeman Incident Tracking System (FITS) from the University of Chicago.
- **http://arti.indiana.edu/ott/technol/techs/0022.html** ITrack from Indiana University. This page claims that a license is available for its use, but doesn't give a download location. You'll have to check out the page and write to them to see if you qualify to use it.
- **www.sans.org/infosecFAQ/intrusion/incident_track.htm** A publication by SANS on the topic of incident tracking.

- **www.securityfocus.com/library/2066** An older paper on the topic from CERT.
- **http://staff.washington.edu/dittrich/talks/security/response.html** A short-and-to-the-point checklist for incident response by Dave Dittrich.

## Miscellaneous

The following are miscellaneous Web resources:

- **www.cybercrimes.net/MCCIP/MCCIP.html** The Model Code of Cybercrimes Investigative Procedure (MCCIP). An exhaustive summary of investigative procedures. Take a look at Article IX, "Processing and Analyzing Evidence" in particular.
- **www.atsweb.neu.edu/uc/w.farwell/guide.htm** "Stand-alone PC Examination Basic Forensic Guidelines," forensic information gathering guidelines from the Court's perspective.
- **www.vogon.co.uk/fc-05.htm** A set of "case studies" on the Web site of a forensics tools vendor. I found these particularly interesting.
- **www.crazytrain.com/dd.html** Another perspective on the use of dd for forensic backups.

# Summary

There are many mistakes to be made and much trouble to get into if you handle intrusions and security incidents without a set response policy. An *incident response policy* will dictate how you will respond to an intrusion, and it codifies all the agreements between concerned parties at your organization as to who is responsible for what.

An *incident response team* is the group of people in your organization who can help respond when an incident occurs. It may include people from the security team, network team, system administration, Legal, Human Resources, and management. This team is responsible for responding to incident reports. Most likely, someone from the security team will be the first line of contact for reports, and bring in other team members as needed. Some members of this team need to be skilled in forensic investigation, or you need to have a relationship with an outside party that can provide those skills.

The forensic aspect of security work is one of the more interesting for technically minded people. Forensics has to do with using the available evidence to build a picture of what has occurred, and possibly trace it back to its origin. Computer forensic investigation requires in-depth knowledge of operating systems and application software. You must first have established what normal behavior is so that you can determine when the evidence suggests that something abnormal has happened.

The first step in any forensic investigation is to make a backup of the evidence. The main question boils down to whether to attempt backup of a live system, or whether to shut it down and boot a different operating system in order to make image backups. There are a variety of tools available for performing backups. Some of the tools don't grab the slack space on a disk, so keep that in mind when choosing a tool. Some companies sell comprehensive forensic toolkits. If you will need all of the functions that such a kit provides, you might consider making the investment in one of these prepackaged kits.

One of the other components you will need to do your job is an incident tracking system. An *incident tracking system* is used to keep track of the various probes and incidents a typical company sees during its normal course of operation. The items you track include the minor probes that you might just ignore, or possibly report to the ISP responsible for the party who sent them. More serious incidents will be assigned a higher priority, and the system will be used to track the pertinent communications, and evidence locations.

# Solutions Fast Track

## Why Is an Incident Response Policy Important?

☑ An incident response policy helps you answer questions crucial to political, logistical, and physical security issues that arise in a crisis. Do you need to contact management or Legal? Do you need to contact the PR department to handle any inquiries about the intrusion? Did the attacker get into the database? What do we need to do to get the Web site back? Should we shut it off so that people can't see the defacement? Are we going to be able to find a system administrator and database administrator to help us clean up?

☑ An incident response policy is not there because you don't know what you are doing; it's there because not everyone will agree with your way of doing things. If you've gotten signoff from all concerned parties ahead of time, and you follow the procedure outlined, then it will be much more difficult to hold you at fault. A well-written policy will tell you what your responsibilities are, and what other people are on the hook for.

## Establishing an Incident Response Team (IRT)

☑ You'll likely need to involve a network person and a systems administrator. You'll probably need a representative from your

Legal department or attorney's office. A system administrator or a dedicated security engineer can handle the forensics work.

☑ You'll need a dedicated security function that will form the core of the team, and tie it together. This may be a dedicated person, or perhaps a portion of a person's time, but the responsibility must belong to one or more individuals. The core person's responsibility will be to call meetings, make sure representation is present from all concerned organizations, coordinate writing policy and getting agreement on policy, arrange for training as needed, and drive actual incident response when the occasion arises.

## Setting the Prosecution Boundaries

☑ The first line you have to draw is the line between attempt and incident. All day long, you will receive probes and scans. These are people trying out new tools, or potential attackers gathering intelligence information, or even automated worms. You may get somewhere between dozens and thousands of these per day.

☑ The chain of custody defines who has access to the evidence during the entire investigation process. Maintaining a chain of custody list isn't difficult; you just have to record several items: who was in custody (possession) of the evidence, where the evidence was, what security measures are in place at that location, and what items of evidence existed at that time. You must write down a new entry each time one of these changes.

## Establishing an Incident Response Process

☑ One fairly common response for relatively benign attempts is to report the attempts to the appropriate ISP, company, or their provider. Some IDS software includes a reporting mechanism to help generate reports and locate the proper e-mail addresses to contact.

- ☑ Once you have a policy in place that dictates how you will respond when an incident occurs, you need to build a set of processes to support your responses. This covers the range from minor attempts to full intrusions.
- ☑ You will first need to understand how the files are stored on disk, how the processes interact, how all the software is configured, and what log information is available to you. And, you have to know this for each different operating system you need to investigate.

## Introduction to Forensic Computing

- ☑ The first step in any forensic investigation is to make a backup of all the information available to you, if possible. Unfortunately, this doesn't just mean backing up the drives. Before you even get to that point, you have to decide how to examine what might be in memory when you arrive. There may be some evidence in memory that you want to get at, and not all operating systems have a provision for dumping RAM to disk.
- ☑ The general problem with backing up a compromised system before you shut it down is that any use of the compromised system damages the evidence to some degree.
- ☑ There are tools that are intended to "image" systems to restore them to a particular state. These tools can be used to create an image of the drives of a compromised system. The advantage is that many of them are designed to boot from DOS, and to send the images across a network.
- ☑ Most professional forensics backup programs include features to do MD5 checksums to verify data integrity. Some of them are entire forensics toolkits, and go well beyond just taking an image of a disk. Some of them even include full scripting languages to help automate the use of their features.

## Tracking Incidents

- ☑ An incident tracking system (ITS) is a collection of programs designed to help an IRT manage the incidents that occur in their environment. These programs range from simple port scans that you do nothing about, to full-blown legal cases with appropriate legal documentation.
- ☑ The variety of products and programs that make up incident tracking systems fall into three main categories: software to assist security incident tracking, software to assist with a help desk function, and software to tracks bugs in a software development environment.
- ☑ Many of the things your IDS will report will be false alarms, but this is totally dependent on your particular environment. You will need to spend some quality time with your IDS, tuning the rules to reduce these as much as possible, and then documenting the ones you can't eliminate entirely.
- ☑ ITS must provide a number of items that must be tracked, including the IP address of the affected system, the IP address of the offender (if known), ports/services scanned, security zone (DMZ, inside, etc.), currently assigned IRT member (if applicable), and the chain of custody.

# Frequently Asked Questions

The following Frequently Asked Questions, answered by the authors of this book, are designed to both measure your understanding of the concepts presented in this chapter and to assist you with real-life implementation of these concepts. To have your questions about this chapter answered by the author, browse to **www.syngress.com/solutions** and click on the **"Ask the Author"** form.

**Q:** Can I buy commercial incident response hardware?

**A:** Several companies have hardware kits available, usually with bundled software as well. There's the Forensic Recovery of Evidence Device ("F.R.E.D.") line from Digital Intelligence (www.digitalintel.com), Forensic-Computers.com (www.forensic-computers.com), and the DIBS line at www.computer-forensics.com.

**Q:** This all seems like a lot of stuff to do. Is there any way to outsource these functions?

**A:** Yes, there are companies called managed service providers (MSPs). The range of services offered varies, but most of them offer some combination of managing your firewall, watching your logs, tracking incidents for you, and making reports on your behalf. Examples of such companies include Counterpane (www.counterpane.com), Guardent (www.guardent.com), @stake (www.atstake.com), and METASeS (www.metases.com).

**Q:** Where can I learn more about forensics, or ask questions?

**A:** One of the better places I've seen is the Forensics mailing list maintained by SecurityFocus.com. You can find their archives and subscribe here: http://securityfocus.com/forums/forensics/intro.html.

**Q:** Where can I find someone to perform forensic investigations for me when needed?

**A:** Most of the big accounting firms offer this as a service, as well as many of the MSPs. Some of the forensic software vendors offer services, too. One directory of smaller investigative types of firms can be found at http://expertpages.com/experts/compevidence.htm.

# Appendix A

# Cisco Solutions for Content Delivery

## Solutions in this appendix:

- Improving Security Using Cisco LocalDirector
- Securing Geographically Dispersed Server Farms Using Cisco DistributedDirector
- Improving Security Using the Cisco Content Services Switch

☑ Summary

☑ Frequently Asked Questions

# Introduction

In the past, it was said that a company's receptionist was the window into a company; they were the first contact people had with the company. Imagine that the receptionist receives more telephone calls than can be handled—calls would be dropped, customers would get frustrated, and money would be lost. Today's reality is that your *Web site* has become that window into your company. Similarly, if your Web site gets too many hits, the same thing would happen—hits would be dropped, customers would get frustrated, and money would be lost.

As the World Wide Web grows and companies expand their presence on the Internet, so the demand increases for scaling Internet traffic, and in particular Web traffic. Cisco Systems has developed a family of products, collectively known as *Content Delivery Devices* that allow you to scale Internet traffic to very large volumes.

Although Cisco's Content Delivery Devices are not the only products that can assist you in scaling your Internet traffic, they are amongst the most innovative and most widely used. By giving you insight into the security features of these products as well as their application and implementation, this appendix explains the options available to you in order to secure your systems from hackers.

Damage & Defense...

## Cisco Systems Security Advisories

Cisco Systems publishes a list of Internet Security Advisories, as well as a list of advisories for vulnerabilities that affect their products. You can find this list at www.cisco.com/warp/public/707/advisory.html.

# Improving Security Using Cisco LocalDirector

Cisco's LocalDirector is a product that allows you to load balance Internet resource requests among multiple local servers. One would typically use this solution to front-end a Web server farm, based in the same location, and load balance Web traffic to the most appropriate server.

Using this technology, LocalDirector allows you to publish a single Web address, with a single IP address associated with that address, and yet have one of many Web servers respond to that resource request.

## LocalDirector Technology Overview

Cisco's LocalDirector uses the Open System Interconnection (OSI) Layer 4 (transport layer) load balancing technology that allows you to publish a single Uniform Resource Locator (URL) and a single Internet Protocol (IP) address for an entire server farm.

The LocalDirector determines which is the most appropriate server by tracking network sessions and server load conditions in real time.

This technology can help decrease your service response time and increase the service reliability. Your service response time is decreased, because resource requests to a URL or IP address are directed to the most appropriate server within the server farm. Your service reliability is increased, because the LocalDirector monitors individual servers in the server farm and does not direct resource requests to servers that are not operating correctly.

Before the inception of this technology, you would have had to know the name or IP address of every individual Web server in the server farm, or you would have had to make use of multiple IP addresses associated with a single Web address. Neither of these techniques were user friendly, nor did they result in appropriate load distribution. They were also not reliable, because no attempt was made at verifying the servers' integrity (their ability to respond).

Cisco's LocalDirector can be compared to an Automatic Call Distributor (ACD) in the telephony world. LocalDirector is similar to an ACD in that incoming telephone calls are routed to a pool of agents and answered as soon as an agent is available.

Figure A.1 depicts a typical LocalDirector implementation. LocalDirector front-ends a Web server farm, and redirects resource requests to the most appropriate server.

**Figure A.1** Typical LocalDirector Implementation

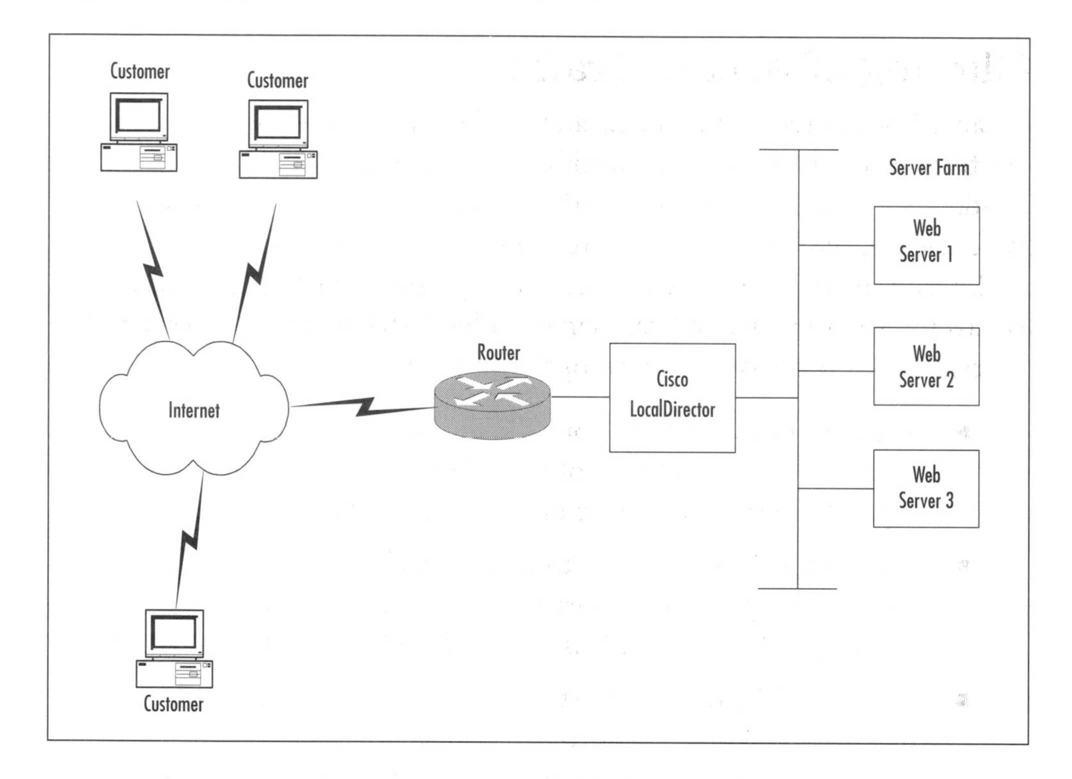


## LocalDirector Product Overview

The LocalDirector product is available in two different ranges:

- **LocalDirector 416** This is both the entry-level product as well as the medium-size product. It supports up to 90Mbps throughput and 7,000 connections per second.
- **LocalDirector 430** This is the high-end product. It supports up to 400Mbps throughput and 30,000 connections per second.

For additional performance, LocalDirector can be used together with Accelerated Server Load Balancing (ASLB) on the Catalyst 6000 series switches to increase throughput to 15 million packets per second (mpps).

## LocalDirector Security Features

The following information about the security features of LocalDirector will allow you to better understand the security mechanisms it uses and enable you to configure or change these features.

## Filtering of Access Traffic

Because LocalDirector maintains and tracks states on all client stations, it can filter or control access to specific servers based on incoming source IP address or service (port number). This allows you to increase security by restricting what resources the request is allowed to access.

LocalDirector protects your network by only allowing specific traffic to pass between virtual and real servers. This restricts both external and internal access to servers. Several options are provided:

- **SecureAccess** Allows you to manipulate a connection based on the source IP address of the client. Traffic can be directed to a specific virtual server or dropped altogether.
- **SecureBind** Allows you to restrict traffic to a specific port. TCP traffic going to a port that is not specified is sent a reset packet (TCP RST). This is not applicable to UDP-based traffic.
- **SecureBridging** If a port is configured to be bridged, clients are allowed direct access to real servers via their registered IP addresses. Bridging can be turned off, thereby forcing client traffic through the LocalDirector virtual address.
- **Secure IP address** This allows LocalDirector to translate the IP address of a real server to a virtual IP address, thereby hiding the IP address of the real server.

## Using *synguard* to Protect against SYN Attacks

A SYN attack is a form of Denial of Service (DoS) attack that occurs when a hacker transmits a volume of connections that cannot be completed. This causes the connection queues to fill up, thereby denying service to legitimate TCP connections.

On host systems, for example on Web servers, you should also employ techniques for minimizing the effect of a SYN attack. One of these techniques is to increase the size of the connection queue (SYN ACK queue) so that the SYN attack has to have more time and use more resources to cause problems. Another is to determine whether or not your host software vendor has any patches that help protect against SYN attacks. Many vendor products, including IBM's AIX, Microsoft's NT, and SUN's Solaris now have these types of patches. Using the **syn-guard** feature, you can set the maximum number of unanswered SYNs to allow before entering into a protection mode.

By default this feature is disabled, the default value is 0, and the maximum allowable numbers of SYNs needs to be configured before the feature is enabled.

The following syntax is used to configure the **synguard** feature (from configuration mode):

```
synguard virtual_id count
```

where *virtual_id* is the virtual server IP address or name and port (if a port-bound server), and *count* is the number of unanswered SYNs allowed before entering **synguard** mode.

To disable **synguard**, either set the count back to 0, or use the **no** command:

```
no synguard virtual_id count
```

Note that the **synguard** command provides limited protection against SYN attacks to the virtual IP address. After the feature is activated, LocalDirector starts to protect the real network and servers from a SYN attack.

Here is an example that illustrates the use of **synguard**:

```
LocalDirector(config)# show synguard

        Machine      Port    SynGuard      Status

   www.test.com  default           0

LocalDirector(config)# synguard www.test.com 500
```

```
LocalDirector(config)# show synguard
        Machine      Port    SynGuard      Status
   www.test.com  default         500
LocalDirector(config)# show syn
        Machine      Port        Conns   Syn Count
   www.test.com  default         648         176
```

The following example shows **synguard** active. Notice how the status changes to Active:

```
LocalDirector(config)# show synguard
        Machine      Port    SynGuard      Status
   www.site.com  default         500      Active
LocalDirector(config)# show syn
        Machine      Port        Conns   Syn Count
   www.site.com  default         892         500
LocalDirector(config)#
```

## Using Network Address Translation to Hide Real Addresses

LocalDirector supports Network Address Translation (NAT). This allows you to use unregistered IP addresses on your inside network (usually the server farm) and prevents hackers from being able to directly target the real server's IP address.

Request for Comments (RFC) 1918 reserves three address ranges—often referred to as *private, internal,* or *unregistered* address ranges—for internal use. These address ranges are not routed on the Internet and packets need to be converted to registered IP addresses before they can be sent to the Internet. NAT performs this conversion from private IP addresses to registered IP addresses, and vice versa, allowing devices access to and from the Internet. This also conserves registered IP addresses.

Increased security is provided through NAT by hiding the internal IP address range and making it more difficult for potential hackers to access as well as learn about the internal structure of your network.

Figure A.2 shows an example of a device performing NAT. The 10.0.0.x IP address range is not accessible via the Internet, without first going through the NAT conversion process where the registered IP address range is converted to the private IP address range.

**Figure A.2** NAT Conversion Process

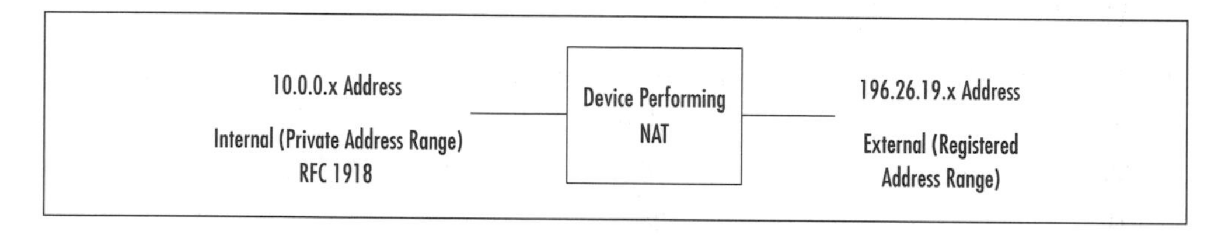


## Restricting Who Is Authorized to Have Telnet Access to the LocalDirector

You may specify who is authorized to have Telnet access to the LocalDirector. This can be either in the form of IP address, or network address. Limiting who can Telnet into the LocalDirector is an easy and highly effective way of keeping hackers from trying to gain access or cause disruption to your systems.

The following syntax is used to configure who has telnet access (from configuration mode):

```
telnet ip mask
```

where *ip* is the IP address or network of the host that is authorized to access the LocalDirector Telnet management interface, and *mask* is the subnet mask for the network specified in this command. Use 255.255.255.255 if you specified an IP address.

To disable this feature, use the **no** command:

```
no telnet ip mask
```

You can use the following syntax to view allowed IP addresses or networks:

```
show telnet
```

**SECURITY ALERT!**

For maximum protection, configure telnet access restriction to allow only one IP address to access LocalDirector. This will greatly enhance LocalDirector's security.

## Password Protection

LocalDirector supports two levels of password protection: *privileged* and *nonprivileged*. The enable password is the privileged level and allows you to view settings as well as make configuration changes, whereas the Telnet password is the nonprivileged level that allows you to view certain settings but not to change them.

**SECURITY ALERT!**

For maximum protection, use a different password for the different password levels. Having the same passwords for different levels of security is a frequently encountered vulnerability and is strongly discouraged.

### *Enable Password*

The enable password is the privileged-level password. There is no default enable password. Be sure to set one before you deploy LocalDirector. The following syntax is used to create an enable password (from configuration mode):

```
enable password password
```

### *Telnet Password*

The Telnet password is a user-level password. The default Telnet password is *cisco.*

**SECURITY ALERT!**

A common security mistake is not to change the default Telnet password for LocalDirector. Be sure to change this before you deploy LocalDirector.

The following syntax is used to change the default Telnet password (from configuration mode):

```
password password
```

where *password* is a password of up to 16 alphanumeric characters, which is not case sensitive.

## Syslog Logging

Often, knowing about an attack is as important as taking steps to protect yourself against the attack. This is where logging plays an important role.

If a syslog server is configured, LocalDirector will log error and event messages to an external syslog server (called *host*). Among others, a syslog message will be generated if LocalDirector enters synguard protection mode.

The following syntax is used to configure the syslog feature (from configuration mode):

```
syslog {host|console} ip
```

where *host* defines which hosts are sent syslog messages, *console* displays syslog messages on the console port, and *ip* is the IP address of the log host.

To disable syslog, use the **no** command:

```
no syslog {host|console} ip
```

You can use the following syntax to view previously sent syslog messages:

```
show syslog
```

# Securing Geographically Dispersed Server Farms Using Cisco DistributedDirector

Cisco's DistributedDirector is a product that allows you to load balance Internet resource requests among geographically dispersed servers. A typical application is for a corporation to make use of Web servers, or Web server farms, in multiple locations to service Web requests.

DistributedDirector does this by redirecting resource requests to servers located closest to the customer requesting that service.

## DistributedDirector Technology Overview

Cisco's DistributedDirector uses routing table intelligence in the network infrastructure to transparently redirect a customer's service requests to the closest responsive server, as determined by the client-to-server proximity or client-to-server latency.

By using this technology, you can decrease the service response time and increase the service reliability, as well as reduce the cost of long distance communication. The service response time is decreased and the cost of long distance communications reduced, because resource requests to a URL or IP address are redirected to the closest server from the customer requesting the service. The service reliability is increased, because DistributedDirector monitors individual servers and does not direct resource requests to servers that are not operating correctly.

Director Response Protocol (DRP) is a protocol that allows DistributedDirector to query routers (DRP Server Agents) for routing table metrics between distributed servers and clients. DistributedDirector uses this information to redirect the customer's service requests to the closest server.

Cisco's DistributedDirector can be compared to a regionalized toll-free number in the telephony world. DistributedDirector is similar to a regionalized toll-free number where incoming telephone calls to a single national toll-free number are routed to agents located in the same region from which the toll-free call originated, thereby saving on long-distance charges that would otherwise have to be incurred if the call were answered in a centralized location.

Figure A.3 depicts a typical DistributedDirector implementation. Web requests are sent to the DistributedDirector, which redirects the requests to the most appropriate Web server. Very often, this is the closest server to the customer. For example, the Web server in San Francisco might best service a Web request from Customer 1 and Customer 2, whereas the Web server in London might better service a Web request from Customer 3.

**Figure A.3** Typical DistributedDirector Implementation

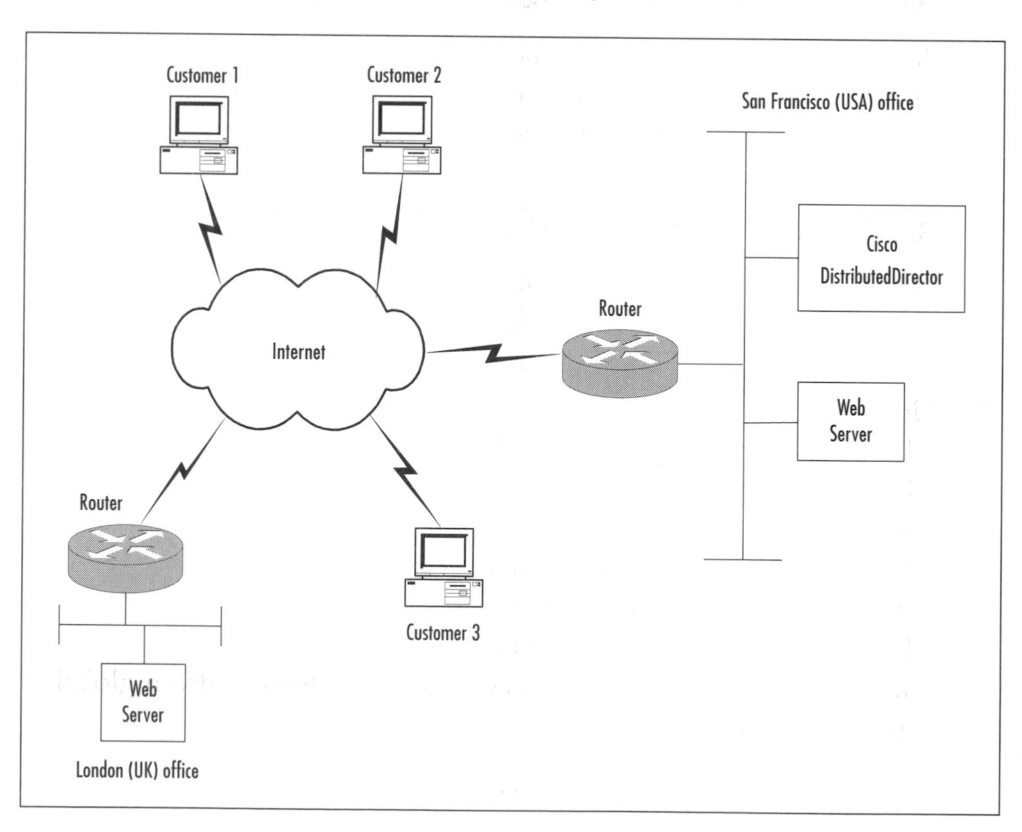

## DistributedDirector Product Overview

The DistributedDirector product is available in three different ranges:

- **DistributedDirector 2501/2502** This is the entry-level product. The DistributedDirector 2501 has a Ethernet interface and the DistributedDirector 2502 has a Token Ring.
- **DistributedDirector 4700M** This is the medium-level product and comes in models that have Ethernet, Fast Ethernet, Token Ring, and FDDI interfaces.
- **Cisco 7200 Series router** This is the high-end product. This product is based on the modular Cisco 7200 router, with the DistributedDirector feature set.

## DistributedDirector Security Features

The following information about the security features of DistributedDirector will allow you to better understand the security mechanisms it uses and enable you to configure or change these features.

### Limiting the Source of DRP Queries

Security can be increased by limiting DRP server agents' access to devices having specific source IP addresses. This is done using standard Cisco Access Control Lists (ACLs) together with the **ip drp access-group** command.

If this feature is not implemented, hackers could exploit this vulnerability by creating forged DRP queries and disrupting the normal DRP process by providing incorrect DRP information. Protection against DoS attacks using forged DRP queries is also provided, because DRP queries that do not originate from authorized DRP sources are discarded even before they can be processed.

The following syntax is used to configure this feature (from global configuration mode):

```
ip drp access-group access-list-number
```

where *access-list-number* is the standard IP access list.

## Authentication between DistributedDirector and DRP Agents

In order to increase security and help prevent DoS attacks based on DRP packets, authentication of DRP queries and responses between the DistributedDirector and the Director Response Protocol (DRP) agents are supported.

By using DRP authentication, DistributedDirector stops hackers from forging DRP queries and disrupting or interfering with the service request redirection function. This authentication is based on Keyed-Hashing for Message (HMAC) – Message Digest 5 (MD5) digital signatures. The following syntax is used to configure this feature (from global configuration mode):

```
ip drp authentication key-chain key-chain-name
```

where *key-chain-name* is the name of the key chain containing one or more authentication keys. The key chain name is a string of characters without spaces.

To disable this feature, use the **no** command:

```
no ip drp authentication key-chain key-chain-name
```

### SECURITY ALERT!

For additional security, use multiple keys on a key chain so that you can expire keys based on time using the **accept-lifetime** and **send-lifetime** commands.

You will also need to configure a key chain, comprising of keys and key-strings. To do this, here is an overview of the key chain, key, and key-string commands.

## *The* key chain *Command*

The *key chain* is the structure that holds the authentication keys and key-strings together. The following syntax is used to configure this feature (from global configuration mode):

```
key chain name-of-chain
```

where *name-of-chain* is the name of the key chain.

To disable this feature, use the **no** command:

```
no key chain name-of-chain
```

Use the following syntax to verify key chain information:

```
show key chain
```

## *The* key *Command*

The *key* is a number used to identify the authentication key on a key string. The following syntax is used to configure this feature (from the key chain configuration):

```
key number
```

where *number* is the identification number of an authentication key on a key chain. The range of keys is 0 to 2147483647. The key numbers need not be consecutive.

To disable this feature, use the **no** command:

```
no key number
```

## *The* key-string *Command*

The *key-string* is used to identify the authentication string for a key. The following syntax is used to configure this feature (from the key chain configuration):

```
key-string text
```

where *text* is the authentication string. The string can contain from 1 to 80 uppercase and lowercase alphanumeric characters, except the first character cannot be a number.

To disable this feature, use the **no** command:

```
no key-string text
```

Here is an example of DRP authentication using a key chain, keys, key-strings, and accept-lifetime, as well as send-lifetime. In this example, the password *barracuda* will always be a valid key for accepting and receiving. The *marlin* key will be accepted from 15:30 to 17:30 (7,200 seconds) on January 14th, 2001 and be sent from 16:00 to 17:00 (3,600 seconds) on January 14th, 2001. The overlap allows for migration of keys or a discrepancy in the router's time. The *swordfish* key-string works in the same way but with different times.

```
ip drp authentication key-chain fish
!
key chain fish
 key 1
  key-string barracuda
 key 2
  key-string marlin
  accept-lifetime 15:30:00 Jan 14 2001 duration 7200
  send-lifetime 16:00:00 Jan 14 2001 duration 3600
 key 3
  key-string swordfish
  accept-lifetime 16:30:00 Jan 14 2001 duration 7200
  send-lifetime 17:00:00 Jan 14 2001 duration 3600
```

## Password Protection

Because DistributedDirector runs a modified copy of Cisco's Internetworking Operating System (IOS), the procedure for changing passwords on DistributedDirector is the same as for regular IOS. DistributedDirector supports three different levels of password protection: *enable secret, enable,* and *telnet.*

**SECURITY ALERT!**

For maximum protection, use a different password for the three different password levels that Distributed Director supports. Although IOS will allow you to set all the passwords the same, this is strongly discouraged for security reasons.

### *The Enable Secret Password*

The *enable secret* password is the most secure, encrypted privileged-level password. This password is used even if an enable password is configured. The following syntax is used to create an enable secret password (from configuration mode):

```
enable secret password password
```

where *password* is the enable secret password.

### *The Enable Password*

The *enable* password is a less secure, non-encrypted privileged-level password. This password is used when the enable secret password does not exist. The following syntax is used to create an enable password (from configuration mode):

```
enable password password
```

where *password* is the enable password.

### *The Telnet Password*

The *telnet* password is a user-level password that allows you to look at some of the configuration information, but not to change any configuration. By default, telnet is not allowed and there is no default telnet password. You will need to configure both the telnet as well as an enable password for you to be able to telnet into the DistributedDirector. The following syntax is used to configure a telnet password (from vty configuration mode):

```
password password
```

where *password* is the telnet password.

## Syslog Logging

Often, knowing about an attack is as important as taking steps to protect yourself against the attack. This is where logging plays an important role.

Because DistributedDirector runs a modified copy of Cisco's Internetworking Operating System (IOS) the procedure for configuring logging to an external syslog server (called host) is the same as with regular IOS.

The following syntax is used to configure the syslog feature (from configuration mode):

```
logging ip
```

where *ip* is the IP address of the log host.

To disable syslog, use the **no** command:

```
no logging ip
```

Use the following syntax to view syslog messages in the buffer:

```
show logging
```

# Improving Security Using the Cisco Content Services Switch

The *Content Services Switch* uses content switching to intelligently redirect service requests to the most appropriate server. The key difference between load balancing and content switching is that content switching makes decisions based on information from Layers 4 through 7 (including URLs, host tags, and cookies) instead of just Layer 4 information such as LocalDirector and DistributedDirector.

Many of you might know this product as the ArrowPoint Content Smart Switch. Cisco Systems acquired ArrowPoint Communications in June 2000 and incorporated their products and technology into Cisco's product range.

A common implementation of this technology is for a service provider to have two types of Web services. The first service is for contracted Service Level Agreement (SLA) customers and the second for non-SLA customers. In this way, customers with SLAs can be guaranteed a faster Web response time than non-contract customers. This would typically be done using cookies. The Content Services Switch recognizes the cookie and processes that flow via the SLA policy to the most appropriate server. The SLA policy might specify more Web servers than the non-SLA policy.

## Content Services Switch Technology Overview

At first glance, the Content Services Switch appears to have similar features to those of LocalDirector or DistributedDirector (if you add the enhanced feature set to the Content Services Switch).

Although this observation is partly correct, Web content switching uses a completely different technology to load balancing, which is what both LocalDirector and DistributedDirector are based on. Load balancing uses OSI Layer 4 (transport layer) technology and content switching is based on OSI Layers 5 through 7 (session, presentation, and application layers) technology.

Content switching optimizes Web traffic by utilizing information at OSI Layers 5 through 7 to better direct the Web request to the most appropriate server. In this way, content switching can make use of URLs, host tags, and cookies to optimize content delivery.

OSI Layer 3 and 4 (network and transport) switching is simply not optimized for Web-based traffic. For a start, Web traffic is largely asymmetric, with much larger flows back out to the customer from the Web servers than inward-bound flows. It is also very different in the way sessions are constantly brought up and torn down, often with little data involved but many concurrent connections.

Figure A.4 depicts a typical Content Services Switch implementation. The Content Services Switch redirects the Web request to the most appropriate server. The enhanced feature set is required to give the Content Services Switch the ability to make use of servers in different locations.

**Figure A.4** Typical Content Services Switch Implementation

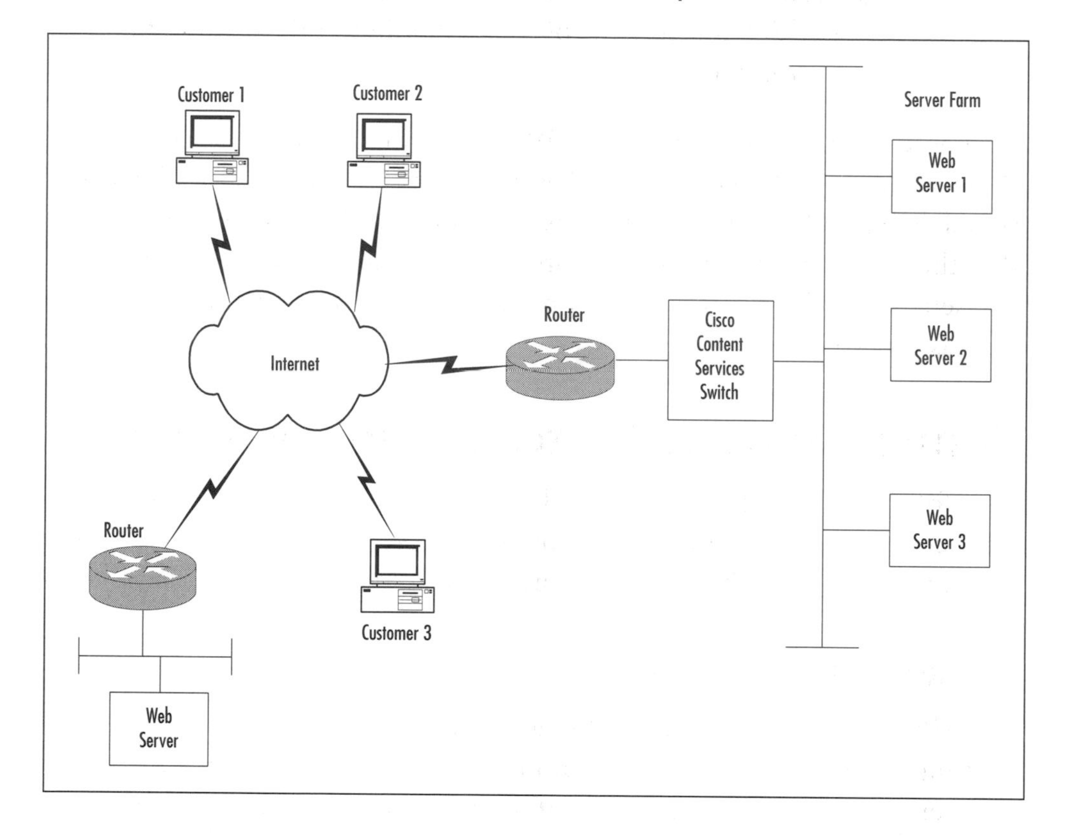


## Content Services Switch Product Overview

The Content Services Switch product is available in three different ranges:

- **CCS 11050** This is the entry-level product and is suitable for small Web sites as well as points of presence (PoPs). It was designed for throughput of up to 5Gbps and has a fixed port configuration. Use for up to eight Web servers or caches.

- **CCS 11150** This is the medium-level product and is suitable for small-to-medium sized Web sites. It was designed for throughput of up to 5Gbps and has a fixed port configuration. Use for up to 16 Web servers or caches.
- **CSS 11800** This is the high-end product, suitable for large, high-traffic Web sites and Web-Hosting infrastructures. It was designed for throughput of up to 20Gbps and has a modular port configuration.

Cisco Web Network Services (Web NS) is the software that runs on these switches and a copy of the basic feature set is bundled with the switches. An enhanced feature set is also available. The key difference is that the enhanced feature set also includes multi-site content routing and site selection, all content replication features, and content distribution as well as delivery services.

## Content Services Switch Security Features

The following information about the security features of the Content Services Switch will allow you to better understand the security mechanisms it uses and enable you to configure or change these features.

### FlowWall Security

*FlowWall* is an integrated firewall that provides wire-speed per flow based filtering of content requests, with no performance penalty. It provides firewall services such as firewall rules, ACLs, and flow admission control.

Using ACLs, policies can be created that are based on actions (include/bypass/block) for traffic matching some or all of the following:

- Source IP Address
- Destination IP Address
- TCP Port
- Host Tag
- URL
- File Extension

FlowWall provides intelligent flow inspection technology that allows it to screen for all common DoS attacks, such as SYN floods, ping floods, smurfs, and abnormal or malicious connection attempts.

It does this by discarding frames that have the following characteristics:

- Length is too short.
- Frame is fragmented.
- Source IP address = IP destination (LAND attack).
- Source address = Cisco address, or the source is a subnet broadcast.
- Source address is not a unicast address.
- Source IP address is a loop-back address.
- Destination IP address is a loop-back address.
- Destination address is not a valid unicast or multicast address.

**SECURITY ALERT!**

FlowWall does not scan for Java and Active-X traffic.

## Using Network Address Translation to Hide Real Addresses

Content Services Switches support wire-speed Network Address Translation (NAT). As described in the LocalDirector section, this allows you to use unregistered IP addresses on your inside network (usually the server farm) and prevents hackers from being able to directly target the real server's IP address.

# Firewall Load Balancing

Content Services Switches can enhance security by load balancing traffic among multiple firewalls. This not only eliminates performance bottlenecks but also guards against having a single point of failure.

This is typically done by deploying a Content Services Switch in front and at the back of the firewalls being load balanced, with the firewalls being in the middle. In this way, traffic for a given flow will traverse the same firewall.

Figure A.5 depicts a typical Content Services Switch implementation to load balance multiple firewalls. This design provides not only firewall load balancing, but also redundancy, while maintaining all the usual firewall security features.

**Figure A.5** A Typical Content Services Switch Implementation to Load Balance Multiple Firewalls

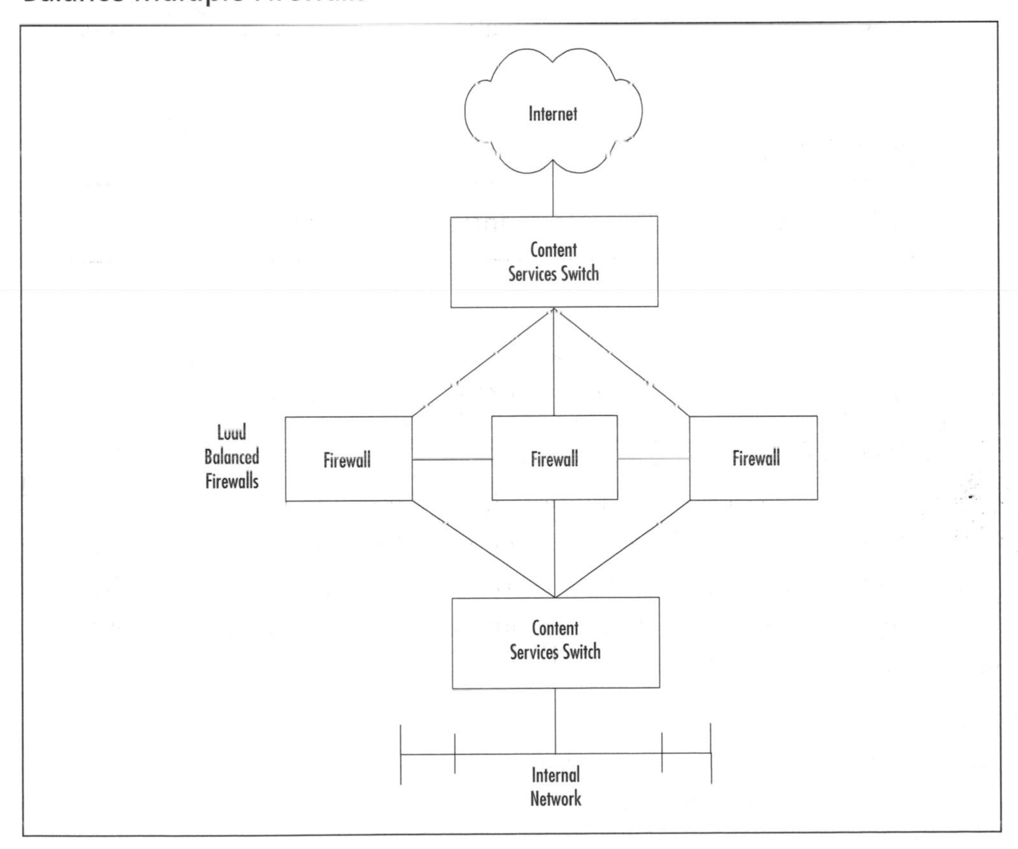

# Password Protection

Content Services Switches support two types of access levels, *User* and *SuperUser,* and up to 32 usernames, including the administrator and technician.

## The User Access Level

This is the user-level user. This type of access level allows you to have access to a limited set of commands that allow you to monitor and display parameters but not change them. The following syntax is used to create a User account (global configuration command):

```
username name [des-password|encrypted-password|password] password
```

where *name* is the username you want to create or change (a text string with a maximum of 16 characters is supported); where *des-password* encrypts the password with Data Encryption Standard, or DES (use this option only when you are creating a file for use as a script or a startup configuration file. The password is case sensitive and is between 6 and 64 characters long); where *encrypted-password* encrypts the password (use this option only when you are creating a file for use as a script or a startup configuration file); and where *password* is the password, which must be between 6 and 16 characters long.

## The SuperUser Access Level

This is the privileged-level user. This type of access level allows you to both monitor and display parameters, as well as change them. The default privileged-user username is *admin* and the default password is *system*.

The following syntax is used to create a SuperUser account (global configuration command):

```
username name [des-password|encrypted-password|password] password
   superuser
```

where *name* is the username you want to create or change(a text string with a maximum of 16 characters is supported); where *des-password* encrypts the password with DES (use this option only when you are creating a file for use as a script or a startup configuration file. The password is case sensitive and is between 6 and 64 characters long); where *encrypted-password* encrypts the password (use this option only when you are creating a file for use as a script or a startup configuration file); where *password* is the password, which must be between 6 and 16 characters long; and where *superuser,* which is optional, creates the user with SuperUser rights. If you don't specify this last command, the user is created as a normal user.

The syntax to list existing usernames is:

```
username ?
```

The syntax to remove users is:

```
no username username
```

**SECURITY ALERT!**

A security mistake that is often made is not to change the default admin password for the Content Services Switch. Be sure to change this before you deploy the Content Services Switch.

## Disabling Telnet Access

Although not feasible for many customers with Content Services Switches deployed in more than one location, disabling telnet access to these switches greatly increases security. Access would then be via the physical console connection.

The syntax to disabling telnet access is:

```
telnet access disabled
```

## Syslog Logging

Often, knowing about an attack is as important as taking steps to protect yourself against the attack. This is where logging plays an important role. If a syslog server is configured, the Content Services Switch will log error and event messages to an external syslog server (called *host*).

The following syntax is used to configure the syslog feature (from configuration mode):

```
logging host ip
```

where *ip* is the IP address of the log host.

To disable syslog, use the **no** command:

```
no logging host
```

## Known Security Vulnerabilities

Content Services Switches have two known security vulnerabilities. Detailed documentation is available on Cisco's Web site at www.cisco.com/warp/public/707/arrowpoint-cli-filesystem-pub.shtml.

### *Cisco Bug ID CSCdt08730*

This vulnerability allows someone with a non-privileged user level account to cause an abnormal event that can cause the switch to reboot, which will prevent normal function for up to 5 minutes. This vulnerability can be continuously reproduced resulting in a DoS attack.

This vulnerability has been resolved in Cisco WebNS software revision 4.01(12s) and revision 3.10(71s).

### *Cisco Bug ID CSCdt12748*

This vulnerability allows someone with a non-privileged user level account to gain access to files on the Content Services Switch that he should not have access to.

There is currently no resolution to this vulnerability, although workarounds include limiting telnet access with access lists as well as disabling telnet access.

Damage & Defense…

### My Systems Are 100 Percent Secure!

Organizations often tell me that their systems are 100 percent secure. I would argue that they have missed the point. I don't believe that a 100 percent secure system can exist.

Security is a process, not an end result. Organizations need to understand that security vulnerabilities can pose a considerable threat to their existence and take precautions to minimize their exposure to these threats.

I'm also often told that their systems are secure because they have bought the latest technological gadget.Real security doesn't come from any particular device or technology, but rather through a security policy that specifies that organizations security requirements and enforces this policy through the deployment of a number of devices, features, technologies, methodologies, and procedures.

Here is what Professor Eugene Spafford, an acknowledged expert in computer security, has to say about security:

*"The only truly secure system is one that is powered off, cast in a block of concrete and sealed in a lead-lined room with armed guards—and even then I have my doubts."*

# Summary

Cisco's Content Delivery Devices provide powerful and versatile technologies that can help you scale your Internet traffic and improve your security measures against DoS attacks and other system compromises.

With every passing day, our reliance on Internet applications and technologies becomes more widespread, and the risks of security vulnerabilities becomes even greater. Our greatest weapon against security attacks is information. In order to protect ourselves from hackers and cyber-terrorists, we have to ensure that we keep ourselves up-to-date with the latest security threats and constantly evaluate these threats against the security of our own systems.

Gone are the days when all you had to do is keep hackers out of our systems. Now you have to stop them from knocking at your door. By flooding your systems with useless service requests, hackers can effectively shut down your systems, degrading your service response time to such a degree that legitimate requests can no longer be serviced.

I hope that this appendix has provided you with insight into the security features of Cisco's LocalDirector, DistributedDirector, and the Content Services Switch and trust that it will encourage you to be ever vigilant and help protect your systems from security attacks. In today's world, nothing could be more true than Thomas Jefferson's words, "Eternal vigilance is the price of liberty."

# Frequently Asked Questions

The following Frequently Asked Questions, answered by the authors of this book, are designed to both measure your understanding of the concepts presented in this chapter and to assist you with real-life implementation of these concepts. To have your questions about this chapter answered by the author, browse to **www.syngress.com/solutions** and click on the **"Ask the Author"** form.

**Q:** Will FlowWall security slow down my network traffic?

**A:** No, FlowWall was designed to provide wire-speed security and will not slow down your network traffic.

**Q:** Where can I get a syslog server?

**A:** A syslog daemon comes standard with most versions of UNIX. For Windows platforms, several freeware and commercial programs are available.

**Q:** Are there any organizations that can help me stay informed about security threats?

**A:** Yes, several. They typically offer security advisories and background information that can help you in securing your systems. Have a look at:

**CERT Coordination Center** www.cert.org

**FIRST** www.first.org

**Bugtraq** www.securityfocus.com

**Q:** Our management sees little value in spending money on computer security. How do I change that?

**A:** Explain to them what the consequences of an attack on your systems would mean to their business, both in monetary terms as well as non-monetary terms. Many organizations suffer huge monetary losses as a result of an attack, often not directly, but rather due to clients losing confidence or trust in the business as well as general negative market perception.

**Q:** Does securing my systems need to cost me a lot of money?

**A:** No, one of the most effective tools in protecting your system is information. Often this information is publicly available and need not cost you a lot of money. However, depending on your specific requirements, you might be well advised to consult a professional.

# Appendix B

# Hack Proofing Your E-Commerce Site Fast Track

**This Appendix will provide you with a quick, yet comprehensive, review of the most important concepts covered in this book.**

# ❖ Chapter 1: Applying Security Principles to Your E-Business

## Security as a Foundation

☑ The primary principles of security are confidentiality, integrity, and availability.

☑ Information is possibly one of the most valuable assets most companies possess; losing it or caring for it negligently could spell disaster and possibly even ruin. The risks to confidentiality do not stop with access to data; credit card details are illegally obtained from Internet facing systems, then used or sold, with alarming frequency.

☑ We assume that the database system we are using will maintain the records of our sales correctly. We believe that our billing system is smart enough to add the items on a customer's bill. Without some form of integrity checking, neither of these situations may be true.

☑ Availability is the lifeblood of any business. In the e-commerce world, where every moment can directly translate to thousands of dollars in sales, even downtimes of less than an hour can do immense financial damage to a company.

☑ Security also entails a three-step process of assessment, revision, and implementation of changes. This continual process of evaluation and feedback is necessary to adapt processes and products to the ever-changing conditions of the online world, as hackers examine existing software and hardware systems and discover new vulnerabilities.

☑ Once you have successfully secured your environment and processes down to the level of your accepted risks, it is time to mitigate those issues through a combination of technology, policy, and awareness. Begin by using your list of accepted risks to create a policy to deal with them. Once you have mitigated your risks, you can begin to bring your systems online and offer access to the public.

**Chapter 1** Continued

## Applying Principles to Existing Sites

☑ The process of applying the three principles of confidentiality, integrity, and availability to existing sites differs a bit from new sites, but many of the concepts are the same. What does change is where and when these tools begin to be applied. For example, beginning the assessment process on your existing site could damage your production systems, so most sites begin by testing their development environment or a mirror of their production environment created just for the purpose of testing.

☑ Fix those vulnerabilities with the highest risk first. Often, it is a good idea to mitigate these risks through additional means (such as by blocking the appropriate ports at the firewall or at border routers) while your staff works toward implementing the patches and modifications. Pay special attention to the popular services such as DNS, HTTP, SMTP, SNMP, FTP, POP, IMAP, and security-related applications such as firewalls or intrusion detection programs.

☑ Migration plans also begin with risks, just like an assessment. The plan outlines which systems and components at your site are considered mission critical and defines the systems that fit into lesser categories as well. The migration plan is used to determine when a vulnerability is of the most urgent nature or when it resides lower in the queue. From there, the plan illustrates how the administrators should handle patches and modifications to each category of system. It defines the steps to be followed for authenticating a patch and backing up a system, as well as the testing required for a patch to be approved for implementation on the production site.

## How to Justify a Security Budget

☑ The yardstick approach uses security and risk as yardsticks to measure the gains that security measures have made for the organization. Try to convert the security processes you have already created into a dollar amount versus the dollar amount of the damage that

**Chapter 1** Continued

we might have faced should we have accepted those risks without mitigation (or use other units of measure such as labor hours).

- ☑ The fear tactic approach raises the level of fear, uncertainty, and doubt in the organization, it is often very successful in raising the level of awareness. Tools such as penetration tests, real-life security incidents, and information warfare scenarios are the basis for this strategy. The bottom line here is to figure out what hurts an organization, and if it is a possibility, either exploit or explain it.

## Security as a Restriction

- ☑ Perception in a company of security being a restriction arises immediately after the implementation of controls or monitoring software is put into place to better manage the use of network resources or performance during business hours. While these technologies are not the cause, they are often seen as being a symptom of a "Big Brother" approach. These images and perceptions cause damage to the security process.

## Security as an Enabler

- ☑ To overcome the restrictive view of security, change the overall image of your team to be seen as enablers. Security as an enabler is best portrayed when the security team takes the role of consultant to the other members of your organization. When other teams begin to see security as a flexible tool that creates options for their projects instead of a tight set of rules that they have to follow, you will have created a partnering image for your team and you will find that other groups begin to actually include your team in the planning and development stages of their projects.

# ❖ Chapter 2: DDoS Attacks: Intent, Tools, and Defense

## What Is a DDoS Attack?

☑ A DoS attack attempts to reduce the ability of a site to service clients, be they physical users or logical entities such as other computer systems. This can be achieved by either overloading the ability of the target network or server to handle incoming traffic or by sending network packets that cause target systems and networks to behave unpredictably.

☑ Resource consumption attacks predominantly originate from outside the local network, but do not rule out the possibility that the attack is from within. These attacks usually take the form of a large number of packets directed at the victim, a technique commonly known as *flooding*. Other forms of resource consumption can include the reduction of connections available to legitimate users and the reduction of system resources available to the host operating system itself. A classic example of this scenario was the Melissa virus.

☑ A SYN flood usually involves a number of packets being directed at the target server, consequently overloading the connection buffer. Unfortunately the SYN flood attack can be quite effective, primarily because it can be launched by a hacker with limited resources and has the added advantage of obscuring the source of the attack in the first place.

☑ An *amplification attack* achieves its effectiveness by enlisting the aid of other networks that act as amplifiers for the attack. This allows hackers with limited resources to target victims with a considerable increase in resources. The networks used in the amplification attacks are usually oblivious to their part in the whole process. Two examples of amplification attacks are the whimsically named Smurf and Fraggle.

☑ A *malformed packet attack* usually consists of a small number of packets directed at a target server or device. The packets are constructed in such a fashion that on receipt of the packet, the target

**Chapter 2** Continued

panics. A *panic* is considered to occur when the device or operating system enters an unstable state potentially resulting in a system crash. A classic DoS malformed packet attack is the Ping of Death.

☑ An often-neglected aspect of securing a site against DoS attacks is ensuring *physical* security. Not only must the physical security of the servers be considered, but also the cabling and power infrastructures.

☑ Indirect attacks could also become more relevant as DoS attacks attain greater subtlety. A savvy hacker could target the weakest link in your business chain instead of mounting a full frontal assault on the business itself.

☑ One of the significant differences in methodology of a DDoS attack is that it consists of two distinct phases. During the first phase, the perpetrator compromises computers scattered across the Internet and installs specialized software on these hosts to aid in the attack. In the second phase, the compromised hosts, referred to as zombies, are then instructed through intermediaries (called masters) to commence the attack. Microsoft became next in the line of bemused businesses subjected to successful DDoS attacks.

## Why Are E-Commerce Sites Prime Targets for DDoS?

☑ The more complex a site and the technologies it uses, the more difficult it is to maintain an aggressive security profile. The complexity of the site can reduce security coverage through human error, design fault, or immature technology implementations. Managing change control can be particularly troublesome for large sites, and each change has the potential to introduce vulnerability.

☑ The media continues to play a significant, though unintended, role. Attacks are intensely scrutinized not only by the IT press, but also by every conceivable TV station, newspaper, and magazine. Using the latest DDoS tools, even a fledgling hacker can bring down well-known international companies and get front-page coverage.

**Chapter 2** Continued

## What Motivates an Attacker to Damage Companies?

☑ Hacktivism is the electronic extrapolation of the right to free speech and expression coupled with modern-day activism. Certain individuals and groups take the ability to express ideals and beliefs a step further by taking direct action, which usually involves damaging or attacking sites with conflicting perspectives. This tactic is often deemed acceptable by the hacktivists due to the publicity such an attack can generate. Most hacktivists are of the opinion that the media attention generates public interest in their causes.

☑ A DDoS attack could force a business to focus attention on resuming normal operations, hackers can compromise the site via an alternate route and gain information such as credit card and bank account details. These details can then be resold on the Internet or used personally by the hacker.

☑ The anonymity provided by the Internet may encourage hackers to project threatening personalities and indulge in extravagant and aggressive role-playing or vandalism. It is impossible to determine the rationale behind attacks motivated purely through a will to deface or destroy.

## What Are Some of the Tools Attackers Use to Perform DDoS Attacks?

☑ Using the open source model allows a significant number of people to contribute to the development of new strains and versions of the DDoS tools. Contributions from hackers from a variety of backgrounds allow the code to develop organically and in surprising directions. Additionally, coding neophytes can pick at the source code used for a particular attack to hone and refine their own burgeoning skills.

## Chapter 2 Continued

- ☑ Trinoo, one of the first publicly available DDoS programs, rose to fame in August 1999 after it was used to successfully mount an attack on the University of Minnesota. Like most multi-tier DDoS attacks, the early stages of a trinoo attack involves the attacker compromising machines to become masters. The masters then receive copies of a number of utilities, tools, and—of course—the trinoo control and daemon programs. The master then compiles a list of machines with specific vulnerabilities (possibly involving buffer overflows in RPC services) targeted to act as zombies in the forthcoming attack. The trinoo daemon is then installed and configured to run on the compromised hosts.
- ☑ The main components of TFN2K after compile time are two binaries, namely *tfn* and *td*. Using a well-defined syntax, the client program (tfn) sends commands to the TFN2K daemon (which can be unlimited in number) installed on compromised hosts. The daemon (td) then carries out the commands as directed by the client. At the most basic level, tfn instructs td to either commence or halt attacks. TFN2K is quite versatile; it works on a number of platforms—even on Windows platforms using UNIX shells such as vmware and cygwin.
- ☑ The compilation of the Stacheldraht source code results in the generation of three binaries. The three binaries are *client*, *mserv*, and *td*, each of which is used in a separate tier in the attack model. Mserv is the *client software* because it runs on the master. Compromised hosts to be used as zombies are then configured to run the td binary, which contains the actual code to assemble attack packets and traffic streams. When the client binary is run, it establishes a telnet-like session with the master running the mserv program. Stacheldraht uses the freely available Blowfish encryption algorithm based on a 64-bit block cipher.

**Chapter 2** Continued

## How Can I Protect My Site against These Types of Attacks?

☑ DDoS countermeasures include *egress filtering* of spoofed addresses and *ingress filtering* of broadcast packets. Egress filtering encompasses the filtering of outbound traffic, whereas ingress filtering relates to the filtering of inward-bound network traffic. Your ISP should be required to implement ingress filtering, which can aid in identifying zombie networks.

☑ Options available to minimize DDoS exposure include keeping the security profile current; profiling traffic patterns; splitting DNS infrastructure; using load balancing; tightening firewall configurations; securing perimeter devices and using traffic shaping; implementing an IDS, vulnerability scanner, and/or proxy server; taking snapshots and conducting integrity checks of existing configurations; configuring sacrificial hosts; increasing network and host management; maintaining a response procedure; and deploying more secure technologies.

☑ Network *choke points* are usually an excellent place to apply egress rules or filters. Choke points requiring egress filtering include all internal interfaces on firewalls, routers, and dial-in servers.

☑ Operating systems should be configured to ignore directed broadcasts, to incorporate SYN flood resilience, to establish strong passwords, and have all unnecessary services turned off.

☑ A profusion of tools are available to aid in the identification and recovery of networks involved in DDoS attacks, including Nmap, Find_ddos, Zombie Zapper, tfn2kpass, RID, DDosPing, Ramenfind, DDS, GAG, and Tripwire.

☑ In case of attack, your response procedure should incorporate information gathering; contacting the ISP; applying more aggressive filters; applying different routing options; attempting to stop the attack; changing the IP address of the target system, and commencing incidence investigation.

# ❖ Chapter 3: Secure Web Site Design

## Choosing a Web Server

☑ The expense of having a private Web server will generally be more costly than it would be to rent space on an ISP's server. Remember that renting such space removes the cost of purchasing servers, software, and T1 lines to the Internet. If problems arise with the equipment, the ISP is responsible for fixing them. However, any choices regarding security, services, or extra software installed on the server will be decided by the third party.

☑ By using a platform your staff is already familiar with, there is less chance they will miss security holes because they may already be aware of them in other operating systems.

☑ Because the Web server runs on top of the operating system like any other software, an operating system with better security features will improve the security of your Web server. For example, although Windows 95 can be used to run Apache Web server, it would be more secure to use Apache on Windows NT Server. Windows 95 has fewer security features and a less secure file system than NT.

☑ In looking at the various servers, pay close attention to certain features, specifically those that control authentication, use of the SET protocol, the setting of rights and permissions, and the use of CGI applications.

## The Basics of Secure Site Design

☑ When developing a site, you should create a security plan that includes the following steps: Identify what needs to be secure; identify the value of what's being protected; identify the risks involved with your site; identify the exposure to those risks; put the plan into action.

☑ Proxy servers can provide additional security measures often not found or easily configured in the Web server application itself, for example, providing inbound and outbound access control, packet

**Chapter 3** Continued

filtering, and dial-in access controls. Port and packet filtering is an effective way of preventing unauthorized access to your network.

☑ A number of Web servers require an SSI executable to have the file extension .CGI for the specified file to be executed. However, you should check your server documentation to see if this is indeed the case. Much of the functionality a hacker could acquire through this command depends on whether permissions have been properly set up on the server. For example, if all users had the read privileges to all files or full access to programs on the server, then SSI could be used to read these files or execute various programs. Evaluate permissions given to users and determine what default permissions are given to newly created directories.

☑ Web design issues dealing with HTML code will require you to: review HTML code in all Web pages posted to your site; remove or revise sensitive information contained in HTML code; ensure that directories on the site have proper permissions; determine whether Server Side Includes are a potential threat to your site; determine whether certain Server Side Includes should be disabled or if Server Side Includes shouldn't be allowed on your site.

## Guidelines for Java, JavaScript, and Active X

☑ Java applets are generally digitally signed or of a standalone format, but when embedded in a Web page, it is possible to skirt around this requirement. Hackers can program an applet to execute code on a machine so that information is retrieved or files are destroyed or modified. Remember that an applet is a program, and it has the capability of performing malicious activities on your system.

☑ A common problem that hackers will use to their advantage regards scripts and programs that trust user input. Scripting languages can also be used to run shell functions. With a properly written and executed script, the cmd.exe could be used to run other programs on a Windows NT or 2000 system. In addition to user input, you

**Chapter 3** Continued

will need to write programs and scripts so that no input is trusted that is passed from a client.

☑ Because of the possible damage a Java applet, JavaScript, or ActiveX component can do to a network, in terms of threatening security or attacking machines, many companies filter out applets. Firewalls can be configured to filter out applets, scripts, and components so that they are removed from an HTML document. By removing such elements from ever being displayed, the Web page will appear different from the way its author intended, but any content that is passed through the firewall will be secure. On the client side, many browsers can also be configured to filter content. By changing the settings on a Web browser, you can prevent such programs from being loaded into memory on a client computer. The user accessing the Internet from your network is provided with the HTML content but isn't presented with any of these programmed features.

## Programming Secure Scripts

☑ Active Server Pages have problems that are similar to those seen in client-side scripting. By embedding the scripts into the Web pages, this allows curious and malicious users to view ASP code. A hacker may be able to acquire usernames, passwords, and identify vulnerabilities in the code.

☑ Any programs and scripts available on your site should be thoroughly tested before they are made available for use on the Web. Determine whether the script or program works properly by using it numerous times. If you are using a database, enter and retrieve multiple records. Have members of your IT staff try the script or program themselves, because they may enter data in a different order or try a task differently.

**Chapter 3** Continued

## Code Signing: Solution or More Problems?

☑ Digital signatures can be used to guarantee the integrity of files and that the package being installed is authentic and unmodified. This signature is attached to the file being downloaded. The signature identifies who is distributing the files and shows that they were unmodified since being created. The certificate helps to keep malicious users from impersonating someone else.

☑ A major problem with code signing is that you must rely on a third-party for checking authenticity. If a programmer provided fake information to a CA or stole the identity of another individual or company, then it would be possible to effectively distribute a malicious program over the Internet. Another problem is if valid information is provided to the CA, but the certificate is attached to software with bad or malicious code.

☑ Using software such as Microsoft Certificate Server, you can create your own digital certificates for use on a network. This allows someone to self-sign their code with their own CA, and make it appear that the code is valid and secure. You should verify the validity of the CA before accepting any files to avoid installing a hacker's code onto your system.

## Should I Outsource the Design of My Site?

☑ You should determine what information will need to be provided for the contractor to do her job right without compromising the security of your network, and you should also determine what security policies will be used for the Web server to keep the contractor from accessing unauthorized data (and whether these policies will impact existing policies).

☑ A very real complication in outsourcing is that who you hire may not be who does the work. When determining whom to hire, you should inquire as to whether they will do the job themselves or use outside contractors.

**Chapter 3** Continued

- ☑ Accept another person's design without checking to see if there are any existing security vulnerabilities or problems is foolish. You will need to go through each page of the site to view the source code and determine whether that information represents a security threat.
- ☑ Before making the site public, you should view content, run scripts, applets, components, and other programs on a test server. You should also use more than one type of browser when checking your site for problems. Last, you should ensure that any software on the machine has the latest patches and security packs applied to them.

# ❖ Chapter 4: Designing and Implementing Security Policies

## Why Are Security Policies Important to an E-Commerce Site?

- ☑ Failing to implement cost-effective security solutions affects the profitability of your site from several perspectives. Insufficient security can lead to expenses from downtime, lawsuit, or data loss; security that is too extreme can inhibit productivity, constrict customer interaction, or require too much in the way of administration costs. Profitability lies somewhere in the middle, and that somewhere is different for every e-commerce venture.
- ☑ Security policies should exist to help others make good decisions, not to get in the way of productivity. Cost effective security doesn't spend more to protect an asset than it's worth to the business, although its value to a particular business may be more or less than the actual market or street value. Security improvements generally have an inverse relationship with productivity, but both end up costing money if taken to the extreme.
- ☑ As you develop the policy, try to be brief. The longer the policy, the less likely that users will read it. The policies need to be clear, doable in your environment, and enforceable. Generally, if the

**Chapter 4** Continued

policy specifies the "what" without specifying the "how," supporting departments are granted greater leeway to develop innovative solutions to problems and still stick to the overall security goals. Defining words in simple terms before they are used prevents differing interpretations later on.

## What Elements Should My Security Policy Address?

- ☑ A comprehensive security policy is actually made up of several individual policies, each of which targets unique lateral aspects of the site's business processes. The individual policies work together to provide three basic assurances for the site: confidentiality, integrity, and availability of data.
- ☑ To be certain that your site is not handing out confidential information to impersonators, you should authenticate customers as well as assuring your site's identity to them. A site SSL certificate doesn't tell the server anything about the client's identity, which could be impersonating your real customer. The security policy defines client authentication requirements for your site.
- ☑ Most external theft of data from Web sites occurs because the data is not properly encrypted or stored after the Web server has received it. Security policy should be clear about requirements for encryption at every stage of processing, from client browser to Web server, to application server, to database. The policy needs to require session management that prevents others from viewing pages that are part of another users session.
- ☑ Protecting information while it is stored on your site means protecting the servers themselves by defining specifically what a secure server, or bastion host, should look like. A bastion host is a computer system with special modifications that fortify its ability to withstand a targeted attack. The security policy specifies the steps to take to produce a bastion host from an initially installed operating system.

**Chapter 4** Continued

- ☑ Quality assurance policies specify enforcement mechanisms that include change control, auditing, reporting, and intrusion detection. Availability of service policies specify uptime requirements, acceptable use guidelines, and disaster recovery procedures.

## Are Any Prewritten Security Policies Available on the Net?

- ☑ The companies that are most successful at implementing security policies are those that avoid the "do it and forget it" mentality and somehow convince all the employees that security belongs to each of them, that it is an ongoing function of doing business, and that success of the company depends on it. Beyond that, the content of the security policies will vary as greatly as businesses themselves do.
- ☑ If you are determined to do the work in-house, start with an outline of items that must be covered somewhere in the policy and begin fleshing it out after obtaining the necessary input from others. The Internet is a good resource for locating templates to begin the process. If you don't have time to write one yourself, you can hire a security company to do the legwork for you. If a security consultant tries to sell you a canned policy without spending considerable time investigating your business culture, management goals, and unique business aspects, run away fast, because you'd be wasting your money.

## How Do I Use My Security Policy to Implement Technical Solutions?

- ☑ The task of enforcing the policy begins by implementing technical solutions to perform that enforcement at every tier of security within the company. Perimeter security primarily concerns itself with lower protocol layers where policy can be enforced by limiting traffic flows at those layers. Host and applications security represents the upper protocol layers, where session controls and

**Chapter 4** Continued

application security can be used for enforcement. Network security mechanisms fill in any gaps between the two and perform logging and auditing enforcement functions.

☑ If a policy requires a certain network transport, enforcement mechanisms include a firewall at the perimeter, access lists on network routers internally, and session-based controls on the host or application.

## How Do I Inform My Clients of My Security Policies?

☑ Electronic selling is still selling, just the same. E-commerce lends itself wonderfully to everything about selling except the first thing customers expect to see when they walk in the door. Disclosure of security policy is a way to build customer confidence by putting a kinder, gentler face on at least a portion of your site.

☑ Disclose the components of your site's security policy that will assure customers of the safety of their transactions, but don't do it with great fanfare. A small link that takes customers to a page detailing what they want to know meets the need without over doing it.

☑ Customers choose to do business with companies that are successful in projecting an image of being the helping hand that guides them, the one that's in their corner, the one that can meet their need and be trusted. In the end, the successful e-commerce ventures will be the ones that sell this same image to their customers as hard and fast as the physical products or services those customers are buying.

# ❖ Chapter 5: Implementing a Secure E-Commerce Web Site

## Implementing Security Zones

☑ Security zones are discrete network segments holding systems that share common requirements, such as the types of information they handle, who uses them, and what levels of security they require to protect their data. They may be the same type of operating system or different operating systems altogether. They may be PCs, or servers, or even a mainframe.

☑ DMZ systems are offered some level of protection from the public Internet while they remain accessible for the specific services they provide. In addition, the internal network is protected by firewall and from the systems in the DMZ. Because the DMZ systems still offer public access, they are more prone to compromise and thus they are untrusted by the systems in the protected network. This scenario allows for public services while still maintaining a degree of protection against attack.

☑ Customer names, addresses, order information, and especially financial data are protected from unauthorized access through the creation of specialized segments similar to the DMZ called *security zones*. Many sites choose to implement a multiple segment structure to better manage and secure their business information.

☑ Access controls also regulate the way in which network conversations are initiated. It is always preferable that DMZ systems do not initiate connections into more secure areas, but that systems with higher security requirements initiate those network conversations.

☑ Creating and managing the security controls such as firewall rules, IDS signatures, and user access regulations is a large task. Start with deny-all strategies and permit only the services and network transactions that are required to make the site function. Carefully manage the site's performance and make small changes to the access controls to more easily manage the rule sets.

**Chapter 5** Continued

## Understanding Firewalls

☑ Packet filtering firewalls make decisions about whether or not to pass network traffic based upon the source and destination information in the headers of the packets being transmitted.

☑ Proxy-based firewalls also make decisions based upon the source and destination addresses of packets, as well as the ports used for the conversation. The additional work done by a proxy firewall is that it is inspects the data load portion of a packet and attempts to decide if the data fits the proxies' requirements for such a conversation.

☑ Hybrids between the two technologies have also emerged and may be a good fit for your organization if you desire the proxy level of control and the speed of a packet filter. These firewall devices integrate both the proxy and packet-filtering technologies to create solutions that monitor data load and achieve high throughput speeds.

☑ The process of designing the rule set for any firewall should always start with a "deny all" attitude. That means that you begin by making the firewall deny any connections that you do not specifically allow. Thus, starting with nothing, you can add in the connections required between each of the security zones to allow the systems on those segments to perform their work and to be administered, but nothing else. This helps to prevent the possibility of allowing unneeded services and additional gateways for an attacker to compromise your servers.

☑ After you have come to terms with the rule sets for your site operation, you need to ensure that you allowed only the required protocols, and only to the servers or segments where they are needed.

## How Do I Know Where to Place My Components?

☑ Evaluate your systems using such criteria as users, sensitivity of data, external visibility, internal access controls required, and encryption requirements.

**Chapter 5** Continued

☑ Using those criteria, decide what systems will be primarily protected by the firewall, what systems will be dependant on internal authentication methods, and what systems will require additional tools for protecting them from unauthorized access.

☑ Group the systems together and assign them to network segments by looking for the commonalities and placing those systems together. Consider also using host-based tools such as IDS, log monitoring, or a customized configuration when for some reason a system should not be placed with its similar peers, or create another network segment specifically for that system.

☑ When you have your systems placed, create your firewall rule set. Generally, start with a basic principle that *everything that is not specifically allowed is denied* and then add in the conversations that you want to allow.

## Implementing Intrusion Detection

☑ Intrusion detection is the name given to a family of products that are deployed to look for suspicious events that occur on a network or system. When the tool notices an event that matches its definition of "suspicious," it will perform some action such as logging the details, alerting an administrator, killing the traffic or process, and/or updating other devices such as firewalls to prevent the problem from happening again.

☑ *Host-based* IDS tools reside on the host and watch events from the view of the computer's operating system. As events occur, they compare those events against their rules base, and if they find a match, they alert and/or take action. *Network-based* IDS products monitor the network traffic streams for suspicious traffic patterns. The system acts as a sensor reading the data flow off of the wire and parsing it against a database of patterns.

☑ Although some IDS tools are very versatile, others may be very difficult to configure and may not be able to recognize patterns outside of those programmed into it by its creators. Most IDS systems

**Chapter 5** Continued

compare traffic or user patterns against databases of known attack fingerprints or signatures. When selecting your IDS, one of the primary questions you should ask is how easy it is to have signatures added to the database.

☑ Open source tools such as Snort!, Shadow, and PortSentry have brought IDS to market as well. Some of the freeware security tools have complete documentation, online support, and a plethora of add-ons, plug-ins, and extensions.

## Managing and Monitoring the Systems

☑ Patches, hot fixes, and workarounds have to be applied as new security issues and other problems are discovered and repaired. Each of these revisions has to be authenticated, tested, and will require re-verification of the security posture of your site. Changes to the content and features of your site will also require ongoing evaluation.

☑ Use automated tools (or agents) that reside on the host computer being monitored and communicate with a management console via a network connection. The agent watches usage patterns, processor workload, log files, disk space, and other items for signs of a problem. If a problem occurs, the agent sends a message to the management console with the appropriate details. The management console often assigns a follow-up task to the appropriate administrator and alerts them to the condition. Some management systems also track the problem through its resolution and log the collected information for trend analysis and other types of reporting.

☑ Automating monitoring processes is usually a good idea as long as a *human* is involved somewhere in the process to evaluate the automated alerts and output and to periodically check for missing events. In addition, if you do choose to automate the security log inspection process, make sure that you have multiple levels of security devices observing your traffic.

**Chapter 5** Continued

## Should I Do It Myself or Outsource My Site?

☑ Consider the feasibility of training a staff member or members to perform the functions against the costs of hiring someone who already has those skills to perform it for you. Look also at the security requirements for your site and determine if your policy and processes allow for outsourcing to hired personnel.

☑ If an ASP assumes the responsibility of providing and maintaining the security of your site, be sure to maintain the rights to audit and inspect the security processes of the ASP you work with. Performing regular vulnerability assessments against your site and the ASP itself will ensure that your policies are being enforced.

☑ Co-location is a service provided by many vendors to allow companies to share the costs of establishing bandwidth and other infrastructure components (such as credit processing systems and the like) while still providing them with the freedom of owning their own servers and support systems; this a popular solution for companies who want control over the day-to-day management and operation of their site, but who may not be able to afford or manage the entire e-commerce network on their own.

# ❖ Chapter 6: Securing Financial Transactions

## Understanding Internet-Based Payment Card Systems

☑ Hackers love credit card data for a number of reasons: It's easy to steal, it's easy to resell, and it's hard to get caught. The best targets are those that are loosely protected, contain large volumes of payment card data, and are easy to access over the Internet.

☑ Credit cards, charge cards, bank cards, and payment cards all relate to a family of payment options that involve relationships rooted in

**Chapter 6** Continued

trust and good faith. You trust that the financial institution that issued you a card will pay the merchant for the goods and services you purchase. Merchants trust that the card issuers will pay them reasonably quickly, and the card issuers trust that you'll pay your bill on time each month.

☑ The processing steps for charge cards and debit cards are identical to those for credit cards, with the exception of the mechanics involved in the authorization request and settlement processing. Because charge cards are not based on preset spending limits, the notion of an open-to-buy is irrelevant. Rather, charge card systems use other means to authorize or decline a charge request. Some companies use risk models, heuristics, patterns of spending, or manual review.

☑ Internet sales can be viewed as seven distinct phases where unique security requirements come into play as data collects and processing commences.

☑ POS processing adds complexity to already vulnerable Internet-attached networks and heightens the need for strict security controls.

## Options in Commercial Payment Solutions

☑ Commercial payment systems appear in three basic forms: outside turnkey solutions, in-house solutions, and combinations of the two.

☑ Commerce Server Providers (CSPs) will lease you access to the system, allocate disk space for you to maintain your products, may offer multiple payment processing options, and may even provide robust site reporting and easy Web-browser-based interfaces for maintenance. Many of them are operated under secure and trustworthy environments and may even offer Web design service. Be careful, though—not all CSPs provide the same levels of service or the same payment processing fee structures.

☑ Hack-proofing a payment-card handling system requires secure architectures to ensure network and server-based security, and they

**Chapter 6** Continued

require the uses of complex cryptography protocols running atop the network layer—primarily at the application layer. Most of today's payment protocols incorporate multiple forms of applied cryptography for its functions.

## Secure Payment Processing Environments

☑ Security experts embrace three-tier systems for Internet, intranet, and extranet applications. When they're present, these three tiers—Web server(s), application server(s), and database server(s)—greatly reduce many of the threats to production back-office systems and networks. Add still more layers of security both between and within each tier.

☑ Secure payment processing environments rely on careful separation of activities where a "defense in depth" approach can help to shield you from threats coming from the Internet.

☑ Diligent and knowledgeable system administrators are essential to maintaining the controls needed for e-commerce success.

☑ Any dynamically generated data (stored billing and shipping information, etc.) should be kept as far out of reach from the Internet as possible. Furthermore, any data that your customers supply via Web-based forms should immediately be removed from the Web server through as many firewalls as needed to safely secure it.

☑ Permitting HTTP routing into the back office places you at risk of hackers tunneling through HTTP to try to take over another server. Consider using protocols like CORBA/IIOP, RMI, socket connections via TCP, or DCOM on Microsoft NT to gain access to services residing on the Application tier.

☑ On the Database tier, consider encrypting the contents at the field level, the row level, the table level, or the entire database level.

**Chapter 6** Continued

## Understanding Cryptography

- ☑ Most of the industry standard methods to secure data at the application layer require robust uses of digital cryptography. POS processing, for example, needs cryptographic processing for securing data while it's in transit and while it's stored and processed within your stewardship.
- ☑ Strong cryptography always produces ciphertext that appears random to standard statistical tests. Because keys are generated for uniqueness using robust random number generators, the likelihood of their discovery approaches zero. Rather than trying to guess a key's value, it's far easier for would-be attackers to *steal* the key from where it's stored, so extra precautions must be taken to guard against such thefts.
- ☑ Using cryptography effectively on a well-designed and well-implemented secure network builds up the layers of defense on the application software layer where merchant operators tend to have the greatest degree of control over processing.
- ☑ Multiple solutions relying on cryptography are needed to address specific needs for security and data integrity on all points of sales processing, from end to end.
- ☑ Any cryptosystem that hasn't been subjected to brutal attacks should be considered suspect.
- ☑ The Secure Hashing Algorithm (SHA-1) and the Message Digest 5 (MD5) algorithm are common with e-commerce systems. SHA-1 is used in the process for creating a digital signature, which is authenticated with a public and private key system. You can't rely on your e-commerce customers to manage their own cryptographic keys—e-commerce requires a Public Key Infrastructure (PKI) for establishing and maintaining trusted digital certificates.
- ☑ Many of the higher-order e-commerce protocols, such as Secure Electronic Transactions (SET), use a robust set of digital certificates

**Chapter 6** Continued

to authenticate people and resources for assurance that all parties possess the rights needed to transact.

## Examining E-Commerce Cryptography

- ☑ The three goals of secure messaging—sender authentication, message integrity, and confidentiality—require complex cryptography if they're to succeed.
- ☑ Hashing is a powerful mechanism to protect user passwords on e-commerce sites. Should your site require IDs and passwords for personalization reasons, you'll want to store the passwords that people create in the form of a hash value. That way, even if a hacker steals your security database records, the hacker won't be able to use the data to impersonate your customers directly.
- ☑ Secure Sockets Layer (SSL) has emerged as the de facto standard for today's private communications on the Internet, but it does not go far enough to meet e-commerce security demands.
- ☑ PGP is a distributed key management approach that does not rely on Certificate Authorities. Users can sign one another's public keys, adding some degree of confidence to a key's validity. Limitations on the informal Web of Trust that PGP relies on makes it impractical for conducting electronic commerce on the Internet.
- ☑ Secure Electronic Transaction (SET) addresses most of the consumer demands for privacy when using a credit card to shop online. SET's uses are specific to the payment acceptance phases of the shopping experience. It covers the steps from the point a particular payment card is selected for use through the point the merchant completes the transaction and settles the batch with its acquirer bank or processor.

**Chapter 6** Continued

## A Virtual POS Implementation

☑ POS products available on the market today have become more and more sophisticated in their features and flexibility.

☑ Any of the in-house virtual POS software that you'll select to implement can't guarantee security unless you deliberately set out to install it securely on secure network resources. While much of the systems' documentation offers advice on secure implementation, it can't provide security automatically. Regardless of the system you choose, it's left up to you to install it, operate it, and maintain its security.

☑ ICVERIFY, one merchant POS software option, is designed to handle in-store, mail, telephone, and Internet-based transactions. Multiple merchant support capability allows more than one merchant ID on a single copy of the software to support multiple e-stores running in a single environment (cybermalls). Most of the commercial implementations of merchant POS software should provide you with a similar set of features and functions as ICVERIFY does.

## Alternative Payment Systems

☑ Alternative payment systems are designed to answer a variety of concerns and problems that plague e-commerce, such as fraud, chargebacks, lack of user authentication, an unwillingness to transact, and escalating processing fees.

☑ Smart cards are credit-card-sized devices that are distinguished from ordinary credit cards by the presence of a microchip on the front or reverse side of the card. EMV specifications define a broad set of requirements to ensure interoperability between chip cards and terminals on a global basis, regardless of the manufacturer, the financial institution, or where the card is used.

☑ MONDEX is one smart-card-based electronic purse applications. E-purses eliminate the requirement to share payment account

**Chapter 6** Continued

information with a merchant, eliminating many of the threats to large databases full of "toxic data." MONDEX uses strong cryptography to transfer value between participants in the scheme. Transfers of value occur in real-time, and the costs to processes are dramatically reduced.

☑ The Common Electronic Purse Specifications (CEPS) defines requirements for all components needed by an organization to implement a globally interoperable electronic purse program.

☑ With a proxy payment service, like PayPal and Amazon Payments, a consumer opens an account with the service and provides information about his or her credit cards or checking accounts. When the consumer wishes to make a payment, he or she logs on to the Web site of the provider and enters information about the sale. The service then provides the interface to the merchant without revealing the personal account information of the buyer.

☑ Funny money, like beenz and Flooz points, relates to payment mechanisms that are generally thought of as points and rewards programs backed by prepaid credit card charges or prepaid corporate accounts. Points may be given through online offerings and incentives.

## ❖ Chapter 7: Hacking Your Own Site

### Anticipating Various Types of Attacks

☑ An information leakage attack is an attack against confidentiality. A classic example of an information leakage problem is the *finger service*. Way back when, most UNIX machines ran a service called *finger*. There was a matching finger client command that would provide information about a particular user on a particular machine. This type of information does not lead directly to compromise, but it's rather disheartening how often a user's password matches their username—finger is a quick way to collect some usernames.

## Chapter 7 Continued

☑ A *file access* attack is an attack against confidentiality *and* integrity. There are any number of subcategories under file access, such as read access, write access, and delete permissions. Read access directly affects only confidentiality, whereas others permit modifications, which affect integrity. For example, UNIX- and DOS/Windows-based operating systems use **..** to represent the parent of the current directory, so that entering **cd ..** will take you up one directory level—some server software fails to take this into account and will allow **..** to be used in the file request, allowing an attacker to step out of boundaries.

☑ A *misinformation* attack is designed to confuse the defender. It's an attack against integrity—not the integrity of the systems themselves, but rather the defender's information *about* the systems. An example of a misinformation attack is an nmap scan that will generate extra traffic aimed at your host alongside the real packets doing the scanning.

☑ A lot of the interesting stuff at a site lives in a database. This is especially true for e-commerce sites. One extremely common programming mistake developers make when developing a Web site is to improperly escape or filter user-supplied data, giving an attacker a way to send SQL commands to a database.

☑ An *elevation of privilege* attack is an attack against the integrity of the security structure, though it often leads directly to other compromises. If an attacker can gain further capabilities beyond what they were supposed to have, then a security mechanism somewhere has been broken. Such a mechanism may be broken due to bad design, a bug, or just because the administrator implemented the mechanism improperly.

**Chapter 7** Continued

## Performing a Risk Analysis on Your Site

☑ Assets at risk can include money and financial information, customer information, products, intellectual property, employees, and reputation.

☑ By carefully watching firewall and IDS logs, you will begin to understand the difference between someone who has tried his trick and moved on, and someone who is sticking around for a little while. You may manage to spot an attacker that looks like he is taking some care to stay below the radar, perhaps by doing a slow scan.

☑ A honeypot is a system that is designed to be broken into. Setting up a honeypot will give you an opportunity to study the tactics of attackers. Your honeypot should be the easiest machine to penetrate on your network. One has to have some familiarity with forensic techniques, log analysis, and protocol analysis to make a honeypot useful.

## Testing Your Own Site for Vulnerabilities

☑ A good change control process can help with minimizing the risks in between full scans. Each time some change is made, make a best effort to determine exactly what will be affected and recheck just those things that are affected. Accurately record and assess any changes made and report the changes to the people who will need to recheck. Some host-based IDS systems will catch some of the changes, but they will never be as effective as accurate records from the people actually making the changes in the first place. Think of these as incremental penetration tests, similar to doing incremental backups in between full backups.

☑ Any tool or testing method could potentially result in false negatives but blindly running exploits will result in a much higher false negative rate. If you're getting caught by attacks of convenience, then you need to take a hard look at your procedures for tracking new vulnerabilities and applying vendor patches.

## Chapter 7 Continued

☑ Types of knowledge you should take advantage of include the following: Trust relationships, IP addresses on all network segments, brands and versions of all your software, what type of network gear you use, and source code for all the software if available (especially custom software).

☑ An attacker may try to use some stealth techniques to evade detection. This may include doing certain types of stealth portscans (these are of limited use, because just about any network IDS will pick these up. Some host-based measures like TCP wrappers may not.) Other techniques are slow scans (doing a port scan slowly over time so as not to set off an IDS threshold and make the red port-scan light go off), packet fragmenting (effective against a number of IDS systems), and finally, various types of misinformation attacks.

☑ The pieces of information needed for targeting known holes and downloading an existing exploit include IP Addresses, names, open ports, OS versions, software versions, network structure, and firewall configuration(s).

☑ Banner scanning is the method of trying to determine what software is running by seeing what kinds of information it will volunteer, somewhat equivalent to connecting to a given port and seeing what kind of output you get. This works fine for TCP, but UDP is a bit harder. Although one can use a simple tool like a Telnet client to connect to many TCP services and get back some output, for UDP you have to issue the right kind of request and see what kind of output, if any, you get.

☑ The default files that come with any Web server often aren't removed, and in many cases, they have had vulnerabilities. For example, all copies of IIS 4.0 Web server contained a sample file called showcode.asp—its purpose is to show the source code for an .asp file rather than running it, a feature any attacker would love to have.

**Chapter 7** Continued

☑ Even if automated scanning tools were 100 percent accurate, the majority of them will not actually carry out a penetration, they will only try to determine if a site is vulnerable or not. It will be up to you to actually exercise the vulnerability.

## Hiring a Penetration Testing Team

☑ Running an external audit, you should expect references and resumes of the individuals that will be performing your audit. You should expect to sign an agreement indemnifying them of any repercussions from a successful penetration. You should expect to outline in detail what you want done, and what you do not want done. You should expect an estimate for the work asked for, and an agreement that you will be contacted for approval if extra time is needed. You should expect a report of findings, both what was tried and failed, as well as what was successful.

☑ There is no reason why your internal people couldn't conduct the same kind of audit as an external team if they have the skillset. There is also no reason why you shouldn't require the same documentation that you would get from an external audit.

☑ If you're going to do both an internal and external audit, it might be smart to do the internal audit first. The ideal is to get rid of any easy problems first so that you get the most for your money from the external auditing team.

# ❖ Chapter 8: Disaster Recovery Planning: The Best Defense

## What Is Disaster Recovery Planning?

☑ A disaster recovery plan in its simplest form can be little more than a spreadsheet with relevant phone numbers and information passed around to staff members. Alternatively, it can be as complex as a published business continuity plan that provides for fully equipped

## Chapter 8 Continued

backup data centers running in continual standby mode, ready to deploy on a moment's notice.

☑ A good e-commerce disaster recovery plan addresses these three areas: loss of trade secrets or critical data; loss of access to hardware and software systems; loss of personnel or critical skill sets. Common to all three is the need to identify key staff members responsible for responding to emergencies, how they should be contacted, what their authority levels should be, and under what circumstances they will be called upon.

☑ If your e-commerce site is a business-to-business site, you may find that ISO certification is required for doing business with foreign organizations, especially those in Europe. However, even if your e-commerce venture is small or you just don't wish to pursue ISO certification right now, it's still good business to self-audit your e-commerce quality standards, think ahead about what might happen tomorrow, and formulate steps you can take today to prevent and plan for emergency situations.

# Ensuring Secure Information Backup and Restoration

☑ The most effective way of assuring the quality of your data backups at restore time is to perform a routine verification of the data as it is backed up, typically by restoring all or a portion of the data back to disk and comparing it to the original. Most backup software provides an automated mechanism for verifying that the data written to the backup media is an exact copy of the data on disk, but it may be up to the backup operator to make sure that feature is turned on. It takes longer to do backups using the verification procedure, but it's well worth the extra time.

☑ Documenting the process for performing data backups and restores is an essential part of disaster planning, because backup and restore procedures may vary slightly from system to system. For example, it

**Chapter 8** Continued

is important to know which software must be stopped before a backup occurs. Most database software has to be stopped prior to backing up the database, or the backup image can be corrupt. The last thing you need at recovery time is corrupt backup media, so you should plan ahead for that possibility.

☑ Your software also needs to allow you to prevent restores to a DMZ in the event it becomes compromised. If a system becomes sufficiently broken to need a restore, it should be taken offline, brought inside, repaired, and then returned to the DMZ. Allowing restores to go out through the firewall is asking for trouble. One way to prevent this is to purchase software that performs backups on one port and restores on another and then block the restore port at the firewall.

☑ If you have two backup operators, where one knows the authentication password, the other knows the encryption passphrase, and it takes both people to do a backup or restore, the risk of either being able to damage backup data alone is diminished.

## Planning for Hardware Failure or Loss of Services

☑ Most businesses have local phone lines that can be utilized for dial-backup solutions when normal network services become unavailable. If you have a leased line as your network connection, chances are the DSU that connects it to your internal network can do dial backup too. Dial backup doesn't have to rely on wired phone services, either. You can implement backup wireless networks or wireless modems to automatically dial out when your normal network provider takes a hit.

☑ Every point end-to-end between every component of your e-commerce site must be examined for single points of failure if you are implementing a High Availability configuration.

## Chapter 8 Continued

- ☑ If your line to one ISP goes down one day, you'll want a second redundant ISP ready to cut over immediately to take its place. You might contract with this second ISP to advertise a low priority route to your site while the first advertises a high priority route. If the first goes down, the other will then automatically pick up the traffic. If your site can't afford two network service providers, the next best thing would be to install either two separate physical lines going to the same service provider or two service providers routing traffic to the same local loop.
- ☑ Redundant Arrays of Inexpensive Disks (RAID) provides several redundancy options for people needing to eliminate single points of failure from disk storage solutions. RAID specifies several methods of writing data to several hard drives at once, also known as "striping." Different levels of striping provide different RAID redundancy options.

# How Do I Protect against Natural Disasters?

- ☑ Just as hardware and network redundancy helps to build fault tolerance into your site, data center redundancy adds fault tolerance to your whole business' operations. In the event of a total unavailability of critical business functions, hot standby data center (hot site) is ready to turn up replacement services with very little downtime, providing computing facilities, equipment, services, security, and living quarters for critical support personnel. Locate it away from your main data center, so it isn't affected by the same event that caused your primary site to be unavailable.
- ☑ A yearly practice disaster drill should be performed to ensure that your DRP is up to date and everyone knows the part they need to play recovering systems and software. Disaster drills force people to think about questions they don't normally have to ask.

**Chapter 8** Continued

## Understanding Your Insurance Options

- ☑ The Internet has introduced new definitions of property, damage, and lost revenue that simply don't fit well with the provisions of traditional general liability policies. To address deficiencies in coverage by these traditional policies, new insurance products have emerged that target the needs of various types of e-commerce businesses. Some of the new insurance product offerings are hybrids of security and insurance that aim to reduce risk prior to underwriting insurance.
- ☑ If your site resells its Web services to other companies, errors and omissions (E&O) provisions of a comprehensive e-commerce package will be an important consideration to protect your business if the services you sell don't meet customer expectation. Specialty e-commerce policies may cover damage to the insured, damage to third parties, or both, and exact provisions vary widely from one underwriter to the next.
- ☑ Perhaps the greatest reason for considering e-commerce coverage is provisions for theft or loss of intellectual property. High-tech companies are becoming increasingly aware that the data stored on their computer systems is far more valuable than the systems themselves.
- ☑ Some policies exclude damage to third-party systems caused by a virus originating from your site, so you should examine the policy or purchase an optional endorsement to ensure that you are covered.
- ☑ So-called "Hacker Insurance," which covers damage done during a security breach, is not included in e-commerce liability insurance by some insurers but is included as an automatic provision by others.
- ☑ Most underwriters will require a security audit before selling e-commerce insurance, but may offer a discount on the insurance that covers the entire cost of the audit if results are within expectations. A security audit can cost as much as $20,000 or higher depending on the provider, if not. If you are a consultant or contractor building e-commerce sites for other client companies, you

**Chapter 8** Continued

likely will be asked to provide a Professional Liability Certificate to the company hiring you.

☑ Many insurers offer a comprehensive package of insurance comprised of several smaller products you can choose individually. Individual products can usually be tailored to suit your needs with optional endorsements.

# ❖ Chapter 9: Handling Large Volumes of Network Traffic

## What If My Site's Popularity Exceeds My Expectations?

☑ A typical e-commerce infrastructure includes Web servers, database servers, e-mail servers, DNS servers, network equipment, and possibly some other specialized servers, such as media servers or financial transaction servers. If any one of these components is at capacity, then your site overall is not working properly.

☑ An overloaded device is often harder to troubleshoot than a device that is down all the way—some of your tests might pass on an overloaded device, whereas they will fail for a down device.

☑ By definition, you can't handle an infinite load, and some piece will always max out first. The term "load" collectively refers mostly to a combination of network throughput, CPU utilization, and I/O.

☑ Determine which component is the current bottleneck. The Web servers are one of the pieces most prone to overload (in addition to the database server.) They are also the most flexible in terms of configuration options and the most complex to measure. Determine current traffic at the router—for proactive monitoring, you will want to use a network management package of some sort that keeps statistics over time and perhaps offers utilization graphs. In general, switches don't have a whole lot to go wrong.

**Chapter 9** Continued

- ☑ Assuming that you've gone through the process of tuning your server-side processing, and you're not stalling out waiting on external bottlenecks, such as a database server, then your only real choice is to upgrade your hardware, whether getting a faster individual machine, or adding an additional separate physical machine to help take on some of the work.

## How Do I Manage My Bandwidth Needs?

- ☑ Bandwidth can either be delivered to your premises, or it might be in the form of a handoff at a co-location facility. The co-location option tends to be cheaper, and it's less convenient. Having the bandwidth delivered to your location is very convenient, but it can also be fairly expensive, especially if you need a large amount of it.
- ☑ Try to estimate ahead of time as best you can what your bandwidth requirements will be. Some services, such as media serving, have fairly fixed bandwidth needs. HTTP traffic isn't quite as smooth to calculate; a good rule of thumb is to take the simple product of byte totals per HTML page times number of simultaneous users you need to support, and double it. Also, a number of network management packages will measure line utilization for you.
- ☑ Leave yourself room to grow into your pipe and try to pick a solution that will allow for expansion with a minimum of notice.

## Introduction to Load Balancing

- ☑ Load balancing permits you to use one virtual IP address for multiple servers. How the connection request is passed to a Web server is one of the major points of difference among all the load balancer vendors. Some of them work by modifying MAC addresses, some of them work by modifying IP addresses, some work by proxying, and some work via custom software on the Web servers or clustering.
- ☑ Load balancers allow for relatively seamless on-the-fly addition and removal of servers.

**Chapter 9** Continued

☑ Drawbacks of load balancers are that they introduce one more single point of failure or bottleneck, and they are as open to compromise by an attacker as any other system on your network.

# ❖ Chapter 10: Incident Response, Forensics, and the Law

## Why Is an Incident Response Policy Important?

☑ An incident response policy helps you answer questions crucial to political, logistical, and physical security issues that arise in a crisis. Do you need to contact management or Legal? Do you need to contact the PR department to handle any inquiries about the intrusion? Did the attacker get into the database? What do we need to do to get the Web site back? Should we shut it off so that people can't see the defacement? Are we going to be able to find a system administrator and database administrator to help us clean up?

☑ An incident response policy is not there because you don't know what you are doing; it's there because not everyone will agree with your way of doing things. If you've gotten signoff from all concerned parties ahead of time, and you follow the procedure outlined, then it will be much more difficult to hold you at fault. A well written policy will tell you what your responsibilities are, and what other people are on the hook for.

## Establishing an Incident Response Team (IRT)

☑ You'll likely need to involve a network person and a systems administrator. You'll probably need a representative from your Legal department or attorney's office. A system administrator or a dedicated security engineer can handle the forensics work.

## Chapter 10 Continued

☑ You'll need a dedicated security function that will form the core of the team, and tie it together. This may be a dedicated person, or perhaps a portion of a person's time, but the responsibility must belong to one or more individuals. The core person's responsibility will be to call meetings, make sure representation is present from all concerned organizations, coordinate writing policy and getting agreement on policy, arrange for training as needed, and drive actual incident response when the occasion arises.

# Setting the Prosecution Boundaries

☑ The first line you have to draw is the line between attempt and incident. All day long, you will receive probes and scans. These are people trying out new tools, or potential attackers gathering intelligence information, or even automated worms. You may get somewhere between dozens and thousands of these per day.

☑ The chain of custody defines who has access to the evidence during the entire investigation process. Maintaining a chain of custody list isn't difficult; you just have to record several items: who was in custody (possession) of the evidence, where the evidence was, what security measures are in place at that location, and what items of evidence existed at that time. You must write down a new entry each time one of these changes.

# Establishing an Incident Response Process

☑ One fairly common response for relatively benign attempts is to report the attempts to the appropriate ISP, company, or their provider. Some IDS software includes a reporting mechanism to help generate reports and locate the proper e-mail addresses to contact.

☑ Once you have a policy in place that dictates how you will respond when an incident occurs, you need to build a set of processes to support your responses. This covers the range from minor attempts to full intrusions.

**Chapter 10** Continued

☑ You will first need to understand how the files are stored on disk, how the processes interact, how all the software is configured, and what log information is available to you. And, you have to know this for each different operating system you need to investigate.

# Introduction to Forensic Computing

☑ The first step in any forensic investigation is to make a backup of all the information available to you, if possible. Unfortunately, this doesn't just mean backing up the drives. Before you even get to that point, you have to decide how to examine what might be in memory when you arrive. There may be some evidence in memory that you want to get at, and not all operating systems have a provision for dumping RAM to disk.

☑ The general problem with backing up a compromised system before you shut it down is that any use of the compromised system damages the evidence to some degree.

☑ There are tools that are intended to "image" systems to restore them to a particular state. These tools can be used to create an image of the drives of a compromised system. The advantage is that many of them are designed to boot from DOS, and to send the images across a network.

☑ Most professional forensics backup programs include features to do MD5 checksums to verify data integrity. Some of them are entire forensics toolkits, and go well beyond just taking an image of a disk. Some of them even include full scripting languages to help automate the use of their features.

# Tracking Incidents

☑ An incident tracking system (ITS) is a collection of programs designed to help an IRT manage the incidents that occur in their environment. These programs range from simple port scans that you do nothing about, to full-blown legal cases with appropriate legal documentation.

## Chapter 10 Continued

- ☑ The variety of products and programs that make up incident tracking systems fall into three main categories: software to assist security incident tracking, software to assist with a help desk function, and software to tracks bugs in a software development environment.
- ☑ Many of the things your IDS will report will be false alarms, but this is totally dependent on your particular environment. You will need to spend some quality time with your IDS, tuning the rules to reduce these as much as possible, and then documenting the ones you can't eliminate entirely.
- ☑ ITS must provide a number of items that must be tracked, including the IP address of the affected system, the IP address of the offender (if known), ports/services scanned, security zone (DMZ, inside, etc.), currently assigned IRT member (if applicable), and the chain of custody.

# Index

# B

## C

# F

## G



## H

# I

## J



## K



## L

# N

# O



# P

# Q



# R

# S

# T

## U

## V

## W



## X



## Y



## Z

## The Global Knowledge Advantage

Global Knowledge has a global delivery system for its products and services. The company has 28 subsidiaries, and offers its programs through a total of 60+ locations. No other vendor can provide consistent services across a geographic area this large. Global Knowledge is the largest independent information technology education provider, offering programs on a variety of platforms. This enables our multi-platform and multi-national customers to obtain all of their programs from a single vendor. The company has developed the unique CompetusTM Framework software tool and methodology which can quickly reconfigure courseware to the proficiency level of a student on an interactive basis. Combined with self-paced and on-line programs, this technology can reduce the time required for training by prescribing content in only the deficient skills areas. The company has fully automated every aspect of the education process, from registration and follow-up, to "just-in-time" production of courseware. Global Knowledge through its Enterprise Services Consultancy, can customize programs and products to suit the needs of an individual customer.

## Global Knowledge Classroom Education Programs

The backbone of our delivery options is classroom-based education. Our modern, well-equipped facilities staffed with the finest instructors offer programs in a wide variety of information technology topics, many of which lead to professional certifications.

## Custom Learning Solutions

This delivery option has been created for companies and governments that value customized learning solutions. For them, our consultancy-based approach of developing targeted education solutions is most effective at helping them meet specific objectives.

## Self-Paced and Multimedia Products

This delivery option offers self-paced program titles in interactive CD-ROM, videotape and audio tape programs. In addition, we offer custom development of interactive multimedia courseware to customers and partners. Call us at 1-888-427-4228.

## Electronic Delivery of Training

Our network-based training service delivers efficient competency-based, interactive training via the World Wide Web and organizational intranets. This leading-edge delivery option provides a custom learning path and "just-in-time" training for maximum convenience to students.

# Global Knowledge Courses Available

## Microsoft

- Windows 2000 Deployment Strategies
- Introduction to Directory Services
- Windows 2000 Client Administration
- Windows 2000 Server
- Windows 2000 Update
- MCSE Bootcamp
- Microsoft Networking Essentials
- Windows NT 4.0 Workstation
- Windows NT 4.0 Server
- Windows NT Troubleshooting
- Windows NT 4.0 Security
- Windows 2000 Security
- Introduction to Microsoft Web Tools

## Management Skills

- Project Management for IT Professionals
- Microsoft Project Workshop
- Management Skills for IT Professionals

## Network Fundamentals

- Understanding Computer Networks
- Telecommunications Fundamentals I
- Telecommunications Fundamentals II
- Understanding Networking Fundamentals
- Upgrading and Repairing PCs
- DOS/Windows A+ Preparation
- Network Cabling Systems

## WAN Networking and Telephony

- Building Broadband Networks
- Frame Relay Internetworking
- Converging Voice and Data Networks
- Introduction to Voice Over IP
- Understanding Digital Subscriber Line (xDSL)

## Internetworking

- ATM Essentials
- ATM Internetworking
- ATM Troubleshooting
- Understanding Networking Protocols
- Internetworking Routers and Switches
- Network Troubleshooting
- Internetworking with TCP/IP
- Troubleshooting TCP/IP Networks
- Network Management
- Network Security Administration
- Virtual Private Networks
- Storage Area Networks
- Cisco OSPF Design and Configuration
- Cisco Border Gateway Protocol (BGP) Configuration

## Web Site Management and Development

- Advanced Web Site Design
- Introduction to XML
- Building a Web Site
- Introduction to JavaScript
- Web Development Fundamentals
- Introduction to Web Databases

## PERL, UNIX, and Linux

- PERL Scripting
- PERL with CGI for the Web
- UNIX Level I
- UNIX Level II
- Introduction to Linux for New Users
- Linux Installation, Configuration, and Maintenance

## Authorized Vendor Training

## Red Hat

- Introduction to Red Hat Linux
- Red Hat Linux Systems Administration
- Red Hat Linux Network and Security Administration
- RHCE Rapid Track Certification

## Cisco Systems

- Interconnecting Cisco Network Devices
- Advanced Cisco Router Configuration
- Installation and Maintenance of Cisco Routers
- Cisco Internetwork Troubleshooting
- Designing Cisco Networks
- Cisco Internetwork Design
- Configuring Cisco Catalyst Switches
- Cisco Campus ATM Solutions
- Cisco Voice Over Frame Relay, ATM, and IP
- Configuring for Selsius IP Phones
- Building Cisco Remote Access Networks
- Managing Cisco Network Security
- Cisco Enterprise Management Solutions

## Nortel Networks

- Nortel Networks Accelerated Router Configuration
- Nortel Networks Advanced IP Routing
- Nortel Networks WAN Protocols
- Nortel Networks Frame Switching
- Nortel Networks Accelar 1000
- Comprehensive Configuration
- Nortel Networks Centillion Switching
- Network Management with Optivity for Windows

## Oracle Training

- Introduction to Oracle8 and PL/SQL
- Oracle8 Database Administration

# Custom Corporate Network Training

## Train on Cutting Edge Technology

We can bring the best in skill-based training to your facility to create a real-world hands-on training experience. Global Knowledge has invested millions of dollars in network hardware and software to train our students on the same equipment they will work with on the job. Our relationships with vendors allow us to incorporate the latest equipment and platforms into your on-site labs.

## Maximize Your Training Budget

Global Knowledge provides experienced instructors, comprehensive course materials, and all the networking equipment needed to deliver high quality training. You provide the students; we provide the knowledge.

## Avoid Travel Expenses

On-site courses allow you to schedule technical training at your convenience, saving time, expense, and the opportunity cost of travel away from the workplace.

## Discuss Confidential Topics

Private on-site training permits the open discussion of sensitive issues such as security, access, and network design. We can work with your existing network's proprietary files while demonstrating the latest technologies.

## Customize Course Content

Global Knowledge can tailor your courses to include the technologies and the topics which have the greatest impact on your business. We can complement your internal training efforts or provide a total solution to your training needs.

## Corporate Pass

The Corporate Pass Discount Program rewards our best network training customers with preferred pricing on public courses, discounts on multimedia training packages, and an array of career planning services.

## Global Knowledge Training Lifecycle

Supporting the Dynamic and Specialized Training Requirements of Information Technology Professionals

- Define Profile
- Assess Skills
- Design Training
- Deliver Training
- Test Knowledge
- Update Profile
- Use New Skills

## Global Knowledge

Global Knowledge programs are developed and presented by industry professionals with "real-world" experience. Designed to help professionals meet today's interconnectivity and interoperability challenges, most of our programs feature hands-on labs that incorporate state-of-the-art communication components and equipment.

## ON-SITE TEAM TRAINING

Bring Global Knowledge's powerful training programs to your company. At Global Knowledge, we will custom design courses to meet your specific network requirements. Call (919)-461-8686 for more information.

## YOUR GUARANTEE

Global Knowledge believes its courses offer the best possible training in this field. If during the first day you are not satisfied and wish to withdraw from the course, simply notify the instructor, return all course materials and receive a 100% refund.

## REGISTRATION INFORMATION

In the US:
call: (888) 762–4442
fax: (919) 469–7070
visit our website:
www.globalknowledge.com

# Syngress Publishing's Sweepstake Terms

## OFFICIAL RULES - NO PURCHASE NECESSARY

### 1) TIMING

The contest (the "Contest") begins March 1, 2001 at 9:00 a.m. EST and ends November 30, 2001 at 11:59 p.m. EST (the "Entry Period"). You must enter the contest during the Entry Period.

### 2) THE PRIZES

Three (3) prizes will be awarded: (a) a Sony DVD Player ("1st Prize"); (b) a Palm Pilot V ("2nd Prize"); and (c) a Rio MP3 Player ("3rd Prize"). One of each prize will be awarded. The approximate retail value of the three prizes is as follows: (a) the Sony DVD Player is approximately $595; (b) the Palm Pilot V is approximately $399; and (c) the Rio MP3 Player is approximately $299.

Sponsors make no warranty, guaranty or representation of any kind concerning any prize. Prize values are subject to change.

### 3) ELIGIBILITY REQUIREMENTS

No purchase is necessary. Contest is void in Puerto Rico, and where prohibited by law. Employees of Syngress Publishing, Inc. (the "Sponsor") and their affiliates, subsidiaries, officers, agents or any other person or entity directly associated with the contest (the "Contest Entities") and the immediate family members and/or persons living in the same household as such persons are not eligible to enter the Contest.

This contest is open only to people that meet the following requirements:

- legal residents of the United States
- Must be at least 21 years of age or older at the time of winning
- Must own a major credit card

**4) HOW TO ENTER:** No purchase is necessary to enter. Contestants can enter by mail (see below) or may enter on the Syngress website located at. www.syngress.com/sweepstake.html. ONLY ONE ENTRY PER PERSON OR E-MAIL ADDRESS PER HOUSEHOLD WILL BE ACCEPTED.

No purchase is necessary to enter. To enter by mail, print your name, address, daytime telephone number, email address and age. Mail this in a hand-addressed envelope to: **Syngress Publishing Contest, Syngress Publishing, Inc., 800 Hingham Street, Rockland, MA 02370**. All mail entries must be postmarked before November 15, 2001.

Sponsor assumes no responsibility for lost, late, or misdirected entries or for any computer, online, telephone, or human error or technical malfunctions that may occur. Incomplete mail entries are void. All entries become the property of Sponsor and will not be returned.

If a prize notification or prize is returned to Sponsor or its fulfillment companies as undeliverable for any reason, it will be awarded to an alternate. If necessary, due to unavailability, a prize of equal or great value will be awarded at the discretion of the Sponsor. Prizes are not transferable, assignable or redeemable for cash.

By entering the Contest on the Sponsor Internet site, you may occasionally receive promotion announcements from Sponsor through e-mail. If you no longer wish to receive these e-mails, you may cease your participation in such promotions by sending an e-mail to promotions@syngress.com with your First Name, Last Name, and your e-mail address.

**5) WINNER SELECTION/DEADLINE DATES:** Random drawings will be conducted by the Sponsor from among all eligible entries. Odds of winning the prize depend on the number of eligible entries received. The first drawing will be for the winner of the 1st Prize, then a drawing will be held from all remaining eligible entries for the winner of the 2nd Prize and finally a drawing will be held from all remaining eligible entries for the winner of the 3rd Prize. These drawings will occur on December 1, 2001, at the offices of Syngress Publishing, Inc., 800 Hingham Street, Rockland, MA 02370. The decisions by the Sponsor shall be final and binding in all respects.

**6) GENERAL CONDITIONS:** Contest entrants agree to be bound by the terms of these official rules. The laws of the Commonwealth of Massachusetts and the United States govern this Contest, and the state and federal courts located in Suffolk and Middlesex Counties in the Commonwealth of Massachusetts shall be the sole jurisdiction for any disputes related to the Contest. All federal, state, and local laws and regulations apply. Winners will be notified via e-mail and/or U.S. Mail within two (2) weeks of prize drawing. Winners will be required to execute and return an Affidavit of Eligibility and Release of Liability and where legal, Publicity Release within 14 days following the date of issuance of notification. Non-compliance within this time period or return of any prize/prize notification as undeliverable may result in disqualification and selection of an alternate winner. Acceptance of prize constitutes permission for Sponsor to use winner's name and likeness for advertising and promotional purposes without additional compensation unless prohibited by law. BY ENTERING, PARTICIPANTS RELEASE AND HOLD HARMLESS SYNGRESS PUBLISHING, INC., AND ITS RESPECTIVE PARENT CORPORATIONS, SUBSIDIARIES, AFFILIATES, DIRECTORS, OFFICERS, PRIZE SUPPLIERS, EMPLOYEES AND AGENTS FROM ANY AND ALL LIABILITY OR ANY INJURIES, LOSS OR DAMAGE OF ANY KIND ARISING FROM OR IN CONNECTION WITH THE CONTEST OR ACCEPTANCE OR USE OF THE PRIZES WON.

**7) INTERNET:** If for any reason this contest is not capable of running as planned due to infection by computer virus, bugs, tampering, unauthorized intervention, fraud, technical failures, or any other causes beyond the control of the Sponsor which corrupt or affect the administration, security, fairness, integrity, or proper conduct of this contest, the Sponsor reserves the right, at its sole discretion, to disqualify any individual who tampers with the entry process, and to cancel, terminate, modify, or suspend the online portion of the contest. The Sponsor assumes no responsibility for any error, omission, interruption, deletion, defect, delay in operation or transmission, communications line failure, theft or destruction or unauthorized access to, or alteration of, entries. Sponsor is not responsible for any problems or technical malfunction of any telephone network or telephone lines, computer on-line systems, servers, or providers, computer equipment, software, failure of any e-mail or entry to be received by Sponsor on account of technical problems, human error or traffic congestion on the Internet or at any Web site, or any combination thereof, including any injury or damage to participant's or any other person's computer relating to or resulting from participation in the Contest or downloading any materials in the Contest. CAUTION: ANY ATTEMPT TO DELIBERATELY DAMAGE ANY WEB SITE OR UNDERMINE THE LEGITIMATE OPERATION OF THE CONTEST IS A VIOLATION OF CRIMINAL AND CIVIL LAWS AND SHOULD SUCH AN ATTEMPT BE MADE, SPONSOR RESERVES THE RIGHT TO SEEK DAMAGES OR OTHER REMEDIES FROM ANY SUCH PERSON (S) RESPONSIBLE FOR THE ATTEMPT TO THE FULLEST EXTENT PERMITTED BY LAW. In the event of a dispute as to the identity of a winner based on an e-mail address, the winning entry will be declared made by the authorized account holder of the e-mail address submitted at time of entry. "Authorized account holder" is defined as the natural person who is assigned to an e-mail address by an Internet access provider, on-line service provider, or other organization (e.g., business, educational, institution, etc.) that is responsible for assigning e-mail addresses for the domain associated with the submitted e-mail address.

**8) WHO WON:** Winners who enter on the web site will be notified by e-mail and winners who had entered via mail will be notified by mail. The winners will also be posted on our web site. Alternatively, to receive the names of the winners please send a self addressed stamped envelope to: Syngress Publishing Contest, care of Syngress Publishing, Inc., 800 Hingham Street, Rockland, MA 02370.

The Sponsor of this sweepstakes is Syngress Publishing, Inc., 800 Hingham Street, Rockland, MA 02370.